Reshaping
the German Right

RESHAPING THE GERMAN RIGHT

Radical Nationalism
and Political Change
after Bismarck

Geoff Eley

YALE UNIVERSITY PRESS
NEW HAVEN & LONDON 1980

To my parents

Designed by Caroline Williamson and set in Monotype Ehrhardt.

Printed in Great Britain by Ebenezer Baylis and Son Ltd, The Trinity Press, Worcester, and London

Published in Great Britain, Europe, Africa and Asia (except Japan) by Yale University Press Ltd, London. Distributed in Australia and New Zealand by Book & Film Services, Artarmon, N.S.W., Australia; and in Japan by Harper & Row, Publishers, Tokyo Office

Library of Congress Cataloging in Publication Data

Eley, Geoff, 1949–
  Reshaping the German right.
  Includes bibliographical references and index.
  1. Germany—Politics and government—1888–1918.
  2. Nationalism—Germany—History.   I. Title.
  DD228.5.E45   320.9′43′084   79-20711
  ISBN 0-300-02386-3

CONTENTS

PREFACE

This is primarily a study in politics. However, while reducing politics neither to economics nor to society and expressly eschewing determinism in that sense, it none the less seeks to understand political developments in a larger context. It is concerned with processes of political change in Germany in the period extending from 1890 into the early years of the Weimar Republic—the changing forms of political life, a general reconstitution of the public sphere, and a specific set of changes in the ideology and practice of the German right. It considers these problems by looking in detail at a particular category of organizations, the nationalist pressure groups or *nationale Verbände*, whose main representatives were the Pan-German League, the Navy League, the Colonial Society, the Society for the Eastern Marches and the Defence League.

My aim has not been to produce formal organizational histories of these groups or blow-by-blow accounts of their development, but to use them to open up larger questions. In particular, their practice exposed certain weaknesses of the established right-wing parties in responding to the demands of a new popular politics. During the 1890s the nationalist pressure groups offered a field of involvement for activists who tended to experience party politics as the closed preserve of notables. As the nationalist groups also had specific conflicts with the government and their party allies (over colonial policy, the pace of naval expansion, treatment of the national minorities, anti-socialism etc.), this led to some tension. In this situation there developed a critique of *Honoratiorenpolitik*—'the politics of notables'—which was felt to inhibit the progress of a popular nationalist revival. The overall setting for this debate was the spectacular advance of the SPD and a more general popular mobilization in the 1890s, which embraced the countryside as well as the towns: fundamentally, the argument was about how an adequate popular politics could be developed by the right, and how the threat of the Socialists could best be met.

Gradually there developed in the nationalist groups a profound disbelief in the ability of the establishment to solve these problems. This provided the basis for a new 'national opposition' to the government, claiming superior access to the 'will of the nation'. In other words, the political dissidence of the nationalist pressure groups developed into a populist attack on the government and the old right. The form of this ideology I have called radical nationalism. It was located mainly in the Pan-German League and in a dominant tendency of the Navy League. It cohered as a political position particularly after 1903 and in the 1907 elections, culminating in a dramatic crisis of the Navy League in 1907–8 and in the Daily Telegraph Crisis of November 1908. Under specific circumstances after 1909, which are discussed in the final part of the book, it became generalized into a party-political opposition to the government of Bethmann Hollweg. This amounted to an important radicalization of the German right, involving a decisive rupture with past traditions and a renewal of the right's popular capability. At the centre of this process was the problem of how the political relations between dominant and subordinate classes, in a context of impressive left-wing advance, could be lastingly reconstructed. The *manner* in which this was tackled—an unstable relationship to the petty bourgeoisie, under extreme nationalist auspices and the impetus of a Pan-German populist offensive—created the *political context* in which the possibility of a German fascism could develop.

In other words, this book is concerned with the conditions under which a particular right-wing ideology—radical nationalism, with a strong populist inflection—was generated. By ideology I mean something more than the formal ideas held by recognizable intellectuals or the systematized doctrine to be excavated from a set of founding literary texts, though each of these is important. I am more concerned with the structured experience of nationalist activists —with the material practices and social relations that bound their loyalties together, and with their attempts to organize their experiences into a coherent system. This implies no disrespect or indifference towards the history of ideas, but simply a necessary forbearance, for to enquire more deeply into the formal development of certain concepts (e.g. the nation, *das Volk*, and so on) would require further expansion of an already lengthy text. My concern in this book is to see how ideas were made to work in directly political ways. This seemed more important than yet another formal discussion of deep-rooted intellectual traditions.

*

This book began life as a doctoral thesis on the German Navy League at the University of Sussex between 1970 and 1974. Accordingly the Navy League figures prominently in the following analysis, though mainly because its centrality to the problem of the *nationale Verbände* demands it. In addition I have added a great deal of further research and the analysis of the Navy League is I hope successfully integrated into the larger project. Some parts of Chapters Four and Five have already appeared in articles in *Social History* and the *Historical Journal* ('Defining Social Imperialism: Use and Abuse of an Idea', *SH*, 1, 3 (1976), pp. 265–90; 'Reshaping the Right: Radical Nationalism and the German Navy League, 1898–1908', *HJ*, 21, 2 (1978), pp. 327–54), and I

am grateful to the editors of those journals for allowing me the opportunity
to try out my ideas.

Since beginning my research I have been helped by many individuals and
institutions too numerous to be listed by name. Special mention should be made
of the archivists and staff at the *Zentrales Staatsarchiv* in Potsdam, the *Bundesarchiv* Coblenz and the *Bundesarchiv-Militärchiv* Freiburg, the *Stadtarchiv*
Augsburg, the *Stadtbibliothek* Mönchen-Gladbach and the *Institut für Zeitungsforschung* in Dortmund, whose help was especially important for the archival
basis of this study. Otherwise the archives visited are indicated in the Bibliography and I would like to express my general gratitude for all the assistance
given. I would also like to thank Herr Gerd Keim for allowing me to use his
grandfather's private papers and for receiving me with such friendliness and
hospitality, and Herr Klaus Werner Schmidt for enabling me to use another
important collection of private papers. At different times I have received
generous financial assistance from the Volkswagen Foundation, the Twenty-
Seven Foundation, the British Academy and the D.A.A.D., for which I remain
extremely grateful.

Many individuals enabled this book to be written and contributed to whatever virtues it may possess. Like any intellectual product it owes its origins to
innumerable readings, discussions and seminars, and specific influences
cannot always be identified. But my first debt in this respect, extending now
over ten years, must be to Hartmut Pogge von Strandmann, who taught me
as an undergraduate, supervised my doctoral work, and has continued to steer
me in the right direction, controlling my worst excesses and leavening his
cautionary advice with occasional praise. At all levels his help always exceeded
the formal obligations of a supervisor and provided the securest of foundations
for my work in the archives. In retrospect his careful guidance formed my ideas
about German history far more than I was immediately aware, though they have
sometimes taken directions he may not have envisaged. I hope very much he is
pleased with the results and that the latter do justice to his efforts.

Many of the ideas in this book first took shape during intensive discussions
with my exact contemporary Fred Taylor, as we braved the rigours of initiation
into the German archives in 1971–2: I owe my understanding of the Imperial
League Against Social Democracy mainly to him, but the more general debt is
incalculable. More recently I have benefited enormously from countless discussions with David Blackbourn (particularly for the ideas in Chapter Two),
Jane Caplan, Gareth Stedman Jones and David Crew, and the weekly meetings
of the Social History Seminar in Cambridge have been immensely valuable.
The probings of my thesis examiners Volker Berghahn and John Röhl helped
establish where further work had to be done, and a detailed exchange of letters
with Wilhelm Deist was also extremely helpful. At different times versions of
the manuscript were read by Hartmut Pogge, David Blackbourn, Jane Caplan,
David Crew, Keith Nield and Jonathan Steinberg. On a number of occasions

1*

Tim Mason has provided verbal and written responses to my arguments. Paul McHugh read the entire manuscript as a British historian and provided a valuable lay response. James Joll identified some much-needed revisions in an overgrown final manuscript. All their comments have been very gratefully received and I hope I have learned from their criticisms. The strengths of this book derive very much from their advice, but they should not be blamed for its faults.

Of course there is more to life than German history alone, though the peculiar isolation of doing doctoral work in foreign archives sometimes made this hard to remember. Living out of a suitcase and three carrier bags was made bearable by the kindnesses and solidarity of a number of friends, and these too made a huge contribution to the production of this book. In the initial months Fred Taylor, Gary and Sally Shellman, Otmar Escher and Marcus Phillips overcame the tedium of a Coblenz winter with their company, Arno and Heide Brauer looked after me in Berlin, and Ulrich Brack shared a pleasant summer in Potsdam. Sue Ostick and Tony Cousins provided a welcome refuge on my trips back to England. Most of all, Eleanor Levy provided constant encouragement, support and companionship and helped immeasurably at every stage of the book, at the cost unfortunately of also sharing the discomfort (the night in Herne, when the roof of our attic flat blew in, was the low point). I owe more to her than I can possibly express and only hope that this book may partly compensate her efforts.

Finally I would like to express my gratitude to the London Office of Yale University Press—to Caroline Williamson for handling the final stages of the manuscript, and to John Nicoll for his confidence in my project, for his patience, and for making the process of publication, at least for the author, such a painless process.

I did the typing myself and, except where otherwise indicated, the translations are my responsibility.

ABBREVIATIONS

AAZ	*Augsburger Abendzeitung*
AdH	Archiv der Hansestadt
AfS	Archiv für Sozialgeschichte
AHR	*American Historical Review*
Alld. Bl.	*Alldeutsche Blätter*
ANN	*Augsburger Neueste Nachrichten*
BA	Bundesarchiv
BA-MA	Bundesarchiv-Militärarchiv
BdI	Bund der Industriellen
BdL	Bund der Landwirte
BHSA	Bayerisches Hauptstaatsarchiv
BK	*Bayrischer Kurier*
BNN	*Berliner Neueste Nachrichten*
CEH	*Central European History*
CVDI	Centralverband Deutscher Industrieller
DAGZ	*Deutsche Arbeitgeberzeitung*
DIZ	*Deutsche Industreizeitung*
DKZ	*Deutsche Kolonialzeitung*
DNVP	Deutschnationale Volkspartei
DortmZ	*Dortmunder Zeitung*
DSB	Deutsche Staatsbibliothek
DTZ	*Deutsche Tageszeitung*
DVC	*Deutsche Volkswirtschaftliche Correspondenz*
DWZ	*Deutsche Wirtschafts-Zeitung*
DVFP	Deutschvölkisch-Freiheitspartei
DZ	*Deutsche Zeitung*
FZ	*Frankfurter Zeitung*
FreisZ	*Freisinnige Zeitung*
GLA	Generallandesarchiv
HA/GHH	Historisches Archiv der Gutehoffnungshütte
HN	*Hamburger Nachrichten*
HSA	Hauptstaatsarchiv
HZ	*Historische Zeitschrift*

JCEA	*Journal of Central European Affairs*
JCH	*Journal of Contemporary History*
JMH	*Journal of Modern History*
JWG	*Jahrbuch für Wirtschaftsgeschichte*
KrZ	*Kreuz-Zeitung*
KVZ	*Kölnische Volkszeitung*
KZ	*Kölnische Zeitung*
LA	Landesarchiv
LNN	*Leipziger Neueste Nachrichten*
LT	Landtag
MAZ	*Münchner Allgemeine Zeitung*
MGM	*Militärgeschichtliche Mitteilungen*
MNN	*Munchner Neueste Nachrichten*
NatZ	*National-Zeitung*
NAZ	*Norddeutsche Allgemeine Zeitung*
NLR	*New Left Review*
NPL	*Neue Politische Literatur*
NSDAP	Nationalsozialistische Deutsche Arbeiter-Partei
P & P	*Past and Present*
PVS	*Politische Vierteljahresschrift*
Rkz	Reichskanzlei
RT	Reichstag
RWZ	*Rheinisch-Westfälische Zeitung*
SA	Stadtarchiv
SH	*Social History*
StA	Staatsarchiv
Sten. Ber.	Stenographische Berichte
TLS	*Times Literary Supplement*
TR	*Tägliche Rundschau*
VDEStI	Verein deutscher Eisen- und Stahlindustrieller
VfZ	*Vierteljahreshefte für Zeitgeschichte*
VMB	Verhandlungen, Mitteilungen und Berichte des CVDI
VSWR	Vereinigung der Steuer- und Wirtschaftsreformer
WA	Werksarchiv
WeimZ	*Weimarische Zeitung*
ZStA	Zentrales Staatsarchiv

1. Introduction

I

During the last fifteen years there has been a remarkable flourishing of historical studies in the Federal Republic of Germany. Partly this has followed a familiar international pattern—the expansion of higher education and the loosening of ideological conformities in the 1960s, new inter-disciplinary contacts with sociology, political science and social anthropology, the burgeoning of interest in social history, and so on. But in the Federal Republic, by a process which is now equally familiar, it was also promoted by a particular set of historio-graphical changes, initiated by the famous 'Fischer Controversy' about the nature of German imperialism and its aims in the First World War.[1] Though increasingly concerned with the details of the July Crisis and diverted by Fischer's opponents into arguments about the role of personalities, this also raised much larger issues. In particular, Fischer's work quickly directed a younger generation to the problem of continuity and the place of Nazism in the longer historical experience between Bismarck and Hitler. The reasoning has recently been described as follows:

> In the first place, if there really were some similarities between Hitler's foreign policy and that of Wilhelm II, then might there not also be some similarities in the *internal* political structure of Germany under Hitler and under the last Kaiser? Indeed, could not some of the longer-term origins of the Third Reich—origins whose existence the older generation of historians had largely denied, ascribing the rise of Nazism solely to the demonic genius of Hitler—lie precisely in developments that took place in Wilhelmine or even Bismarckian Germany? Furthermore, if Germany really did launch the First World War, then must there not have been powerful internal social and economic influences prompting her to do so—influences more profound

[1] The Fischer Controversy is best approached through the following: A. Sywottek, 'Die Fischer-Kontroverse', in I. Geiss and B. J. Wendt (eds.), *Deutschland in der Weltpolitik des 19. und 20. Jahrhunderts* (Düsseldorf, 1974), pp. 19–47; I. Geiss, 'Die Fischer-Kontroverse', in *Studien über Geschichte und Geschichtswissenschaft* (Frankfurt, 1972), pp. 108–98; J. A. Moses, *The Politics of Illusion* (London, 1975). For a useful guide to recent developments, see R. J. Evans, 'Introduction: Wilhelm II's Germany and the Historians', in Evans (Ed.), *Society and Politics in Wilhelmine Germany* (London, 1978), pp. 11–39.

than the mere incompetence of her diplomacy or the blinkered technical
rigidity of her military men?[2]

Armed with these questions, the new generation (who themselves graduated
into senior posts during the early 1970s) achieved a root-and-branch re-
examination of conventional truths, involving everything from Bismarck's
colonial policy to the so-called 'parliamentarization' of German politics before
1914. In so doing they drew on the over-arching interpretations of German
political development available in the social sciences and simultaneously reinstated the neglected writings of radical outsiders from the inter-war years.
Quite apart from adding immeasurably to our general knowledge of the
Kaiserreich, moreover, this battery of new work has generated a larger view of
the German past. Though reformulated in terms of social structures and political
relations, the latter broadly accords with an older Anglo-Saxon explanation—
the view that German history between the early nineteenth and mid-twentieth
centuries was principally the record of an unfolding authoritarian tradition
which repulsed or co-opted any movement of liberal opposition, whether in
1848, the 1860s, on the eve of the Great War or during the Weimar Republic,
and which supplied the vital condition of Nazi success. At the centre of this
view is an unmistakable commitment to the notion of continuity between
Bismarck and Hitler.[3]

In what is that continuity held to exist? Originally, of course, the Fischer
Controversy drew attention to formal similarities in the annexationist programmes of the two World Wars, amounting to a continuity of German
imperialist ambition. But Fischer's successors soon took this further, arguing
that these similarities had a common structural explanation. One of the concepts
used to express this deeper continuity was 'social imperialism'. Taken to mean
'the diversion outwards of internal tensions and forces of change in order to
preserve the social and political status quo', and a 'defensive ideology' against
the 'disruptive effects of industrialization on the social and economic structure
of Germany', this was an attempt to understand Germany's aggressive foreign
policy as the consequence of serious faults inside German society.[4] Beginning

[2] Evans, 'Introduction', pp. 12f.
[3] The older Anglo-American work tended to concentrate on intellectual history and the
'German mind'. E.g.: H. Kohn, *The Mind of Germany* (London, 1966); F. Stern, *The
Politics of Cultural Despair* (Berkeley, 1961); G. L. Mosse, *The Crisis of German Ideology*
(London, 1966).
[4] The main architect of this view has been Hans-Ulrich Wehler. The quotations are taken
from his *Bismarck und der Imperialismus* (Cologne, 1969), p. 115. I have discussed the ante-
cedents of this idea of social imperialism and its limitations in two essays: 'Defining Social
Imperialism: Use and Abuse of an Idea', *Social History*, I, 3 (1976), pp. 265–90, and 'Social
Imperialism in Germany: Reformist Synthesis or Reactionary Sleight of Hand?', in I. Geiss
and J. Radkau (Eds.), *Imperialismus im 20. Jahrhundert. Gedenkchrift für G. W. F. Hallgarten*
(Munich, 1976), pp. 71–86.

with Bismarck's colonial policy, it is argued, popular nationalism was consistently exploited as a 'long-term integrative factor which helped stabilize an anachronistic social and power structure'. Support for expansion abroad was used to 'block domestic progress' and 'social and political emancipation', an effective 'technique of rule' for defeating 'the advancing forces of parliamentarization and democratization'.[5] For the leading voice among recent German historians, Hans-Ulrich Wehler, this casts important light on the origins of Nazism:

> If this single line of development is pursued—the social-imperialist resistance to the emancipation-process in industrial society in Germany—then in historical terms we may draw a connecting-line from Bismarck, through Miquel, Bülow, Tirpitz, as far as the extreme social imperialism of National Socialism, which once again sought to stem domestic progress and divert attention from the absence of freedom at home by breaking out to the East.

'If there is a continuity in German imperialism', Wehler has argued, then it consists in 'the primacy of social imperialism from Bismarck to Hitler.'[6]

Carrying the enquiry further, recent work has also tried to examine the social interests and 'relations of domination' which these 'diversionary techniques of rule' were meant to defend. At the institutional level of the state these are easy to identify: the monarchy and its traditions of military and bureaucratic independence; the relative freedom of the executive from parliamentary controls; the special position of Prussia in the Empire; the restricted franchise in most of the individual states; the socially weighted tax system; and so on. But within this framework of institutions historians have normally detected a particular social interest, namely 'the predominance of the feudal aristocracy'.[7] The social basis of Germany's constitutional authoritarianism, according to this view, was the ability of a 'pre-industrial élite' of landowners to preserve the essentials of its power by subordinating the state machinery to its interests. The instruments of aristocratic power were the domination of the military and bureaucratic apparatuses of the state, a privileged position in the Prussian Landtag, vital fiscal immunities, and a transmuted seigneurial authority over a dependent rural population east of the

[5] H.-U. Wehler, 'Industrial Growth and Early German Imperialism', in R. Owen and B. Sutcliffe (Eds.), *Studies in the Theory of Imperialism* (London, 1972), pp. 89, 87, 88.

[6] H.-U. Wehler, 'Bismarcks Imperialismus 1862–1890', in *Krisenherde des Kaiserreichs 1871–1918. Studien zur deutschen Sozial- und Verfassungsgeschichte* (Göttingen, 1970), p. 161; H.-U. Wehler, 'Probleme des Imperialismus', ibid., p. 131.

[7] This phrase is taken from a chapter-heading in S. Mielke, *Der Hansa-Bund für Gewerbe, Handel und Industrie 1909–1914. Der gescheiterte Versuch einer antifeudalen Sammlungspolitik* (Göttingen, 1976), p. 17: 'The Political System: Preservation of the Predominance of the Feudal Aristocracy'.

Elbe. To these may be added a preferential treatment in the area of economic protection. Accordingly, despite the capitalist transformation of German society and the growing predominance of industry in the economy, it is argued, 'political power remained in the hands of the economically weakened pre-capitalist ruling strata (Junkers, bureaucracy, military)'.[8]

To maintain its power, of course, the landed interest required political allies, particularly in view of its diminishing economic base. To deal with this dimension, therefore, the concept of social imperialism has normally been accompanied by a second concept, that of *Sammlungspolitik*. A term of contemporary usage which has enjoyed a great historiographical vogue since the end of the 1960s, *Sammlungspolitik* refers to a defensive alliance of capitalists and landowners, convergent protectionist forces united by fear of foreign competition and democratic reform—'the compromise-ideology of the ruling strata of industry and agriculture, with its basis in the common . . . anti-liberal and anti-Socialist calculation', as one historian has called it.[9] Though the germs of this bloc were present earlier, its final coalescence in the late 1870s was facilitated by several key developments: the temporary resolution of the national question, the onset of the depression after 1873, and the rise of the organized working class. The Bismarckian settlement of 1878–9, with its twin pillars of protective tariffs and the Anti-Socialist Law, marked its first appearance as a firm political coalition.[10] After a slight interruption in the 1890s, when the Chancellorship of Leo von Caprivi saw a growth of tension between industrialists and agrarians, *Sammlungspolitik* was revived in the years 1897–1902 under the guidance of the Prussian Finance Minister Johannes von Miquel. The motive force was provided by a new movement for protective tariffs, stimulated by German agriculture's declining position in the world market and the erection of new

[8] Ibid., p. 181. Despite the importance given to the landed interest in the existing literature, there is still no good study of its social history to compare with F. M. L. Thompson's *English Landed Society in the Nineteenth Century* (London, 1963)—an absence which enables talk of a 'feudal aristocracy' still to persist. The best existing work still considers the landowning interest only as a political or ideological phenomenon without considering its real social character, its relation to industrial capital, and its place in rural society. The most influential works are: A. Gerschenkron, *Bread and Democracy in Germany* (2nd ed., New York, 1968); H. Rosenberg, 'Die Pseudodemokratisierung der Rittergutsbesitzerklasse', in *Probleme der deutschen Sozialgeschichte* (Frankfurt, 1969), pp. 7–150; H.-J. Puhle, *Agrarische Interessenpolitik und preußischer Konservatismus im Wilhelminischen Reich 1893–1914* (Hannover, 1966).

[9] D. Stegmann, *Die Erben Bismarcks. Parteien und Verbände in der Spätphase des Wilhelminischen Deutschlands. Sammlungspolitik 1897–1918* (Cologne, 1970), p. 13. Literally, *Sammlungspolitik* simply means 'the politics of rallying-together'.

[10] Here the key works are the following: H. Rosenberg, *Große Depression und Bismarckzeit* (Berlin, 1967); H. Böhme, *Deutschlands Weg zur Großmacht. Studien zum Verhältnis von Wirtschaft und Staat während der Reichsgründungszeit 1848–1881* (Cologne-Berlin, 1966); I. N. Lambi, *Free Trade and Protection in Germany 1868–79* (Wiesbaden, 1963); M. Stürmer, *Regierung und Reichstag im Bismarckstaat 1871–1880: Cäsarismus oder Parlamentarismus* (Düsseldorf, 1974).

tariff walls in Europe and North America. Increased unionization and the growth of the SPD strengthened the call for right-wing unity, and the elections of June 1898 gave some added impetus. The collaboration of industry and agriculture was consummated in a new high tariff settlement in 1902.[11]

Besides this basic protectionist impulse and the underlying anti-Socialist orientation, historians have tended to see a structural connection between *Sammlungspolitik* in 1897 and the proclamation of *Weltpolitik* ('world-policy') at about the same time. The government changes in the summer of 1897 produced not only a new protectionist commitment, but also a more aggressive pursuit of German interests in the world, of which the First Navy Bill and the seizure of Kiao-Chow were the main symbols. The 'social interest aggregate' of the *Sammlung*, so the argument runs, was forged from 'a sort of package-deal' in which heavy industry and agriculture received 'economic and political benefits' from each other.[12] Eckart Kehr, the most important exponent of this view, rationalized the arguments into a convenient formula: 'for industry the fleet, *Weltpolitik* and expansion, for the agrarians the tariffs and the upholding of the social supremacy of the Conservatives, and as a consequence of this social and economic compromise, for the Centre Party the political hegemony'.[13] Reinforced by the findings of several contemporaries and belatedly taken up by the recent generation, Kehr's analysis has now become conventional. The expansion of the Navy in the two Laws of 1898 and 1900 is now seen as an integral part of a system of economic and political compensations designed to bolster up the existing system of power, terminate progress towards social reform, and keep the working class in a state of subjection. The fleet allegedly gave heavy industry the incentive to join in the arrangement, provided an object for the frustrated nationalism of the German bourgeoisie, and offered a means of channelling working-class support into the parties of the right.

The most significant development of this view may be found in the work of Volker Berghahn, who sees the 'Tirpitz-Plan'—the construction of a big Navy freed of parliamentary control—as the leading instrument of *Sammlungspolitik* in 1897 and the essential key to government policy before 1914. Thus the Navy was 'the catalyst which was supposed to facilitate a *Sammlung*' between industry and agriculture, 'a vehicle for the introduction of a new period of

---

[11] See Stegmann, *Erben*, pp. 63ff., 80ff., and the same author's later essay, 'Wirtschaft und Politik nach Bismarcks Sturz. Zur Genesis der Miquelschen Sammlungspolitik 1890–1897', in Geiss and Wendt (Eds.), *Deutschland in der Weltpolitik*, pp. 161–84. See also my essay '*Sammlungspolitik*, Social Imperialism and the Navy Law of 1898', *MGM*, 15 (1974), pp. 29–63.

[12] V. R. Berghahn, *Germany and the Approach of War in 1914* (London, 1973), p. 26. The idea of the 'social interest aggregate' derives from G. W. F. Hallgarten, *Imperialismus vor 1914* (Munich, 1963), II, p. 1422.

[13] E. Kehr, *Battleship Building and Party Politics in Germany, 1894–1901* (Berlin, 1930; trans. Chicago, 1975), p. 217.

stabilization' after the uncertainties of the 1890s.[14] Tirpitz's naval policy 'was nothing less than an ambitious plan to stabilize the Prusso-German political system and paralyze the pressure for change'.[15] With the aid of Bülow and Hohenlohe he managed to impose it after 1897, it is argued, as official government policy. For Berghahn, *Sammlungspolitik* began 'at the same time with and through the construction of the fleet'.

The Navy was to act as a focus for divergent social forces which the government hoped to bribe into a conservative *Sammlung* against the "Revolution". Promises of a great economic and political future were made with the aim of maintaining the big landowners, the military and the bureaucracy in their key positions within the power structure.[16]

Hardened by usage into a dogma, this thesis has now passed into the common vocabulary of German historiography, invoked as a matter of course by monographs and general works alike.[17] It clearly depends on a particular understanding of political mobilization, in which the concept of 'manipulation' has a central place. Wedded to a functionalist notion of political integration and the operation of ideology, it is this idea which carries the burden of explaining why the bourgeoisie and the other subordinate classes allowed themselves to be assimilated so easily to the alleged aristocratic predominance.[18] The bourgeoisie accepted its junior partnership with the aristocratic élite, it is argued, partly because it backed away from confrontation with the military-bureaucratic state and partly because it feared a more radical challenge to its left, but partly also because it became integrated by ideological means. The *Kulturkampf*, anti-Socialism and war scares, it is suggested, were all examples of how Bismarck

[14] Berghahn, *Germany and the Approach of War*, p. 24, and the same author's *Der Tirpitz-Plan. Genesis und Verfall einer innenpolitischen Krisenstrategie unter Wilhelm II* (Düsseldorf, 1971), p. 157.

[15] Berghahn, *Germany and the Approach of War*, p. 29.

[16] Ibid., pp. 29f.

[17] It would obviously be fruitless to provide an exhaustive list of examples. The best illustration is probably the simple incorporation of the argument into text-books, general essays and the introductory sections of monographs: e.g. H.-U. Wehler, *Das Deutsche Kaiserreich 1871–1918* (Göttingen, 1973), pp. 100ff.; P.-C. Witt, 'Innenpolitik und Imperialismus in der Vorgeschichte des 1. Weltkrieges', in K. Holl and G. List (eds.), *Liberalismus und imperialistischer Staat* (Göttingen, 1975), pp. 7–34; D. Groh, *Negative Integration und revolutionäre Attentismus. Die deutsche Sozialdemokratie am Vorabend des Ersten Weltkrieges* (Frankfurt, 1973), pp. 81ff.; Mielke, *Hansa-Bund*, pp. 11ff.; H.-P. Ullmann, *Der Bund der Industriellen. Organisation, Einfluß und Politik klein- und mittelbetrieblicher Industrieller im Deutschen Kaiserreich 1895–1914* (Göttingen, 1976), pp. 165ff.

[18] The other major factor which requires mention, of course, is that of repression, or at least the fear of repression, whether in the form of laws against the SPD and the trade unions, or a general *Staatsstreich* or coup d'état. Evans distinguishes *four* methods of social control as outlined by recent Wilhelmine historians—repression, manipulation, diversion and negative integration—but the latter three are arguably only variations on a single theme. See Evans, 'Introduction', pp. 17–20.

employed the technique of 'secondary integration' to cement the loyalty of the bourgeoisie to a state it did not control.[19] In each of these cases a specific campaign of carefully mounted propaganda was required, but in essence the operation of the major 'socializing institutions' (e.g. the education system, the conscript army, the churches) is accorded a similar function by recent work.[20] This institutionalized 'manipulation' secured the 'stabilization of the system' in the short term, it is argued, but the artificial character of this 'secondary integration' left the Second Empire structurally prone to periodic political breakdown. The cracks in the fabric could only be papered over by a fresh diversionary emphasis on foreign affairs, and this 'social-imperialist' mechanism led to the ultimate gamble of July 1914.

Putting the above comments together, we derive a general picture of conservative stasis—a continuity of 'authoritarian and anti-democratic structures in state and society', as Karl Dietrich Bracher has put it.[21] Moreover, these structures long outlived the formal constitutional edifice of the Hohenzollern monarchy and its supports: they persisted beyond the collapse of the Empire in 1918, survived the years of revolutionary upheaval, and subverted the foundations of the Weimar Republic. In other words, the recent analysis of the Second Empire's 'mis-development' also contains an important argument about the nature and origins of German fascism. Its exponents explain the latter, it seems, by a series of long-term structural factors: 'the consequences of delayed national unification and delayed industrialization, and the effects of the absence of bourgeois revolution and parliamentarization'.[22] This stress on the survival of 'pre-industrial traditions' as the vital condition in the emergence of National Socialism as a successful political movement introduces a powerful note of structural determinism, and effectively redefines the problem of fascism as the more general problem of political backwardness.[23]

Thus in characterizing the importance of continuity between Second and Third Reich, Wehler refers to a 'long catalogue of historical handicaps' which

[19] See in particular: W. Sauer, 'Das Problem des deutschen Nationalstaats', in H.-U. Wehler (Ed.), *Moderne deutsche Sozialgeschichte* (Cologne, 1966), pp. 407–36; M. Stürmer, 'Konservatismus und Revolution in Bismarcks Politik', in Stürmer (Ed.), *Das Kaiserliche Deutschland. Politik und Gesellschaft 1870–1918* (Düsseldorf, 1970), pp. 143–67.

[20] E.g. the classic statements in Wehler, *Das Deutsche Kaiserreich*, pp. 118–31.

[21] K. D. Bracher, 'The Nazi Takeover', in *History of the 20th Century*, 48 (London, 1969), p. 1339.

[22] H.-J. Puhle, *Von der Agrarkrise zum Präfaschismus. Thesen zum Stellenwert der agrarischen Interessenverbände in der deutschen Politik am Ende des 19. Jahrhunderts* (Wiesbaden, 1972), p. 53.

[23] See esp. the contributions of Kocka and Winkler to the 1973 Bochum Symposium, H. Mommsen, D. Petzina, B. Weißbrod (Eds.), *Industrielles System und politische Entwicklung in der Weimarer Republik* (Düsseldorf, 1974): H. A. Winkler, 'Vom Protest zum Panik: Der gewerbliche Mittelstand in der Weimarer Republik' (pp. 778–91), and J. Kocka, 'Zur Problematik der deutschen Angestellten 1914–1933' (pp. 792–811); see also the discussion pp. 836ff.

burdened the Weimar Republic: 'the susceptibility to authoritarian politics; the hostility to democracy in education and party-politics; the influence of pre-industrial leadership groups, norms and ideals; the tenacity of the German ideology of the state; the mystique of the bureaucracy; the manipulation of political anti-semitism'.[24] Where exactly this leaves the definition of fascism itself is unclear, for it seems to collapse the latter entirely into a description of its origins. At any rate, Wehler argues, that in 1918 'continuity undeniably prevailed in the bureaucracy and the army, in education and the parties, in the economy and the interest-groups etc., ensured at least one thing: the traditional power-élites could hold the stirrups for Hitler'; and without the stirrups 'he could never get into the saddle'.[25]

II

The general emphases of this approach to Wilhelmine history have been salutary. Under the banner of the *Primat der Innenpolitik* ('primacy of domestic policy') recent historians have finally buried the *Primat der Außen-politik* ('primacy of foreign policy'), with its inordinate concern for the dictates of diplomacy and the logic of Germany's position in the world. The work of Fischer and his successors has decisively ruptured the old Rankean tradition of German historiography.[26] Though the problems of definition have certainly been under-estimated, the idea of social imperialism at least fixes our attention on the vital relations of economy, politics and social structure. Moreover, while misconstruing the partial subordination of the bourgeoisie and exaggerating the archaism of the Imperial Constitution, the stress on aristocratic survivals in a period of rapid industrialization—the 'deep discrepancy between the social structure and the political system', in Bracher's phrase[27]—still identifies the central contradiction of Wilhelmine politics: the persistence of a state structure which guaranteed the historic privileges of a landowning interest, at a time when the capitalist transformation of German society, the diminishing role of agriculture in the economy and the antagonism of capital and labour were all demanding an adaptation of that state to entirely novel situations.

However, as will become clear in the main body of this book, my own reading of politics under the Empire differs considerably from the view sketched

[24] Wehler, *Das Deutsche Kaiserreich*, pp. 238f.

[25] Ibid., p. 226.

[26] Wehler has been most prominent in this offensive: see his edition of Eckart Kehr's essays, *Der Primat der Innenpolitik* (Berlin, 1965). For a magisterial reply to his recent critics, see H.-U. Wehler, 'Kritik und kritische Antikritik', *HZ*, 225 (1977), pp. 347–84. For general discussions of the historiographical background, see G. Iggers, *The German Conception of History* (Middletown, 1968).

[27] K. D. Bracher, 'Kaiser Wilhelm's Germany', in *History of the 20th Century*, 5 (London, 1968), p. 119.

briefly above. In particular, the general belief that the Wilhelmine period was characterized mainly by 'the defence of inherited ruling positions by pre-industrial élites against the assault of new forces', establishing a continuity which culminated in 1933, is not without its problems.[28] It raises difficulties at both a theoretical and empirical level. Most fundamentally it contains a number of assumptions about the efficacy of 'pre-industrial traditions', the 'aristocratic' character of the dominant class and the 'feudalized' subordination of the bourgeoisie, which can only be tackled properly at a level of theory; in contrast to this historicist approach I have preferred to emphasize the specific features of the Wilhelmine conjuncture after 1890 and the new structure of politics determined by the capitalist mode of production. Though the detailed adjudication of these alternative perspectives must await another occasion, I have tried to consider them at different points in the ensuing analysis and in the Conclusion. In addition there are two further points of disagreement which deserve some prefatory explanation.

The first of these concerns the nature of political mobilization and the role of ideology. As suggested above, recent work has argued that a backward political structure (in which 'pre-industrial élites' had the dominant place) was maintained in Imperial Germany by a repertoire of manipulative interventions from above, which mobilized new popular support for the '*status quo*'. One of the strongest bearers of this mechanism is taken to be the Agrarian League, founded in 1893 under Junker leadership. Now, it is perfectly true that to maintain an effective political presence under conditions of universal suffrage aristocratic landowners needed new popular support, and that the independent peasantry west of the Elbe eventually provided it. But the nature of the political relationship this involved was quite complicated. There was no simple subordination of the peasantry determined by 'pre-industrial traditions' of deference, because the central and south German peasantries had long traditions of vigorous political independence, often with a strong radical-democratic and anti-Prussian tinge. In fact, peasants and landowners were combined into a single 'landed interest' only by a long and complex process of political struggle, which was actually initiated by the spontaneous action of the peasants themselves, under conditions set by the specific conjuncture of the 1890s.[29]

That being the case, it makes more sense to focus *not* on the authoritarian traditions of aristocratic power, but on the texture of the political relations constructed between landowners and peasants beginning in the 1890s. Moreover, it is extremely important not to approach this problem through the concept of 'manipulation'. The momentum for change—for adaptation to new conditions of popular politics—came from the widespread self-activation of the subordinate classes at the start of the 1890s, on an independent basis which seemed to

[28] Wehler, *Das Deutsche Kaiserreich*, p. 14.
[29] This theme will be taken up in the next chapter. My general understanding of rural politics owes an incalculable debt to long discussions with David Blackbourn.

threaten the 'natural' leadership of the traditional rulers in town and country. The growth of trade unions and the electoral victories of the SPD were the obvious instances of such a threat, and at the level of national politics they were decisive in setting a new pattern of political life. But in the early 1890s there was also a crucial mobilization amongst the rural population, covering most of central and south Germany, which largely pre-dated the launching of the Agrarian League. In the protectionist agitation of 1893–1902, as we know, the Junkers quickly tried to turn this popular discontent to their own advantage. But it would be wrong to see the emergence of a single 'agrarian interest' embracing both landowners and peasants as a 'manipulative' achievement of the former which simply guaranteed their power in the old form. On the contrary, it involved an arduous adaptation extending over many years, was regionally uneven, and brought the peasants real advantages.[30]

A major aim of this book is to assess the new forms of politics which emerged from encounters of this type. One of its main arguments is that the 1890s witnessed a popular challenge to the patrician forms in which public life was then constituted. The origins of this challenge were mixed: the SPD naturally, but also political Anti-Semitism in Hessen, Thuringia and Saxony, Catholic radicalism in Baden and Württemberg, the Peasants' Leagues in Bavaria, and diverse forms of rural and *Mittelstand* protest.[31] The political parties responded with varying success. As already suggested, the Conservatives eventually absorbed much of this popular material through the agency of the Agrarian League, though at the cost of being thoroughly 'agrarianized' and taken in tow by a demagogic practice not entirely to their taste. In the Centre Party the greater elasticity of Catholicism as a social ideology allowed similar antagonisms to be resolved inside the party itself, with the partial exception of Bavaria. By contrast, as we shall see, the National Liberal Party was the real casualty of

[30] The manipulative view of agrarian mobilization is most closely associated with the works of Hans-Jürgen Puhle. For useful correctives: J. C. Hunt, 'Peasants, Grain Tariffs and Meat Quotas: Imperial German Protectionism Reexamined', *CEH*, VII (1974), pp. 311–31; I. Farr, 'Populism in the Countryside: The Peasant Leagues in Bavaria in the 1890s', in Evans (Ed.), *Society and Politics*, pp. 136–59, esp. 146ff.

[31] We are still extraordinarily ignorant of the varying local context of German politics in the nineteenth century. A start may be made with the following: D. S. White, *The Splintered Party. National Liberalism in Hessen and the Reich 1867–1918* (Cambridge, Mass., 1976); K. Möckl, *Die Prinzregentenzeit. Gesellschaft und Politik während der Ära des Prinzregenten Luitpold in Bayern* (Munich, 1972); K. Simon, *Die württembergischen Demokraten: Ihre Stellung und Arbeit im Parteien- und Verfassungssystem* (Stuttgart, 1969); J. C. Hunt, *The People's Party in Württemberg and Southern Germany, 1890–1914. The Possibilities of Democratic Politics* (Stuttgart, 1975). For a study which brilliantly combines region and locality, with a keen sense for the nation as well, see David Blackbourn's forthcoming study of Württemberg politics, based on his dissertation, 'The Centre Party in Wilhelmine Germany: the Example of Württemberg' (Cambridge Ph.D., 1976). On a more modest scale: H. Büsch, *Die Stoeckerbewegung im Siegerland. Ein Beitrag zur Siegerländer Geschichte in der zweiten Hälfte des 19. Jahrhunderts* (Siegen, 1968).

this process, for it failed to effect a comparable organizational and ideological reorientation to stem the flow of its defecting rural support. Taken together these events helped erode the foundations of traditional *Honoratiorenpolitik*— i.e. the politics of notables, which could previously subsist on the natural solidarities of the squirarchy and local bourgeoisie, without the extra sustenance of an organized apparatus of popular agitation. Later on, after 1900, the radical nationalists delivered a further blow to this patrician mode by fracturing its ideological authority.

Once we set the politics of the right in this social context, it becomes clear that a simple notion of authoritarian continuity obscures far more than it explains. Moreover, the concept of manipulation is singularly inappropriate for describing the uneven transition from one mode of politics to another. Most obviously, such a term implies direction from above, in a devious managerial way, which misleads people as to their 'real' interests. Hans-Jürgen Puhle's study of the Agrarian League is a good example: its focus is the latter's national apparatus and leadership, and the League's success as a popular movement is ascribed almost entirely to 'the extraordinary integrative power of the militant new conservative-agrarian, *völkisch*-national ideology of economic harmony, with its social-darwinist, *mittelständisch* and anti-semitic strains'.[32] But there is no discussion of how that ideology was mediated, no exploration of the interior relations between leaders and led, and no understanding of the League's relation to rural society. The peasants themselves appear only as the passive objects of propaganda, responding to initiatives rather than taking them. Thus while recent work may have emancipated itself from German historiography's older preoccupation with the state in the narrower sense, it remains entrapped by the broader frame of organizational history and high politics.[33] Above all, as currently used the concept of 'manipulation' entails an extraordinarily crude view of how political mobilization occurs, how ideology is constructed, and how consciousness is formed.

My second point of difference concerns the problem of continuity. As remarked above, this has usually been linked to a particular political structure —*Sammlungspolitik* and the alliance of 'iron and rye'—which was re-consolidated during 1897–1902 by the efforts of the Prussian Finance Minister Miquel and his ally at the Imperial Office of the Interior, Arthur von Posadowsky. By using the negotiations for a new tariff settlement which began in September 1897, Miquel hoped to build both a stable governing majority in the Reichstag and a workable coalition of parties for the 1898 elections. Moreover, though the role of the naval policy adopted around the same time is more contentious, this political conception lent some unity to government policy in these years and was taken over by Bernhard von Bülow when he succeeded to the Chancellorship

[32] Puhle, *Agrarkrise*, p. 41.
[33] A similar point was brilliantly made in the important review essay, 'The Coming of the Nazis', *TLS*, Feb. 1st 1974, pp. 94f.

in 1900.[34] Yet while Miquel's policy re-convened the scattered remnants of the Bismarckian power bloc, articulated the dominant ideology of the right and provided a structure of practice for government, it also had clear limitations. In general *Sammlungspolitik* proved incapable of performing the two vital functions required of the right in the post-Bismarckian era: that of re-integrating the different fractions of the power bloc on a long-term basis after the conflicts of the Caprivi years; and that of re-establishing the power bloc's popular legitimacy.

Recent work has tended to stress the constancy of the industrial-agrarian alliance after 1897, but in a number of key areas the *Sammlung* proved badly fitted for the emerging context of political life at the turn of the century. Thus the attempt to provide an economic rallying-point through the slogans of protection showed limited returns in the party-political sphere: the so-called 'Economic Manifesto' of March 1898 had a mixed reaction and the elections in June were characterized more by the disunity of the putative right coalition.[35] Moreover, if it proved hard to devise adequate organizational forms for the co-operation of the right while the individual parties kept their separate identities, the latter were also badly lacking in popular support: the new white-collar strata remained an untapped reservoir; most successful appeals to small property-owners occurred on the margins of the established right-wing parties or in direct opposition to them (e.g. the Christian-Socials in Berlin and parts of Westphalia, Anti-Semites in Hessen, *Mittelstand* groups in Thuringia and Saxony, and in many areas the Agrarian League); and in general the 1898 *Sammlung* failed to produce an equivalent popular movement. In addition, *Sammlungspolitik* failed to accommodate the political forces generated by the adoption of an imperialist foreign policy, namely the radical nationalists. Finally, it sidestepped the major long-term issue of this period, namely how the agrarians were to be reconciled to the prospect of an urban industrial-capitalist society, where protection of landed incomes was no longer the main priority.[36]

In all of these ways the decisions of 1897 failed to create an enduring framework for right-wing politics in the rest of the Wilhelmine period. They aspired to reconstruct an older Bismarckian practice in an environment which was rapidly making it obsolete: Miquel was forced to adjust his thinking to the relatively stable conditions of a parliamentary politics which Bismarck had hoped to supersede, and the dictates of this step exposed the declining relevance of the policy in the new context. It was the very backwardness of *Sammlungs-politik*—i.e. the fact that it was tied so closely to the 'social dominance of a

[34] Unfortunately there is no space to discuss the political departures of 1897–1902 in any detail. The broad lines of my thinking may be found in Eley, '*Sammlungspolitik*, Social Imperialism and the Navy Law of 1898'.

[35] Ibid., pp. 48ff.

[36] Each of these themes is developed in detail in the main body of this book.

ruling group which was economically no longer viable', the big landowners[37]
—which ensured that the politics of the right would soon outgrow it. In that
sense it certainly structured the terms of political debate in the following years,
not by resolving contradictions as historians have tended to argue, but by
exposing them. In other words, in each of the areas mentioned above it placed
specific questions on the agenda: how to budge the agrarians from an intransigent defence of all their positions; how to assimilate the forces generated by
support for imperialism; how to find a new framework for rallying the forces of
the right; how to mobilize new sources of popular support; and finally, how to
operate under conditions of open competition in a parliamentary framework.

Thus in seizing on concepts like social imperialism, secondary integration,
Sammlungspolitik and the like, recent historians have tended to sacrifice
interpretative caution to the pursuit of an overall thematic unity. It is now
commonly accepted that there was little room for political movement within
the Wilhelmine political system—that the parties were incapable of outgrowing
'the traditional framework of order', and that 'from the 1860s until 1929' they
'remained bound to their original communities of sentiment and their inaugural
conflicts', as Wehler has put it.[38] In this view the supposed absence of bourgeois
revolution between the 1840s and 1870s had frozen political life in a 'pre-
industrial' authoritarian mould and the chances of a genuine 'modernization'
of the state were already foreclosed. Yet so far from revealing a static and
inward-looking continuity, the history of the parties between the 1860s and
1929 reveals a far-reaching process of decomposition and regroupment, with
an initial phase centring on the 1890s and a later more protracted one beginning
after 1909. In each of these two phases the bourgeois parties were reconstituted
in a radically different relationship with a vital popular constituency, first with
the peasantry and then with the petty-bourgeoisie.

At the same time, of course, the forms of public life underwent some dramatic
transformations, with an expanding electorate, new technologies of propaganda
and communication and new levels of organization. Thus, by stressing stability
and the unchanging constancy of conservative attitudes, previous work has
tended to obscure the structural changes in the right—radical discontinuities
of ideology and practice—which endowed some of the possibilities for a German
fascism. It delivers an over-simplified view of linear continuity between the
Second and Third Reichs which skates over all the interesting problems of the
transition from one kind of right-wing politics to another. Part of my aim is to
recover some of these lost complexities by considering the dynamics of political
change. This study seeks to reinstate the importance of change across time,
not as a linear progression, but through the resolution of problems in an un-

---

[37] Kehr, *Battleship Building*, p. 278.
[38] See Wehler, *Das Deutsche Kaiserreich*, p. 80. The idea originates with M. Rainer Lepsius,
'Parteiensystem und Sozialstruktur: Zum Problem der Demokratisierung der deutschen
Gesellschaft', in G. A. Ritter (Ed.). *Deutsche Parteien vor 1914* (Cologne, 1973), pp. 56–80.

predictable succession of conjunctures. Above all, it is concerned with those movements of political change generated inside Wilhelmine society itself.

III

This study explores these general problems—the position of big landed property in the structure of the Wilhelmine state, the texture of political relations between dominant and subordinate classes, the forms and extent of continuity between 'Bismarck and Hitler'—by analysing the particular phenomenon of the nationalist pressure groups. My aim is not to provide formal organizational histories of the individual groups or a blow-by-blow narrative account of their development, for in some ways this need is already covered by a relatively extensive secondary literature.[39] Instead, my concern is to use these specific histories to clarify the larger political relationships in which they were situated. Consequently, the form of the enquiry is conceived as a series of structural analyses, located in an overall perspective of change between the 1890s and 1913–14, through which the political contribution of the nationalist pressure groups may be assessed: the conditions of their formation in the 1890s, their internal social relations, the character of their ideology, their mode of political practice, and the internal dynamic of their development.

By using the *nationale Verbände* to shed light on more general problems I have tried to avoid exaggerating their contribution. At the very least they have a vital symptomatic importance; without necessarily being consciously about the problems of a viable right-wing politics at all times, their activities can none the less tell us a great deal about how the latter were posed. In other words, what the nationalist pressure groups were doing reveals much about what the existing

[39] The best introduction to the *nationale Verbände* is through the appropriate articles in D. Fricke (Ed.), *Die Bürgerlichen Parteien in Deutschland*, 2 vols. (Leipzig, 1968–70), esp. the following: A. Wulf, 'Deutscher Flottenverein 1898–1934', I, pp. 432–49; H. Müller and H.-J. Fieber, 'Deutsche Kolonialgesellschaft 1882 (1887)–1933', I, pp. 390–407; F.-H. Gentzen, 'Deutscher Ostmarkenverein 1894–1935', I, pp. 502–12; G. Haude and K. Possekel, 'Verein für das Deutschtum im Auslande 1881–1945', II, pp. 716–29. Otherwise see the following: M. Wertheimer, *The Pan-German League, 1890–1914* (New York, 1924); A. Kruck, *Geschichte des Alldeutschen Verbandes 1890–1939* (Wiesbaden, 1954); E. Hartwig, *Zur Politik und Entwicklung des Alldeutschen Verbandes von seiner Gründung bis zum Beginn des Ersten Weltkrieges 1891–1914* (Jena, 1966); K. Schilling, *Beiträge zu einer Geschichte des radikalen Nationalismus in der wilhelminischen Ära 1890–1909* (Diss. Cologne, 1967); R. Pierard, 'The German Colonial Society 1882–1914' (Ph. D. Thesis, Iowa, 1964); R. W. Tims, *Germanizing Prussian Poland. The H-K-T Society and the Struggle for the Eastern Marches in the German Empire 1894–1919* (New York, 1941); A. Galos, F.-H. Gentzen, W. Jacobczyk, *Die Hakatisten. Der Deutsche Ostmarkenverein 1894–1934* (Berlin, 1966); K. Klauß, *Die Deutsche Kolonialgesellschaft und die deutsche Kolonialpolitik von den Anfängen bis 1895* (Diss. Berlin, 1966); H. Pogge von Strandmann, 'The Kolonialrat, its Significance and Influence on German Politics from 1890 to 1906' (D.Phil. Thesis, Oxford, 1970); G. H. Eley, 'The German Navy League in German Politics 1890–1914' (D.Phil. Thesis, Sussex, 1974).

right-wing parties were not. The most self-conscious exponents of an independent radical nationalism directly addressed a series of problems for which the party-political right had no answer at the turn of the century: the special position of the Junkers, the domestic importance of empire, the forms of anti-Socialist unity, the need for a new popular politics, and the constraints of universal suffrage. In so doing—but by a protracted and complex process—they provided an impetus for important changes, whereby the right adjusted unevenly to the changing conditions of political life. In this way the *nationale Verbände* were constituted by a field of tension with the ideology and practice of the old right. They simultaneously reproduced the contradictions of existing right politics and contributed constructively to their uneven resolution.

In the following pages the particular analysis of the nationalist pressure groups is intentionally located in a much wider discussion of Wilhelmine politics and society. This contextual analysis is necessarily stronger at the outset and the conclusion, but as far as possible I have tried to maintain the commitment throughout the book. Somewhat against the grain of much Wilhelmine historiography, I have conceived the post-Bismarckian period—inaugurated by processes of accelerated capitalist development, the end of the depression and the passage to imperialism—as one of far-reaching political change, in which the entire structure of the public domain was re-ordered. The particular history of the nationalist pressure groups only makes sense in this context of change: namely, the decomposition of one structure of politics, and its gradual, uneven replacement by another. I have tried to present this as a long-term crisis of *Honoratiorenpolitik* (the 'politics of notables'), in which the latter is understood not just as a particular form of social oligarchy or the rule of some 'pre-industrial élite', but as a relationship, a field of political and ideological relations between dominant and subordinate classes. That crisis contained a direct threat to the continued viability of *Sammlungspolitik* as a strategy of government, for this was strongly rooted in exactly the same structure of politics. Moreover, in the end the effects of the crisis ran much deeper, to the very foundations of the Wilhelmine state. This concentric progression of the analysis—from the *nationale Verbände* to the crisis of *Honoratiorenpolitik*, to the limitations of the Bismarckian alliance of 'iron and rye', and finally to the structure of the Wilhelmine state—is crucial to the organization of the argument.

This study contains other important arguments—e.g. concerning the character of German liberalism, the forms of a 'modern' popular politics, the analysis of nationalist ideology, and so on—but its main commitment is to an understanding of the German right and its changing relationship to the Wilhelmine state. Its underlying focus is a long-term structural problem of that state, created by the declining position of the landowning class and its diminishing ability to control the government. This posed new problems for the right at a time when the new class relations of capital and labour were also imposing pressures of a very different kind. This was the crucial particularity of the Wilhelmine conjuncture, in which the politics of the bourgeoisie were constituted from a double contradiction—hostility to the independent politics of the Social Democratic working class, but also a growing impatience with the remaining aristocratic survivals of the Prusso-German monarchy. This particularity clearly formed the character of German liberalism, and set definite limits to the chances of a decisive reforming departure before 1914. But it also provided the ultimate context of the nationalist pressure groups, and in the final analysis determined the surprising radicalism of their ideology.

PART I

2. *Honoratiorenpolitik* and the Crisis of National Liberalism

I

The 1890s witnessed a general decomposition of the Bismarckian system. By this is meant not just the dismissal of the great man, the break-up of the Cartel, and the unstable eclecticism of the new course, but a general rearrangement of political life. The 1890s were a vital decade of political flux, in which one pattern of politics began to be replaced by another. The important feature of the change was this: between the 1860s and the end of the 1880s the dominant fraction in the Bismarckian power bloc had been *liberal*—even after 1879 national politics had still been structured by the parliamentary strength of the various liberal groupings—but by the start of the 1890s this liberal predominance was already starting to decompose, and by 1900 it was in fragments. In 1887—the last elections in which the National Liberals recovered something like their former strength of the 1870s before sinking in subsequent elections to a fairly even plateau of some fifty seats[1]—the party possessed a continuous belt of seats stretching from Baden in the south-west through the Palatinate, Prussian and Grand Ducal Hessen, Prussian Saxony and Hannover, flanked by Thuringia and Saxony, and culminating in Schleswig-Holstein in the north. By 1898 that predominance had fragmented, with the permanent loss of some forty seats. The 1890s saw a similar crisis in the regions: as White observes, 'After 1896, when the Hessian National Liberals lost their broad margin in the second chamber, no regional liberal party in south Germany exclusively controlled its state legislature'.[2]

It is vital to stress that in electoral terms the National Liberal predominance was rural as much as it was urban. The National Liberals had come to power at the end of the 1860s as the leaders of popular regional coalitions against aristocracy and reaction: this applies to Prussian Hessen and Hannover as well

[1] In the first elections under the Empire the National Liberals won 125 of the 382 seats, rising in 1874 to 155 out of 397 or 39% of the total. Under the pressure of the protectionist and anti-Socialist agitation their representation declined to 128 in 1877 and 99 in 1878, and by 1884 the rather confused alignments amongst the liberal groupings as a whole left the National Liberals with only 51 seats. The National Liberal share of the vote fell from its peak of 29·7% in 1874 to 12·9% in 1884. After 1887 (99 seats, 22·3% of the vote), the party averaged at 48 seats and 13·7% of the popular vote.

[2] White, *Splintered Party*, p. 151.

as to the more obvious cases of Bavaria, Württemberg and—pre-eminently—
Baden.[3] In Hessen they were the beneficiaries of unification in 1870-1, which
swept the liberals to office with forty-one of the fifty seats in the election of
1872.[4] There resulted a close symbiosis, which was characteristic of the
regions just mentioned, between liberal *Honoratioren* (or notables) and state
officials, in which the social primacy of the former was given institutional shape
in the dispatch of administrative functions through the provincial commissions,
district committees, school boards, chambers of commerce, agricultural
associations, and so on. Discriminatory property franchises, both for the Landtag and for the provincial and district assemblies, were enough to add some
extra legal security to the 'natural' leadership of this liberal oligarchy. Ideologically the coalition was cemented by the *Kulturkampf*, which was fundamental
in consolidating its popular legitimacy during the 1870s.[5] In the towns it all
went together with a flourishing social milieu, where inter-marriage, kinship
networks, business contacts, associations from school and university, religious
observance, philanthropy, cultural events and the social arena of the club
combined to keep the mechanisms of influence well oiled.[6] Though present in
the countryside, these associations could not be as effective there, and here the
liberal predominance rested far more on the initiative of a handful of leading
personalities. The Oberhessian village of Lindheim provides a good example.
Like most villages in the Wetterau it was dominated by the estate of an absentee
noble, whose lessee the National Liberal Richard Westernacher was the largest
farmer in the community. Westernacher, who took over the lease from his

[3] For this social formation of National Liberalism in the struggles of the 1860s and 1870s:
H. Schwab, *Aufstieg und Niedergang der Nationalliberalen Partei. Zur Geschichte in Deutschland
1864-1880*, Habil.schrift (Jena, 1968), M. Gugel, *Industrieller Aufstieg und bürgerliche
Herrschaft. Sozioökonomische Interessen und politische Ziele des liberalen Bürgertums in Preußen
zur Zeit des Verfassungskonflikts 1857-1867* (Cologne, 1975); L. Gall, 'Liberalismus und
"bürgerliche Gesellschaft". Zur Charakter und Entwicklung der liberalen Bewegung in
Deutschland', in *HZ*, 220 (1975), pp. 324-56; G. Schmidt, 'Die Nationalliberalen—eine
regierungsfähige Partei? Zur Problematik der inneren Reichsgründung 1870-1878', in
G. A. Ritter (Ed.), *Deutsche Parteien*, pp. 208-23.

[4] White, *Splintered Party*, pp. 23-35.

[5] This point is also made by Schmidt, 'Die Nationalliberalen—eine regierungsfähige
Partei?', p. 120. See L. Gall, 'Die partei- und sozialgeschichtliche Problematik des badischen
Kulturkampfes', in *Zeitschrift für die Geschichte des Oberrheins*, 113 (1965), pp. 151-96;
U. Tal, *Christians and Jews in Germany. Religion, Politics and Ideology in the Second Reich,
1870-1914* (Ithaca and London, 1975), pp. 81-120.

[6] Some detailed social-historical studies of local associational life in late 19th-century Ger-
many are badly needed. At present there are two important general essays but little else:
T. Nipperdey, 'Verein als soziale Struktur in Deutschland im späten 18. und frühen 19.
Jahrhundert, in *Gesellschaft, Kultur, Theorie. Gesammelte Aufsätze zur neueren Geschichte*
(Göttingen, 1976), pp. 176-205; O. Dann, 'Die Anfänge politischer Vereinsbildung in
Deutschland', in U. Engelhardt, Volker Sellin, Horst Stuke (Eds.), *Soziale Bewegung und
politische Verfassung* (Stuttgart, 1976), pp. 197-232. See also H. Freudenthal, *Vereine im
Hamburg* (Hamburg, 1968).

father in 1872, was a veteran Landtag deputy and ran unsuccessfully for the Reichstag in Hoechst-Homburg in 1893. As village notable he was joined by the owner of the old castle Major Kuno von Arnim, the priest Möller, the innkeeper Voß, and several of the better-off peasants.[7]

In destroying the *dominance* of the National Liberals in German politics, the collapse of this historic rural constituency was far more important than the SPD's gains in the towns.[8] In this sense the major solvent of the existing political alignments in the 1890s was an unprecedented agrarian radicalism, which could already be detected in 1890, but which is normally associated with the foundation of the Agrarian League in 1893. In fact, this agrarian mobilization was initiated not by the classic Junker grievances—hostility to Caprivi's commercial treaties or the threat of lower tariffs—but by the distinctive long-term problems of the smaller farmer, and above all by indebtedness and its sources, rural depopulation, the erosion of ancillary enterprises like brewing and rural crafts, and the apparent cultural bias of government in favour of the towns. In 1891-2 these were exacerbated by the disastrous foot-and-mouth epidemic, of which the smaller farmer bore the brunt, and the severe drought of 1893 helped maintain a continuity of crisis. The threat of higher taxes from the Army Bill also added to peasant grievances. Moreover, the activation of the peasantry occurred not only at a time of quickening social change, but also when the institutional consolidation of the rural class structure was ensuring that the peasantry bore most of the costs and few of the gains. Small producers had little hope of sharing the potential benefits of a growing economy without the benevolent intervention of the state in the form of tax-relief, cheaper credit or the construction of railway branch-lines. But the new consultative arrangements between government and the organized interests, let alone the larger power structures of which they were a part, normally excluded such people.[9]

---

[7] See K. E. Demandt, 'Leopold von Sacher-Masoch und sein Oberhessischer Volksbildungsverein zwischen Schwarzen, Roten und Antisemiten', in *Hessisches Jahrbuch für Landesgeschichte*, 18 (1968), pp. 180-4.

[8] This is naturally not to deny that the National Liberals were formed primarily in the cultural image of the urban bourgeoisie. But to achieve the necessary electoral resonance and to consolidate their social primacy the support of the countryside was essential. See the remarks in A. Rosenberg, *Imperial Germany. The Birth of the German Republic 1871-1918* (New York, 1970), pp. 28f. (note 2).

[9] On the general situation of the peasantry, see S. Dillwitz, 'Die Struktur der Bauernschaft von 1871 bis 1914. Dargestellt auf der Grundlage der deutschen Reichsstatistik', in *Jahrbuch für Geschichte*, 9 (1973), pp. 47-127. The most sensitive discussions of peasant politics are in three essays by D. G. Blackbourn: 'The *Mittelstand* in German Society and Politics', in *SH*, 4 (1977), pp. 420, 426ff.; 'The Political Alignment of the Centre', in *HJ*, XVIII, 4 (1975), pp. 831-42; 'Class and Politics in Wilhelmine Germany', in *CEH*, IX, 3 (1976), pp. 233-7. For the specific problem of the agricultural associations: Puhle, *Agrarkrise*, pp. 21-8; White, *Splintered Party*, pp. 40, 141f.; G. Frfr. von Schrötter, 'Agrarorganisation und sozialer Wandel (dargestellt am Beispiel Schleswig-Holsteins)', in W. Rüegg and O. Neuloh (Eds.), *Zur soziologischen Theorie und Analyse des 19. Jahrhunderts* (Göttingen, 1971), pp. 123-44.

For this reason peasant protests normally took the form of an anti-plutocratic populism, in which the nobleman, the priest, the big city, the educated gentleman and an unfeeling distant government were all increasingly conflated into a single image of oppression. Invariably this was also accompanied by a symbolic demonization of the Jew as the immediate agent of financial exploitation, and anti-semitism was a dominant motif in the rhetoric of peasant radicalism. The scenario of peasant unrest these factors produced was common to most of central and southern Germany, with slighter traces in the rest of the country. The exact forms varied, from political Anti-Semitism in Hessen to independent peasant radicalism in parts of Bavaria and a redeployed social Catholicism in Baden. In Württemberg the launching of an independent Centre Party coincided with the climax of traditional radical democracy in the shape of the People's Party, and both seem to have taken much of their popular impetus from rural aspirations. In each of these cases National Liberalism (or its regional equivalents) was the main object of party-political hostilities, though in Bavaria the Centre also came in for its fair share.[10] In general this amounted to a spontaneous self-activation of rural voters beyond the frontier of party-political control, in ways which threatened to destroy the hold of existing parties on their traditional support.

The radicalism of the challenge to the established parties derived not just from its social and ideological character—the parallel movements of rural populism and urban Social Democracy, fleetingly correspondent in their hostility to artistocracy, militarism and reaction—but also from the popular mode of its organization. A new style of politics was being inaugurated. This can be gauged generally from the expansion of the electorate, rising rates of participation, the intensity of electioneering, growing numbers of second ballots, the increasing costs of campaigning and so on.[11] In particular the hustings were a novel experience in most though by no means all constituencies. Georg von Hertling drew a sharp contrast between his uneventful return for a Rhineland constituency in the 1880s and the intensive village campaigning needed in his new Bavarian seat in 1896.[12] In the first two decades of the Empire constituency politics were conducted by small groups of big notables, who were bound together more by social prestige than by any organized party

---

[10] For Hessen: R. Mack, 'Otto Böckel und die antisemitische Bauernbewegung in Hessen 1887–1894', in *Wetterauer Geschichtsblätter*, 16 (1967), pp. 113–47; White, *Splintered Party*, pp. 134–48. Bavaria: Farr, 'Populism in the Countryside'; Möckl, *Prinzregentenzeit*, esp. pp. 446ff. Baden: C. H. E. Zangerl, 'Courting the Catholic Vote: The Centre Party in Baden, 1903–13', in *CEH*. X, 3 (1977), pp. 220–40. Württemberg: Blackbourn, 'The Political Alignment of the Centre'; J. C. Hunt, 'The "Egalitarianism" of the Right'.

[11] The most important general study is T. Nipperdey, *Die Organisation der deutschen Parteien vor 1918* (Düsseldorf, 1961). But see also H. Fenske, *Wahlrecht und Parteiensystem. Ein Beitrag zur deutschen Parteiengeschichte* (Frankfurt, 1972), pp. 106–47.

[12] G. von Hertling, *Erinnerungen aus meinen Leben*, 2 vols. (Munich, 1919–20), II, p. 176 (cit. Blackbourn, '*Mittelstand*', p. 428).

contact, who met only a few weeks before the poll to choose a candidate, and who rarely bothered with any serious campaigning. The absence of any organized context for a local political life was a counterpart to the post-unification National Liberal hegemony. Thus when Gerson von Bleichröder was briefly nominated in the constituency of Brunswick in 1878, he scarcely even bothered to visit the place and announced that he would be making no speeches as the strain would be too great. This Olympian detachment from the vulgarities of electioneering would have been far less feasible by the 1890s, when winning a seat normally entailed 'working' a constituency well in advance.[13]

Otto Böckel's victory in Marburg in 1887 was the classic case in which the old politics collided head on with the new. Here a small clique of leading personalities had previously managed the entire election campaign without a major rally, and Böckel's opponent now proceeded as before, appearing three weeks before the poll 'to address influential merchants, teachers and professionals' behind closed doors.[14] Meanwhile Böckel was stumping the villages instead, achieved maximum visibility amongst the peasants, and carried the seat on a much higher poll. More significantly, he maintained the momentum of his movement and in the ensuing years injected it with a sense of corporate identity and *élan*, which at the time could be found in few areas other than in the SPD. There was a conscious attempt to re-appropriate the iconography of 1848, and by presenting himself as a colourful 'man of the people' Böckel was making a play not only for the local peasantry's democratic populism but also for its Hessian patriotism. The institutional sinews of the movement were provided by the Central German Peasants' Union and its auxiliaries, but Böckel's tireless agitational drive was the real key to his success. In the first four months of 1890 he held a total of over sixty rallies. Style was crucial. His progress was accompanied by 'marching-bands' or 'torchlight processions which marched from village to village singing Lutheran hymns and patriotic songs. Mounted peasant youths guarded his wagon while hosts of followers, all wearing the blue cornflower as an identifying party badge, trailed along behind.' Politics here were popular and celebratory, and cannot be interpreted outside their specific local context.[15]

Nor can they be regarded as 'manipulative' in origin. The popular origins of this rural radicalism become clearer if we recognize that the SPD was also making considerable gains in the countryside during the 1890s. By 1898 the SPD took 26·5% of its total vote from small communities of less than 2,000 people, or some 15% of the votes cast there. Clearly many of these were in

[13] F. Stern, *Gold and Iron. Bismarck, Bleichröder and the Building of the German Empire* (London, 1977), p. 199.

[14] R. S. Levy, *The Downfall of the Anti-Semitic Political Parties in Imperial Germany* (New Haven, 1975), pp. 55f.; H. von Gerlach, *Von rechts nach links. Erinnerungen eines Junkers* (Zurich, 1937). p. 59.

[15] Levy, *Downfall*, p. 56.

industrial Thuringia and Saxony or the hinterlands of the great urban strongholds such as Hamburg, Berlin, Nuremberg or Königsberg. But this should not
obscure a marked success in the rural areas proper. By 1898 the SPD was 'not
only the strongest party of the town, but also the third strongest party in the
village'.[16] This was especially striking in two types of area with little developed
industry: in Mecklenburg and the province of East Prussia where big-estate
agriculture predominated, and in peasant areas like Hessen, central Württemberg and the northern Palatinate. The entry of the SPD into parish-pump
politics could often be dramatic in its disruption of old solidarities. Thus in
1888 in Lindheim, the Oberhessian village mentioned above, a left candidate
contested the re-election of the local mayor, who had normally been presented
as a matter of course by Westernacher and the other National Liberal notables;
the left victory split the village down the middle, leading to breakaways in the
choir and the savings-bank, two camps in the church and open feuding.[17]
National Liberals might be forgiven for conflating the problem of the SPD
with that of the Anti-Semites, for they were both associated with overturning
the comfortable certainties of local politics. By 1898 the SPD had entered the
run-offs in three of the six Hessian rural constituencies, and these were precisely
the centres of Anti-Semitic advance: in Giessen the SPD vote rose from 19%
to 33%, in Friedberg-Büdingen from 17% to 34%, and in Bensheim-Erbach
from 11% to 27%. In 1887 the National Liberals had won all three of these
seats on the first ballot, yet they were now reduced to 30%, 35% and 44%
respectively. In Hessen as a whole the National Liberal share of the poll fell
from 42% to 31% between 1893 and 1898, while the SPD's climbed from
22% to 35%.[18]

II

The abolition of the Anti-Socialist Law in 1890 challenged the adaptability
of the bourgeois parties, for as the SPD expanded its range of public activities
it became increasingly dangerous to take the old mechanisms of political
conformity for granted. The problem was least urgent—and the dominant
party least capable of an enterprising response—in the Conservative strongholds
east of the Elbe. When the SPD issued the slogan 'Out into the Countryside!'
in October 1890, one Conservative statement retorted that 'If the enemy comes
we want to meet him with fist and flail, in the good old German way', and this

---

[16] H. Hesselbarth, *Revolutionäre Sozialdemokraten, Opportunisten und die Bauern am
Vorabend des Imperialismus* (Berlin, 1968), pp. 247f. See also: H. G. Lehmann, *Die Agrarfrage
in der Theorie und Praxis der deutschen und internationalen Sozialdemokratie* (Tübingen, 1967).

[17] Demandt, 'Leopold von Sacher-Masoch', p. 182.

[18] For a detailed breakdown of the SPD's performance in rural constituences, see Hesselbarth, *Revolutionäre Sozialdemokraten*, pp. 241–50. See also K. Saul, 'Der Kampf gegen das
Landproletariat', in *AfS*, XV (1975), pp. 167–77.

blunt refusal to acknowledge the SPD's rights of access to the rural people continued to distinguish Junker attitudes in the coming years.[19] It was underpinned by a distinctive set of class relations. On the one hand, the Junkers still wielded enormous social power, secured not only by the economic subordination of an agricultural proletariat, but also by the legal transmutation of old seigneurial jurisdictions. Despite the local government reforms of 1872 and later, the productive unit of the estate still formed the unit of local administration, and the owner or his henchman was still self-selecting as the local mayor. As such he controlled the lives of the inhabitants not just as an employer, but also through the essential governmental functions, including police powers, taxation, welfare and education. In 1910 masses of people were still subject to this mode of domination in the seven eastern provinces, ranging from 5·3% in Saxony to 28·1% in Posen and a remarkable 35·8% in Pomerania.[20] But the corollary was an ideological resistance to properly political activity: so long as an administrative closure of the discourse was available —through police harassment of SPD organizers, seizures of propaganda, denial of rooms for meetings—Conservatives turned to an agitational activity of their own with extreme reluctance. As one official statement put it, the latter would destroy the 'entire political outlook of the common man', for instead of being 'smashed down with a firm blow' the revolution would be given 'friendly encouragement' once the natural rulers started taking it seriously as a political rival.[21]

The commonest form of Conservative initiative at this early stage were the so-called 'Protection Societies', combinations of agricultural employers in the guise of paternalist welfare agencies. Though a general propaganda intent was also announced, they were mainly concerned with the labour shortage and the openings this created for job-changing and wage-bargaining amongst the agricultural workers: much of the discussion aimed at devising a new form of the master-and-servant laws. The first to be founded was the 'League for the Improvement of Rural Labour Relations' in provincial Saxony in early 1891. But though others followed in Posen and Schleswig-Holstein, efforts in Brandenburg, Silesia, Pomerania and royal Saxony produced little tangible result. There were no traditions of association. Even the Agricultural Associations—service agencies for the larger landowner—were poorly developed in the east. Only 8·6% of farmers with over 5 hectares of land were members of the East-Prussian Association, 17·8% in Pomerania, 20·7% in Brandenburg and

---

[19] Ibid., pp. 190f.

[20] Full details from ibid., pp. 180f. See also R. M. Berdahl, 'Conservative Politics and Aristocratic Landholders in Bismarckian Germany', in *JMH*, 44 (1972), pp. 1–20. In one East Prussian *Kreistag*, 163 estate-owners controlled 163 votes, a city of 10,000 had one vote and 62,000 peasants 3 votes (H. Heffter, *Die deutsche Selbstverwaltung im 19. Jahrhundert*, Stuttgart, 1950, p. 131).

[21] *Conservative Correspondenz*, cit. Saul, 'Kampf', p. 177.

24·1% in Silesia, whereas the figures further west were much higher—36·4% in Saxony, 47·3% in Schleswig-Holstein, 51·7% in Hannover.[22] It was no accident that the most successful Protection Society was that for the province of Saxony, where the East-Elbian pattern of transmuted seigneurial authority was least extensive and industry was closest. By 1893 the Agrarian League was subsuming these efforts. Several of its leaders had been active in the infant Protection Societies. Ruprecht-Ransern, whose manifesto in December 1892 spoke of going down amongst the Socialists to fight for agrarian interests, was prominent in the Silesian League for the Improvement of Rural Labour Relations; Gustav Roesicke was involved in the Brandenburg equivalent; Heinrich Suchsland, the Agrarian League's first Director, had been highly active in 1891–2 as the Saxon Protection Society's organizing Secretary.[23]

After 1893 the administrative protection of the rural proletariat against the SPD—which was achieved more by sealing it off in cultural quarantine than by active political agitation—fell increasingly to the Agrarian League. It was clearly fairly successful in the eastern backwaters, because in 1898 the meagre SPD vote in West Prussia, Posen and Pomerania sank even further. But this victory was deeply inscribed in the economic and social relations of big-estate agriculture and owed little to imaginative political intervention. In the Catholic agricultural regions, on the other hand, where the SPD vote also slumped in 1898 from its already modest 1893 totals, the anti-Socialist counter-attack was far more of a creative political achievement: in Baden, Württemberg and Bavaria (and to some extent in Rhineland–Westphalia) the Centre Party was faced not with a subordinated class of landless labourers, but with a vigorous independent peasantry. When it began expanding its organization in the early 1890s, therefore, the Centre was partly responding to a new volatility in the southern countryside, where agrarian self-interest conjoined with traditions of parish-pump radicalism to produce a far more complex political formation than in the Prussian east. But the development of an elaborate Catholic sub-culture of party, trade union, self-help and cultural agencies was also partly the conscious achievement of the leadership. The Centre managed far more rapidly than any other bourgeois party to reconstitute itself for full-scale competition with the SPD after 1890. The old guard hankered for a new Anti-Socialist Law. But the coming generation around Ernst Lieber appreciated the need to fight the Socialists on their own ground. The construction of the People's League for a Catholic Germany in autumn 1890 on broad ideological foundations (rather than narrow confessional ones, as some older voices had wished), the parliamentary opposition to fresh exceptional laws, and the gradual move towards Christian trade unionism were all symptoms of this trend. As the Hessian leader Philipp Wasserburg, a self-styled 'clerico-democrat', put

[22] A. Backhaus, *Agrarstatistische Untersuchungen über den preußischen Osten im Vergleich zum Westen* (Berlin, 1898), pp. 277ff.
[23] See Saul, 'Kampf', pp. 220ff.

it when opposing the 'Revolution Bill' in 1895: 'Police and Church are for once irreconcilable opposites'.[24] It was no accident that, when the government finally opted for stable co-operation with the Centre in summer 1897, it was simultaneously abandoning its lingering flirtation with a *coup d'état*.

The National Liberals were by comparison far less adaptable. They failed to emulate the Conservatives and Centre by going on to the offensive as a national and regional party. Where the latter were busily constructing an organizational apparatus for moderating the rugged independence of the new agrarian movements, the National Liberal Party failed to generate a comparable response. Both the Conservatives and the Centre reconstituted themselves in a new representative relationship to old rural constituencies; ideologically this involved a far-reaching process of innovation, through which a diverse movement of rural discontent was gradually rationalized into a single 'agrarian interest' and the *Mittelstand* simultaneously constructed as an object of right-wing attentions. But not only did the National Liberals fail to create new popular organizations for recovering lost ground in rural areas; they also formed a dangerous alliance with the newly founded Agrarian League, which certainly brought short-term advantages in the 1893 elections, but which simultaneously gave a hostage to fortune. When the Agrarian League sank roots in Hannover and Hessen during spring 1893, for instance, it turned naturally to National Liberal farmers: almost without exception the leaders were prominent liberal notables and the League's local structures enmeshed neatly with those of the Agricultural Associations.[25]

The contrast with the Centre is revealing. The problems confronting the National Liberals in Hannover, Hessen and the Palatinate were much the same as those of the Centre in Bavaria and the south-west. Both were faced with a new kind of popular activity in rural areas which outgrew the conventional framework of *Honoratiorenpolitik* and demanded innovation. Both were also anxious to defend their existing character as parties of disinterested principle, 'reconciling and harmonizing the opposed economic aspirations in our midst', as one National Liberal put it.[26] But whereas the Centre maintained its own integrity as a party, the National Liberals in effect sub-contracted with a potentially hostile independent partner—the Agrarian League—with its own national apparatus and a special relationship to another party, the Conservatives. This was an absolutely crucial turning-point; rather than adapting their own organization, the National Liberals had vacated vital political space to an

---

[24] H. Gottwald, *Zentrum und Imperialismus* (Diss. Jena, 1966), pp. 96f.

[25] See for instance: White, *Splintered Party*, pp. 143f.; Hunt, ' "Egalitarianism" of the Right', pp. 515ff. In 1893 seven of the nine National Liberal candidates in Hessen during the Reichstag elections were endorsed by the Agrarian League, and the other two were broadly sympathetic.

[26] Arthur Hobrecht in June 1897, quoted in L. F. Seyffardt, *Erinnerungen* (Leipzig, 1900), p. 595.

agrarian movement which would eventually strike out on its own in decidedly *non-liberal* directions. In some ways the ability of the Agrarian League to insert itself politically *between* the National Liberal Party and its historic rural constituency was the most significant development of the 1890s. Arguably the impact of the League was far greater here, in the central belt from Hannover down to Württemberg, than ever it was east of the Elbe. In the east it merely serviced an existing system of neo-seigneurial domination; in the other areas it delivered new allies into the Conservative camp and fractured the political confidence of the National Liberals.

To illustrate the National Liberal predicament, it is worth looking again at Lindheim. In small villages like this, with only a few hundred people, the liberals' prestige needed little organization beyond the usual savings-club for the smaller farmers. A more elaborate initiative followed two normal courses. One was the arbitrary presence of a particularly vigorous philanthropist such as Leopold von Sacher-Masoch, who arrived in Lindheim in 1887 and launched his short-lived 'Oberhessian League for Popular Education' in January 1893.[27] But this kind of activity died down almost as quickly as it began. More commonly the notables were stirred into action by the intrusion of an unwelcome competitor, whether Anti-Semite, Socialist or some other kind of radical. Thus the bitter village election for the Lindheim mayor in 1888 was followed the next year by the establishment of a farming school for girls under the auspices of the Oberhessian Agricultural Association and inspired directly by Richard Westernacher. Similarly, when the Agrarian League was launched in the province in 1893 it was no surprise to find Westernacher on its committee together with other leading National Liberal farmers.[28] In these circumstances National Liberal activity had a natural agrarian direction once challenged for traditional village support. Badly in need of a local apparatus to fight the Anti-Semites and SPD, it was scarcely surprising that the National Liberals welcomed the sudden appearance of the Agrarian League.

By using the League's resources National Liberals in both Hessen and Hannover (in the latter with far more difficulty) managed to arrest the electoral decline: between 1898 and 1903 the total liberal vote in these areas rose from 31·9% to 35·5% and from 27·3% to 29·2% respectively. But in the towns, where the threat came from the SPD, the needs were rather different, and there was no urban equivalent of the Agrarian League to do the work of organization. In Darmstadt the National Liberal vote plummeted disastrously from 49·3% in 1893 to only 32·7% in 1898, whilst that of the SPD rose from 31% to 45·4%. By 1898 each of the three big urban constituencies in Baden—Pforzheim, Mannheim and Karlsruhe—had fallen to the SPD. Moreover, National Liberal problems were compounded in south-west Germany by a notable invigoration of the local Centre Parties. In Hessen the latter polled 10·4% in 1893, but

[27] Demandt, 'Leopold von Sacher-Masoch', pp. 177f., 182, 192ff.
[28] Ibid., pp. 185f.

13·1% in 1898 and 17·1% in 1903, whilst for Baden the figures were 29·9%, 35·5% and 40·7% respectively. In the Palatinate, finally, each of these factors coincided to create a crisis of dramatic proportions. In 1898 the National Liberals divided on the agrarian issue when faced with an aggressive intervention by the Agrarian League, and at the same time had to cope with a much stronger challenge from the SPD and a firm bloc of Centre votes. The outcome was the loss of two of the six seats held in 1893 and a drop from 47·7% to 34·5% of the total vote.

Elsewhere the National Liberals became increasingly dependent on alliances with other parties, especially in industrial regions like the Ruhr, the two Saxonies and Thuringia. Here the commonest alignment was a regional continuation of the Cartel with the Conservatives and Free Conservatives, in which the three parties aimed for a common list of candidates. In the two Saxonies this enabled the National Liberal vote to hold up quite well after 1887, though it tended to be redistributed across different constituencies with the shifting terms of the electoral pact.[29] However, in the neighbouring Thuringian states matters were seriously complicated by a strong left-liberal presence, which originated in the National Liberal secession of 1881. Here the National Liberal electorate always pulled two ways, either before the poll itself when parties tried to agree on a common nomination, or actually during the voting. In the 1893 Coburg election, for instance, a left liberal defeated the National Liberal in a three-way contest largely by uniting around himself the votes of the defeated Socialist. But by 1898 the National Liberal had disappeared to be replaced by an Anti-Semite and an Agrarian Leaguer, who seem to have divided his former votes between them, with a smaller third share probably going to the left liberal; this time the latter defeated the Socialist in the run-off. In 1903 a National Liberal candidate again appeared and won the seat. The same pattern was repeated in Gotha, where in 1898 the former supporters of the absent National Liberal gravitated towards a Conservative and the left liberal in a ratio of two to one. In 1903 in Schwarzburg-Sondershausen the intrusion of an Anti-Semite attracted so much former National Liberal support that the left liberals abandoned their independent candidacy and united with the National Liberal rump. In Schwarzburg-Rudolstadt there were two left liberals facing the Socialist in 1893, and a left liberal and a National Liberal in 1898, but in 1903 the intervention of the Agrarian League cut the National Liberal share of the vote by over 65%.

[29] In 1893 the Conservatives fielded candidates in Mittweida, Chemnitz, Zwickau and Reichenbach, but deferred to the National Liberals in 1898 and 1903, whilst in rural Leipzig and Glauchau the arrangement worked the other way. In 1893 a clash of Conservatives and National Liberals occurred in only 3 of royal Saxony's 23 constituencies and in only 2 of the 20 in the Prussian province; in 1898 the figures were 3 in each; and in 1903 1 in the former, 5 in the latter. See T. Klein, 'Reichstagswahlen und –Abgeordnete der Provinz Sachsen und Anhalts 1867–1918', in W. Schlesinger (Ed.), *Zur Geschichte und Volkskunde Mitteldeutschlands. Festschrift für Friedrich von Zahn* (Cologne-Graz, 1968), I, pp. 65–141.

2*

In this sort of area, where industry had penetrated deep into the countryside, and agricultural, handicrafts and industrial production coexisted in jumbled proximity, the dangers of agrarian mobilization for the National Liberals' mixed sociology of rural and urban *Honoratioren* were especially sharp. In an area like Hessen the loss of support in town and country could be confronted separately, and to some extent it was possible for the party's development in these different environments to assume different trajectories. But in Thuringia the two processes intersected inside individual constituencies, and local National Liberals were finding it much harder to manoeuvre independently between both a strong left liberal tradition and a new agrarian presence. This completed a national picture of some complexity, in which National Liberal relations with the Agrarian League covered everything from outright hostility (e.g. parts of the Palatinate, Baden, Hannover and Schleswig-Holstein) to harmonious co-operation (Hessen). Most commonly this diversity introduced a powerful element of internal conflict into the party's counsels, leading to frequent local splits and much acrimony. At all events it was imperative that National Liberals devise a popular practice adequate to the needs of the new situation.

III

Yet astonishingly, there were no obvious efforts in this direction. Political defeats had provided some impetus, first in 1881 with the Secession and apparent recovery of the left liberals, and then in 1890 when the elections returned only forty-two instead of the previous ninety-nine National Liberals. On both occasions the party was galvanized into limited action: in 1883 the central office was properly institutionalized for the first time, with a General Secretariat, a Managing Committee and a Central Executive; beginning in 1890 regional secretariats were set up in most of Germany; and in 1892 relations were regulated by the adoption of the party's first Constitution. But throughout this process the Reichstag and Landtag groups kept a strict control over events. Where regional executives existed they comprised the appropriate parliamentary representatives and such regional notables as they chose to co-opt. The 1892 Constitution made no attempt to define the relations between party organs and actual membership. Until the revised Constitution of 1905 the National Liberal leadership remained a self-constituted oligarchy of party *Honoratioren*. By 1900 the vague 'committees' which came together for elections were being replaced by formal Associations at the constituency level, but the Agents who conducted their relations with the centre had no guaranteed access to the policy-making bodies. Provision was made for occasional Delegate Meetings, but they had no rights of influence over party organs or policy and rarely met.[30]

[30] Nipperdey, *Organization*, pp. 102f.; K.-P. Reiss (Ed.), *Von Bassermann zu Stresemann: Die Sitzungen des nationalliberalen Zentralvostandes 1912–1917* (Düsseldorf, 1967), pp. 12–17.

The most interesting aspect of this organizational consolidation, in other words, was the extent to which the ordinary National Liberal membership was left largely uninvolved. In a way the old *Honoratiorenpolitik* was simply reproduced at a slightly higher level of constitutional formality. The reforms merely facilitated formal consultations between descending, informally con-stituted levels of notables—at the national, regional and municipal levels of conventional liberal politics—for the purposes of occasional high-level co-ordination. Even here there was no guaranteed representation on the Central Executive for the non-Prussian regions. For the existing leaders nothing more was strictly necessary: as White has said of the Hessian Progressives, 'politics was one more arena in which they worked together with the same men they knew and respected through business, social contact, community involvement, or often enough, family ties'.[31] It was only with the rise of the Young Liberals as a distinct ginger group inside the party after 1900 that fresh pressure for more represen-tation materialized. Thus in September 1902 the Young Liberal Delegate Meeting called for an invigoration of party life by a far-reaching democratization of the Constitution. Specifically it demanded annual meetings of elected constituency delegates rather than the existing occasional assemblies called at the whim of the Executive and nominated from above. The Delegate Meeting should become the party's supreme body, with rights to elect the Central Executive and vote on an annual report. This major demand made some progress in the revised Constitution of 1905, but the Central Executive again largely perpetuated its own oligarchic authority: it still comprised the two major parliamentary fractions (Reichstag and Prussian Landtag), but the other states and the Prussian provinces could now send their spokesmen on the basis of electoral performance—one for every 20,000 votes recorded, making a total of fifty-five regional representatives on the basis of the 1903 figures. This made little imprint on the dominance of the *Honoratioren*, because regional represen-tatives were still nominated by regional executives, who still formed themselves by co-option.[32]

The reluctance of the National Liberals to develop a constituency apparatus for involving wider circles of supporters in the local life of the party—indeed their reluctance to create such a party life in the first place—is clearly revealed in White's study of Hessen. Here the party existed in precisely the interlocking networks of rural and urban notables indicated above, who selected themselves for political leadership by virtue of property and education, a mixed cultural predominance experienced by local inhabitants as a diversified moral authority, but normally guaranteed by some form of successful capitalist enterprise. The most striking Hessian case was Cornelius Heyl, who sat for the Reichstag in Worms fairly continuously from 1874, the beneficiary of his grandfather's conversion of the family leather firm in the 1840s for the large-scale manufacture

[31] White, *Splintered Party*, p. 41.
[32] Reiss, *Basserman zu Stresemann*, pp. 15ff.

of patent-leather. Immeasurably the largest employer in Worms, one of the
few non-titled members of the Hessian upper chamber until his ennoblement
in 1886, and highly connected at the Grand Ducal Court, Heyl naturally
accumulated communal responsibilities—'charitable foundations, the local
historical society, committees for flood prevention or for restoration of the
Romanesque Worms cathedral, the chamber of commerce'.[33] Less exalted
instances of natural eminence within their respective communities were men
such as Gustav Böhm, a successful manufacturer of perfumed soap in Offenbach, or Arthur Osann, who ran a flourishing legal firm in Darmstadt and
chaired the Hessian party. Their rural counterparts were men like Albert
Möllinger of Pfeddersheim, who came from a long line of improving farmers
in Rhinehessen: he was President of that province's Agricultural Association,
a Landtag deputy, Mayor of Pfeddersheim, member of the Worms district
committee, and so forth.[34]

Examples could be multiplied, both for Hessen and elsewhere. Thus in the
two Anhalt constituencies and most of Thuringia the National Liberal primacy
of the 1870s was doubly rooted in the heroic days of 1848 and the pioneering
commercial activity of the 1840s and 1850s, and the leading personalities had
pedigrees to match. The dominant figure in Bernburg-Ballenstedt in the 1860s
and 1870s was the local sugar magnate Baldamus, the son of a Magdeburg
leather manufacturer, who built the first Anhalt sugar factory in 1850 and
quickly accumulated an empire of beet estates and refineries. Likewise, the
co-founder and Chairman of the Magdeburg National Liberal Association,
Otto Duvigneau, who sat for the Reichstag from 1887 to 1890, chaired the
party's provincial committee and sat on its Central Executive, built his reputation from small beginnings on the successful manufacture of earthenware in the
1850s and 1860s. Of Calvinist background, he was also a church elder and
member of the provincial synod, provided sickness and retirement benefits in his
works, sponsored the plans for a Magdeburg museum, ran the arts and crafts
society, and was active in 'numerous civic societies'.[35]

The magic circles of respectable society in which such personalities moved
were not necessarily party-exclusive. They followed the natural contours of
prestige in a class society and were consequently fully capable of accommodating
some degree of dissidence. Thus 'in Heilbronn, as in all such towns, there was
a society, the Harmony, to which the leading industrial and commercial
families, the gentlemen from the law courts and other state officials and the
army officers belonged', housed in its own 'building with club rooms, reading
rooms and a library', and set in a park called the 'Shareholders' Garden'.
When Theodor Heuß's father was appointed building inspector in the town

[33] White, *Splintered Party*, pp. 43, 129; G. Kriegbaum, *Die parlamentarische Tätigkeit des
Freiherrn C. W. Heyl zu Herrnsheim* (Meisenheim, 1962), pp. 15–20, 28–36, 40–5, 18–51.
[34] White, *Splintered Party*, p. 44.
[35] Klein, 'Reichstagswahlen und –Abgeordnete', pp. 132, 104.

in 1890 he applied to join as a matter of course, even though his support for the radical People's Party offended political sensibilities in certain influential quarters. The army officers threatened to resign *en bloc*, but in the event backed down and Heuß was absorbed easily enough.[36] Moreover, this miniature high society was by no means inward-looking or isolated from wider social inter-course, but was surrounded by a fine web of organized activity, with strong lines to the community radiating from its centre. The visible performance of civic duties was vital to a notable's moral authority, whether they involved sitting in charitable or philanthropic societies, improving public amenities, patronizing the arts, promoting education, organizing public festivals or commemorating great events.[37]

Instances might range from the multiple tenure of public offices on the grand scale, as with Heyl in Worms or Duvigneau in Magdeburg, to the more modest benefactions of a Richard Westernacher in the village of Lindheim.[38] In Heilbronn the Harmony Society included many charitable activities in its programme, and Heuß's father naturally involved himself in this direction, helping to form 'a family welfare society', sponsoring the education of a 'poverty-stricken tailor's son', and propagating the ideas of municipal housing.[39] But this sort of activity normally had little bearing on national politics. Whereas the associational fabric of municipal public life might provide a meeting-place for wide circles who were outside the inner sancta of the élite itself, it rarely gave a point of entry into the more serious business of national or even regional party-politics. There remained a vital gap between these two levels of the public realm. Though the National Liberal Central Office was certainly trying to build up a network of local agents in the constituencies after the adoption of the Constitution in 1892, these rarely did anything between elections and never implanted themselves very deeply in the potentially fertile ground of local club life.

Moreover, the question can be turned on its head: if the National Liberal Party badly needed constituency activists, there was no shortage of energy to be harnessed. The informal mechanisms of recruitment whereby the notables added discreetly to their ranks made it hard for initiatives to rise from below, and where ordinary National Liberal supporters tried to become active outside this network of patronage, they invariably did so in the 1890s outside the party altogether. As mentioned above, much of the expanded local activity of the National Liberals in the mid-1890s actually took place under the auspices of the

[36] T. Heuß, *Preludes to Life. Early Memoirs* (London, 1955), p. 34.

[37] The great classic amongst historical analyses of this particular structure of politics is a work on Britain: J. Vincent, *The Formation of the British Liberal Party 1857–68* (Harmonds-worth, 1972), esp. pp. 93–176. See also S. Yeo, *Religion and Voluntary Organizations in Crisis*, (London, 1976) pp. 29–50, 211–52.

[38] As well as founding a farming school for girls, Westernacher also sponsored the building of a monument in the village. See Demandt, 'Leopold von Sacher-Masoch', pp. 185f.

[39] Heuß, *Preludes to Life*, pp. 34f.

Agrarian League, and this already provided an alternative pole of loyalty in areas like the Palatinate, Hessen and Hannover. This introduced an element of unpredictability and dissension into the party's local life without providing a framework for higher levels of continuous participation by the members at large. It could also easily get out of control. In the Hannoverian constituency of Otterndorf the bulk of National Liberal agents still supported Dietrich Hahn in 1898 even though he had been expelled from the party's Reichstag fraction, whilst in the adjoining seat of Stade an Agrarian League attempt to impose its own candidate instead of the leftish Carl Sattler was defeated only with great acrimony.[40]

More dramatic defections occurred to the Anti-Semites in Central Germany. Otto Böckel had shown the way by utilizing the radical idealism of Marburg and Giessen students for his village campaigning—a branch of the League of German Students was formed in Marburg in 1886[41]—and he soon attracted the support of young farmer-politicians who felt shut out from the exalted counsels of the *Honoratioren*. Philipp Köhler, himself a 'local power in the classic mould—mayor, jury foreman, civil registrar, postmaster, and founder and director of the savings and lending bank' in his native village of Langsdorf in Oberhessen, was a typical case. Of a strong Reform-Protestant background, he began farming in Langsdorf at the age of twenty-four in 1883, and in both 1884 and 1887 his name could be found amongst the backers of the National Liberal candidate in Giessen. Yet by 1890 he had become Böckel's most forceful collaborator in the Grand Duchy and was busily engaged in building an independent power base for himself in the Central German Peasants' Union, eventually breaking with Böckel in 1894.[42] It was only by striking out independently like this that the inhibiting effects of social precedence might be overcome. But Köhler and others like him would have been the natural architects of a flourishing National Liberal activism comparable to that of the Centre or

---

[40] Nipperdey, *Organisation*, p. 93. Dietrich Hahn (b. 1859) was the most extreme of the Agrarian League's national agitators, becoming the organization's Director in June 1897. Of humble Hannoverian farming stock but with an academic education, he was the original Chairman of the new League of German Students in 1881. A committed 'Bismarckian', he represented the constituency of Kehdingen-Neuhaus in the Reichstag and Prussian Landtag from 1893, and originally joined the National Liberal fraction. After voting against the Russian commercial treaty in 1894, however, he was excluded from the party and gravitated generally towards the Conservatives. Committed to an extreme nationalist and anti-semitic ideology, he stood outside the existing tradition of Conservative agrarian politics and represented a new type of professional politician, a characteristic product of the new rural politics. See A. Vagts, 'Dietrich Hahn—ein Politikerleben', in *Jahrbuch des Bundes der Männer von Morgenstern* (n.p., 1965), pp. 155–92; Puhle, *Agrarische Interessenpolitik*, p. 298.

[41] See Levy, *Downfall*, pp. 58f. Amongst the students recruited by Böckel in Giessen was Heinrich Claß, later the Chairman of the Pan-German League (H. Claß, *Wider den Strom. Vom Werden und Wachsen der nationalen Opposition im alten Reich*, Leipzig, 1932, p. 26).

[42] White, *Splintered Party*, pp. 145f.; Demandt, 'Leopold von Sacher-Masoch', p. 190; Levy, *Downfall*, pp. 48, 107f.

the Anti-Semites. By tolerating their local defection the National Liberal oligarchy was vacating a vast area of important political space, and by failing to organize its supporters in the constituencies it was denying itself in the long run the materials of political survival as a popular party.

By 1900 the more perceptive observers had recognized this. Thus in a long reflection on the meaning of the 1903 elections the radical journalist Eugen Katz argued that by neglecting their relations with the ordinary liberal voters both the National Liberals and left liberals had failed to educate them into genuine civic responsibility. The workers had already been lost to the SPD, and, given the prevalent anti-Socialist temper amongst most liberals, 'a viable party which was at the same time both liberal and social' along the lines envisaged by Barth and Naumann was 'in Germany a thing of the impossible'. An 'anti-Socialist bourgeois-party . . . extending from Richter to Kröcher' was far more likely, because on trade union matters there was little to separate left liberals in Bremen or Lower Silesia from 'say a Conservative peasant or an Anti-Semitic master-artisan'.[43] In the long term a two-party system was inevitable, and radical liberals would have little option but to enter the SPD. But in the meantime—'One must say, as Naumann does, that Germany needs a reformed Social Democracy, but one must also say, as Barth does not, why we cannot be Social Democrats today'—the task was 'to unite civilization (intelligentsia) and Social Democracy', by gradually convincing the 'educated stratum' that the only hope for the future lay with the working class, just as in an earlier period it had lain with the 'emancipation of the peasants'. In the short run radical liberals must also strengthen their hand by recovering ground in the countryside by building 'an independent movement of small peasants'. The latter had at least been aroused from indifference by the Agrarian League and were now ready material for a skilful leader. Moreover, this was the only means of shifting the National Liberals from their immobility, for the party's leaders had only survived the above processes of liberal decay by skilful tactical compromises with the Conservatives: 'as a semi-agrarian bourgeois party they are unassailable so long as there is no independent peasant movement at their back'.[44]

This idea—that the 'liberal party of the future' could only emerge from a new type of reform-coalition (a 'bloc from Bassermann to Bebel' as it became known) based on the simultaneous conciliation of the right wing of the SPD and the detachment of the small peasants from their existing agrarian affiliations —was increasingly popular in radical-liberal circles. Between the 1890s and

[43] Eugen Richter (1838–1906) was the leader of the *Freisinnige Volkspartei*, the less flexible and more dogmatic of the two left liberal parties formed from the split of 1893: he remained a resolute opponent of all forms of state intervention, whether in arms spending, colonies or social reform, and rejected any course of rapprochement with the SPD. Jordan von Kröcher was an East Elbian estate-owner and Conservative Reichstag deputy.

[44] Katz to Brentano, Dec. 12th 1903, BA Coblenz, Brentano Papers, 32.

1909, of course, it had little real striking-power in party terms, and after 1909 was only adopted by a wider grouping in a greatly truncated form. But it at least pinpointed fairly accurately the nature of the National Liberal dilemma and brought it to the forefront of the discussion. As Naumann said in October 1899: 'The agrarian peasant on whom they rely is certainly not becoming liberal, but the liberal burghers will not stand for an agrarian attitude. So, with whom do the gentlemen want to make liberalism?'[45]

IV

By allowing the Agrarian League in 1893 to mediate their relations with the peasantry, the National Liberals abandoned the field to an untrammelled sectionalism and failed to develop a distinctive liberal policy towards the land. To some extent the regional parties could be left to work out their own solutions, but as soon as agrarian issues were discussed as matters of national policy the dissatisfaction of 'the liberal burghers' would be given full rein. Thus in 1897–8, when the government announced its new commitment to an agrarian tariff policy, the party could scarcely avoid an official response, especially after the release of the Economic Manifesto in March 1898. In reaction to the latter a meeting of the Central Executive was hastily convened on March 7th 1898, specially enlarged to include the committees of the Reichstag and Prussian Landtag groups and spokesmen for the industrial and agrarian wings of the party. The proceedings revealed two strongly opposed positions: that of the extreme anti-agrarians like Ernst von Eynern, who wanted the full retention of the Caprivi commercial treaties with no increase in agricultural tariffs; and that of the agrarians themselves, led by the Hessians Heyl zu Herrnsheim and Waldemar Graf von Oriola, who insisted that all positive reference to the commercial treaties be omitted from any party statement.[46] It was unclear how these positions might be reconciled. In the end a declaration was issued recognizing the special needs of agriculture and expressing 'approval for the general aim' of the Economic Manifesto, but with two important reservations. The first was a clear refusal to let 'the independence of our party and the national, idealist and liberal ideas from which our party has grown to be forced into the background'. But secondly, the statement insisted that future concessions to agriculture should not pre-empt the need of industry for commercial treaties of long duration.[47]

When the Delegate Meeting approved an Election Manifesto on May 1st 1898, this papering-over of disagreements was repeated with more assurance. The parts dealing with economic policy acknowledged that agriculture required

[45] Naumann to Brentano, Oct. 30th 1899, BA Coblenz, Brentano Papers, 45.

[46] See the record of the meeting in BA Coblenz, Friedberg Papers, Kl. Erw., 303/9.

[47] For a copy of the statement, see HA/GHH, 3001071/3 (it was published in the press on Mar. 9th 1898). For the background, see Eley, '*Sammlungspolitik*', pp. 52–7.

greater security than Caprivi's treaties had provided, but at the same time reaffirmed industry's need for treaties of long duration. Similarly, it distinguished the protection of the peasantry and *Mittelstand* as a 'main task' of the party, specifically mentioning the entire run of *Mittelstand* grievances: organization of the crafts, laws against usury and hawking, better facilities for agricultural and commercial training, assistance for co-operatives, availability of cheap credit, improvement of communications, and support for internal colonization. Yet these commitments were hedged by the obligatory reminder that the National Liberals were 'not a one-sidedly economic party, but had a duty to represent all classes which were active in the life of the state and economy, and by balancing their interests to direct their attention to the common good'. This amounted to a necessary evasion of clear choices on economic policy, for the party was constrained by the diversity of its social and regional base.[48]

In the discussion both Max Ludwig Goldberger, the respected Berlin merchant, and Struckmann, the Mayor of Hildesheim, where the local party was besieged by an independent Agrarian League candidature, adopted an aggressive anti-agrarian position, arguing that in its current form the Election Manifesto would 'forfeit the support of broad circles of the commercial and industrial *Mittelstand*'.[49] As Goldberger said: 'In the beginning the bourgeoisie was the bearer of the national idea, and not the agrarians.' But this was offset by the majority's more pragmatic willingness to deal with the increasingly vocal agrarian movement. Hermann Paasche gave a frank admission of this effect: 'You know that in many cases we are being attacked in the country . . . and calumnied as enemies of agriculture. To this we oppose the statement that we are willing to give agriculture "better" guarantees for the conclusion of new commercial treaties, but that at present we are in no position to commit ourselves in detail.' Theodor von Möller, who had helped draft the Economic Manifesto, added the strategic gloss:

Do we want to repeat what happened in England in the thirties and forties, when the Anti-Corn Law League emerged simultaneously with the related agitation for (a parliamentary reform) which would have guaranteed greater influence to the broad masses of workers? Should we want this struggle— which certain elements among us are seeking to provoke—there would be a fight to the death between agriculture and trade, a fight in which one of the contestants must be defeated and seriously hurt . . . A first attempt to deflect

[48] For the full manifesto, see *Allgemeiner Delegiertentag der Nationalliberalen Partei* (Berlin, 1898), pp. 4–7.

[49] Ibid., p. 55. This usage of the term *Mittelstand* is a salutary reminder of its ambiguities of meaning: in the context it clearly comes close to the English 'middle class', and though by this time such a meaning was mainly vestigial, it also suggests that as yet the term does not automatically imply the backward strata of the traditional petty-bourgeoisie. For the best discussion of the latter, see Blackbourn, '*Mittelstand*'.

this grave struggle is the goal of *Sammlungspolitik*. Its goal is to soften the contradictions and in the long run to make the excesses of certain agitators impossible.[50]

Confronted by the dissolution of the party's unity into hostile sectionalisms, its leaders retreated into a celebration of the National Liberal heritage. Bennigsen had already taken this line at the emergency Executive meeting of March 7th, and in the Delegate Meeting on May 1st each of the three introductory speeches by Bassermann, Hammacher and Bennigsen followed suit: the party had originated in the conflicts of the 1860s as the champion of liberalism, national unity and compromise, and now—as Germany's historic *Mittelpartei* —its role was once again to mediate between the different economic interests, both for the sake of the nation as a whole and for its own survival as a party.[51] Another senior spokesman, Albert Bürklin, took the same view: ' . . . we recruit our members from all parts of our German fatherland, from all occupational estates, from all social strata . . . We represent all social strata, the people, we represent the German *Bürgertum*.' When politics had been dominated by constitutional questions, in the 1860s, this diversity had been a source of strength, but now that 'economic questions are in the foreground, questions that is, in which we don't feel so united, there is a certain weakness in our position'. The only recourse, he argued, was to continue stressing the unifying political factors by searching for the 'middle ground'.[52] At its most grandiloquent this meant invoking the party's character as an historic community of sentiment, what Arthur Hobrecht called 'the cement of history, the cement that a long period of common effort in great tasks and of common struggles over great questions necessarily produced'.[53] But more prosaically, it meant a stronger emphasis on 'national questions', including both the strengthening of the state fabric and the defence of the 'idealist heritage of the German people'.[54] One example was the continuing adherence to the maxims of the *Kulturkampf*—the German equivalent of the 'bloody shirt'—and in the late 1890s the most enthusiastic celebrants of the National Liberal past tended to cling most stubbornly to the old 'anti-ultramontane' slogans. But it also produced a stronger interest in foreign policy, in naval armaments and colonies, in the subordination of the national minorities, and in the aggressive 'defence of German civilization'.

Faced with the gradual dissolution of the old social coalitions against reaction which had laid the foundations of its brief period of national hegemony in the

---

[50] *Allgemeiner Del.tag*, pp. 52, 48f.

[51] Ibid., pp. 9f., 13, 15–26.

[52] Ibid., pp. 57f.

[53] Seyffardt, *Erinnerungen*, p. 595.

[54] Statement by Prof. Wilhelm Kahl of Berlin (1849–1932) to the Delegate Meeting, *Allgemeiner Del.tag*, p. 72.

1870s, and which persisted in regional politics down into the 1890s, the National Liberal Party took increasing refuge in a process of nationalist self-congratulation which did little to solve its immediate problems. The above discussion has tried to illustrate the difficulties of the party in a period of rapid political transition, caught between the comfortable drawing-room informalities of *Honoratiorenpolitik* and the newer, more exacting requirements of constituency agitation, with its stress on local interests and soap-box oratory. It offers striking evidence that the adjustment to a new style of mass politics was by no means a natural stage in the life of parties, in which they brought their practice automatically into line with the demands of a new age and its technologies. When the National Liberals encountered demands for a stronger local rooting of political life, in fact, they responded very slowly and with extreme reluctance. By comparison both the Centre and the Conservatives managed a far quicker response—the former through the political elasticity of the Catholic Church and its social relations, the latter by a remarkable improvisation during a crisis of its moral authority in the countryside. The larger context of these innovations, deriving from the separate radicalizations of the peasantry and labour, failed to elicit a comparable response from the National Liberals, whether on the level of organization or on that of ideology.[55]

One further comparison may be offered in conclusion, namely that with Britain, because this directs us to deeper structural weaknesses of National Liberalism in Germany. For the National Liberals never experienced that fundamental process of renewal which was so crucial to the political vitality of British liberalism after the 1860s, in which the parliamentary party became newly constituted as the national representation of a flourishing undergrowth of local political cultures. As Vincent has said, there were really two processes at work: not only 'the slow adaptations of the Parliamentary party', but more

[55] Why they failed to respond is a massive question which lies beyond the scope of the present enquiry. We know next to nothing about the details of the process of decomposition. One priority for future work would be to examine those regions (such as Schleswig-Holstein, Oldenburg, Rhinehessen or parts of Pomerania) where liberals did manage to survive as a popular political force in the countryside, because this would tell us much about their failures elsewhere. The answer will almost certainly lie with the systems of landholding, the forms of peasant emancipation, and the degree of political independence enjoyed by the peasantry in the past. At all events this problem can only be resolved at the regional and local levels, not by further studies of the National Liberals' parliamentary leadership (though we remain fairly ignorant about even this). White's study of Hessen, *Splintered Party*, is an important pointer in this direction. The literature on the Weimar period is much better developed in this respect, and R. Heberle, *From Democracy to Nazism. A Regional Case Study of Political Parties in Germany* (new ed. New York, 1970), remains a classic. For some interesting general reflections, see K. Rohe, 'Liberalismus und soziale Struktur—Überlegungen zur politischen Gesellschaft und zur politischen Kultur des Ruhrgebiets', in *Liberal*, 18, 1–2 (Jan.–Feb. 1976), pp. 43–56, 113–21; and for an indication of the *type* of work that needs to be done, T. Judt, 'The Origins of Rural Socialism in Europe: Economic Change and the Provençal Peasantry, 1870–1914', in *SH*, 1 (1976), pp. 45–66.

importantly 'the adoption of that Parliamentary party by a rank and file'.[56] If the National Liberals failed to effect the equivalent adaptations, they also lacked the benefit in the 1890s of a rank and file, which in the British case came from the political activation of 'militant dissent' and the self-improvement of radical artisans. The reasons are naturally deeply historical, and are to do with the far longer sedimentation of political culture in Britain under parliamentary auspices, the absence of a German equivalent to the Nonconformist tradition, and the effects of the political rupture in the 1860s between German liberals and the infant labour movement. But they do point to a vital question, which younger generations of National Liberals were increasingly asking after 1900: if they were denied the obvious rank and file of both the working class and the peasantry, then from whom would the rank and file come?

[56] Vincent, *Formation of the British Liberal Party*, p. 19.

3. The Emergence of the Nationalist Pressure Groups

A. THE BASIC PATTERN

As a distinct category of organizations the so-called *nationale Verbände* are at first glance easy to enumerate. They ranged from groups like the Pan-German League or the much smaller and more eccentric German-Union, which held a general brief for the country's nationalist integrity, to those which campaigned on single issues, like the Navy League, the Colonial Society, the Society for the Eastern Marches or the Defence League. To them may be added organizations operating mainly in the cultural sphere such as the Christian Book League and its sibling the Fatherland League, or the Society for Germandom Abroad (originally known as the General German School Society). The military and naval veterans' clubs are also normally grouped under the same heading, as too are the various youth groups which affiliated with the Young Germany Union after 1911. In addition the anti-Socialist labour organizations often acted in an equivalent manner, from the Evangelical Workers' Associations, to the various types of company union and the so-called patriotic workers' associations sponsored by the Imperial League Against Social Democracy. Taken together they are often seen by historians to represent a powerful current of popular nationalism which was consciously promoted by both government and right-wing parties as a political counterweight to the growing parliamentary strength of the left. As such they suggest a political demonology which has become increasingly familiar in recent historiography: viz. the agencies of an organized manipulation of popular sentiments, calculated to stabilize the *status quo* and distract attention from pressing domestic problems.[1]

Conventional thinking about the agitational pressure groups has two principal features. On the one hand, they are regarded as an important structural component in the alleged political backwardness of the *Kaiserreich*, because the 'impotence of the parties' under the Constitution clearly favoured the application of pressure directly on the governmental bureaucracy itself rather than

---

[1] See esp. Wehler, *Das Deutsche Kaiserreich*, pp. 90–5, 107–10; M. Stürmer, 'Machtgefüge und Verbandsentwicklung im wilhelminischen Deutschland', *Neue Politische Literatur*. 14 (1969), pp. 490, 503–7; H.-J. Puhle, 'Parlament, Parteien und Interessenverbände 1890–1914', in Stürmer, *Das Kaiserliche Deutschland*, esp. pp. 346ff.

through the potential organs of representative democracy. As Wehler has said: 'Precisely the authoritarian *Kaiserstaat* enabled the pressure groups to swarm into the crevices of the Constitution, precisely the castration of the German parties provoked the predominance of the interest groups, precisely the Imperial parliament's absent faculty of co-ordination . . . promoted the egoism of the pressure group.'[2] The result was an 'anti-democratic pluralism', a modern caesarism in which the nationalist groups lent themselves easily to plebiscitary manoeuvres against the democratic left.[3] But secondly, these organizations are normally seen as the best political instruments of the 'ruling strata' in their efforts to 'preserve the *status quo*' and have been given a central place in recent discussions of 'social imperialism' before 1914. The latter has been defined as a Machiavellian 'technique of rule' by which pressure for democratic change was diverted on to harmless foreign objects, 'a cool and calculated instrumental-ization of foreign policy for domestic purposes'.[4] Within this general schema the *nationale Verbände* are implicitly linked to the leading politicians of the right and the class interests of the ruling industrial-agrarian bloc. They are attributed a major significance in socializing people into the dominant authori-tarian value-system of the Empire (as it is normally described), and are held to exemplify the manipulative and diversionary character of conservative politics.

Unfortunately, these twin approaches simplify both the function of the nationalist pressure groups in the political system and the nature of their relations to the state and the parties. There are two errors in particular. First, the simple category of the nationalist pressure group can disguise some impor-tant differences between the organizations in question. There are several ways of dividing them up. If we do this by function, for instance, we arrive at a four-fold classification: the agitational pressure groups proper (Pan-Germans, Navy League, Colonial Society, Eastern Marches Society, Defence League); cultural groups (e.g. German-Union, Society for Germandom Abroad, the various publishing and propaganda agencies); para-military groups (veterans' clubs and youth groups); and finally anti-Socialist organizations. Even this method of differentiation is not a sufficient one, for each organization clearly performed more than one function in social-historical terms. If we distinguish them by the form of their political practice, moreover, we arrive at a rather different classification: those which were fairly closely subordinated to the state, like the veterans' clubs and youth groups or the Christian Book League; those directly beholden to the right-wing parties, like the Imperial League Against Social Democracy; those operating in the cultural domain, offering less scope for co-operation with the government but likewise no serious threat (e.g. German-Union, Society for Germandom Abroad); those agitational groups

---

[2] Wehler, *Das Deutsche Kaiserreich*, p. 94.

[3] Ibid., p. 90. See also M. Stürmer, 'Bismarckstaat und Cäsarismus', *Der Staat*, 12 (1973), pp. 467–98. The problem of caesarism is discussed in more detail in Ch. 6 below, pp. 206ff.

[4] Wehler, *Bismarck und der Imperialismus*, p. 115, and *Das Deutsche Kaiserreich*, p. 177.

which were formally independent of the state, but whose activities dovetailed neatly into the existing administration of the latter's priorities and rarely caused it much political trouble after the mid-1890s (Colonial Society, Society for the Eastern Marches); finally, those agitational groups who pursued their objectives even at the cost of serious conflict with the government.

It was this final category which, in the terms of the current enquiry, contained the primary vehicles of a fully developed radical-nationalist politics. Pre-eminent here was the Pan-German League, followed by the Navy League and later the Defence League. Naturally the categories cannot be exclusive— e.g. at different points in its life the Navy League oscillated between co-operation with the government and opposition, while the Colonial Society and Eastern Marches Society each contained vocal radical-nationalist minorities bent on a course of conflict—but they may provide a better guide to the political status of the different organizations than the existing tendency to group them under a single heading. Thus for the veterans' clubs the term pressure group is clearly a misnomer, for they were almost exclusively organs of sociability. Though there were intermittent efforts by government to use them for political propaganda, the breadth and diversity of the membership's political affiliations left these a conspicuous failure.[5] In this and other cases the conventional category of the *nationale Verbände* can easily suggest a higher level of nationalist agitation and commitment than was actually given by the mass of the ordinary members.

Moreover—this raises the second weakness of the conventional approach— the nationalist groups were rarely in direct conflict with the party-political system as such until the years immediately before the First World War. They were certainly hostile to individual parties before that time and frequently exhibited anti-democratic sentiments. But on the whole, in the period between the 1890s and 1908–11, they were happy to operate within the system as then constituted and to accept pragmatically its parliamentary and representative features. It makes no sense to construct a simple dichotomy between the parties and the pressure groups, or more specifically between the National Liberals and the nationalist organizations, because leading members of the bourgeois parties were always prominent amongst the leaderships of the various groups. Thus the original Colonial League of 1882 was called into life mainly by leading National Liberals and Conservatives, while in the 1890s the Pan-Germans still enjoyed significant patronage of this kind, as did also the Society for the Eastern Marches and the Navy League. It was not until after 1900 that the Pan-Germans became identified with that disreputable politics of 'national opposition' which led many established politicians to reconsider their support.

Moreover, when the more extreme radical nationalists did start attacking the

---

[5] See H. Henning, 'Kriegervereine in den preußischen Westprovinzen. Ein Beitrag zur preußischen Innenpolitik zwischen 1860 und 1914', *Rheinische Vierteljahresblätter* 32 (1968), pp. 430–75, and K. Saul, 'Der "Deutsche Kriegerbund". Zur innenpolitischen Funktion eines "nationalen" Verbandes im kaiserlichen Deutschland', *MGM*, 6 (1969), esp. pp. 112ff.

parties, they aimed their fire not only at the parliamentary left but also at the moderate or traditional right. Far from being the simple tools of the 'ruling strata', the *nationale Verbände* were riddled from the start with dissatisfaction with the governmental orientation of their highly connected leaders. The colonial movement was divided from its inception, at first into two separate organizations, and then by the internal factionalism of the united Colonial Society which emerged from the fusion of 1887. The Pan-German League was in effect an organizational focus for the more radical of the Colonial Society's two factions, but it too was subject to the same internal difficulties later in the 1890s, while its supporters also took care to maintain their own factious presence inside the Colonial Society. Similar rivalries divided the Navy League—in its pre-history of early 1898, again in late 1899 with residual effects in spring 1901, and then in a more developed form in 1905–8. As in the agrarian movement, the lines of antagonism ran through and not between the two political complexes of the parties and *Verbände*.

To make sense of this factionalism it is worth outlining its formal political basis. In the first place, of course, its extent must not be exaggerated, particularly between the 1880s and 1908, for both sides argued their differences from a ground of common ideological assumptions and class location, certainly with respect to the primary contradiction with the Socialists and their suspected allies. As has often been said, the nationalist groups sprang at one level from a major preoccupation which motivated most tendencies of the right, namely the creation of a stronger framework of consensual ideology for containing sectional conflicts and for confronting any group (such as the SPD) which chose to set itself outside the fold. Bülow, speaking from the relative freedom of retirement, gave a good statement of the arguments to which his contemporaries were increasingly prone. The only means of rising above the debilitating disunity of domestic sectionalism, he argued, was the constant emphasis of key national issues—'foreign relations, colonial policies, armaments'.[6] As his predecessor in the Chancellory put it, it was necessary to create 'a field of activity for the strengthened national sentiment'.[7] The aim was the isolation of the SPD and the steady erosion of its support. As Bülow argued: 'We must fight steadily for the souls of our workmen, must seek to win back the Social Democratic workmen to the state and the monarchy, and to keep the non-Social Democratic workmen away from the danger of imbibing such views.' Accordingly, 'the idea of the nation as such must again and again be emphasized by dealing with national problems, so that this idea can continue to move, to unite and to separate the parties'.[8]

For Bülow the supreme vindication of this stance was the passage of the

[6] H. Stretton, *The Political Sciences. General Principles of Selection in Social Science and History* (London, 1969), p. 83. This is an excellent analysis of the type of thinking.

[7] Hohenlohe: RT, Dec. 11th 1894, p. 21.

[8] B. von Bülow, *Imperial Germany* (London, 1914), pp. 195f., 199.

Defence Bill in 1913 by the votes of every party but the SPD. At about that time Paul Fuhrmann, a leading right-wing National Liberal, reaffirmed the political moral:

> If we look for a great common aim for all political, economic and national activity, then we must point to an area of tasks whose magnitude completely overshadows the significance of domestic disputes, tasks which can only be resolved in opposition to Social Democracy . . . I mean that great problem of German foreign policy for which the not entirely appropriate term of imperialism has now become customary.[9]

For the exponents of this position, 'struggles between strata of the same nation' were 'nothing more than fever and decomposition of the organism'.[10] As August Keim saw it, the sole solution was 'a great, common, *national* goal'. The only means of immunizing the workers against Socialism was the assiduous cultivation of the 'national pride and love of the fatherland', 'a marked German consciousness and the spirited feeling of national fellowship'.[11] This type of thinking denied any real basis of social inequality to the success of the SPD amongst the working class. The Socialists were just 'unscrupulous agitators and seducers' robbing Germany of 'its national strength', 'everywhere at hand to hold down the national idea'.[12]

The question, of course, was where exactly to draw the line of anti-national anathema. Men like Bülow drew it unequivocally only around the SPD itself. But others desired not only the exclusion of the Socialists from the national bunker, but also an uncompromising hostility to any other party whose nationalist credentials they considered less than perfect—the Catholic Centre, many left liberals, even certain agrarian Conservatives. In a curious way this mirrored the Socialist debate between the reformist advocates of co-operation with the bourgeois left and their unbending revolutionary critics. Thus the more pragmatic conservatives like Bülow laid out the rather modest objective of a united nationalist front which drew its common purpose from the principle of anti-Socialism, but took practical cognisance of the divergent sectional interests to which the individual parties were committed—'the pairing of the conservative with the liberal spirit' on the 'basis of national questions', as he once put it.[13] The more radical spirits on the right, by contrast, wanted much more than this. They resented the tactical accommodation of sectional interests for what they

---

[9] Cit. Stegmann, *Erben*, p. 279.

[10] *Reichsbote*, Mar. 14th 1913, cit. K. Stenkewitz, *Gegen Bajonett und Dividende. Die politische Krise in Deutschland am Vorabend des Ersten Weltkrieges* (Berlin, 1960), p. 298.

[11] A. Keim, *Erlebtes und Erstrebtes* (Hannover, 1925), pp. 154, 155.

[12] Ibid., p. 152, and Keim's statement in the Cassel Congress of the Navy League, Jan. 19th 1908, *Verhandlungen*, p. 25. GLA Karlsruhe, 69P, 8.

[13] Bülow to the Colonial Policy Action Committee, Jan. 19th 1907, cit. G. Crothers, *The German Elections of 1907* (New York, 1941), p. 159.

saw as some lowest common denominator of nationalist commitment. The latter
should be dominant and overriding, proclaimed in all its purity, rather than
diluted by messy domestic agreements. The nationalist appeal should be
wielded aggressively, slicing through the empty phrases of the party politicians,
fixing the public eye on the 'real issues' and not the selfish trivia of the 'cattle-
trading' in the Reichstag.

This was a conflict that permeated the politics of the right in the two decades
before the First World War. On the one side stood those who demanded the
'primacy of the national' and the ruthless subordination of all other issues. On
the other were those like Bülow, who appreciated that agreement on national
questions, from the prosecution of an aggressive foreign policy to the struggle
against Socialism, could only be achieved through the simultaneous conciliation
of entrenched sectional interests. Though taking different forms and present
in varying degrees, this was a potential source of disruption in most of the
nationalist pressure groups before 1914. Thus, as already mentioned, the Colonial Society of 1887 was a somewhat uneasy union of two earlier groups, the
Colonial League of 1882 and the Society for German Colonization of 1884.
Though differences over colonial policy were clearly important, many of these
were also motivated by more basic ideological disagreements which now remained to disturb the new Society's stability. The backbone of the 1882 League
was formed largely from the establishment world of big business and the
parties. The Colonization group which followed two years later, on the other
hand, was interested less in the possibilities of large-scale capital investment
than in the sponsorship of peasant settlement overseas. This second group
was altogether more radical, with economics blending subjectively into the
fiercer language of world power politics. Tensions persisted beyond the merger
of 1887, and though the attempt to foist further colonial obligations on to a
reluctant Bismarck recreated a temporary unity of purpose, this failed to outlast
the latter's demise in 1890. A number of dissatisfactions became jumbled
into a colonialist critique of Bismarck's policies from within the government
coalition, joining 'moderates' who wanted the state to bear the costs of colonial
administration to 'radicals' pressing for further territorial acquisitions. Although
the former were appeased by the prospect of a colonial department (half-
realized under the aegis of Caprivi in the form of the Colonial Council) and a
normalization of relations with the British, the latter were unimpressed and
retreated into formal opposition.[14]

The result was a new organization, the General German League of 1891,

[14] The best account of the early colonial movement in the late 1870s and 1880s is now
K. J. Bade, *Friedrich Fabri und der Imperialismus in der Bismarckzeit. Revolution – Depression
– Expansion* (Freiburg, 1975). Otherwise see the following: Klauß, *Deutsche Kolonialgesell-
schaft*, esp. pp. 43–50, 99ff., 168ff.; Pierard, 'German Colonial Society', pp. 8–95; Wehler,
Bismarck und der Imperialismus, pp. 139ff., 333ff.; F. F. Müller, *Deutschland – Zanzibar –
Ostafrika. Geschichte einer deutschen Kolonialeroberung 1884–1890* (Berlin, 1959), pp. 35–66,
97ff., 134ff., 177ff.; Pogge von Strandmann, 'Kolonialrat', pp. 13ff.

later renamed the Pan-German League in 1894. In one way this was simply a reconstitution of the former Colonization group, and the freebooting activities of Carl Peters (very much the heroic figure of Wilhelmine radical nationalism) had provided both the immediate stimulus for the new foundation and a continuing focus of aspirations during the preceding five years.[15] The more radical colonial politics had always threatened to become generalized into a larger statement of principle—e.g. in the 'General German Congress' of 1886 which momentarily spawned an earlier but abortive General German League[16]—and the lasting initiative of 1891 announced a set of aims which clearly outgrew the colonial framework: 'competition with the Colonial Society will not be undertaken, but the association will rest on deeper foundations, supplementing those to which the aims and composition of the Colonial Society do not reach, particularly with respect to propaganda activities'.[17] The basic aim was the 'rallying of nationally minded citizens, without consideration of party, in the thought that the accomplished unification of the German race is only the foundation of a larger national development; that is the development of the German people into a cultural and political world power, as the English people already are and the Russians will doubtless become'.[18] The new organization's brief would encompass not only matters of foreign, colonial, naval and military policy, but also those concerning the national minorities inside Germany, the outposts of German nationality in Central and Eastern Europe, Latin America, Africa and anywhere else in the world, the preservation of all the artifacts of German culture, and the continuing propagation of all such ideas amongst the German public.

The above discussion contains, in the barest outline, a general scenario for the emergence of radical nationalism. At its centre was a dynamic and complicated relationship between the *nationale Verbände* and the political parties. Leading spokesmen for the latter were always involved at the highest levels in the deliberations of the pressure groups, both at their foundations and later, and radical nationalists were always conscious of the parliamentary arena in which legislation was formed. But the pressure groups also contained many activists who lacked firm party affiliations, who regarded their nationalist activities as a primary loyalty, and showed little respect for the tactical niceties of party-political life. Thus the internal disputes in the pressure groups between moderate and radical nationalists normally followed the distinction

[15] For Peters, see the disappointing thesis by H. Bair, 'Carl Peters and German Colonialism', unpub. Ph.D. Thesis (Stanford, 1968), and Wehler, *Bismarck und der Imperialismus*, pp. 333–366. For the foundation of the Pan-German League: Kruck, *Geschichte*, pp. 1ff.; Hartwig, *Zur Politik*, pp. 6–26; D. Guratzsch, *Macht durch Organisation* (Düsseldorf, 1974), pp. 22–6.

[16] Very little is known of this affair. The fullest account may be found in Müller, *Deutschland – Zanzibar – Ostafrika*, pp. 177–91. See also Bade, *Friedrich Fabri*, pp. 297ff.

[17] Hugenberg's circular of Aug. 1st 1890, cit. Wertheimer, *Pan-German League*, p. 34.

[18] Petition to Carl Peters, ibid.

between those members who were simultaneously active in conventional
party politics and those who were not. This political antagonism also contained
a social contradiction between 'old' and 'new' men, for the moderate nationalists
were invariably established at a pinnacle of achievement and social prestige
(normally inherited), while their opponents were invariably outsiders with
a reputation and political career still to make. The object of this chapter is
to explore these dimensions of the relations between parties and *Verbände*
in the 1890s and to establish the exact meaning of the tensions between
them.

B. THE PAN-GERMAN LEAGUE

The foundation of the Pan-German League brought a new factor on to the
political stage: the first coalescence of a grouping for whom the 'primacy of the
national' was an insistent actuality, not as an occasional consequence of severe
national crisis or the exceptional condition of wartime unity, but as a structural
imperative of political life in general. The Pan-Germans saw themselves as the
purest embodiment of the nationalist cause, standing above the political parties
and their conflicts, the supreme co-ordinator of individual nationalist campaigns. In fact, this claim was never a reality until the period after 1908: the
Pan-Germans watched their functions gradually being usurped by a succession
of separate organizations—the Colonial Society naturally remained, but
unwelcome competition also arrived with the Society for the Eastern Marches
in 1894, the German-Union in 1895, and the Navy League in 1898. Individual
Pan-Germans entered the new groups, but in general were forced to play a
frustrating waiting game, affirming the doctrinal purity of Pan-German ideas
until changed circumstances brought them closer to the centre of the stage.
They called for firmness, consistency and aggression in all matters of 'national'
policy, and this led to tension not only with moderates in each of the rival
organizations, but also with the government of the day. Causing great resentment, in other words, the Pan-German League constituted itself as a 'national
opposition'.
    This describes a central motif of the pre-war scene, and helps make sense of
an apparent confusion of factional disputes. Such disputes proved a recurring
problem of the Colonial Society, for instance, and the difficulties of the 1880s
resurfaced in a number of internal wrangles, the most serious occurring in
1895 and 1907–8. The ultimate goal of the Pan-Germans was to sublimate
this factionalism in the eventual fusion of the *nationale Verbände* under their own
auspices. There is an important continuity, in fact, which links a series of
abortive projects of this type, from the short-lived 'General German League
for the Furtherance of German National Interests Overseas' in 1886, to the
abortive National Party in 1892–3 and the so-called 'overseas syndicate' of

1908, with the actual unity of the war years. But the Pan-Germans only began to establish their moral and intellectual ascendancy amongst the other 'patriotic associations' after 1908. In the intervening period this position represented the ideal which they claimed to embody, but to which in practice they could only aspire.[19]

Organizationally the Pan-German League in its early years should not be presented as a radical departure. At first it threatened simply to reproduce the familiar patterns of *Honoratiorenpolitik* which still marked the practice of the parties. Under the initial Presidency of Karl von der Heydt from 1891 to 1893 the League's activities were very much Berlin-centred, with very little attempt to stimulate the formation of local branches and no political rapport between the national executive and the localities.[20] The Presidium had an unmistakable honorific tinge, comprising figures of high prestige but no necessary commitment to a distinctively Pan-German politics of any vigour: Ludwig von Fischer, the National Liberal Mayor of Augsburg; Wilhelm von Kardorff, the leader of the Free Conservatives; Julius Graf von Mirbach-Sorquitten, the leading East-Elbian Conservative; Alexander Lucas, a Director of the *Deutsch-Ostafrikanische Gesellschaft*; and Johannes Wislicenus, Professor of Chemistry at Leipzig and a highly regarded National Liberal.

But the conventional concerns of the group around von der Heydt were revealed most clearly by the manoeuvre for a new 'National Party' in the autumn of 1892. Though little is still known of this affair, it appears that the Free Conservative group in the League (Heydt, Wilhelm Schröder-Poggelow, possibly Otto Arendt, Hermann Graf von Arnim-Muskau and Kardorff) together with their party friends (mainly Silesian magnates like Guido Fürst Henckel von Donnersmarck) were the moving spirits behind this, and by the start of 1893 a wider circle of sympathisers had been attracted, including the banker Adolph von Hansemann, the military intriguer Alfred Graf von Walder-

---

[19] The Pan-German League's relation to the other *nationale Verbände* will be discussed in detail in subsequent chapters.

[20] Karl von der Heydt (1858–1922) was head of a family bank in Elberfeld from 1881–99, moving to Berlin in 1891 and founding the Berlin Bank v. d. Heydt & Co. in 1895. He was an early associate of Carl Peters and played a key part in the financing of the *Deutsch-Ostafrikanische Gesellschaft* in 1885. Prominent in the Colonial Society, he was a natural figurehead for the dissident nationalist initiative which produced the General German League in 1890-1: though resigning as President in 1893, he remained a member of the Executive until 1900. Politically he had a Free Conservative background in Elberfeld, and in 1892-3 combined with Schröder-Poggelow to float the idea of the National Party, partly to provide a platform for Peters. He was involved in launching the Central Association of German Navy Leagues Abroad in 1898, became its Treasurer, and later became the Treasurer of the Navy League itself during the latter's reconstruction in 1908. Commercially he accumulated extensive colonial holdings in Africa (e.g. through railway finance), founded the German Palestine Bank, and became deputy chairman of Mannesmann. For full details, see Pogge von Strandmann, 'Kolonialrat', pp. 97f.

see, Friedrich Alfred Krupp and some National Liberals.[21] But whereas the principles inscribed in the group's manifesto were close to the basic aims of the Pan-Germans, the party political nature of the enterprise—in effect a re-combination of the Cartel into a single party at a time when the Conservative Party seemed beneath the control of Christian-Socials, Anti-Semites and radical agrarians—was very different. Such a far-reaching realignment clearly exceeded the intentions of the purer idealists like Alfred Hugenberg, who stood outside the ranks of this highly connected circle.[22] In particular, the supra-party credentials of the Pan-Germans were threatened. In the event the project for a new party came to nothing. But without necessarily directly inspiring the rationalization of the League's affairs, it at least re-emphasized the need for a clarification of its priorities, not least because of an impending financial crisis.[23] The latter had been precipitated by the failure of an ambitious publishing venture—a *Kalendar aller Deutschen* compiled by Karl Prell—which showed a deficit of 6,000 marks. During 1893 membership sank from 21,000 to a mere 5,000, and there was no obvious sense of future political direction to rectify this parlous state of affairs.[24]

Clarification was achieved in two meetings in the summer of 1893 in Frank-furt and Berlin, called against the wishes of the central leadership, with the express purpose of deciding either the 'dissolution or reorganization of the League'.[25] Heydt resigned after making good two-thirds of the deficit on the publishing venture and passed the Presidency over to Professor Ernst Hasse of Leipzig, a close associate of Wislicenus and a veteran of the early colonial associations of the late 1870s. Hasse appointed Dr Adolf Lehr business manager of the League's affairs, and together their achievement was considerable. They placed the administration on a sound financial footing, equipped the movement with a regular organ of opinion (the *Alldeutsche Blätter*, which began publication in January 1894 under Lehr's editorship), outlined a systematic programme for implanting the organization in the localities, and created the broad ideological framework within which the agitation was conducted during the next decade. This shake-up was a decisive repudiation of the ulterior motives which the party politicians around Heydt seemed to have invested in the League and reaffirmed the non-partisan intentions of the original founders. The moving spirit behind the latter had been Alfred Hugenberg, then a twenty-five-year-old law graduate in Hannover. The new reforms were very much a return to his

---

[21] The fullest account is in Stegmann, *Erben*, pp. 106ff. See also: Hartwig, *Zur Politik*, pp. 38ff.; A. von Waldersee, *Denkwürdigkeiten* (Berlin-Stuttgart, 1922), II, p. 265. There is a copy of the circular letter canvassing the idea of the party in BA Coblenz, Harden Papers, 140, H.1.

[22] Hugenberg was among the firmest opponents of the proposed National Party. See Guratzsch, *Macht durch Organisation*, p. 25.

[23] Guratzsch, ibid., suggests that the abortive episode was the direct stimulus to reform.

[24] For details: Hartwig, *Zur Politik*, pp. 26–49.

[25] Wertheimer, *Pan-German League*, p. 40; Guratzsch, *Macht durch Organisation*, pp. 24f.

original ideas: the local association of particularly committed nationalists completely outside the party framework.[26] The name was now changed to Pan-German League.

At this early stage two factors were especially important in demarcating the Pan-Germans both from the sympathetic parties and from their own previous practice between 1891 and 1893. The first was a self-denying ordinance confining the movement's operations to the sphere of foreign affairs, broadly defined to encompass matters such as the treatment of the national minorities and the protection of the German language and culture. The second was an avowed decentralization which broke decisively with the existing patterns of party politics. Hasse personally assisted this process by continuing to reside in Leipzig, while Lehr co-ordinated the administration from Berlin. But beyond this he insisted on the special importance of setting up local branches and of promoting a regular exchange of views between executive and localities. Henceforth the meetings of the Managing Committee and the annual Convention had a crucial representative function in the life of the organization, and the opinions of the membership were always actively canvassed in advance. Relations between Council, Managing Committee, Executive (as the Presidium was now named) and Convention were carefully codified in a new Constitution formally adopted in 1903.

The sovereign body was the Council, comprising honorary members of the League, the members of the Executive and Managing Committee, the chairmen of district and local branches together with the local contact-men where the latter had not yet been formed, ordinary members co-opted by the Council itself, and additional representatives from local branches with over a hundred members. This rather unwieldy body met twice a year to determine policy and had the power to change the Constitution by a two-thirds vote. The twenty-person Managing Committee met more often and tended to be the real policy centre of the movement; it controlled the *Alldeutsche Blätter* and handled standing relations with the branches. Its boundaries tended to be fluid and other key individuals were often invited to its meetings, particularly when important matters were being discussed. The Executive was a standing committee of three to six members elected for a term of three years to assist the

[26] See Hugenberg's draft for the form of the organization, winter 1890, cit, ibid., p. 24. Ernst Hasse, the son of a Saxon pastor, had studied in his youth for the ministry, served in the unification wars as an officer, and resigned his commission in the Saxon Army in protest at the anti-Prussian feeling there. In the late 1860s he was already the founder of an early geographical society in Leipzig. During the 1870s he made an academic career, becoming head of the Leipzig statistical office. In 1879 he established the Society for Commercial Geography and Colonial Policy in Leipzig and in the 1880s established himself as a prominent speaker and publicist in the early colonial movement. In 1890 he was elected as a National Liberal for one of the Leipzig constituencies and became known in the Reichstag primarily as a Pan-German. He chaired the League from 1893 until his death at the start of 1908. The best source for his early activity is Bade, *Friedrich Fabri*, pp. 105, 117, 136ff.

Chairman and Vice-Chairman in the running of the organization. The Convention was to meet at least once every three years, but in practice met annually with the exceptions of 1895 and 1901.

The provision of a formal structure for the regular involvement of the membership was a new departure. This becomes particularly clear if one compares the situation still pertaining inside the National Liberal Party at both a national and a state level. As suggested above, even the greater activity of the 1890s left the newly forming constituency Associations and local Agents of the National Liberals without any guaranteed access to the party's national decision-making bodies, and the 1892 National Liberal Constitution certainly established nothing like the carefully regulated representative framework shown by the Pan-German Statute of 1903. The previous chapter tried to stress the predicament of the National Liberals in a situation of unprecedented political mobilization in town and country, and suggested that unlike the Conservative and Centre Parties they proved unable to adapt their organization for a more popular style of politics. Instead they clung to the older conventions of *Honoratiorenpolitik*, which hampered the initiation of new recruits into the life of the party at the very time when they were most needed. In particular, the National Liberal Party failed to organize its traditional supporters in the rural constituencies and accordingly left an invaluable opening for a more energetic agency like the Agrarian League. Of course, in an area like Hessen the National Liberals were quite happy to work through the Agrarian League for the purposes of elections and in the short run this proved a rewarding arrangement. But, as argued above, in the longer term this denied them the materials of survival as a popular party.

A less obtrusive effect of the same political abdication was the independent activity of the Pan-Germans and other radical nationalists. Moreover, the Hessian case is particularly useful here for being the home stamping-ground of Heinrich Claß, who succeeded Hasse as Chairman of the Pan-German League in 1908 after long being one of its leading activists. Significantly, Claß came to the Pan-Germans through a disillusioning experience with the National Liberals. Formed intellectually in a strongly National Liberal family—his maternal grandfather was a senior official in the Hessian Ministry of Justice with responsibility for prosecuting the *Kulturkampf* until his retirement in 1875—he went to Berlin in 1887 to study law, mainly to have the opportunity of listening to Treitschke.[27] Having completed his studies at Giessen he returned to Mainz in 1891 for practical training at the district court, qualifying at the end of 1894. In the 1893 election he assisted his immediate superior, the later Hessian Finance Minister Braun, in the National Liberal campaigning, and emerged with poor impressions of the party's Mainz leadership. The usual problems of political access were accentuated in this case by Claß's powerful anti-semitic

[27] For the details of Claß's family and early intellectual background: H. Claß, *Wider den Strom*, pp. 1–19.

feelings, which led him to explain the party's lack of vitality by the prominence of Jews in its counsels.[28]

It was therefore not surprising to find Claß directing his energies elsewhere. After renewing an old student acquaintance with a philologist at a local *Gymnasium*, Karl Berger, who had introduced him to the ideas of Friedrich Lange at Giessen, Claß gathered together a group of like-minded nationalists, 'mainly young lawyers and philologists', who later formed the kernel of the local Pan-German branch.[29] In April 1894 this group responded to Friedrich Lange's manifesto for the formation of the German-Union, recognizing in this a stronger ideological commitment to nationalist and 'Bismarckian' politics than the National Liberals were willing to give: 'the moral rebirth of our people, the defence of its culture and to this end a decisive struggle against Jewry'. In the autumn a *Gemeinde* (as the German-Union's branches were called) was formed under the chairmanship of Berger, and in October 1894 Claß went as a delegate to the German-Union's founding conference in Berlin, where he met Lange for the first time. With the Mainz group as a base, wider support for the movement's ideas was secured, and fresh *Gemeinden* were set up in Worms and Darmstadt. During a further conference organized by Lange in February 1897 Claß was approached by Adolf Lehr for the Pan-Germans, and after detailed discussions the Mainz network was converted into the basis of a more ambitious Pan-German organization.[30]

This situation, in which the Pan-Germans and National Liberals were not so much directly hostile to each other as inhabiting different planes of political activity, was probably fairly typical of areas similar to the Grand Duchy of Hessen, where the location of National Liberal politics in a provincial coalition against aristocracy and reaction survived relatively intact from the 1860s to the turn of the century. This might apply to Baden, Württemberg and the Palatinate, and to Prussian Hessen and Hannover. Here there was no reason for radical nationalists like the Pan-Germans to look elsewhere, certainly not to the other parties. The Conservatives were either too traditional or narrowly agrarian, the left liberals too democratic, and the Anti-Semites too vulgar. Accordingly, it was perfectly possible for persons like Claß to dismiss the National Liberals as inadequate for the formal pursuit of Pan-German ideals without yet finding it necessary to regard the Pan-German League as an exclusive alternative. In the 1903 election Claß was able to run as a joint candidate for the Agrarian League and the National Liberals, though the experience did nothing to allay his scepticism concerning the latter. The two allegiances could be held in non-antagonistic tension less easily where the old popular hegemony of National Liberal notables was disintegrating far more rapidly into agrarian and industrial sectionalisms under simultaneous pressure

[28] Ibid., p. 38.
[29] Ibid., pp. 30f.
[30] Ibid., pp. 31ff.

3

from the left, or where it had scarcely been consolidated in the first place due to political Catholicism or because National Liberalism was more directly a vehicle for the political interests of large capital. Here the clearer direction of National Liberal politics also clarified the implications of a Pan-German position and imposed choices which could be fudged elsewhere. Thus in Bavaria the particularist terms of the discourse necessarily identified the more coherent Pan-Germans, with their German-national stress on the Reich and centralism, with a specific section of the political spectrum. Similarly in Hamburg, where the liberal business oligarchy enjoyed a far more exclusive and formalized monopoly of political authority than was possible in central Germany (with the obvious exception of Frankfurt), the local Pan-Germans, who recruited mainly from the lesser bourgeoisie in the city, were more obviously excluded from the liberal establishment.[31]

It was thus the *specific* character of the local situations into which the Pan-Germans were inserted that determined the speed at which they adopted a distinct position inside the party-political system. A good illustration of this effect was provided by Theodor Reismann-Grone, an original signatory of the Pan-German founding manifesto. Appointed General Secretary of the Ruhr Mineowners' Association in 1891 at the age of twenty-eight, and resigning several years later to devote all his time to the ownership of the *Rheinisch-Westfälische Zeitung* in Essen, Reismann-Grone stood right at the centre of a vital network of political relations. Quickly acquiring a small chain of local papers, he used them to subsidize the *Rheinisch-Westfälische* as a Pan-German platform. He already enjoyed some experience from before 1891 as an organizer of Ruhr industry's press relations and now established himself as one of the most important pro-industrial newspaper proprietors.[32]

Politically he set out to promote the unity of the anti-Socialist parties within a strong Pan-German setting and saw the local 'National Party' in Essen as a natural focus for his efforts. A unitary constituency framework for the activities of the 'national parties' at the municipal and electoral levels, this seemed a ready-made arena for some unobtrusive Pan-German work. But Reismann-Grone soon discovered that the controlling faction—led by Wilhelm Hirsch in the general interests of the city's business oligarchy—was unwilling to brook any interference in its preserve.[33] In 1903 Reismann and a group of sympathizers

[31] See E. Böhm, *Überseehandel und Flottenbau* (Düsseldorf, 1972), pp. 67ff., and passim.

[32] These details are taken mainly from Reismann-Grone's own autobiographical references in his manuscript diaries, SA Essen, Reismann-Grone Papers, 10. See also Guratzsch, *Macht durch Organisation*, pp. 23, 417, 258–65.

[33] Wilhelm Hirsch (1861–1918) was born the son of a mine-foreman in Goslar, attended university at Leipzig and Berlin, and emigrated for a time to the USA. In 1887 he took up a position under Bueck at the CVDI, and during the following twenty years made himself into one of the leading functionaries of the West German heavy-industrial interest, marrying Bueck's daughter on the way. In 1897 he became Secretary of the Essen Chamber of Commerce. During the same period he developed into a leading political spokesman for the same

('*die Völkischen*', as he later called them)[34] made common cause with a liberal grouping under the lawyer Niemeyer to try and dislodge the 'clique', and set themselves up as a separate committee. Reismann took care of organization while his colleagues handled the public propaganda, with a view towards preventing the re-election of Hirsch to the Prussian Landtag in late 1903. Despite the efforts of the Hirsch group to patch up a compromise, the new opposition went ahead and contested the election as an independent 'National Association', winning some two-thirds of the electors in Essen in the process. However, Hirsch still carried the electors in Mülheim and Duisberg, and some last-minute equivocations by the Niemeyer group prevented the dissidents from capitalizing on their strength. This proved the summit of Reismann-Grone's success, for in February 1904 the independent committee voted, against his sole opposition, to reunite with the Hirsch group and on March 3rd dissolved itself. Niemeyer admitted later that Albert Müller, head of the *Essener Credit-Anstalt* and closely connected with the Krupp interest, had threatened to cut him off from the bank's business.[35]

This was a classic illustration of the difficulties of breaking into the closed shop of municipal *Honoratiorenpolitik*—even for the best-connected of radical nationalists. Reismann-Grone continued to involve himself in the Essen National Party, despite this defeat and his personal antipathy towards Hirsch, and in 1905 was elected on to its Council. But he had given up ideas of fighting for the acceptance of overtly Pan-German perspectives and hoped instead 'to revolutionize it slowly in a national direction'.[36] Working closely with his own chief editor, Heinrich Pohl, a former teacher and chairman of the Pan-German branch in Mülheim, he argued consistently for bourgeois unity against the SPD in every election. In general he retreated far more than before into Pan-German propaganda work, resuming his commitments in the national Managing Committee after the hiatus of 1903–4, and engaging himself heavily for the radical nationalists in the Navy League. The main conclusion he drew from the disappointments in Essen was that the time was not yet ripe for direct political interventions. In November 1908 when the pressure was mounting amongst his Pan-German colleagues for a decisive public initiative by the League, he recorded his scepticism: 'I stand by the view that the Pan-German League is far too insignificant to sweep the people along with it. So, first keep on working.'[37] He later commented of his views at this time that 'I understood that

interests: 1901–18 town councillor in Essen, 1901 National Liberal Landtag deputy, 1916 Reichstag deputy. He was also a close associate of Hugenberg, with membership in both Pan-German League and Navy League (though this seems to have been largely formal). He died in Oct. 1918, and there was a suspicion of suicide. Details supplied by SA Essen, but otherwise see Guratzsch, *Macht durch Organisation*, pp. 97ff., and passim.

[34] SA Essen, Reismann-Grone Papers, 10, IX. 03. 11.
[35] Ibid., IX, 03. 11ff., IX. 04. 1ff.
[36] Ibid., IX. 05. 4.
[37] Ibid., IX. 08. 6.

we can *never* win unless we educate the masses into the nation', and to this end he and Pohl had started a 'workers school' in the company, where they gave instruction in geography, history, constitutional law, and so on.[38] Like Heinrich Claß, therefore, Reismann received his political education in a disillusioning encounter with the National Liberals.[39] Though his retreat into 'educational' propaganda work was predicated on a realistic appraisal of the limited short-term possibilities for the Pan-German League of rectifying the situation, this in no way lessened his scorn for the National Liberal establishment.

It is hard to know just how typical this experience was, because the evidence is so closely tied to personal biographies. But the main point is this: in the conditions of the 1890s the newly consolidated Pan-German organization offered opportunities for action which were poorly served by the existing party framework. As suggested in the previous chapter, the parties were *occasional* institutions as they entered the 1890s, geared overwhelmingly to the demands of an election—loose and informal associations of notables, bound together by common ownership of rank, wealth and privilege, rather than by organizational procedures or by regular formal contact. As such they gave little scope at the local level for a more continuous involvement, for between elections the discussion of policy or legislation remained confined to the narrow circles of the party leaders, in direct negotiation with the state apparatuses or the functionaries of business. By the 1890s the threat of the SPD began to highlight the dangers of this situation, where the 'parties of order' were ill-equipped to deal with political mobilization and a mass electorate. But the old structures of *Honoratiorenpolitik* could not be dismantled overnight, and the party leaders proved reluctant to open their ranks to wider sections of the populace. As suggested above, the National Liberals were perhaps especially prone to this exclusiveness and the political backwardness that accompanied it. In the absence of any serious attempt to place the party on a more popular footing, it was hardly surprising that energetic individuals like Claß or Reismann-Grone should seek an alternative outlet in the so-called 'patriotic associations' or *nationale Verbände*.

The foundation of the Pan-German League proved to be the most self-conscious outgrowth of this situation, through which the difficulties of political access were articulated into a full-scale ideological critique. The League increasingly defined its politics only *via* an angry repudiation of the existing parties and their partial commitment to 'national goals'. The Pan-German lawyers, teachers, doctors and managers who railed against the 'fraction-philistine' with such passion were precisely the people to whom the National Liberals customarily looked for their natural support; yet these people professed

[38] Ibid., IX. 07. 1.

[39] Though the Essen National Party was technically a coalition of the Cartel parties, the National Liberals were by far the dominant grouping. As remarked above, from 1901 Hirsch was an important member of the National Liberal Landtag fraction.

nationalist beliefs with a totality of commitment which was quite foreign to the liberal establishment of the 1890s. They might also have little desire for assimilation within any of the existing parties, but on the contrary claim a separate existence, patrolling the nation's conscience and proclaiming their own higher virtue, asserting their independence of the parties and their moral superiority. Partly this reflected the constitutional structure of the Empire and the parties' limited power in the Reichstag; the real source of influence was often the bureaucracy itself, and this could be an obvious justification for by-passing the parties. But the ideology of the *Primat des Nationalen* was also important. The primacy of nationalist goals expressed by the distinctive German formula of *nationale Politik* determined a doctrinaire hostility to the process of sectional negotiation and compromise which was central to the conventional political process. Many aspiring bourgeois and petty-bourgeois politicians felt a genuine revulsion from 'party politics' in this sense, and accordingly sought a practical surrogate through the Pan-Germans and the other *nationale Verbände*.

In the most pronounced cases, therefore, like those of Claß and Reismann-Grone, this might take the form of explicit animosity against the existing parties, normally the National Liberals. But at the early stage of the 1890s it resulted more frequently in a kind of ecumenical nationalism, in which the propagation of nationalist values was elevated to a superior level of activity, which was unconnected but not at all incompatible with a diversity of sectional interests and politics. Hermann Rassow, senior master at an Elberfeld *Gymnasium* before moving to become headmaster of a school near Magdeburg in 1901, provides one of the best examples of this disinterested political eclecticism. A member of the Pan-German Council, he used all manner of organizations as a public platform in the later 1890s—not only local branches of the League itself, but Young Men's Associations, groups of his former pupils, the Elberfeld Christian-Social Association, the Elberfeld Evangelical Workers' Association, the Royalist Association of Railway Craftsmen, the Provincial Conference of Conservatives in the Rhineland, the Elberfeld 'Tuesday-Society', and all manner of workers' clubs and 'patriotic associations'.[40] As he showed later in his work for the Navy League, Rassow was one of the most relentless and ingenious of the nationalist agitators, immensely skilled in the full range of propaganda media, well-connected and adept in the difficult arts of securing industrial and official patronage. But unlike Claß and Reismann-Grone he made no attempt to place these skills at the service of a coherent party-political strategy. Instead he occupied an indeterminate middle ground of radical nationalism, feeling equally at home with populisms of the right and the left, animated above all by the

[40] See Rassow to Navy Office, Mar. 6th 1897, Rassow to Hollmann, Mar. 15th 1897, and Rassow to Navy Office, May 13th 1897, all BA-MA Freiburg, 3136, I. 2.1. 4d; Rassow to Haßler, Jan. 12th 1898, SA Augsburg, Haßler Papers, 13; Rassow to Delbrück, Sept. 8th 1896, DSB Berlin, Delbrück Papers.

desire to 'win back the embittered masses with the aid of the naval question'.[41] In the 1890s he was a political admirer simultaneously of Adolf Stöcker, Friedrich Lange and Friedrich Naumann.[42]

This pointed to a central difficulty of the Pan-Germans in the mid-1890s. Though the attempt to co-opt the League's high ideals of non-partisanship into the party-political project of the 'National Party' had been scotched, and though Hasse and Lehr had successfully rationalized the administration, it was by no means clear what, in concrete political practice, the League should be doing. Because it imposed no strict criteria of domestic political affiliation on its members it ran the danger of becoming a refuge for all manner of eccentric non-political nationalisms. Even if the League successfully distanced itself from such elements—the exponents of 'anti-semitism, the *Los-von-Rom* movement, the Wodan-cult, the anti-alcohol movement, purification of the language, the promotion of so-called German writing', as Hasse once listed them[43]—it still faced the problem of defining a clear position of its own. Though the disinterested propagation of the 'national idea' in the style of Hermann Rassow was an important ideological enterprise, it was difficult to quantify its material political effect. In Rassow's case it came close to a kind of displaced middle-class philanthropy, akin perhaps to temperance campaigning and similar ideologies of moral improvement. To specify the content of a Pan-German commitment, in other words, and to bind the rather disparate expectations of its members into some more coherent overall perspective, the League badly needed an important issue to focus its activity.

C. THE SOCIETY FOR THE EASTERN MARCHES

The activities of the Society for the Eastern Marches (also known as the 'H-K-T Society' after the surnames of its three founders, Ferdinand von Hansemann, Hermann Kennemann and Major Heinrich von Tiedemann-Seeheim) shed some interesting light on the situation of the Pan-Germans in the 1890s. Founded in November 1894, this organization owed much to the same bundle of nationalist discontents that had already spawned the Pan-German League four years before. Most obviously, it was a reaction against Caprivi's conciliatory Polish policy, which signalled a major departure from the stern centralist nationalism (or at least, greater Prussianism) of Bismarck's last years. Minor concessions were made to the Polish language in the schools, the harassment of Polish agrarian organization was relaxed, as was the discrimination against

---

[41] Rassow to Tirpitz, Apr. 12th 1898, BA-MA Freiburg, 2223, 93943.
[42] See Rassow's correspondence with Delbrück during 1895–6, and Rassow to Delbrück, Jan. 24th 1900, DSB Berlin, Delbrück Papers.
[43] Hasse's opening address to the Eisenach Convention, May 25th 1902, *Kundgebungen, Beschlüsse und Forderungen des Alldeutschen Verbandes 1890–1902* (Munich, 1902), p. 94.

Poles in public employment, and a gesture to Polish cultural autonomy of considerable symbolic power was made in 1892 when the Polish Landtag deputy Florian Stablewski was appointed to the Archbishopric of Posen and Gnesen.[44] The actual extent and overall coherence of these concessions should certainly not be exaggerated, because the local administration of the Polish-speaking areas in the provinces of Posen and West Prussia continued much as before under the same personnel. But at a time of increasing demographic pressure on the German minority in Posen (maximized by the general flight from East to West), they easily fuelled alarmist predictions concerning the erosion of German culture and morale in a crucial border area.

Moreover, this nationalist dissatisfaction fed directly into a general 'Bismarckian' critique of the Caprivi administration. The manifesto of the abortive National Party in the autumn of 1892 had itemized the grievances: the change of course in foreign policy, the terms of the commercial treaties, an educational policy which neglected the basic interests of the state, and now a Polish policy which abdicated political leadership in the Eastern Marches 'to the Polish clergy and nobility'.[45] Without personally agitating for such a position Bismarck was re-emerging by 1893 as a focus for right-wing opposition to the existing government. His supporters were well-equipped with major organs of opinion, an influential circle of Free Conservative and National Liberal politicians gathered around him, and the pilgrimage to Varzin or Friedrichsruh became a regular feature of dissident nationalist politics.[46] Concurrently, and in mutual interaction with this, the Conservative Party began to establish a far more pronounced agrarian presence, and although their dependence on seasonal Polish labour made many Junkers heavily ambivalent towards the more extreme anti-Polish programmes (e.g. for closing the borders), in the short term the nationalist charges against Caprivi had an obvious atttaction. Inevitably, Caprivi's opponents regarded his reliance on Polish votes in the Reichstag, particularly in the case of the commercial treaties, as an affront and a provocation. By the spring of 1894, therefore, nationalist hostility to the Poles had broadened to cover all sections of the right-wing opposition to Caprivi, and it was no accident that the reconstituted Pan-German League

[44] For the 'era of conciliation' in Polish policy between 1890 and 1894: M. Broszat, *Zweihundert Jahre deutscher Polenpolitik* (Frankfurt, 1972), pp. 152ff.; Tims, *Germanizing Prussian Poland*, pp. 16–21; H. K. Rosenthal, 'German-Polish Relations in the Caprivi Era', Ph.D. Thesis (Columbia, 1967).

[45] Copy in BA Coblenz, Harden Papers, 140.

[46] For the development of the 'Bismarck Fronde', see J. A. Nicholls, *Germany After Bismarck* (Cambridge, Mass., 1958), pp. 101ff., 132f.; E.-T. P. W. Wilke, *Political Decadence in Imperial Germany. Personnel-Political Aspects of the German Government Crisis 1894–97* (Urbana, 1976), pp. 76f., 83f. For the institution of the Bismarck pilgrimage: A. Galos, 'Der Deutsche Ostmarkenverein von 1894 bis 1900', in *Die Hakatisten*, pp. 33f. For Bismarck's politics in the 1890s in general: H. Hofmann, *Fürst Bismarck, 1890–1898*, 3 vols. (Stuttgart, 1914).

chose the Polish question for its major public interventions in that year.[47]

In the first place, accordingly, the foundation of the Society for the Eastern Marches must be seen in the general context of the backlash against Caprivi. The organization was connected to the *Bismarck-Fronde* through the personality of one of the three co-founders, Ferdinand von Hansemann, the son of the Berlin financier Adolph von Hansemann and a member of the consortium which converted the *Berliner Neueste Nachrichten* into a Bismarckian organ in 1893.[48] But more specifically, the idea of the Society took shape during a short-term manoeuvre of the agrarian opposition. Hansemann, the owner of a massive estate at Pempowo in the south of Posen, had already gone on record as an opponent of the commercial treaties, and during the summer of 1894 he now combined with some fellow estate-owners to organize a public deputation to Bismarck's Pomeranian residence at Varzin.[49] As Tims said, Bismarck was to be adopted as 'the visible symbol in a great public demonstration which should at once rally the German population of the eastern provinces to greater unity of action, stimulate their patriotism, advertise the interests of the Prussian East to the entire Reich, and incidentally serve as handwriting on the wall for the Chancellory and the Imperial Palace'.[50] Preparations were conducted in private without public appeals, and on September 16th 1894 a procession of some 1,700 Posen landowners and their camp-followers made the envisaged trek to Varzin. A week later a similar delegation from West Prussia repeated the occasion, marching six abreast from the station to Bismarck's residence, singing songs and making presentations, before receiving Bismarck's address. Nationalist concern for the Polish question was clearly experiencing an upswing—the Posen expedition had been sandwiched between two major speeches by the Kaiser in Königsberg and Thorn (September 6th and 22nd)—and it was fairly natural for the minds of the organizers to turn to the idea of a permanent association.[51]

The upshot was the launching of the Society for the Eastern Marches on November 3rd 1894, after the previous formation of an executive and the issue of a public manifesto. The meeting was attended by eighty persons, mainly from the province of Posen. It appointed an Executive composed of ten representatives from Posen and a further three from West Prussia. A General Committee was also formed, with 104 members from Posen and West Prussia,

[47] Galos, 'Ostmarkenverein', p. 33; Kruck, *Geschichte*, p. 11. See also Hugenberg's three articles, 'Der Preußische Staat als Polonisator', *Alld. Bl.*, Apr. 15th, July 19th and Oct. 14th 1894, repub. in *Streiflichter aus Vergangenheit und Gegenwart* (Berlin, 1927), pp. 300–6.

[48] Adolph von Hansemann was President of the *Disconto-Gesellschaft* and was ennobled in 1872. The family claimed an eminent liberal tradition. See H. Münch, *Adolph von Hansemann* (Munich-Berlin, 1932).

[49] F. von Hansemann, 'Commercial Treaties and Polish Policy', *Deutsches Wochenblatt*, Nov. 16th 1893, and 'On the Political Circumstances of the Province Posen', ibid., Mar. 22nd 1894.

[50] Tims, *Germanizing Prussian Poland*, p. 24.

[51] For the details of this pre-history: ibid., pp. 24ff.; Galos, 'Ostmarkenverein', pp. 35ff.

113 from the rest of Germany: some sixty per cent of the former came from the ranks of the Junkers and the related social categories, whilst in the case of the latter the percentage of Junkers sank to less than fifteen, well behind both the civil servants (30%) and the teachers (25%). At this stage it was envisaged that the Society would be a Posen organization, though room was left for a possible extension of its scope to West Prussia and Silesia (the other two provinces with a larger Polish population). According to the Constitution, the aim was the 'strengthening and rallying of Germandom in the Eastern Marches through the revival and consolidation of German national feeling and the economic strengthening of the German people'. This also mapped out a series of practical tasks: the systematic monitoring of the Polish-language press; promotion of German settlement and productive immigration to the East; 'the strengthening of the German *Mittelstand* in town and country through the guarantee of custom and credit'; the organization of German festivals; the 'promotion of the German curriculum in schools'. The general justifications advanced for the new organization were the fatalism and passivity of the German population in the East: in the Bismarckian era the latter had grown used to relying on the government for a firm response to the growth of Polish nationalism, and the change of course under Caprivi had consequently left them leaderless and without direction. The spokesmen for the Society insisted upon its defensive character: it was to work for the Germans rather than against the Poles.[52]

Superficially, from the identity of the co-founders (three of the biggest landowners in the East) and the social composition of the initial leadership the H-K-T Society would seem to have been a classic organization of the East Elbian aristocracy. Yet on closer inspection this impression proves to be extremely misleading. In the first place none of the co-founders conforms easily to the stereotype of the *Krautjunker*, the East Elbian backwoodsman immersed in his parochial defence of a traditional social order, setting his shoulder against the modern world and clinging to his feudal status. Hansemann, for instance, came from a Rhineland banking family with impeccably liberal credentials during the middle third of the century; his father had been ennobled in 1872 and the estates in Posen were acquired shortly afterwards. Though well set to follow in his father's footsteps (reading law at Heidelberg, marrying an academic's daughter), Ferdinand opted instead for 'the life of a gentleman-farmer and amateur politician', settling on the new family estate at Pempowo and devoting himself to horse-breeding and cheesemaking. Only thirty-three in 1894, he was clearly ambitious, and his family's social standing combined with his father's business contacts to provide him with a political base in Berlin. The second member of the triumvirate, Hermann Alexander Kennemann, was an immensely successful career-farmer, who had gradually accumulated the largest landholding in Posen after acquiring a bankrupt Polish estate at Klenka, ten miles from the Russian border, in 1840, at the age of twenty-five. An

[52] Ibid., pp. 44–7; Tims, *Germanizing Prussian Poland*, pp. 29–35, 40–2.

3*

incoming colonist and practising farmer, who turned down the chance of
ennoblement, he was 'the type *par excellence* of the non-noble agrarian capitalist
of the Prussian East'. The third co-founder, Heinrich von Tiedemann, was
closer to the stereotype of the Junker and his family was deeply rooted in the
East; after serving as an officer in the Army for eighteen years he retired in
1881 and bought an old Polish estate south-west of Posen, renaming it Seeheim.
But even Tiedemann reproduced in his later career the characteristic effects
of the growing inter-penetration of industrial and agrarian capital: he married
into a successful Berlin merchant family and in 1898 became a part-owner of
its exporting business. Increasingly resident in Berlin, he united in his own
person complementary networks of political influence.[53]

In our present state of ignorance about the structure of East Elbian agriculture during the transition to capitalism, it would be dangerous to pronounce
these three cases either typical or untypical of the landowning class in general.[54]
But they are certainly rather unusual in their willingness to become involved
so vigorously in a nationalist venture such as the H-K-T Society. Most of the
evidence suggests that after the inaugural period, when the latter had a
transitory importance for the struggle against Caprivi, most agrarians treated
it with indifference, not to say occasional hostility. Hansemann and Tiedemann
had already found it difficult to interest the East Elbian luminaries of the
Conservative Party during the foundation itself: a week before the Society
was launched Hansemann commented that 'Stolberg-Wernigerode is the only
one of his kind who has not turned us down', 'whilst with few exceptions the
Conservative landowners of the old Prussian provinces are treating us with
reserve'.[55] Indeed, they had to thwart a separate initiative from Endell, the
Chairman of the Agrarian League in Posen, who envisaged the new organization
as an auxiliary of the League rather than an independent nationalist pressure
group pursuing general goals: though the triumvirate successfully scotched this
rivalry some weeks before the foundation, Endell had to be accommodated in
the original Executive, and his potential agrarian factionalism was only finally
removed by his resignation in January 1895.[56] During this contest Tiedemann
had successfully mobilized his connections in Berlin to intercede with the

[53] Details mainly from ibid., 35–40, 216–18; also Galos, 'Ostmarkenverein', pp. 34ff.

[54] It is sometimes forgotten that the highly influential essay by Hans Rosenberg, 'Die
Pseudodemokratisierung der Rittergutsbesitzerklasse', in *Probleme der deutschen Sozialgeschichte* (Frankfurt, 1969), pp. 7–50, is only a suggestive introductory essay. The best
general works on agriculture are: H. Haushofer, *Die deutsche Landwirtschaft im technischen
Zeitalter* (Stuttgart, 1972), and H. W. Graf Finck v. Finckenstein, *Die Entwicklung der Landwirtschaft in Preußen und Deutschland 1800–1930* (Munich, 1960).

[55] Hansemann to Bismarck, Oct. 27th and Nov. 18th 1894, BA Coblenz, Bismarck Papers,
349.

[56] For this episode, see the discussion in Galos, 'Ostmarkenverein', pp. 40f., 103f. A
proposal also surfaced during Sept. 1894 from the Conservative Association in Bromberg for
a 'Society for the Furtherance of Germandom'.

Agrarian League's leaders and in the following years a *modus vivendi* was reached with the agrarian Conservatives in Posen. But the figures spoke for themselves: whereas two-thirds of the original Executive were the owners of a *Rittergut*, by 1914 there were only four such amongst a total of fifty; similarly, amongst the eighty-five chairmen of local branches in Posen in 1908 there were only eleven farmers, none of whom owned a *Rittergut*, whilst the comparable figures for West Prussia and Silesia were two out of forty-nine and three out of fifty-seven.[57] Whatever the formal relations between the Society and the Conservative Party, as individual landowners the latter held themselves aloof.

In terms of its ordinary membership, the Society was clearly not an organization of the landed interest. In one sample of twenty-six branches from the years 1894–1900 only 10·7% of the 951 members were landowners, with a further 2·7% Army officers; the largest groups were civil servants (26·6%), artisans (17·6%), businessmen (15·7%), and teachers (14·0%), whilst the professions counted for 6·5%, clergymen 4·2%, rentiers 0·7%, and those with no designation 1·3%.[58] This was still the case later, when the total membership was more: in Posen in 1907 only 2·0% of the membership were landowners, whilst for West Prussia the next year none were specifically listed; in both cases the largest groups were the civil servants (39·8% and 36·3% respectively), peasants (22·1% and approx. 20·2%), artisans (22·1% and 17·7%), and teachers (9·4% and 11·1%).[59] As time went by, the Society clearly became increasingly dependent on state employees for its support, a fact which partially reflected the top-heavy character of the public sector in the local economy.[60] The closest consultations with the ministerial bureaucracy had certainly been fundamental to the initial growth of the organization in 1894–5, when Tiedemann had at once established contacts at the highest level in Berlin, and the goodwill of the provincial apparatus was considered an essential precondition for an effective recruitment campaign in the localities. The normal procedure for putting down roots in a new town or rural district was to confer with the highest provincial officials on the spot. Where the solicited support was not forthcoming the Society found itself forced to operate in an atmosphere of scepticism and indifference from the general German-speaking population. Thus in East Prussia, where the authorities adhered to more conciliatory programmes of gradual Germanization until after the turn of the century, the Society received no concrete assistance from local officialdom: a major recruiting effort in 1898 produced only a handful of new branches, and of these only the one in Königsberg managed a public meeting before 1900; at a recruiting meeting called in Gumbinnen in April 1898 only fourteen people turned up, comprising a few

[57] Figures quoted by Tims, *Germanizing Prussian Poland*, p. 219.
[58] Galos, 'Ostmarkenverein', p. 77.
[59] Computed from figures in ibid., pp. 148, 157.
[60] See Broszat, *Zweihundert Jahre*, pp. 169f.

teachers, a doctor, two ladies and a journalist, and no branch could be formed.[61]

To acquire a large membership a local branch required the patronage of either a sympathetic landowner or the local bureaucracy, and in either case the mechanism of recruitment must cast serious doubt on the level of real commitment amongst the ordinary members: thus one of the largest branches was at Klenka, Kennemann's own seat, where he simply commanded dependent tenants and estate officials into the Society; similarly at Deutsch-Krone, where the branch chairman was Wolff, the Governor of the prison, the great majority of members were actually prison officers and the like, many of whom left when their superior retired.[62] Where it existed a mass membership rarely carried much real meaning, and the average size of local branches was quite small if this is borne in mind: thus in 1908 the average number of members of the sixty-two West Prussian branches was 144, but only 114 if the largest three were subtracted.[63] There were often bitter complaints about the inactivity of the membership, particularly the notables, who were then accused of perpetuating the 'caste-spirit', of importing outworn conventions of social precedence and hierarchy into a movement technically committed to the classless solidarity of all Germans.[64] Local branches often had to fight directly against the obstructionism of local landowners, as in Gnesen (Posen), where the Conservative Junker Wendorf tried to hinder the Society's progress, or in Witkowo, where the Agrarian League successfully closed off the rural population. The annual report of 1907 commented pointedly: 'the leading upper stratum of the German population, the larger landowners and the senior civil service, apart from certain pleasing exceptions, either hold themselves completely aloof from the Society or at the very best content themselves with paying the membership fee, but participate in not one of the meetings of the local branch'.[65]

In this respect—its relative isolation from the interlocking rural power structure of the squirarchy and its bureaucratic allies, and its relative dependence on the activist involvement of teachers, professional men and middle-ranking civil servants—the Society for the Eastern Marches was fairly close to the Pan-German League. In both cases, for instance, teachers were disproportionately important in the life of the branches: in 1901 24·3% of the Pan-German membership consisted of teachers, and in 1906 the latter accounted for 36% of the League's local officers; in the H-K-T Society teachers seem to have been

---

[61] Galos, 'Ostmarkenverein', pp. 66f. For the special problems of East Prussia: ibid., pp. 65ff., 160–2. For the process of establishing contact with sympathizers in a town: ibid., pp. 89ff., and for the procedure in setting up a branch: ibid., pp. 59ff.

[62] Both examples from ibid., pp. 53f.

[63] W. Jacobczyk, 'Der Deutsche Ostmarkenverein von 1900 bis 1914', in *Die Hakatisten*, p. 157.

[64] For a good selection of these complaints, see ibid., pp. 153ff. But see above all the tract by Hans Semrau, *Der Deutsche Ostmarkenverein und die völkische Erziehung der Ostmarkendeuschen* (Lissa, 1907).

[65] Jacobczyk, 'Ostmarkenverein', pp. 148 (note 49), 153f., 159.

between 9% and 14% of the membership and around 22% of the functionaries (e.g. in Posen in 1914 forty-four out of a hundred and seven branch chairmen).[66] Moreover, both organizations shared an ideological populism which, though cautiously expressed in the 1890s, had some disquieting implications for the traditional rulers: the commitment to the strengthening of small peasant property in the East goes a long way towards illuminating the tensions between the agrarians and the *Hakatisten*, for given the historic form of the rural class structure east of the Elbe, this could only be done in the long term by expropriating the latifundia. Both the Pan-Germans and the H-K-T Society tried officially to soft-pedal on this issue, but the logic of a populist intervention into the Polish question constantly restated the contradiction, particularly in the practice of the rank-and-file ideologues. Moreover, there were also echoes of a related Pan-German syndrome, for the demonstrable passivity of the notables was redeployed by their critics into a swingeing *social* critique, which demanded that all members, whatever their social status, be admitted to the decision-making in the branches. This was an important step. The notables were no longer being attacked just for their lack of personal commitment; they also stood accused of damaging the nationalist cause, even of deliberately retarding its development, by their élitism and social exclusiveness. At the very least, one critic declared, it would 'do no harm at all if for once the wealthier and more educated sat down for a beer with the man in the work-blouse'.[67]

But in other respects the Society for the Eastern Marches and the Pan-Germans were very different. It is clear, for instance, that the former enjoyed much closer relations with the government and had developed a special relationship with the bureaucracy which the uneven reversal of Caprivi's softer policies in the field could not disguise. Thus, it is true that the Society received little succour from the Governors of East Prussia and Silesia until after 1900, and that relations with the Governor of Posen, Wilamowitz-Moellendorf, remained uneasy until his retirement in 1899. But during this early period Tiedemann had cultivated a close feeling with Miquel, and as the latter consolidated his central position in the Ministry of State between 1894 and 1897 the Society became an indirect beneficiary: the regularization of its relations with the provincial apparatus was a more distant effect of Miquel's rising influence and his vital ministerial axis with Posadowsky.[68] The end of Caprivi's new course was strongly felt in Polish affairs, initially by piecemeal shifts in administrative practice: the sensitivity of the authorities to the most prosaic

[66] Pan-German figures from Wertheimer, *Pan-German League*, pp. 65ff., and those for the Eastern Marches Society from Galos, 'Ostmarkenverein', p. 77, Jacobczyk, 'Ostmarkenverein', pp. 148, 157, 167, and Tims, *Germanizing Prussian Poland*, p. 224.

[67] Prof. Hoffmann at a meeting of the Danzig branch in 1908, cit. Jacobczyk, 'Ostmark-verein', p. 159. The clearest and most radical statement of this critique is Semrau, *Der Deutsche Ostmarkenverein*.

[68] Details: Galos, 'Ostmarkenverein', pp. 66–70, 83ff., 94–8; Jacobczyk, 'Ostmarkenverein', pp. 160–72.

manifestations of Polish cultural life markedly increased over 1894–5 and the flow of reports from the provinces was quickly matched by a more efficient system of card-indexing at the centre. This extension of surveillance culminated in 1898–9 in a cluster of executive decisions: the settlement fund was increased, a new fund was created for the Eastern Governors, the important 'Instructions for Officials' was published in April 1898, plans were hatched for a restrictive language law, and an inter-ministerial working-party set up.[69] The *Hakatisten* had obviously made their contribution here, but it would be wrong to present them as the main instigator. The Society was not involved directly in the government's deliberations, and on the whole it was the latter's requirements that determined the pace and terms of the relationship.[70] For example, though Tiedemann made much of his ability to bring ministerial sanctions against unco-operative local officials, the long campaign against Polish postal workers showed only small returns, whilst attacks on individuals rarely succeeded.[71] But whatever the exact parameters of the Society's influence, there can be no doubt that it was exerted within a framework of constructive co-operation with the government, and this was further strengthened by Bülow's final emergence in 1901–2.[72]

This stood in sharp contrast to the situation of the Pan-German League, which never achieved this degree of political integration with the priorities of the government. There were moments of close co-operation in the mid-nineties, principally over naval policy as we shall see, but the state never deployed the Pan-German organization and membership as an additional resource as it did with the Society for the Eastern Marches. This was partly a matter of the organizations' respective scope, for where the Pan-Germans were simultaneously committed on a number of political fronts, some compatible with government policies and others not, the *Hakatisten* were exclusively concerned with a single area, which coincided almost exactly with a current preoccupation of the government itself. But beyond this there was a deep ideological gulf between the Pan-German leadership and the government, produced by the former's belief in the 'primacy of the national' and a populist notion of citizenship, which certainly animated parts of the H-K-T Society's membership, but which played

[69] Ibid., pp. 86ff. For details of the 'Instructions', see Tims, *Germanizing Prussian Poland*, p. 69. Note that plans for a new language law were not actually realized for another decade.

[70] This point is rightly stressed by Galos, 'Ostmarkenverein', p. 93.

[71] Ibid., p. 100. The case of Paul von Roëll, the district official in Pleschen who obstructed the founding of a branch there, was fairly typical. Tiedemann had immediately protested at the Ministry of the Interior, but Roëll (original editor of *DVC* 1876–82, co-founder of *Das Deutsche Adelsblatt* and editor of *Neue Politische Korrespondenz*) was too highly connected for this intervention to work. In any case the Prussian Government was unlikely to allow itself to be dictated to in such a fashion.

[72] Ibid., pp. 70f., 130–2, 144f. With the demise of Miquel between 1899 and 1901 there had been fears in the Eastern Marches Society that a strong anti-Polish policy would die with him.

no part in Tiedemann's own conception.[73] Moreover, this populist nationalism had an organizational dimension which marked a further difference between the two movements. As we saw, the Pan-German League was notable in the 1890s for its formal emphasis on the full rights of the ordinary membership to regular participation in discussions about policy and tactics; this had been one of the issues in the crisis and regroupment of 1893–4, and was meticulously explored in the new Constitution adopted in 1903. The Society for the Eastern Marches, on the other hand, was organized strictly around the personal leadership of Heinrich von Tiedemann, in which an overbearing autocratic centralism was the characteristic feature. All the threads of administration ran through Tiedemann's hands, including relations with the government and the traffic with the provincial secretariats in Posen, Graudenz, Königsberg and Breslau. He insisted on the strict subordination of the full-time officers and maintained an obsessive commitment to secrecy. He regarded the branch chairmen as the mere agents of his will and barely tolerated any autonomous local initiative.[74] This again contrasted with the leadership of the Pan-German League, where Hasse kept a self-effacing provincial residence in Leipzig, set a premium on internal discussion and took care to involve the membership in all important decisions.

This discussion of the Eastern Marches Society is intended to cast the newly-established Pan-German presence in the mid-1890s into political relief. It is also meant to highlight some of the diversity in the structure and practices of the so-called *nationale Verbände*. Most obviously, one was a single-issue pressure group, while the other counted that issue as only one amongst many. But they were also separated by a differing relationship with the state, a contrasting style of political leadership and a different understanding of political participation. On the other hand, they were motivated by similar ideological commitments to the primacy of nation over class or confession as the primary loyalty of a citizen. They also tended to appeal to the same kind of person as far as active commitment was concerned—to the Protestant petty-bourgeoisie of teachers, professional men, moderately successful businessmen and middling civil servants, occasionally to artisans and peasant-farmers. They experienced indifference and sometimes hostility from the traditional *Honoratioren*, particularly the big landowners, and existed in an uneasy relationship with the conventional political parties. The paradox of the H-K-T Society was that this distinctive social physiognomy of radical nationalism coexisted with a *modus operandi* which denied its populist potential. In this way it exemplified both the future direction of radical nationalist politics and the nature of the constraints which they currently observed. Though the more active local branches were prepared to question the social complacency of the notables and the

[73] This is fully discussed in Ch. 5 below, pp. 160ff.
[74] For good descriptions of Tiedemann's leadership: Galos, 'Ostmarkenverein', pp. 48ff., and Jacobczyk, 'Ostmarkenverein', pp. 136ff.

dictatorial leadership of Tiedemann, the movement as a whole lacked the vitality and popular momentum to escape this contradiction.

D. *WELTPOLITIK* AND THE GERMAN NAVY LEAGUE

The foundation of the Society for the Eastern Marches exemplified in immediate political terms a central difficulty of the Pan-German League. For the appearance of yet another specialized organization was an ironic commentary on its claim to a general leadership in nationalist politics and helped prolong the uncertainties from which the Pan-Germans were trying to escape. Even before the official appearance of the Eastern Marches Society the League approached the organizers for a possible demarcation of interests: Hasse hoped to confine the new organization to the province of Posen, where its work would in any case be concentrated, and where the Pan-Germans lacked a firm presence of their own. For his own part Tiedemann regarded the Pan-Germans with some scorn as 'fanciful idealists' notable for 'fuzziness and lack of vigor'. When an entire Pan-German branch joined the anti-Polish crusade in Plauen, he remarked that 'six hundred Pan-Germans *en bloc* in our Society might well be cause for real discomfort'. Though the Statutes included specific provision for 'amicable co-operation' with the League, the relationship was for many years an uneasy one. More than anything else it re-emphasized the lack of any clear definition of the *raison d'être* of the Pan-German League. There was no uniformity in the Pan-German response: branches in Hagen, Mainz and Karlsruhe willingly helped the Society get off the ground with facilities and speakers, but the one in Mülheim merely gave one of its spokesmen a few minutes in one of its own meetings.[75]

This adumbrated the nature of the Pan-Germans' tactical dilemma: despite Hasse's stress on the vitality of the local branches, the latter could hardly establish themselves as the natural focus of radical nationalist energies until the *national* organization had won for itself a public position which clearly distinguished it from competitors. The H-K-T Society was not the only new foundation in the aftermath of the shake-up which brought Hasse and Lehr into office. The appearance of Friedrich Lange's German-Union around the same time, for instance, was potentially very confusing, particularly as Lange already commanded a wide following from his activities at the *Tägliche Rundschau*. His quarrel with the latter and the launching of his own paper the *Deutsche Zeitung* led to a bitter struggle for local subscribers in 1896 which further added to the confusion.[76] For purely accidental reasons individuals might

[75] See Galos, 'Ostmarkenverein', p. 106, and Tims, *Germanizing Prussian Poland*, p. 250. See also *Die Post*, Oct. 17th 1894, for discussion between the Eastern Marches Society and the Pan-Germans.

[76] See esp. the following letters from Rassow to Delbrück: Feb. 25th 1896, early July 1896 and June 11th 1897, DSB Berlin, Delbrück Papers.

choose one rather than the other of two similar organizations, and at least two prominent Pan-Germans, Heinrich Claß and Georg Freiherr von Stössel, passed first through the ranks of the German-Union.[77] Moreover, it was still unclear exactly how the Pan-Germans differed from the Colonial Society, for given their origins the former were publicly identified mainly with a more extreme colonialism. This impression was enhanced by the maintenance of a noisy Pan-German presence inside the Colonial Society, particularly in its important Berlin Section. Hasse was alive to these difficulties. In his first confidential circular to the membership after the crucial Council of July 1893, he argued that the previous 'weakness of the League (consisted) in the absence of a definite long-term practical object', by contrast with groups like the Colonial Society which already had such a permanent goal. Experience taught that it was not enough simply to gather together 'German-minded people of the more decisive cast'; it was also necessary to provide concrete goals and to wait on real events before giving substance to the general principles expressed in the programme of the movement.[78]

In January 1896, first with the Krueger Telegram and then with the Kaiser's famous *Weltpolitik* speech, 'real events' did their job for the Pan-Germans. There was already some pressure for an expansion of Germany's naval armaments in order to strengthen her position in the world market—in 1893-4 the Colonial Society was shifting rather unevenly between conventional calls for more cruisers and the more novel demand for a battlefleet[79]—and news of the Jameson Raid provided the necessary stimulus for a more vigorous upswing in public discussion. On January 7th Johannes Grunow, the Editor of *Grenzboten*, called for a voluntary subscription for the Navy in a Pan-German meeting in Leipzig, and on January 19th—the day after the Kaiser's speech—the League endorsed this officially.[80] On January 24th the Colonial Society set its propaganda machinery in motion with a circular to the local Sections. Significantly, the most decisive Pan-German intervention occurred within the Berlin Section of the Colonial Society: on February 17th Hasse and Peters managed to displace Prince Arenberg, the Centre deputy, from the Chair during a public meeting, and together with their supporters railroaded through a radical naval resolution. A few days later Hugenberg delivered a calculated indiscretion in a speech at Celle, in which he claimed that the Pan-Germans had been asked to start a propaganda campaign by Senden-Bibran, the Head of the Kaiser's Naval Cabinet, in order to prepare the public for a navy bill in the autumn. In the

[77] Claß, *Wider den Strom*, pp. 30ff.; U. Lohalm, *Völkischer Radikalismus* (Hamburg, 1970), pp. 32ff.

[78] Schilling, *Beiträge*, p. 371.

[79] H. Pogge von Strandmann, 'Nationale Verbände zwischen Weltpolitik und Kontinentalpolitik', in H. Schottelius and W. Deist (Eds.), *Marine und Marinepolitik im kaiserlichen Deutschland 1871 bis 1914* (Düsseldorf, 1972), p. 303.

[80] Schilling, *Beiträge*, pp. 70f.

ensuing outcry both Hasse and Hugenberg issued a retraction, but the statement
had served its purpose in appropriating to the Pan-Germans the public thunder
of the naval campaigning.[81]

Quite apart from Hasse's professed intention to find a concrete agitational
object, the League needed to move quickly in order to pre-empt competitors.
As well as the Colonial Society there were signs that a special naval organization
might be formed: in April 1895 a German Navy League had been founded in
Baden Baden with a purely local resonance, but at the end of January 1896
Hans Delbrück called in the *Preussische Jahrbücher* for 'the formation of a
league for the strengthening of the war fleet that should proceed with petitions
and popular assemblies'.[82] Accordingly—but not without opposition from the
prominent party politicians amongst its members—the Pan-German Council
endorsed the previous initiatives in two sittings in April and June 1896, issuing
a resolution to proclaim its leadership of the naval movement.[83] This decisive
response to events had clearly shown returns: in April 1896 the moderates
in the Berlin Colonial Society retreated into a newly-formed Section for Berlin-
Charlottenburg, thus abdicating from the political fight with the radicals, and
in February the mercantile establishment in Hamburg likewise established its
own Section of the Colonial Society to anticipate a similar move by the Pan-
Germans there. These defensive manoeuvres spelt a clear success for the Pan-
Germans: towards the end of March Hasse addressed the Hamburg branch of
the Pan-German League and presented the Kaiser's January speech as a
Pan-German declaration.[84]

Having placed the executive of the Colonial Society under pressure, correctly
sensed the activist temper of rank-and-file enthusiasts and generally established
its political leadership in the movement for a bigger Navy, the Pan-German
Executive had few objections to reinforcing its own efforts by also working
through the Colonial Society. In the spring of 1897, when the parliamentary
difficulties of the naval estimates prefigured a fresh cycle of naval agitation, the
pace was set by Reismann-Grone. In May 1897 the latter received a visit from
Dr Korn, Krupp's Secretary, who confided that a new Navy Bill was definitely
in the offing and requested his assistance in preparing public opinion. He began
work at once, collected a fund of nine thousand marks, and proposed a vigorous
naval campaign to the Pan-German Managing Committee on June 9th 1897.
He was strongly backed by Alfred Hugenberg (then working in the Posen
Settlement Commission), Bruno Weyer, the famous naval writer, and Paul

[81] For details: Kehr, *Battleship Building*, pp. 49ff.; Anderson, *The Background of Anti-
English Feeling in Germany, 1890–1902* (New York, 1969), pp. 181ff.; Pierard, 'German
Colonial Society', pp. 168ff.; Pogge von Strandmann, 'Nationale Verbände', p. 304. For events
in the government, see Röhl, *Germany Without Bismarck*, pp. 166ff.

[82] Kehr, *Battleship Building*, p. 55.

[83] Schilling, *Beiträge*, pp. 76f.

[84] Böhm, *Überseehandel*, p. 81; 'strictly confidential' circular, Apr. 1896, signed by 22
prominent members of the Colonial Society in Berlin, BA Coblenz, Bismarck Papers, A20.

Simons, the Elberfeld industrialist, who was also under strong pressure from Hermann Rassow in his local branch.[85] After winning the necessary approval, Reismann and Weyer left for Munich the next day to canvass the Colonial Society, whose annual Congress was about to convene. They received ready backing from Heinrich von Kusserow, who helped Reismann frame a composite resolution calling for a full-scale naval campaign. The backlog of internal difficulties associated with previous Pan-German initiatives complicated the easy acceptance of a resolution which might implicate the colonial movement in political agitation against a Reichstag majority. But on this occasion the favourable political context, in which most committed nationalists acknowledged the need for an expansion of the Navy, enabled the establishment of a suitable consensus. The proposals submitted by Reismann and Kusserow were thrashed out in committee on June 11th and accepted by the full Congress the following day.[86]

The resolution called for naval construction to the limits of the shipyards' capacity, and a special 'Agitation-Committee' was set up by the Colonial Society to finance and co-ordinate the propaganda. As a result of the joint initiative of Reismann and Kusserow and suitably boosted by the announcement of Tirpitz's ambitious Navy Bill, an impressive campaign unfolded during the winter months of 1897–8: the Colonial Society held 173 lectures and distributed 140,000 leaflets and pamphlets, including 2,000 copies of Mahan's *The Influence of Sea Power in History* supplied free of charge by the Navy Office.[87] The Pan-Germans conducted a parallel activity, especially in the West where Reismann himself provided the inspiration. The Pan-Germans concentrated on large public gatherings addressed by the movement's naval experts, often resulting in large accretions of membership or the formation of a new branch, and attracting as many as six or seven hundred people.[88] A similar campaign occurred in Hessen under the direction of Claß: in the spring he had taken the German-Union *Gemeinden* into the Pan-German League and inaugurated the new affiliation with a public meeting on the Navy addressed by Weyer on May 9th. Branches were launched in Alzey, Worms, Sprendlingen, Wöllstein, Wiesbaden, Frankfurt, Offenbach, Hanau and so forth. By the end of 1898 the

[85] SA Essen, Reismann-Grone Papers, 10, IX. 1895. 5. Weyer, a retired naval officer, was the author of the widely circulated *Taschenbuch der Kriegsflotten*.

[86] SA Essen, Reismann-Grone Papers, 10, IX. 1895. pp. 7f.; *Germania*, July 16th 1897; Kehr, *Battleship Building*, pp. 99f.; Pogge von Strandmann, 'Nationale Verbände', p. 304. Kusserow was the retired Foreign Office specialist on colonial affairs, whom Kehr rightly describes as 'the driving-force' behind the naval propaganda in the Colonial Society.

[87] Kehr, *Battleship Building*, p. 100; Pierard, 'German Colonial Society', pp. 176ff.; Kusserow to Tirpitz, Feb. 19th 1898, BA-MA Freiburg, 2222, 93941.

[88] See the regular reports in *RWZ*, including the following: Jan. 21st 1898 (Stolberg); Jan. 25th 1898 (Rheydt); Jan, 26th 1898 (Hagen, Hohenlimburg, Hamburg); Jan. 27th 1898 (Haspe, Wetter); Jan. 30th 1898 (Barmen); Jan. 31st 1898 (Altendorf); Feb. 1st 1898 (Elberfeld). Attendances were large, reaching 6–700 in Rheydt and Altendorf. See also the large collection of resolutions and petitions in BA-MA Freiburg, 2222, 93939.

Mainz branch had over seven hundred members, whilst a Rhine-Main-*Gau* had been constituted with a membership of 3,600.[89] Much attention was also given to the Hagen constituency of Eugen Richter, leader of the *Freisinnige Volkspartei* which was opposing the Navy Bill: at one stage or another at least seven Pan-German agitators (Reismann, Simons, Weyer, Paul Neubaur, Hans Graf von Bernstorff, Hermann Rassow and a Dr Rumpe) were working there.[90]

All this was financed largely by private sponsors, for which Reismann-Grone's business connections proved invaluable, but some support was also received from the Navy Office.[91] The degree of collaboration and overlap in the two campaigns of the Pan-Germans and the Colonial Society was very high. Many local meetings were held jointly and the same team of speakers serviced both organizations—Bruno Weyer, Paul Neubaur, Rassow, Bernstorff, and so on. The Colonial Society's largest and best publicized meeting, held in Berlin on September 13th 1897, was addressed by Kusserow and two of the leading Pan-German speakers, Neubaur and Weyer.[92] The Pan-Germans could regard the results of the campaigning when it ground to a halt after the passage of the Navy Bill in April 1898 with much satisfaction: it led to a big expansion of the organization and enabled later observers to pick out the naval issue as one of the movement's most effective propaganda vehicles. From the depths of 1893–4 the membership had tripled, rising from 5,742 at the end of 1894 to 15,401 in April, 1898, and 17,364 by the end of the year. Almost 60% of that overall increase had come in the two years between April 1896 and April 1898. In the same four-year period the number of local branches rose from only 33 to 129, and the subscribers to *Alldeutsche Blätter* from 2,507 to 6,664.[93] The Navy Bill of 1897–8 was regarded with some justification as a vindication of Pan-German politics during the past five years, and in addition had successfully galvanized the colonial movement into political activity under Pan-German auspices.

But on the other hand, the experience of the first Navy Bill brought fresh evidence of Pan-German limitations. The threshold of real political authority was still to be crossed, and two factors conspired to hold the Pan-Germans back during the naval agitation, one deriving from the priorities of the government, the other from within the ranks of the radical nationalists themselves. Superficially, for instance, the campaign also brought the League closer to the seats of power. There is no doubt that August von Heeringen, the head of the Navy Office's new Information Bureau, was in constant touch with Adolf Lehr

[89] Claß, *Wider den Strom*, pp. 33ff.

[90] Lehr to Hasse, Jan. 7th 1898, ZStA Potsdam, ADV, 181: 611f.

[91] In addition to 9,000 marks raised in the summer of 1897, Reismann-Grone kept a steady stream of money entering the Pan-German coffers, including 4,000 marks in Jan. 1898 and a further 2,000 at the end of Feb. 1898. Hermann Rassow found similar sources of finance in Elberfeld. For detailed reference, see Eley, 'German Navy League', pp. 39f.

[92] Ibid., pp. 40f.

[93] Figures from Wertheimer, *Pan-German League*, pp. 54ff., 121.

during the crucial months, and the Navy Office made willing use of both Pan-Germans and the Colonial Society for the distribution of literature and the provision of speakers.[94] But Heeringen's response was mixed. From the start he was highly sceptical of the agitation's political value and afraid that the Pan-Germans might drive their demands well beyond the politically desirable. An agitation which demanded too much too quickly might alienate party opinion and create international difficulties into the bargain. The general view at the Navy Office was that 'these people do more harm than good'. The Colonial Society, with its larger contingent of political moderates, offered fewer potential embarrassments, but Heeringen still expected little to come of its local propaganda. His attention was drawn to other objects: 'It would be much more helpful to us if the Rhineland industrialists would get together with the Hamburg people to start a movement which would also include Bremen.'[95] This admission revealed the rather different concerns of the government and of the pressure groups in the area of propaganda. The priority of the Navy Office was the direction of pressure into the legitimate channels of the parties and the Reichstag rather than the creation of any extra-parliamentary movement. In particular, Heeringen aimed to pile up statistics, learned articles, resolutions from Chambers of Commerce and public demonstrations by economic corporations, to show the economic importance of power at sea. His main efforts in autumn 1897 were directed towards a massive display of business opinion, and for him the extensive grass-roots activity of the Pan-Germans took a poor second place. Thus he took up Reismann-Grone's offer of support not for his influence in the Pan-German League, but for his extensive connections in the business world. Though local meetings of the Pan-Germans and the Colonial Society might influence the occasional deputy, a public demonstration embracing all the institutions of the business world might have a far more dramatic impact on the party fractions in Berlin.[96]

On the whole the Navy Office showed itself to be fairly indifferent to a more popular propaganda amongst 'the great masses' in 1897–8. Its definition of public opinion proved to be socially extremely restrictive and was confined largely to the so-called 'educated classes'. Tactically it was concerned with an even narrower band of 'opinion-makers'—the daily press, influential political journals, academics and key figures within the parties. The priority was to create a parliamentary majority for the passage of the Navy Bill, and the

[94] Heeringen to Tirpitz, Aug. 6th and 14th 1897, and Tirpitz's notes for an audience with the Kaiser, Sept. 5th 1897, BA-MA Freiburg, Tirpitz Papers, N. 253, 4. See also Lehr's daily correspondence with Hasse, ZStA Potsdam, ADV, 181.

[95] Heeringen to Tirpitz, Aug. 6th 1897, BA-MA Freiburg, Tirpitz Papers, N. 253, 4; Hollweg, 'Ergebnisse der Erfahrungen 1900–1901', ibid., 2284, 92472.

[96] This difference between official and unofficial propaganda during 1897–8 is not sufficiently brought out in recent work, which tends to stress unduly the ambition and 'modernity' of the former, in the sense of its 'plebiscitary' character. This question is taken up more fully below in Ch. 6, pp. 206ff.

propaganda was intended to strengthen the commitment of parties already sympathetic to the Navy rather than to break the opposition of its enemies. More precisely, it was aimed at the two groups currently engaged in withdrawing from their earlier opposition, the Centre Party and the *Freisinnige Vereinigung*. The official campaign was meant to influence decisions within the circle of the parties, not to mobilize popular opinion against them. It was an attempt to convince waverers in the Reichstag and to coax the Centre out of its ambivalence, to persuade rather than to coerce. The alternative—the creation of wider, extra-parliamentary support, a swell of popular feeling which could be used against the Reichstag in a plebiscitary manner—was not attempted. Because a full-scale exploitation of the naval issue's ideological potential might pander to anti-agrarian feelings amongst businessmen and conversely aggravate agrarian suspicions that their interests were being forced aside by the government's attempts to foster trade and industry, there were political objections inside the government itself to such a course.[97] But the latter was also inhibited by a limited conception of agitational priorities on the part of Tirpitz himself, who was careful at all times to keep a tight control over the discussion of policy. Though he reckoned with the possibility of a dissolution and fresh elections over the naval issue, there was no attempt to prepare the ground amongst the electorate at large as opposed to the notables and the educated minority. Even within the latter, he had little time for the small businessmen, teachers, doctors and small-time lawyers who flocked to Pan-German meetings in the provinces.

First-hand evidence of this indifference to the popular aspirations of radical nationalists was provided on the very occasion of Heeringen's most striking success, namely the impressive demonstration of business opinion orchestrated in the *Kaiserhof* Hotel on January 13th 1898. Plans for a 'mass meeting of the interests' were formulated by Heeringen as early as August 1897 and became the backbone of the campaign for the Navy Bill.[98] After some mutual suspicion, an adequate basis was found for co-operation between the shipping interests of the north coast and the heavy industrialists of the Rhine-Ruhr, and by mid-December 1897 a twenty-six man committee had been formed from the major business associations, including the CVDI, BdI and *Chemieverein*, the Hamburg, Bremen and Lübeck Chambers of Commerce, the corporate organizations of the sugar and textile industries, and the Committee of the United Guilds of Berlin; though the DHT was not officially represented its President was there in his private capacity. The rally itself on January 13th seemed a convincing demonstration of the naval issue's much-vaunted 'unifying power'. A declaration issued on December 19th 1897 carried 251 signatures, including

[97] For a detailed justification of this view, see Eley, '*Sammlungspolitik*', pp. 33–48, and 'German Navy League', pp. 27ff.

[98] Heeringen to Tirpitz, Sept. 10th 1897, BA-MA Freiburg, Tirpitz Papers, N. 253, 4. See also W. Deist, *Flottenpolitik und Flottenpropaganda* (Stuttgart, 1976), pp. 110ff., 148.

those of the Presidents of seventy-eight Chambers of Commerce and the chairmen of all important non-agrarian economic organizations. As argued above, this type of public intervention was not without its problems for the government, because at a time when it was doing its best to conciliate the landed interest the spokesmen for the latter were conspicuous at the *Kaiserhof* only by their absence; moreover the most enthusiastic patrons of the rally had been attracted not least by the possibilities of converting the naval issue into the vehicle for a new anti-agrarian front. But despite this note of qualification, the rally was clearly a major success for the official campaign as conceived by Heeringen and Tirpitz.[99]

For our purposes the affair had an interesting aspect not visible to the public eye. As well as posing problems by implication for the industrial-agrarian alliance from the left, the *Kaiserhof* rally also attracted elements which threatened to outflank it from the right. On January 6th 1898 the organizing committee received a letter from J. E. Stroschein, an unknown cod-liver oil manufacturer from Berlin, requesting permission to announce in the meeting that a so-called *Reichs-Marineverein* was to be launched. Stroschein urged that the *Kaiserhof* assembly should declare itself 'in perpetuity' as a 'permanent association' for the propagation of the naval idea. He had got the idea, according to his own account, from two articles in the *Berliner Neueste Nachrichten* in July 1897 about navy leagues in Britain, France and Italy. He now requested twenty-five minutes after the official address to announce his proposed organization. Three days later he met Henry Axel Bueck personally and gave him full details of the plan. The reception was cool and permission for the announcement was not forthcoming. Undeterred, he suggested calling a second meeting, formally separate from the first but beginning immediately afterwards, and the committee again refused. Bueck, Hassler and their colleagues had no intention of admitting Stroschein to their privileged circle. The day after the rally Bueck discussed the matter with Tirpitz, who agreed that such an important venture could not be entrusted to a man like Stroschein. The latter had been in touch with the Navy Office, but Tirpitz claimed that there had been no mention of a possible naval organization: Stroschein had spoken only of charity for the German troops in Kiaochow. Moreover, Tirpitz could see no point in the idea. As Bueck reported:

> The Secretary of State regards the formation of such an organization as completely unnecessary. Those organizations which already exist, as yesterday's rally has shown, are fully capable, if another occasion should arise, of staging future campaigns to meet all wishes and purposes.

Though the real nature of Stroschein's early contacts with the Navy Office is unclear, the official attitude was now final. After conferring with Heeringen,

[99] For full details and detailed references: Eley 'German Navy League', pp. 43ff.

Tirpitz decided that the Navy Office would have nothing to do with the idea. He commented tersely: 'The man is a fantast.'[100]

Though bitter, Stroschein proceeded with his plans. To learn from the experience of naval groups abroad he visited Villafrance and Genoa and in March 1898 produced a pamphlet which he sent to several thousand public personalities. On March 15th he formed a steering committee with two factory-owners from Bernau called Jasper and Pohl, who agreed to share the financial burden. By April the support of 121 individuals had been won for a founding committee, and the constituent meeting for the putative body, successively renamed *Deutsche Flottenliga* and *Deutscher Flottenbund*, was set for May 15th 1898. The support came from none of the big monopolies organized in the CVDI nor from the northern shippers. The founding members included only a few important businessmen: Dannenbaum (Director of the *Preussische Pfandbriefbank*), Küp (Director of the *Versicherungs-Gesellschaft Securitas,* Berlin), Oscar Caro (a general manager in Berlin), Carl Lindemann (Chairman of the *Export-Verein* in Saxony), Freiherr von Pechmann (Director of the *Bayrische Handelsbank*), and Hermann Wirth (Chairman of the BdI). The only members of the *Kaiserhof* committee to join Stroschein were Caro and Wirth: significantly they were both associated with the light-industrial and exporting sector of the economy, as were the other businessmen. Accordingly, although Stroschein won the backing of several well-known figures—the two admirals Mensing and Werner, and two important journalists, Hugo Jacobi of the *Berliner Neueste Nachrichten* and Heinrich Rippler of the *Tägliche Rundschau*—his committee consisted mainly of lesser businessmen, retired officers and members of the professions. In some ways Stroschein himself set the tone for the whole group. After serving an apprenticeship he had bought his own pharmacy and gradually built up his capital for a move into the chemical industry. In 1893 he set up a factory for the manufacture of cod-liver oil. Sociologically speaking, he was a rising petty-bourgeois. Tirpitz remarked snobbishly: 'The man has the narrow mind of a typical chemist.'[101]

Stroschein's initiative and the reactions it provoked cast an interesting light on the triangular relationship between the Pan-German League, the conventional party establishment and the larger milieu of radical nationalism. For it represented precisely the type of spontaneous intervention by unattached nationalist idealists which owed nothing to deliberate manipulations by the state or to the direction of the parties. In fact, its public rhetoric was defiantly

---

[100] See Tirpitz's note of Jan. 14th 1898, BA-MA Freiburg, 2276, 94227.

[101] Tirpitz's note on Stroschein's letter of Jan. 15th 1898, BA-MA Freiburg, 2276, 94227. Stroschein's career is described in his letter to Tirpitz, Jan. 20th 1898, ibid., and the progress of his initiative is described in some detail in his later account, *Bericht über die am 14. Dezember 1898 im Hotel Bristol stattgefundene erste Sitzung des Gesamtvorstandes des Deutschen Flottenvereins, sowie eine persönliche Mitteilung* (Berlin, Mar. 1899), copy in BA-MA Freiburg, 3476, 67692.

anti-party, and Stroschein personally viewed his organization as some kind of morally superior alternative to the diseased sectional bickering (as he would have called it) of party-political life.[102] But if the Stroschein initiative had its origins—both politically and socially—outside the conventional framework of parliamentary *Honoratiorenpolitik*, it was not directly inspired by the available Pan-German alternative to this. On the contrary, it presented the Pan-German League with a serious political problem. As we saw, in the eighteen months after the Kaiser's speech of January 1896 the Pan-Germans had much success in establishing their leadership of the unofficial naval movement: without the latter the naval issue would lose its value as a concrete object of agitation, for the League needed above all to register its moral authority over the other nationalist pressure groups. But now the appearance of Stroschein's group threatened to repeat an all too familiar scenario of radical nationalism: the Pan-Germans made all the running on a specific issue, only to be rewarded by the foundation of yet another specialized organization.

The dilemma was obvious. On the one hand, Stroschein's *Flottenbund* would simply steal the Pan-German thunder just at the point when the final passage of the Navy Law was to realize the political investment of the past two years' agitation. A new naval pressure group would hive off another area of nationalist intervention which the Pan-Germans regarded as legitimately their own. For these reasons Lehr advised Hasse that they decline Stroschein's invitation to join the founding committee. But on the other hand, if they abstained they might end up simply vacating a vital area of Pan-German interest and abandoning it to political innocents with no great understanding of Pan-German aims. To make matters worse a number of individual Pan-Germans had already joined, including Hermann Rassow, Admirals Mensing and Werner, Heinrich Rippler, Erwin von Dessauer and J. F. Lehmann. As well as exposing the major contradiction between the political establishment and the exponents of a new type of petty-bourgeois nationalism, therefore, Stroschein's intitiative also registered two related weaknesses of the Pan-German League: it had certainly not established itself as a natural organizational focus for nationalist politics, and was incapable of imposing any effective political discipline on its own activists. At present it remained a heterogeneous assortment of enthusiasts, whose relations both with the parties and with the other pressure groups were ambivalent and indeterminate, whose nationalism was far too inclusive and who lacked a coherent perspective on domestic politics.[103]

Both these points—the insensitive persistence of traditional *Honoratiorenpolitik*, and the political immaturity of radical nationalism—were re-emphasized

---

[102] See esp. Stroschein's original pamphlet, *Manuskript: Die Begründung des deutschen Reichsmarine-Vereins, sowie die persönliche Empfindung eines im öffentlichen Leben gänzlich unbekannten Mannes (Über die gegenwärtige politische Situation unseres Vaterlandes)* (Berlin, 1898), esp. pp. 5ff., copy BA-MA Freiburg, 2276, 94227.

[103] For detailed Pan-German references: Eley, 'German Navy League', pp. 68f.

by the fate of Stroschein's plans. A fortnight before his *Flottenbund* was due
to see the light of day, it was suddenly rendered redundant by the foundation,
in secret, of a completely new organization, the German Navy League, which
held its constituent meeting on April 30th 1898. The exact circumstances of
this were unclear. Victor Schweinburg, the new group's Secretary, later claimed
that the responsibility was his own—that he had formed the idea of a Navy
League quite independently, with no knowledge of Stroschein's activities.
According to this account, the idea was hatched in February 1898 during an
after-dinner conversation in which Schweinburg described the success of the
British Navy League: one of those present later wrote to him suggesting a
similar organization for Germany. He showed this letter to Fürst Wilhelm zu
Wied and at the latter's prompting agreed to undertake the task of launching
such a movement. Prince Alexander von Hohenlohe, the son of the Reich
Chancellor, also gave his support, as did Bueck, and together they canvassed
wider opinion, particularly from the members of the now-defunct *Kaiserhof*
committee. This account was almost certainly broadly correct, and the un-
named initiator of the idea may have been Krupp. But Schweinburg's claim
to have known nothing of Stroschein until told by Lucanus, the head of the
Kaiser's Civil Cabinet, *after* the actual foundation of the Navy League, was
disingenuous. Both Bueck and Carl Busley, who also worked closely with
Schweinburg, were kept fully informed by Stroschein and it is inconceivable
that they should have kept their colleague in the dark. In fact, the invitation to
the foundation meeting took great pains to point out that the proposed organization had nothing to do with Stroschein's plans.[104]

Previous historians may well have been right that Krupp and his heavy-
industrialist colleagues intervened to prevent political embarrassment: an
organized naval movement committed to the ideology of sea power might
disrupt attempts to reunite with the agrarians.[105] But an élitist conviction that
the matter was too important to be left to an outsider with no connections was
probably the primary motive, whether or not Schweinburg had arrived at the
idea independently. Tirpitz certainly subscribed to this view: Stroschein was
not 'the appropriate person to call the planned organization into existence'.[106]
Hassler agreed: Stroschein was quite unsuitable.[107] The Stroschein initiative,
drawing its support from lesser businessmen, retired officers and petty-
bourgeois nationalists, was clearly regarded as some sort of threat by 'the
group of Conservatives, large industrialists and their allies' which stepped in
to launch the Navy League.[108] The one factor in no doubt is that the group
responsible for the *Kaiserhof* rally was unwilling to surrender control of an

[104] Full details and references: Eley, 'German Navy League', pp. 55ff.
[105] Kehr, *Battleship Building*, pp. 177ff.; Wulf, 'Deutscher Flottenverein', p. 434.
[106] Tirpitz to Bülow, Apr. 2nd 1898, BA-MA Freiburg, 2276, 94227.
[107] Haßler to Kalle, May 6th 1898, SA Augsburg, Haßler Papers, 13.
[108] Hans Delbrück, in *TR*, Dec. 1st 1899.

institutionalized naval movement to an unknown petty-bourgeois animated by an undisciplined idealism.

The preparations for the Navy League's foundation brought together a group of eighty-three individuals, of whom forty-four attended the constituent meeting on April 30th 1898. The meeting appointed an Executive Committee, later renamed Presidium, comprising a President (Wied), two Vice-Presidents (Alexander von Hohenlohe and Bueck), a Secretary (Schweinburg), a Treasurer (the Berlin banker Robert von Mendelssohn) and three ordinary members (Busley, Oktavio von Zedlitz und Neukirch, Lieutenant-General Friedrich von Dincklage-Campe). It also elected a Council of thirty by acclamation: it included leading members of the CVDI and the heavy-industrial interest (Bueck, Hassler, Jencke, Krupp, Ritter, Vopelius, van der Zypen), the the Hamburg-Bremen shipping interests (Plate, Wiegand, Woermann), the shipbuilding industry (Busley, Sartori, Schlutow, Ziese), and the Berlin banking houses close to the CVDI (Delbrück, Mendelssohn). The numbers were made up by the CVDI's moderate agrarian allies (Schwerin-Löwitz, Manteuffel), other politicians closely associated with this alliance (Zedlitz, Schweinburg), and a number of individuals from South Germany to provide a full geographical spread (Linde, Lucius, Pflaum, Schneider, Tucher, Wurtzbürg). Of the Council's thirty members twenty-four attended the foundation: though the other twenty present included a few landowners, a university teacher and a large Berlin publisher, the majority inhabited the upper reaches of the business world. The same was true of the fifty-three nominated as local agents.[109]

As Schweinburg said, those invited to Berlin had been scrupulously selected from 'the circle of my close acquaintances'.[110] In this rarefied atmosphere there was little place for Stroschein and his associates. The product of the alternative deliberations of Schweinburg, Wied and Bueck was one from which non-establishment voices were carefully excluded, and precautions were taken to keep outsiders from any say in the running of the new organization. This was reflected in the first Constitution, which was 'thoroughly centralist'.[111] The sovereign body, the General Meeting, was to consist of the Agents alone— i.e. those local representatives already nominated by Wied and those the leadership saw fit to co-opt to their ranks. This was an explicit attempt to confine decisions within a tightly drawn circle.[112] Independent initiatives for

[109] For details of the foundation see the official *Stenographischer Bericht*, Wied Papers. A shortened *Protokoll* was also distributed to the participants, copy in BA Coblenz, ZSg. 1, 195/2.

[110] Schweinburg to Kusserow, June 14th 1898, ZStA Potsdam, Kusserow Papers, 42: 22f.

[111] Circular to the membership from Wied and Schweinburg, late 1899, copy StA Hamburg, DFV, III, 3. See also the address of Paul Schmid, an Augsburg businessman, to the constituent meeting of the local branch: 'The basic idea of the organization is a thoroughly centralist one', *ANN*, Feb. 21st 1900.

[112] See esp. Wied's explanatory remarks on Apr. 30th 1898, *Sten. Ber.*, p. 22, Wied Papers.

the formation of local branches were frowned upon, and the utmost care was taken to ensure that authority in the Navy League was exercised by men 'qualified by their social rank to undertake a certain role of leadership'.[113] In this, both in the spirit and in the actual practice of its internal relationships, the Navy League was sharply at variance with the new pattern of nationalist politics which the Pan-Germans were trying to establish. Instead, and on a rather more impressive scale, it came much closer to the Society for the Eastern Marches. Going further back still it seemed reminiscent of the original Colonial League in 1882, and given the unhappy existence of Stroschein's stranded committee, threatened to reproduce that early organization's factional conflicts with the more radical colonizers around Carl Peters, from which the Pan-German League had originally derived.

The Navy League was launched by its founders, then, as a dampener on the broader-based, more undisciplined initiative of Stroschein, a tactical intervention to bring the naval movement under safe control by excising the populist phraseology and eliminating the anti-party rhetoric. It was a defensive, pre-emptive gesture to forces which threatened to produce something far worse. Although the exporting interests of the north coast were well represented amongst the founding committee, this could not disguise the dominance of the protectionist, politically more conservative industrialists, whose patient efforts to construct a working alliance with the agrarian Conservatives were placed at risk by the possibility of a demagogic agitation around the naval issue. Their control over the Navy League was secured by the executive power of Victor Schweinburg, who supervised the organization's growth in 1898–9 and made it very much his own creation. An archetypal insider with his foot in many doors, Schweinburg was ideally equipped to bring together a broad group of high-ranking sponsors, procure the necessary finance and protect the interests of both government and business. He was ably assisted in the entrenchment of the CVDI's political interest by his close friend and associate Zedlitz-Neukirch, a typical product of the Prussian bureaucratic milieu and a classic adherent of the *Sammlungspolitik* which it systematically fostered.[114] In general

[113] District Official in Melsingen to the Cassel Deputy Governor, Nov. 15th 1898, StA Marburg, 150, 650.

[114] In later 1899 Oktavio Frhr. von Zedlitz und Neukirch (1840–1919) concluded a long career in the state service, during which he had twice been a candidate for ministerial posts. After retirement he devoted himself completely to politics and became the effective leader of the Free Conservatives. In the course of the 1890s he attached his own star to that of Miquel and closely identified himself with the latter's *Sammlungspolitik*, eventually to the detriment of his own bureaucratic career. The concept of *Sammlung* lends a basic unity to his entire political career. See R. Martin, *Deutsche Machthaber* (Berlin-Leipzig, 1910), pp. 382ff., and P. Merbach, 'Oktavio von Zedlitz-Neukirch', in H. von Arnim and G. von Below, *Deutscher Aufstieg* (Berlin, 1925), pp. 361–5. See also *KVZ*, Oct. 10th and 12th, Dec. 7th 1899. Victor Schweinburg stood at the centre of a vital network of press relations, linking government, CVDI industry and the Cartel parties. An influential journalist of Moravian Jewish background, he owned and edited two news sheets heavily used and subsidized by the CVDI and

the concerns of *Sammlungspolitik* were clearly present in the setting-up of the Navy League. But the naval movement was not a logical outgrowth of the *Sammlung*: the two were on the contrary at serious cross purposes. Most industrialists assumed that the job was done after the massive *Kaiserhof* rally, certainly after the passage of the Navy Law at the start of April, and not a few eyebrows were raised when Bueck began canvassing for this new venture.[115] Bueck himself, another characteristic exponent of Miquel's *Sammlungspolitik*, was typical of this attitude. His execution of the decision to frustrate Stroschein's project was purely tactical. Once the latter had been blocked he showed minimal interest in the activities of the Navy League, and though nominally Vice-President withdrew from all active membership.[116] His lack of interest is indicative of the Navy League's marginal relevance to the mainstream of *Sammlungspolitik*. But this again emphasized the character of the organization: the impetus for its foundation came from the desire to pre-empt an earlier move. Its members were concerned to hold back the naval enthusiasm, not to drive it forward to its logical political conclusion.

This expressed itself in a cautious governmentalism. Wied stressed that the foundation had taken place three weeks after the passage of the Navy Bill so that the new organization could then proceed 'without political agitation' and 'without directing itself against the Reichstag': 'Complete abstention from all politics must be the motto of the organization.' Schweinburg echoed this point: 'The first principle for the Navy League to establish if it is to fulfil its proper role will be: to follow no political tendency whatever and to give preference to no one political direction.' The definition of the Navy League as a 'non-political' organization, which was inserted at the top of the first Constitution, was dictated partly by law, partly to admit members of all parties but the Social Democrats. But it was mainly an expression of extreme political caution. Though both Wied and Schweinburg stressed the need to sharpen 'the national consciousness', especially of the younger generation, they were also careful to defuse its political potential. Schweinburg said that 'the Navy League must not be an agitational organization with an aggressive purpose'. The movement should relate its propaganda strictly to the government programme. A clause

---

the government from the 1880s on, the *Berliner Politische Nachrichten* and the *Neue Reichs-korrespondenz*. He was one of only three journalists admitted to the Committee meetings of the CVDI, and received an annual subsidy from the CVDI Directorate. For these and other details: Stegmann, *Erben*, pp. 168f., and H. Kaelble, *Industrielle Interessenpolitik in der wilhelminischen Gesellschaft* (Berlin, 1970), pp. 17, 19, 45, 162.

[115] e.g. Carl Lueg (Gen. Manager of *Gutehoffnungshütte*) to Bueck, Apr. 17th 1898, HA/GHH, 300 1073/2. Lueg protested that he had no time, and in any case there was no need for a naval pressure group now that the Reichstag had passed the Bill; but if Bueck thought it in the general interest he would join. Lueg's name eventually appeared amongst the original fifty-three local representatives. See also Schweinburg's remarks on Apr. 30th 1898, *Sten. Ber.*, Wied Papers,

[116] Schweinburg to Haßler, June 15th 1898, SA Augsburg, Haßler Papers, 13.

which spoke of exerting pressure on the government for the attainment of the Navy League's aims was struck out of the proposed Constitution on the grounds that it was too 'provocative'. One participant commented that 'it would be a sad moment if it should ever be necessary to pressurize the government into fulfilling its naval obligations'; personally, he could not imagine 'that we would ever find ourselves in such a situation'. This unquestioning governmentalism reinforced the decision to abstain from politics. Wied declared: 'At this point it is absolutely essential to be satisfied with what the government has defined as sufficient for the size of the fleet.' The League must confine itself to 'complete confidence in the government's standpoint'. Its role was merely to explain the importance of the fleet to the population at large. When the fine words of the foundation meeting were reduced to their concrete reality, in other words, it is hard to discover anything more ambitious than a few 'educative' lecture tours. Certainly nothing was to be done without official approval. As Wied said to Tirpitz, the new group would attempt nothing without the approval of the Navy Office: the movement was appointed in the first instance 'to learn from the experts'.

The character of the Navy League, in its view of the political uses of the naval enthusiasm, its attitude towards the parties, its social exclusiveness and cautious governmentalism, contrasted sharply with that of Stroschein's movement. Above all, it reflected no deep commitment to the political importance of an ongoing naval agitation. Schweinburg and his associates were too closely identified with the reconstruction of the party-political Cartel in the Reichstag and the proclamation of a new programme of protective tariffs. There was no direct, constructive or necessary connection between these preoccupations and their participation in the naval movement, and the former claimed an unquestioned priority on their time and interest. Beside such matters the Navy League was a very poor relation. To purer souls, moreover, the first loyalty of men like Schweinburg and Bueck was transparently sectional, and even worse, governed by motives of economic self-interest. It was easy enough to scrape away the rhetorical veneer of patriotic ardour and expose the profit motive of the arms industry beneath. This contrast, between the populist bluster of Stroschein's original idea and the closed doors of the organization which suddenly superseded it, stated a conflict of perspectives which runs through the history of the naval movement like a red thread, and recalled the older dichotomies of the colonial agitation. Though Stroschein allowed his planned *Flottenbund* to merge formally with the Navy League on May 15th 1898, the unfortunate circumstances of the foundation bequeathed an unhappy legacy to the movement and suggested the doubtful compatibility of the two strains from which it was currently constituted.[117]

Stroschein's reaction to the news of the Navy League's foundation had been bitter. He claimed angrily to Tirpitz that his idea had been stolen by the same

[117] Detailed references from Eley, 'German Navy League', pp. 59–61.

'clique of businessmen' which had debarred him at the *Kaiserhof*. After he had generously informed Bueck and Busley of his moves, they had cynically repaid him by reappropriating his plans for their own self-seeking purposes. The news that a naval group had been set up in secret had struck him 'like a bolt from the blue'.[118] Despite his being co-opted to the League's Council his bitterness rankled throughout the year. Besides, his sense of personal injustice was hardened by the evident gulf of political principle. In so far as a strong commitment can be found at all, the group behind Schweinburg saw the League simply as a means of reinforcing official policy through quiet propaganda with no agitational content. Under certain exceptional circumstances it might be used to provide the government with 'nationally-minded' auxiliaries, or, as the Kaiser put it, 'voting-fodder'.[119] Stroschein's group, on the other hand, saw things in a different light. They were firmly committed to the ideological power of the naval idea, regarding it as a so-called integrative, 'national' factor capable of mobilizing the 'masses' behind the state and immunizing the working class against the influence of Socialism. This was true above all of the Pan-German elements, especially of men like Hermann Rassow and Heinrich Rippler. For such figures the form of the Navy League's foundation had the effect of severely aggravating their sense of injured patriotism and of being excluded from the centre of the political stage. 'In the interests of my *cause*,' Stroschein incanted bitterly, 'I have suffered humiliations of every kind, but I have borne them for my fatherland, which I regard as nothing more than my extended family.' This disinterested nationalism was again contrasted with the cynical manipulations of Bueck and Schweinburg: 'For *this* clique a man evidently becomes worthy of respect only when he is a big businessman.'[120]

Not surprisingly the Pan-German leadership felt a special sense of grievance. As suggested above, their campaign for the Navy Bill had been rewarded with a marked upswing in the life of their movement, both in membership and morale. Their natural response to Stroschein's overtures had thus been a negative one: Hasse and Lehr saw their own organization as a perfectly adequate base for future naval agitation and to emphasize this point the Managing Committee had voted to continue the propaganda even after the passage of the Law. None the less, the presence of several Pan-Germans amongst Stroschein's founding committee suggested that there was still room for discussion. The question gave fresh life, in fact, to a recurrent debate in the Pan-German League concerning the correct attitude towards other more specialized nationalist groups—whether to defend the Pan-German primacy by principled dissociation, or to seek a wider platform for Pan-German ideas by careful infiltration. As Lehr said, if they agitated against the proposed naval group they would be accused of acting like a 'dog in the manger', if they did nothing

[118] Stroschein to Tirpitz, May 3rd 1898, BA-MA Freiburg 2276, 94227.
[119] Wilhelm II to Bülow, Aug. 30th 1905, cit. in *Berliner Tageblatt*, Oct. 14th 1928.
[120] Stroschein to Tirpitz, Jan. 13th 1898, BA-MA Freiburg, 2276, 94227.

another field of activity would be lost. The foundation of the Navy League seemed in this way to herald a familiar process. As Reismann-Grone commented with some bitterness: 'as always the Pan-Germans are the pathfinders and the pioneers; when everything else had been settled, along came the Navy League under Fürst Wied'. Hasse made the same point: 'And where, pray, were Messrs Woermann, Krupp etc., *before* the acceptance of the Navy Law?' Things were made much worse by the identity of the Navy League's founding group, drawn as it was from the political establishment, of which the Pan-Germans' very existence constituted a critique. For Lehr, 'Working with Bueck and Schweinburg is not to my taste,' whilst Hasse remarked that 'Whenever I see Bueck's name I always go completely wild.' Though the Pan-German group made an effort to secure their influence in the merger meeting of May 15th, the proceedings were tightly controlled by Schweinburg and Hohenlohe. The Pan-German League was left with little recourse but to enter the new movement and 'win as much influence as possible'. Under the prevailing circumstances little more could be expected than uneasy coexistence.[121]

Events in the naval movement are worth describing at some length because they illustrate rather better than those in the colonial or anti-Polish movements the main features of the evolving relationship between the nationalist pressure groups and the existing system of politics. As argued in the previous chapter, the main context of German politics in the 1890s was characterized by the activation of new social strata at a time when the existing party framework was ill-equipped to absorb their impact. In the countryside, it was suggested, this amounted to a decomposition of those political relations which had predominated at least since the 1860s. In the towns the cultural hegemony of notables —*Honoratiorenpolitik*—was being subjected to strains from another quarter, that of the Socialist working class. But at the same time (though far less seriously in numerical terms) the older right-wing parties were also faced with another movement of independent activity in the towns. Here the impulse came from the proliferating nationalist associations—the autonomous cultivators of Hohenlohe's 'field of activity for the strengthened national sentiment'[122]— which offered a focus of activity for large numbers of energetic middle-class idealists. The threat to the party establishments was far less urgent in this case, for by deliberately designating this area of nationalist agitation as non-party such groups enabled their supporters to maintain an existing party affiliation. This was further assisted by the diffuseness of nationalist politics at this stage, for as yet only a small minority of pronounced activists united their membership of the pressure groups with a coherent domestic perspective. Still, this could not hide the fact that the new engagement was occurring outside the institutional parameters of party-political life, that in the absence of proper constituency organizations the natural leaders of the latter were busily involving themselves

---

[121] Detailed references: Eley, 'German Navy League', pp. 67ff.
[122] Hohenlohe, RT, Dec. 11th 1894, p. 21.

elsewhere. By attempting to appropriate to itself one area of this nationalist politics—the naval agitation—in a particularly insensitive manner, the party-political grouping around Schweinburg threatened to convert the uneasy parallelism of parties and pressure groups into an open conflict.

E. THE NAVY LEAGUE'S FIRST CRISIS

The terms in which such a conflict would be conducted were partially given in the manner of the Navy League's insertion into the independent discourse of the *nationale Verbände*. For instance, it was Stroschein's special pride that his own initiative had come 'from the very heart of the people' rather than being imposed from above by a clique of big businessmen.[123] But on the other hand, both the *Sammlungspolitiker* and the Navy Office saw his proposal as a potentially dangerous initiative from below. During its first two years, therefore, the Navy League was hardly more than a safe front for vested interests and a subsidiary for the official propaganda machine. This difference reflected alternative images of the naval movement's legitimate role in the political system, themselves suggesting deeper levels of ideological conflict. In fact, the efforts of the political heavyweights to elbow Stroschein out of the way, and the sharp internal crisis eighteen months later in which he took his revenge, threw up the raw material which was hammered during the next decade into a far-reaching critique of the conventional values of the German right.

A foretaste of things to come was provided straight after the Navy League's foundation when it failed to gain the backing of the so-called 'naval professors'. Many academics had been goaded into public support for the first Navy Bill, partly at the prompting of Heeringen, partly under social-imperialist imperatives of their own, and it was natural for Schweinburg to solicit their goodwill. To this end negotiations were opened in June 1898 with Gustav Schmoller (as Rector of Berlin University) and Hans Delbrück, who in turn consulted with their 'social-political friends'. Schmoller's first reaction was favourable, but he insisted on a broadening of the League's party-political base: at present it was just 'an association of big industrialists looking after their business'. After detailed discussions with Delbrück and Max Sering, the Professor of Agriculture, a clear demand was formulated. Representatives of three political tendencies were to be co-opted on to the executive: the *Freisinnige Vereinigung*, the National-Socials, and the so-called 'academic-social-political group', all on the social-reformist left of the spectrum. As Delbrück told Schweinburg: 'The Navy League can only prosper if all the parties and groups which support the Navy are represented in its organs.' If any were omitted the League would automatically assume a party-political character:

---

[123] Stroschein, *Manuskript: Die Begründung*, p. 3, BA-MA Freiburg, 2276, 94227; see also Stroschein's *Bericht*, ibid., 3476, 67692.

4

Whenever a committee is formed outside the parties, whether for a statue of some kind of fund, it always keeps as strictly as possible to the principle that from the very beginning all the different groups or estates concerned are represented. In the foundation of the Navy League this has unfortunately been neglected . . . [124]

This controversy revealed once again the party location of the early Navy League: it was above all a foundation of governmental and industrial interests. Moreover, although the shipping interests tended towards the left liberals, most of the original Council members came from the right wing of the National Liberals, the Free Conservatives or the Conservatives. Not surprisingly this worked against the acceptance of Schmoller's terms. A big gap separated men like Bueck, Zedlitz and Jencke from Barth, Delbrück and Naumann, which could not be bridged by a momentary convergence on the single issue of the Navy.[125] Moreover, whereas the academics and Naumannites agreed to nominate someone, Theodor Barth refused for the *Freisinnige Vereinigung* because of the Navy League's exclusively 'governmental character', and the three groups had agreed to make any decision unanimous. The divisions between the bourgeois parties ran too deep: Schweinburg and Sering, Zedlitz and Barth, Bueck and Naumann, would make strange bedfellows indeed. As Heinrich Rippler later observed, it was hard for Schmoller and his colleagues to sit down with the League's leaders when they had been 'pelted with mud for years by Schweinburg and his newspapers because of their social [reformist] convictions'.[126] The Navy League's leadership rejected the full-scale reconstruction required by Schmoller and Delbrück. Constitutional pretexts were cited, but the real reason was clearly a political one. To allow left-liberal, free-trading, social-reformist, above all *anti-agrarian* elements a platform in the naval movement was too dangerous at a time when the renegotiation of the grain tariffs was the overriding political priority.[127]

Further problems arose when Stroschein resigned from the Council in a blaze of fury at the end of 1898. The occasion seemed innocuous: he had organized a write-in campaign for an illustrated naval magazine and the Berlin Office had been deluged with postcards and letters. But whereas several years later this might have been greeted as an expression of popular enthusiasm, it was now made the object of sarcastic complaints when Schweinburg reported to the Council on December 14th 1898. This produced an apoplectic response

---

[124] Detailed references from Eley, 'German Navy League', pp. 65f.

[125] Theodor Barth, a leader of the *Freisinnige Vereinigung*, and Friedrich Naumann, the driving-force of the National-Social Association, had been suggested by Delbrück as possible candidates for co-option. If Naumann proved unacceptable to the Navy League, Sering proposed Prof. Rudolf Sohm, a member of the National-Socials' conservative wing. Frentzel, President of the DHT and a member of the *Freisinnige Vereinigung*, was also mentioned, as was Theodor Mommsen.

[126] *TR*, Nov. 30th 1899: '*Vorwärts* and Herr Schweinburg'.

[127] See esp. *DTZ*, Apr. 25th 1900.

from Stroschein, who delivered a torrential indictment of the entire Executive and ended by announcing his resignation. The substance of his complaints was the same: the original initiative had come 'from the very heart of the people', this popular impulse had now been betrayed. On December 16th Stroschein wrote to Schweinburg accusing him of intrigues and of trying to buy him off with expenses and decorations. The next day he sent similar letters to Bueck and Busley, alleging a secret conspiracy to displace his planned *Flottenbund* earlier in the year.[128] There is no indication that this personal resentment reflected any more general discontent in the membership, but it restated the issues and gave an important focus for any future opposition. Moreover, the potential hostility of the Pan-Germans could not be forgotten: for the moment they were anonymous, but if any larger movement of opposition to the leadership should develop, they would gladly twist the knife.

These three strands of discontent—the naval professors and the groups of the liberal reformist left, Stroschein, the Pan-Germans—came together at the end of 1899. As the campaign for the Second Navy Bill swung into top gear at the end of October Schweinburg became the butt of a powerful press vendetta, in which his relations with Krupp and the CVDI were paraded before the public. The opening shot was fired from Munich, where the SPD press somehow acquired a copy of the circular sent out by Wied and Schweinburg to set the propaganda work in motion.[129] Attacks from this quarter were expected and hardly very damaging. They became more serious when taken up by pro-naval organs of opinion, and the campaign began in earnest with an article by Stroschein himself in the *Tägliche Rundschau* on November 12th 1899, endorsed editorially by Heinrich Rippler. The old complaint was wheeled out once again: under Schweinburg the Navy League was only a mouthpiece for heavy industry and high finance, and had been alienated from the popular base which had first called it into life. But Rippler's journalism now gave the attacks a much sharper edge. His remarks amounted to the first systematic statement of a populist programme which was to give the Navy League its agitational drive during the coming years. The aim, Rippler argued, was to 'carry the naval idea into the people' and not confine the efforts to the 'highest ten thousand'. Many people had long been dissatisfied with the Navy League's leadership, the article continued, and after consulting with prominent friends of the Navy Rippler had now decided that Schweinburg should resign. The latter's connections with Krupp and the CVDI were mentioned, but the general tone was fairly moderate: it was conceded that his abilities might still be put to use, though in a less prominent position. Three days later the paper published a fresh statement by Stroschein asserting that he was not concerned with Schweinburg's personality, only 'the popular nature of the Navy League'.

[128] See Stroschein, *Bericht*, BA–MA Freiburg, 3476, 67692.
[129] *Münchner Post*, Nov. 4th 1899. For a copy of the offending circular (which was actually quite innocuous by the later standards of 1904–7), see SA Augsburg, Haßler Papers, 13.

The next day Rippler repeated his demand: Schweinburg must resign as his presence played into the hands of the Navy's opponents. This time his heavy-industrial connections were given greater prominence.[130]

By this time the issue had become a major story throughout the daily press. The accusation of 'business patriotism' was levelled at the Navy League from all sides, not only by the SPD but from virtually every organ of bourgeois opinion except those directly aligned with the CVDI.[131] The opposition ranged from Eugen Richter's *Freisinnige Zeitung*, which exploited the issue remorselessly for its campaign against the Bill, through the other Berlin liberal papers, the provincial National Liberal press, the organs of the Centre, the Conservatives, the Agrarian League and the anti-Semitic right.[132] Then on November 16th 1899 a new organization, the Free Union for Naval Lectures, issued its manifesto to the press. Its aim was the holding of 'popular lectures' all over Germany, to be inaugurated with a series of six in Berlin itself.[133] The sponsors included many leading academics: Schmoller, Delbrück, Ernst Francke, Wilhelm Oncken, Carl Rodenberg (Professor of History at Kiel), Dietrich Schäfer (Professor of History at Heidelberg), Max Sering, Adolph Wagner (Professor of Political Economy at Berlin). They also included prominent naval and military writers, such as the retired Pan-German Admiral Reinhold Werner, Max Jeans, Dagobert von Gerhardt-Amyntor and Albert von Boguslawski; the theologians Beyschlag and Harnack; and a group of well-known artists, authors and poets, including Max von Liebermann, Richard Strauss, Julius Stinde, Hans Hopfen, Julius Rodenberg and Wilhelm Rabe. The organization, such as it was, worked closely with the Navy Office, and in one sense may be seen as an attempt to institutionalize the mobilization of the academics and intellectuals of two years before. Its office received long lists of suitable speakers from the Information Bureau of the Navy Office. It had its own secretary, Julius Lohmeyer, who if not actually a member was intellectually close to the Pan-Germans, and a rudimentary regional apparatus.[134] But the

---

[130] *TR*, Nov. 12th, 15th and 16th 1899.

[131] A striking exception was Reismann-Grone's *RWZ*. Otherwise the only major papers to abstain from the attacks on Schweinburg were *BNN* and *Die Post*, both of which were under heavy-industrial control. See Stegmann, *Erben*, pp. 166ff.

[132] Many right papers dwelt on Schweinburg's Jewish origins: e.g. *Berliner Blatt*, Nov. 16th 1899: 'Victor Schweinburg'. See also the annotated leaflets returned anonymously to Wied, copies in Wied Papers: e.g. 'A Jew-free Germany which didn't have to support Jewish parasites, could build a new battlefleet every year.'

[133] Probably little was done in the provinces, though Schmoller did give two addresses in Strasbourg and Hannover. See the material in BA-MA Freiburg, 2377, 94732.

[134] From 1900 Lohmeyer published a periodical called *Deutche Monatschrift für das gesamte Leben der Gegenwart*, which served as a platform for mainly Pan-German writers. In addition to the academics and Berlin intellectuals, the Free Union attracted at least two personalities who later played active roles in the life of the Navy League: Breuer, a Wiesbaden headmaster, and Weitbrecht, a Stuttgart professor. For a report of a meeting in Wiesbaden, see *Rheinischer Kurier*, Feb. 12th 1900.

real purpose of the Free Union was a polemical one. Its very existence was meant to emphasize that the Navy League was inadequate for the mobilization of popular opinion (especially in view of the abortive negotiations between Schmoller and Schweinburg in June 1898), and though it had little effect itself on this score, it made a point the Navy League could not afford to ignore.

The aim of Schweinburg's opponents, from Stroschein and Rippler to the naval professors, was to highlight the narrowness of the Navy League's party-political base and the emptiness of its claim to stand higher than the parties. The force of their attacks was greatly sharpened when Friedrich Naumann and his National-Social Association entered the fray: for the first time the objections to Schweinburg were incorporated into an open and systematic critique of the forces he represented. Naumann's position took the form of a novel social-imperialist synthesis of 'power abroad and reform at home', in which support for the Navy was joined to the demand for tax-reform and trade union rights, the whole being advanced as an alternative to the prevailing policy of *Sammlung*.[135] The government's decision to finance the Second Navy Bill from the proceeds of higher grain tariffs gave Naumann one line of attack in this respect, while the attempt to introduce anti-strike legislation through the so-called 'Hard-Labour Bill' provided another. Moreover, in the autumn of 1899 the dominant coalition of industry and agriculture seemed in some disarray: the agrarians were opposing the Canal Bill, a measure supported mainly by West German heavy industry, whilst a section of the National Liberals had resisted the pressure of their heavy-industrial right wing by opposing the Hard-Labour Bill. In this situation the Second Navy Bill, with its implied promotion of industrial growth at the further long-term expense of the landed interest, threatened to exacerbate the differences.[136] Naumann seemed to see in this apparent state of flux a chance for political realignment: at the very least he hoped to lay the foundations for a broad anti-agrarian front against the likely increase of the grain tariffs, and at most it might be possible to split the National Liberals. In a meeting on November 15th, just as the attacks on Schweinburg were reaching a first height, Naumann developed this idea especially sharply.

[135] See the programme adopted at the constituent meeting of the National-Socials, Erfurt, Nov. 25th 1896, cit. D. Fricke, 'National-Sozialer Verein', *Die Bürgerlichen Parteien*, II, p. 378. The most systematic statement of Naumann's politics at this time is probably his pamphlet *Flotte und Reaktion* (Berlin, Nov. 1899), but see also the more detailed *Demokratie und Kaisertum* (Berlin, 1900). For an extended discussion of his politics in the context of the National-Social experiment, see D. Düding, *Der Nationalsozialer Verein 1876–1903* (Munich, 1972), which fails to grasp the strategic importance of the commitment to imperialism. For a longer treatment of the problem: Eley, 'German Navy League', pp. 74ff., and '*Sammlungs-politik*', pp. 44ff.

[136] See esp. the argument in Naumann, *Flotte und Reaktion*, and the speech by Helmuth von Gerlach, reported in detail by *RWZ*, Nov. 16th 1899. Tirpitz certainly perceived this logic, and may have pursued it through the policy of the Navy Office, though this latter point is still rather obscure. The best discussion of this field of relations is Böhm, *Überseehandel*, pp. 235–63.

After virulent attacks on Miquel, the architect of the conventional coalition on which government was still based, and after a detailed analysis of the interdependence of the Canal, Hard-Labour and Navy Bills, he laid out the political alternatives supposedly facing the government: it would either 'have to go yet again with the Conservatives', or else with 'the Left which is beginning to form from the mass strength of Social Democracy and its upper layer, the industrial entrepreneurs'. The demands were then repeated: rejection of the anti-strike legislation, and support for the combined programme of canal, financial reform and fleet.[137]

Naumann stood on the left flank of the populist front against Schweinburg. He also used this speech for a scornful attack on the latter, and his comments on the political function of the Second Navy Bill pinpointed the wider significance of the opposition in the naval movement. Schweinburg was a sitting target. He was the owner and editor of two press-sheets subsidized by the CVDI; he was one of three journalists admitted to the CVDI's Committee meetings; he was until the end of 1899 Business Manager of the *Berliner Neueste Nachrichten*, in which Krupp then held a controlling interest; he was a close political collaborator of Miquel, and moved freely in Berlin's political society. Moreover, his friend and colleague in the Navy League Executive, Zedlitz-Neukirch, had conducted a long campaign against the Canal Bill through the pages of *Die Post* from an agrarian standpoint, and this was widely interpreted as a revelation of Miquel's own position.[138] Schweinburg and Zedlitz were left in a dangerously exposed position by their long association with the practice of *Sammlungspolitik*, and their opponents in the Navy League spared no opportunity to press this home. The wider implications were carefully drawn out. As Naumann said: 'We have scarcely had a more intense secret enemy of the social [reform] movement than Herr Victor Schweinburg.'[139]

By the start of December 1899 the agitation against the ruling clique in the Navy League had moved towards a peak. It was spearheaded by Heinrich Rippler and the *Tägliche Rundschau*, with the aid of Stroschein. This had produced a response in the League's membership and the Executive was starting to receive resolutions calling for Schweinburg's resignation.[140] The

---

[137] Naumann, *Flotte und Reaktion*, p. 15. Naumann's expectations were naturally unrealistic. Their importance, however, was twofold: to identify the necessary logic of an opposition to *Sammlungspolitik* which was to be effective, and to accentuate the subversive implications of the opposition to Schweinburg in particular.

[138] See the article in *KVZ*, Dec. 7th 1899, which considered these relationships in much detail.

[139] Naumann, *Flotte und Reaktion*, p. 4.

[140] On Dec. 2nd 1899 the Heidelberg branch, with 600 members under the Chairmanship of Dietrich Schäfer, issued a declaration to this effect, and on Dec. 5th 1899 it was circulated to the League's membership in general. For copies, see SA Augsburg, Haßler Papers, 13. Similar movements arose in Munich and Solingen, and there were doubtless many more. See *FreisZ*, Dec. 9th 1899; *KZ*, Dec. 16th 1899.

naval professors and the National-Socials had added their voices, and the Pan-Germans also joined the fray. The possibilities of a juncture between these rather disparate elements could already be glimpsed. Rippler, for example, was himself a Pan-German, and after the collapse of the Naumannite daily *Die Zeit* in 1897 the National-Socials had been using the *Tägliche Rundschau* as a make-shift mouthpiece. Though disagreements over the tariff question later led to a separation, the common ground of the Navy had enabled a high degree of co-operation between Rippler and Naumann, particularly in view of the paper's Evangelical connections.[141] Hans Delbrück, through whom the *Freisinnige Vereinigung*, Naumann and the Berlin academics had negotiated with the League in 1898, was now a leading light in the Free Union for Naval Lectures, and had been a close associate of Naumann since the early 1890s. The same was true of many other academics involved in the Free Union, such as Sering, Harnack, Schmoller, Sohm and Wagner.[142] Dietrich Schäfer, who demanded Schwein-burg's resignation in the name of the Navy League's large Heidelberg branch, was a Pan-German and member of the Free Union, whilst Dessauer and Lehmann, who led the internal opposition in Munich, were both Pan-Germans. Hermann Rassow, who had taken part in Stroschein's original movement, was a cousin of Delbrück, a member of the Pan-German Council and an admirer of Naumann. The circle was completed when Stroschein was made honorary chairman of the Free Union and presided over its first meeting in Berlin.[143]

The political possibilities of these personal links were suggested on November 18th 1899 when Helmuth von Gerlach, the former Christian-Social and now National-Social speaker, shared a platform with Ernst Hasse, the Pan-German leader, during a meeting for the Navy Bill. Both attacked Schweinburg for betraying the ideals behind Stroschein's first initiative. Gerlach reiterated the Naumannite line: the essential corollary of the Bill must be a comprehensive tax reform, for otherwise the workers would not be inclined to support it. Moreover, Schweinburg was a damaging influence in the Navy League, for at this time he was busily publishing articles in his press-sheets calling for an agrarian tariff settlement. Hasse, who by now had also been elected to the Reichstag in Leipzig as a National Liberal, at first tried to evade the issue, but finally admitted that he had personally been concerned with the problem of a liberal finance reform for several years. He closed his remarks with the ominous (for the agrarians) slogan: 'For the moment—ships; for the future—tax reform.'[144] On December 1st 1899 Delbrück used the pages of the *Tägliche Rundschau* to develop a detailed critique of the Navy League: it was controlled

[141] T. Heuß, *Friedrich Naumann* (Stuttgart-Tübingen, 1949), p. 153.
[142] See Delbrück's correspondence with Naumann, BA Coblenz, Delbrück Papers, 32.
[143] Stroschein to Wied, Dec. 23rd 1899, Wied Papers.
[144] *TR*, Nov. 19th 1899. There is some evidence that attempts were made to explore co-operation between the National-Socials and Pan-Germans on a more formal basis, but the differences on other issues proved too deep. See Hasse to Lehr, Nov. 11th 1899, ZStA Potsdam, ADV, 181: 922.

'exclusively' by 'the group of Conservatives, large industrialists and their allies'. Rippler had presented such a critique consistently over the previous three weeks and he now repeated his main demands: the Navy League must cease to be an 'agitation team' for heavy industry and government and become instead 'a free association of all nationally-minded German men friendly to the fleet, a *Volksverein*'.[145]

The reaction of the Navy League's inner leadership to all this had been cautious and restrained. It seems that Schweinburg had no great personal stake in the movement and had tried at an early stage to withdraw from his commitments: he had remained at the request of Wied to guide the organization through its birth pangs, and would now be happy to retire to protect the League from further attacks. As early as November 10th he submitted his resignation, but the Executive Committee voted unanimously that he stay. The statements by Delbrück and Rippler on December 1st, however, threatened to generalize the attacks into an assault on the entire existence of the Navy League. The conversion of the campaign into a full-scale critique of the premises of *Sammlungspolitik* led Schweinburg's political friends to urge him to take decisive action. After conferring with Zedlitz, Jencke, Lucanus and Posadowsky, Schweinburg told Wied that his resignation was unavoidable. A few days later this was confirmed when he found on the admission of Gercke, the League's Business Manager and a former naval officer, that the Navy Office and Tirpitz were deeply implicated in the campaign. Despite Lucanus' assurances that his credit with the Court and the government was still the same, he was concerned for his political reputation: as he said to Wied, his opponents were now trying 'to destroy my entire civil existence'. On December 10th 1899 Schweinburg's resignation was accepted. He was succeeded by Freiherr von Beaulieu-Marconnay, a serving army officer recommended by Schweinburg himself.[146]

But Rippler and the larger movement behind him were now demanding much more than this. In the second of two leading articles reviewing the new situation on December 19th he returned to Delbrück's demand of June 1898 for representation of the Barth left liberals and the National-Socials in the Navy League's leading organs:

> The Navy League Council could do nothing better than to co-opt not only the liberals Rickert or Barth, but also Pastor Naumann, or even better still the worker, lithographer Tischendörfer. If seats on the Navy League's Council are given not just to the spokesmen of property and power, but also finally to those of the trading *Mittelstand* and the working people, the fruits will be quite different from those of the past. For this would avoid even the faintest impression that the Navy League is a creation of rulers and business interests.

[145] *TR*, Dec. 1st 1899.
[146] Detailed references from Eley, 'German Navy League', pp. 80f.

It was only by these means, Rippler continued, that the movement could live down its unfortunate past and return to its 'founding idea', the creation of a genuine *Volksverein*, 'which unites all strata of the population'. Rippler concluded: 'As a national education association, as one of our nation's most important aids to political education, this is how we regard the organization, and that is why we regarded the necessary reform as a general political matter of the utmost importance . . . '[147] It was a measure of the strength of the opposition to the old leadership that this demand was met. The ranks of the Executive Committee were extended to make room for Professor Max Sering, as a representative of the 'academic-social-political group' and the Free Union.[148]

This was an enforced concession, not just to an internal opposition and to public opinion, but also to an alternative view of the role of the naval movement in German politics. Moreover, the victors wished to carry their success even further. After his co-option Sering opened discussions with Max Maurenbrecher for the admission of someone from the National-Socials to the Executive. These discussions broke down because of Wied's resistance and because Maurenbrecher's colleagues pitched their demands too high. Similar plans for a comprehensive indictment of Schweinburg and his methods in the forthcoming General Meeting had to be abandoned when Krupp and 'his friends' threatened to leave the Council *en masse*. But the opposition could afford to feel well satisfied with its achievements. Beaulieu-Marconnay, Schweinburg's successor, was thought to be 'thoroughly modern' in his approach, with ideas 'miles apart from those of Stumm' in the area of social policy; he even spoke of helping to bring together the capital for reviving *Die Zeit*, Naumann's defunct daily newspaper.[149] Naumann himself placed the seal of approval on the reconstructed Navy League, because 'the élitist, anti-worker attitudes which previously dominated the movement now seem to have been definitively removed'.[150] A success for the opposition, of course, was also a defeat for the political forces which had earlier been in control: the heavy-industrial political operators and their Conservative allies, the major adherents of Miquel's *Sammlungspolitik*. One of the unpublicized demands of Sering's backers, in fact, had been the resignation of Zedlitz-Neukirch and on December 18th the latter obliged. He told Wied that the attacks were directed 'even more against big industry than at Schweinburg' and issued a public statement explaining his resignation as a protest against the co-option of Sering and the demands for the further admission of a National-Social.[151] The next day *Die Post* emphasized the chagrin of

[147] *TR*, Dec. 19th 1899.
[148] *FreisZ*, Dec. 22nd 1899. The Free Union merged with the Navy League in early 1900.
[149] Detailed references from Eley, 'German Navy League', p. 82.
[150] *Die Hilfe*, Jan. 21st 1900.
[151] In early November 1899 Bueck had also resigned, to be replaced by Admiral Hollmann, but this had nothing to do with the campaign against Schweinburg. Full references from Eley, 'German Navy League', p. 83.

4*

Miquel's apostles by delivering a bitter denunciation of both the *Freisinnige Vereinigung* and the National-Social Association: it warned the supporters of 'national' policies 'to keep their eyes skinned in case free-trading and Socialist contraband is smuggled in under the flag of the naval movement'.[152]

F. THE LIMITS OF *SAMMLUNGSPOLITIK*

The first crisis of the Navy League exposed two rival conceptions of what the movement should be doing. On one side stood the actual founding group, composed of representatives of large industrial, merchant and finance capital, who drew the support of their moderate agrarian allies and enjoyed the co-operation of both the Navy Office and the official bureaucracy in general. At this early stage the regional leadership was composed of the same elements. This group saw the Navy League essentially as an auxiliary of the Navy Office, whose propaganda should fulfil the latter's requirements. It was conscious of the value of the naval idea for mobilizing popular support amongst the petty-bourgeoisie, and if at all possible in the working class as well. But these popular elements were to receive no access to the movement's leading organs or to the making of decisions regarding the size of the Navy or its rate of expansion. Any propaganda was to stay broadly within the limits drawn by the experts of the Navy Office. The second group in the naval movement, on the other hand, which shaded into other groups of radical nationalists like the Pan-Germans, harboured a more ambitious conception, though its full implications were still unclear. Here the populist rhetoric of the foundation meeting was taken seriously, and rationalized into an ideological system. The naval idea was to supply an ideological bond stronger than party, confessional or social divisions within the nation, which could restore the national spirit of 1870-1. Above all, it was to reach down into the working class, 'the masses' or the 'fourth estate', and win them back from the pernicious, anti-national influence of international-ist Social Democracy.

Hermann Rassow described this as the motive passion of his political activity, the ulterior attraction of the naval question. In the later 1890s he formulated the populist goal at its most coherent and made it the *leitmotif* of his political practice during the ensuing years. As one of the Navy League's most important propagandists, moreover, known particularly for his annual publication *Deutschlands Seemacht* with its accompanying tables and posters. Rassow succeeded in establishing his methods as a paradigm of intensive local agitation. He was active first in Elberfeld and later in Burg and Potsdam, and in each of these contexts found ways of making his commitment to a vigorous activity amongst the industrial working class quite concrete. In Elberfeld he directed his activities through the Evangelical Workers' Association, and in Burg through

[152] *FreisZ*, Dec. 23rd 1899.

the Workers' Association of Tack & Co., a large shoe factory. He financed them from the donations of local businessmen. In Burg he built up the membership of the local branch to a figure of 400 by 1902 (with about 100 factory-workers), and 600 by 1905.[153] Moreover, Rassow united in his own person the various strands of the opposition to Schweinburg in 1899: he had been an original supporter of Stroschein, he was one of the Pan-German League's leading speakers at this time and a member of its Council, he had strong links with Naumann and the National-Socials, and was a cousin of Hans Delbrück.

The broad coalition of loose populist forces which unseated Schweinburg and Zedlitz-Neukirch in December 1899 raised demands which not only questioned the non-partisan credentials of the Navy League's early leaders, but also surpassed this immediate aim to probe the legitimacy of Miquel's neo-Bismarckian coalition of heavy-industrial and agrarian capital. The involvement of Naumann and his associates in this campaign highlighted the threat which these entrenched interests perceived: the systematic coupling of an expansionist foreign policy with extensive social reform signified an opposition going far beyond the objections to Schweinburg as an individual. For Naumann such objections were inseparable from Schweinburg's general politics, particularly from his history as an enemy of organized labour. For this left wing of the populist front the anti-Socialist orientation of *Sammlungspolitik* disqualified its practitioners from any successful appeal to the working class. As one statement put it: 'Anti-Socialist law, Revolution Bill, Hard-Labour Bill—these are the three steps which lead our workers along the path of hostility to the state.' Then, explicitly invoking a model of supposedly successful social imperialism in Britain, it declared:

> The workers need *Weltpolitik* for a permanent improvement in their conditions of work. Therefore they should be in favour of the fleet. The state needs the workers for the pursuit of *Weltpolitik*. Therefore she should treat them justly and advance them socially. The one is just as important as the other. No social policy without *Weltpolitik*. But also no *Weltpolitik* without social policy.

In general, 'German *Weltpolitik* means the policy of the future for German workers.'[154] Naumann and his co-thinkers clearly had a firm belief in the persuasive power of the naval propaganda. As Rassow put it: 'that the fleet is *useful* to the workers, in that it protects trade and therefore the chance to work, is surely as clear as sunlight'.[155] But they also believed that this must be complemented by some movement towards meaningful social reform, or at least

[153] Rassow to Witzleben, Mar. 13th 1902, BA-MA Freiburg, 2379, 93943; Rassow's speech at the Navy League's Stuttgart Congress, May 27th 1905, *Protokoll*, pp. 15ff., ibid., 2276, 94230.

[154] Undated cutting, *Welt am Montag*, BA-MA Freiburg, Heeringen Papers, 7622, 4.

[155] Speech to the Stuttgart Congress, May 27th 1905, *Protokoll*, p. 15, BA-MA Freiburg, 2276, 94230.

the vigorous defence of existing rights. As Gerlach observed, the twin demands of the National-Socials were acceptance of the Navy Bill and rejection of the Hard-Labour Bill. Only then would the way be clear for 'the German *Weltpolitik*'.[156]

At the end of 1899, therefore, the debate in the Navy League became a vehicle for the discussion of much wider issues and the presentation of much larger demands. The resolution of the crisis registered a first victory for the populist tendency which broadly dominated the movement till the resolution of a later crisis in 1908.[157] A final reconstruction of the leadership did not take place until the spring of 1901, when Beaulieu-Marconnay and Wied were pushed out to the accompaniment of accusations of mismanagement and corruption. But the basic lines of internal conflict had already been sketched out, and the major slogans—*Regierungsverein* or *Volksverien*—had already been coined, though the later split of 1905–8 was naturally compounded of many other issues and disagreements. In particular, the call for a linkage of *Weltpolitik* and social reform was heard less often after 1900, and the National-Socials became less prominent in the movement after the passage of the Second Navy Law. Other issues, like the struggle against the higher tariffs, began to preoccupy Naumann, though some of his associates stayed to play a leading role: Hermann Rassow, Heinrich Oberwinder, Ludwig Weber.[158] Above all, figures entered the leadership after 1900 who held a different view of the political purpose of popular mobilization around the naval issue, although

---

[156] *Die Zeit* (Vienna), Nov. 25th 1899.

[157] However, it would be quite wrong to construct a simple line of continuity between the opposition to Schweinburg and the emergence of a more coherent radical nationalism after 1904. A dynamic process of self-realization and clarification was necessary before radical nationalists in the Navy League reached the ideological position they occupied by 1908. Thus the concept of *Volksverein* as it emerged from the practice of those later years was *not* present in 1899, even though people like Rippler already used the term. Similarly, the presence of Naumann and his colleagues make the populist critique of 1899 a more complicated affair. What can be said is that elements were present in the campaign against Schweinburg—those mainly characterized by Rippler and Pan-Germans like Hasse—which clearly anticipated the later development.

[158] Oberwinder had a chequered political career, beginning as a student of Lorenz von Stein and a supporter of the liberal National Society, progressing through the Lassallean labour movement in the later 1860s to Stöcker's 'Berlin movement' in the 1880s. He also had a spell in the 1870s and 1880s as a police informer in Germany and France, providing information about the activities of the SPD. In 1895–6 he was a member of Naumann's circle, but broke with the National-Socials at an early stage. He was later editor of the *Dresdner Anzeiger*. Politically his later attitudes are unclear, and he may have concerned himself exclusively with the Navy League. See the flyleaf of his pamphlet *Nationale Politik und Parteipolitik. Ein Beitrag zur Geschichte des Deutschen Flottenvereins* (Dresden, 1907), for most of these details. Weber was the Chairman of the Evangelical Workers' Movement, the *Gesamtverband evangelischer Arbeitervereine*. For a time he was also an associate of Naumann in the 1890s, but diverged after the turn of the century. See A. Böhmer, 'Pfarrer Dr. Ludwig Weber', *Beiträge zur Heimatkunde der Stadt Schwelm und ihre Umgebung* (1961), pp. 77–89.

the principle of mass politics remained axiomatic. In a sense, the radical naval programme and an aggressive approach to foreign policy began to serve in this period as a surrogate for the sophisticated social imperialism expounded by Naumann, and the process of transition may be concretely exemplified by the careers of men like Weber and Oberwinder.[159]

But the crucial influence of the 1899 controversy, as suggested above, lay in its implication of rival paths of development for the naval movement: on the one hand, a role as an 'auxiliary', a virtual extension of the Navy Office's own propaganda section; on the other hand, a medium for transmitting the wishes of the *Volk*, and an instrument for its mobilization, if necessary against the government, should the latter resist these demands. In this way the Navy League began to provide an important refuge for the political outsider, who claimed to speak for the independent views of the neglected non-Socialist masses. The original group convened by Stroschein had harboured this sort of idea, and their supersession by the Navy League's actual founders had been a powerful demonstration of the reluctance of the existing political establishment to abandon an élitist conception of political organization and admit these vocal, frequently petty-bourgeois elements to a say in their counsels. The first crisis of the naval movement marked a resurgence of this displaced group, a reassertion of their demands and a significant shift in the orientation of the organization. As Heinrich Rippler—in a real sense the manager of the campaign against Schweinburg—said in his retrospective on the crisis:

> A greater Germany cannot be sent down to us from above: that would be unworthy and impossible for a mature people. Instead the idea must capture the imagination of the whole German people so completely that it becomes a reality, *even if obstacles are put in its way from above*.[160]

Rippler's remarks succinctly communicated the essence of the opposition's demands and intimated the long-term significance of their populist content. The convergence of Rippler's Pan-German nationalism with Naumann's nascent social liberalism united two hostile judgements on the conventional *Sammlungspolitik* of Miquel into a common critique, and by so doing suggested that in the final resort they were separated by far less than was immediately apparent. They formulated the critique from different directions. Naumann attacked the entire framework of *Sammlungspolitik*, refused the claims of the Junker for special protection, and demanded that workers be given a share of power in the state. Rippler, on the other hand, implicitly accepted the legitimacy of the *Sammlung* and at this stage failed to perceive any contradiction between the latter and his own radical nationalism: he called for social concessions to the working class and the *Mittelstand*, but only to transform them into reliable

[159] For detailed discussion of this problem: Eley, 'Defining Social Imperialism'.

[160] *TR*, Dec. 19th 1899 (emphasis in the original). See also *DZ*, Nov. 18th 1899: 'The Movement for the Strengthening of the Fleet'.

patriots. Their co-operation illustrated the elasticity of the naval issue in this early period, and the dual source of its disruptions for Miquel's policy. It mobilized both those to the left, who wished to replace the *Sammlung* with an anti-agrarian front of forward-looking forces, *and* those to the right, who were not hostile in principle, but demanded that Miquel's coalition abandon its closed-door élitism and open its ranks to men from the *Volk*. The arguments of many of Schweinburg's opponents, moreover, of whom Stroschein was a typical example, passed the *Sammlung* completely by: it was not so much that they demanded admission to its ranks as that they implicitly denied the relevance of its preoccupations.

This was the final significance of the Navy League's first crisis: it exposed the essential narrowness of Miquel's coalition and of the mode of patrician politics through which it was constituted. It also points towards the limitations of *Sammlungspolitik* as an explanatory key to the political events of these years. As suggested above, the naval issue must be regarded as fundamentally separate from the mainstream of *Sammlungspolitik*, because it mobilized forces which could not be accommodated to its framework of class alliance. But this was not only true of expansionist industries and liberal-reformist politicians. It also applied to elements, amongst whom the Pan-Germans were ideologically the most advanced, who at this stage had little quarrel with the character of the state or the pro-agrarian, anti-Socialist premises of the *Sammlung*, but who demanded the more vigorous prosecution of 'national' responsibilities and the translation of the latter on to a more popular basis. It was this fact, the existence of a growing bloc of right-wing forces outside the ranks of the *Sammlung*, which gave the naval movement its special significance after 1900 and specified the importance of the *nationale Verbände*. In the long run this signalled the obsolescence of Miquel's *Sammlungspolitik* as the political instrument of the German right.

PART II

4. Inside the Pressure Groups

A. From an Honorific to an Activist Organization

I

It is no accident that the Navy League began to occupy an increasingly prominent position in the last chapter. It was incomparably the largest of the various nationalist groups. The Colonial Society, having boosted its membership from 14,838 to 18,250 between 1887 and 1892, experienced a mild stagnation in the mid-1890s (its membership was 16,264 in 1894) before benefiting from the new imperialist boom after 1895–6. But although membership climbed to 36,000 by May 1900, in the next years it stagnated around 34,000, and showed no real increases until the 'Hottentot elections' brought it up to 36,956 in 1907. As we saw, Pan-German membership climbed steadily in the later 1890s until it reached 21,735 at the end of 1900. But the rate of increase had already slowed down in 1899, and after a further marginal increase to 21,924 in 1901 the membership showed annual losses of several hundred, dropping to 18,445 in 1906. The Society for Germandom Abroad had registered 36,000 members by 1890; by 1895 this was down to 26,524, and it was not until 1900 that the earlier total was again in sight at 32,000. In 1905 the figure stood at 34,774. Because of the rather special contingencies of Polish affairs, the Society for the Eastern Marches showed a rather different trajectory. The 20,000 members registered at the end of the first full year had dwindled to 18,500 by the end of 1896 and plummeted to only 9,400 in 1897. But by 1900 they had recovered the earlier peak of 20,000 and the more energetic Polish policy inaugurated by Bülow in 1902–3 quickly redounded to the organization's advantage: membership rose to 29,300 in 1903, 40,500 in 1906 and 53,000 in 1910.[1]

By comparison the Navy League's absolute membership was very much bigger, and grew far more quickly. In 1907 it had reached a total of 324,372,

---

[1] Figures are taken from the following: Pierard, 'German Colonial Society', p. 106; Wertheimer, *Pan-German League*, p. 54; Haude and Poßekel, 'Verein für das Deutschtum im Ausland', p. 716; Galos, Gentzen, Jacobczyk, *Hakatisten*, p. 57. Later, after 1908 or so, memberships tended to rise with the general international conjuncture. Thus the Defence League is not mentioned here, partly because it was not formed until 1912, but also because different determinations were at work. The German-Union was too small for inclusion.

or eight and a half times that of the Colonial Society in the same year. After its first eighteen months the Navy League had already far surpassed the modest totals of the other groups, recording 86,675 members at the end of November 1899. The Second Navy Bill provided the impetus for a massive influx of new support. The campaign of vilification against Schweinburg held it back slightly (between the start of November and the end of 1899 membership rose from 84,810 to 93,991), but his resignation seems to have opened the floodgates: during 1900 it shot to 269,370. Moreover, despite a lack of concrete aims to focus enthusiasm after the passage of the Second Law, a net increase was still shown of some 27,000 at the end of 1901, and during 1902 this figure was consolidated—though 11,640 people left, they were compensated by 11,794 newcomers. During 1903 there was a slight drop from 238,921 to 233,487, but in 1904 the adoption of a new agitational programme restored it to a new record of 249,241. The movement was then steadily upward: 275,272 in 1905, 315,420 in 1906, 324,372 in 1907. When the members of corporately affiliated organizations are also added in, this brings the total well over 900,000.[2] By most criteria the Navy League was in a class of its own. Thus by the end of 1900 it already claimed 1,091 branches and a further 1,343 local agents, and by 1906 the corresponding figures were 3,006 and 2,924 respectively: by comparison, the Pan-Germans could muster only 190 local branches in 1906 and the Society for the Eastern Marches 404. Similarly, the Navy League's official organ *Die Flotte* had a subscription order of 270–280,000 after 1900, whereas the *Kolonialzeitung* could manage only 45,000 and the *Alldeutsche Blätter* only 8,000 during its peak years of 1899–1902.[3]

As a genuine mass movement the Navy League was unique amongst the *nationale Verbände*. Its internal history was defined by the dynamics of this popularity. Where both the Pan-Germans and the Colonial Society suffered stagnation after 1900, the Navy League could always solve the problem of political direction by setting itself new agitational targets. The timing of the government's own naval programme between 1900 and 1908 provided a natural rhythm for the Navy League and this undoubtedly conferred on it a somewhat privileged position. To a large extent the tribulations of the other groups derived from the general political primacy of the naval question in the period 1897–1908: significantly, both the Pan-Germans and the Colonial Society

[2] In 1905 the organizations with corporate membership of the Navy League included 714 veterans' clubs, 92 sailing, rowing and sports clubs, 20 choirs, 13 women's and children's societies, 22 student societies, 9 sections of the Colonial Society, 25 civil servants' associations, 16 workers' associations, and a wide miscellany of other groups, including many town councils. See *Jahresbericht* 1905, BA Coblenz, ZSg. 1, 195/2.

[3] Details from: Navy League *Jahresberichte*; Wertheimer, *Pan-German League*, pp. 55, 121; Galos, Gentzen, Jacobczyk, *Hakatisten*, pp. 135ff.; K. Wernecke, *Der Wille zur Weltgeltung. Außenpolitik und Öffentlichkeit im Kaiserreich am Vorabend des Ersten Weltkrieges* (Düsseldorf, 1970), p. 319.

enjoyed their most impressive expansions between 1895 and 1900 when campaigning mainly on this issue. Moreover, the extraordinary growth of the Navy League in 1900 posed specific organizational tasks of its own, and the problems of consolidation expanded conveniently to fill a potentially dangerous interlude of inactivity. This was not simply a matter of rationalizing an organized framework for the new mass membership, but also entailed a far-reaching shift of character from an *honorific* to an *activist* organization. This was the main dynamic of the Navy League's internal life. It helps illuminate not only the changing composition of the leadership and the local officers, but also the constitutional structure, the forms of agitation and the themes of ideological conflict which stamped the movement's history after Schweinburg.

The rapid growth of 1900 outstripped both the interest and capabilities of the original founding-group, and Beaulieu-Marconnay's brief tenure of the key executive post marked a confused interlude in the Navy League's early history.[4] The original members were in the process of dropping out or taking a back seat; new ones had yet to establish their claims. Some of the former (Bueck, Zedlitz, Schweinburg himself) had retired under duress in autumn 1899, but the majority discovered that their interest in the Navy was not commensurate with the demands of a full-scale involvement. Only two of the original thirty members of the Board, and only twelve of the sixty listed on August 15th 1900, were amongst the forty-four who made up the Board on April 21st 1901; of the latter some thirty had become members since the end of 1899. Similarly, amongst the ninety-seven members who attended the General Board in 1904 there were only fourteen of the sixty listed in 1900, and at least half of them had entered after December 1899. The case of Adolf Frentzel was probably typical: entering the Presidium in early 1900 as a candidate of the left liberals, he left it in December because of business commitments. Many kept a nominal membership of the Board until 1903, when the implementation of the new Constitution gave them a chance to withdraw. This right was exercised by eighteen members: twelve were in the original Board, and all the others were co-opted straight after the foundation except one, Frentzel, who was co-opted in December 1899. They were all leading businessmen, big landowners or prominent party politicians.[5] Only three (Hohenlohe, Linde and Schlutow) had

---

[4] Beaulieu-Marconnay's period at the Navy League was distinguished by singular mismanagement of the organization's resources, during which it became massively over-extended in big prestige operations (e.g. the so-called 'China Expedition' of 1900 and an ill-fated cable-laying enterprise) of no political value. After much disquiet in the rest of the leadership he was eventually forced out in March 1901, under allegations of serious financial malpractice. For full details, see Eley, 'German Navy League', pp. 95-100.

[5] The 18 in question were: Ballin, Drenkmann, Frentzel, Hohenlohe-Schillingsfürst, Hubbe, Jencke, Knorr, Linde, Lucius, Sartori, Schlutow, Schwerin-Löwitz, Teschendorf, Tietgens, Tucher, Wiegand, Zedlitz-Neukirch and Zypen. They included eight aristocrats. Only nine of the 44 personal members of the General Board bothered to attend the meeting of Mar. 28th 1903. See the list in BA-MA Freiburg, 2276, 94228.

attended the General Meeting in 1901, and only two (Sartori and Schlutow) that of 1902.[6]

Between 1900 and 1901 there was an infusion of new blood. Most of the men who held leading positions until 1908 entered the Presidium during this period. As described above, Max Sering was co-opted in December 1899, and he was followed by Fürst Otto zu Salm-Horstmar who succeeded Hohenlohe as first Vice-President in June 1900, and Major-General August Keim who was co-opted in October. Graf Eckbrecht von Dürkheim-Montmartin (March), Wilhelm Menges (May) and Erwin von Bressensdorf (October) became members in 1901, and in February 1902 they were joined by Louis Ravené, General Sarwey, Walter Kyllmann and Louis Freiherr von Würtzburg. Conversely, the remaining dead wood was lost: Alexander von Hohenlohe bowed out in the summer of 1900, and in August 1901, at a respectable length of time from the enforced resignation of Beaulieu, Wied handed over the Presidency to Salm-Horstmar. Dincklage-Campe clung on until February 1902 before vacating the second Vice-Presidency to Würtzburg.

Moreover, the new Constitution of 1902, with the greater participation by delegates from the regions, gave the local activists a chance to penetrate the General Board. Here the General Board of 1903 proved to be the watershed: an explicit attempt was made to elect 'particularly deserving' individuals and the next day the open Congress chose a completely new list of personal members by acclamation. Not surprisingly this brought many new faces to the fore, who proceeded to play a big part in the national life of the movement: they included Becker of Darmstadt (a retired officer), Dietrich of Ludwigshafen (an industrial chemist), Gwinner (an Augsburg lawyer), Dr Hopf (a Pan-German doctor from Dresden), Major-General von Rodewald of Detmold, Major Schwarzzenberger of Danzig, and Hermann Rassow. The regional delegations also provided a vehicle for regional and local activists to assert themselves nationally. In 1904 these included Flintzer (a Weimar lawyer), Walther Hammerstein (a banker from Mülheim a.d.R.), Gustav Heimendahl of Crefeld, von Holleben (a bank official in Essen), Major-General von Kleist of Rudolstadt, Lieutenant-General von Liebermann of Cassel, Oscar Martens (Secretary of the Dortmund Chamber of Commerce), Heinrich Oberwinder, Riesebieter (a public prosecutor in Oldenburg), von Salmuth (a retired officer from Brunswick), Heinrich Schilbach (a worsted manufacturer from Greiz), and Otto Stern, at that time a junior judge in Gleiwitz.[7]

These changes gave the Navy League a new face. After 1905 only five of the forty-four individuals who had attended the foundation meeting in 1898 retained any real interest in the affairs of the movement: Busley, Manteuffel,

---

[6] Full references from Eley, 'German Navy League', pp. 100f.
[7] Lists of participants in BA-MA Freiburg, 2276, 94228 (Mar. 28th 1903), and BA Coblenz, ZSg. 1, 195/2 (Apr. 16th 1904).

Vopelius, Carl Theodor Deichmann and Walther vom Rath.[8] The new faces also showed a much higher level of engagement: twenty-one of the Board's personal members attended the meeting of April 16th 1904, as against a mere nine the previous year, ten in 1902, and a miserable six at the crucial meeting of April 21st 1901. At Stuttgart in 1905 twenty personal members attended, and although the number dwindled to 16 the next year in Hamburg, the heightened controversy of 1907–8 pushed it up again: the three General Board meetings of 1908 attracted thirty-seven, thirty-one and thirty-one respectively.[9] This expressed less the rise of any particular faction than the influence of the genuine activists with the time, money and energy to run the affairs of a large pressure group. For this reason they also tended to be older men of independent means: retired officers, a few landowners, successful independent businessmen, and members of the professions able to organize their own time. But while the enthusiasts who entered the leading organs between 1901 and 1904 tended to provide the backbone of the radical nationalist tendency in 1907–8, their political engagement emerged largely from the agitational practice of the intervening years. At this earlier stage their concerns were more mundane: consolidating the organization, mastering the techniques of agitation, penetrating new areas of support.

II

Interestingly, the new activists often lacked formal commitments in the parties or even an interest in parliamentary affairs. Added to the ideological primacy of the nationalist consensus, this freedom from external loyalties gave credence to the Navy League's 'non-political' status and facilitated the co-operation of many later antagonists. Beaulieu-Marconnay was openly greeted as a man of this type, though his supporters were soon disappointed. Max Sering, the Presidial candidate of Schweinburg's opponents in December 1899, was also unaffiliated. Though his contacts with Naumann and the *Kathedersozialisten* brought pointed attacks from the orthodox right, he was never totally a part of this social-reformist milieu.[10] He shared some of Naumann's hostility to the Junkers as a degenerate, privileged social class and believed in the need to strengthen the independent peasantry, but this was accompanied by a doctrinaire adherence to the concept of the *Agrarstaat* and support for the grain tariffs of 1902.[11] His marriage of keen support for the Navy with principled opposition to a full capitalist transformation of German society was further

---

[8] Membership of the Presidium or the Board, tenure of regional office, or attendance at meetings are taken here as indications of 'real interest'.

[9] Eley, 'German Navy League', p. 103.

[10] e.g. Zedlitz to Wied, Dec. 15th 1899, Wied Papers; *FreisZ*, Dec. 22nd and 23rd 1899.

[11] See K. D. Barkin, *The Controversy over German Industrialisation 1890–1902* (Chicago, 1970), pp. 147ff.

testimony to the complexity of his position. Sering, like Beaulieu but unlike their predecessors, could not be fitted very easily into the conventional party-political spectrum.

This shift of complexion was confirmed by later accessions to the leadership. Keim, Menges and Sarwey were all retired soldiers, as was Major Toegel who joined the Presidium for 1902–3. None had relations with any particular party. Dürkheim-Montmartin, a Hannoverian aristocrat of Bavarian provenance, retained many agrarian contacts from the campaigns of the 1870s, but his full-blooded support for the colonies and the Navy placed him on the fringe of orthodox Conservatism. Erwin von Bressensdorf, the wealthy Leipzig merchant who joined the Presidium in October 1901, had no apparent party connections, and neither did another rich businessman, Marx of Danzig, who was a member for a few months in 1901, nor the successful Berlin architect Walter Kyllmann, who joined in February 1902. Würtzburg, who became second Vice-President in 1902, is best seen as a Bavarian liberal-conservative, but with no fixed party. This judgement may be extended to Carl Theodor Deichmann, the successful Cologne banker, and Admiral Thomsen, who joined in 1904 and 1906 respectively. Some members may be located more precisely: Gustav Williger (1902) supported the parties of the Cartel; Schorlemer-Alst and Loe-Wissen (1900–5 and 1901) were both conservative Catholics; Hollmann remained an influential member of the Court circle, in close touch with key men in the government. But the second President of the Navy League, Otto zu Salm-Horstmar, typified the new Presidium. From an old West German noble family with vast Westphalian estates, his prominence in the Conservative fraction in the *Herrenhaus* was a bow to tradition more than anything else. By contrast the Navy League was his primary interest between 1900 and 1908, and this was also true for most of his active colleagues.

To some extent this characterized the other nationalist groups as well. Thus although the Colonial Society was dominated by party notables, many of the latter had a direct stake in colonialism and occupied positions which were far from being merely honorary; the Colonial Council was also an obvious focus for lobbyists, and it is possible around 1900 to detect the emergence within it of a strong group of colonial activists, for whom party was less important and who were much closer to an independent Pan-German position.[12] Similarly, the Eastern Marches Society was quickly penetrated by men of an activist temper, less interested in serving the political needs of the agrarian movement than in reconstituting the latter under nationalist auspices on a broader popular footing. The most important members of the Berlin-based twenty-five-man Central Council were its two deputy chairmen, the lawyer Franz Wagner and the ex-diplomat Ludwig Raschdau, and the three professors Dietrich Schäfer, Manfred Laubert and Otto Hoetzsch, whilst in Posen Leo Wegener increasingly

[12] See Pogge, 'Kolonialrat', pp. 257–338.

set the tone.[13] The best evidence of all came from the Pan-Germans, where the firm political guidance of both Hasse and Lehr gave the independent nationalists more headway and placed the conventional party-politicians under pressure. Hugenberg's initiatives over the naval question in 1896 had already encountered resistance from the latter, and the agitation for a pro-Boer position between 1898 and 1902 proved even more embarrassing for individuals with a senior party position to keep up. In 1900 the resignations of Arnim-Muskau and Stolberg-Wernigerode from the Pan-German Executive were nicely offset by the rise of Heinrich Claß to the position of Hasse's effective deputy.[14]

These activists were a new breed of professional politician. They owed their rise only partly to a general bureaucratization of political life. As we saw, the 1890s were certainly a decade in which the parties began their adjustment to conditions of popular politics by devising new permanent organizations for the cultivation of their supporters' loyalties. This produced many changes of personnel. One of the best examples is the decline of the traditional aristocratic leaders in the Centre Party and their replacement by a new generation of parliamentary specialists, invariably lawyers by training, whose new style of pragmatic collaboration with the government stamped them 'as political brokers rather than political leaders' in Blackbourn's telling phrase.[15] It was also a time of proliferating economic pressure groups and the more elaborate organization of business lobbies, and this too determined a novel context for political activity. In the cases of both parties and pressure groups new kinds of salaried officials were needed: Dietrich Hahn in the Agrarian League, August Pieper in the People's League for a Catholic Germany or Gustav Stresemann in the organs of the light-industrial business lobby—all made a successful career from the new opportunities of political mobilization. New avenues of political initiation short-circuited the protracted and unpredictable processes of *Honoratiorenpolitik*. Max Weber's celebrated distinction between living 'for' and living 'off' politics does make a certain sense of this phenomenon, and contains a valuable insight into the quality of political commitment in this new careerist mode.[16]

But as Weber himself recognized, 'By no means is this contrast an exclusive one.' Most of the nationalist enthusiasts spanned both categories, drawing

---

[13] Tims, *Germanizing Prussian Poland*, p. 219; Gentzen, 'Deutscher Ostmarkenverein', p. 504. Wagner was also involved in the Imperial League Against Social Democracy (K. Saul, *Staat, Industrie, Arbeiterbewegung im Kaiserreich* (Düsseldorf, 1974), p. 470). Wegener was perhaps a special case amongst the non-party independents, as he inhabited the Hugenberg network of civil service, co-operative, credit and commercial institutions in the East. See Guratzsch, *Macht durch Organisation*, pp. 26–62.

[14] The changes in the Pan-German League are discussed in more detail in Ch. 7 below, pp. 242–53. Claß replaced Adolf Lehr, who died in 1901.

[15] Blackbourn, 'Problem of Democratization', p. 172. See also Weber's comments in 'Politics as a Vocation', H. H. Gerth and C. Wright Mills (Eds.), *From Max Weber* (London, 1948), pp. 94f.

[16] Ibid., p. 84.

income from their activities, but at the same time actuated by powerful ideological commitments. Bearing this in mind, we can probably
distinguish three types amongst the activists in the *nationale Verbände*:
a group of ambitious ideologues who had often completed one career, normally
in the armed services or the state bureaucracy, who occupied quite high social
positions, and who therefore entered the organizations at the top; the group
of paid functionaries, who might be totally dependent on their positions for a
livelihood, and who transferred quite commonly from one organization to
another; and thirdly, a group of freebooters, normally journalists but also
teachers and academics, who likewise lived 'off' their nationalist activities, but
normally enjoyed regular employment elsewhere and regarded their involvement as an instrument of personal advancement. Again, these categories are
not mutually exclusive and are to be used as a rough guideline. They emphasize
that the new activism was not the manifestation of one specific social group on the
rise, but a politico-ideological phenomenon of diverse social origins. This was
notably true of the first category, which included big nobles, petty aristocrats,
dynamic capitalists and respectable *Bildungsbürger*, whilst the functionaries and
freebooters included both the sons of the petty-bourgeoisie on the make,
déclassé aristocrats and bourgeois veterans of the nationalist movement.

Both Salm-Horstmar and Dürkheim-Montmartin, aristocratic men of leisure
with plenty of time for dabbling in politics, were good examples of the first of
the three types, as were Tiedemann and Hansemann in the H–K–T Society.
But the classic instances were the two political generals, August Keim and
Eduard von Liebert.

Keim had a chequered career, spanning the entire Wilhelmine era. From an
old Hessian military family, he served in various Hessian regiments and fought
in the wars of 1866 and 1870 before being called to the General Staff in 1881.[17]
A prolific military historian of some repute, he took up a natural position in
the historical section and lectured at the Military Academy as an exact contemporary of Hindenburg and Goltz-Pasha.[18] By the end of the 1880s he was
writing regularly for the daily press, and it was one of these journalistic excursions, a newspaper article criticizing official defence policy, which interrupted
a successful career in 1889: despite some powerful protectors (or because of
them), Bismarck suspected an intrigue and Keim was banished to a field position.[19] In 1892 Caprivi recalled him by placing him in charge of the government's
campaign for the Army Bill of 1892–3, and after some intensive lobbying of
Reichstag deputies, extensive propaganda and fresh elections, Keim had the

---

[17] A. Keim, *Erlebtes und Erstrebtes* (Hannover, 1925), p. 35.

[18] Ibid., p. 40. Keim published his first work of military history in 1872 and produced a
steady stream of writings during the 1870s. In 1908 on the basis of an international reputation,
he was asked to write a chapter on the War of 1809 for Vol. IX of the *Cambridge Modern
History*.

[19] Ibid., pp. 42ff.

satisfaction of seeing the disputed Bill passed; it was here that he acquired the experience, contacts and skills which were so useful to the Navy League after 1900.[20] In eclipse again with the fall of Caprivi in 1894, and further compromised by identification with Bronsart von Schellendorf, the ill-fated Minister of War, there seemed little future for him in the Army. As Keim himself said: 'As a "Caprivi man" and a "Bronsart man" I was in certain circles no longer *persona grata*.'[21] He retired from the Army in 1899 with the rank of Major-General at the age of fifty-four.

There were obvious similarities in the career of Eduard von Liebert. Five years younger, he was, like Keim, of bourgeois origins, and saw active service in the war of 1866 as a sixteen-year-old cadet. A talent for languages brought him preferment into the General Staff, where he worked in the Russian section. In the 1880s he developed an interest in colonial affairs and was associated with the radical Peters-wing of the early colonial movement. In 1890 he attended a protest meeting against the Zanzibar Agreement in full uniform.[22] In 1897 he was appointed Governor of German East Africa and this was generally regarded as a concession to the radicals in the colonial movement. His term was character- ized by harsh laws against miscegenation, the brual repression of native unrest and an authoritarian labour law. On the economic front he encouraged the cultivation of cotton in the colony, and after retirement retained many links with colonial enterprise. Returning to Germany in 1900 he was rewarded by ennoblement, but then found his further military progress blocked by obscure mechanisms of discrimination. Like Keim, Liebert had been closely linked to Bronsart von Schellendorf and this seems to have been the reason. At the early age of fifty-one, two years after Keim, Liebert retired from the Army.

Both men shared a powerful ideology of the national interest. Though their respective careers had brought them contacts with the National Liberals— Liebert in the colonial movement, Keim in negotiations over the Army Bill[23] —neither were 'party men'. In Keim's case this independence took the form of pronounced hostility to the principle of party-politics, which he stigmatized as a sham, an elaborate game in which opportunist manoeuvres for short-term sectional advantage masqueraded as displays of political principle. Here the experience of the Army Bill was crucial, for the initial opposition of the Reichstag majority confirmed the 'anti-national' rottenness of party politics, just as the successful elections of 1893 vindicated his belief that the 'national interest' was the ideal campaigning slogan. This left an indelible imprint on Keim's subsequent practice in the Navy League: the oppositional front of Centre, left liberals and

[20] Ibid., pp. 49–77; Hallgarten, *Imperialismus vor 1914*, I, pp. 335ff.; Nicholls, *Germany After Bismarck*, pp. 229–64.

[21] *Erlebtes*, p. 95. For the Bronsart affair, see J. C. G. Röhl, *Germany Without Bismarck* (London, 1967), pp. 182ff.

[22] These and other details of Liebert's career are taken from his autobiography, *Aus einem bewegten Leben* (Munich, 1925), pp. 122ff.

[23] Ibid., p. 174; Keim, *Erlebtes*, pp. 60ff.

SPD became the constant bane of his nationalist aspirations, while the electoral defeat of the Centre made him aggressively intolerant of the government's future attempts to conciliate that party over the Navy. Whenever the Navy Office pleaded its need to deal cautiously with the Centre during the years 1903–6, Keim always invoked the experience of 1892–3, insisting that it showed both the party's unreliability and its vulnerability at the polls.[24]

There were two further legacies of this common experience. First, both Keim and Liebert believed the post-Bismarckian administrations to be lacking in nationalist conviction. This was already apparent in the latter's associations with the Pan-German critics of Caprivi, but the effect was again much sharper in the case of Keim, who had painful first-hand experience of official infirmity. Though drafted from the outside specially to co-ordinate the campaign for the Army Bill, he was denied the money, staff and co-operation necessary for the job and was thrown back largely on to his own resources. In the process he pioneered a new type of propagandist intervention, and in the absence of official finance constructed a network of private patrons which proved invaluable to the Navy League ten years later.[25] But secondly, this produced a particular political psychology. Keim imagined himself an outsider on the margin of the establishment, slighted and misunderstood, a Cassandra with his finger on the pulse of the nation, appointed for acclaim by posterity but not by his contemporaries. Both men were denied a promising military career whilst apparently on the verge of lasting achievement, and in Keim's case the sense of injustice was aggravated by a stormy personality and his somewhat unusual admiration for Caprivi. He was already known for a certain bloody-minded independence in his dealings with authority, and at the Navy League his personality seemed to grow more abrasive with advancing years.[26] He flouted conventions of respect for high officers of state, defied attempts to restrain him even at the highest level, and by 1908 had deliberately placed himself at odds with the Court, the government and the wider political establishment.[27] This was not the result of a flawed temperament, clumsiness or lack of tact. Keim eagerly embraced his own exclusion from high-political grace. In so doing he assumed a characteristic posture of radical nationalism before 1914.

Keim and Liebert had a further similarity: fresh out of uniform and ideologically disposed to a non-partisan view of the national interest, they were ideal recruits for the nationalist pressure groups. They typified the growing

[24] See Keim to Witzleben, Feb. 15th 1904, BA-MA Freiburg, 2277, 94234; Keim to Sering, Dec. 20th 1907, ibid., 3476, 67693.

[25] e.g. Beaulieu to Wied, Oct. 5th 1900, Blum to Wied, July 16th 1900, Wied Papers.

[26] For some commentaries on Keim's personality: Junius Alter (Franz Sonntag), 'Kampfjahre der Vorkriegszeit', MS, p. 70, BA Coblenz, Junius Alter Papers, 6; Claß, *Wider den Strom*, p. 157; Boy-Ed to Egidy, Jan. 28th 1907, and Boy-Ed to Tirpitz, Mar. 14th 1907, BA-MA Freiburg, 2282, 94257.

[27] e.g. Keim to Sering, Dec. 20th 1907, BA-MA Freiburg, 3476, 67693; Boy-Ed to Rassow, Feb. 14th 1906, ibid.

body of activists who entered national politics through the back door, not through the lengthy apprenticeship of the parties and local *Honoratiorenpolitik*, but via the open house of the *Verbände*. Keim wasted little time before getting involved in the naval movement: in early 1900 he sent some articles on events in China to *Die Flotte* and in July Wied asked him to join the Board. In October the energy of his commitment carried him into the Presidium and after April 1901 he assumed effective control of agitation and propaganda.[28] Until 1908 he remained exclusively committed to the Navy League, but when forced into resignation he quickly made contact with the Pan-German League and joined its Executive. He now threw himself whole-heartedly into general nationalist commitments, launching three new organizations of his own (the Patriotic Book League, the German Youth League and the General German Writing Association), became a provincial chairman for the Imperial Anti-Ultramontane League, and in 1912 launched the Defence League.[29] Liebert, by contrast, had been active from the beginning in a wide variety of contexts: he was already a member of the Colonial Society Board, he joined the Pan-German Executive in 1904, he gave a major lecture tour for the Navy League in the winter of 1903–4, and became the Chairman of the Imperial League Against Social Democracy in May 1904.[30]

The second category of activists, the salaried officials or functionaries, were analogous to the first type, with the obvious difference of being more exclusively dependent on the immediate remuneration of their work. The easiest way of describing them is again by concrete example. Dr Albert Bovenschen is a case in point: a journalist by profession, having moved gradually through papers of the bourgeois left to those of the agrarian right, he was appointed to the Posen Secretariat of the H-K-T Society in 1897 and the next year took up the national Secretaryship in Berlin, where he also edited the Society's journal *Die Ostmark*; in 1904 he resigned to become Secretary of the newly-formed Imperial League Against Social Democracy, but remained an officer of the Berlin branch of the H-K-T Society for many years; much later, in 1929, he eventually returned to an official post in the latter.[31] Far more than a mere employee, he had strong political views and played a constructive part in the establishment of both organizations.

Alfred Geiser, who exchanged the Secretaryship of the Pan-German League for that of the Society for Germandom Abroad in 1908 is a case of the same sort.[32] The world of the pressure groups and the press offered a rich source

[28] For the details of this, see Eley, 'German Navy League', pp. 97ff.

[29] Keim, *Erlebtes*, pp. 153ff.

[30] See Liebert to Hasse, Jan. 17th 1904: 'I am being frankly exploited by all the national leagues and cannot take much more on my shoulders' (ZStA Potsdam, ADV, 188: 31). See also Liebert, *Aus einem bewegten Leben*, p. 175.

[31] Galos, Gentzen, Jacobczyk, *Hakatisten*, p. 50; Tims, *Germanizing Prussian Poland*, pp. 234, 239.

[32] Haude and Poßekel, 'Verein für das Deutschtum im Ausland', p. 718.

of employment and opportunity for the enterprising publicist, and individuals might pass swiftly through a number of different positions. Thus Ludwig Schaper, a National Liberal functionary in Bochum, became Secretary of the Hamburg Economic Defence League in January 1905, Chairman of the new Union of Patriotic Employees in the same city in January 1906, and then Chairman of the Union of Patriotic Workers' Associations in May 1907; he had given these offices up for health reasons by the end of 1908, becoming successively an official of the Imperial League Against Social Democracy in Kiel and the editor of a Free Conservative weekly there.[33]

In cases such as this we are already moving into the third category of activist, that of the freebooters and mavericks, who either lived from their pens or aspired to do so, a kind of Grub-Street of the *Verbände*, where both amateurs and professionals tried to cash in on the nationalist upswing after 1895–6, hawking their pamphlets and essays to the press, the pressure groups and the government. This milieu contained some genuine talents. Ernst Graf zu Revent-low, a former naval officer who left the service under a cloud and made his way by full-time journalism, was one of these: he was unashamedly ambitious and by 1908 his ebullient and sensational attacks on the government had lifted him into the inner circles of the Pan-German League.[34] But others, lacking Revent-low's high connections and political flair, appeared erratic and transparently careerist. One such example was Bruno Wagener, who edited a succession of provincial newspapers in Hamburg, Hannover and Breslau and offered his ser-vices to the Navy Office and the Navy League as a propagandist: despite evident literary talents he was known to be both politically unstable and heavily in debt, and neither agency gave him their complete confidence.[35] Other cases were those of Gustav Adolf Erdmann, an important naval writer used extensively by the Navy League, who taught at the School for Non-Commissioned Officers in Weißenfels, and the Catholic cleric F. H. Schütz who ran a private school near Cologne: the former was disqualified from favour by his gushing political

---

[33] Saul, *Staat, Industrie, Arbeiterbewegung*, p. 466; information supplied by F. Taylor.

[34] Reventlow was quite candid about his motivations in correspondence with Maximilian Harden: e.g. Reventlow to Harden, Dec. 25th 1906, BA Coblenz, Harden Papers, 87, H. 5.

[35] As Editor of the *Hamburg-Altonaer General-Anzeiger* Wagener identified with the National-Socials and Damaschke's Land Reform movement, and when editing *Hann. Tageblatt* for six months in 1902 he followed a broadly left liberal line. In 1903 he contested Lauenburg for the *Freisinnige Vereinigung* and in the run-off supported the Social Democrat against the Free Conservative. In 1905–7 he edited the *Hann. Anzeiger*, which was originally left liberal, and veered wildly between Conservative, liberal and even SPD positions. He was also known to have supported Anti-Semitic and Guelph politics as a journalist, and was not afraid to attack the local civil servants and even the Kaiser. The Ministry of the Interior thought him 'an unscrupulous politician', but the Navy Office knew him as a 'keen naval propagandist', and were willing to use him sparingly. See the report on his character, June 17th 1907, Boy-Ed's memo of Oct. 9th 1907, and the additional material, all in BA-MA Freiburg, 2258, 94066.

naïveté, the latter by shady entrepreneurial transactions and illegitimate use of an academic title.[36]

Examples of this kind can be multiplied indefinitely. Fairly typical perhaps was Heinrich Fränkel. Born in 1859 he obtained his first employment with the Chemnitz Chamber of Commerce and then worked for most of the 1880s as a roving speaker for the Liberal Society for the Spread of Popular Education. In 1889–90 he set up the CVDI-sponsored Society for the Mass Distribution of Good Writings, and in the next two decades worked mainly as a freelance author of anti-Socialist tracts. In 1903 he was involved in the early initiatives which led to the Imperial League Against Social Democracy, and his work was widely used by both industry and the state. Later he was a regular contributor to the journals of the patriotic workers' movement and was also active in the Defence League. During the war he wrote for the *Alldeutsche Blätter*.[37]

To return to a general theme of this study, a career like Fränkel's illustrated just how much of an organizational deficit the National Liberal Party now had to make up. *Nationale Verbände*, anti-Socialist groups, patriotic propaganda agencies—all these might well work to the advantage of the National Liberals in many areas, but none of them were generally and integrally constitutive of the party's local practice. On the contrary, like the Agrarian League in the countryside they tended to siphon off the available talent and inserted themselves between the National Liberals and their normal supporters. Significantly, many of the activists discussed above moved into their new positions from a liberal past. As we saw earlier, men like Claß and Reismann-Grone were drawn to the Pan-German League partly by unhappy encounters with their local National Liberal oligarchies, and many of the pressure-group functionaries seem to have travelled a similar route. Schaper, Wagener, Bovenschen and Fränkel all drifted out of older liberal affiliations as either journalists or officials and into a rather unspecified nationalist commitment. More often than not they were also of a particular generation, that born in the 1860s, for whose freshly formed nationalist convictions the fall of Bismarck and Caprivi's 'new course' came as a deep ideological shock. In 1890 Claß was only twenty-two, Hugenberg twenty-five, Reismann-Grone twenty-seven, Bovenschen twenty-six, Fränkel thirty-one, Leo Wegener twenty, and so on.

Moreover, the next generation of activist recruits were already being formed in an intellectual environment heavily influenced by the Pan-Germans and their fellow radical nationalists. Here the trajectory of Albert Dietrich, lawyer and member of the Hugenberg circle, who succeeded Wegener as head of the Posen Secretariat of the Eastern Marches Society, was probably typical: he was born in 1877, his views were formed in the League of German Students, he was

---

[36] For Erdmann, see ibid., 2259, 94146–7, and for Schütz, 2224, 93948.

[37] Details from Saul, *Staat, Industrie, Arbeiterbewegung*, p. 449; F. Taylor, 'Foundation and Early Development of the Imperial League Against Social Democracy', unpub. MS., pp. 3ff.

active in the colonial movement and the Society for Germandom Abroad, and on going to work for the Posen co-operative movement in 1905 he naturally got involved in the H-K-T Society.[38] His equivalent in the Navy League was the mysterious Dr Gerhard. Qualified in theology, the latter migrated to America with his family but returned in 1903 to begin a career as a journalist. After publishing an abortive news-sheet specializing in news from America, he obtained a post in the Navy League central office. A vigorous agitator, he identified himself closely with Keim and helped orchestrate the latter's press campaign in 1908. Finally forced out by the victorious moderates in October 1908, he immediately succeeded Geiser as Secretary of the Pan-German League. He was also recommended by Keim to the Anti-Ultramontane League and in 1909 joined its regional executive for Berlin-Brandenburg.[39]

These examples are meant to illustrate the kind of person who sank their political ambitions in the Navy League during the transitional phase of consolidation between 1900 and 1903. They do not exhaust the full range of activists, for the latter also included many conventional politicians who worked for the movement in their spare time. But they do point to the source of a radical-nationalist impulse. There was some continuity between the new full-time activists described above and the critics of the original leadership in 1898 and late 1899, but this was not linear or direct. The earlier attacks on the Schweinburg group had certainly identified their honorific status and narrow party-political base as the decisive obstacles to a more popular type of movement. But that opposition had always relied too much on a vacuous populist rhetoric, was politically disparate and lacked an obvious candidate to succeed Schweinburg.[40] It had cleared the way for the appearance of new activists—a new strain as it were, of 'indigenous' naval agitators—but the latter were generated spontaneously by the more intensive propaganda of 1900. They had a hard-headed commitment to the naval movement in its own right, whereas many of the earlier critics had been more interested in the ideological uses of the naval idea, either in a general idealist way (e.g. university intellectuals like Hans Delbrück or Dietrich Schäfer), or for the victory of Pan-German perspectives (Ernst Hasse, Heinrich Rippler), or for unlocking the reactionary party front of big industry and agriculture (Friedrich Naumann). These earlier critics had often viewed the reform of the naval movement from a slightly detached position, proffering the disinterested advice of concerned onlookers, whereas for

[38] Details from Guratzsch, *Macht durch Organisation*, p. 41.

[39] Hansemann to Knorr, Feb. 17th 1909, BA-MA Freiburg, Knorr Papers, 7593; Samassa to Hasse, May 14th 1904, ZStA Potsdam, ADV, 188: 320f.; Gerhard to Claß, Dec. 22nd 1908, ibid., 192: 547; Würtzburg to Boy-Ed, Apr. 11th 1907, BA-MA Freiburg, 2277, 94235.

[40] The most coherent of Schweinburg's critics, such as Heinrich Rippler, were committed elsewhere. Moreover, the Pan-Germans were still undecided over the correct attitude towards the Navy League even when reformed, while Naumann and his supporters were too far to the left.

the newcomers after 1900 the Navy League often represented their primary commitment.

III

The counterpart to this process of renewal was the adoption of a new Constitution in 1902, the fourth in as many years.[41] The new stratum of activists was a consequence and cause of this step, for the massive growth of membership left successive makeshift constitutions obsolete and created new pressure for involving the fresh recruits. At the head of the League stood the Presidium, comprising the President, two Vice-Presidents, an Executive Chairman, his deputy, the Treasurer and nine ordinary members. The new Presidium was conceived as 'the supervisory board of a joint-stock company', and its main purpose was to ensure that the Executive Chairman carried out the policy of the General Board and Congress. In practice the larger non-Prussian states had permanent representation: Bavaria had one of the Vice-Presidencies in 1902 (Würtzburg), while Saxony (Bressensdorf) and Württemberg (Sarwey) both had ordinary seats. Decisions were taken by a simple majority, with a quorum of five. The Presidium convened the General Board and the annual Congress, though emergency meetings could also be called by at least half the regional executives. The Presidium also ran the movement's organ *Die Flotte*, and was guaranteed fifty per cent of regional revenues to cover the costs. All correspondence with government was to pass through the Central Office, which was run by a salaried Secretary. These provisions formed the administrative basis for an effective agitation and assisted a concentration of authority and resources in Berlin.

Predictably the real distribution of power was slightly different. In practice authority lay with those members permanently resident in Berlin: the Presidium met only five to ten times a year and attendance was seldom more than five. In 1902 four of the six national officers lived in Berlin (Hollmann, Menges, Busley and Ravené), but only four of the nine ordinary members (Keim, Kyllmann, Sering and Sarwey). Between 1902 and 1908 their number was augmented by only two others, Thomsen and Vohsen. Not surprisingly the structure favoured dynamic personalities ready to attend meetings, master the machinery, control the flow of information, build up contacts in the localities and cultivate relations with the press and parties. Of those resident in Berlin in 1902 only Keim and Menges gave their whole time to the movement: Busley, Kyllmann and Ravené were in business, Sering was an academic, and Hollmann stayed clear of administration. Moreover, though Menges was officially sole responsible executive officer, in practice he divided his job with Keim, the latter taking agitation, the former relations with the government. Busley, Menges' official

---

[41] The following is based on the account in Eley, 'German Navy League', pp. 107–20, where detailed references may be found.

deputy, was not interested. Once Menges was gone (at the end of 1905), there was no check on Keim's appetite for work, and he tolerated neither of Menges' fleeting successors.[42] He was strengthened further by the consistent support of Salm-Horstmar, the President. While the Constitution *permitted* centralization, therefore, practical circumstances worked strongly in its favour. Keim's inveterate opponent, Freiherr von Würtzburg, was always hampered by the distance from Munich to Berlin.

However, this necessary centralization of resources was matched by the principle of participation in the sphere of policy. Sovereignty was poised somewhere between the annual Congress and the General Board. Initially the Navy League had reflected the prevailing norms of *Honoratiorenpolitik*: a leadership long familiar to each other from the daily intercourse of business, politics and society, bound by shared social prestige rather than formal responsibility to a national movement and its ordinary members. Executive power was originally concentrated in the hands of Schweinburg to see 'how far we can expand', as he put it. But this was also dictated by the limited commitment of his colleagues, and still more by the desire to keep tight political control. For this reason, local Agents were to be appointed only by the Board, while independent local initiatives were discouraged. In all this was a clear note of social exclusiveness. Wied assured the founders that the right to vote in a General Meeting could not be given to ordinary members; it should lie with those of high standing with a sense of political decorum. Accordingly, it was vital 'that the Agents always keep the decisions in their hands'.

This 'thoroughly centralist' organization hardly survived Schweinburg's fall. Demands for devolution of authority were a natural consequence of the Navy League's rapid expansion, which soon created greater self-consciousness in the regions. (By the end of 1900 only three small Thuringian states still lacked an executive.) The tension between centre and periphery focused on the matter of money, which nicely encapsulated the movement's organizational dilemma: the Presidium could not support the growing bureaucracy of the Central Office, still less organize nationwide propaganda, without access to the bulk of subscriptions; conversely a healthy regional movement required a large portion of its revenue for local use. This problem, with its implied opposition of centralism and federalism, gave increasing concern. At the General Meeting of January 12th 1900 which modified the original Constitution, there was already talk of establishing 'autonomous branch organizations', and this went hand in hand with special pleading for the South, where the confessional situation imposed a particular set of regional tactics. Here Freiherr von Würtzburg led the attack, threatening to reorganize the Bavarian naval movement on a virtually independent basis which reproduced Bavaria's federal status in the Reich.

---

[42] Menges' two successors were Hentig (a retired Gotha Minister of State), and Pfaff (a retired General): neither properly claimed the position. For full detail: Deist, *Flottenpolitik*, pp. 195f., 200; Eley, 'German Navy League', p. 382.

Würtzburg articulated the most extreme anti-centralist position and was joined only by the spokesman for Berlin-Brandenburg. In these quarters the call for regional autonomy was less an expression of the new activism than the reflex of *Honoratiorenpolitik* under duress. The leadership in Berlin-Brandenburg, like that in Bavaria, was dominated by prestigious public figures who moved freely in Court circles and enjoyed the ear of government: its two senior officers were Hollmann (Tirpitz's predecessor at the Navy Office) and Manteuffel (a leader of the Conservative Party). They were concerned above all that an over-mighty Presidium might use its power to embarrass the government or its allies. Accordingly, Berlin-Brandenburg proposed a straightforward primacy of the regional executives, so that all important activity was wholly regionalized and the Presidium reduced to an occasional forum for national consultation; in addition the main register of activism, the General Board, should be abolished. This represented not so much a decentralization as a determined relocation of the centralist moment on to the regions, where the paternalist supervision of the movement by notables might be better guaranteed. It was not a blow for greater participation of the membership, but a defensive manoeuvre by precisely the circles for whom Schweinburg had originally acted.

Deep inside the constitutional argument, in fact, was a political charge. Spokesmen for Bavaria and Berlin-Brandenburg opposed the application of pressure for concrete naval demands; instead they wanted an exclusively 'educational' propaganda. That being the case strong direction from the centre was unnecessary. By contrast the alternative view of the Navy League—that it should be a kind of pacemaker for the Navy Office, formulating new demands and preparing the public for a fresh move forward—clearly necessitated a strong central authority, with access to the movement's financial resources, which could co-ordinate agitation in the regions for a common political goal. As Dürkheim-Montmartin, an advocate of centralization, put it: 'the tasks which still fall to the German Navy League are quite enormous. They demand a united advance by the movement, its organs and subsidiaries. The movement's leadership must provide the great ideas and the regional executives are there to carry them out.' There was little doubt that this second view would prevail. It was inseparably tied to the populist momentum which had borne the movement through the attacks on Schweinburg and the campaign for the Second Navy Bill.

In fact the arguments of Berlin-Brandenburg were decisively rejected by the General Board of February 18th 1902 which preceded the adoption of the new Constitution. At least half the revenue of all regions should go to the central Treasury, and the main burden of financing (and hence organizing) meetings and other events should fall on the Central Office. But if the principle of regional autonomy was defeated, the regional context of activism was handsomely acknowledged. Henceforth the General Board comprised the Presidium, a maximum of fifty members elected by the Congress, and one representative of each regional executive, either the Chairman or a delegated deputy; the Congress

5

comprised the Presidium, General Board, and two further delegates per region. It became customary to fill the Board's personal seats with deserving activists from the regions: at Hamburg in 1906 this was done systematically by asking regional delegates to submit their recommendations. Authority was divided uneasily between General Board and Congress. But in practice there was little chance of a serious clash: the Board met the day before the Congress, and regional delegations were fully informed of discussions.

IV

The Navy League's 1902 Constitution laid the organizational foundations of the subsequent expansion. The decision-making structures it laid down survived intact till the outbreak of war in 1914: a clear hierarchy of local, district and regional committees, with the Presidium at the apex. Though the policy-making bodies were strictly speaking the General Board and annual Congress, in practice this function passed increasingly to the Presidium and the most active elements in its ranks. Access to information, control of the agitational apparatus and residence in Berlin all contributed to this process. The key to the Navy League's structure between 1902 and 1908 was an effective blend of centralization of resources and participation by regional activists in the central organs. The former allowed the Presidium to organize a nationwide agitation, the latter the membership to feel involved in the movement. By the next Congress of 1903 the Navy League already possessed the 'firm organization' which, as August Keim put it, was 'the indispensible basis for [its] further development into a great movement of a truly popular kind'.[43]

B. Who Joined, Why, and What did it Mean?

I

Historians have shown surprisingly little curiosity about the internal world of the pressure groups. This may seem a sweeping statement given the centrality of the *Verbände* in recent discussions of the Wilhelmine political system. But there are still very few comprehensive explorations of individual movements, and what there is tends to stop short at a formal description of the organizational structure and the simple recitation of membership figures, range of activities, size of propaganda output, and so on.[44] Thus the very existence of organizations

[43] *WeimZ.*, Apr. 29th 1903.

[44] This is true of Klauß, *Deutsche Kolonialgesellschaft*, and Pierard, 'German Colonial Society', Kruck, *Geschichte*, and Hartwig, *Zur Politik*, Schilling, *Beitrage*, and Saul, 'Der "Deutsche Kriegerbund" '. It is also true of older works like Wertheimer, *Pan-German League*, and Tims, *Germanizing Prussian Poland*, and even of Galos, Gentzen, Jacobczyk, *Hakatisten*, which is otherwise very good. Eley, 'German Navy League', also fails to do this side of the problem justice.

like the Colonial Society and the Navy League tends to be taken as an historical 'fact' in itself and their paper membership as a sufficient demonstration that they decisively influenced the formation of public opinion. In this way the *nationale Verbände* are reduced to mere institutional factors in an existing 'system of domination', functionally fitted for the 'defence of the status quo' and directly related to the ruling bloc and its state power.[45] Wilhelmine historians tend to write about the pressure group as though it were 'a corporate historical actor' with its own living personality, but one which adhered carefully to a script provided by the 'ruling strata'. Attention is rarely devoted to the internal relations between leaders and led, Berlin and the branches, the centre and the periphery. Thus the problem of analysing the impact of the *Verbände*—of trying to establish how, concretely, they affected the consciousness of the people who joined them or read their literature—is collapsed into a series of assumptions about their relation to the orthodox politics of the government and the right. Above all, there is seldom any attempt to uncover what it meant to be a member, the quality of experience involved rather than just the number of people affected.[46]

It was suggested earlier in this study that there was some variation in the internal character of the different nationalist organizations. In particular, the Pan-German League was distinguished by a relatively strong commitment to involving the ordinary members in important decisions: this could be seen in the detailed provisions of the 1903 Constitution and in the practice of Ernst Hasse's leadership. The key to this lay in Hasse's conception of the League as an independent nationalist forum, which kept alive certain ideas by educational propaganda and acted as a kind of nationalist watchdog on the policies of the government. Hasse's aim was to gain a hearing for the Pan-German 'point of view', and neither he nor Adolf Lehr harboured further-reaching designs on the party system. The Navy League revealed a similar commitment to involving the membership, though the movement's much greater size necessitated a higher degree of delegation and disciplined centralization of resources. By contrast, local initiatives were kept tightly under control by Heinrich von Tiedemann's dictatorial administration of the Eastern Marches Society: some local branches were extremely active, but their members seldom penetrated to the inner sancta of the national leadership. The internal relations of the Colonial Society were particularly lifeless. Its leadership was the most conventionally honorific amongst the *nationale Verbände* and made no attempt to strike a

[45] The most representative and systematic rendition of this view: Wehler, *Das Deutsche Kaiserreich*, pp. 90ff.

[46] One of the few exceptions is Henning, 'Kriegervereine', which makes a genuine effort to understand what the veterans' clubs meant to their different groups of members. See also H. Cunningham, *The Volunteer Force. A Social and Political History, 1859–1908* (London, 1975), and R. Price, *An Imperial War and the British Working Class* (London, 1972). The general methodological point has been made with great force by the important review essay 'The Coming of the Nazis', *Times Literary Supplement*, Feb. 1st 1974, esp. pp. 94f.

close rapport with the membership of the local Sections. At the 1907 Council meeting it was roundly attacked for this by a discontented minority, which made unfavourable comparisons with the Navy League. A month later an emergency General Meeting of the Pan-German-dominated Berlin Section called on the forthcoming Congress to inject new life into the Colonial Society by amending the Constitution to give the members more control over policy.[47]

In fact the Congress did the opposite. The existing Constitution adopted in 1887 was on paper quite close to the Pan-German ideal of a participating membership, linked to the elected leadership by avenues of regular consultation and bound by a community of radical nationalism. By contrast the changes of 1907 deprived the annual Congress of certain key rights, including those of amending the Constitution and approving the accounts, both of which now passed to the Council. Similarly, the Executive Committee lost control of ordinary business (e.g. the treasury, central office, propaganda work) to the Presidium (the President and his two deputies). Though the Council continued to be elected by the Congress, the co-optive element was much enlarged, and whilst both the Presidium and the Executive Committee were likewise still elected by the Council from inside its own ranks, the President was now allowed to nominate six out of the Committee's twenty-one members. There was thus a clear structural shift of authority in the Colonial Society from the annual assembly of the Section delegates to the President himself. The effect of this centralism was more or less to remove the leadership—which had largely perpetuated itself from the 1880s with some attrition from deaths and retirement—from the potential criticisms of its rank-and-file.[48]

This distance, which in the case of the Colonial Society amounted to a virtual isolation, of the executive, must seriously qualify the significance of the movement's popular support. Although the 1907 Congress made some concessions to the opposition by permitting the local Sections greater latitude in the organization of propaganda, the vitalizing effects of this reform were largely negated by the simultaneous entrenchment of executive authority in the area of policy-making. In the Colonial Society the main centre of activity was located firmly in the Berlin headquarters rather than in the localities. In its public activities the Society was more exclusively a national agency for the distribution of propaganda than the other nationalist groups: naturally the distribution of leaflets required considerable voluntary assistance on the ground, as did the organization of local lectures, but on the whole these were operations initiated and conducted from the national centre rather than the natural emanations of

[47] See the reports in *DortmZ*, May 3rd 1907, June 19th 1907.
[48] This point is also made by K. Hausen, *Deutsche Kolonialherrschaft in Afrika. Wirtschaft und Kolonialverwaltung in Kamerun vor 1914* (Zurich and Freiburg, 1970), p. 45. For details of the Constitution, see *DKZ*, 1887, pp. 704–7; 1907, pp. 449–53, 512; 1898, pp. 195, 255.

a vigorous branch life. Moreover, after the fall of Caprivi the Colonial Society became increasingly embedded in a network of national consultative arrangements with both government and business, for which the Colonial Council and the Colonial-Economic Committee were the organizing instances.[49] After the exceptional propaganda effort for the two Navy Bills in 1897–1900, the energies of the Society were consumed in the more technical task of demonstrating the economic viability of the existing colonies. In this period its constituency was less the radical-nationalist enthusiast from the provinces than a wide miscellany of specialists, from colonial merchants and investors, to the religious missions, colonial administrators, academics and explorers. After the turn of the century the Colonial Society successfully turned itself into the most important independent source of technical expertise in colonial affairs, and the bombastic sponsorship of colonial expeditions rapidly receded before the organization of botanical, medical and geographical research, experimentation with new crops, endowments of university chairs, promotion of colonial knowledge in the schools, the mounting of colonial exhibitions and a general technical concern with the economics of colonialism.[50]

In other words, to demonstrate the impact of the *nationale Verbände* it is not enough to enumerate their large membership, the size of their literary output and the range of their propaganda, or even to establish their social composition, though all of these are clearly important. It is necessary to enquire after the character of the internal relations which held each of the organizations together, the content of their activities as well as their outer form. In the case of the Colonial Society one suspects that after 1900 there was little sense among the ordinary members of belonging to a vigorous national movement which made real efforts to harness their abilities and commitments for creative agitational work. This was partly because the leaders set great store by close relations with the government, particularly during the life of the Colonial Council between 1891 and 1908, when the national instances of the Society became virtually an adjunct of the state colonial apparatus.[51] The absence of significant tensions with the government removed what was the greatest single impetus towards independent agitations in the cases of the Navy League and the Pan-Germans. From a political point of view this makes the Colonial Society the least interesting of the nationalist groups, at the opposite pole from the Pan-German League. The latter, with its ideological commitment to the cultivation of nationalist beliefs in the local arenas of social and political life, provided the opportunity for whole-hearted involvement in the local branches. More than anything else it is this factor, the exact nature of the relationship between the

---

[49] Pogge, 'Kolonialrat', pp. 188ff.
[50] Pierard, 'German Colonial Society', pp. 242ff.; H. R. Rudin, *Germans in the Cameroons 1884–1914. A Case Study in Modern Imperialism* (New Haven, 1938), pp. 166ff.; Müller and Fieber, 'Deutsche Kolonialgesellschaft', pp. 393–7.
[51] See Pierard, 'German Colonial Society', pp. 212–93.

national and local moments of the pressure group's activity, which enables us
to work out the proper significance of its apparent popularity.

II

On the whole the nationalist pressure groups shared a common sociology,
drawing their members from the same categories of people: professionals, civil
servants, businessmen, less frequently artisans and peasant-farmers, more
rarely the big landowners. As we saw, both the Pan-Germans and the Eastern
Marches Society relied heavily on these groups, and they figured even more
disproportionately amongst the branch officers.[52] This was scarcely surprising,
for these were the classic 'joiners', qualified by education and social status for
a respectable place in the public life of such voluntary associations, yet excluded
from the highest circles of municipal *Honoratiorenpolitik*.[53] They were the
natural leaders of the local branches. As Tims said of the average small-town
branch of the Society for the Eastern Marches, it 'might consist of the local
postmaster, the pastor of the Evangelical Church, one or two school teachers,
a doctor and a lawyer, the *Landrat* of the district, the editor of the country
paper, the railway station master, possibly the innkeeper and a few tradesmen,
a magistrate, one or two of the more sociable and democratic *Rittergutsbesitzer*
of the neighbourhood, a farm foreman from a neighbouring estate, and possibly
several peasant colonists if the Royal Colonization Commission had established
a village near at hand'.[54]

The Colonial Society largely conformed to this pattern. The earliest colonial
groups at the end of the 1870s and the start of the 1880s had drawn their support
overwhelmingly from the upper orders, including the Colonial League of 1882
which began life as 'a pure *Honoratiorenverein*'.[55] In 1883, when the Colonial
League's membership had risen to 3,260, a slightly broader spread had been
achieved, but this still consisted mainly of 'middling entrepreneurs and
businessmen . . . academics, mayors, aldermen, high officials'. The fusion
with the Society for German Colonization in 1887 introduced a stronger

---

[52] See the comments in Ch. 3 above, pp. 61–5. See also Haude and Poßekel, 'Verein für
das Deutschtum in Ausland', p. 720.

[53] However, it is dangerous to assume that these groups were somehow 'naturally' right-
wing—i.e. to read off a specific set of ideological positions from their social status. Chickering
found exactly the same sort of people in the German Peace Society: tradesmen, teachers,
physicians, lawyers and municipal officials. He concludes that 'the bulk of the membership
. . . was drawn from a nonrural, middle to lower middle-class constituency—that it consisted
of people who, in the words of one police-report, "belong to the middle *Bürgerstand* but occupy
no prominent position in society" '. R. Chickering, *Imperial Germany and a World Without
War. The Peace Movement and German Society 1892–1914* (Princeton, 1975), p. 75.

[54] Tims, *Germanizing Prussian Poland*, p. 238.

[55] Klauß, *Deutsche Kolonialgesellschaft*, p. 112 (also for the following). Also see the details
for the various geographical societies and the West German League for Colonization and
Export, in Bade, *Friedrich Fabri*, pp. 102–5, 139ff., 302ff.

petty-bourgeois element, but by 1893 the respectable total of 18,000 members broke down in much the same way: the largest group were the businessmen with 40·5%, followed by the civil servants with 13·1%, Army and Navy officers with 8·3%, the legal profession with 8·3%, doctors with 4·7% and teachers with 6·1%. Farmers made up only 2·4%, and neither artisans nor workers appeared as a separate category; though a residual category of miscellaneous occupations accounted for some fourteen per cent, it was unlikely to contain many of the latter.[56] As time went on the national leadership was also broadened slightly, but this stopped well short of the subaltern groups amongst the ordinary member-ship. In 1898 the elected Council consisted of seventeen businessmen, seven big landowners (most of whom were high noblemen with extensive commercial holdings), nine senior civil servants, senators and diplomats, five former officers in the Army and Navy, three lawyers and two teachers, two academics and two explorers, a single engineer and a single cleric. Moreover, these were extremely prestigious individuals: the officers included two former colonial governors and a vice-admiral, most of the businessmen were nationally known personalities, and in all there were eight Reichstag deputies.[57]

By social designation the leadership of the Navy League appeared much the same. Notwithstanding the populist rhetoric, the original executive had consis-ted of a leading political journalist, a retired general, a major banker, heavy industry's leading functionary, a technical advisor to the shipbuilding industry, the leader of the Free Conservative Party, and two princes. This underwent little change: of twenty-six Presidium members between 1900 and 1908, ten were big businessmen, five landed aristocrats, two admirals, seven ex-Army officers, one a professor and one a retired civil servant. Moreover, the regional leaderships reflected exactly the leadership at the centre in their overall composition. The setting-up of the regional executives, as Pan-German critics never tired of observing, had proceeded 'from above' rather than 'from below'. The relevant circulars sent out in summer 1898 had stressed that the Navy League could not succeed 'without the energetic co-operation of the Prussian state-service', or, in the non-Prussian areas, without the aid of the German Princes.[58] The procedures were fairly uniform: the respective Governor or Ministry of State would seek out the 'appropriate' personalities in the region, make the necessary preparations and then retire into the background. This was like the experience of the Eastern Marches Society, only far more compre-hensive.

Events in the Rhineland were typical. On June 20th 1898, less than two

[56] Müller and Fieber, 'Deutsche Kolonialgesellschaft', p. 393; Pierard, 'German Colonial Society', pp. 108ff.
[57] Details from Anderson, *Background*, p. 180.
[58] e.g. circular from Wied and Schweinburg, June 30th 1898, StA Marburg, 150, 650; Wied to Fürst von Schaumburg-Lippe, Sept. 25th 1898, StA Bückeburg, Schaumburg Des., L. 4, 10896.

months after the foundation, Wied and Schweinburg sent a request to Nasse, the Governor in Coblenz, asking for the formation of a regional committee. Encouraged by the Minister of the Interior, Nasse went ahead and contacted Julius van der Zypen, the Cologne steel industrialist and a founder-member of the Navy League's Board. Zypen responded by bringing in Gustav Michels, the Secretary of the Chamber of Commerce. Nasse then contacted other personalities, including Hans Jencke (Krupp General Manager), Richard Vopelius (Saar glass industrialist and member of the CVDI Directorate), and Wilhelm Becker (liberal Mayor of Cologne). He next compiled a list for a preliminary meeting in Cologne on November 11th 1898: it included twenty-four senior officials from all branches of the provincial bureaucracy, from the three deputy governors to the head of the post office; four senior Evangelical clergymen; twenty-three of the most important businessmen; and thirteen large landowners. Though a few names changed later, its social character remained the same. The final circular announcing the formation of a regional executive was signed by Nasse himself, Becker, Jencke, Michels, Zypen, Vopelius, five other businessmen and two senior civil servants.[59]

This process followed the normal by-ways of *Honoratiorenpolitik*. It was broadly repeated in the other Prussian provinces and in the larger states.[60] The prominence of the respective bureaucracies varied, but they always began the soundings and later provided the ruling Prince as honorary patron. In Hamburg, Bremen and Lübeck the initiatives were borne by the commercial oligarchies: in Bremen the League's officers were the Mayor, the President and Secretary of the Chamber of Commerce, the latter's deputy and the Secretary to the Senate. In Saxony the main work was done by von der Planitz, the newly appointed head of the Exchequer and brother of the Minister of War. In late November 1899 the first meeting of the executive for Berlin-Brandenburg was convened by the *Reichsbank* President and the Governor and met on official premises. The provincial bureaucracy was used especially blatantly in East Prussia. Here as usual the initiative came from the Governor and a manifesto appeared in the press on November 5th 1899. After a decent lapse of three weeks, he then instructed the district officials to set up local groups. Meanwhile the other provincial officers were galvanized into action: the provincial post office, for instance, instructed all postmasters to compile a composite list of members from amongst their employees.

Further down, the local leadership—the branch officers—were generally drawn from the bourgeoisie and petty-bourgeoisie. In this sense the Navy League's leadership was based on descending élites: industrialists, merchants, senior officers of state and the more successful professional men in the larger towns; the lesser and middling civil servants, the professions and the commercial

[59] The relevant correspondence is in StA Coblenz, 403, 9661.

[60] For comprehensive details of the following, with full archival references, see Eley, 'German Navy League', pp. 124ff.

petty-bourgeoisie of hoteliers and small businessmen in the smaller towns; the local and district officials, landowners and village notables (teachers, priests, tradesmen) in the rural areas.[61] In a total of 9,158 branch officers in 1912, by far the largest categories were higher government officers including mayors (19·9%), middling and lower officials including civilian clerical workers (17·6%), and teachers (18·5%). Large landowners and ex-Army and Navy officers (8·4%), industrialists and managers (7·7%), bankers and tradesmen (6·2%), and the professions (8·6%) came next and beneath these came the commercial petty-bourgeoisie of hoteliers and shopkeepers (4·9%) and the master-artisans and farmers (together 4·5%). In addition, there were considerable numbers of priests and other churchmen (2·7%). In all there were twenty-six workers occupying offices in the Navy League, making 0·2% of the total.

III

Though the mass membership itself was spread fairly evenly across the country, the Navy League did reveal some interesting variations. In 1907 the crude figures ranged from 42,000 members in the Rhineland, 27,000 in Berlin-Brandenburg, 25,000 in Bavaria and 23,000 in Westphalia and royal Saxony, to only 335 in Coburg, 454 in Schaumburg-Lippe, 471 in Hohenzollern and 527 in Lübeck.[62] When expressed as a percentage of the total population, however, the membership in Westphalia fell below that in Schaumburg-Lippe (the least populous state)—0·7% as against 1·0%. In these terms the highest figure was 3·0% in Reuß ä.L. and the lowest 0·2% in Hannover. Eleven regions claimed a figure of 1·0% or more: Reuß ä.L. (3·0%), Schwarzburg-Rudolstadt (2·1%), Reuß j.L. (2·0%), Saxe-Weimar-Eisenach (1·3%), Saxe-Altenburg and Mecklenburg (1·2%), Anhalt, Oldenburg, Hessen-Nassau, Shcaumburg-Lippe, and Waldeck-Pyrmont (all 1·0%). On the other hand, eleven areas showed a figure of less than 0·5%: Bavaria, Posen, Saxe-Meiningen and Schwarzburg-Sondershausen (0·4%), Baden, Alsace-Lorraine, Hamburg, East Prussia, Silesia, Saxe-Coburg-Gotha (0·3%), and Hannover (0·2%). In general these levels stayed fairly constant across the years, but at one stage or another most showed some fluctuation. One characteristic distinguished the higher percentages: they were all located in Northern Germany, mainly in the small states of Thuringia and the Central belt.[63]

Moreover, in certain areas the organization was poorly developed. Thus in

---

[61] The following calculations are based on the occupations listed in the *Handbuch* of 1912 against the names of local officers. They provide only a rough rule of thumb, as the simple designation 'merchant'/'tradesman', 'factory-owner' or 'landowner' inevitably conceals great differences in wealth and social standing. For this reason the occupational analysis cannot claim tremendous accuracy in detail.

[62] *Jahresbericht* 1907, BA-MA Freiburg, 2276, 94230.

[63] These were also the areas of greatest radicalism during the internal crisis of 1907–8.

5*

Schleswig-Holstein, Aachen and Trier the branch offices were held almost exclusively by either mayors or district officials. In Schleswig-Holstein the local apparatus was also formed by Agents rather than branches, and the vast majority of these (some 300 or 64·1% of the total officers) were either the stewards of landed estates or the chairmen of the village councils; the pattern was broken only in the towns, where landowners (5·6%), teachers (5·3%) and higher civil servants (8·8%) were also prominent. In Trier forty-five out of seventy-two Navy League officers were government officials: in the rural district of Trier itself thirteen out of the fourteen branch chairmen were mayors, and the fourteenth was a senior station master. A similar pattern also appeared in East Prussia, Pomerania, Posen and parts of Westphalia. In Prussia as a whole 30·5% of the Navy League's local offices were held by senior civil servants, as against a national figure of 19·9%. The only other regions to approach this level were the Upper Palatinate (24·4%) and Lower Franconia (31·3%) in Bavaria, Alsace-Lorraine (23·2%), Lippe-Detmold (42·8%), Mecklenburg (30·6%), and Schwarzburg-Sondershausen (26·9%). In addition, these were also regions where the executives were dominated by civil servants. In three Prussian provinces—West Prussia, Schleswig-Holstein and Saxony— the Chairman of the executive in 1912 was the Governor himself. In two more —Pomerania and Posen—the Navy League's office was housed in the Governor's building and staffed by his assistants.

In this way it is possible to distinguish different regional patterns in the Navy League's organization. The first, just described, could be found in rural parts of Prussia and Bavaria, often Catholic, where the local apparatus of the League was poorly developed and devolved largely on to the shoulders of local civil servants and their equivalents. In the worst cases (Schleswig-Holstein, Trier, Aachen, to a lesser extent Hannover and most of Bavaria except Lower and Central Franconia and the Palatinate) the regional executives were also dominated by representatives of the state. In others, where the regional economy was more mixed, the ranks of the executive were extended to take in prominent members of the industrial, commercial and professional bourgeoisie: this combination of high provincial bureaucracy and urban bourgeois élite was clearest in Silesia and West Prussia, but also appeared in Posen, East Prussia, Hessen-Nassau, Prussian Saxony, Baden and Württemberg. A second broad type of region was provided by those in which the leading role passed almost exclusively to the civil élite, with the state officials retiring into the background. In Prussia this was true of Westphalia and the Coblenz, Cologne, Düsseldorf and Essen areas of the Rhineland, in Bavaria of the Palatinate and Central and Lower Franconia. It was especially marked in Essen, which was a separate office precisely because the local business community showed such strong interest, and in Westphalia.[64] It was self-evidently true in Hamburg, Bremen

---

[64] For further detail and references, see Eley, 'German Navy League', pp. 126ff.

and Lübeck, where the leadership continued to reflect the structure of the city oligarchies.[65]

But thirdly, we can distinguish those areas which were both highly industrialized and extremely diverse, with low levels of industrial concentration and an emphasis on light-industrial manufactures, and which were at the same time Protestant and non-Prussian. This meant the broad central belt running from royal Saxony in the East through Thuringia and the other small states to Hessen and the Palatinate in the West, together with parts of Württemberg and Hessen-Nassau. Here the regional executives tended to be both larger and more broadly based: that in Saxony had thirty-two members, that in Hessen thirty-five, the small states of Anhalt and Brunswick twenty-one and seventeen respectively. In Saxony this was expressed in a larger contingent of middling civil servants and professionals, but in Hessen the latter reached further into the ranks of the petty-bourgeoisie and pushed out the higher civil servants almost completely.[66] This was clearer in the smaller states. In Anhalt the offices were held by a rear-admiral, a naval captain and two court officials, but the ordinary seats were held by a banker, a tradesman and a factory-owner, a priest, a bookshop-owner, two headmasters, two officers, two mayors, four district officials and one central government officer. Moreover, the same diversity appeared in the leadership of the branches. The central belt accounted for all those regions showing fewer than ten per cent senior civil servants among the branch officers (i.e. well below the national figure of 19·9% and massively below the Prussian average of 30·5%), and the only central German states not to fall below the national average were Schwarzburg-Sondershausen with 26·9% and the freak case of Lippe-Detmold with 42·8%.[67] The groups figuring more prominently varied. In Reuß ä.L. they were industrialists and managers (18·9%), teachers (27·3%), and craftsmen (12·6%). In Saxe-Altenburg they came from religion (8·9%) and education (42·2%); in Saxe-Meiningen industrialists (13·3%), traders and bankers (23·3%) and the professions (20·0%); and in Schwarzburg-Rudolstadt landowners (18·0%), traders and bankers (10·6%), religion (7·4%) and craftsmen (10·6%).

From this it seems that the Navy League in the central German states drew on a slightly wider range of social categories for its activists. In particular, though this was not exclusive to these regions and did not appear uniformly

---

[65] Böhm, *Überseehandel*, pp. 173–83.

[66] In 1912 the positions on the Hessian executive were held by Wilhelm Merck of the large Darmstadt chemicals firm, a professor, a serving admiral, a retired officer, and a high government official. The ordinary members comprised four teachers, three headmasters and a professor, eight professionals (two doctors, a pharmacist, an industrial chemist, a senior librarian, a lawyer, an engineer, an architect), an industrialist, five officers (mostly retired), five district officials, a district judge, and only two central government officials.

[67] Those states showing fewer than 10% senior civil servants were: Reuß ä. L. (4.2), Saxe-Altenburg (1·1), Saxe-Meiningen (3·3), Schwarzburg-Rudolstadt (5·7), and Württemberg (4·0).

within them, the petty-bourgeoisie of smaller employers, shopkeepers, small traders, Protestant clergy, teachers and professionals played a leading role in the life of the organization. In other words, it reproduced a pattern which was already familiar from the Pan-German League and the Society for the Eastern Marches, and broadly typical of other nationalist organizations.[68] But in 1906–7 the Navy League was at least eight times the size of the Colonial Society, Eastern Marches Society and Society for Germandom Abroad, and over sixteen times the size of the Pan-German League. If any of them was likely to broaden its social base appreciably into the ranks of the artisanate, trading *Mittelstand*, peasantry and industrial working class, then it was the Navy League. As we saw, the Navy League also managed the difficult transition from the honorific to the activist style of organization more successfully than its counterparts. In both these respects, therefore—the social identity of its supporters and the type of involvement it gave them—the Navy League provides by far the best material for measuring the impact of the *Verbände*.

We have already seen that in late 1899 the Navy League was rent by an ideological antagonism between the *Honoratioren* and those who claimed to be speaking for the masses, and that in an important sense this conflict corresponded to the conditions of the Navy League's birth in spring 1898. We have also seen that in the next three years there was an extensive renewal of the national leadership, in which personalities of a more activist temper gradually infused the Presidium and the General Board. The period inaugurated by the fall of Schweinburg was also the one when the movement made the qualitative jump from the membership normally expected amongst the *nationale Verbände* to one which placed it squarely in the ranks of the genuine mass organizations of Wilhelmine politics: from some 85,000 at the start of November 1899 to 269,000 at the end of 1900. Given these three levels of transition, therefore—of ideology, personnel and organization—and the general context of massive numerical expansion in which they took place, it will be interesting to see if a further process of change occurred at the level of the movement's grass-roots sociology. In view of the articulation which the other processes were given in the public commentaries of their bearers—namely, that the League was being transformed into a *popular* movement based in the ordinary people rather than the notables—it is vital to establish the exact reality of the new leadership's populist claims.

IV

The ability to break away from the conventional model of the *Honoratioren-Verein*—to be something more than just another 'society of notables'—was

[68] In this context 'playing a leading role' is taken to mean the tenure of official positions in the movement and dispatch of its agitational functions. The question of what it meant to be a member and/or activist is taken up later in this chapter, pp. 133ff.

essential to the claims which the Navy League made for itself. Its spokesmen insisted constantly, from its foundation right through to the outbreak of war, that it was a *Volksverein*, a genuine popular movement with support from 'all occupational groups' and its feet planted firmly amongst the ordinary people. The Navy League's fundamental aim, it was constantly reiterated, was to mobilize the masses and to rouse the *Volk*.[69] More concretely this meant winning the support of the *Mittelstand* and the working class. 'The education of the workers' was a 'special task of the organization', for this alone would complete the 'unifying work' of the 'naval idea' and give the League its final justification. It was a 'splendid aim to extend the patriotic efforts of the German Navy League into the working masses by showing how necessary the protection of a strong fleet is for the very bread of the worker'. This was also the best means of reawakening 'the love of the fatherland' in the hearts of the working class.[70] In the light of this aspiration it becomes a point of considerable importance whether the movement actually did succeed in penetrating the ranks of the working class.

The evidence we possess suggests that skilled artisans often joined the branches with their small-master employers, but that the Navy League experienced great difficulty in attracting factory and other industrial workers without the help of special circumstances extraneous to the naval question itself. In Versmold, a small town in north-west Westphalia, the Navy League's sixty-one members in 1906 numbered eight hoteliers, four bakers, two shoemakers, joiners, tinsmiths and tailors, and a single locksmith, watchmaker, gardener, blacksmith, mason, bookbinder, miller, distiller and dyer. In addition there were also three teachers, eight larger tradesmen, two manufacturers, and a brickyard-owner, a pharmacist, a retired Army officer, a policeman, a postman and two local officials, one of whom acted as branch chairman.[71] There were no industrial workers amongst the members, but then Versmold was only a small town with little developed industry. A similar pattern emerges from other branches in the same area. In Rheine, which claimed seventy-five members in February 1901, there were six butchers, eight hoteliers, two pharmacists, bookbinders and locksmiths, and a single watchmaker, shoemaker, barber, mason and chimney-sweep. This petty-bourgeois contingent was broadened by the presence of three clerks, three policemen, four minor officials, and the familiar groups of the professions (a doctor, a surveyor and a professor), the senior officials (five in all, including the chief of police and the mayor), and

[69] e.g. Schweinburg's comments in the foundation meeting, Apr. 30th 1898, *Sten. Ber.*, p. 10, Wied Papers; Bressensdorf's statement to the Gen. Meeting, Jan. 12th 1900, *Die Flotte*, Jan. 1900, p. 15; Presidium circular, Oct. 1900, StA Münster, Kr. Steinfurt, Landratsamt, 454; Presidium circular, Oct. 1904, BA-MA Freiburg, 2276, 94229; Presidium circular, Dec. 16th 1911, ibid., 2277, 94231.

[70] Address by von Spies to the Munich branch General Meeting, June 17th 1907, reported in *AAZ*, June 18th 1907.

[71] Membership list, StA Detmold, M. 2 Halle, Amt Versmold, 867.

the entrepreneurial element (fifteen in all). In addition there were eight engine-drivers and seven stokers, i.e. state employees and members of the uniformed working class. Two years later the membership had dropped to sixty-four, but had gained an extra six engine-drivers and four stokers.[72]

On this evidence, therefore, the mass of the League's ordinary members came from the petty-bourgeoisie, especially from the sector of craftsmen, small masters, shopkeepers and petty employers. In other parts of north-west Westphalia the same effect could be seen: in the branches of Borghorst, Wettringen and Emsdetten the League built its following from the *Mittelstand* rather than the proletariat. Although a number of factory-owners appeared amongst the membership, there was no sign of their employees. In the large branch of Ochtrupp near the Dutch border, on the other hand, there was some success: the League claimed twenty-four factory-workers in a total of 235 in 1900, and though the total strength had declined to 229 by the next year the allegiance of this group was kept. The absence of similar lists unfortunately makes it harder to assess the performance in the more industrial parts of Westphalia. But the evidence of local officers, conference delegates, public statements and occasional correspondence suggests rather limited success among industrial workers.

It would certainly be surprising if some workers did not join the Navy League in the industrial belt of the Ruhr and the lower Rhine. But their conspicuous absence from the 9,000 local officers of the League suggests that the incumbents found it difficult to treat them as social equals. This contradiction was often striking, as in the case of Richard Carstanjen, a Duisburg industrialist responsible for building the League's branch in the city up to a strength of some 6,800 by 1902 (2,300 individual members, 4,500 in affiliated organizations). The central aim was restated: the Navy League must 'penetrate into the broadest masses of the people', for 'the great mass must swear allegiance to our banner, and the worker, the "little man", must learn to think in a national way'. He continued in the same vein: 'Before God we are all men, in the German Navy League all Germans, united in our striving for the greatness of the fatherland.' Yet in the same breath he could argue that 'the social status' of the leaders was crucial: they should 'come from the best quarters of the town, be well-liked in society, and where possible should have acquired a privileged position through amiability and excellence in their profession.[73] The Navy League branch in Elberfeld, which numbered 349 members in 1904 and prided itself on the extent of its work in the working class, had no workers among the sixteen members of its executive: they comprised six traders, three industrialists, the mayor and two further senior officials, two teachers, a banking official and Henry

[72] Membership lists, StA Münster, Kr. Steinfurt, Landratsamt, 454, also for the following.
[73] R. Carstanjen, *Erfahrungen über die Bildung einer Ortsgruppe in einer größeren Fabrikstadt* (Berlin, 1904). The pamphlet was published by the Navy League's Central Office for the guidance of members.

Boettinger the National Liberal Landtag deputy and director of Bayer chemicals.[74]

When workers did join, we may need an explanation beyond the attractive power of the Navy League's own propaganda. This would often depend, for instance, on a particularly energetic individual who saw his work for the Navy League in a broader perspective of social conciliation. One such personality was Richard Carstanjen, who stressed the need to treat even the worker as a 'gentleman', and another was Otto Stern, who concentrated on welding a class solidarity in Lower Silesia against the 'Slav peril'.[75] The classic example was Hermann Rassow. He was already active amongst the working class in association with the Christian-Social Party when the naval question assumed its pressing importance in the mid-1890s. He worked mainly through the Elberfeld Evangelical Workers' Association (one of the largest of its kind with about 700 members in 1897), but also utilized the so-called Royalist Association of Railway Craftsmen which had about 200 members.[76] By early 1896 he was also conducting a weekly history class for members of these associations.[77] When the time came these contacts provided an admirable vehicle for the dissemination of Rassow's sophisticated naval propaganda. On moving from Elberfeld to Burg he continued this practice. Here he channelled his efforts through the Workers' Association of *Tack & Co.*, a large shoe factory, which helped in recruiting about 100 factory-workers for the local Navy League and gave him facilities for organizing slide-shows and films on the plant's premises.[78]

Rassow placed special stress on the need to treat the working man as an intelligent human being and an adult, to coax him tactfully into a nationalist position rather than bludgeoning and cajoling him. Thus he took pride in the fact that Socialist workers often came to his meetings: it was vital that such opponents were given the chance to hear the arguments rather than being alienated by harsh polemics. This stress on a political style of conciliation, though it made him less typical amongst the Navy League's most active propagandists, was clearly a key factor in his success. But although he doubtless aroused much respect amongst his Socialist opponents and won the allegiance of many individuals, even Rassow enjoyed limited returns. In 1897, for instance, he complained that the members of the Evangelical Workers' Association

[74] SA Wuppertal, P. III, 191.

[75] For Carstanjen, see his *Erfahrungen*, p. 2, and for Stern, see his *Die Bedeutung der Flottenbewegung für Oberschlesien* (Breslau, 1906), esp. p. 8.

[76] Rassow to Hollmann, Mar. 6th 1897, BA-MA Freiburg, 3136, II.2.1.4d. For the Evangelical Workers' Association in Elberfeld, see the material in HStA Düsseldorf, Zweigarchiv Kalkum, Reg. Düss., Polizei, 30434, which includes membership lists from 1890. See also the material in HStA Stuttgart, E. 151, c. II, 238, including the pamphlet by Ludwig Weber, *Zur Geschichte der Arbeitervereine* (n.p., 1899).

[77] Rassow to Delbrück, Jan. 28th 1896, DSB Berlin, Delbrück Papers.

[78] Rassow to Navy Office, Oct. 29th 1902, BA-MA Freiburg, 2257, 94136; Rassow to Witzleben, Mar. 13th 1902, ibid., 2379, 94742.

comprised 'unfortunately only one third real *factory*-workers'.[79] Similarly, his weekly history class numbered only 6–8 participants, and these included only one worker, a stoker on the railways. His most promising protégé, moreover, was a master-baker.[80]

Rassow's experience suggested the need for additional allies. The yellow trade unions, evangelical workers' associations and later the so-called 'national' workers' associations might all be media of recruitment, and a paternalist and authoritarian system of industrial relations also helped.[81] Fear of victimization or reluctance to incur the disfavour of the management could be a potent factor: it was one which was clearly operating in 1899–1900, when large numbers of postal workers, telegraphists and railway employees were pressed into joining by the government bureaucracy.[82] It could be particularly important in regions like Silesia, where industrial paternalism was particularly strong.[83] This was one of the few areas where workers appeared amongst the branch officers (but only nine in all, 1.6% of the total), and many branches, particularly in the industrial empires of figures like the Prince of Pleß, were dominated exclusively by managers, foremen, estate-officials and the closely allied local bureaucrats.[84] Thus in 1904 Otto Stern was able to revive the flagging branch of Ruda by winning the support of the Ballestrem mining estate: the General Manager Pieler

[79] Rassow to Hollmann, Mar. 6th 1897, ibid., 3136, II.2.1.4d.

[80] Rassow to Delbrück, Sept. 8th 1896, DSB Berlin, Delbrück Papers; Rassow to Navy Office, May 13th 1897, BA-MA Freiburg, 3136, II.2.1.4d.

[81] The historical literature on this subject in Wilhelmine Germany is now considerable: e.g. Saul, *Staat, Industrie, Arbeiterbewegung*, pp. 51–187; K. Mattheier, *Die Gelben. Nationale Arbeiter zwischen Wirtschaftsfrieden und Streik* (Düsseldorf, 1974); G. Heidorn, *Monopole – Presse – Krieg* (Berlin, 1960), pp. 26ff.

[82] See *FreisZ*, Nov. 15th, 26th 1899. See also the allegations made in the Reichstag by Bebel and Singer, RT, Dec. 12th 1899, p. 3320, and Jan. 30th 1900, p. 3834; and again by Singer, RT, Feb. 19th 1901, pp. 1437, 1453. In 1900 the Navy League's Railway Committee had 3,890 members before being disbanded the following year. See *Jahresbericht 1901*, BA Coblenz, ZSg. 1, 195/2. For the surveillance and disciplining of railway employees, see K. Saul, 'Konstitutioneller Staat und betriebliche Herrschaft. Zur Arbeiter- und Beamtenpolitik der preußischen Staatseisenbahnverwaltung 1890–1914', in D. Stegmann, B.-J. Wendt, P.-C. Witt (Eds.), *Industrielle Gesellschaft und politisches System. Beiträge zur politischen Sozialgeschichte* (Bonn, 1978), pp. 315–36.

[83] See *Eine Abrechnung mit den Fürstlich Pless'schen Grubenverwaltungen Niederschlesiens. Zur Aufklärung für Reichstags- und Landtagsabgeordneten, Behörden, Bürger und Arbeiter* (Waldenburg, 1911). This was a systematic SPD indictment of the coercive practices of the Pless management and provides useful insight into the conditions under which the various 'national' organizations recruited their working-class members in the Silesian mining belt. More generally, see L. Schofer, *The Formation of a Modern Labour Force. Upper Silesia 1865–1914* (Berkeley and Los Angeles, 1975).

[84] e.g. the Friedrichshütte branch, where the offices were held by three senior foremen and a senior smelter; the Bismarckhütte branch, where they were held by a General Manager, a foreman, a local bureaucrat and a police officer. Similar complexions appear in the branches of Hochwald-Neulieberdorf, Lipine, Schlesiengrube, Proskau, Pless (where all the officers were senior officials of the Pless industrial estate), Rothenbach, etc.

became the Honorary Chairman and his son ordinary Chairman.[85] In Kattowitz Gustav Williger, the General Manager of the *Kattowitzer AG*, was especially active in recruiting for the Navy League, helped by the firm's doctor, Arendt.[86]

But a favourable context was no guarantee of instant success. In Sulzbach in the heart of the Saar there was only one worker, a miner, in a branch of fifty-five, although there were many managers and foremen.[87] The Navy League agitators often complained of the poor response from working people. Despite persistent efforts amongst the forestry workers of Lower Franconia, during which he furnished free copies of *Die Flotte*, Professor Englert failed to entice a single one into the movement.[88] In Schaumburg-Lippe 'the lower orders' showed small enthusiasm for 'an idea which apparently they don't really understand'.[89] Whatever the size of the working-class membership, it was manifestly a passive one. As shown above, the number of working men who held local office in the Navy League was negligible. No manual worker, even a skilled artisan, ever attended a national Congress of the Navy League. In a list of 238 individuals who made themselves available for lectures, and who may be counted amongst the movement's most vigorous activists, there was not a single worker.[90] In terms of the social identity of its leadership, formal and actual, at the national, regional and local levels, the German Navy League was clearly a movement of the middle classes, if that rather diffuse term is used to encompass the industrial, professional and petty-bourgeoisie.

V

What did it mean to be a member? Perhaps the simplest way of broaching this question is to describe the procedures of one of the Navy League's more vigorous branches. Like most of the latter, the Duisburg branch derived much of its vitality from the dynamic leadership of a particular person, in this case the successful businessman Richard Carstanjen. To expedite the retention as well as the initial recruitment of members the branch depended on a fine net of local agents, appointed by urban district with the aid of a street-plan: apart from anything else this ensured the punctual and efficient distribution of *Die*

[85] Stern to the Presidium, Apr. 23rd 1907, BHSA Munich, II, Ges. Berlin, 1158.

[86] In March 1901 Williger and Arendt organized the first large-scale naval film-show in Kattowitz. The 19 performances were attended by a total of 24,000 visitors, and the branch took a profit of 5,000 marks. Williger's company co-operated closely in the undertaking. See *Jahresbericht* 1901, BA Coblenz, ZSg. 1, 195/2. For details of Williger's career, see A. Perlick, *Oberschlesische Berg- und Hüttenleute* (Kitzingen-Main, 1953), p. 172.

[87] Membership list, LA Saarbrücken, Best. Depositum Sulzbach.

[88] Englert to Navy Office, Jan. 3rd 1902, BA-MA Freiburg, 2379, 94742.

[89] Wasserschleben to Feilitzsch, Feb. 15th 1900, StA Bückeburg, Schaumburg Des., 1. 4, 10896. See also the annual report of the Weimar branch (printed in *WeimZ*, May 29th 1903) for 1902, which complained of the indifference amongst factory-workers.

[90] *Jahresbericht* 1904, p. 4, BA Coblenz, ZSg. 1, 195/2.

Flotte, whose monthly arrival was the one secure point of contact with the ordinary members. The agents also constituted the branch council, which met fortnightly two weeks before the monthly public meeting, to prepare the form of the latter and to discuss the latest communications from Central Office. Carstanjen himself took charge of the financial and secretarial tasks.[91] Great stress was placed on close and regular contact with the local press, through informal cultivation of the editors, the provision of reporting facilities and unsolicited news about the movement, use of the letters column, and so on.

Carstanjen was not entirely happy with the recommended methods for winning members: i.e. 'welding together a core of the patriotically minded who are in sympathy with the efforts of the German Navy League, and working through lectures, meetings and agents so that a slow but continuing growth of the membership is achieved'. Instead he opted for lavish public events, heavily subsidized to make them accessible to the less well-off. His favourite example was an organized outing to the Dortmund naval exhibition in 1901, for which he negotiated an all-in ticket of one mark fifty covering the rail journey and entrance: forty carriages were filled, each with a steward who gave out copies of the League's Constitution, badges and invitations to the next open meeting, which was to discuss a proposal for a 'winter festival'. The branch membership rocketed from 200 to 1,400 as a result. When the Winter Festival was finally held on January 18th 1903 it lasted from late afternoon to the early hours of the morning, and as well as the illustrated lecture on 'The Rhine and its Relations to the Sea' included music, tableaux, a choir, a gymnastic display, a one-act entertainment and a late-night ball. It was attended by some 4,000, with a further 5,000 turned away by the police. Branch membership now stood at around 2,300, with a further 4,500 in corporately affiliated organizations (e.g. the veterans' clubs, gymnastic clubs, etc.).[92]

This kind of large-scale celebration was common in most of the larger branches, and it is worth describing one of them in detail to communicate something of the atmosphere in the movement. In January 1905 the *Weimarische Zeitung* carried a portentous announcement from the local branch of the Navy League: 'Great events cast forth their shadow.' The object of this hyperbole was a proposed Naval Festival:

> 'Poets and Philosophers, composers and librettists, artists and engineers, directors and choreographers, *Fournisseure* and *Traiteure*, *Monteure* and *Dekorateure*, have all been at work now for weeks, arranging and adorning the Festival so that its shining glory will long emblazon the memory. For the Weimar Navy League this is certainly the most important event of the new century.'[93]

---

[91] Carstanjen, *Erfahrungen*, p. 6.
[92] Ibid., pp. 3–5. Carstanjen may well have exaggerated the size of the surplus audience.
[93] *WeimZ*, Oct. 8th 1905: 'A Naval Festival in Weimar.'

The occasion eventually arrived on March 18th 1905, and the press account was florid and enthusiastic. The 'spacious beer-hall' had not displayed 'such an exciting and colourful picture' since the Singing Festival in June 1903. The hall was decked in flags and banners, the side-rooms were made up as tea-rooms and dockside bars, and the guests appeared in fancy dress and naval costume. The evening began with 'an evocative prologue' from the Court Player, written by 'our esteemed fellow-citizen Hans Hoffmann', 'in which he urged the naval responsibilities of the German people on the attentive audience'. This was followed by a choral entertainment and a 'naval fantasy' by Fritz Jacobs called 'Appeal to the Sea-Bottom', in which the perils of naval service were dramatized on a sunken ship. There followed two songs from Fräulein Runge, a 'Sailors' Quadrille' performed by the Grand Ducal Ballet Company, and a comedy called 'The Friend of the Fleet'. Dancing began at eleven p.m. Finally, in the early hours of the morning, 'one left the intoxicating atmosphere in the certain belief that business had been combined with pleasure and that by taking part in the Festival one had done one's bit for the highly esteemed endeavours of the Navy League.[94]

The political purpose of events like the above was decidedly secondary. Like other voluntary organizations the Navy League had to offer its membership something more than the bare diet of naval propaganda which was formally inscribed in its Statutes. To this extent the ancillary vehicles of sociability which tended to cluster around the body of the local branches were a necessary accoutrement of the Navy League's status as a large popular pressure group, enabling at least some contact with the daily lives of its members. As Carstanjen put it, the League had an 'obligation . . . to interest its members . . . in its activities, i.e. by entertainment and instruction of every kind to make it worthwhile for the members to belong to the organization'. For unless this was tackled, the main aim of the Navy League—'to raise the national consciousness and to strengthen the interest in the fleet'—would not be met. To this end a series of sub-groups had formed in the Duisburg branch: a Dramatic Society of some fifty members, men and women, 'who for every monthly meeting delight us with a new show'; a Society for the Presentation of Tableaux; a Choral Society which met each week; and finally the Gymnastic Societies, which normally entertained the monthly meetings with folk-dancing and athletics displays. This range of activities ensured variety in the ordinary business of the branch and converted the monthly meetings into enjoyable social occasions.[95] The most successful interventions of the Navy League were precisely those with added attractions. This was true of the naval exhibitions, the organized school-trips to the coast, and above all the extensive use of film.

But having made allowance for these efforts, it must be said that the organization's impact on ordinary life was very limited. At the national centre it was

[94] *WeimZ*, Mar. 21st 1905.
[95] Carstanjen, *Erfahrungen*, pp. 7f.

clearly a permanent fixture of the political system. But locally its impact was more sparse. Another large urban branch, that in Nuremburg with some 1,500 members, provides a useful insight into the general levels of activity. In 1900, the foundation year, it met in all capacities nine times, but by 1901 this had sunk to five, and before 1908 meetings of all descriptions rarely exceeded four.[96] There were only two lecture meetings in 1900, one in each of the next two years, and two in 1903; the new national campaigning brought the figure up to three in 1904 and 1905, but by 1906 it was down again to a single meeting. Duisburg notwithstanding, even the most vigorous branches had to struggle to exceed this modest performance.[97] Participation in organized public activity was an occasional experience. The ordinary member would receive the monthly journal and attend the odd lecture. If lucky he might see a film-show. He might also use the 'mutoscope' (slot-machine with moving pictures) on the station and would almost certainly see the so-called 'Rassow-Tables' in the booking-hall or the doctor's surgery.[98] During special campaigns he might read a few leaflets. If rich enough he might join a trip to view the fleet, and would doubtless buy the organization's handbooks, postcards, posters and emblems. But in general these acts made few demands on an individual's time, intellect or political commitment. Quite the contrary in many cases; the movement's statutory obligation to preserve party-political neutrality favoured a built-in tendency for branches to take refuge in lavish social events with minimal political content.[99]

In itself, to join the Navy League was not a very significant act. When the movement was getting off the ground in 1898–1900, it was an almost routine acknowledgement of existing loyalties. In Pomerania, for instance, the 'Governor called fifty men together and asked them to sign a manifesto. These men regarded themselves as a committee . . . and formed a provincial executive

---

[96] These comments are based on an analysis of the branch's minute-book. The high level of activity in 1900 resulted from the special needs of the foundation, and in 1908 the number of meetings rose sharply due to the Navy League's internal crisis. See SA Nuremberg, Vereine 19, 1: *Protokollbuch*.

[97] In 1904 the Weimar branch, a major centre of activism in the League, held only three meetings: a concert, the annual general meeting, and a lecture evening addressed by Liebert on 'The Influence of Sea Power on the Development of a Nation's Strength'. See *WeimZ*, Feb. 16th, May 14th and Nov. 9th 1904. In 1905 there were still only two lecture meetings (*WeimZ*, June 6th and Dec. 15th 1905). These remarks are based on an exhaustive survey of the *WeimZ*.

[98] The 'Rassow-Tables' were representations of naval strength in poster form, compiled by Rassow. They were also issued as leaflets and as part of a larger pamphlet.

[99] See Erdmann to Boy-Ed, Apr. 7th 1908 (concerning the Weissenfels branch), BA-MA Freiburg, 2259, 94147: '. . . *nothing* has happened for ten full years apart from the worthless film-shows for the children'. See also Geiser to Hasse, Mar. 23rd 1904 (report on a recruiting tour), ZStA Potsdam, ADV, 188: 219–21: although the Navy League was stronger in many places than the Pan-German League on paper, 'in general it also exhibits a prevailing mood of great indolence'.

which enlarged itself by co-option. The district officials and mayors were asked to form local committees.'[100] The process was much the same throughout the country. Prospective committee-men came from a select circle of businessmen, landowners and other dignitaries. One meeting to form a branch in Crefeld consisted of farmers convened by the district official, another in Schwelm attracted some thirty representatives of 'the first ranks of society, from post-master to lieutenant of the reserve, foreign consuls, factory-owners, senior teachers and so on'.[101] Such people made little contribution subsequently to the movement's active life, lending only the prestige of their names, a larger subscription and perhaps some extra facilities like office space and clerical personnel.[102] Their patronage was often transparently selfish. The Navy League presented annual rolls of honour for decoration by the Kaiser, and inclusion was often a reward for services rendered. The Berlin tycoon Friedländer offered to assume the organization's entire financial responsibility if this brought ennoblement in return.[103]

Prevailing social norms rather than precise political commitments brought large numbers of the 'upper ten thousand' into the Navy League. Lying outside the everyday practice of political and economic struggle, it was necessarily rather tangential to the main concerns of capitalist and worker, landlord and peasant, merchant and *Mittelständler* alike. This is a vital point, because the nationalist pressure groups performed quite different functions from many of the other mass movements of the day. Organizations like the trade unions or the economic defence leagues of the peasantry and *Mittelstand* were located at the very centre of their members' social existence, with a variegated practice closely attuned to their social needs, from organized protection by strike and boycott to the formation of co-operatives, the provision of insurance, the organization of opinion through an independent press, and the general arrange-ment of leisure. They interlocked with political movements: the SPD and the Centre each intervened in the educational and recreational lives of their supporters through music, song and sport, evening classes, and not least through the effective control of ale-houses. For the non-Catholic peasantry and *Mittel-stand* there were choral and athletics clubs, veterans' clubs and later the Young Germany Union, which were similarly often linked with a particular Con-servative or Anti-semitic party. All were an organic part of their members'

---

[100] Statement to the General Board by Hagen, a senior official in the Pomeranian provincial administration, Feb. 18th 1902, *Verhandlungen*, p. 14, BA-MA Freiburg, 2276, 94228.

[101] *FreisZ*, Dec. 16th and 23rd 1899.

[102] e.g. the Essen branch was based in the offices of the *Essener Credit-Anstalt*, its business manager was an official of the bank, and its Honorary Chairman the bank's head Albert Müller.

[103] Undated note, summer 1900, Wied Papers. For the Navy League's annual honours list, see the general material in BA-MA Freiburg, 2312, 94423. For a cynical comment on this type of motivation, see Claß, *Wider den Strom*, p. 83.

lives, deeply embedded in the social fabric of their daily existence.[104]
The same can rarely be said of pressure groups like the Navy League or the
Colonial Society, which impinged less directly on the ordinary affairs of their
membership: once a month with the arrival of the journal, perhaps half a dozen
times a year with an organized event. This was partly because they were single-
issue pressure groups, but even where they pooled resources in informal local
cartels they still remained occasional discussion circles of activists and hangers-
on. To break this barrier something like the more continuous interventions of
the Imperial League Against Social Democracy was needed, with its more
systematic penetration of the working class, its sponsorship of patriotic fronts
on socio-economic matters, its speakers' schools and its labour secretariats.
Otherwise, they would continue to draw most of their support from a class
whose solidarity required little formal organization but arose naturally from
the conditions of abundance to which it was accustomed, moulded by common
ownership of power, wealth and cultural privilege. They reinforced the more
pompous symbolism of patriotic occasions like Sedan Day, the Bismarck
Festivals or the Kaiser's Birthday.[105] The Navy League was far less exclusive
than most of its sister-organizations, but it remains to be shown that the various
subaltern groups amongst its members left any decisive plebeian stamp on its
make-up. The above remarks have argued that they did not.

These observations suggest some vital modifications to the model of social-
imperialist mobilization currently accepted by most Wilhelmine historians.
There is no doubt that the Navy League was one embodiment of an attempt to
demonstrate the overriding economic and cultural value of empire and thereby
to bind to the 'status quo' the subordinate classes of Wilhelmine Germany:
the peasantry, the *Mittelstand*, the industrial proletariat. But the efficacy of
this offensive seems to have been very limited. The rural population was
apparently largely indifferent to the attractions of *Weltpolitik*, and the same
may also have been true of parts of the urban *Mittelstand*.[106] Workers were

---

[104] For two useful studies which touch on the associational life of the bourgeoisie: W.
Henning, *Das westdeutsche Bürgertum in der Epoche der Hochindustrialisierung 1860–1914*
(Tübingen, 1972), and W. Hofmann, *Die Bielefelder Stadtverordneten. Ein Beitrag zur
bürgerlichen Selbstverwaltung und sozialem Wandel 1850 bis 1914* (Hamburg and Lübeck,
1964).

[105] Retzlaw has left a good atmospheric description of such social rites in Schneidemühl,
a garrison town and railway junction in Pomerania: K. Retzlaw, *Spartakus: Aufstieg und
Niedergang. Erinnerungen eines Parteiarbeiters* (Frankfurt, 1971), p. 15. See also K. Stenke-
witz, *Gegen Bajonett und Dividende. Die politische Krise in Deutschland an Vorabend des ersten
Weltkrieges* (Berlin, 1960), pp. 77–95; N. Birnbaum, 'Monarchs and Sociologists: A Reply to
Professor Shils and Mr. Young', in *Toward a Critical Sociology* (Oxford, 1971), pp. 57–80;
E. J. Hobsbawm, 'Inventing Traditions in 19th Century Europe', in *Past and Present Society
Annual Conference 1977*, pp. 1–24.

[106] See Böhm, *Überseehandel*, pp. 183–263; Gellately, *Politics of Economic Despair*, pp. 92,
96; Blackbourn, 'Problem of Democratization', p. 178; Farr, 'Populism in the Countryside',
p. 142.

certainly heavily under-represented in the membership and played little part in the movement. Craftsmen had a proportionately larger presence, but again had little visible impact. Moreover, because of a public activity confined at the local level to desultory and fitful interventions, it probably made little constructive contribution to the mental formation of the mass of members whatever their social origin. The political consciousness of the bourgeois strata from which the latter were mainly recruited was formed elsewhere, in family, school, Church, Army and Navy, university, professional life, and in negative definition against the uncomfortable pressures exerted by the subordinate classes.

VI

To identify the real contribution of the naval movement to the political life of the *Kaiserreich* we must turn to a very specific group of highly conscious politicians who comprised a small minority of the overall membership: those who shouldered the real burdens of agitation by filling the key posts and by throwing themselves whole-heartedly into the minutiae of propaganda in the branches, the genuine activists who attended congresses, gave lectures, wrote pamphlets and lobbied the parties. In other words, we should examine not so much the *general* level of commitment as the *particular* engagement of those who tried to exploit the opportunities of the nationalist pressure groups for some more concrete purpose. These were invariably men who gave their whole time to the cause, supporting themselves from a salary provided by the movement itself or the proceeds of a multifarious journalistic activity. They might also have a pension or a successful business. A new type of political functionary, they moved readily between organizations. August Keim, Albert Bovenschen, Friedrich Hopf, Ludwig Schaper and the mysterious Dr Gerhard all, in their different ways, typified this milieu. It was in cases like these, where energy combined with a coherent ideology of the *Primat des Nationalen*, that the movement threatened to achieve a wider impact. Thrown together largely by their experience in the Navy League itself, they came to form a radical-nationalist phalanx united by impatience with the tempo of official naval policy and contempt for the political parties which obstructed its acceleration. After a bitter crisis in 1908 these elements fused with the Pan-Germans, who showed an analogous commitment, to form the kernel of a so-called 'national opposition' on the right of the government and its former natural allies.

Finally, having stressed the limitations of *individual* membership in the Navy League, it is important to re-emphasize the latter's relative strengths as an *organization*. For instance, although groups like the Pan-Germans or the German-Union might obtain a higher level of continuous involvement from the membership in general, this necessarily took the form of intensified petty labour—e.g. repeated fund-raising operations and the collection of small donations through the equivalent of coffee-mornings and jumble-sales. In this case a genuine community was achieved through the shared burden of *Kleinarbeit*: at one level a rather trivial, self-perpetuating activity which always threatened to become the organization's only grass-roots reality, but at another a sense of self-sacrificial commitment and of everyone pulling together to hold the organization above water. In this sense the Pan-Germans and German-Union (like the Society for Germandom Abroad and the Eastern Marches Society in the same way) were instances of the typical minority organization unable to 'take off' into sustained large-scale agitation. On the other hand, the Colonial Society was much more of a technocratic organization, closely integrated into the state apparatus and financed directly by big capital: its major activities consisted not of the Pan-Germans' self-sustaining local *Kleinarbeit*, but of sponsoring research and promoting public awareness by large-scale administrative interventions (e.g. by the mounting of colonial exhibitions). The Navy League was different again, combining strong elements of both, but subordinating them to the larger capability of a mass agitational organization. The Navy League had the resources to launch nationally co-ordinated propagandas, in which political pressure of all types was concentrated on the appropriate parts of the political system, and which allowed far more scope for the nationally-focused involvement of local activists. In other words, its practice contained an uneasy tension between the tendency of its local organs to routinize activity into unpolitical social events and the much greater opportunity for a highly politicized version of radical-nationalist activity. The crisis of *Honoratiorenpolitik* originated in this contradiction.

C. FINANCE

Finance is the acid test of the 'manipulative' model of nationalist mobilization. All the *nationale Verbände* kept permanent offices run by full-time staff, they all mounted big literary operations, and they all engaged in specific campaigns of agitation. To do this they needed money. The scale of activity was limited by the ability to mobilize resources quickly. Not only is the question of finance an important general measure of the degree of interest shown in the nationalist groups by the 'ruling strata', therefore, but a large financial commitment was also inseparable from any attempt to use them for ulterior political purposes. If the social-imperialist argument is to hold any water, in other words, it must be shown that the financial means of 'manipulation' were actually provided, for otherwise setting up an agitational pressure group would be futile, rather like digging a garden without a spade. Arguably, to justify talk of 'manipulative social imperialism', 'caesarism' and 'plebiscitary techniques of rule', the financial involvement would need to be systematic rather than just occasional or individual. Thus even where substantial involvement by capital (or individual capitalists), the state or the right-wing parties *can* be identified, the meaning must be extracted with great care.

Motivations might vary widely. Thus heavy-industrial and commercial sponsorship of the Colonial Society may be interpreted as an investment for the future, through the sponsorship of biological, medical and geographical research and a general encouragement of interest in the colonies; in any case, given the low agitational profile of the Society, such largesse can hardly offer much evidence for the 'manipulative' interpretation of the role of the *Verbände*.[107] Similarly, though firms like Krupp and individual capitalists like its proprietor might contribute regularly to the funds of the Eastern Marches Society, their reasons probably had more to do with strengthening the state fabric in the vulnerable East than with any conscious manipulation of popular nationalism.[108] As the war years revealed, strategically placed Pan-Germans like Alfred Hugenberg could mobilize vast sums of money for ambitious programmes of Eastern settlement, but not for specific nationalist agitations amongst the German populations of Posen and West Prussia before the war.[109]

Until the changed political circumstances immediately before the war, the Pan-Germans continually found it difficult to secure financial donations of any size. Under Hasse the League's headquarters had been based deliberately in Leipzig, but after his death in 1908 the new Chairman Heinrich Claß remained in Mainz largely because the official funds would not bear the move to Berlin, and when the Berlin premises were finally acquired in 1916 a massive appeal to industrial sponsors had been necessary.[110] Otherwise the League survived financially on a mixture of special appeals and self-taxation by the members. The League's ordinary running costs were met from membership dues, which accounted for 43,228 marks in 1900, dropping slowly to 31,593 by 1905.[111] With advertising revenue the journal *Alldeutsche Blätter* (4 marks to members, 6 to the general public) proved largely self-supporting. But for special campaigns and the production of propaganda the Pan-Germans were heavily dependent on special appeals. One of these was launched in 1898 in memory of Bismarck and by 1903 reached the modest total of 13,538 marks. Then in 1903 the 'Pan-German Defence Fund' was launched at the instigation of J. F. Lehmann,

[107] See Pierard, 'German Colonial Society', pp. 116, 178, 184, 212–41.

[108] The firm of Krupp gave an annual contribution of 1,000 marks, while in 1905 Friedrich Krupp made a personal donation of 5,000 marks in response to a special appeal. See Gentzen, 'Deutscher Ostmarkenverein', p. 508.

[109] e.g. Guratzsch, *Macht durch Organisation*, pp. 441ff.

[110] In 1915 the Pan-German deficit stood at 19,571 marks. To wipe this out and finance the politically urgent move to Berlin, Claß obtained donations of some 62,000 marks, largely through the good offices of Emil Kirdorf. See Stegmann, *Erben*, p. 490.

[111] The national subscription was raised in 1899 from one to two marks. In general Wertheimer's chapter is an excellent guide to the visible public finances of the Pan-Germans, and unless otherwise stated, this is the source of detailed information. See Wertheimer, *Pan-German League*, pp. 75–89.

producing in the first year 19,424 marks specially earmarked for agitation as opposed to general administration. It was a considerable success and by the end of 1910 reached a grand total of 206,948 marks.[112] By far the largest of the special operations was organized in support of the Boers in 1899–1902, producing the impressive sum of 634,111 marks. Beyond these visible efforts much money was clearly donated at a local level for *ad hoc* aims—e.g. between May 1897 and February 1898 Reismann-Grone raised some 15,000 marks for the naval agitation in the Ruhr[113]—but on the whole the Pan-Germans were severely constrained by the natural limits of their own members' generosity. The classic patron of the Pan-Germans was the small subscriber, the disinterested patriot who dug into his own pocket for a modest donation. Understandably, this ruled out massive propaganda operations like those mounted by the Navy League.[114]

Because of its much greater size the Navy League provides a better opportunity for assessing the financial involvement of the 'ruling strata'.[115] Moreover, there can be no doubt that the Navy League needed such support, for its needs were never covered by the ordinary subscriptions of the membership. In 1898 dues were deliberately fixed at a low minimum of fifty pfennigs to enable people of small means to join, and to make up the deficit it was hoped that wealthier members would voluntarily pay a higher rate. The original members of the Board each gave 1,000 marks.[116] However, others were not so generous and from an early stage the League became heavily dependent on special donations from industry and private persons. There is no record of 1898–9, but in 1900 extraordinary contributions of this kind accounted for some 411,000 marks, as against 348,000 marks in members' dues.[117] Both the money needed to launch the China Expedition in summer 1900 and that required to meet its huge losses were raised by special appeals. In 1901 special contributions (168,350 marks)

[112] *Alld. Bl.*, 1911, p. 125. Between 1911–13 the Fund actually doubled to a total of 413,808 marks, which is an index of growing industrial support. See Wertheimer, *Pan-German League*, p. 81.

[113] For detailed references: Eley, 'German Navy League', p. 41 (note 125).

[114] Wertheimer, *Pan-German League*, p. 78, makes the point that the Pan-Germans simply could not afford to flood the country with leaflets and propaganda. In 1898 more money was spent on the League's oak-leaf badge than on pamphlets.

[115] Unless otherwise stated, all references are taken from Eley, 'German Navy League', pp. 142–56, and particular citations will not be given.

[116] Busley's statement to the General Board in Kiel, June 3rd 1909, proceedings, ibid., 2278, 94239. Busley also claimed that this had been the original function of the Board, and it had certainly influenced the choice of members. Wied committed himself to an annual payment of 300 marks after his initial contribution, but reduced this to 50 marks after resigning the Presidency. See his instructions to his estate, May 11th 1898 and Nov. 19th 1902, Wied Papers. Haßler, on the other hand, paid an annual subscription of only 20 marks. See his membership card, SA Augsburg, Haßler Papers, 15.

[117] See the Presidium's *Rechenschaftsbericht* for 1900, BA Coblenz, ZSg. 1, 195/2. Later figures are taken from appropriate annual reports. See also Kehr, *Battleship Building*, pp. 474–481.

fell below ordinary revenue (225,350 marks), and the next year they dwindled to a mere 410 marks. In 1903 they rose again to 23,000 marks, but in 1904 were down to 1,317 marks, and in later years the item disappeared from the published accounts. According to these the Navy League financed its national activities—production of *Die Flotte*, other literary operations, organization of lectures, provision of material and equipment for the branches, the general costs of administration—overwhelmingly from the ordinary subscriptions of the membership.[118]

However, large amounts of money raised privately did not pass through the official accounts. Propaganda was subsidized far in advance of the figures officially designated at the start of each year.[119] Thus in January 1900 Beaulieu-Marconnay, who had just taken over the chief executive position from Schweinburg, warned the General Meeting that at least one million marks would be needed to cover the costs of the campaign for the Second Navy Bill, and four days later the Presidium sent out an appeal to the regional executives for funds: it suggested that a confidential letter be sent to 'the better-off industrialists, bankers, merchants and other well-to-do inhabitants of the individual areas'. The appeal was clearly a success. Donations from the area around Saarbrücken, for instance, ranged from 124 marks (G. F. Grohé-Heinrich & Co.) to 30,000 (Hermann Röchling). Though the detailed evidence is fragmentary, there is enough to suggest that Beaulieu's target was met with ease: Salm-Horstmar gave 1,400 marks, Carl Funke of Essen 3,000, and the Cologne factory-owner Ludwig Stollwerck 30,000. The Berlin businessman Fritz Friedländer even offered to take responsibility for the entire costs of the League. The ill-fated China Expedition was funded in a similar fashion: 7,000 marks was obtained from the German Princes, Stumm-Halberg gave 1,000 marks, Max Goldberger 40,000 and Marx of Danzig 85,000. Goldberger and Louis Ravené also negotiated a six-month interest-free loan of 150,000 marks.[120]

This was probably indicative of the kind of aid on which the League could draw. Beaulieu-Marconnay bore much of the credit for opening up connections with business, especially with 'Berlin high finance', while Dincklage-Campe and Hollmann had 'excellent relations with Herr Krupp'.[121] In autumn 1900 Beaulieu proposed a so-called 'financial committee' to institutionalize these contacts: consisting of four or five key businessmen, this would take responsibility for finding extra sources of income, and Max Goldberger expressed

[118] Regional executives kept some revenue to meet their own costs. Initially the proportion varied by region, but after 1902 the Presidium was guaranteed at least 50% of regional income. In 1901 it received 224,000 out of 381,000, in 1902 246,000 out of 405,000, and in 1903 262,000 out of 416,000. See Eley, 'German Navy League', pp. 110ff.

[119] The figure normally set aside for lectures was 10,000 marks.

[120] Information taken from a series of undated notes and correspondence in Wied Papers. For full references, Eley, 'German Navy League', pp. 388f. (notes 113–15).

[121] Blum to Wied, Aug. 13th 1900; Beaulieu to Wied, June 23rd 1900 and Oct. 10th 1900; Schweinburg to Wied, Nov. 3rd 1899, all in Wied Papers.

himself willing to take the matter in hand. The scheme came to nothing. It smacked too much of manipulation by self-seeking industrialists and financiers at a time when the Navy League's credibility required a denial of such links. The populist allegations of 'business-patriotism' against Schweinburg and his backers had damaged the League's idealist credentials, and though the new regime under Beaulieu claimed a clean slate, suspicions still lingered in some quarters. In June 1900 it was felt necessary to issue a public statement that no contributions had been accepted since December 16th 1899 from 'industrialists and businessmen who want to make money out of the naval expansion'. At the General Meeting of January 1901 Dietrich Schäfer demanded the rejection of financial gifts from all individuals and organizations who stood to gain from the shipbuilding programme, and proposed that the names of all donors be published in *Die Flotte*. Many industrialists, highly sensitive about their public image, thought twice before risking this kind of allegation. Krupp responded by stopping all further 'extraordinary donations'.[122]

Although Krupp and many of his colleagues in the CVDI were clearly reluctant to attract public attention by overtly supporting ventures like the Navy League, there is no evidence that this dried up the general flow of unofficial income.[123] In this respect August Keim proved especially useful: entering the Board in summer 1900 he brought a wealth of contacts accumulated eight years before in the campaign for the Army Bill of 1892–3. He knew Goldberger extremely well and played a key role in negotiating the financial backing for the China Expedition.[124] In October 1900 he toured all the shipyards and shipping companies and with his friend Kurt Freiherr von Reibnitz mobilized a wide range of contacts for the future. Between the end of 1903 and the Stuttgart Congress of 1905 Keim found about 240,000 marks for agitation outside the official budget.[125] Sturtz, the League's secretary for 1904–8, left a graphic description of Keim's method: he would ask a contact to arrange a meeting of the richest people in an area; on arrival he would give a short address and then put a 'pistol to their heads: "You give 2,000, you 1,500", and so on'. Sturtz claimed that each new excursion of this kind brought 15–20,000 marks into the League's coffers. Financial support like this was crucial to the massive agitation of 1904–8, particularly to Keim's activity after leaving the Presidium in January 1908. Money was also raised by formal appeals. In the winter of 1904–5 the executives for Essen and Westphalia approached firms in their respective areas for a contribution measured either by size of

[122] Krupp to Wied, July 14th 1900, Wied Papers.

[123] Shortly afterwards Krupp also severed his links with another political enterprise which badly burned his fingers in public—viz. the daily paper *BNN*. See Boelcke, *Krupp und die Hohenzollern*, p. 154; Stegmann, *Erben*, pp. 167f.

[124] Blum to Wied, July 16th 1900, Wied Papers. Ravené may have been introduced to the Navy League by Keim.

[125] Note by Holleben on a talk with Sturtz, June 2nd 1905, BA-MA Freiburg, 2277, 94234, also for the following.

work-force or by amount of invested capital in the case of banks and commercial houses: this brought in 12,000 marks in Essen and a gift of 1,741 marks from Phoenix AG to the Westphalian executive.[126] But the best source of extra income was undoubtedly the informal contacts: those cultivated by Keim, and those provided by rich businessmen with a special commitment to the naval propaganda.

A second type of unofficial donation occurred at the local level. The branches were heavily dependent on external sponsorship for the mounting of film and slide shows, exhibitions and the distribution of literature, and local appeals often raised money which did not pass through the public accounts. The activities of Hermann Rassow provide an instructive example.[127] Although he received much financial support from the Presidium and a considerable amount from the Navy Office and the Prussian Ministry of Culture as well, the League's own resources were limited and he was often thrown back on to private sponsorship. In late 1901, for example, he proposed appending his naval tables to *Die Flotte* in order to give them maximum exposure. The Presidium required an additional subsidy to cover the cost of postage, however, and Rassow had to rely on his own resources. He proceeded to mobilize his extensive contacts in Elberfeld. In 1899 the latter had raised 2,000 marks, and the year before 1,000 marks. Rassow had also persuaded about 150 individuals, including the two Landtag deputies Böttinger and Weyerbusch, to promise at least 100 marks for future occasions. However, Rassow observed that it was dangerous to tax the generosity of such people too often, and his caution seems to have been well-advised: his appeal went to 200 people but produced only 200 marks; the common reply was that the responsibility for such things had now passed to the Navy League. None the less, Rassow successfully repeated the pattern in Burg after 1901. He built up a strong circle of industrial patrons, amongst whom the large shoe-factory of *Tack & Co.* proved especially fruitful. Thus in the spring of 1902 one local manufacturer sponsored the publication of a leaflet as an appendix to two local newspapers in 5,000 copies at a cost of 80 marks.

Although Rassow's experience was surely representative of many other branches and their activists, its political significance is by no means clear. Any view which seeks to explain the foundation of the Navy League as a manipulative venture of heavy-industrial capital, or to attribute later changes in the movement's orientation to shifts in the relative influence of the CVDI and BdI in the Presidium, is misleading.[128] The response of CVDI firms to the League's appeals for financial support varied from concern to concern, and from time

[126] Essen executive to Presidium, Feb. 9th 1905, with copy of circular sent to local firms in Nov. 1904, SA Essen, Rep. 102, Abt. 1, 823. See also the comments in the letter from the Mines Dept. of *Phoenix AG* to Head Office, Apr. 20th 1909, WA/Mannesmann, P. 8, 25, 93, 4. The total contribution from Westphalia is unknown.

[127] Following details mainly from BA-MA Freiburg, 2257, 94136f. Otherwise see Eley, 'German Navy League', pp. 146ff.

[128] e.g. Stegmann, *Erben*, pp. 50, 112; Wulf, 'Deutscher Flottenverein', p. 441.

to time. Figures such as Vopelius, Martens or Schweckendieck clearly showed great interest in the aims of the Navy League, but it is dangerous to generalize too ambitiously on their example. The appeal of the Essen and Westphalian executives in 1904–5 is sufficient evidence of sizeable support from the heavy industry of the Rhine-Ruhr before the war. But this was also described as a non-recurrent donation and many firms were reluctant to repeat the gesture. This was the only time *Phoenix AG* contributed until February 1914, when it gave 300 marks to the League's invalid home for ex-sailors. In 1909 the Chairman of the branch in Meiderich appealed for help in covering the costs of providing *Die Flotte* for the membership—since many members came from the working class these could not be met from the ordinary dues. Superficially this might have been an admirable opportunity for 'manipulative social imperialism', but *Phoenix* failed to respond: all the management offered was a friendly reply 'in recognition of the deserving and patriotic efforts of the naval organizations'. It would be equally wrong, of course, to generalize from the example of *Phoenix*: the same correspondence reveals that the *Rheinische Stahlwerke* made an annual donation of 250 marks to the Meiderich branch, and the heavy implication of subsequent correspondence is that Emil Kirdorf and the *Gelsenkirchener Bergwerks AG* likewise gave the Navy League considerable support.[129] In the same way, it is also possible to identify prominent representatives of the BdI-interest amongst the Navy League's most committed supporters: Gustav Stresemann, Alexander von Pflaum, Heinrich von Wiedenmann, Emil Wichmann, Heinrich Schilbach, and many others.[130] The League seems to have provided one common platform, at least, on which the spokesmen of conflicting economic and political views could meet.

But this should indicate precisely the secondary importance of such corporate affiliations, not their centrality. Stresemann was present in the Navy League's counsels only partly as the leading functionary of the BdI and the exporting interests of Central Germany: he was also present as a rising National Liberal acutely conscious of the nationalist predilections of his party's electorate. Similarly, men like Kirdorf, Hugenberg and Hirsch had political as well as business reasons for joining the regional executive for Essen. There are certainly clear instances in which the Navy League's Presidium responded to industrial pressure for fresh naval agitation.[131] But these spasmodic interventions were no evidence of any continuous corporate involvement on the part

---

[129] WA/Mannesmann, P. 8, 25, 93, 4. On the other hand, there is no evidence that another big concern, *Gutehoffnungshütte* in Oberhausen, gave the League any money at all.

[130] Stresemann was Secretary to the League of Saxon Industrialists, the BdI's most important constituent organization, and in many ways the leading functionary of the light-industrial interest. Pflaum and Widenmann were close business associates in Stuttgart, with wide holdings in the light industry of the Neckar Valley; Wichmann was a banker in Bernburg with an interest in the engineering industry; and Schilbach was a worsted manufacturer in Greiz.

[131] See Kehr, *Battleship Building*, pp. 474ff.

of either the CVDI or the BdI. As far as anti-Socialist interventions are concerned, the big concerns like Krupp, M.A.N., Siemens, *Gutehoffnungshütte* or *Bochumer Verein* were far more interested in financing their own paternalist apparatus of company unions, welfare and surveillance, or at most the more ambitious political operations of the Imperial League Against Social Democracy: by comparison the less tangible ideological activity of the Navy League had far less to offer. On the other hand, the patronage of smaller businessmen, as secured by men like Rassow in the branches, probably did signify something more serious. It was in cases such as these that support for the Navy League was more closely related to a notion of changing the consciousness of the working class.[132] Similarly, in analysing the deeper involvement of individual big businessmen like Böttinger, Schweckendieck, Kirdorf, Martens, Deichmann, Schilbach, Ravené or Vopelius, it is for particular ideological explanations that we must look.

D. THE RADICAL-NATIONALIST MILIEU

I

How do we situate the *nationale Verbände* in relation to the social formation as a whole? Part of the answer to this must await the conclusion of this study. But certain general implications may be drawn out of the preceding discussion. A clear composite picture of the Navy League's character begins to emerge. In organization it put the emphasis on centralization, but left plenty of room for regional activists to join in the formulation of policy. Geographically, the membership was spread fairly evenly across the whole of Germany, but there is reason to think that the movement was more active in some areas than in others. In some parts of Prussia and Bavaria, for instance, the Navy League's branch organization was poorly developed: it had few active supporters amongst the local population and the official functions tended to pass to the government bureaucracies by default. This tended to be true of areas which were both rural and Catholic: the extreme east and west of Prussia, most parts of Bavaria except the Rhine Palatinate and the Protestant north. On the other hand, the movement seems to have been at its most vigorous in the manufacturing belt of central Germany, which was both industrial and Protestant. In these areas, as in the rest of the country, the Navy League was primarily a movement of the urban middle class, ranging from the *haute bourgeoisie* of the big towns to the petty élites of small villages. This is a generalization which requires some qualification, for the Navy League numbered representatives of every social group among its

[132] e.g. Franz Ohm (owner of the firm *Em. Krause* and member of the Chamber of Commerce for Glogau-Sagan) to Tirpitz, Dec. 6th 1907, BA-MA, 2258, 94141. The letter requested that the Navy Office send a speaker to accompany a slide-show to be given to the Evangelical Workers' Association on Feb. 2nd 1908, the Kaiser's Birthday.

members, including landed aristocrats, peasant farmers, rural *Mittelstand* and industrial workers. But these groups were certainly under-represented in relation to their numbers in the general population. In terms of the active membership—those who occupied formal positions in the branches, attended meetings and bore the burden of agitation—the generalization still holds. It emerges unmistakably from the registry of local officers,[133] from the lists of participants in general meetings,[134] and from lists of voluntary speakers.[135]

How typical of the other nationalist groups was this picture? Like the Navy League the others also managed to sink roots in most parts of the country, but likewise had to observe certain regional constraints. The Society for the Eastern Marches was the obvious case: in 1906 67% of its members came from the four Eastern provinces of Posen, West Prussia, East Prussia and Silesia, and in 1913 the figure was 74·6%. West of the Elbe its support was negligible: nine branches with 454 members in Thuringia, eight branches with 608 members in the Rhineland, five with 557 in Baden, four with 205 in Bavaria, and so on.[136] The organization found it hard to create much enthusiasm in Western areas, for the Pan-Germans, Navy League, Colonial Society and Society for German-dom Abroad already held the stage. Similarly, though the Colonial Society had supporters in most parts of Germany, in Catholic agricultural regions like Bavaria it was normally dependent on civil servants, officers and men with a particular commitment to the national idea—'National Liberals, the supporters of a unitary Reich and migrants from North Germany', as Freiherr von Würtzburg put it.[137] This was even truer of the Pan-Germans, with their heavier ideological emphasis.

[133] See the Navy League's *Handbuch*, produced in 1900, 1902, 1905, 1909, 1912.

[134] e.g. at the Dresden Congress in 1904, these consisted of 30 businessmen, 25 profes-sionals, 24 senior civil servants and 23 military and naval officers. There were only 10 aristocratic landowners (though 11 of the officers and 4 civil servants had titles) and a mere handful from the middle and lower ranks of the bourgeoisie (2 journalists, 2 priests and a hotelier). There were no peasant farmers, shopkeepers or master-craftsmen, let alone working men. See the full list of participants, Apr. 17th 1904, BA Coblenz, ZSg. 1, 195/2.

[135] In 1904 they included 86 members of the professions (including 42 teachers), 43 officers (26 military, 17 naval), 26 businessmen, 21 protestant clergy, 30 civil servants, 8 writers and journalists, 6 landed aristocrats, a gardener and a hotelier. See *Jahresbericht* 1904, pp. 4f., ibid.

[136] See Galos, Gentzen, Jacobczyk, *Hakatisten*, p. 147. The only significant membership West of the Elbe was in Westphalia, with 15 branches and 1,550 members.

[137] Würtzburg to Heeringen, Dec. 12th 1899, BA-MA Freiburg, 2379, 94741. See also the appeal of the Colonial Society's Section in St Avold in Alsace-Lorraine in July 1902, com-plaining that although the Society had more members per head of the population in Alsace-Lorraine than anywhere else, it had still failed to attract the natives: 'The Lorraine sections consist almost entirely of civil servants and officers; to them may be added the immigrants from old Germany; industrialists are relatively badly represented; but the civic personalities (*Bürgerkreise*) are absent altogether.' The Section officials were two lieutenant-colonels, the mayor and the head of the local school. See BA-MA Freiburg, 2224, 93950. A later circular in Dec. 1903 noted a small advance in this respect.

Organizationally, the Eastern Marches Society was almost dictatorially centralist, and in 1907 the Colonial Society moved further in this direction; only the Pan-Germans aimed for the high involvement of the branch activists we noted in the Navy League, and in fact took this much further before Hasse's death brought Claß into the Chair in 1908. In this respect the Colonial Society was most compatible with the existing party framework, for it reproduced in its own internal relations the classic syndrome of exclusive *Honoratiorenpolitik* which confined significant participation to a narrow band of privileged dignitaries and assigned the rest to passivity. The Pan-Germans stood at the other pole, and set great store by the equality of all patriots. The Eastern Marches Society stood somewhere in between: Tiedemann's authoritarian control of the organization inhibited participation by local activists, but at branch level its populist programme (e.g. land reform) tended to scare off many of the local notables who might otherwise have dominated the proceedings.

At this point it is worth re-emphasizing the importance of the Navy League's much greater size. For it was this which made possible a more decisive fracture in the existing legitimacy of *Honoratiorenpolitik*. By 1900, for instance, the Pan-German League was fast becoming identified with a particular ideological position, and to join it (certainly as an activist) increasingly required conscious political choices. Where the latter were articulated openly as a dissenting conservatism the Pan-Germans tended not to pose a very serious challenge to the established parties: the League's small size enabled the latter to dismiss it as a movement of the lunatic fringe, confined to a small corner of the political system with little prospect of influencing those who were not already converted. In these circumstances the Pan-Germans' critique of the conventional parties became a self-fulfilling prophecy of their own higher patriotism, which gave them little hope of jolting the 'fraction-philistine' and his supporters out of their complacency. Where local Pan-Germans failed to make such a clear political commitment, they tended to become just another nationalist discussion circle with little direct impact on local politics.

The Pan-German League drew upon exactly the same strata which were dominant in the Navy League. In December 1902, for instance, Claß reported to Hasse that recruitment was meeting with much enthusiasm in the Hessian countryside. Country people were '*to be had for us*. Naturally not in masses, but certainly in their entire upper stratum: mayors, clergymen, judges, doctors, teachers etc.'[138] But in the Navy League such people were brought directly into contact with members of the subordinate classes as well, or at least were forced to confront the political problem of how to mobilize them. This raised within the framework of the naval movement itself the problem of the limitations of *Honoratiorenpolitik* and how they were to be transcended. The Pan-German critics of the latter attacked the *status quo* from the organizational

---

[138] Claß to Hasse, Dec. 22nd 1902, ZStA Potsdam, ADV, 186: 35.

6

isolation of doctrinal purity and enabled the party notables to continue much as before. But the huge membership of the Navy League brought such patricians into direct contact with their less prestigious middle-class colleagues. This rarely led at once to ideological tension, but created conditions under which it might arise. The special importance of the Navy League amongst the the *nationale Verbände* was that it provided a context in which the potential contradiction between insiders and outsiders could become properly antagonistic.

II

To illustrate this point it is worth returning to the local arenas of political life, to the texture of the social relations into which the nationalist pressure groups were inserted. Earlier in this study some emphasis was placed on the importance of a general transition in the structure of public life towards the end of the nineteenth century, which can perhaps be dated with some precision to the decade between the later 1880s and 1890s. This took place in a general context of accelerated capitalist development, demographic upheaval and higher levels of political mobilization amongst previously dormant strata, particularly in the countryside. It took the form of an attempted formalization of party allegiance and organization, at a time when the old pattern of electoral politics was decomposing. The parties could no longer be certain of the traditional support of subordinate classes, for the latter were defecting both to the SPD in the towns and to new agencies of rural protest in the country. In order to halt the decline the parties had to transform themselves from loose associations of notables with little permanent organization into stable bureaucratic structures with a reliable apparatus for recruiting, holding and involving a new mass membership. Moreover, the socio-political flux also affected the local undergrowths of association in which party life was embedded. As we saw, the commonest matrix of local *Honoratiorenpolitik* was a social club like the Heilbronn Harmony, which was a natural feature of most German towns by the mid-nineteenth century. Normally formed from the confluence of older eighteenth-century associations (Reading Societies, Patriotic Societies, political discussion circles, Freemasonry, other secret societies),[139] they quickly acquired their own buildings, were composed of the town's most prestigious families, admitted new members only by election, provided a wide range of social facilities and organized balls, banquets, concerts and lectures. They were the obvious centres of political discussion, and around them clustered a variety of charitable, recreational and philanthropic agencies. To some extent changes in

---

[139] For a typology, see Dann, 'Anfänge politischer Vereinsbildung', pp. 202–19. One estimate puts the number of reading societies around 1800 at 270: I. Jentsch, *Zur Geschichte des Zeitungswesens in Deutschland* (Leipzig, 1937), cit. by J. Habermas, *Strukturwandel der Öffentlichkeit* (Neuwied, 1971), p. 93.

this associational fabric preceded the tightening-up of party organization.

One of the few studies to open a window on this process of change is Hofmann's survey of municipal politics in Bielefeld.[140] In the earlier nineteenth century the town was dominated by some thirty textile merchants and their families, a handful of associated lawyers and doctors, and leading officials such as the Mayor and the local magistrates. This oligarchy was strongly integrated by common education, intermarriage and shared activity in the Chamber of Commerce, presbytery and town council. This was assisted by the slow pace of concentration and mechanization in the textile industry: the putting-out system persisted well into the twentieth century, as did the structure of the family firm in which the owner was directly involved.[141] The centre of social integration was the *Ressource*. It was founded in 1795 by nine merchants, originally to provide an opportunity for social contact on a regular footing: they would meet for drinks in the evening, to read the newspapers, and to discuss both the town and affairs of state. Gradually, the club began to organize social events on a larger scale and also assumed a more direct political function. It crystallized factional groupings in municipal politics and increasingly provided a kind of social ante-room to the council chamber. This shift was reflected in a stricter separation from the home, for until 1825 the members' families were also admitted to the proceedings. Membership was highly valued and was regulated by ballot. It was the acid test of social acceptance into the oligarchy. In 1853 there were 125 members, in 1880 around 200.[142]

As Hofmann has said, 'without being political in the narrower sense, the *Ressource* still represented the emancipatory drive of the big bourgeoisie at a time when there were no fixed party organizations'.[143] In the 1840s, for instance, the ruling sentiment was liberal, leading to serious tensions with the Prussian state apparatus and the local Army, and this remained the case until the start of the 1880s. But from the middle of the century a number of related processes damaged the status of the *Ressource* as an agency of social integration in municipal life. The most important was the growth and economic diversification of the town in the later nineteenth century (its population grew from 6,077 in 1811 to some 12,000 in 1857 and 82,000 in 1914). The progress of mechanization from the 1860s by the formation of new joint-stock companies introduced a new group of managers and technicians and gave a stimulus

---

[140] Hofmann, *Bielefelder Stadtverordneten*. The changes described were naturally bound up with more fundamental processes of economic and social change, literacy etc. Here I am concerned mainly with political effects.

[141] Ibid., pp. 17–19, 33–7. *Buddenbrooks* is brought easily to mind.

[142] Ibid., pp. 41f. Similar clubs had been formed elsewhere in the region around the same time: the Barmen *Concordia* in 1801, the *Union* in Unterbarmen, the *Ressource* in Minden, the *Sozietät Nr. 5* in Crefeld, the *Vereinigte Gesellschaften von 1828* in Essen, the *Gesellschaft Heideblümchen* of 1852, and so on.

[143] Ibid., p. 41.

to the engineering industry.[144] This diluted the exclusiveness of the town's upper stratum and confronted the oligarchy with a growing discrepancy between the new economic reality and its own composition. The directors of the new mills were admitted fairly easily to the *Ressource* as were those in engineering branches which were closely allied to the former. Other new arrivals were accepted less easily, especially if they came out of the lesser bourgeoisie or *Mittelstand*. The self-taught mechanic Nikolaus Dürkopp, who by the 1880s had won a key position in the engineering branches, only entered the *Ressource* in 1890 after losing an earlier ballot, and was widely resented. The same was true of August Oetker, the baking-powder magnate, who by 1914 ran the largest business in the town.[145] In 1914, when there were well over 300 industrial enterprises and the engineering branches heavily predominated over textiles, the town's economy had far outgrown the integrative capabilities of the old *Honoratiorenverein*.[146]

Secondly, there was a process of sharper political differentiation. This began as early as 1850, when a competitor to the *Ressource*, the *Eintracht*, was launched by a mixture of professional men, manufacturers and the better artisans; in 1859 it was paralleled by the formation of the choral society *Arion* by thirteen artisans as a secession from the establishment *Liedertafel*. This was politically motivated and 'both societies...were the organizational platform of "Progress"'. Similarly, the Rifle Club (founded 1831), with 670 members in 1858, was appropriated increasingly during the 1850s as a meeting-point for the 'democratically-minded bourgeoisie'. In the 1870s the left liberal group in the *Eintracht* predominated in the town and in 1874 even carried the Reichstag constituency.[147] Until 1884 the smaller National Liberal group was content to ally itself with the left liberals, but in that year the latter adopted a stricter line of demarcation against the right. Consequently, the National Liberals joined the Conservatives. At the same time, however, the SPD was advancing from the left: in 1877 it had already polled 32.6% in the town itself, and in 1890 the figure was 65.2%. As well as the growth of trade unions, this was also accompanied by the familiar apparatus of cultural and recreational instances, amongst which the local People's Theatre was especially notable.[148]

There were two clear effects of this greater differentiation. On the one hand,

---

[144] The most important branches were sewing-machine manufacture and machine tools, both of which were integrated quite closely with the textiles industry, and then from the 1880s bicycles.

[145] Ibid., pp. 37f., 157.

[146] See Hofmann's comment: 'the engineering industry was heavily under-represented ... and the *Ressource* limited itself on the whole to the old families and their allied circles'. Ibid., p. 42.

[147] The rural districts of the Bielefeld-Wiedenbrück constituency normally negated the large votes achieved in the town by the liberals and later the Socialists. Before 1890 the seat normally went to the Conservatives, after 1890 to the Centre.

[148] Ibid., pp. 42–4, 69–74.

the social organs of left liberalism shed their popular radicalism, became depoliticized and effectively closed themselves against the working class. The Rifle Club confined itself to the mounting of exclusive festivities and moved into the orbit of the Cartel parties. Under the lawyer Emil Adriani between 1886 and 1899 the *Arion* was consciously directed into anodyne domestic music. Social life became more class-based than before: from the mid-nineties the working class had its own choral and gymnastic clubs, whilst the bourgeoisie withdrew into a similar network. Between 1880–1901, for instance, nine new veterans' associations were formed, all with a pronounced animus against the SPD. On the other hand, as part of the same process, the *Ressource* and *Eintracht* also lost much of their political character to formal party committees. The differences between the two clubs were not completely obliterated. As one of Hofmann's sources said, 'the *Eintracht* sings itself, the *Ressource* summons the singers to it', a nuance which speaks volumes for the original social distinction.[149]

The greater formalization of party organization entailed by the above processes had the short-term effect of creating a greater distance between the party leaderships and their supporters. Once National Liberals and Progressives ceased to inhabit a common universe of general belief—a 'community of sentiment'—the selection of candidates could no longer be entrusted to general assemblies of liberal voters. Instead they were more carefully vetted in committee, where policy was also determined. Though the left liberals continued for some time to submit committee decisions regarding election tactics for the approval of general meetings, this could not disguise the fact that 'important decisions had been displaced from the rank-and-file on to the committees'.[150] This problem—how to prevent a necessary tightening of the organization from creating a gap between the new bureaucratic structure and the party's wider popular constituency—vexed most of the bourgeois parties towards the end of the century.[151] It was particularly acute for the National Liberals as we saw, for, deprived of their urban supporters by the SPD and unable to cope with the agrarian conquest of the countryside, they lacked a popular movement to moderate the effects of a more formalized *Honoratiorenpolitik*. In Bielefeld their long-term realignment with the local Conservatives also failed to bring much succour in these terms: though the latter had been previously rooted in a

[149] Ibid., p. 42.
[150] Ibid., p. 76.
[151] Even the Centre, which maintained organic links with its agrarian and *Mittelstand* support more successfully than most, experienced this difficulty: though the party responded skilfully to the needs of popular organization in the 1890s, it was simultaneously passing under the leadership of a new grouping of professional politicians, invariably lawyers, who could easily provoke resentment from the rank and file in the villages. Both phenomena—grass-roots rural radicalism and professionalization of the leadership—were vital to the party's success, but could not always be held in smooth equilibrium. For an excellent analysis of this problem, see Blackbourn, 'Problem of Democratization'.

flourishing sub-culture of Evangelical associations in the surrounding country-side with close links to the urban artisanate, the agrarian turn of the 1890s both subsumed the former and eroded the latter.[152]

In these circumstances the appearance of a large popular organization like the Navy League (and to a lesser extent the other nationalist groups) had a double importance. On the one hand, its populist commitment to a classless politics of national solidarity which embraced all social strata represented a noteworthy intervention at a time when the Protestant bourgeois parties were demonstrably failing to realize the same objective. The National Liberals certainly still claimed to be a classic 'party of the centre', committed to ideals rather than interests and in which no one social group called the tune. But there was little attempt to *practise* this organizationally, as the exclusivist Constitution of 1892 and the élitist social demarcation of club life only too clearly revealed. The veterans' associations, superficially an ideal instrument of social integration with their efforts to re-create the patriotic community of the Army in civilian life, provide a good example of the declining effectivity of the established institutions.[153]

Analysis of their membership reveals that neither the professions nor higher civil servants (i.e. those with an academic education) were very strongly represented, and that amongst the latter the district officials (under instructions from their superiors) predominated. The commonest groups tended to be *nouveau riche* businessmen, junior civil servants, artisans and workers, i.e. precisely the groups who were excluded from élite clubs like the Bielefeld *Ressource*. But these groups were rarely uniformly integrated, and more often than not industrial workers were confined within their own homogeneous associations: in other words, the petty-bourgeoisie 'closed ranks against the workers just as firmly as the *Honoratioren* had done against themselves'.[154] This contrasted with the situation in the Navy League. Its attempts to involve the working class showed only modest success, as we saw, but at least produced a sizeable working-class presence amongst the paper membership, however passive and invisible. Given the practice of other organizations of public life, the ability to recruit workers at all was a considerable achievement. The ideological commitment to do so, moreover, was still more significant. Whatever their success, the Navy League's major activists often believed passionately in a mission of social harmony. It was no accident that the mainstay of the Bielefeld branch was Johann Klasing, whose family was most deeply associated

---

[152] Hofmann, *Bielefelder Stadtverordneten*, pp. 65–8.

[153] The extent to which the veterans' clubs were successfully used as instruments of anti-Socialist integration or agitation is not dealt with directly here. The two main accounts differ strongly: Saul, 'Der "Deutsche Kriegerbund" ', p. 96; Henning, 'Kriegervereine', p. 447.

[154] Henning, 'Kriegervereine', p. 468. The petty-bourgeoisie might often leave and form their own club, as in Langendreer (ibid., p. 469). Details of social composition from ibid., pp. 459–72.

with the popular Evangelical Conservatism which was eclipsed in the mid-1890s by the party's ascendant agrarian wing.[155]

Secondly, the Navy League provided a local forum for the discussion of national politics. As argued earlier in this study, opportunities for charitable and philanthropic work or for municipal improvement were often available within the framework of local *Honoratiorenpolitik*: it was mainly the linkage of that municipal arena with the national scene which proceeded behind closed doors. Matters like the selection of a Reichstag candidate, the lobbying of the government and general relations with the national party leaders were reserved for the notables. As also argued above, it would be wrong to present the *nationale Verbände* as such as complete substitutes for local party organization: there was certainly no conscious antagonism of this kind and the notables would normally provide some of the officers in the Navy League's local branches. But if by its example the Navy League might sometimes expose the social exclusiveness of the existing institutions, it also closed the gap between the local and the national levels of the public realm. In the Navy League we encounter an attempt to implant a *nationally* oriented politics at the *local* level, by people whose frame of reference was the national rather than the local arena. In this as in the commitment to a non-élitist popular membership, the practice of the Navy League amounted to an oblique, double-edged critique of the established parties, normally the National Liberals. It suggests, especially given the usual recruitment of their leaders from within the ranks of the notables themselves, that the primary significance of the nationalist pressure groups is to be sought at the ideological level. They were inserted into local political cultures whose earlier integration was decomposing along class lines, and attracted as activists a group of people whose special ideological commitment was more important than their similar social origins.

III

In concluding this discussion of the radical-nationalist milieu it is important to dispose of one potential misunderstanding, which is present in much existing work as a half-stated thesis, implied rather than systematically expounded. This is the idea that the *nationale Verbände* constituted a well-integrated, interlocking, self-contained system of politics. The social-imperialism hypothesis, with its imputation of overtly anti-parliamentary purposes to the nationalist groups (i.e. as a system of right-wing popular mobilization standing both outside the parties and against them), encourages this mistake, because it is only a short step from this basic position to the misleading assumption that the groups represented some kind of unity. The very term 'ideological holding-company' given by Kehr to the Pan-German League and largely taken over by recent historians ascribes a coherence and a unity to the milieu which in

[155] Hofmann, *Bielefelder Stadtverordneten*, pp. 65–8; Nipperdey, *Organisation*, pp. 157f.

reality was not there. Moreover, the mistake is commonest not so much in the work specifically about the nationalist organizations (which in any case is fairly sparse) as in the incidental references of text-books and work on other subjects. This is a good example, in fact, of the way in which an orthodoxy can accumulate by default, by the failure to confront a problem systematically, rather than by organized presentation of a thesis. When assumptions are smuggled in by the side-entrance like this, real relationships can be obscured. For instance, August Keim's membership of the Navy League and Pan-German League is often mentioned in the same breath, implying that these were co-terminous and that the Pan-German affiliations necessarily affected and probably determined Keim's radical stance in the naval movement. In fact, the reverse was true: Keim joined the Pan-Germans only after his resignation from the Navy League in 1908, and this step is impossible to understand without the prior experiences of 1900–8.[156]

Consequently, it is important to establish exactly what connections *did* exist between the respective groups and what was their status. At an official level the prevailing relation was one of fraternal cordiality. Some of the *Verbände* may have been corporately affiliated with each others' national organizations, but this is unclear. They certainly sent delegations to each other's national congresses. The Navy League, Society for Germandom Abroad, Defence League, League of German Students and six other organizations were all represented at the 1912 Convention of the Pan-German League.[157] The annual reports of the Navy League usually picked out such relations for special mention: in 1905 it singled out the Colonial Society, the military and naval veterans' associations, the Pan-Germans, the Society for Germandom Abroad, the Eastern Marches Society and the German Language Society.[158] Corporate affiliation was common at the local level. The Berlin branch of the Eastern Marches Society numbered amongst its members the German Language Society, the Berlin League of German Students and two other student groups, four gymnastic clubs and a rowing club, the historical society and an agricultural association. Altogether the Navy League claimed the affiliation in 1905 of 714 veterans' associations, ninety-two sailing, rowing, gymnastic and sports clubs, twenty choral societies, thirteen women's and children's groups, twenty-two students' groups, nine sections of the Colonial Society, twenty-five civil servants' associations, sixteen patriotic workers' associations, and 372 others, including

---

[156] For a representative illustration of how the *nationale Verbände* tend to be run together into a single category, see Wehler, *Das Deutsche Kaiserreich*, pp. 92–4. See also Stürmer, 'Machtgefüge und Verbandsentwicklung', esp. pp. 503ff., and Puhle, 'Parlament, Parteien und Interessenverbände.' pp. 346ff.

[157] *Alld. Bl.*, 1912, p. 333. The others were: the Evangelical Society for German Settlers, German National-Society for the Aid of Commerce, Rüdesheim Union of German *Burschenschaften*, the Union of Germans in Bohemia, Society of the Southern Marches, and the German National-Society from Krems on the Danube.

[158] *Jahresbericht* 1905, p. 2, BA Coblenz, ZSg. 1, 195/2. See also *Die Ostmark*, 1899, p. 19; Tims, *Germanizing Prussian Poland*, p. 250.

many town councils.[159] There are also major instances of formal co-operation at a national level. The combination of the Pan-Germans and Colonial Society for the Navy Bill of 1897–8 and the unobtrusive assistance given by the Imperial League Against Social Democracy to the Navy League in 1905–6 are two of the most important.[160]

There were also many cases of personal overlap. One form which this took has already been discussed above, namely the frequent passage of salaried officials from one group to another, as in the examples of Albert Bovenschen, Alfred Geiser and Dr Gerhard. Many leading radical nationalists also maintained membership in several groups at once. Eduard von Liebert, as we saw, was simultaneously active in the Colonial Society, Navy League, Pan-German League (in which he was a potential Chairman), and Imperial League Against Social Democracy (which he actually chaired); politically amphibious, from 1907 he also sat in the Reichstag for the Free Conservatives. Alfred Hugenberg was both an evil genius for the Pan-Germans, the co-ordinator of a sophisticated apparatus of political influence in the Eastern Marches, and from 1909 the manager of an even larger power structure based on his Chairmanship of Krupp in Essen, where he also sat on the Navy League executive.[161] Wilhelm Hirsch, Secretary of the Essen Chamber of Commerce and a close lieutenant of Hugenberg, sat on the Board of the Imperial League Against Social Democracy, was a member of the Pan-German League and was Secretary of the town's Navy League.[162]

Individual examples may be easily duplicated: Hermann Heydweiller, the district official in Altena, was simultaneously Chairman in the local Navy League and Colonial Society, and the same was true of Major von Hagen in Weimar. In the Navy League's branch in Nuremburg in 1908, one of the thirteen executive members was simultaneously a member of the town Colonial Society, Society for Germandom Abroad and Society for the Eastern Marches, namely the merchant Carl Nold: amongst his colleagues, four had membership in two of the other three groups, and another five in at least one; only three members of the Navy League local executive abstained from nationalist involvement elsewhere.[163] But this sort of personal overlap is in itself hard to evaluate.

---

[159] *Jahresbericht* 1905, pp. 1f., BA Coblenz, ZSg. 1, 195/2.

[160] In December 1905 Liebert was invited to attend the Navy League's General Board, played a leading part in the discussions of tactics for the campaign over the current Navy Bill, and placed a team of the Imperial League's speakers at the disposal of the Navy League. See the Presidium's circular of Dec. 2nd 1905, and the record of discussion in the Board, also Dec. 2nd 1905, *Verhandlungen*, p. 6, BA-MA Freiburg, 2277, 94234.

[161] For a brief account, see Leopold, *Alfred Hugenberg*, pp. 1ff., and for greater detail, Guratzsch, *Macht durch Organisation*, pp. 26ff., 66ff., 95ff.

[162] Ibid., p. 98.

[163] For Heydweiller: *RWZ*, Nov. 8th 1899; Heydweiller to Sachse, Jan. 15th 1900, BA-MA Freiburg, 2379, 94741. For Hagen: *WeimZ*, Feb. 22nd 1903; May 29th 1903; Jan. 21st 1904. For Nuremberg: SA Nuremberg, Vereine, 19, 1 (Navy League); Vereine, 487 (Colonial Society); Vereine, 75 (Society for Germandom Abroad); V D 15, 2787.

6*

If membership of one group could be honorific rather than activist, there is no reason why the same could not be true of several. To establish the political significance of multi-membership in the *nationale Verbände* we have to look more closely at the particular motivations involved.

One way of doing this is to find instances of regular and close co-operation at a local level. In February 1898, for instance, a local branch of the Pan-Germans was formed in Posen, with seventy-five members, under the Chair of Hugenberg, and set itself 'the immediate task of vigorously promoting all measures directed at the strengthening of Germandom in the Eastern Marches in close co-operation with the other national associations'. By November 23rd 1900 it was finally possible to convene a meeting at which the choral and rowing societies, the civil servants' rowing club, the Society for the Eastern Marches, the Navy League and the Pan-Germans were all represented: taking the so-called 'German Evenings' established in Munich, Potsdam and elsewhere as a model, it was agreed to hold regular joint events with a nationalist inflection and an executive committee was set up for this purpose.[164] It is difficult to know how common such 'German Evenings' were. One of the earliest was that in Lübeck, inaugurated by the Society for Germandom Abroad, Language Society and Colonial Society in 1892, and joined later by the Pan-Germans in 1896, Evangelical Union in 1899 and Navy League in 1901. By 1902 there was evidence of similar arrangements in at least Potsdam, Magdeburg, Dresden, Cassel, Stuttgart, Munich, Mainz, Dortmund and Barmen.[165] The one in Potsdam seems to have been particularly vigorous.[166]

The normal form was a monthly lecture meeting in which the participant groups took turns to preside. In Elberfeld in 1909–10, where there were seven member organizations (Pan-Germans, German Union, Language Society, Society for Germandom Abroad, the Schiller-Union, German-National Commercial Assistants' Association, Evangelical Workers' Association), these meetings drew audiences of a hundred and covered such topics as 'Germany's Foreign Policy' (Heinrich Pohl), 'The Significance of Germandom Abroad for the German Empire' (Alfred Geiser), 'The Greater German Reich of Kaiser Wilhelm II' (Paul Langhans), 'Bismarck to Dernburg' (Wilhelm Lattmann), 'Bismarck and Goethe' (Max Bewer), 'Is Alsace-Lorraine ripe for Federal

---

[164] Details from Galos, Gentzen, Jacobczyk, *Hakatisten*, pp. 151f.

[165] See *Der Deutsche Abend in Lübeck in den ersten zehn Jahren seines Bestehens* (Lübeck, 1902), copy in AdH Lübeck, DFV, 3. For evidence of co-operation between the Eastern Marches Society and other groups, especially the Society for Germandom Abroad, in Erfurt, Gelsenkirchen, Posen, Merseburg, Mühlhausen, Salzwedel, Obornik, Oranienburg, see Galos, Gentzen, Jacobczyk, *Hakatisten*, p. 105 (note 368).

[166] See Stössel to Claß, Jan .19th 1908, ZStA Potsdam, ADV, 192: 10f.; manifesto issued by Potsdam branches of Navy League, veterans club, Pan-Germans, electoral committee of the united national parties, and the so-called *Verband nationaler Vereine*, Jan. 1909, in BA-MA Freiburg, 2257, 94137. For the involvement of the Society for Germandom Abroad in Potsdam, see Haude and Poßekel, 'Verein für das Deutschtum im Ausland', p. 719.

Status?' (Prof. Hermann Bäcker, Chairman of the local Workers' Association and pseudoanonymous author of the novel *Hohentaun*).[167] Collaboration might also occur more on an *ad hoc* basis. During the campaign for the Navy Bill of 1905–6 the Navy League often held joint meetings with the Colonial Society and Pan–Germans.[168] In May 1910 the Dresden Pan-Germans joined with the Eastern Marches Society to organize a memorial evening for a deceased activist: as well as the national and local representatives of the two host-groups, it was also addressed by spokesmen for the veterans' associations, the Imperial League Against Social Democracy and the Society for Germandom Abroad.[169]

Examples such as these make it clear that the individual groups felt themselves to be part of a general ideological community, which could sometimes be roughly identical with the local establishment of the bourgeois parties, but was more frequently a separate sub-culture within them. But the uses to which this nationalist consensus was to be put—its precise political significance—depended very much on the larger motivations of the participants. It has earlier been emphasized that the ordinary membership of the Navy League may have been only marginally involved in any larger ideological commitment, and that to identify the latter we must turn to a smaller group of highly motivated activists. This was equally true of the German Evenings, though these obviously signified in themselves a higher level of nationalist consciousness. Max Freiherr von Stössel, an old associate of Friedrich Lange and close collaborator of Heinrich Claß, is a good illustration of how a specific type of Pan-German commitment might give some extra shape to the local activities of the *nationale Verbände*.[170] We normally find that a particular activist and his supporters played the key role in getting local co-operation off the ground: Stössel himself in Potsdam, Senator Johannes Neumann in Lübeck, W. Niemann in Barmen, Reismann-Grone and Carl Klingemann in Essen, J. F. Lehmann and Erwin von Dessauer in Munich, Friedrich Hopf in Dresden, and so on. To make sense of their activities and to evaluate the radical-nationalist milieu they helped to create, therefore, it is to the internal structure of their ideology that we must now turn.

[167] *Alld. Bl.*, 1910, p. 15.

[168] See the material in BA-MA Freiburg, 2260, 94153, which includes petitions and resolutions: e.g. meetings with the Pan-Germans and Colonial Society in Eßlingen on Nov. 25th 1905, in Höchst on Jan. 10th 1906, and in Osnabrück on Jan. 12th 1906.

[169] *Alld. Bl.*, 1910, p. 190.

[170] For a full statement of his political credo, see Stössel to Claß, Jan. 2nd 1903, ZStA Potsdam, ADV, 187; 2f., and also Stössel to Claß, Mar. 10th 1904, ibid., 188: 201f.

5. The Ideology of Radical Nationalism

I

There are a number of older approaches to the study of radical nationalism in the Wilhelmine period. The most familiar is probably that of the conventional history of ideas, whose exponents deal in carefully constructed intellectual genealogies, plotting the passage of nationalist beliefs through several generations of published writings. A common version locates the origins of nationalist doctrine in the reactions of the German romantic intellectuals against the French Revolution. This circumstance, it is held, had already imparted a distinctive 'anti-democratic' quality to German nationalism, for the 'revolt against the West' tended to substitute a mystical 'organic' notion of the nation for the strong associations with popular sovereignty established by the French Revolution. The idea that a nation was defined by a unique cultural individuality, made manifest in its language, customs, religion, institutions and history, constituted the nation as the new subject of history and subsumed the notion of individual freedom beneath the superior ideal of national self-realization. This powerful tradition coexisted uneasily with ideals of liberal self-government during the first half of the nineteenth century, but after 1848 the declining prospects of parliamentary reform raised it to an undisputed primacy in the political programme of the German bourgeoisie. In this way Wilhelmine nationalism is seen to evolve naturally out of the liberal nationalism of the earlier nineteenth century once the latter had lost the natural arena of parliamentary institutions for its self-realization. As one influential text-book puts it: 'In the same measure that German nationalism lost, indeed suppressed its liberal elements after 1848 (and here again the failed revolution signifies a deep break), the antagonistic elements expanded, until finally the anti-attitudes were completely dominant.'[1]

Apart from its obvious idealism, this approach is notable for a concern with the intellectual origins of National Socialism—with excavating a specifically German tradition of authoritarianism through whose influence the appeal of the Nazis might be rendered more intelligible. Its effect is to submerge the specific qualities of Wilhelmine nationalism beneath a series of general assumptions

[1] Wehler, *Das Deutsche Kaiserreich*, p. 108.

about the longer-term historical formation of the German political culture.[2] For the exponents of this approach the emergence of a radical-nationalist movement in the 1890s presents no special problem: it is explained simply by the inherited cultural dispositions of a German bourgeoisie which had failed to produce a vigorous native liberalism after the failures of the 1840s and 1860s.[3] Rather than being investigated in its own right, radical nationalism is plotted along an ideological continuum between the Romantic era and that of the Nazis. This produces a kind of mirror-image of the liberal-democratic teleology so familiar in the historiography of Britain, France and the U.S.A., for the *absence* in Germany of a bourgeois revolution in the classic liberal-democratic mould is made to structure the entire history of the ensuing century. The failure of the German bourgeoisie to generate a triumphant tradition of heroic liberalism is made to determine, step by step, a disastrous accumulation of right-wing attitudes: extreme nationalism, but also violent anti-Socialism, hostility to parliamentary reform, anti-semitism, and so on. In other words, instead of being interpreted in the determinate context of the Wilhelmine conjuncture itself, notably between the end of the depression in 1895–6 and the start of the First World War, radical-nationalist ideology simply disappears into the linear continuity of 'pre-industrial' authoritarian traditions.

Without discarding this longer perspective, recent historians have also shown an interest in the particular effects of the changing organization of the economy. The Great Depression, the breakthrough to imperialism and the transition to monopoly capitalism are all held to have formed the expression of nationalist belief under the Second Empire.[4] A series of one-to-one relationships is uncovered in which nationalist ideology is made to correspond functionally to a succession of interests and developments: the imperialist competition of the great powers, the need for ideologies of racial superiority, the calculated manipulation of nationalist sentiments for integrationist ends (e.g. during elections), and so on. Moreover, the 'social-imperialist' exploitation of nationalism was facilitated, it is claimed, by the existence of a disoriented popular mass, which lacked the security of traditional communities. Thus 'broad social strata' responded to social-imperialist initiatives, including 'the petty-bourgeoisie of craftsmen and small businessmen, parts of the industrial labour-force, of the

---

[2] e.g. this statement by K. D. Bracher, cited by G. Barraclough, 'Mandarins and Nazis', *New York Review of Books*, Oct. 19th 1972, p. 42: the 'ultimate cause' of Nazism goes right 'back to the beginning of the nineteenth century', and derives from 'the deep schism between German and Western political thought'. See also the two essays by Talcott Parsons: 'Some Sociological Aspects of the Fascist Movements', and 'Democracy and Social Structure in Pre-Nazi Germany', in *Essays in Sociological Theory* (Glencoe, 1964), pp. 104–41.

[3] A typical and influential example is F. Stern, 'The Political Consequences of the Unpolitical German', in *The Failure of Illiberalism* (London, 1972), pp. 3–25.

[4] e.g. Wehler, 'Der Aufstieg des Organisierten Kapitalismus und Interventionsstaates in Deutschland', in H. A. Winkler (Ed.), *Organisierter Kapitalismus, Voraussetzungen und Anfänge* (Göttingen, 1974), pp. 36–57.

rural *Mittelstand* and of the larger landowners'.[5] The activation of such groups is normally linked to the impact of the Great Depression and the strains of industrialization. Here radical nationalism is associated with the 'status anxiety' of traditional small producers and other elements hit by the rapid growth of industrial capitalism.[6]

Such formulations have a certain descriptive value. German governments were acutely conscious of the need for integration—both to legitimate the Empire's institutions against Socialist attack and to establish new forms of national cohesion over the older particularist, confessional and parochial solidarities. The growth of imperialist rivalries sharpened the urgency of this drive. These motivations were clearly at work in the two Prussian School Conferences of 1890 and 1900.[7] They could also be seen in the treatment of the national minorities. But however illuminating when applied to particular policies or institutions, the functionalist view of nationalism substitutes a description of effects for analysis of the conditions under which different types of nationalist commitment were formed. This is particularly clear where recent historians try to explain how processes of legitimation actually worked, because on the whole their analysis moves uneasily from nationalism's general functions to the production of nationalist ideology in particular individuals and institutions. Either they stress the manipulative aspect by focusing on the propaganda of organizations like the *nationale Verbände*, or else they resort to a simple sociological model of 'primary . . . and secondary . . . socialization', which stresses the unconscious acquisition of norms, particularly through the educational system. Normally both are employed to assert the 'lasting internalization of domination' on the part of the general population. The concert of propaganda groups and government apparatuses produced an 'institutionalized control of behaviour', which 'preserved external control instead of encouraging individual responsibility' and enables us, it is argued, 'to speak of structural hostility to democracy'.[8] But the problem is explored only at the level of the institutions and their organized activity. How they acted on the consciousness of their members and intended audience is rarely discussed.

This betrays a certain reluctance to take ideology seriously. Where it is not reduced to a mere instrument of political conformity (nationalism as 'one of the ideological tools which enables the bourgeoisie to maintain its domination over the proletariat', in the vulgar-Marxist formulation of the same

[5] Wehler, *Bismarck*, pp. 480f. It should be noted that in Wehler's case these are mere assertions backed up by no empirical research.

[6] This bears close affinities with much American work on the 'status anxiety' of groups threatened by 'modernization'. See D. Bell (Ed.), *The Radical Right* (New York, 1963), and R. Hofstadter, *The Paranoid Style in American Politics and Other Essays* (New York, 1967), pp. 3–92.

[7] See H.-J. Heydorn and G. Koneffke, *Studien zur Sozialgeschichte und Philosophie der Bildung. II. Aspekte des 19. Jahrhunderts in Deutschland* (Munich, 1973), pp. 179–238.

[8] Wehler, *Das Deutsche Kaiserreich*, pp. 105, 122ff.

approach),[9] it is treated 'as a sort of *deus ex machina* of cohesion' which somehow establishes the stability of the 'social structure'. Most historians of Wilhelmine nationalism oscillate between these two positions. Neither is very informative about the detail of how ideology is constructed: 'methodologically', they work 'forward from structural trends towards the ideological response, which is then invoked mechanically'.[10] They reduce ideology to the status of an effect: an effect of the government's manipulations, an effect of attempts to preserve the status quo and an effect of the social needs of people hit by industrialization. A certain sociological reductionism is also present, for the appearance of specific political commitments is explained either by the social backgrounds of the actors or by the notional 'needs' of their society. Putting this together, radical nationalism becomes the precipitate of a political reaction between two sets of factors: the historic 'authoritarianism' of the German political culture and the particular need to 're-integrate' a society riven by the shocks of industrialization. A number of other factors—imperialism, the electoral success of the SPD, 'social-imperialist' manipulations by the government—then helped to make it more extreme.

Against these existing approaches, two general points must be made. The first concerns their understanding of 'domination', i.e. of the processes whereby the existing distribution of economic and political power in a society (the 'status quo') is maintained. Here, as suggested above, most Wilhelmine historians rely on a functionalist model of 'social control', in which the maintenance of a 'traditional value-system' occurs as an unproblematic one-way transmission of authoritarian values downwards into the general populace, orchestrated through the management of key institutions, from the Army, police and courts to the church, the school and the media.[11] But the moral authority of a ruling class is not automatically or spontaneously generated by its economic power, nor even by the control and manipulation of such key institutions. On the contrary, that authority has first to be constructed and reconstructed by material processes which are open to contest and hence unpredictable. To avoid a simple model of 'domination-subordination', therefore, in which the dominance of a set of ideas follows naturally from another set of social and economic facts, something like Gramsci's notion of hegemony becomes essential.[12]

As an idea of *negotiated consent*, in which the dominance of a ruling class is constructed ideologically through a continuous process of resistance and intervention, this has some clear advantages. It provides an alternative to ideas of

[9] M. Löwy, 'Marxists and the National Question', *NLR*, 96 (Mar.–Apr. 1976), p. 82.

[10] A. D. Smith, *Theories of Nationalism* (London, 1971), pp. 53f.

[11] For the classic example: Wehler, *Das Deutsche Kaiserreich*, pp. 105–40.

[12] Gramsci's own writings on the subject of hegemony may be found in A. Gramsci, *Selections from the Prison Notebooks* (London, 1971), pp. 206–76, 55ff. The best introductions are now the following: S. Hall, B. Lumley, G. McLennan, 'Politics and Ideology: Gramsci', in *Working Papers in Cultural Studies. 10. On Ideology* (Birmingham, 1977), pp. 45–76; P. Anderson, 'The Antinomies of Antonio Gramsci', *NLR*, 100 (Nov.–Jan. 1977), pp. 5–55.

diffusion for understanding the spread of ideologies and frees us from the simple idea that they somehow merely 'permeate' the 'value-system' of a society. It allows us to see a society's dominant ideas as the object of an ideological struggle whose precise outcome is never fixed. In Gramsci's thinking it also directs us to 'civil society' as a clear domain of public life: the *site* of hegemony, the location of political struggle, where the potential antagonism of the subordinate classes is contained, but where the legitimacy of the power bloc is also subjected to their political scrutiny. Viewed like this, the extension of hegemonic rule entails a certain contraction of repressive intervention, until state power comes to rest on an 'equilibrium of hegemonic and coercive institutions'.[13] State apparatuses still extend into civil society of course (notably in education, welfare and religion), but in so doing provide a terrain where the legitimacy of the system may be queried as well as enforced. More than anything else hegemony has 'to be won, secured, constantly defended'. It is 'a struggle to win over the dominated classes in which any "resolution" involves both *limits* (compromises) and *systematic contradictions*'.[14] It requires that the dominance of a ruling class be continually renegotiated in accordance with the shifting strength (economically, culturally, politically) of the subordinate classes.

The construction of hegemony is also an historical process, in which areas of bureaucratic and repressive control are steadily constrained. European historiography has traditionally seen this as a movement towards parliamentary democracy, while the social sciences have rationalised it into 'modernization theory' and 'political development', where 'industrial societies' advance naturally towards 'citizenship' and 'participation'.[15] Where this official itinerary is not taken (e.g. Germany) the answer is normally sought in the survival of 'pre-industrial traditions' which blocked the road.[16] But this liberal–democratic teleology constructs a false polarity between authoritarian and parliamentary paths of development, assuming that the obstruction of one necessarily entails the victory of its direct opposite. In fact the ideological consolidation of capitalist social relations is an unpredictable process which has no given or fixed destination (parliamentary democracy), but which on the contrary is both uneven and reversible, particularly in its early stages.

[13] E. J. Hobsbawm, 'The Great Gramsci', *New York Review of Books*, XXI, 5 (Apr. 1974), p. 42.

[14] Hall, Lumley, McLennan, 'Politics and Ideology', p. 68.

[15] For a recent affirmative discussion, see H.-U. Wehler, *Modernisierungstheorie und Geschichte* (Göttingen, 1975). For two critiques: A. G. Frank, *Sociology of Development and Underdevelopment of Sociology* (London, 1971); A. D. Smith, *The Concept of Social Change. A Critique of the Functionalist Theory of Social Change* (London, 1973), pp. 60–95.

[16] For a critical discussion of this mode of analysis, see G. Eley, 'Capitalism and the Wilhelmine State: Industrial Growth and Political Backwardness in Recent German Historiography, 1890–1918', *The Historical Journal*, 21, 3 (1978), pp. 737–50, and the important forthcoming study by D. F. Crew, *Industry and Town. The Social History of Bochum, 1860–1914* (New York, 1979).

Moreover, hegemony should not be thought of mainly as the conscious achievement of a ruling class, a grand strategy of manipulation and ideological containment, for this would merely return us to the comforting simplicities of 'social control'. Rather, it is determined by a diversity of pressures, some consciously directed, but others emerging more haphazardly from fields of economic and political conflict. It is no grand design, but a series of struggles from which a pattern only gradually coheres, a process only partially subject to direct political control, in which first one and then another fraction of the ruling class gains ascendancy. The complexity comes not only from a diversity of strategies for containing popular opposition, but also from the need to resolve and accommodate antagonism within the ruling class itself. These two sets of contradictions—those of the struggle for a negotiated equilibrium of the dominant and subordinate classes, and those of the internal fractioning of the ruling bloc—determine the varying forms of political rule in different periods and countries.

The particular interest of the Wilhelmine period in Germany is that the general process of hegemonic construction (i.e. the enrichment of coercive or repressive state power by conciliation and consent) was in its early stages. In the 1890s, for instance, we can see it proceeding on two distinct levels. The more obvious was that of policy towards the SPD. The abolition of the Anti-Socialist Law in 1890 introduced a period of transition in which the general legalization of Socialist activities was combined with harassment of individual trade unionists, speakers and journalists, periodic calls for restrictive legislation against strikes, pickets and Socialist agitation, and in some quarters even resort to *Staatsstreich* (coup d'état). The end of this period may be dated to the autumn of 1899, when the Hard-Labour Bill was defeated in the Reichstag: the piece-meal retreat of the National Liberals from a course of repressive anti-Socialism combined with the Centre Party's populist constitutionalism and the acute political vision of key individuals like Bülow to help force the fight against the SPD on to the level of propaganda and electoral politics. The announcement of Miquel's *Sammlungspolitik* in 1897 simultaneously inaugurated a series of attempts to recompose the unity of the power bloc on the basis of the given Constitution.

But secondly, beneath this primary struggle against the SPD, a further impetus to popular politics came from the need of the non-Socialist parties to find new ways of holding the allegiance of a mass constituency. As we saw, in their different ways both the Centre and the Conservatives were relatively successful in the latter, whilst the National Liberals fared notably worse: confronted by the defection of customary rural voters in the 1890s they simply hitched their fortunes to the Agrarian League and hoped for the best. Thus, whilst at the high-political level of the government and parties the power bloc proved relatively stable until 1909, at the popular level its legitimacy was badly flawed. In this way the inability of the National Liberals to organize their support in the constituencies remained a source of instability in the working of the power bloc during the Bülow years, for it created a vacant political space, not only for the Left, but also for independent initiatives of the Right. It is in this double context of unstable hegemonic construction—the tentative transition from repressive to propagandist anti-Socialism, and the divided efforts of the right to find some purchase on popular legitimacy—that the emergence of a distinctive radical-nationalist ideology between the 1890s and 1908 must be located.

The second general point is the need to respect the relative independence of ideology, where the latter is taken to mean 'an objective systematized representation of social relations embodied in real material institutions and practices'.[17] It is vital to recognize that membership of the *nationale Verbände* had its own internal logic for activists. It was conceived by them as an autonomous sphere of political engagement. It cannot be reduced to the functional requirements of the so-called 'ruling strata' and their 'strategies of stabilization'. The clause of the Navy League's Constitution which outlawed partisan alignment with individual parties and committed the organization to 'non-political' activities was no mere fiction meant to mask the real relations with a hidden power structure of big business, state bureaucracy and party establishment. Nor was it mere self-deception, a mechanism of 'false consciousness' which duped the naval enthusiasts into serving the interests of the 'ruling strata', 'objectively' and unbeknown to themselves. On the contrary, it denoted the real idiom in which they thought through and acted out their political beliefs, the real terms in which they understood their membership and its relation to the party-political arena. As such it had an effectivity in its own right in Wilhelmine politics. The ideology of the national interest was the primary instance around which the self-understanding, political activity and internal life of the Navy League was organized, and the same was even truer of the Pan-Germans.

It is vital, therefore, to consider radical-nationalist ideology on its own terms —not as the descendant of a disembodied intellectual tradition or as a closed system of formal ideas, but as a mode of commitment which articulated a series of antagonisms within the existing political structures of Wilhelmine Germany's ruling bloc. Those antagonisms certainly originated in the social consequences of Germany's capitalist transformation, in the sense that the latter first allowed their possibility. But the dominant moment of antagonism between old and new right in the nationalist pressure groups was ideological rather than social, and this conflict must not be reduced to direct social determinations. The division between moderate and radical nationalists did not correspond to different social groupings, nor to different fractions of industrial capital, as has sometimes been suggested. In many ways the attack on *Honoratiorenpolitik* came from persons who were themselves *Honoratioren*: they might indeed be less wealthy and prestigious than their opponents, but the form of

[17] R. McDonough, 'Ideology as False Consciousness: Lukacs', in *Working Papers 10*, p. 41.

their opposition was given principally at the level of ideology. The conflict disclosed alternative ideals of political order and competing modes of political practice. It was only secondarily concerned with inequalities of social access on the part of the radical nationalists themselves. Because the terrain of the conflict was primarily political, therefore, we should not be surprised to find some archetypal notables on both sides. The radical nationalists were constituted as a distinctive political grouping not by their similar social origins, but by a shared political experience and its ideological formulation.

II

The strongest of the conventional analyses of Wilhelmine nationalism is the integrationist one. At one level, after all, nationalism is intrinsically an integrative ideology: it stresses the common identity of all citizens by reference to language, history and shared traditions, and raises it to the highest loyalty in the state. Moreover, the fact that political practice has been shaped by the linguistic, institutional and territorial extent of the nation-state has been of incalculable political importance, for it has held political imagination in a structure of limited possibilities and heavily constrained the expression of dissent. Increasingly, circumstances were admitted in which political conflict would not be pushed to an extreme. As 1914 revealed, war was the most dramatic of these, but governments quickly discovered that similar advantages might be obtained by political rather than military means, by deliberately manufacturing a 'moral equivalent to war' in which a comparable sense of national solidarity might arise.[18] This might encompass everything from war scares and diplomatic coups to the identification of fifth columns or subversives (e.g. racial minorities, immigrants, revolutionaries, 'extremists'), the utilization of national symbols, rituals and ceremonial (the 'invention of tradition'), and the political appropriation of the scientific, artistic and sporting achievements of individual nationals.[19] Though the growing stress on national communities could never eliminate political conflict, the tangible material reality of the nation endowed appeals to the 'national interest' with a seductive credibility. They were skilfully used to moderate disagreements and in certain circumstances to suspend them altogether.

This placed an enormous weapon in the hands of government. To recognize that state apparatuses (most notably the school and the conscript Army) were

[18] The phrase 'moral equivalent to war' comes from William James's essay of the same name, in *Memories and Studies* (New York, 1917), pp. 267–306.

[19] See Max Weber's much-quoted dictum: 'Every successful imperialist policy of force abroad normally strengthens likewise, at least initially, the domestic prestige and consequently the power and influence of those classes, castes and parties under whose leadership the success has been obtained' (*Wirtschaft und Gesellschaft*, Berlin and Cologne, 1964, p. 673). It must be said, however, that this is a fairly obvious insight. See the discussion in Eley, 'Defining Social Imperialism', pp. 282ff.

consciously used by government to propagate a 'national view' is certainly not to reinstate the functionalist account of nationalism criticized above. The latter moves illicitly from a general description of the formal properties of nationalist ideology to a series of unproven assumptions about its material effect in society. The problems of exploiting a shared national tradition were far more complex than this, particularly in a young state like Wilhelmine Germany, where both the temporal proximity of unification and the rapidity of industrialization permitted the survival of powerful particularist loyalties, and class antagonisms continued to articulate nationalist perceptions into diverse ideological positions. In other words official nationalism was just one ideology amongst many, allied to a particular political practice. In purely formal terms a wide spectrum of nationalisms may be distinguished at the turn of the century, from official doctrines of dynastic continuity and federalism, to south German particularisms and the defence of states' rights, biologically founded racisms, the intellectualized ethnic populism of the Pan-Germans, and the radicalism of South-west German democracy, shading imperceptibly into the democratic patriotism of the SPD. In other words, hostile political groupings competed vigorously with each other precisely to appropriate to themselves the 'true' heritage of the nation. In fact, rather than working to the advantage of the government or the 'status quo' as functionalists would claim, nationalism provided the terrain on which hegemony, the right to speak for 'the people in general', was contested.

By using the educational system and conscription to inculcate a sense of national belonging, therefore, the government was not simply 'manipulating' a system of 'socializing agencies' to 'stabilize' the 'status quo', but was engaging in a political struggle whose terms could not be dictated from the ministerial drawing-board. These were political interventions into territory already occupied by independent confessional, cultural, trade-union and political organizations which could not be dislodged without a fight. Indeed, it was precisely the success of these agencies that prompted government interventions in the first place. To gauge the effectiveness of the latter it is necessary not only to measure the popular reception, but also to uncover the process of manoeuvring which preceded and accompanied them.

To take one example, we know that from an early stage after the end of the Anti-Socialist Law some government circles were highly sensitive to the difficulties of protecting young people against Social Democratic ideas. In particular, means were sought of bridging the gap between two periods of direct institutional surveillance, namely school and conscription, between the ages of fourteen and twenty. Various methods were mooted, from the sponsorship of sporting festivals and physical training, continuation schools and charitable youth work, to uniformed youth groups like the scouts, the Young-Germany-Union in 1911 and some form of compulsory military training between school and conscription. Yet these efforts were not conspicuously successful at creating a unified machinery for the propagation of a single 'national' view. The striking thing was a continued diversity of practice and its resistance to standardization: plans for a German Olympiad were finally shipwrecked in 1899 on the jealousy of the Gymnastics Movement; further education suffered from lack of money until 1911, when the required legislation was successfully defeated by an alliance of heavy industry, artisans and the Centre Party; a higher measure of co-operation between the state and private agencies after 1907 was achieved only by explicitly conceding the autonomy of the latter, especially of those that were religious; and although 1911 definitely began an upsurge of paramilitary youth work, the much-vaunted legislation for compulsory military training continued to elude a badly divided government. Irrespective of whether or not these were an effective means of combating Socialist ideas, in other words, the government was faced with the prior problem of first constructing an adequate infrastructure.[20]

Similar strictures apply to the educational system proper: existing literature speaks much about the anti-Socialist directives of the educational bureaucracy, but rather little about the actual practice of schools and teachers, and still less about the real effects on children.[21] But providing we remember that the government's nationalist interventions had to observe political constraints of the above kind, we can now point to certain areas of congruence in the activities of state and *national Verbände*. As already remarked, this had something to do with the essential properties of nationalism as an integrative ideology, in stressing what united the Germans rather than divided them. In the propaganda of all the nationalist groups there was a particular stress on national integration and the national idea, and within certain limits this was bound to redound to the advantage of the state. Moreover, it had a definite anti-Socialist and normally an anti-parliamentary inflection, which was also welcome to the government at a time of encroaching parliamentarization. By the turn of the century the government was passing through a period in which independent nationalist agitation was of particular value. It both contributed to the general popularity of *Weltpolitik* and added to the repertoire of anti-Socialist techniques. As the histories of the Colonial Society and the Society for the Eastern Marches showed, this potentially made for a relationship of harmonious and productive co-operation between state and *Verbände*.

One area in which this generally worked was that of education. At the two

---

[20] K. Saul, 'Der Kampf um die Jugend zwischen Volksschule und Kaserne. Ein Beitrag zur "Jugendpflege" im Wilhelminischen Reich 1890–1914', *MGM*, 9 (1971), pp. 97–143; Stenkewitz, *Gegen Bajonett und Dividende*, pp. 65ff.

[21] For typical assertions, see Wehler, *Das Deutsche Kaiserreich*: 'the perpetuation of the social structure and the social power relationships through the education system' (p. 124); 'On this terrain it is possible to recognize in all its clarity the manipulative application of nationalism for the purpose of stabilizing the social power structures and by that means for internalizing sublimated power relations' (p. 126).

Prussian School Conferences in December 1890 and June 1900 there was much talk of making school more relevant to the needs of the new German state as an industrial and a world power by reorganizing the curriculum and its content. As the Kaiser's old tutor Dr Hinzpeter said at the outset of the 1900 proceedings: ' . . . the whole educational ideal has significantly shifted. Previously the educated man was distinguished by knowledge of the old languages and the culture and history of antiquity; now he is distinguished by knowledge of the modern languages, of German culture and history, and of the natural sciences.'[22] Accordingly, the Wilhelmine period saw a gradual movement away from the classical humanist education towards a stronger emphasis on modern languages and literature and on German history, whilst older concerns with physical education and the sciences were strengthened. At the opening of the 1890 Conference the young Kaiser insisted that the education system lacked a 'national basis. We must take German as the foundation of the Gymnasium; we should educate young national Germans and not young Greeks and Romans,' whilst one of the subsequent speakers remarked that 'the claims of Germany's world position on the education of its youth speak for themselves'.[23] Such statements were an open invitation to groups like the Colonial Society and Navy League to help educate German youth in 'a pronounced German consciousness and a vigorous feeling of national solidarity', and 'to train the coming generation as sensible advocates of our overseas tasks'.[24] Thus in 1902 the Navy League joined in a comprehensive rewriting of school textbooks by producing a collection of naval essays for the guidance of historians, geographers and other authors.[25] In November 1904 the Colonial Society embarked on a similar project: a committee was established for the compilation of a book of colonial readings for schools and in February 1905 the educational ministries were asked to incorporate these into the curriculum; in February 1906 ministerial circulars were dispatched to this effect.[26]

The Navy League set special store by the involvement of teachers and devised a particular category of agitational literature for their use. They were often the most active propagandists: one thinks of Hermann Rassow in Elberfeld, Burg and Potsdam, of his associates Richard Stoldt and Johannes Dieckvoß (*Gymnasium* professors in Bromberg and Eutin), Jakob Couvreur of Weimar,

---

[22] Heydorn and Koneffke, *Studien*, p. 216.

[23] Ibid., pp. 188, 185.

[24] Keim, *Erlebtes*, p. 155; Navy League *Jahresbericht* 1902, p. 7, BA Coblenz, ZS g.1, 195/2.

[25] The project was edited by Hüttemann, a Westphalian headmaster from Ohligs, and the collaborators included Gercke (the Navy League Secretary), Rassow, Georg Wislicenus, Dau (a senior civil servant from Neisse), Holleben (a retired naval officer from Bad Honnef), and two teachers, Rattke of Wilhelmshaven and Rohwedder of Ellerbek. See *Jahresbericht* 1903, BA Coblenz, ZSg. 1, 195/2; Menges to Witzleben, Oct. 13th 1903, BA-MA Freiburg, 2276, 94229.

[26] Pierard, 'German Colonial Society', pp. 279f.

of Ludwig Kemmer, professor at the *Luitpoldgymnasium* in Munich. Exhibitions and film-shows were always mounted with the co-operation of the schools in the locality concerned: in 1904 at least half of the 650,000 visitors to the Navy League's film-shows were schoolchildren. A guide to careers at sea was published in 1901 and issued on request to teachers and parents for remittance of postage: by 1903 26,000 copies had been given out. In addition the higher naval ranks were presented in a poster, and after sales of 2,000 in 1901 and 18,000 in 1902 this was distributed by the educational ministries to practically all *Mittelschulen*. Another major device was the organized trip to the coast, the first of which took place in 1903. In 1905 over 4,800 boys visited the major naval installations in 15 different parties.[27]

This kind of activity was welcome to the government. In fact, it was exactly what the latter expected, namely a voluntary back-up to the state's own ideological apparatus, formally independent yet acting broadly in consonance with official wishes. It might encompass both a general licence to 'educate' the populace in a 'national direction' and more specific actions on individual issues. How far government made direct use of the pressure groups varied with the issues concerned and the extent of the latter's radical-nationalist commitment. When the Colonial Society moved away from the sponsorship of speculative expeditions, *via* the naval campaigns of 1897–8 and 1899–1900, towards technical problems of colonial development, for instance, the possibilities for co-operation with the government accordingly increased. But if here co-operation was eased by the gradual recession of radical-nationalist activity, in the case of the Eastern Marches Society the movement was the other way, for in the special area of policy towards the Poles the government came closest to an overtly radical-nationalist position. This was already apparent in late 1897, when several Ministers had urged protection of the German population against the Poles by the full range of measures advocated by the *Hakatisten* and Pan-Germans.[28] This correspondence increased with the ministerial ascendancy of Miquel and the later accession of Bülow to the Chancellorship in 1900, while the appointment of Konrad von Studt as Minister of Culture in September 1899 heralded a heavier emphasis on 'Germanization' in matters of language and education. The latter development in particular pushed the government and the Eastern Marches Society closer together, especially under the dramatic impetus of the Wreschen incident of spring 1901 and the school strike of 1906. The relationship was vitally mediated by the Hugenburg connection, whose members had by 1908 entrenched themselves deeply inside the central and provincial bureaucracy.[29]

[27] For detailed references: Eley, 'German Navy League', pp. 152, 161–3.
[28] See Röhl, *Germany Without Bismarck*, pp. 256ff.
[29] See especially Guratzsch, *Macht durch Organisation*, pp. 39–47; but also Tims, *Germanizing Prussian Poland*, pp. 76–103. The Hugenberg connection were particularly important in framing the Polish legislation of 1908.

In this cultural domain, therefore, the activities of the *nationale Verbände* complemented those of the government, particularly under Bülow, who had a keen eye for the general importance of national integration. The search for an adequate political response to the SPD's gains in the 1903 elections, to which the Imperial League Against Social Democracy was a first solution, was a special form of this concern and, as we shall see, the 1907 elections were a clear illustration of how nationalism and anti-Socialism mutually reinforced each other. But here the nationalist groups were operating on the very heartland of the nationalist consensus by attacking those obvious outsiders (the Socialists and national minorities) who directly questioned the primary loyalty of the citizen to the state. Though certain party politicians might dislike the extremism of the radical-nationalist approach, in these areas there was a fair amount of common ground. But in other matters, such as foreign policy, armaments, religion and social legislation, a radical-nationalist position entailed conflict not just with the *Reichsfeinde* but with important groupings inside the consensus itself. Both the Pan-Germans and the Navy League provide good evidence of this effect. But before exploring the sources of conflict within the right it is worth looking more closely at the integrationist aspect of nationalist agitation. This can be done most conveniently by taking two key individuals, first Hermann Rassow and then Freiherr Louis von Würtzburg.

Rassow, a cousin to Hans Delbrück, a member of the Pan-German Council and an early admirer of Naumann, was one of the most interesting of the naval propagandists. A well-connected *Bildungsbürger*, he was in many ways a prototype of the disinterested nationalist intellectual, committed to an ideal of social conciliation under the banner of national community, a man formed ideologically by the experience of unification, for whom loyalty to the new nation-state was paramount. Though he showed a lively interest in the 'social problem' and believed that Socialists should be reasoned with rather than simply suppressed, he assumed that the answer to working-class discontent lay with an expanding capitalist economy and natural rises in the standard of living rather than specific remedial interventions by the state. In these two respects—the primacy of his nationalist loyalty to the state and his acceptance of Germany's changing social reality—Rassow was truly a child of the Empire, in this sense a *Wilhelminian*, who was attracted neither by the anti-capitalist counter-utopias of conservatives nor by the prospect of a more democratic state.[30] Moreover, precisely because he saw himself as a nationalist missionary to the working class he was not strictly identified with any single political tendency. Instead he moved along a fine web of political contacts, with liberal-conservative academics like Delbrück, with the Pan-Germans and other radical nationalists like Friedrich Lange, with the industrialists of Rhineland-Westphalia, with the Christian-Socials, the Evangelical Workers' Movement

[30] The idea of a specific 'Wilhelminian' ideology was first suggested to me by Hartmut Pogge, who has now explored the problem in his forthcoming study of Rathenau.

and the Naumannites, and with the club world of the local *Honoratioren*.[31] In this respect he was an ideal auxiliary for the government.

Rassow seems to have made serious contact with the Navy Office for the first time in March 1897, when he volunteered information about his activities and solicited some material for use in a lecture.[32] Here he voiced the opinion that the naval issue was ideally suited to raise 'the German national consciousness', and we know from other sources that this reflected an involvement in a larger political project. In the mid-1890s, when the challenge of Hammerstein and Stöcker for the leadership of the Conservative Party was finally scotched and the supporters of Naumann were moving towards an open break with the Christian-Socials, Rassow entertained thoughts of a new 'conservative people's party' in west Germany.[33] The popular evangelical Conservatism of Westphalia, which had helped sustain Hammerstein and Stöcker in the early 1890s, gave this idea some credibility, and provided the context of Rassow's earliest propaganda excursions. The main problem, he argued, was to find some basis like the naval question

> on which we intellectuals (*Gebildeten*) . . . could re-unite with the big industrialists. At the moment they simply regard us as Social Democrats and if we can work *with* them on this, then afterwards it will be easier to bring them back to the idea of social reform as well. The contact had actually almost been lost . . . Then the naval question came along just at the right moment.

The difficulty was getting the industrialists 'to abandon their childish identification' of social reform with Social Democracy, for Naumann's name in particular was like a 'red rag' to a bull.[34] The best hope in the short term, he thought, was to gain the support of the Kaiser for a linkage of imperialism and social reform, and in the meantime the workers could be given a healthy dose of patriotism. As time went on, however, the latter became more and more dominant. In April 1898, after the passage of the Navy Law, Rassow told Tirpitz that the future problem was to ease the workers' 'return to patriotism'. After the acceptance of the Navy Bill itself,

> this, winning back the embittered masses with the aid of the naval question, which benefits them in the *very highest* degree, was always the second aim I had in mind with my agitation. This hope, which I have nurtured for years, has been converted into the *firmest confidence* by the many valuable experiences of this year. Without this prospect who could believe in a really great future for Germany?[35]

[31] Rassow's agitational practice is also discussed extensively at several points elsewhere in this study, e.g. pp. 52f., 94f., 131f., 172–4, 225f.

[32] See Rassow's three letters of Mar. 6th, Mar. 15th and May 13th 1897, BA-MA Freiburg, 3136, I.2.1.4d.

[33] Rassow to Delbrück, Feb. 25th 1896, DSB Berlin, Delbrück Papers.

[34] Rassow to Delbrück, Jan. 28th, June 13th and Feb. 25th 1896, ibid.

[35] Rassow to Tirpitz, Apr. 12th 1898, BA-MA Freiburg, 2223, 93943.

In the following years Rassow threw himself wholeheartedly into this task. To some extent his liberal-imperialist affiliations remained: at several points he was associated with plans for reviving a Naumannite daily paper, whilst in December 1906 he welcomed the left-liberal electoral front and relished the prospect of Naumann's election to the Reichstag.[36] But on the whole he was more interested in pulling the adherents of Eugen Richter towards state-interventionist imperialism than in promoting social reform: thus in both 1897–8 and 1899–1900 he campaigned in Altena-Iserlohn against Lenzmann, and in 1903 helped swing the left liberals in Burg round to support for the Navy. Throughout this time he worked closely both with the Prussian provincial bureaucracy and with the Navy Office, receiving materials, technical information and financial subsidies, and providing regular reports on the progress of his agitation. After 1901 he was one of only five civilians who were sent regular copies of the *Marineverordnungsblatt*.[37] During the Navy League's crisis in 1907–8 Rassow proved an invaluable ally for the Navy Office, supplying it with detailed information as to the progress of the factional manoeuvring and lending the considerable prestige of his name in the movement to the moderate cause.[38] In this individual case, therefore, the pursuit of nationalist goals seemed to work almost wholly to the advantage of the state. No propagandist could be more assiduous or imaginative than Hermann Rassow, but his activity carried no specific political charge.

If Rassow's integrationist nationalism was mainly cultural, however, Freiherr von Würtzburg's had a more direct political implication. Arguing from a specific set of 'Bavarian conditions' (viz. the predominantly Catholic and rural population, together with the regional dominance of the Centre Party), he insisted that the Navy League's aim must be the construction of the broadest possible consensus which excluded only the SPD. Specifically, he argued the primary importance of conciliating the Centre. There followed from this a series of positions. Most obviously, it required a conciliatory style of propaganda which concentrated on the simple transmission of 'educational' information and avoided programmatic demands for fresh naval expansion, on the grounds that the latter would only alienate an already sceptical Catholic peasantry.[39] Secondly, this coincided closely with Tirpitz's own thinking and laid the basis

[36] Rassow to Delbrück, Jan. 24th 1900 and June 18th 1903, DSB Berlin, Delbrück Papers; Rassow to Boy-Ed, Dec. 13th 1906, BA-MA Freiburg, 2257, 94137.

[37] Jacobsen's note of June 21st 1901, BA-MA Freiburg, 2284, 94272.

[38] See in particular: Rassow to Delbrück, Apr. 21st, Apr. 22nd and May 20th 1907, DSB Berlin, Delbrück Papers; detailed correspondence with Boy-Ed in BA-MA Freiburg, 2257, 94137, and 2278, 94236 (esp. Rassow to Boy-Ed, 'Confidential', Jan. 20th 1908).

[39] Peasant hostility—normally with a pronounced parochial and particularist inflection—to the financial and other burdens of higher spending on the Army and Navy was the main material foundation of Centre Party opposition to the military estimates of 1887, 1893 and 1899, and (in a more fragmented way) to the Navy Bills of 1897–1900. See Farr, 'Populism in the Countryside', p. 142.

for a fruitful alliance between the Navy Office and the Bavarian leadership in the Navy League. Thirdly, it also reflected a powerful commitment to federalism, as the organizing constitutional principle of both the Empire and the Navy League. Fourthly, Würtzburg also subscribed to a traditional notion of social hierarchy which located him firmly in the camp of conventional *Honoratiorenpolitik*. An ingrained belief in the social exclusiveness of power set him solidly against the populist demands of the radical nationalists and oriented his politics towards the establishment. His attentions were confined to a narrow sector of society: the royal family, the liberal–conservative ministerial bureaucracy, the landed Catholic aristocracy, senior officers in the Bavarian Army, the upper reaches of the Catholic Church. Finally, each of these positions demanded that the Navy League's activities be formally 'non-political'. Würtzburg's ideal was a naval rally attended by 'the greatest number of Centre voters and clerics'. Prince Rupprecht, the son of the Regent, would take the chair and the Archbishop of Bamberg would deliver 'a patriotic speech'. 'That', he added, 'would have been an achievement of national significance.'[40]

Würtzburg took the principle of non-partisanship to an extreme, arguing that the Navy League should envisage a time when *every* German was a member.[41] This represented the integrationist aspiration at its most inclusive, but leaving aside the special political coloration that Würtzburg gave it, some ideal of this kind motivated most active supporters of the Navy League. The ability of the naval idea to cut across sectional barriers within the nation was for most of its adherents 'the strength of the entire agitation', as one government memorandum put it.[42] Not only could the League remove the Navy from party conflict, it could also provide a model of 'national unanimity', as Stroschein had phrased it. Many believed with Heinrich Claß that 'the joy in a proud, powerful foreign policy . . . will not miss its healthy rallying effect on the domestic quarrelling'.[43] In this way exaggerated hopes were invested in the naval movement. It was expected to break down old parochial loyalties by stressing the importance of the Reich, 'to express the feeling in the German nation that all German tribes and all parties belong together in the struggle to strengthen the instruments of imperial power'. As the Prussian Ambassador in Munich said, 'interest in the fleet provides the ground on which the imperial idea wins friends from the camp of its enemies'. It was the Navy League's 'value as a national factor and a bond between North and South' which made it so attractive—its importance 'for the cultivation of the national sentiment and the federal unity of the German nation', for the 'high and handsome aim of

---

[40] Würtzburg to Boy-Ed, Sept. 21st 1908, BA-MA Freiburg, 2278, 94238.

[41] A remark attributed to Würtzburg by Rassow at the Stuttgart Congess of the Navy League, May 27th 1905, *Protokoll*, p. 15, ibid., 2276, 94230.

[42] 'Ergebnisse der Erfahrungen 1900–1901', ibid., 2284, 94272.

[43] Stroschein, *Manuskript: Die Begründung*, p. 8, ibid., 2276, 94227; *Alld. Bl.*, 1911, p. 314.

national concord', and for the union of 'the German tribes of North and South'.[44]

This aspiration, common to both moderate and radical nationalists, fostered the illusion that the Navy League could somehow achieve an ideal unity of the nation, reaching across geographical, confessional, party-political and social barriers. The movement saw itself as a tidy 'community', where businessmen and landowners rubbed shoulders with teachers, doctors and lawyers to keep a paternal eye on peasants, workers and shopkeepers. The belief that the League embraced 'all parts of our nation, from the very cream right down to the ordinary worker',[45] received the seal of contemporary legitimacy in the institution of the royal protector or patron. The convention whereby each of the regional sections enjoyed the formal patronage of its ruling house was intended to bind the movement to the existing political order, to reflect the federal structure of the Reich, and to symbolize traditional bonds between ruler and ruled.[46] The entire existence of the Navy League as a mass movement was conceived as a polemical refutation of the class analysis of the Socialists. Thus Würtzburg celebrated the 1903 Congress in Munich as a supreme demonstration of the organic unity of the nation: 'beginning with the royal princes and ministers, all estates and classes were present, right down to the simplest artisan.'[47]

III

At this point it becomes essential to deploy the concept of ideological struggle outlined above. In other words, we are dealing not just with a natural or neutral process of national integration, but with a series of problematic interventions into a zone of *contested* ideological territory. It is easy enough to freeze the analysis at the pious affirmations of social solidarity voiced by Würtzburg by viewing the *nationale Verbände* as defenders of the existing social and political order and nationalism as its ideological cement. But government could not count on the political advantages of nationalist agitation quite as easily as that: once a licence was conceded to independent propaganda agencies in the name of

[44] Sources of quotations: Flintzer (Weimar) in the Gen. Board, Apr. 16th 1904, *Verhandlungen*, p. 6, BA Coblenz, ZSg. 1, 195/2; Braun (Augsburg) in the Cassell Congress, Jan. 19th 1908, *Verhandlungen*, p. 37, GLA Karlsruhe, 69P, 8; Pourtales to (prob.) Hamman, Mar. 15th 1905, BA-MA Freiburg, 2277, 94234; Würtzburg to Boy-Ed, Feb. 10th 1907, ibid., 94235; Boy-Ed for Tirpitz, Dec. 20th 1907, ibid.; Boy-Ed to Würtzburg, May 5th 1906, ibid., 94234; Franz von Bodelschwingh (Schwarzenhasel), in *DTZ*, July 22nd 1908. Such quotations could be multiplied indefinitely.

[45] Klewitz (Brandenburg) in the Cassel Congress, Jan. 19th 1908, *Verhandlungen*, p. 40, GLA Karlsruhe, 69P, 8.

[46] It should be noted that the phenomenon of the royal patrons does not appear in the other nationalist pressure groups, principally because of the Navy League's far greater popular membership: the other groups did not possess such highly developed regional organizations.

[47] Würtzburg, ibid., p. 10.

'national integration', an ideological space was created in which alternative political programmes might be advanced, not always to the advantage of the government. The most interesting feature of the attempts to manufacture a stronger sense of national belonging during the 1880s and 1890s, in fact, was the extent to which particular parties and organizations tried to appropriate the newly inaugurated German-national tradition for their own purposes. At the most elementary level there were of course certain universal symbols and marks of nationality, of which the language and the national literature were perhaps the most important. But by 1900 most parties, from the Social Democrats to the most traditional Conservatives, were seeking to identify themselves with the 'true' soul of the nation. We can see this in the rich iconography which proliferated at the turn of the century, some of which was certainly created by the state itself (e.g. national festivals like Sedan-Day or the Kaiser's Birthday, ceremonial in schools, historical motifs in postage stamps and so on),[48] but which often also originated independently and which was invariably disputed. 'Kaiser-Wilhelm-Monuments' competed both with the 'Bismarck-Monuments' of the independent right and the surviving symbols of an older liberal or democratic nationalism.[49] This element of contest appeared most sharply in the centenary celebrations of Napoleon's defeat in 1815. Official efforts to glorify dynastic traditions were attacked not only by the SPD and the left liberals, but also by the Pan-German right, who charged the government with misrepresenting the popular character of the fight against Napoleon.[50]

In other words, the 'integrationist' analysis of Wilhelmine nationalism is not very helpful in uncovering a distinctive radical-nationalist position, though it clearly distinguishes an important aspect of it. Part of this difficulty stems from the over-emphasis of the idea of the 'status quo'. In recent work this tends to obscure far more than it explains by assuming that those participating in Wilhelmine politics can be divided almost wholly into two camps: those who wished to change the 'status quo', and those who wanted to defend it.[51] But this understanding of the idea of the status quo is extraordinarily static. It seems to embody some notion of authoritarianism and of aristocratic or feudal power which bears little relation to the actual political fabric of German capitalism as it developed between the 1870s and 1914. In the final instance, surely, the Wilhelmine status quo meant the capitalist mode of production,

[48] Hobsbawm, 'Inventing Traditions', p. 19.

[49] See T. Nipperdey, 'Nationalidee und Nationaldenkmal in Deutschland im 19. Jahrhundert', in *Gesellschaft, Kultur, Theorie*, pp. 133–73.

[50] Stenkewitz, *Gegen Bajonett und Dividende*, pp. 77–96; see also *RWZ*, Dec. 13th 1911: '1812–1912'.

[51] For accessible summary statements of this approach: Wehler, *Das Deutsche Kaiserreich*, pp. 78ff., 100–5; Berghahn, *Germany and the Approach of War*, pp. 5–24, 211–14; Berghahn, *Tirpitz-Plan*, pp. 11–20, 592–604; H. A. Winkler, 'From Social Protectionism to National Socialism: The German Small-Business Movement in Comparative Perspective', *JMH*, 48 (1976), pp. 1ff.

and politically it encompassed not only residual enclaves of 'feudal' privilege in the military and bureaucratic apparatus of the state, but also the general rule of law and a relatively advanced Constitution. The partial realization of mid-century liberalism's legal programme between the 1860s and 1890s, together with universal suffrage and embryonic parliamentary forms, cast the left in the role of defending, the right in that of questioning the status quo. From the political point of view, in other words, the latter implies not some abstract tradition of 'authoritarianism', but a specific set of constitutional and institutional relationships, which changed across time and were continually exposed to renegotiation through political action. Its character was redefined by successive conjunctures and cannot be reduced to a single authoritarian 'essence'. The 'status quo' in this sense might evoke the enmity of the right rather than their support. The actuality of Wilhelmine Germany was far more complex and ambiguous than the term's current usage allows.

With these remarks in mind it is dangerous to assume that the right could be easily united around the status quo in general. From our point of view the case of federalism is a particularly interesting one. In this respect the settlement of 1866–71, with its dynastic compromises and guarantees for states' rights, had produced on paper a delicate balance of jurisdictions. For some time this also worked in practice, but by the 1890s the governing system was gradually becoming more centralist: this was apparent in the relative weight of the Reich against the Prussian bureaucracy, in the increasing location of government business in the Reichstag, in the growth of national expenditure, and in the rising pressure for a Reich finance reform.[52] Though in administrative terms the centre of gravity was clearly shifting, however, the government remained committed to operating the federalist Constitution, for the vested interests of royalism and particularism were far too strong.[53] In such a situation the political articulation of a *German-national* ideology might easily become embarrassing for a government which had to observe a variety of federal constraints. Radical nationalists in the Pan-German League were highly impatient of the latter, insisting on the exclusive primacy of the citizen's loyalty to the nation-state and denying the legitimacy of older allegiances, whether dynastic, confessional or regional. When opportunity arose for strengthening the Reich against the states Pan-German support was uncompromising, as in the sensitive question of the Brunswick succession in 1913,

[52] At present this remains something of an open question, which badly needs systematic investigation. In the meantime see: P. Molt, *Der Reichstag vor der improvisierten Revolution* (Cologne, 1963); M. Rauh, *Föderalismus und Parlamentarismus im Wilhelmischen Reich* (Düsseldorf, 1977); P.-Chr. Witt, *Die Finanzpolitik des Deutschen Reiches von 1903 bis 1913* (Lubeck, 1970).

[53] Bismarck had flirted with *Staatsstreich* (or coup d'état) in 1878–9, but this form of coup was never seriously contemplated again at a governmental level (i.e. against the federal nature of the Constitution). See M. Stürmer, 'Staatsstreichgedanken im Bismarckreich', *HZ*, 209 (1969), pp. 566–615.

when Guelph particularism enjoyed a brief resurgence.[54] Radical nationalists were unimpressed by the political etiquette of monarchism, and as we shall see from events in the Navy League were perfectly willing to criticize the royal families if they obstructed a vigorous nationalist practice.

In the case of federalism, therefore, the government was forced to observe a set of necessary tactical restraints which the radical nationalists prided themselves on repudiating. The government's relationship to the Centre Party suggested a similar contrast. For most of the period after 1890, certainly from 1897, the Centre's decisive parliamentary position had been pivotal to the government's political strategy. A succession of tightly negotiated parliamentary deals culminating in the passage of the 1902 tariffs had gradually installed the party at the heart of the governing majority in the Reichstag. In no case was this truer than in that of the naval legislation, for from the start Tirpitz had based his thinking on the conciliation of the Centre, and to a great extent the tempo of the naval programme depended on how far the accommodation of the party's leadership could be pushed. Moreover, the Navy League had to cope with a special form of the Centre's political dominance, for in South Germany it contended with a Catholic peasantry whose political representatives were only lukewarm and often directly hostile to the Navy. In 1898 a third of the Centre deputies voted against the First Navy Bill, and most of these came from Bavaria. In 1900 the Second Bill had an easier passage, but the hostility of the South German group had changed little.[55] Bavaria's population was almost seventy-five per cent Catholic and this enabled the Centre to build an almost monolithic bloc of safe seats, which in 1903 counted thirty deputies in a national strength of 103; adding those from Baden and Württemberg, the South German group comprised over forty per cent of its parliamentary strength. This Bavarian dominance was broken only by the SPD in Munich itself, a few independents from the Bavarian Peasants' League, and a sizeable enclave in the more Protestant north running from Ansbach to Hof which was normally contested by the Conservatives, Liberals and Socialists. The picture was similar in the Landtag: in 1905 the Centre controlled 102 of the 157 seats

[54] In 1884 the exiled Duke of Cumberland, son of the dispossessed King of Hannover, acquired a title to the Duchy of Brunswick, but was prevented from succeeding to this in 1885 because he refused to renounce his claims to Hannover. Brunswick was governed by a Prince Regent until 1906, when the latter's death again reopened the question. Johann Albrecht von Mecklenburg took over the Regency until 1913, when the Duke of Cumberland's son was married to the Kaiser's daughter and installed in Brunswick. Throughout the controversy the radical-nationalist press remained bitterly opposed to any compromise with Guelph claims. See especially the leading articles in *RWZ*, Oct. 9th 1913, and *LNN*, Oct. 16th 1913. See also Stenkewitz, *Gegen Bajonett und Dividende*, pp. 53–66.

[55] See H. Gottwald, 'Der Umfall des Zentrums. Die Stellung den Zentrumspartei zur Flottenvarlage von 1897', in F. Klein (Ed.), *Studien zum deutschen Imperialismus vor 1914* (Berlin, 1976), pp. 181–224; J. K. Zeender, *The German Centre Party 1890–1906* (Philadelphia 1976), pp. 63ff.

in the lower chamber.[56] Unless the Navy League was to isolate itself from potential support in the Catholic masses, it was clearly compelled to take some account of this special situation.

Indeed, these special 'Bavarian conditions' supplied the main imperative in the tactics of the Bavarian executive. In December 1899, for instance, Freiherr von Würtzburg accused the Presidium of pressing prematurely for the formation of a Bavarian section. This step should only be taken when the ground had been thoroughly prepared, for 'the conditions here are well-known to be very special—there are prejudices . . . to be overcome in certain quarters, and certain matters cannot be rushed'.

> In my view there is no point whatsoever in launching a naval movement in Bavaria which consists only of National Liberals, the supporters of a unitary Reich and migrants from North Germany. It is not simply a question of the number of members and the amount of money, but of *who* belongs to the organization. The essential thing must be to . . . win over those with little sympathy for the national cause. In this way we can try to raise matters of national defence above the bustle of the parties.

It was useless preaching only to the converted: to survive in Bavarian conditions the Navy League needed 'personalities from a different background, especially from the Centre and the particularists'. At the very least it needed 'a certain number of people from the circles currently dominant in Bavarian politics'.[57] Moreover, the foundation must be delayed until the official patronage of Prince Ludwig was secure, for this would be an indispensable aid to winning the sympathy of Catholics.[58] In the event the Bavarian executive was launched in March 1900 and although Prince Rupprecht, Ludwig's son, agreed to become Patron, Würtzburg's ideal conditions were hardly realized. The executive comprised mainly National Liberal businessmen, Bavarian officers, Pan-Germans and nationalist academics. The Navy League *was* preaching largely to the converted and only a handful of Centre supporters proved ready to join.[59]

To Würtzburg's later opponents this only showed the wrong-headedness of his conciliatory approach. Radical nationalists believed that the Centre would never commit itself properly to nationalist policies, regardless of how far the latter were diluted. In March 1903 August Keim stated this argument at some length. He told the Navy Office that all half-measures were useless and

[56] The most important recent study of the Centre in Bavarian politics is Möckl, *Prinzregentenzeit*.
[57] Würtzburg to Heeringen, Dec. 12th 1899, and Monts to Heeringen, Dec. 1st 1899, BA-MA Freiburg, 2379, 94741.
[58] Würtzburg to Heeringen, Dec. 12th 1899; Monts to Hohenlohe, Jan. 23rd 1900 and Feb. 7th 1900; Monts to Heeringen, Mar. 24th 1900, ibid.
[59] See the *Protokoll* of the constituent meeting, Munich, Mar. 4th 1900, and that of the larger Delegate Meeting on May 27th 1900, BA Coblenz, ZSg. 1, 195/2; Monts to Heeringen, Mar. 25th 1900, BA-MA Freiburg, 2379, 94741.

all 'so-called "tactical" considerations' irrelevant: they sacrificed fundamental principles for momentary advantage and were normally counter-productive. The Centre was the true obstacle to a rapid expansion of the Navy and was unreliable as a parliamentary pillar of government policy. 'The parliamentary situation', Keim argued, 'has a great deal in common with the time in autumn 1892 before the introduction of the Army Bill.' Then too the Centre had abused its parliamentary strength to deter the government from bringing in a vital measure for national defence, and then too the latter had been reluctant to test the strength of nationalist feeling by forcing new elections. Tirpitz's current difficulties in the Budget-Committee were merely the first signs that the Centre was preparing to desert the government again. But far from shirking an electoral confrontation, the Navy Office should gladly embrace it, for as in 1893 the government would return victorious from the polls, bearing a popular mandate for a new Bill.[60] As Tirpitz learned from one informant later that month, there were clearly elements in the Navy League pressing for an agitation *against* the government. Men like Keim were tired of playing 'servant to the Centre'. 'They miss energy, purpose and gravity in the leading personalities, including the Secretary of State, the Imperial Chancellor and His Majesty the Kaiser, the All-Highest Himself.'[61]

An important point begins to emerge from this juxtaposition of moderate and radical positions in the Navy League, namely that the national idea could be put to work in strikingly different ways, even within the limited context of a nationalist pressure group. The profound antagonism of the radical nationalists towards the Centre was a highly complex phenomenon. Partly it came from residual liberal hostility to the temporal power of the Catholic Church, above all its control of education; and the desire of 'liberal patriots' to secure 'freedom from the yoke of the Church' was clearly an important factor for many Navy League radicals.[62] A stronger motive was the desire to strengthen the authority of the state by eliminating the surviving intermediate jurisdictions of the Church, resolving the problem of divided loyalties between Church and State, and adapting the educational system to the needs of the latter as an instrument of conformity. Radical nationalists found it intolerable that the Catholic Church could still interpose itself between the nation-state and the undivided allegiance of its citizens.[63] But the immediate object of resentment was the

[60] Notes by Varrentrapp and Witzleben, Feb. 15th 1904, and Keim to Witzleben, Mar. 4th 1904, BA-MA Freiburg, 2277, 94234. See also Deist, 'Reichsmarineamt und Flottenverein', pp. 123f.

[61] Wenckstern to Tirpitz, Mar. 31st 1904, BA-MA Freiburg, 2277, 94234.

[62] See Stern to Tirpitz, Dec. 16th 1906, BA-MA Freiburg, 2244, 94040, for one of the clearest such formulations.

[63] For a powerful statement of this resentment, ibid. See also Claß, *Wider den Strom*, p. 9. This vigorous anti-clericalism in education made an interesting contrast with Würtzburg's Catholic traditionalism. He believed that 'the clergyman alone has the necessary general education . . . to instruct our youth and our people on these matters in the correct way'. See

7

Centre's power in the Reichstag—its ability to obstruct naval and military legislation. To Keim the party was purely confessional in its loyalties, owing respect to Rome rather than the Reich, belonging in the same category as the SPD, with which it often went 'arm-in-arm'.[64] It was 'anti-national' and opportunist, giving its votes to government and opposition in turn, depending on the source of greater sectional advantage. Radicals attacked Tirpitz most bitterly of all for allowing naval policy to become part of this 'cattle-trading' with the Centre, whilst the Bavarian executive were similarly maligned as tools of the party.[65]

The political sum of radical frustrations with the government was the demand for a showdown with the Centre. A big Navy programme should be announced, obstruction by the Centre should be met with an immediate dissolution, and new elections should be fought on the 'national issue' of support for the Navy. After a 'dissolution of the Reichstag under a naval slogan', Otto Stern argued, any dissident left liberals would 'simply disappear' and the Centre would be 'seriously weakened'. By neglecting the chance to solve his parliamentary problems once and for all, Tirpitz was 'evidently unfamiliar with the mood of his *own nation*'. He had surrendered 'his business to the masters of cattle-trading' and 'allowed the river of our national feelings to run into the sands'.[66] This drive towards confrontation reflected a vital difference between radical and moderate nationalists: whereas a style of political conciliation was axiomatic to Würtzburg and his allies, the radicals based their practice on a broad philosophy of struggle. Keim—the 'archetype of the dare-devil fire-eater' and a 'man of violence', who thought in military metaphors and believed that 'war is the father of all things'—was similar to his followers.[67] He saw the Navy League not as an instrument for carefully integrating the Centre within a broad national front, but as a weapon for driving it from its decisive parliamentary position. The ideology of *Weltpolitik* was to reduce the Centre's popular constituency and ensure a better mobilization of the other parties against it.

Boy-Ed's memo on Würtzburg for Tirpitz, Aug. 22nd 1906, BA-MA Freiburg, 2277, 94234. Keim, interestingly, also had a Catholic family background, with two sisters in convents. See Keim to Cardinal Fischer of Cologne, May 24th 1907, StA Coblenz, 403, 9529.

[64] Stern to Tirpitz, Dec. 16th 1906, BA-MA Freiburg, 2244, 94040.

[65] For a classic statement of the liberal and nationalist case against the Centre, see R. Böhmer, *Die Bedeutung und Aufgabe des nationalen Blocks im Reichstag, zugleich ein Beitrag zur Beurteilung und zum Verständnis in der Centrumspolitik* (Munich, 1907). See also Lerchenfeld to Podewils, June 5th 1905, BHSA Munich, I, M. Inn., 73547.

[66] Stern to Holleben, Nov. 19th 1905, BA-MA Freiburg, 2276, 94229.

[67] Junius Alter (Franz Sonntag), 'Kampfjahre der Vorkriegszeit', MS, p. 70, BA Coblenz, Junius Alter Papers, 6; Erdmann to Boy-Ed, July 8th 1908, BA-MA Freiburg, 2278, 94238. For good examples of Keim's manner of thinking: address to the Gen. Board, Berlin, Dec. 2nd 1905, *Verhandlungen*, pp. 1f., ibid., 2277, 94234; 'The Naval Question in Germany and England', in *Tag* (*rot*), Dec. 28th 1904; *Die Friedensbewegung und ihre Gefahren für das deutsche Volk* (Berlin, 1914); Keim to Bethmann Hollweg, Feb. 13th 1914, ZStA Potsdam, Rkz., 1415: 94.

For Würtzburg, by contrast, the Navy League's role was to draw the Centre into the nationalist consensus —gradually, peacefully and by careful persuasion. It was absurd, he insisted, to exclude an entire category of people from membership because they belonged to a particular party; it was equally rational to exclude people from a particular region, or farmers, or people who lived in the hills.[68] It was crude and short-sighted to 'brand' the supporters of the Centre 'permanently as national traitors'. It was only necessary to think of the 'history of the Thirty Years' War' to see the damage wrought by 'the exploitation of confessional differences for political ends', because hatred of the Centre was based on 'nothing less than this'. The Navy League's statutory aim was 'to unite all Germans without exception in a common effort for the interests of the fatherland'.[69] To succeed it needed to abstain from partisan agitation, for only thus would sceptics be rallied to the national flag. Likewise, particularist loyalties would disappear 'only through gradual habituation and economic adjustment, not in response to compulsion and abrasive criticism'.[70]

Mainly because of its much greater popularity and the political centrality of the naval question between 1897 and 1908, the Navy League generated this conflict of perspectives far more sharply than the other *nationale Verbände*. Formed in 1898, as we saw, from the nervous coalescence of separate initiatives and convulsed by a sharp crisis eighteen months later, it was then constantly the scene of bitter disputes between the radical majority and their moderate opponents; these ended in 1908 only with the withdrawal of the most pronounced radical nationalists, alienated by the enforced centrist manoeuvring of the governmental conservatives, and rapidly propelled into a coherent Pan-German philosophy of opposition. In many ways this reproduced the lines of conflict between the *Volkskolonialismus* of Carl Peters and the staider economic projections of the Colonial League in the 1880s: though the former was relocated in 1890–1 in the independent organization of the Pan-Germans, it still lingered in certain sections of the Colonial Society and resurfaced intermittently, in 1895–6, in 1904 and in 1907.[71] Taken as a whole, the history of the *nationale Verbände* contains an interesting pattern of right-wing dissidence which frequently proved acutely uncomfortable for the government: the Boer War agitation and the naval radicalism of 1903–8 were the two major instances. This again re-emphasizes the limitations of an integrationist notion of nationalism, because for every simple affirmative impulse which deferred to the government's tactical needs, there was a disruptive radical-nationalist counterpart which deliberately repudiated them. It suggests the political diversity of nationalist initiatives in public life, nationalism's disruptive as well as its

---

[68] Statement to the Bavarian Delegate Meeting, Munich, Dec. 29th 1907, reported by *MNN*, Dec. 31st 1907.
[69] Würtzburg to Boy-Ed, Aug. 21st 1908, BA-MA Freiburg, 2278, 94238.
[70] Hindenburg to Bülow, Apr. 8th 1908, ibid., 94237.
[71] See Pierard, 'German Colonial Society', pp. 170ff., 286ff., 312ff.

integrative potential, its ability to divide as well as unite the nation, even within the limited spectrum of the right. The nationalist factor in Wilhelmine politics cannot be easily reduced to a 'stabilizing' factor in the political system. On the contrary, it led to all sorts of conflicts within the right as to how far and in what ways the national idea could be exploited as an integrative force.

B. POPULISM

I

Earlier in this study it was observed that radical nationalists, particularly in the Navy League, were much more likely to be free of other political commitments than their moderate opponents, who by contrast were invariably active in party politics, often at a high level. This difference was sometimes articulated into a politico-ideological antagonism, through which the latter were arraigned as the representatives of an archaic *Honoratiorenpolitik*, unresponsive to the needs of popular politics. The previous chapter has also stressed at some length that the conscious nationalist commitments of activists in organizations like the *nationale Verbände* must be given proper weighting when trying to evaluate the political significance of their agitation. Putting these points together, we obtain a picture of the radical nationalists as a group of people for whom conventional orientations towards the parties or older 'corporate' institutions like the Army or the Civil Service were secondary concerns: their primary political loyalty was to an idea of the nation materially embodied in an agitational practice which was certainly anti-Socialist and potentially anti-parliamentary. But in trying to understand how such nationalist enthusiasts developed their commitments, existing approaches are not especially helpful, for they fail to identify what was special about radical nationalism as a Wilhelmine phenomenon. Instead they collapse it into an argument about the origins of nationalism in general.

To some extent the radical nationalists may be identified with a particular political generation, that for which unification (meaning not just the military struggles of 1864–71, but also the *Kulturkampf* and the Anti-Socialist Law) was a formative ideological experience. They passed through school and university during the Bismarckian years and qualified professionally at the onset of Caprivi's 'new course'. Their political maturity coincided with both the ideological shock of Bismarck's fall and the aggressive cultural expectations released by the end of the depression and the inauguration of *Weltpolitik*. Given the difficulties of the National Liberals in adjusting to the needs of the new popular politics, moreover, it is perhaps easy enough to see radical nationalism as the political ideology of a marginal generation, disoriented by the removal of Bismarck and denied political access by the ingrained etiquette of *Honoratiorenpolitik*.

There is much biographical evidence for this view. Thus in his autobiography Heinrich Claß reflected that three ideals characterized the liberalism of his father's generation—'patriotism, tolerance, humanity'—and all three contributed to the principle of the 'equality of all citizens before the law'. However, 'we youngsters had moved on: we were national pure and simple. We wanted nothing to do with tolerance if it sheltered the enemies of the people and the state. Humanity in the sense of that liberal idea we spurned, for our own people were bound to come off worse.'[72] Claß's own generation retained a belief in progress, economic growth and cultural mission, and continued to vote for the National Liberals. Yet on the other hand they displayed a pervasive commitment to the intellectual and political primacy of nationalist goals which made them very different from, say, the post-Gladstonian generation in Britain. In explaining this *Primat des Nationalen* the idea of generational anomie can take us only so far, for the latter might send people in any number of political directions. To pin the radical nationalists down we must look more closely at the content of their ideas and the circumstances under which they were formed.

In so doing it is very easy to relapse into a purely descriptive survey of right-wing beliefs in general. Again, the existing literature is not very helpful on this score. A common procedure has been to concentrate on those ideas in the Wilhelmine period which seem to have presaged the beliefs of the Nazis: e.g. 'nineteenth-century racial doctrine, Germanic Christianity, nature mysticism, sun worship and theosophy'.[73] Traces are then uncovered in every corner of Wilhelmine literary culture, so that racists, anthropologists, folklorists, *Heimatkünstler*, land-reformers, communitarians, educational visionaries, free-thinkers, aesthetes, prophets of youth, mystics, Swedenborgians, occultists, new romantics, anti-semites and Pan-Germans are all co-opted willy-nilly to form a wholly artificial composite of 'the German ideology', which is then identified with the political culture in general.[74] Quite apart from the problems of measuring and interpreting the influence of the ideas concerned, this does enormous violence to their actual meanings in the Wilhelmine context. The desire to make Wilhelmine intellectual history obey an iron logic of proto-Nazi development is clearest and most pernicious in Anglo-American discussions of the idea of the *Volk*, which have normally reflected the belief in a peculiar mystical tradition of thinking about racial or national matters in Germany linking Nazism to early nineteenth-century romanticism. In this vein historians normally speak of *völkisch* or 'folkish' ideology. Yet in reality the term *Volk* had the same double connotations of 'national' and 'popular' that can be found in other countries as well. When German politicians referred to the *Volk* at the turn of the century they meant the 'people', though as in other countries the specific ideological charge this carried varied widely. In other words,

---

[72] Claß, *Wider den Strom*, p. 17.
[73] Quoted from the blurb of Mosse, *Crisis of German Ideology*.
[74] Ibid., pp. 13–148 ('The Ideological Foundations').

different circumstances and a complex process of ideological transformation were needed before the Nazis could appropriate the term and inject it with their own meanings. If we talk too uncritically of some distinctive *völkisch* ideology before 1914, this process of ideological struggle may be obscured and later Nazi meanings may be misleadingly read back into an earlier and different discourse.[75]

This slight digression is necessary because the temptation is enormous to assimilate the ideas of the radical nationalists (especially those of the Pan-Germans) to this kind of catch-all 'tradition'. There is of course no question that racist and irrationalist forms of *völkisch* ideology existed in Wilhelmine Germany, whether in the Pan-German League and the German-Union, in the organs of intellectual Anti-Semitism, or in the apparatus of the Agrarian League.[76] But it is doubtful whether they carried the weight of explanatory importance some historians have tried to attribute to them. These efforts misdirect our attention to idealist continuities and make it far harder to appreciate that the dominant ideologies of the Wilhelmine right were actually generated by specific political conflicts *inside* the Wilhelmine period itself. Moreover, they also stereotype radical nationalism as an ideology which was backward-looking and 'anti-modern' in that it supposedly embraced the superior morality of 'pre-industrial' values, anti-urban feelings and organicist notions of traditional community. Yet this stereotype, though it clearly has some purchase on large parts of the agrarian movement and the *Mittelstand*, is singularly inappropriate when applied to the nationalist pressure groups and their ideology.

This can be shown quite easily by the example of Friedrich Lange, a central figure in the world of the *Verbände* before 1914. Anti-semite, and believer in a Germanic 'aristocracy of race', author of a well-known racist tract and founder of the German-Union, the small Pan-German-like sect that managed to combine mystic crankiness with the clear-headed pursuit of anti-Socialist unity, Lange was superficially a prime candidate for the proto-Nazi pantheon.[77] Yet on closer inspection he turns out to have been a far more complex figure. Thus he specifically repudiated that 'ecstacy of habitual German patriotism' and 'beloved self-deception' which looked backwards to the tradition of 'Arndt, Jahn and Körner', and insisted that the nationalist tasks of the Wilhelmine era were fundamentally different.[78] He denied that the German-Union was 'a refuge for *Deutschtümelei*' and countered that 'it knows how to think *modern*'.[79] One of his favourite issues was that of school reform, initiating the movement

---

[75] For useful guidance on this matter, see W. Emmerich, *Zur Kritik der Volkstumsideologie* (Frankfurt, 1970), and K. Lenk, *'Volk und Staat'. Strukturwandel politischer Ideologien im 19. und 20. Jahrhunderten* (Stuttgart, 1971).

[76] For a useful introduction: Lohalm, *Völkischer Radikalismus*, pp. 27–77.

[77] See *Reines Deutschtum. Grundzüge einer nationalen Weltanschauung* (3rd ed., Berlin, 1904), which is the best source for Lange's ideas and career.

[78] Ibid., pp. 338f., XV.

[79] Ibid., p. 375.

in the 1880s and helping to launch the Society for School Reform in 1889: this was partly a desire to 'Germanize' the classical education, but the central demands for a modern syllabus and the unitary grammar school also reflected more technocratic concerns with national efficiency.[80] Moreover, his critique of Christianity and search for a new secular religion of nationality, with its stress on the 'native idealism of our popular stock', had much in common with the cultural criticism of the non-SPD Left: in 1893 his anti-capitalist and anti-clerical play *Der Nächste* was performed by the New Free People's Theatre in Berlin.[81] Lange's advocacy of a 'national socialism', which he characterized as 'economic nationalism combined with a better balance between work and leisure', certainly had a prophetic ring. But when we also find him speaking of 'natural science and socialism' as 'the main levers of recent time', we should perhaps pause before assimilating him too easily to an irrationalist pre-history of Nazi ideology.[82] His ideas are not to be located midway on a continuum between Romanticism and Nazism. They were a complex amalgam of 'progressive' and 'reactionary' motifs which was *sui generis* in the sense that it was determined by a particular set of historical pressures between the 1880s and 1914.

The aim of this chapter and of the following one is to explore this specificity. This will not be done descriptively, because any 'total' account of the ideas held by radical nationalists in general would rapidly turn into the mere mélange of disparate sub-ideologies mentioned above, which provides no insight into the source of their operative cohesion at the higher level of politics. In other words, the aim of what follows is to uncover the common preoccupation which constituted radical nationalism as a distinctive political formation. This takes us right to the heart of the problem of this book. As we saw, the 1890s began a far-reaching process of political redefinition, through which a diverse movement of rural discontent was gradually rationalized into a single 'agrarian interest' under conservative auspices, and the *Mittelstand* simultaneously constructed ideologically as an object of conservative politics.[83] As Puhle has shown, for the

[80] Ibid., pp. 287–346. Lange enjoyed close links with the Society of German Engineers. The contrast with, say, Treitschke on this matter is striking: see for instance the passages on education in H. Kohn (Ed.), *Politics. Heinrich von Treitschke* (New York, 1963), esp. pp. 153–60. E.g. 'Not one of the errors of modern Liberalism is more ridiculous than the idea of unified schools' . . . 'No substitute will ever be found for an education in Latin and Greek' . . . 'Creatively it (the State) can do very little; its main object must be to discover genius.'

[81] R. Pascal, *From Naturalism to Expressionism. German Literature and Society 1880–1918* (London, 1973), p. 88. See Lange, *Reines Deutschtum*, pp. 110ff.

[82] Ibid., pp. 147, 72, X, VIII. Lange's career reveals a highly complex ideological formation which requires extended analysis of its own beyond the confines of this study.

[83] i.e. the *Mittelstand* was fetishized by conservative politics into a social category which bore no necessary resemblance to the real social relations which defined the traditional petty-bourgeoisie at this time. It was an irony of Wilhelmine politics that the *Mittelstand* was idealized by the right as a source of social stability just at the moment that it was ceasing to constitute a stable social grouping. See above all Blackbourn, *'Mittelstand'*.

Conservative Party this movement into popular politics represented both a broadening of the social base and a radicalization of political style.[84] If we are to explain how, in spite of the National Liberal Party's half-hearted involvement until after 1907, the urban bourgeoisie and petty-bourgeoisie were similarly won in large numbers for the right, then it is on an equivalent process of *ideological construction* that we must focus. The more exotic mystic ideologies and racial doctrines clearly brought many individuals into the right in this sense, and both anti-semitism and the different forms of land settlement both had a broader appeal to large numbers of urban craftsmen, small businessmen and white-collar employees. But if the latter were to join arms with the more fastidious members of the *Bildungsbürgertum*, some larger unifying vision would be required.

In other words, it is important to establish clear priorities when examining the formal beliefs of the Wilhelmine right. It is less important to discuss the considerable permutations of particular ideas than to uncover the *process* which articulated them into a fully political position, i.e. one which was capable of catching not only the relatively conscious ideologues, but also the more diffuse commitments of ordinary teachers, lawyers, civil servants and other professional and managerial types. To do this it is worth looking in more detail at the problem of populism. An appeal to the will of the people was an organizing theme in the history of radical nationalism before 1914. At each point of serious conflict with the government or the political establishment the higher legitimacy of the people's purpose tended to be invoked. This was something quite new for the right. Appeals to the national interest were naturally the common stuff of German politics, but in the official language of Wilhelmine conservatism these normally appeared as references to a harmony of interests or 'estates'. The rhetorical syntax of *Sammlungspolitik* left no room for any notion of popular legitimacy as such. The political novelty of radical nationalism was not only that it instated such a notion in the practice of the right, but that it did so in antagonism against the latter's existing institutions. The nature of this antagonism is the object of the following discussion.

II

For reasons already outlined in previous chapters the Navy League provides the best material for exploring this problem. Whereas the Pan-Germans formulated an ideology of national opposition more consciously and systematically, for instance, they also demarcated themselves quite sharply from the political establishment. In the Navy League, by contrast, the conflict between old and new right occurred inside the ranks of the movement itself, generated originally by relatively unpromising arguments over naval policy and propaganda tactics:

[84] Puhle, *Agrarische Interessenpolitik*, pp. 274–89, and 'Der Bund der Landwirte im Wilhelminischen Reich', in Rüegg and Neuloh, *Zur Soziologischen Theorie*, pp. 145–62.

because the antagonism was born of political experience itself, it touched people who might otherwise have remained indifferent to formal appeals of a Pan-German kind.

The conflict in the Navy League began with different interpretations of the organization's 'non-political' status.[85] One group in the movement, moderate and governmental by inclination, took this to mean total abstention from political involvement, demanding that the Navy League confine itself to purely 'educational' propaganda based on the dissemination of given information. 'Technical' matters involving the details of naval policy and relations with the parties were the preserve of government. However, acquiescence in the superior technical competence of the Navy Office was itself clearly a political stance. The underlying anti-Socialist bias was clear, but it also worked to the advantage of the Centre Party and of an official strategy of conciliating the latter rather than opposing it. This was particularly marked in Bavaria, as we saw, where the Centre's regional dominance imposed a clear pattern on the Navy League's public policy. Unless the League tried to accommodate the Centre's predilections, it would simply isolate itself from the potential support of the Catholic population. Accordingly, the movement had to move with 'a certain *prudence and consideration*', as Würtzburg put it. It should not merely reinforce the sympathies of supporters, but should aim for the 'great crowd of voters' who were still hostile. This implied restraint, tactical caution and a systematic attempt to convince waverers, sceptics and critics, or 'to fish on the edges of the opposition', as Hermann Rassow put it.[86]

This was where conflict arose. On both scores—accommodation of the Centre, a propaganda style of political conciliation—the moderates were in a clear minority, based mainly in the Catholic South and those areas directly accessible to government influence. The radical majority, which controlled the Presidium from around 1901, took a very different view of their role. Where the moderates coaxed and conciliated, the radicals preferred to coerce. As one of them put it: ' . . . the path to the national consolidation and integration of all Germans . . . leads not through the utopia of peaceful conciliatory persuasion, but only through the violent destruction of the Centre Party'.[87] Radical-nationalist hostility went further to embrace antagonism to the parliamentary system and to the entire institutional fabric of the conventional party-political process. The Centre was attacked as the most obvious instance of a larger system of parliamentary 'cattle-trading' which sacrificed the national interest for the sake

[85] The 'non-political' clause in the Navy League's Constitution was partly an ideological demarcation from the sphere of 'party-political' activity, and partly a technical concession to the law of association. For a contemporary discussion: G. Kuttner, *Politische Vereine und der Deutsche Flottenverein* (Hannover, 1909).

[86] Address to Bavarian Del. Meeting, Munich, May 29th 1904, *Verhandlungen*, p. 20, BA-MA Freiburg, 2276, 94229; Hermann Rassow in the Gen. Board, Dresden, Apr. 16th 1904, *Verhandlungen*, p. 16, BA Coblenz, ZSg. 1, 195/2.

[87] Stern to Presidium, Apr. 23rd 1907, BHSA Munich, II, Ges. Berlin, 1158.

7*

of momentary sectional advantage. Radical statements were full of rhetorical animus against this 'disagreeable fraction-dogmatism' and the power of the 'German fraction-philistine' to obstruct Germany's nationalist revival. Party debate was stigmatized as 'feeble-minded dogmatism', which militated against a true nationalist consciousness.[88] This was sometimes carried to extreme lengths, as in this statement by a Wiesbaden headmaster: 'Parties cramp the personality of man, parties circumscribe freedom, parties subject us to the will of another. That's why I would like us all to get out of the parties. No more parties! We are not *party-political*.'[89]

The conflict worked on several different levels. At that of formal debate it involved such issues as the amount of consideration due to government policy and to the predilections of the Centre, the exact meaning of the 'non-political' status, the correct style of propaganda, and so on. But these conflicts also implied deeper ideological divisions. As suggested the radicals evolved a general philosophy of confrontation and an angry critique of ordinary parliamentary politics. They gradually incorporated these attitudes into a larger offensive against the political establishment as a whole, whom they accused of debilitating caution, social élitism, blindness to Germany's national needs, and a refusal to obey the dictates of the new mass politics. In turn the moderate minority threw these accusations back and denounced the politics of the radicals with several broad pejoratives: chauvinist because they poisoned Germany's relations with the British; demagogic because they overrode opposition with extravagant appeals to imponderable popular sentiments; and, most interestingly of all, democratic because they appealed over the heads of the government and party leaders to the masses and threatened to erode popular belief in the monarchy.[90] This last was especially important, because the tendency of the royal patrons to enter the conflict on the side of the minority drew the fire of the radicals upon them, and began a debate which brought into question the very strongest of conventional loyalties. Radical spokesmen accused Würtzburg and his fellow moderates of hiding behind the backs of the patrons, and flung out the politically explosive taunt of 'Byzantinism', or subservience to established royal authority, the persistence of a 'narrow subject-mentality'.[91]

[88] The phrases are taken partly from Stroschein, *Manuskript: Die Begründung*, BA-MA Freiburg, 2276, 94227, and partly from the following: Stern to Holleben, Nov. 19th 1905, ibid., 94229; circular letter by Heydweiller, May 1907, StA Hamburg, DFV, III, 49.

[89] Breuer (Wiesbaden) in the Danzig Congress, June 14th 1908, *Protokoll*, p. 12, BA-MA Freiburg, 2278, 94237.

[90] For more detail, see Eley, 'German Navy League', pp. 201–33. But see especially the explicit statements in Würtzburg to Boy-Ed, Apr. 5th 1908, and the three undated memoranda sent by Würtzburg to Boy-Ed on Mar. 15th 1908, all ibid.

[91] See for instance Keim's comments in the Gen. Board, Berlin, Dec. 2nd 1905, *Verhandlungen*, p. 6. ibid., 2277, 94234. It was ironic that liberal Anglo-American critics of the German government system during the First World War used the same term of 'Byzantinism'. Thus to characterize German authoritarian mentalities they appropriated precisely the term used

The readiness of the radical nationalists to question old sources of political legitimacy by evincing the principle that 'above the person must stand the dynasty, and above the dynasty the welfare of the people', as one of them put it, suggested the deeper significance of the conflict.[92] Their attacks on the 'Byzantinism' of the moderates only drove the latter to further extremes of élitist hostility to calls for 'popular' participation. Thus Würtzburg described these as 'nauseous' suggestions, which 'mocked the holiest sentiments of the nation' and played directly into the hands of the Socialists.[93] Another moderate bemoaned the 'deplorable spectacle of such a momentous national organization, beneath the leadership of an aristocratic President, being driven into the democratic waters—as if there were not enough destructive forces at work in the German Reich, already engaged in undermining the existing order.'[94] The moderate position was guided by an unequivocal élitist suspicion of the masses. Their opposition to radical nationalism sprang from a profound social conceit. Important decisions, delicate issues, vital problems of national security —serious politics—must be left to people qualified by experience, understanding and social rank to solve them. Würtzburg bared the social assumptions of his politics in one intemperate outburst in January 1908: 'I did not form my opinions in the Munich *Hofbräuhaus*, but thought it my duty to talk things over with the Secretaries of State for the Navy and the Treasury before coming to a conclusion.' Before opposing the Presidium he had been sure to discuss things with 'other statesmen' and 'outstanding members of the movement'.[95] This contrasted sharply with the self-image of the radicals, one of whom declared in reply: 'I am a man from the people, who grows his cabbage, and sometimes also speaks.'[96]

III

How do we characterize the ideological significance of this conflict in the Navy League? In the first place it registered a break with the previous thinking of radical nationalists. The Pan-Germans had certainly stressed the importance of the *Volk* and the centrality of popular mobilization for any genuine nationalist

---

by the most radical wing of the German right. E.g. W. H. Dawson, *What is Wrong with Germany?* (London, 1915), pp. 89–112 (Ch. V, 'Kaiserism and Byzantinism'). See also E. zu Reventlow, *Wilhelm II und die Byzantiner* (Berlin, 1906).

[92] Reismann-Grone in the Pan-German Committee, Leipzig, Nov. 4th 1908, *Protokoll*, ZStA Potsdam, ADV, 62: 32.

[93] See the statements by Würtzburg and Braun in the Cassel Congress, Jan. 19th 1908, *Verhandlungen*, pp. 10, 37ff., GLA Karlsruhe, 69P, 8.

[94] Röper (Berlin–Brandenburg) to Bülow, Dec. 21st 1907, ZStA Potsdam, Rkz., 2261: 203ff.

[95] Statement to Cassel Congress, Jan. 19th 1908, *Verhandlungen*, p. 11, GLA Karlsruhe, 69P, 8.

[96] Heydweiller, ibid., p. 14.

revival. But after the early optimism of the 1890s a mixture of factors—the stagnation of membership, competition from other nationalist groups, the hostility of the government, and so on—had shaken their confidence in popular intelligence. By 1904 Hasse had come to regard the prospects of immediate Pan-German success with some resignation: 'For in the end every people has the government it deserves. We have to work on our dull-witted, politically child-like German people. And for the forseeable future that will be the life-work and *raison d'être* of the Pan-German League.'[97] Moreover, the corollary of this was an increasing recourse to educational work—'the literary cultivation of the educated classes in a Pan-German direction'[98]—which militated against direct political activity. Despite an important debate in 1904 concerning the means of re-politicizing Pan-German propaganda, there was no genuine upswing in the political morale of the movement until 1908. Here the contrast with radical nationalists in the Navy League could not have been greater. Where Hasse and his colleagues bemoaned the political immaturity of the German nation and scaled down their expectations of nationalist regeneration, August Keim and his supporters revealed naïve but unbounded confidence in popular vitality. In the opinion of the latter huge reserves of popular enthusiasm were waiting to be tapped by enterprising politicians, but this was unfortunately prevented by an alliance of self-seeking parliamentarians and a faint-hearted government.

By displacing responsibility from the nation itself on to a corrupt parliamen-tarism, radical nationalists in the Navy League restored a faith in the short-term potential of popular nationalism at a time when the morale of the Pan-Germans was at a low ebb. Their answer to moderate calls for political conciliation and unobtrusive 'educational' work was scathing. For Eduard von Liebert this was just *Vereinsmeierei*—'clubbery', or an effete messing-around with the formalities and rituals of voluntary association, a trivial, frivolous occupation, in which 'aesthetic lectures' were given before an 'educated audience of invited guests'.[99] Too often the Navy League's meetings degenerated into colourful social occasions, where naval plays, sea-shanties, exotic slides and late-night dancing replaced serious discussions about the Navy. Victor Schweinburg, writing at a safe distance from any formal association, attacked the attempt to depoliticize the Navy League at some length. It 'was not founded', he said, 'in order to make a big noise once a year, to send a telegram to the Kaiser, and at the end of the great feast to sing *Lieb Vaterland, magst ruhig sein* through a drunken haze'. On the contrary, 'the real object was to unite everyone who call themselves national in order to lead them at the right moment into

---

[97] Hasse to Petzold, Apr. 5th 1904, ZStA Potsdam, ADV, 188: 303f.; also Hasse to Ellen-beck, Nov. 10th 1903, ibid., 187: 300ff.

[98] Langhans to Hasse, Mar. 19th 1904, ibid., 188: 216f.

[99] Comments in the Gen. Board, Berlin, Dec. 2nd 1905, *Verhandlungen*, p. 6, BA-MA Freiburg, 2277, 94234.

the struggle against the anti-national and treasonous Social Democrats'. If the League held back from vigorous agitation because it might offend vested interests and involve the movement in 'politics', it would negate its own real aim. 'This whole *Vereinsmeierei* of ours, that calls itself national and royalist and whatever else, is a farce if it refuses to get involved in politics on the grounds that it is unconstitutional.'[100]

To postulate a clear political goal in this way, whether anti-Socialism or a larger naval programme, required a different kind of agitation. The movement had to break the bounds of the closed lecture meeting and carry its message into new territory. As Keim said at the crucial General Board meeting in December 1905 which inaugurated a new agitational line, 'the German Navy League cannot prosper as a shrinking-violet; it is also a movement of struggle and therefore, when necessary, it must go over to the offensive.'[101] The Navy League was to be converted into an instrument of political pressure. It should cease to be a mere vehicle for the transmission of a predetermined orthodoxy, for the dissemination of ideas legitimated in the government and the Reichstag. Instead it should conceive its own ideas, formulate its own policy, and fight for its acceptance by the government and the parties. As Liebert said: 'We must influence the people, the great masses, and not only the intelligentsia, who sometimes don't even bother to vote in elections'; the efforts should be concentrated on workers' associations and veterans' clubs.[102] As another radical put it: 'We must get involved in politics. Lantern-slides and dancing are of no use to the movement, they lead only to the castration of the *Volk*.'[103]

This constant reference to the 'people' in the political vocabulary of the radical nationalists is extremely important. It was counter-posed deliberately as an ideal alternative to the established institutions—the Reichstag, the parties, and then eventually also the federal states, the princes and by extension the Kaiser himself—which had allegedly inserted themselves between the people and its government. The latter was accused of failing to detect the popular mood and, even worse, of deliberately ignoring the manifest popular will. This belief, that government has been alienated from its proper source of final legitimacy, the people's will, was implicit in the polemical dichotomy of *Regierungsverein* and *Volksverein*, which had already been formulated in 1899. Radical statements were riddled with intimations of this kind, in which homage was paid to the 'free will of the people'.[104] It explained the repeated juxtaposition of 'the independent national consciousness of the free man' with 'courtly Byzantinism'

[100] *Berliner Politische Nachrichten*, cit. by *DortmZ*, Feb. 27th 1907.

[101] Statement to the Gen. Board, Berlin, Dec. 2nd 1905, *Verhandlungen,* p. 7, BA-MA Freiburg, 2277, 94234.

[102] Ibid., p. 6.

[103] J. Couvreur in the Gen. Board, Berlin, Apr. 12th 1908, Cancrin's report for Stabel, Apr. 15th 1908, GLA Karlsruhe, 69P, 1.

[104] H. Oberwinder, *Nationale Politik und Parteipolitik. Ein Beitrag zur Geschichte des Deutschen Flottenvereins* (Dresden, 1907), p. 54.

in their arguments.[105] For radical nationalists the Navy League was a genuine *Volksverein*, capable of carrying the naval idea 'to every quarter of the German people, right down to the tiniest hut', and of realizing the idea 'that each individual shares in the responsibility for the fate of the German people far into the distant future'.[106] It would show the government 'what the German people needed—courtly sneaks, empty-headed jingoes and undignified sycophants, or independent citizens, intrepid patriots and responsible tribunes of the people?'[107]

For radical nationalists the essential component of the organization's make-up was its popular character—its *Volkstümlichkeit*. Without this it would be 'degraded more and more into an organization of crawlers' until it was just an exclusive social club, rather like the 'Imperial Automobile Club of Berlin'.[108] A notion of popular intervention in politics, however symbolic, was central to their commitment. Their idea of the *Volk* derived its special force from a comparison with the political values of their moderate opponents. The radicals constructed their ideology from an angry revulsion against 'political careerists and wire-pullers, tub-thumpers, phrase-mongers without aim, warmth, clarity', from a disillusioning encounter with a conservative governing class, steeped in tradition, breathing circumspection, nervous of the vulgarities of mass politics.[109] They castigated their opponents for ignoring the fact that 'the masses have come of age (through elementary schooling, mass conscription, universal suffrage and the cheap oil-lamp)'.[110] 'Parts of our fatherland', Heinrich Oberwinder observed, 'are unfortunately still dominated by traditional bureaucratic residues of the "narrow subject-mentality".' The radicals accused their opponents of obstructing 'the *elevation* of all parts of our nation to consultation and *participation* in national matters'. For many this was more than the aggregate of their experiences in the Navy League alone. Oberwinder had a long history of involvement in popular movements, from the Lassallean labour movement to the abortive populist excursions of Stöcker and Naumann twenty-five years later.[111] For Reismann-Grone, on the other hand, the Navy League was always a secondary concern, subordinate to the higher vision of building the Pan-German League into 'a powerful *Volksverein*'.[112] But despite the diversity of

---

[105] 'A Victory for the Independents' (leading article), *RWZ*, June 15th 1908; statement by Oscar Martens to the Cassel Congress, Jan. 19th 1908, *Verhandlungen*, p. 40, GLA Karlsruhe, 69P, 8.

[106] Statement by Völzing to the Danzig Congress, June 14th 1908, *Protokoll*, p. 12, BA-MA Freiburg, 2278, 94237.

[107] 'The Victory in Danzig' (leading article), *RWZ*, June 16th 1908.

[108] 'The Catastrophe in the German Navy League' (leading article), *DVC*, Jan. 14th 1908.

[109] Comment by Reismann-Grone in his diary, SA Essen, Reismann-Grone Papers, 10, IX. 1897. 7f.

[110] Rassow to Tirpitz, Apr. 12th 1898, BA-MA Freiburg, 2223, 93943.

[111] Oberwinder, *Nationale Politik*, pp. 17, 21, 43ff.

[112] SA Essen, Reismann-Grone Papers, 10, IX. 1898. 12.

their backgrounds, the radicals united against the conventional politicians, who would 'not understand that the caste-spirit in the upper strata has nourished the class-spirit in the lower, and that an obstinate persistence in the old mistakes has aided and abetted the alienation of the masses from the state and the monarchy'.[113]

This was not mere rhetoric, but an accurate representation of the way in which radical nationalists experienced their relation to the governing bloc and its politics. That empirically they did *not* speak for 'the people' is in this context hardly the point. By virtue of the Navy League's mass membership they claimed an access to the people's purpose which the government had in their view lost and which the latter's allies were attempting to block. In this situation to invoke the legitimacy of the people was implicitly to query that of the government. Moreover, radical nationalists insisted that the Navy League was constitutionally organized for participation, and when the moderate minority started to disobey Congress resolutions there was much talk of majority decisions and their binding character. This meticulous attention to procedural correctness in recording the membership's views in resolutions and votes was a salient feature of the lengthy crisis in 1907–9. In this and other ways the political invocation of the people became embodied in a practice which at the very least posed new tasks for the governing bloc and at worst challenged the latter's political authority. In other words, by constituting 'the people' as an independent factor in such a central matter of government policy as the naval programme, the radical nationalists ceased merely 'educating' the populace in the value of sea-power and inaugurated a new mode of political practice for the right.

This commitment to popular independence was at its sharpest in the attempts to rebuff royal interference in 1907–8, when the Patron of the Bavarian Navy League Prince Rupprecht tried to prevent the election of August Keim to a leading position in the national Presidium. J. F. Lehmann, the Pan-German publisher in Munich, argued that the Presidium had been 'guided by the conviction that a *Volksverein* must have the absolute right to take decisions according to its feelings. Otherwise it exposes itself to the danger of acting after the wishes of its twenty royal patrons rather than its own convictions.'[114] As another of Keim's backers put it: 'When German citizens work together for a great goal, they should not burden their cause with too much royal sponsorship.'[115] At a general meeting in Anhalt one speaker, a retired officer called Bismarck, deplored the fact 'that one had to make allowance for royal persons; he wished he could get rid of them. In this case the royal patronage had really shown itself a liability to the cause.'[116] It only required the gross indiscretions

---

[113] Oberwinder, *Nationale Politik*, p. 20.
[114] Minutes of the Gen. Meeting of the Munich branch, Lehmann to Boy-Ed, Dec. 20th 1907, BA-MA Freiburg, 2277, 94235.
[115] *Westfälische Politische Nachrichten*, statement reprinted in *DortmZ*, Dec. 23rd 1907.
[116] Report in *Anhaltischer Staats-Anzeiger*, Jan. 5th 1908.

and political ineptitude revealed by the Daily-Telegraph Affair in November 1908, immediately after the crisis in the Navy League, for the fire of the radical nationalists to be trained on the person of the Kaiser himself. Ludwig Redebold, a Pan-German teacher in Dortmund, captured the political logic of such attacks quite well. After quoting Gobineau on the rights of a people to overthrow a failed leader, he invoked 'the right to rise against the monarch (see the English Revolution) lest he overturn all the positive value that the monarchy has created'.[117]

IV

To make sense of this pattern of popular politics on the right, it is worth exploring the concept of populism, even though it is notoriously hard to define. At one level it is perfectly possible to construct a general typology broad enough to cover most recognized examples of populist movements. One such attempt proposes a familiar check-list of factors, describing populism as: 'moralistic rather than programmatic'; 'loosely organized and ill-disciplined', with a mystical notion of leadership; 'anti-intellectual'; 'strongly opposed to the Establishment', particularly the military and church; hostile to science and technology, with 'a strong tendency to mild racialism'; normally but not necessarily rural, bound to 'tradition and small enterprise', with ideals of economic co-operation between small owners; and so on. Together they may be condensed into the 'major premise' that 'virtue resides in the simple people, who are the overwhelming majority, and in their collective traditions'.[118] A slightly different definition identifies populism with two basic themes: the supremacy of the people's will 'over every other standard, over the standards of traditional institutions and over the will of other strata'; and the belief in a direct relationship between the people and its government, uncluttered by mediating institutions.[119] This set of attitudes—'a syndrome, not a doctrine', in Wiles's phrase—may appear in movements of such widely differing social bases and under such a variety of historical conditions, it is argued, that no reliable generalizations about its social determination can strictly be advanced. But the problem with such definitions, which try to evaluate populism mainly as ideology, is precisely their descriptive character. They enable us to recognize populist appearances without helping to explain their existence. They are silent as to why and how the discrete characteristics in the typology combine together in specific historical situations.

---

[117] Redebold to Claß, Nov. 3rd 1908, ZStA Potsdam, ADV, 67: 19ff.

[118] P. Wiles, 'A Syndrome not a Doctrine: Some Elementary Theses on Populism', in E. Gellner and G. Ionescu (Eds.), *Populism. Its Meanings and National Characteristics* (London, 1969), pp. 167–71, 166.

[119] E. Shils, *The Torment of Secrecy. The Background and Consequences of American Security Policies* (London, 1956), pp. 98–104.

However, within such descriptive definitions there is invariably a series of assumptions which effectively reinstates a sociological interpretation.[120] For instance: populist movements are held to be composed mainly of 'traditional' elements caught in a process of 'modernization' (e.g. peasants and farmers, artisans and small traders, recent migrants to the towns), or of 'marginal groups' in more developed societies who become disadvantaged or disoriented by some form of crisis.[121] By far the commonest approach, in fact, has been a sociological search for similarities in the social bases of populist movements, or at least in the 'social situations', 'levels of development' etc. at which such movements have occurred. The most sophisticated version has defined populism as 'an aberrant phenomenon produced by the asynchronism of the processes of transition from a traditional to an industrial society'.[122] In Western Europe, it is argued, this transition was successfully negotiated through two stages of political integration: 'democracy with limited participation and democracy with total participation'. In the second such stage the ability of a society to 'modernize' itself politically is determined by the 'degree of correspondence between the gradual mobilization of an increasing proportion of the population . . . and the emergence of multiple mechanisms of integration—trade unions, education, social legislation, political parties, mass consumption—capable of absorbing these successive groups, providing them with means for adequate self-expression'. When the masses were mobilized too quickly, in advance of the adaptive mechanisms, political instability and crisis were the result. In this view, populism emerged when 'the premature incorporation of the masses into . . . political life created a pressure which went beyond the channels of absorption and participation which the political structures were able to provide'.[123] This left the masses without suitable autonomous organizations for representing their interests in the political system, it is argued, and left them easy prey to the manipulative designs of 'traditional élites'.

There are recognizable echoes of this approach in Wilhelmine historiography. On the one hand, it approximates superficially to what actually happened to

---

[120] This is particularly true of Macrae's contribution to the Gellner and Ionescu symposium: 'But surely we will automatically and correctly use the term populist when, under the threat of some kind of modernization, industrialism, call it what you will, a predominantly agricultural segment of society asserts as its charter of political action a belief in a community and (usually) a *Volk* as uniquely virtuous, is egalitarian and against all and any elite, looks to a mythical past to regenerate the present and confound usurpation and alien conspiracy . . .' In the quotation the operative phrase is 'under the threat of modernization'. See D. Macrae, 'Populism as an Ideology', in Gellner and Ionescu, *Populism*, p. 163.

[121] See A. Stewart, 'The Social Roots', ibid., pp. 180–96.

[122] E. Laclau, 'Towards a Theory of Populism', in *Politics and Ideology in Marxist Theory*, p. 147, contains an excellent critique of this approach, from which the following exposition is mainly taken.

[123] G. Germani, *Politica y Sociedad en una epoca de transicion* (Buenos Aires, 1965), p. 154, cit. by Laclau, 'Towards a Theory of Populism', pp. 149f.

the political system between the late 1880s and 1914: social change did out-
strip the capacities of the Bismarckian parties to absorb its impact, and until
they had reformed their practice to accommodate the aspirations of freshly
mobilized strata there was much instability in the system—inside individual
parties, in the relations between them, and in the parliamentary affairs of the
government. On the other hand, German historians have for some years used a
similar notion of 'asynchronism' to explain the much-vaunted persistence of
'authoritarian and anti-democratic structures in state and society' in a period
of industrial growth.[124] Here the argument is given an interesting twist:
German society failed to develop the necessary 'mechanisms of integration'
('modern political institutions') due to the entrenched resistance of 'traditional
élites', but the more far-sighted spokesmen of the latter (Bismarck, Tirpitz,
Bülow) recognized the need for an efficient substitute ('secondary integration')
in order to prevent the alienation of the masses from the system; consequently,
they resorted increasingly to artificial remedies and 'diversionary techniques
of rule', from the *Kulturkampf* and the Anti-Socialist Law through to the manipulation of popular feelings through the *nationale Verbände*. This book has tried
to argue consistently against any view of the nationalist pressure groups which
sees them as the simple agencies of national and social integration in this way,
whether as conscious strategy or objective process. However, to extract something of value from the concept of populism for our purposes, it is necessary to
dispose briefly of this view: namely, that it was somehow the ideological
response of traditional or marginal strata freshly introduced into the political
system.

   Many writers have associated the radical right with movements of the
depressed petty-bourgeoisie, drawing their support from 'the despairing
legions of petty officialdom, small shopkeepers, micro-entrepreneurs, respec-
able people (e.g. retired middle class) on fixed pensions and other inflexible
sources of income'.[125] In normal times conventionally conservative, these
groups can be radicalized, it is claimed, into extreme rightist activity by
political or economic disaster. This is also reminiscent of an influential analysis
of German nationalism before 1914: a defensive reaction by threatened strata
to the socio-economic pressures of the Great Depression.[126] This typology is
superficially recognizable in the Navy League, overwhelmingly an organization
of the bourgeoisie and petty-bourgeoisie, in which managerial, professional
and bureaucratic elements tended to play a leading role, but which had strong

---

[124] K. D. Bracher, 'The Nazi Takeover', in *History of the 20th Century*, 48 (1969), p. 1339.
One of the best brief statements is in Wehler, 'Industrial Growth'.

[125] Worsley, in Gellner and Ionescu, *Populism*, p. 241. Note that Worsley himself queries
this approach.

[126] As well as the work by H. Rosenberg, Wehler, Puhle, Winkler, see also S. Angel-
Volkov, 'The Social and Political Function of Late 19th Century Anti-Semitism: The Case
of the Small Handicraft Masters', in H.-U. Wehler (Ed.). *Sozialgeschichte Heute. Festschrift für
Hans Rosenberg zum 70, Geburtstag* (Göttingen, 1974), pp. 416–31.

roots in the *Mittelstand* and weaker ones in the working class. The stereotype of the small-town provincial *Mittelstand*, distracted by the prospect of economic decline and the rise of Socialism, might seem easy to identify among some of its supporters. In Weimar, for instance, at least three members of the branch executive apparently conformed to its specifications: Flintzer, the Chairman, who presided over the foundation of the Weimar *Mittelstand* Association in 1904, and could be found demanding the protection of 'the German handicrafts in town and country against being crushed by the ruthless application of big capital' and the rise of Social Democracy; his deputy in the *Mittelstand* Association, the merchant Hermann Gruner, who was also Treasurer in the Navy League; and Major Toegel, who in January 1905 could be found addressing the small branch of Allstedt on 'The German Mittelstand and the Fleet'.[127]

However, the suggestion that the mass support for populist movements comes mainly from traditional strata who are suddenly and inadequately incorporated into urban political life is not borne out by the example of the Navy League. Such a view simplifies the relationship between social pressures and ideology. It distorts the buoyant optimism which characterized the attitudes of the radical nationalists at the peak of their influence in the League and undervalues 'the cheerfully ascendant German bourgeoisie' in an epoch of dramatic economic growth.[128] By tying populism to a specific stage in social development and a particular dysfunction of 'normal' processes of change, this misdirects our attention to the alleged survival of 'traditional' attitudes which no longer fit the new institutional structure. Yet this scarcely explains the beliefs of the wealthy Cologne banker Carl Theodor Deichmann, the successful Berlin architect Walter Kyllmann, the prosperous iron merchant Louis Ravené, the worsted manufacturer Heinrich Schilbach, or the Stuttgart businessman Alexander von Pflaum.[129] Heinrich Claß, whose professional career reflected the upward mobility of his parents, and J. E. Stroschein, who rose from being an apprenticed pharmacist to a successful cod-liver oil manufacturer between 1870 and the 1890s, were typical of the social profile of the radical nationalists.[130] They were more often rising than declining petty-bourgeoisie, the confident beneficiaries of Germany's capitalist transformation rather than its victims.

[127] See the following issues of the *WeimZ*: June 23rd 1904, Nov. 20th 1904, Feb. 24th 1905, and Jan. 27th 1905.

[128] Karl Barth in 1919, cit. by L. Albertin, *Liberalismus und Demokratie am Anfang der Weimarer Republik* (Düsseldorf, 1972), p. 18 (note 25).

[129] Deichmann had a vast range of diverse interests, concentrated in insurance, property, construction, iron manufacture and transport. Kyllmann had designed numerous important buildings in Berlin, was a city councillor and held interests in property and transport. Ravené was a key man in the iron and steel industry and also sat on the Board of the *Disconto-Gesellschaft*, one of the big four banks; he bought himself into land in Brandenburg and Trier, owned an art gallery, sponsored the building of an Evangelical church in Cochem (a Catholic area), and owned the castle in the same town.

[130] See Claß, *Wider den Strom*, pp. 2–9; Stroschein to Tirpitz, Jan. 20th 1898, BA-MA Freiburg, 2276, 94227.

Their collective self-portrait as 'the type of free independent man, whose commitment is unswerving to what he believes is right',[131] suggests an ideological formation which deserves careful consideration.

Two points can be made about the *form* of the Navy League's populism. First, it did not identify popular vitality with any one social group, like the peasantry in Russia or the independent farmers in America: 'the people' appeared as a diffuse, generalized myth rather than a precise social category. Both moderates and radicals saw the Navy League as a showpiece of 'national concord between worker and prince, between Right and Left, North and South', a popular movement based on neither class, party, confession nor interest, but on the nation as a whole.[132] This non-sectarian impulse was integral to radical nationalism. Most other political organizations sought to identify themselves with a specific social group, elevating it to the status of a universal class, the real source of the nation's character and strength. But the Navy League and the Pan-Germans were unusual in denouncing any appeal of this kind, and this subjective dissociation from a definite social base made their appeals to the 'solidarity of the classes' rather different from those of the German *Mittelstand* Association or the Imperial League Against Social Democracy.[133] In general the Navy League and other radical nationalists refused to be tied down by social preferences, defining their constituency with catholic simplicity as 'the little man'.[134]

Secondly, the prominence of concepts like 'the people', 'freedom', 'responsibility' and 'independence' in the political vocabulary of the radical nationalists suggests a certain relationship to the liberal tradition, and some of their debates bear a formal similarity to the discourse of the German Liberals at mid-century.[135] Indeed, leading radical nationalists invariably came from a strong liberal background, either personally or by family. Heinrich Oberwinder's passage from the liberal *National-Verein* in the 1860s, through the Lassallean labour movement, Stöcker's demagogic Conservatism and Naumann's National-Socials, to the Navy League at the turn of the century, provides a characteristic trajectory.[136] This memory also illuminates the vigorous individualism of men

---

[131] 'The German Navy League Remains a *Volksverein*' (leading article), *Neue Hessische Volksblätter*, Dec. 7th 1908.

[132] Boy-Ed to Erdmann, Jan, 13th 1908, BA-MA Freiburg, 2259, 94147.

[133] Oberwinder, *Nationale Politik*, p. 54. Oberwinder specifically contrasted the Navy League with the Imperial League Against Social Democracy in this respect, describing the latter as a one-sided employers' organization, alien to the Navy League's own disinterested national idealism. Ibid., p. 23.

[134] Statement by Jasper (Bernau) to the Gen. Board, Berlin, Feb. 18th 1902, *Verhandlungen*, p. 10, BA-MA Freiburg, 2276, 94228.

[135] See J. J. Sheehan, '*Partei, Volk* and *Staat*: Some Reflections on the Relationship between Liberal Thought and Action in Vormärz', in Wehler, *Sozialgeschichte Heute*, pp. 163ff.

[136] See Oberwinder, *Nationale Politik*, pp. 43ff.

like Hermann Heydweiller, who declared their personal independence in no uncertain terms: 'We are not vassals, but free citizens who are come of age.'[137] It was a residue of liberalism which led Otto Stern to demand priority for winning over 'the Left side of the German bourgeoisie'.[138] The radicals repeatedly stressed the Navy League's independence, its need to articulate the feelings of the people without fear of official interference, and its function as the voice of a responsible citizenry. If the Navy League proved incapable of 'strengthening the character of the people', it would become 'superfluous' and 'degenerate into a coterie of careerists and honour-chasers', a 'satellite of the Navy Office'.[139] Statements like these suggest that the development of *völkisch* ideas before 1914 was rather more complex than some intellectual historians, obsessed with the 'revolt against the West', romantic irrationalism and 'cultural despair', have been willing to admit.[140] On the evidence of the Navy League's radical nationalism the mainstream of *völkisch* ideas flowed partly from a polluted rationalist source and showed coherent traces of the idea of man's free political nature.

If radical nationalism obeys neither the descriptive ideological definition of populism nor its common sociological counterpart, how then are we to understand a movement such as this, which made an appeal to 'the people' the centrepiece of its public ideology? The liberal past just mentioned provides an initial clue. It signifies that the radical nationalists were composed not of the casualties of Germany's over-rapid but distorted 'modernization', but precisely of those who by family, education and general cultural background were most comfortably integrated into Wilhelmine society. But though formed in the confident cultural milieu of unification-liberalism, the radical-nationalist generation were compelled to deploy their newly-acquired professional skills and political ambitions in an environment—*Honoratiorenpolitik*—which denied them anything but a subordinate place and a long political apprenticeship. Moreover, in the case of the National Liberals this was exacerbated by a vital organizational

[137] Statement to the Cassel Congress, Jan. 19th 1908, *Verhandlungen*, p. 42, GLA Karlsruhe, 69P, 8.

[138] Stern to Presidium, Apr. 23rd 1907, BHSA Munich, II, Ges. Berlin, 1158. See also Paul Helbeck (an Elberfeld Young Liberal and supporter of Keim), 'The Struggle for the Fleet', *Jungliberale Blätter*, Jan. 19th 1908: 'We believe that every liberal man should be delighted that such men stand at the head of the Navy League, who will not allow the organization to be degraded into a directionless tool, but want to give it the role of a vigilant protector, an energetic and careful sponsor of Germany's defensive power at sea.' See also Meinecke's comments on Keim: 'At one time I corresponded occasionally with him, and know that he possesses a powerful liberal heart—liberal in the sense of the Scharnhorst tradition, which is certainly compatible with a little chauvinist hotheadedness.' Meinecke to Goetz, Feb. 16th 1908, in F. Meinecke, *Werke* VI (Stuttgart, 1962), p. 31.

[139] Stern's circular letter to fellow radical nationalists ('old fellow fighters and honoured friends'), Jan. 21st 1908, BA-MA Freiburg, 2278, 94236.

[140] See especially: Stern, *Politics of Cultural Despair*; Mosse, *Crisis of German Ideology*; Kohn, *Mind of Germany*.

deficit which had been accumulating since the early 1890s: their failure to emulate the Centre or the Agrarian League by developing an extensive apparatus of political recruitment deprived the radical nationalists of a natural political outlet. Given the larger absence of an official parliamentary opposition, recourse to the populist legitimacy of the *Volk* was perhaps the natural ideological surrogate once the radical nationalists began activating themselves independently and eventually in opposition to the government. Crucially, the latter occurred precisely when the government and its allies (i.e. the makeshift power bloc of *Sammlungspolitik*) were most under pressure from the left under novel conditions of popular mobilization, relatively free from state repression. The electoral failure of the *Sammlung* in 1898 was followed by the greater SPD gains of 1903, and the more vigorous radical nationalists had no confidence in the government's ability to recover this lost popular ground. In this context the populist form of the radical-nationalist critique signified a crisis of confidence in the current politics of the power bloc. It was a symptom of disunity. Most importantly of all, it proposed a strategy for re-establishing the government's threatened popular legitimacy.

We are now closer to an understanding of the circumstances in which populist appeals may occur. Basically, they are a signal that the ability of the dominant classes to speak for the 'people in general' has become impaired, normally through a powerful challenge from below or a breakdown of internal cohesion at the level of the power bloc or the state. In such situations attempts are made to find a new universalizing vision, in this case an ideal of national community amongst citizen-patriots. This exposes the unnecessary narrowness of the sociological approach, with its stress on the inadequate integration of 'traditional' strata. On the other hand, Peter Worsley's suggestion that 'populism is better regarded as an emphasis, a dimension of political culture in general, not simply as a particular kind of overall ideological system or type of organization', is far more helpful. One way perhaps of approaching a solution is to unite this with the sociological notion of a 'crisis of integration', whilst freeing the latter from its functionalist relation to 'modernization theory'. All governments, for instance, necessarily lay claim to represent the people in general, and political stability normally depends on the ability of the power bloc to neutralize the potential antagonisms of the popular forces by transforming them into objects of compromise. The ability 'to articulate different visions of the world in such a way that their potential antagonism is neutralized', in fact, rather than simply *suppressing* those visions beneath 'a uniform conception of the world', is precisely an index of the hegemony of a ruling class.[141] Following Laclau, we might argue that *specifically* populist interventions occur when the ability of the power bloc to dispatch its hegemonic functions enters a crisis, either of its own internal cohesion or of its ability to neutralize the dominated sectors.[142]

[141] Laclau, 'Towards a Theory of Populism', p. 161.
[142] Ibid., pp. 172–6.

In this situation there occurs an open struggle to appropriate the leadership of the people in general.

V

Wilhelmine society experienced such a crisis during the decomposition of the Bismarckian bloc in the 1890s. To resume the discussion of earlier chapters, there were two basic conditions of that decomposition: the first was the novel organization of the subordinate classes on an independent and antagonistic basis, not only of the working class, but also of the peasantry and to a lesser extent of the petty-bourgeoisie; the second was a partial failure of adaptation to this process on the part of the existing bourgeois parties. The gradual disintegration of the power bloc's claims to exercise leadership over the subordinate classes had a number of consequences at the level of ideology. These amounted to a succession of efforts during the 1890s by minorities, both inside and outside the power bloc, to appropriate the vacant popular leadership. Friedrich Naumann's was theoretically the most ambitious of these, if in the short-term the least successful. The most effective sectoral offensives were mounted under the auspices of new agrarian organizations: after the turn of the century the evident beneficiaries of these turned out to be the Agrarian League and the Centre Party, who predominated on opposite sides of a confessional divide. After the tariff settlement of 1902 the internal unity of the power bloc seemed to have been reconstituted on a relatively stable basis, though the outcome of the 1903 elections revealed that its ability to exercise hegemonic leadership over the popular forces was far from undisputed.

The most interesting aspect of this process of decomposition and recomposition, which could be observed both in the state itself and in the individual parties, was that liberals were least successful in reorienting their practice to the needs of popular politics. It was both ironic and understandable that the fraction which had previously dominated the power bloc between the 1860s and later 1880s should also be the one which singularly failed to offer an adequate response to the crisis of the 1890s. It was precisely this failure, notably on the part of the National Liberals, which created a space for radical nationalism, both ideologically and organizationally. There was a striking contrast in the 1890s between the urban and rural arenas of politics: while in the latter both the Agrarian League and the Centre were busily engaged in creating a structure of practice for moderating the rugged independence of new agrarian movements, in the towns the National Liberals were unable to cope with the advance of the SPD. In the earlier period of the 1860s, of course, during the construction of the liberal-dominated Bismarckian system, liberal politics had themselves been populist, in the sense that they articulated popular aspirations into a political antagonism against the feudal bloc they were seeking to supplant. As late as 1881 the slogan 'Junkers and priests together/Put townsmen and peasants in tether' had still been possible.[143] In the changed conditions of the 1890s, however, liberals failed to devise a new populist formula for accommodating new popular aspirations, whether of the working class or of the peasantry.

Most concretely, the National Liberals failed to generate a flourishing party organism in the constituencies to absorb the energies of their rank-and-file supporters. One consequence of this absence was a certain flux of allegiance, which enabled the natural activists of the National Liberals to drift in and out of a wide variety of liberal, philanthropic, anti-Socialist, economic and patriotic organizations. A more specific effect was the success of the *nationale Verbände* in acquiring a firm body of local activists, who were pre-eminently committed to themselves rather than to any of the political parties. Given the inflexibility of municipal *Honoratiorenpolitik* until well after 1900, it was hardly surprising that the most conscious of such activists should begin to clash with the local National Liberal establishments and their Conservative allies. In a sense the pronounced radical-nationalist politics which emerged from those clashes may be seen as the attempts of displaced National Liberal activists to regain some purchase on popular credibility at the local level. It was significant that when a more concerted attempt was made by the National Liberal Party to define a coherent strategy after 1907 or so, it consisted in large part of trying to appropriate the popular enthusiasm generated by the *nationale Verbände*. Stresemann, a principal architect of that new line, had been a close associate of the radical nationalists in the Navy League between 1905 and 1908.[144]

This, then, was the meaning of the Navy League's populism: it was one consequence of a prolonged crisis of the internal unity and hegemonic capability of the Wilhelmine power bloc, which began in the 1890s and was only briefly resolved after 1902 for a few years before reappearing more acutely after 1909. The extent of radical-nationalist opposition to the power bloc as such should not be exaggerated, for this was directed mainly at the current mode of politics through which the latter was constituted. However, the assertion during 1907–8 from a right-wing perspective that the interests of the nation were not always identical with government policies, that the needs of the *Volk* might diverge from the wishes of the Kaiser, was a necessary condition for the emergence of a 'national opposition' after 1908 which did lay more serious charges against the government. It makes most sense perhaps to regard radical nationalism before this time as a symptom of the disunity of the power bloc. From an inadequate material base it raised in ideological terms the need for a massive populist offensive if that long-term disunity was to be overcome. The history of the German right after the 1890s was the history of unsuccessful attempts to reconstitute the political and ideological unity of the power bloc and simultaneously its leadership over the subordinate classes. Between 1912 and 1914 it seemed that a fraction of the ruling class might detach itself for a more

---

[143] White, *Splintered Party*, p. 100.
[144] Stresemann's politics are discussed in more detail in Ch. 8 and 9 below, pp. 262f., 304–12.

radical populist attack on this problem, embracing a stronger alliance with the petty-bourgeoisie and a revision of the Constitution, but in the end this was interrupted by the war. In the longer term, one might say that the possibility of a German fascism became inscribed in the political and ideological structures of the power bloc at that moment when the struggle to recompose its unity became displaced on to populist terrain. Here radical nationalism made a vital preliminary contribution.

6. The New Terrain of Popular Politics

I

It has become fashionable recently to attribute 'plebiscitary' characteristics to the Wilhelmine political system. By nurturing popular loyalties to the state *as such* in the form of monarchism or nationalism, the argument runs, it was hoped that the prevailing sectionalism of parliamentary life might be overcome, for as it was the latter tended to prevent the construction of stable government majorities in the Reichstag. The constitutional gap between Reichstag and executive—the inability of the parties to translate their parliamentary strength into governmental authority—opened up direct avenues of pressure and influence between the bureaucracy and the organized interests, and by the same virtue created a propensity in government towards the direct manipulation of public opinion. Beginning with Bismarck a range of techniques were institutionalized in the government's practice: emphasis on the national interest as opposed to the narrower sectional interests of the parties, dramatic appeals to the country on issues like armaments and colonial spending, boosting the mystique of monarchy, attacking the national minorities, settling domestic conflicts by invoking the higher urgencies of foreign policy, and the general demonization of the SPD. In pursuit of these ends the official management of opinion soon encompassed the entire repertoire of possible interventions, from the hidden manipulation of the press and the subsidization of nationalist literature, to the use of the educational system, religious and cultural bodies and the nationalist propaganda groups.[1]

Some historians have tried to generalize these interpretations into the concept of 'caesarism' (sometimes also formulated as 'Bonapartism') to describe the political system as a whole.[2] Yet as we have already seen, the claim that extra-

[1] Some aspects of this view have already been discussed in the previous chapter. See Wehler, *Das Deutsche Kaiserreich*, pp. 78ff., 90ff.; Puhle, 'Parlament, Parteien und Interessenverbände', and *Agrarkrise*, esp. pp. 5–19; H. A. Winkler, *Pluralismus oder Protektionismus? Verfassungspolitische Probleme des Verbandswesen im deutschen Kaiserreich* (Wiesbaden, 1972); G. A. Ritter, 'Gesellschaft und Politik im Kaiserreich 1871–1914', in Ritter, *Arbeiterbewegung, Parteien und Parlamentarismus* (Göttingen, 1976), pp. 10–20, and Ritter, 'Politische Parteien in Deutschland vor 1918', ibid., pp. 102–15.

[2] Above all: Wehler, *Bismarck*, pp. 180ff., 455–74, 488; Sauer, 'Problem des deutschen Nationalstaates'; Stürmer, 'Bismarckstaat und Cäsarismus'; E. Fraenkel, 'Die repräsentative und die plebiszitäre Komponente im demokratischen Verfassungsstaat', in *Deutschland und*

parliamentary sources of popular support were deliberately cultivated as an anti-parliamentary weapon by the state does not stand up terribly well when measured against the actual history of the *nationale Verbände*. To justify talk of 'plebiscitary mechanisms' and 'caesarism' we need evidence of a systematic and continuing attempt to place the mobilization of mass opinion on a constant footing, in distinct and conscious opposition to the conventional framework of party politics in the Reichstag. Yet none of the *nationale Verbände* ever achieved this level of 'plebiscitary' activity, nor were they structurally capable of achieving it. They were occasional organizations which declared a public presence only very sporadically: the average branch might meet in public only two or three times a year, hardly enough to justify talk of plebiscitary rule. Likewise, despite Bülow's talk of a 'royalism *sans phrase*' in the 1890s,[3] there is no evidence that the person of the Kaiser or the institution of the monarchy were used to focus the agitation of these organizations. On the contrary, the government's relative moderation on 'national' issues and the resulting conflicts with radical nationalists tended to discredit the monarchy in such quarters. Moreover, though there was plenty of hostility to certain parties and a general animus against the parliamentary system, there was no systematic campaign against the Reichstag by either government or pressure groups: the emphasis was far more on lobbying the sympathetic parties and getting the individual supporters to the polls in an election.[4]

Tied up with this is a tendency to concentrate far too much on the manipulative genius of the politicians at the top. Bedazzled by the achievements of this or that government agency, recent authors have easily fallen into a disregard for the larger contexts (historical, international, technological, cultural) which might help establish the precise relative significance of their subjects. For instance: several major works have described the naval propaganda begun under Tirpitz in 1897 as a crucial breakthrough into the modern era of opinion management and public relations. It marked a 'new beginning . . . in which

---

die westlichen Demokratien (4th ed., Berlin, 1968), pp. 81–112; D. Groh, 'Cäsarismus', in O. Brunner, W. Conze, R. Koselleck (Eds.), *Geschichtliche Grundbegriffe*, II, (Stuttgart, 1972), pp. 726–71; H. Boldt, 'Deutscher Konstitutionalismus und Bismarckzeit', in Stürmer, *Das kaiserliche Deutschland*, pp. 119–42. Whereas the idea has been specified in some detail by Wehler and Stürmer in relation to Bismarck, it remains unclear how it works for the Wilhelmine period. See the attenuated remarks of Puhle, 'Parlament, Parteien und Interessenverbände', p. 349, who sidesteps the issue by talking simply of a 'caesarism without a caesar'. See also the more recent exchange between Mitchell and Stürmer, in *JMH*, 49 (1977), pp. 181ff.

[3] Bülow to Eulenburg, Dec. 4th 1896, BA Coblenz, Eulenburg Papers, 44, pp. 797f.

[4] The best specific example is that of Salm-Horstmar's two circulars to the Navy League membership exhorting them to vote for the 'national parties' in the 1907 elections, one in his official capacity as President, the other as a more personal statement: circular to all regional executives, Dec. 19th 1906, and circular to Navy League members, Dec. 28th 1906, both BA-MA Freiburg, 2276, 94230.

for the support and legitimation of government policy the masses were courted, convinced and whipped up by comprehensive and unceasing influence by the state, so that it could then be claimed that the government activity had been stimulated by a previously existing popular opinion, as if driven compulsively by the will of the masses'. The achievements of the Naval Propaganda Office made Tirpitz 'the first Propaganda Minister of the modern stamp', who created a new awareness of 'the importance of public opinion in the life of the state' and 'raised the great masses, to an unprecedented extent, . . . into a novel and highly influential factor in the political process'.[5] As Deist's work has shown, the operations of the Naval Propaganda Office were indeed impressive. But there is a danger in much recent work of simply accepting such efforts at face value, without measuring their effectiveness against the practice of other government departments, the full range of propagandist opportunities provided by the evolving technology and economics of communications, and the actual receptiveness of the intended audience.

When situated in these three contexts, the pioneering enterprise of the Navy Office appears rather less striking. Most obviously, very similar operations were conducted by other government departments around the same time. At the Foreign Office Otto Hammann put together some equally impressive machinery for monitoring and influencing the press, and together with the interlocking network of contacts administered by Friedrich Wilhelm Loebell at the Chancellory this formed an invaluable political instrument during Bülow's time.[6] All government departments were engaged in propaganda to some extent and from 1898 the Literary Office of the Ministry of the Interior was given the job of co-ordinating the flow of information to the regions and localities.[7] It was at this point, moreover, that a large mass of material flowed into the system from independent agencies, for the state also used its local officials for the distribution of literature from sympathetic organizations. If this sort of activity, which noticeably increased at election time, is also counted as state-directed propaganda, then its scale and content begin to outweigh those of the more technical operations at the Navy Office. There was much blurring of the boundaries between the state and civil society, as the government acted both through and for a range of formally independent agencies: the close co-operation of the Christian Book League and other religious bodies, the use of para-military organizations like the veterans' clubs,

---

[5] J. Meyer, *Die Propaganda der deutschen Flottenbewegung 1897–1900* (Bern, 1967), pp. 25f. This view has been taken over by recent work: Berghahn, *Tirpitz-Plan*, pp. 120ff.; Deist, *Flottenpolitik*, pp. 7ff., 71ff. It has now passed into general currency: e.g. Wehler, *Das Deutsche Kaiserreich*, pp. 165ff.

[6] See: O. Hammann, *Der neue Kurs* (Berlin, 1918), esp. pp. 72–90; Heidorn, *Monopole, Presse, Krieg*, pp. 41ff.; K. Koszyk, *Deutsche Presse im 19. Jahrhundert* (Berlin, 1966), pp. 229–66; Wernecke, *Wille zur Weltgeltung*, pp. 19–25.

[7] See A. Hall, 'The War of Words: Anti-Socialist Offensives and Counter-Propaganda in Wilhelmine Germany, 1890–1914', *JCH*, XI (1976), pp. 17ff.

and the gathering interest in youth-work were all major examples.[8]

It is only when considered against this general background of increasing involvement by the state in the cultural world of its citizens that the real significance of the naval propaganda may be properly grasped. For the latter was not just the product of an exceptional intelligence, the accident of the right man in the right office at the right time; on the contrary, the changing structural conditions of political life in the 1890s virtually imposed the necessity of an extensive propaganda if the naval programme was to succeed. In this respect we may point briefly to the shifting demographic balance from country to town, the growing weight of industry in the economy, the presence of a literate and expanding electorate, the upsurge of political mobilization in the 1890s, and new technologies of mass communications. Given this novel expansion of a national 'public sphere' and especially in view of the unabated rise of the SPD, no minister could afford to ignore the importance of public opinion, least of all if he was defending a major new departure against the confirmed suspicions of a Reichstag majority.[9]

Tirpitz did not raise public opinion to a new importance in the life of the state: it had raised itself and compelled even the most somnolent of traditional bureaucrats to adjust their practice for political survival. As von der Recke, Minister of the Interior at the time of the First Navy Bill, said: 'No government can do without an effective representation of its views and interests in the press for any length of time, without doing damage to its position and prestige.'[10] Naturally some perceived these trends more quickly than others, and here Tirpitz explored the implications with great acuity. But then again, once the basic need for propaganda had been recognized, most of the particular methods —influencing the press, commissioning pamphlets, support for independent publicists, the provision of facilities for journalists, and so on—suggested themselves. The Navy Office may have worked these into a system more success-fully than many of its sister-agencies, but individually they were now unavoid-able conditions of an adequate political practice, certainly by 1900. Even the role of the pioneer, the distinction of having cottoned on to these developments at an early stage, belongs less to Tirpitz than to August Keim, who ran the successful campaign for the Army Bill in 1892–3.[11]

---

[8] The distribution of literature from the Christian Book League and its subsidiary the Fatherland League may be traced through the records of the Prussian provincial administra-tion: e.g. StA Marburg, 150, 662; 165, 46; 165, 47; etc. For more detail: K. Saul, 'Der Staat und die "Mächte des Umsturzes". Ein Beitrag zu den Methoden antisozialistischer Repression und Agitation vom Scheitern des Sozialistengesetzes bis zur Jahrhundertwende' *AfS*, XII (1972), pp. 332–50.

[9] See Eley, 'German Navy League', pp. 28ff., and Eley, 'Sammlungspolitik', pp. 33–48. For the dynamics of official naval propaganda: Deist, *Flottenpolitik*, pp. 71–146.

[10] Hall, 'War of Words', p. 19.

[11] Nicholls, *Germany After Bismarck*, pp. 229–64; Keim, *Erlebtes*, pp. 49–77; Hallgarten, *Imperialismus vor 1914*, I, pp. 335ff.

In other words, before we can devise a suitable measure for the propaganda operations of this or that government department, we need to consider them both in relation to the state as a whole and to the relevant developments in economy and society at large. One way of doing this is to construct a general framework of communications history.[12] The growth of a national reading public, the massive expansion of the popular press between the 1860s and 1900, the establishment of a comprehensive postal service and the later introduction of the telephone, the building of minor roads and railway branch-lines, the spread of libraries, the efflorescence of voluntary associations and the unprecedented availability of cheap reading-matter provide the rudiments of such a general framework, and to them must later be added the new technologies of printing, radio, film and eventually television. One means of considering these factors abstractly is to isolate two central processes: the expanding size of the overall audience and the changing structure of ownership.

As suggested above, the former was a prior determinant of the propagandist 'innovations' of the 1890s whose impact was maximized by universal suffrage and high levels of political mobilization. By 1900 the increasing organization of opinion by trade-union, agrarian and *Mittelstand* organs had ensured that the national public also encompassed the subordinate classes of Wilhelmine society. Exactly how the Navy Office and other state apparatuses defined their own potential audience in relation to these larger facts has a crucial bearing on the 'modernity' or otherwise of their efforts. Secondly, the growing concentration of ownership of the means of communication, which was accelerated by the mass circulation dailies, diminished the importance of small printers and family concerns; it obviously had profound implications for the forms of state intervention in the press. It silenced oppositional voices through the rising importance of capitalist business methods, with dependence on advertising, fast sales and large-scale distribution machinery, and converted the press into a political weapon which was potentially far more dangerous if it were to fall into the wrong hands. Here again, this imposed a structure of relations within which government was constrained to operate, and over which it had very limited control.[13]

In defining the scope of propaganda, a further distinction is required: that between formal propaganda which presents itself openly *as* propaganda, in the form of direct interventions to convey information or influence opinion, and on the other hand the informal propaganda of hidden messages, the

[12] The best guidance is provided by work on Britain: R. Williams, *Communications* (2nd ed., Harmondsworth, 1966), and *Television: Technology and Cultural Form* (London, 1974); G. Murdock and P. Golding, 'For a Political Economy of Mass Communications', *Socialist Register 1973* (London, 1974), 205–34; J. Curran, M. Gurevitch, J. Woollacott (Eds.), *Mass Communication and Society* (London, 1977).

[13] The most important recent study is Guratzsch, *Macht durch Organisation*, pp. 183–343. It does, however, concern the special circumstances of the war. For a British work: A. J. Lee, *The Origins of the Popular Press, 1855–1914* (London, 1976).

dissemination of ideology in ways which are not overtly propagandist. In practice, of course, the latter can be both consciously and unconsciously perpetuated, occurring not only as the deliberate insertion of political messages between the lines of a school textbook, a sermon or a novel, but also as the unreflected transmission of consensual values which can be so uncontroversial as to be embedded in the expressive fabric of the media themselves. By posing the problem of propaganda, its conditions and changing forms, therefore, we return to the problem of ideology: the question of how a system of rule is perpetuated, modified or overthrown, how a ruling class consolidates its cultural dominance or hegemony, and how the terms of public discussion are structured and restructured so as to redraw the possible limits of political action. Once the scope of propaganda is extended this far, it becomes important to consider *all* areas of cultural life: not simply the press and the written word, but also the educational system, religion, recreation, popular fiction, the theatre, film, and latterly radio and television. These are all areas in which values, beliefs and ideas may be proposed and contested. It is in these areas that recent talk of 'plebiscitary' rule and 'caesarism' must be tested, for unless it penetrated to these levels of ideological practice the state would be unable to offer a viable alternative to the existing articulations of political loyalty in the political parties.[14]

Once the much-vaunted work of the Navy Office is considered in relation to these factors—an expanding popular audience, increasingly limited ownership of the means of communication, the larger cultural domain in which consciousness is formed—its limitations become much clearer. Most obviously, its content was very narrowly focused on *naval* matters, and partly by necessity and partly by choice large areas of political life lay beyond its competence. It was only by carefully dissociating the battlefleet programme from any one set of political positions that Tirpitz stood any chance of removing it from the hazards of political controversy and making it just another conventional attribute of Great Power status, like an efficient educational system, a rail network or an Army. The chances for ideological work of a more general kind were limited, and in the content and scope of its propaganda the Navy Office was less penetrating than either the Army, the Ministry of Culture or the Ministry of the Interior. In the audience it defined for itself, moreover, the Navy Office was unambitious. From an early stage it confined its propaganda work to 'the educated classes', with special emphasis on certain well-defined groups of 'opinion-makers', including parliamentary deputies, journalists, academics, and so on.[15] There was no attempt to reach the masses directly,

[14] In particular: S. Hall, 'Culture, the Media and the "Ideological Effect" ', in Curran Gurevitch, Woollacott, *Mass Communication*, pp. 315–48; R. Williams, *Marxism and Literature* (Oxford, 1977), esp. pp. 75–144; H. M. Enzensberger, 'Constituents of a Theory of the Media', *New Left Review*, 64 (Nov.-Dec. 1970), pp. 13–36.

[15] Eley, 'German Navy League', pp. 36ff.; Deist, *Flottenpolitik*, pp. 100ff.

or to devise a means of popular mobilization.[16] There was no attempt to *organize* either workers or petty-bourgeoisie. Methods were likewise conventional, for the more popular media of the public meeting, the petition and door-to-door agitation were neglected. The new technologies of advertising and film were untapped. Mainly for departmental reasons the Navy Office lagged behind some other state apparatuses in these respects.[17]

By contrast, it was precisely their willingness to enter this larger domain of ideological struggle that characterized the more vigorous agitational pressure groups. Thus from an early stage the Navy League was deeply committed to the principle of popular mobilization and nurtured a fixed ambition to win the support of the working masses for the Navy. Similarly, though it lacked the resources of the Navy League and was consequently thrown back on to the more restricted audience of *Bildung und Besitz*, the Pan-German League also escaped the technical limitation of its agitation to naval affairs: hence it waged a broadly conceived campaign of 'national education' which covered most aspects of nationalist concern, both foreign and domestic. Despite the narrow focus of its obsessive anti-Socialism, the Imperial League Against Social Democracy went some way to combining both sorts of activity, aiming a broadly based propaganda at a more popular audience. For different reasons, because they spoke for an immediate popular constituency, the agrarian and *Mittelstand* movements opened up similar opportunities. Popular agitation *created its own methods*, and it was this dynamic, in which the forms of propaganda followed logically from the broader definition of its intended audience, that was absent from the limited publicity of the Navy Office.

II

The preceding pages have raised a number of massive problems, concerning the character of the Wilhelmine state and the best way of describing its polity, the history of mass communications in Germany, and the relation of propaganda to ideology, which exceed the modest terms of the current enquiry. However,

[16] A slight exception was the campaign for the Second Navy Bill in early 1900. Thus Heeringen addressed the Navy League's local representatives on Jan. 16th 1900 on the importance of reaching the working class and stressed the 'high social-political significance of the naval question'. As a result of this meeting 3,300,000 copies of a leaflet entitled *Arbeiter und Flotte* were distributed, including 710,320 put out through the Navy League's 'Railway Committee' in a four-day operation. More enterprisingly, Heeringen co-ordinated an attempt by Navy League speakers, 'naval professors', National-Socials and Pan-Germans to contest the Socialist resolutions in a series of nineteen simultaneous rallies called by the SPD on Feb. 7th 1900. For further detail: Eley, 'German Navy League', pp. 9off.

[17] This argument should not be misunderstood. It is not meant to dispute the scale and ambition of Navy Office intentions by older standards, but merely to keep these in proportion by pointing to parallel developments in other areas of the state, and by identifying the structural rather than the accidental personal reasons for them. Before claiming Tirpitz as the 'first propaganda minister of the modern stamp' we should also remember what came after him.

it is important for our purposes to consider one particular problem in which they intersect, namely the changing requirements of an effective right-wing response to the rise of Social Democracy. For the end of the Anti-Socialist Law in 1890 and the continuing growth of the Socialist movement faced the dominant classes and their political spokesmen with the problem of devising new ways of legitimating capitalist social relations. The forms of capital's domination over labour, both in production and society at large, were undergoing modification, with simple mechanisms of repression making way for more sophisticated processes of ideological containment. Wide circles—in industry, the bureaucracy, the parties, and above all in the Army and on the land—still clung to old coercive habits, but the creeping legitimacy of parliamentary forms could not be ignored. The new technology of mass communications dramatized the fact that Wilhelmine politics were fast becoming the scene of a battle for *consent*, to implant the popular legitimacy of bourgeois values in their specific *German* form.[18] The efforts of new mass organizations like the Navy League to wage a battle or *words* and *ideas* meant partly that the right had cynically 'modernized' its politics. But in practice it also meant that concessions were being made to new popular forces and that the SPD was being fought increasingly on its own ground.

Bearing this in mind, it is useful to distinguish three modes of propaganda. The first was associated with the state itself. Leaving aside the routine administration of education and justice, we are concerned here mainly with government interventions into the public sphere at large: either with a view to general considerations of 'national efficiency' and the 'spiritual welfare of the nation', or else for specific items of legislation or official policy. Promoting military virtues through the veterans' clubs or after 1911 through the Young-Germany-Union would be a good example of the former, while the propaganda for the Army Bill of 1892–3 was an instance of the second. Moreover, though it clearly carried other meanings for sections of the public itself (i.e. the radical nationalists), much of the naval propaganda took this latter form as well. It was orchestrated mainly for the passage of successive Navy Bills in 1898, 1900, 1906, 1908 and 1912, it was primarily technical in content (in the sense of its limitation to naval affairs), and was confined largely to a fairly narrow audience of 'opinion-makers'. Though its level of organization was impressive, the Navy Office worked mainly through the cultivation of personal contacts in the press, pressure groups and parties, the 'placing' of newspaper articles and the commissioning of literature. It made no attempt to 'agitate' public opinion by organizing support directly or by mobilizing pressure against the Reichstag. The closest it came to this was in its relations with the Navy League. But it saw the latter mainly as an independent agency for 'enlightening' the public, not as an agitational instrument, and when it started to outstep this official brief between

[18] This is a carefully chosen formulation, intended to avoid easy identification of 'bourgeois values' with a classic liberal outlook.

8

1903 and 1908, the Navy Office did its best to haul it back. At most it was willing to use the League as a 'pacemaker' for future official departures, but even this was seen as a risk by most of the responsible authorities.[19]

A better instance of government propaganda is given by the Christian Book League, for this concerned itself with a wider range of operations with fewer restrictions on content. Though formally independent, it in practice functioned as the propaganda arm of the Prussian state. Formed in 1880 and administered till his death in 1901 by Pastor Ernst Hülle in close understanding with the Berlin Consistory of the established Evangelical Church, it had the sole function of distributing Christian, patriotic and anti-Socialist literature. It did this in 1900 with a central office of seventy-seven officials and a hundred employees, growing by 1907 to eighty and two hundred respectively. It had only a small membership (898 in 1889, 2,650 in 1898, 686 in 1899), and was dependent for money on large subsidies from a variety of sources: direct grants from government and industry (e.g. three donations of 10,000 marks each from the Interior Ministry at the end of 1895, one of 12,000 procured from the CVDI by the Reich Office of the Interior in 1899), indirect support from the massive purchase of the organization's literature, and *ad hoc* contributions from local notables and individual firms. The hidden subsidy of distribution through the state apparatus was invaluable and leaflets were often produced for specific government needs: elections were the most obvious, but it was also done for specific items of legislation, such as the Hard-Labour Bill of 1899. In addition, the work of distribution was borne by an army of voluntary helpers (12,000 by 1896), including large numbers of teachers and Protestant clergy. The role of the state was central, being regulated by a royal Ordinance of 1896 which instructed all departments to give the Book League every assistance. High officials of the Ministry of Culture sat on its committee, the Ministries of War and Public Works used its publications for soldiers and railwaymen, as did the Ministries of Interior and Agriculture for the countryside. The Christian Book League had the advantage of being an independent agency 'which was nonetheless completely beneath the control of (the government)'. This allowed the latter 'to participate more freely in the political struggle without having to take responsibility for the content of its statements.'[20]

The hallmark of the Book League's activities was the 'tailoring of its leaflets and calendars to the age, sex and occupation of the subscribers and to the local and regional particularities of the distribution area'. By the mid-1890s there were weekly newspapers for factory-workers, agricultural labourers, railwaymen, soldiers, peasants, the self-employed in the towns, members of youth groups and

---

[19] For detailed discussions: Eley, 'German Navy League', pp. 179–91; Deist, *Flottenpolitik*, pp. 163ff.

[20] These details are taken mainly from Saul, 'Der Staat und die "Mächte des Umsturzes" ', pp. 336–50, which has brought this important organization to our attention. See also Hall, 'War of Words', pp. 23ff.

veterans' clubs, working women and ladies of leisure, and for general entertainment. At a normal cost of ten pfennigs for four issues and under 235 separate title-heads, these had reached a total of 695,555 subscribers by 1901. In 1913 the League distributed over seventy-one million copies of its publications. It worked best with a captive audience, as when a sympathetic employer gave the leaflets to his work-force. In general employees of the state were most vulnerable to disciplinary sanctions if they resisted such ideological pressure. Thus the introduction of the League's special paper for soldiers, *Nach Dem Dienst*, at the express request of the Ministry of War in 1891 directly complemented the stricter ideological supervision of recruits then under way. In 1892 the Minister of Public Works prompted a similar intervention on the railways to combat suggestions of trade-union activity: in 1904 the League was made responsible for the monthly organ of the newly set up railway employees association.

In both cases these literary efforts were seen as a way of strengthening the moral resistance of state employees to the wiles of the SPD. The same calculation appeared in the League's work in the countryside, which by 1900 was its main priority. Besides the appropriate weekly paper *Ländlicher Arbeiterfreund*, this led to two special subsidiaries: a body for promoting 'People's Libraries' in 1899 and the Fatherland League in 1894. The latter obliged its members to distribute leaflets once a fortnight, and in 1899 its thousand-odd subscribers managed a record of 840,000 leaflets. Finally, special value was put on the annual calendar, which was invariably the only essential reading-matter in most rural households apart from the bible. Reaching an edition of half a million by 1901 the League's calendar showed most of the typical features of the organization's propaganda. It was aimed mainly at the rural population. It was massively backed by the money and labour of the state apparatus. Its content was carefully tailored to the needs of particular regions, appearing in some twenty separate editions. Its primary content was an unqualified anti-Socialism. It was conceived with some success as a means of displacing from the countryside an SPD agitation then only in its early stages.

However, for the same reasons it also revealed the Christian Book League's characteristic limitations. For all its literary output its goals were extremely conventional. The tacit acknowledgement of the need to fight the SPD on its own terms—i.e. with words rather than bayonets—certainly registered a crucial shift in the terms of the political discourse. But in the Book League's propaganda the more traditional preoccupations of nineteenth-century conservatism were still recognizably present. On the one hand the approach was nakedly paternalist. The intended recipients of the literature were presumed to inhabit a deferential universe of pre-political innocence in which the traditional virtues of family, work, throne and altar remained, thankfully, intact. This self-contained world of stability was threatened by Social Democracy—a pollution of the subject population's natural loyalties, rather like the wastage of primitive communities by an unknown disease. To negate the effects of Socialist agitation, immunities had to be strengthened by the injection of an equal volume of 'healthy' literature. On the other hand, the healthy elements which were still uncorrupted by modern influences were identified mainly with the countryside. The efforts of old-style conservatives to win the support of urban workers, though often considerable in the 1880s, were always tinged with fatalism.[21] These two factors were heavy constraints on the League's approach: its propaganda was concentrated in the safe zones of the countryside and the analogous groups of the relatively immune, like military conscripts and state employees, while its confinement to the mere distribution of literature virtually ruled out independent organizing initiatives from within the citizenry, which might have sparked off some larger movement of opposition to the SPD. In fact, similar limitations appeared in other areas of state propaganda as well. The veterans' associations and state youth groups reproduced much the same authoritarian syndrome. Moreover, though the Navy Office gave more latitude to civilian initiative, the narrower social range of its work combined with the technical content to lessen the potential impact of this greater liberality.

In other words, the government's own propaganda suffered from a lack of political imagination. This was a lack of enterprise directly conditioned by the character of the German polity itself, because the absence of clear lines of ministerial responsibility to parliament meant that the successive governments of Caprivi, Hohenlohe, Bülow and Bethmann Hollweg were not underpinned by any popular movement in the country. Unlike a classic parliamentary administration, they owed no allegiance to a wider constituency whose organizations might help transmute a purely literary propaganda into agitation which was properly political. In a sense the state was its own constituency, subsidizing a vast apparatus of ideological conformity whose primary purpose was to rally the loyalties of the state's own personnel: not just the higher grades of civil servants, but also the clerical workers, teachers, clergy, uniformed working class of railwaymen, postmen and foresters, and conscripts to Army and Navy.[22] Here the unit of organization, the context in which opinions could be formed, was built into the conditions of state employment themselves, and consequently the government had less incentive to start manufacturing new agencies of popular mobilization.

Moreover, this same lack of political enterprise—to distinguish now the second major instance of propaganda activity—was reproduced in the non-Socialist parties as they entered the 1890s. As we know from the work of

[21] The Army's preference for rural as against urban recruits suggests an interesting parallel here: e.g. M. Kitchen, *The German Officer Corps 1890–1914* (Oxford, 1968), pp. 147f.

[22] However, we should not assume that the desired conformity was necessarily achieved, or that all state employees can be reduced to a familiar stereotype of 'statolatry'. For some important reflections on this problem: J. Caplan, 'Bureaucracy, Politics and the National Socialist State', in P. Stachura (Ed.), *The Shaping of the Nazi State* (London, 1978), pp. 234–56.

Nipperdey, initially the parties were loose associations of notables held together by common loyalty to a set of great ideals rather than by any firm organizational structure, and existing in the localities only as self-constituted committees of leading personalities, with no rights of representation in the national party and normally meeting only for the nomination of a candidate in elections. Such organizations were hardly suited to the conduct of an agitational type of propaganda aimed at creating new reserves of constant support. Like the state they confined their attentions to a safe traditional clientele—the National Liberals by fine networks of paternalist relations, the Conservatives by the blunter sanctions of landlordism, the Catholic Centre by the parochial authority of the priest.

When a more enterprising mode of propaganda began to emerge in the 1890s, therefore, it did so very often outside the purview of the government and the established parties. There were isolated moments when the state seemed poised for innovative public mobilization. But these were normally one-off initiatives on specific policies, often entrusted to heterodox individuals without lasting influence in the government's inner circles. August Keim's activities in 1892-3 for the Army Bill were a good example of a striking innovation by the government which left no permanent traces in the structure of its relations with the public. This was a dissipation of plebiscitary opportunities rather than their realization. Likewise, though the campaign for the 1898 Navy Law produced an impressive level of public activity, in the localities this owed far more to the enterprise of the Colonial Society and the Pan-Germans than to the direction of the Navy Office, and in fact the latter saw the rallying of local opinion as a much lower priority than the private cultivation of business opinion and the press.[23] When Stroschein's initiative for institutionalizing the naval agitation materialized in January 1898 Tirpitz was conspicuously unenthusiastic; by the time the safer 'front' organization of the original Navy League took public shape at the end of April, Stroschein, the Pan-Germans and those who had borne the burdens of rallying opinion in the constituencies were disillusioned with the government's limited interest in their efforts. The Navy Office naturally co-operated with the Navy League by providing information, subsidies and technical personnel. But this rarely went as far as direct involvement in the work of agitation itself. The Navy Office was normally in the position of responding to popular initiatives rather than starting them, whether in the case of Stroschein and the later history of the Navy League, in the provision of facilities for independent naval enthusiasts like the redoubtable *Hofrezitator* Neander and his travelling slide-show, or in the more serious backing for popular educators like Hermann Rassow.[24]

When judging the propaganda of the pressure groups—the third major instance of activity together with the state and the parties—it is important to

[23] For a detailed justification of this view, see Eley, 'German Navy League', pp. 35ff.

[24] Deist, *Flottenpolitik*, pp. 100ff., attributes a much more constructive role to the Navy Office than this.

remember that we are dealing with something more than technical innovation. New techniques of agitation were made possible—were determined in that sense—by the incursion of new social groups into the public sphere, and often resulted from the political friction this entailed. In fact, the most radical and ambitious attempts to construct 'public opinion' as we now understand that term occurred either on the margins of party life proper or in the course of a full-scale assault on it. The most familiar example of this process has been established by Puhle's work on the Agrarian League, and it now seems clear that by the end of its first decade the latter had been successfully superimposed on the old Conservative Party. But this transformation of political style resulted not from the manipulative self-modernization of the existing leadership (though this explanation obviously works for individual Conservatives). It came much more from the self-activation of subaltern groups and the unprecedented demagogic campaigns they waged against the authorities during the 1890s, invariably *against* the counsels and sometimes the vigorous opposition of older-style Conservatives. The new levels of popular mobilization were precipitated, in other words, by a political conflict.

III

To illustrate the particular contribution of the *nationale Verbände* to the search for a more effective anti-Socialist propaganda, it is worth looking once more at the Navy League. Most obviously, and by contrast with the Christian Book League for instance, it was a membership organization, so that a large part of its literary activities were devoted simply to servicing the needs of the members. Thus the production of the monthly organ *Die Flotte*, which went to all fee-paying members, was by far the biggest item in the official budget, and the problem of getting it to the members efficiently was one of the movement's major preoccupations between 1900 and 1903. By 1904 it was also supplied to 1,132 newspapers inside Germany and 150 abroad, while a further 3,600 copies were deposited in railway waiting-rooms, dining-cars, ferries, passenger-steamers, hotels and coffee-houses, and 600 bound volumes donated to schools and public libraries. There were many other regular publications, including the official *Handbuch*, a guide to the organization of local meetings (with administrative hints, lists of recommended speakers and digests of suggested lectures), a manual of careers at sea, and a holiday guide to the seaside. A portrait of the Kaiser was produced in 1904 and sent in ten copies to all regional executives, and in the same year an album of naval photographs was also made available. The Navy League also produced naval postcards under the management of Major Toegel in Eisenach, a range of posters, and a library of naval literature in Berlin which by 1905 totalled 900 volumes.[25]

[25] For full details and references: Eley, 'German Navy League', pp. 151–3, 107ff.; *Jahresbericht* 1904, BA Coblenz, ZSg. 1, 195/2.

The most widely distributed item in a broad range of agitational literature was the so-called *Rassow-Tafeln*—depictions of German naval strength in poster, pamphlet and leaflet form which Hermann Rassow had been producing since the mid-1890s. In 1899–1900, 1,200,000 of these were put out in all three forms. In autumn 1901 Rassow produced a new edition, and the next year it sold 12,000 copies of the poster, 11,500 of the pamphlet and 99,000 of the leaflet. In 1905, 800,000 copies of the pamphlet were produced to coincide with the new Navy Bill under the name of *Deutschlands Seemacht*, and this was excerpted into two leaflets, in editions of 470,000 and 516,000 copies. Amongst the purchasers were the Ministries of Education and the Prussian Railways. In late 1901, at a low ebb in the Navy League's general agitation, Rassow himself gave a detailed description of the extent of his work. In Burg and its surrounding villages the posters hung in the classrooms of all *Volksschulen*, newspaper offices, hospitals, doctors' surgeries and lawyers' waiting-rooms. They were also given to the twenty most important inns and hotels in the town.[26] The *Rassow-Tafeln* were naturally only a part of the Navy League's output, and vast quantities of other leaflets were churned out, especially at moments of peak agitation. In 1904 the Central Office handled at least thirteen separate leaflets and pamphlets. Some of these had general themes, others contained specific demands, and others concentrated on appeals to specific groups of people, such as the working class, the peasantry or teachers. In the same year a number of regional and local executives produced their own leaflets with a particular regional bias: they included Cologne, Straßburg, Augsburg, Berlin, Rostock, Ludwigshafen, Hannover and Bavaria.[27]

So far, this was not too distant from the conventional literary operations of the Christian Book League. But the Navy League really distinguished itself by the use of the lecture meeting, the principal vehicle of agitation as against mere propaganda. This took a number of forms. First there was the event organized by the branches themselves which carried most of the weight of establishing the movement as a local presence, a special social occasion with limited political content, whose symbolism and accoutrements projected a dual image of patriotic jollity and bourgeois *Gemütlichkeit*. In this elaborate form the larger branches might manage three or four happenings a year: of the three public meetings in Weimar in 1904 one was a concert, another was the A.G.M., and only the third, addressed by Liebert on the 'Influence of Sea Power on the Development of a Nation's Strength', was called specifically as a lecture meeting.[28] But many of the larger branches spread their efforts over the surrounding countryside and the smaller towns. In 1902 the Navy League in Saxe-Weimar-Eisenach sent a team of twelve speakers to a total of thirty-six small villages, while in the first

[26] Rassow to Navy Office, Nov. 5th 1901, BA-MA, 2257, 94136. Figures from respective *Jahresberichte*.
[27] For full details: Eley, 'German Navy League', pp. 153f.
[28] *WeimZ*, Feb. 16th 1904, May 14th 1904, and Nov. 9th 1904.

three months of 1906 it organized a total of twenty-seven such lectures.[29] In addition the Presidium itself organized more ambitious programmes. It had sponsored extensive speaking tours for the Second Navy Bill in 1900, and this became even more important once the League began advancing its own demands after the end of 1903.[30] A crucial impetus for the latter was provided by Eduard von Liebert's highly successful excursion of the winter of 1903–4, which took him through most parts of Germany. In the winter of 1905–6 a particularly intensive campaign unfolded. Liebert was again active, as was Keim himself, and systematic campaigns were mounted in the regions. In Baden, for example, General Korwan spoke in Karlsruhe and Mannheim, while Neander of Hannover visited eighteen towns and villages; in addition, Sublieutenant Kraus gave sixteen talks in the state's *Mittelschulen*.

A special version of the lecture meeting, with added novelty and greater popular impact, was the film-show. The Navy League's early use of film in its several rudimentary forms was a good illustration of its greater propagandist imagination. Within six years of the cinema's birth the League was already exploring the potential of the new medium and was one of the first agencies to realize its political uses.[31] The success of a series of film shows organized by Gustav Williger (General Manager of the *Kattowitzer AG* and a Presidium member for a few months in 1902) in Kattowitz in Silesia did much to prompt the Presidium's interest: in nine days in March 1901 24,000 people, including many parties of schoolchildren, visited nineteen performances to be informed of life at sea in ways which lay beyond the conventional lecture form. Armed with the enthusiasm of this experience, the Presidium concluded an agreement with the infant *Deutsche Biograph- und Mutoskop-Gesellschaft* for a further series of performances in Rostock, Brunswick, Eisenach, Danzig and Stuttgart. These took place in the autumn of 1901 and drew a total audience of 32,000. This was surpassed in January 1902 by a series of shows in a single town: performances organized in Witten-on-the-Ruhr by Schramm, a local factory-owner, were seen by 34,000 in eight days, including 18,000 schoolchildren.

---

[29] Annual report of Major von Hagen to the Gen. Meeting, *WeimZ*, Feb. 22nd 1903, and the executive's *Tätigkeitsbericht* for 1906, copy in AdH Lübeck, DFV, 8.

[30] In 1900 Adolph von Wenckstern held a total of 25 lectures in 12 weeks across the whole of north and central Germany, Dr Ebeling gave 22 lectures in 24 days in Westphalia in March and April, and Heinrich Oberwinder was highly active in Alsace-Lorraine and the South-West. Detailed references from Eley, 'German Navy League', p. 158, also for the following.

[31] Despite the immense proliferation of publications on the cinema and film, there are no good studies of their political uses before 1914. Some general hints may be found in the following: W. Fritz, *Geschichte des österreichischen Films* (Vienna, 1969), pp. 19–25; J. Leyda, *Kino. A History of the Russian and Soviet Film* (London, 1960), pp. 17–35; R. Low and R. Manvell, *The History of the British Film 1896–1906*, and R. Low, *The History of the British Film 1906–1914* (both London, 1973). One of the few adequate historical treatments is T. Gutsche, *The History and Social Significance of Motion Pictures in South Africa 1895–1940* (Cape Town, 1972).

The Witten branch claimed accessions of one thousand new members.[32]

In 1902 the Presidium extended and refined this activity. As well as large film-shows using the sophisticated but expensive Biograph, it also organized mobile shows for the countryside using the cheaper Kinematograph. In the autumn of 1902 a film-show of this second kind toured villages in Hannover, Pomerania, the Rhineland, Silesia, royal Saxony and the Bavarian regions of Swabia and Central Franconia. In all some 57,900 people were enthralled by primitive films of battleships and naval installations, bringing a new membership of six or seven hundred. In 1903 similar tours were organized for Hessen, Brunswick, Baden and Schleswig-Holstein: in Hessen, Becker, a retired officer from Darmstadt, organized performances in fourteen branches in twenty-eight days, drawing a total of 30,000 visitors; in Brunswick, von Salmuth, likewise a retired officer, organized forty showings with an audience of 12,000 and an accession of 300 members. The larger towns were not neglected. In 1902 extended showings using the Biograph were given in twenty-eight towns all over Germany, with a total audience of 373,180, of whom at least half were schoolchildren, providing a new membership of 2,035. Each performance was introduced by a short talk on the aims of the Navy League, and the Presidium advised that films achieved their maximum effect when accompanied by martial music and appropriate noises like cannon-blasts and ships' whistles. The annual report for 1902 was rapturous: 'It is the unanimous verdict that there is scarcely a better means for filling the inlander with love and understanding' for the importance of sea power.[33]

By 1904 it was conventional to carry the naval message to the people by film wherever possible. At the very least lectures were to be accompanied by slides: by 1904 the Navy League had assembled fifty-four different sets, with titles such as 'The Russo-Japanese War', 'Service on Board' and 'A Tour of a Modern Battleship'; by 1905 they had increased to sixty-two and the Presidium received 388 applications for their use.[34] Many of these sets were commissioned by the Presidium itself, and the League also financed several of its own films.[35] In

---

[32] Details from respective *Jahresberichte*.

[33] *Jahresbericht* 1902, p. 7, BA Coblenz, ZSg. 1, 195/2. For an indication of the size of the venture and the degree of organization involved, see the correspondence concerning the visit of a mobile film-show in Versmold on Mar. 19th 1905, especially that with the local schools, StA Detmold, M. 2 Halle, Amt Versmold, 867. See also the detailed instructions sent by the Presidium, *Winke für Kinematographische Vorführungen*, ibid.

[34] *Jahresbericht* 1904, p. 5, BA Coblenz, ZSg. 1, 195/2. For a surviving collection of slides, on the theme of a visit to the South Seas: SA Nuremberg, Vereine, 19, 20.

[35] e.g. in 1909 the League commissioned the film *Bunte Bilder von der deutschen Flotte* from *Deutsche Bioscop GmbH* in Berlin. (G. Lamprecht, *Deutsche Stummfilme*, I, Berlin, 1969, p. 39.) In addition the League seems to have participated in producing the following films during the First World War: *Stolz weht die Flagge Schwarz-Weiss-Rot* (1916); *Hoch klingt das Lied vom U-Boot-Mann* (1917); *Wenn frei die Meere für deustche Fahrt . . . !* (1917). All three films were scripted by Fritz Proschnewsky, a full-time official in the Navy League's Central Office. I am grateful to Marcus Phillips for this information.

8*

addition, contracts were signed for the installation of mutoscopes in railway stations and other public places: these were small machines which provided moving pictures for the insertion of ten pfennigs and the turn of a handle. By 1903 484 had been installed. But 1905 seems to have been the peak year for the Navy League's use of film. In 1904 there had been a total of 1,400 performances in 512 towns with about 650,000 visitors; in 1905 there were 1,599 performances in 572 towns with a total audience of 873,385. But subsequently these figures were hard to sustain. The Presidium complained that audiences were growing bored with the same old pictures of battleships, and branches were requesting more entertaining subject-matter. Moreover, growing numbers of small kinematographs were touring the country as the commercial possibilities of the new medium became more obvious, and the League found it difficult to beat the counter-attractions of comedy and drama which the alternative films provided. In 1905 income from mutoscopes sank to only half the previous year's figures and sixty-five machines were wound up as a consequence.[36] But despite this falling-off, the League continued to exploit film with great profit, and there can be small doubt as to its effectiveness.

Film, of course, was a *popular* medium, and it was precisely this that attracted the Navy League. One detailed presidial directive pronounced in no uncertain terms that agitation should be aimed 'not only at the so-called educated classes, but even more at the broad mass of the economically active part of the nation, in the first instance, that is, at the workers'. The Navy League went to some lengths, from devising special categories of literature to deliberately instructing local branches (without notable success) to co-opt workers on to their executives, to convert this imperative into a demonstrable reality.[37] It was no accident that the leaflet aimed at the working class in 1905 was distributed in 300,000

[36] Jahresbericht 1905, p. 7, BA Coblenz, ZSg. 1, 195/2. See also the statement by Simonis to the Kiel Congress, June 4th 1909, *Protokoll*, p. 52, BA-MA Freiburg, 2277, 94231. The mutoscopes were not always used for patriotic purposes. In April 1907, at the height of the Centre Party's resentment against the Navy League, the *Deutsche Reichszeitung* in Bonn reported with righteous indignation that the machine maintained by the League on Cologne station was being used for the perpetration of anti-Catholic slanders. Far from producing pictures of life at sea, it bore the inscription 'The Monastery Don Juan', and offered scenes of clandestine clerical seduction. At about the same time the SPD *Münchner Post* reported that one of the League's machines on the Anhalt Station in Berlin provided 'A Peep into a Lady's Bath'. See the cutting sent to Bülow by Anton Rederer, probably Apr.–May 1907, BA-MA Freiburg, 2276, 94230 .

[37] e.g. the Presidium's circular of Oct. 1900, StA Münster, Kr. Steinfurt, Landratsamt, 454: 'In order to express the German Navy League's character as a great *Volksverein*', it was essential to bring 'workers, artisans and peasants' on to the executives at a local level, and the same was true of teachers, doctors and lawyers. Virtually no branches seem to have responded successfully to this injunction. Though the Nuremberg branch tried without success to find a suitable artisan and teacher, for instance, it forbore to search out an eligible worker. See SA Nuremberg, Vereine, 19, 1.

copies whereas that for the peasantry ran to only 40,000.[38] In the same year the Navy League ran two larger pamphlets, *Meister Thesen* and *Auf dem Elbdampfer*, aimed specifically at workers.[39] Commissioned by the Presidium from Gustav Adolf Erdmann in 1904, *Meister Thesen* contained in a fictionalized form all the typical arguments used to attract working-class support, and for that reason is worth a more detailed examination.

The story in the pamphlet centres around a working-class couple, Franz and Frida Lahr. It opens with the distraught Frida tearfully explaining to the sympathetic wife of Thesen, a foreman at the steelworks, that Franz has been laid off with two hundred of his workmates. Frau Thesen assures her patiently that the factory is not to blame: there is simply not enough work to go round. Later that day Frida tries to dissuade an excited Franz from attending an SPD protest meeting to be addressed by the Reichstag deputy Rupprecht. She warns him that a strike would be an unmitigated disaster for the workers and their families, and follows through with a bitter denunciation of Rupprecht: he has never been a worker himself, is an intellectual with no understanding for the worker's situation, and like his party comrades wants only to manipulate the discontent for his own selfish purposes; the real friend of the worker was 'old Master Thesen'. With some effort she convinces him to pay Thesen a visit *en route* to the meeting. In the Thesen household they naturally receive the warmest of welcomes, and after the opening greetings Thesen proceeds to read them a letter from his son, who is serving in the Caribbean with the Navy. This describes the parlous state of the Latin American republics ('There it's a matter of being constantly on your guard for the protection of German interests'), and details a recent incident in one state where the cruiser *Gazelle* was summoned for the defence of German nationals and their property. Sadly, this 'one little ship' could do little by itself, and only a last-minute intervention by the British and Americans secured the interests of 'Germandom'. The incident badly exposed Germany's naval weakness, the letter continues, and damaged German prestige, especially by comparison with the British. The humiliation was completed by the appearance of *two* Italian cruisers on the scene. The son's letter provides the cue for a detailed argument about the naval question, and Thesen proceeds to ask Franz for his opinion.

In the ensuing discussion, of course, Thesen wins hands down. He begins by expounding the first principle of the naval movement's credo: that the naval question is not an object of sectional politics, but a 'question for the entire people and plays a role in the life of every single individual, however rich or poor'. Franz responds with orthodox SPD arguments, but sees them demolished one by one. Big government orders for the shipbuilding industry, for instance,

[38] *Jahresbericht* 1905, pp. 6f., BA Coblenz, ZSg. 1, 195/2. The leaflets in question were *Der deutsche Arbeiter und die Flotte*, and *Der deutsche Bauer und die Flotte*.

[39] The first was by Gustav Adolf Erdmann, the second by Hermann Rassow. They were issued in 5,000 and 30,000 copies respectively, ibid., p. 7.

provide thousands of workers with much-needed employment. The claim that Germany cannot afford a big Navy is also dismissed by invoking the large quantities of money spent on alcohol. Likewise, poverty is discounted as a social problem: material need results from inefficiency and lack of thrift; the poor unlike the frugal Franz and Frida, spend all their money on beer and spirits. Driven rapidly into a corner, Franz starts to deny that the workers oppose the fleet totally, and expresses disbelief when Thesen points out that many Social Democrats oppose giving any money to the Navy at all. Finally when Thesen describes the horrors of a blockade (' "For God's sake, Herr Thesen!" cried Frau Frida, leaping up in great excitement, "Is it possible that even we could experience such a fearful misfortune?" '), Franz concedes that the workers need the protection of a fleet. The substance now conceded, Franz argues that Germany already has a fine Navy. The discussion is now conducted entirely on the Navy League's own ground, and in a final climactic flourish Master Thesen spreads out one of Hermann Rassow's wall-charts on the table. The 'facts' and the naval idea are now triumphant. As a parting shot Thesen tells the Lahrs that their immediate problem has also been solved: he has heard that next day the management of the steelworks will find work for the two hundred laid off workers by shortening hours. As they wend their way home, Franz remarks to his wife 'in a breath of the deepest conviction: If only a Master Thesen could speak to every German worker!'[40]

The pamphlet is a classic example of Navy League propaganda. The anti-Socialist orientation is basic: the pamphlet opens with a description of recession, unemployment and the incipient threat of SPD-inspired strike action; in this context the naval idea is conceived as a means of replacing unthinking discontent at momentary hardship with a rational belief in the long-term inevitability of material prosperity, fostered by skilful intervention by the state and secured by the protective screen of a strong navy. Put slightly differently, it might help form a compliant workforce and a quiescent working class. The familiar right-wing stereotype of the Social Democrat is also present: he is an alien intruder, an intellectual (not yet a Bolshevik or a Jew), invariably from a comfortable bourgeois background, often a small businessman himself on the quiet. He speaks fine words from the rostrum of a political meeting, but has never done anything concrete for the working class; he takes their money to support him in the Reichstag, and is interested only in exploiting their problems for his own ends.[41] The story is informed by an implicit hostility to the independent industrial and political organization of the workers, and stresses the futility

[40] For a copy of the pamphlet, BA-MA Freiburg, 2299, 94351.

[41] For good examples: 'Arminus', *Die Sozialdemokratie, wie sie liebt und lebt!* (Berlin, 1911); H. F. Bürger, *Soziale Tatsachen und sozialdemokratische Lehren* (Berlin, 1900); Baron Falkenegg, *'Wenn die letzte Krone wie Glas zerbricht'. Zeitgemässe Betrachtungen* (Berlin, 1903); F. S. Neumann, *Die Sozialdemokratie als Arbeitgeberin und Unternehmerin* (Berlin, 1909); J. Vorster, *Fürst Bismarck. Ein Freund des deutschen Arbeiters* (Cologne, 1896).

and irrationality of industrial action: 'a strike is the greatest of stupidities for a family man and a misfortune for us all'. Unemployment comes from an iron law of the economy, and workers have no recourse but the benevolence of the employers and the eventual improvement of their situation. For guidance in their predicament they should look to 'old Master Thesen', whose benign petty-bourgeois serenity offers a paradigm of working-class quiescence. He has risen from the shop-floor through intelligence, hard work and frugality, achieving a position of respect with the whole community. He has nothing to do with the Social Democrats. In fact, he is the antithesis of the frivolous, anti-national, Socialist subversive.

The pamphlet's production also reveals something of the Navy League's approach to the working class. Its general appearance was thought to be very important: it should be 'handsomely decorated' with lots of 'coloured pictures' which caught the eye at first glance. It should be intelligible to the ordinary working man, addressing him in his own language and dealing with familiar matters from everyday life.[42] This stricture, though clearly an elementary principle of popular agitation, also reflected a particular view of working-class psychology which found its clearest expression, as in so many aspects of the League's propaganda, in the practice of Hermann Rassow.[43] The pamphlet *Auf dem Elbdampfer*, in many ways very similar to Erdmann's *Meister Thesen* and likewise commissioned by the Presidium in 1904 was typical of this. It consisted of a long conversation, in fictional form, between several workers (a journeyman tailor, a Social Democratic cigar-maker, a foreman) and a peasant about the implications of the Russo-Japanese War for Germany's naval armaments. Before submitting the final draft for publication Rassow gave it to several 'little people' to read, made many changes as a result of their recommendations, and then went through the whole thing, 'sentence by sentence', once more with a factory-worker.[44]

Above all, Rassow insisted that workers be pursued with literature and information at every available opportunity. It was vital to follow them into their own haunts and to take the portable slide-projector into their pubs. He himself never went anywhere without a supply of leaflets or pamphlets, and made a point of handing them out to any worker he happened to meet, whether porters, ticket-collectors, waiters or navvies. Whilst setting out early one morning during

[42] Presidium's circular, Oct. 1904, BA-MA Freiburg, 2276, 94229. See also Rassow to Varrentrapp, Nov. 27th 1904, ibid., 2257, 94136; Rassow's address to the Stuttgart Congress, May 27th 1905, *Protokoll*, pp. 15ff., ibid., 2276, 94230.

[43] 'The little man and his thought patterns certainly interest me in the highest measure.' Ibid.

[44] Ibid. By the end of 1904 the Presidium had distributed 50,000 copies of the pamphlet, and Rassow himself had secured its publication in eight local papers around his home town of Burg. The Presidium also procured its publication by Naumann's *Hilfe* in 8,000 copies. See Rassow to Varrentrapp, Nov. 27th 1904, ibid., 2257, 94136. In 1905 a further 30,000 were distributed. See *Jahresbericht* 1905, p. 5, BA Coblenz, ZSg. 1, 195/2.

a cycling holiday in Thuringia, for instance, he carefully put thirty copies of *Auf dem Elbdampfer* into his satchel: when he passed a crowd of factory-workers on their way to work he handed these out as he passed; as he later commented, the whole thing happened so quickly that they had no choice but to take the pamphlet or let it drop at their feet. His sons assured him that every copy was picked up. Everything depended, Rassow argued, on treating the worker as an intelligent human being:

> No ticket-collector, porter or waiter . . . escapes his naval leaflet; if at all possible he gets a verbal explanation to go with it. The man then feels treated like a 'gentleman', for he has been credited with the ability to *understand* something. And he *can* understand it when I begin as follows: Look here at Table XXI. Costs: Germany 3.50 per head, France 7 (he: that's double). Yes, right, but the French don't enjoy paying taxes any more than we do. And the English actually pay *16* marks (he: Shame!). And in Germany we call that 'boundless naval plans'. But if it's only 3.50 that's nonsense (he: . . . You're right there, *I never thought of it like that at all*). —That is the introduction that constantly recurs in all its variations.

It was this kind of consideration that led the Presidium to select a subtler method of distribution for *Meister Thesen*. Each branch would persuade local 'employers, factory-owners, the managers of businesses etc.' to purchase a quantity at cost price of forty pfennigs. They would then be given to carefully chosen workers 'who exercised a particular influence on their colleagues'. It was important that other workers should want to read the pamphlet on their own initiative: if distributed in this way it would win more attention 'than if the factory-owner gave out copies indiscriminately to every worker'. As Rassow said: '. . . everyone can be made to feel like a "fellow-citizen" if he is credited with enough education to read a piece of literature'.[45]

IV

The burden of this discussion has been to distinguish the special features of the *nationale Verbände*, the innovations and particularities which set their politics apart from those of the government and the conventional right. One of the arguments running through the particular analyses of this study has been that the ideology and practice of radical nationalism simply cannot be assimilated to the so-called 'strategies of stabilization' which recent historians have tried to attribute to Wilhelmine government in the period of Bülow and Tirpitz. I have tried to argue at some length that the primary importance of the *nationale Verbände* cannot be grasped through an 'integrationist' understanding of nationalist ideology: their politics did not correspond to the interests of the Wilhelmine 'power élite' or 'ruling strata' in any simple or direct way,

[45] For detailed references, Eley, 'German Navy League', pp. 168ff.

either by conception, effect or 'objective' function; on the contrary, those politics were defined by an antagonism to the establishment. The twin compulsions of imperialism and anti-Socialism naturally created broad identities of interest at the most general level, but to regard the nationalist pressure groups as somehow contributing to the defence of an ill-defined 'status quo' is a reductionist mis-reading of the radical-nationalist experience and the populist ideology it generated. The same point needs to be made just as forcefully in the area of propaganda. Superficially, there seems little to separate the three instances of activity discussed above, namely those of the state, the parties and the new agitational pressure groups of the 1890s. They all appear to have reflected a general tendency towards the intensification of public life, formed by a common context of expanding publicity and popular literacy, and simply using the new materials of propaganda as a kind of shared operational necessity. Yet if we look more closely, some interesting variations may be diagnosed.

In other words, much the same pattern of inflexible *Honoratiorenpolitik* and radical-nationalist dissidence reappears in the area of propaganda. The propaganda interventions of the state tended to stay firmly within a traditional bureaucratic mode, and were concerned mainly to isolate an existing constituency from the harmful effects of political life. Whether through the Christian Book League, through the Army and veterans' clubs, through the educational system and post-school, pre-conscription youth organizations, or through the disciplining of its own employees, the state was mainly concerned with the paternalist protection of a subject population whose loyalties had been left vulnerable to 'modern' influences. The Navy Office was slightly different in that it moved with greater confidence in the more open discourse of parliament and the press. But the content of its propaganda was too much limited by the technicalities of naval policy and its chosen constituency too restricted for it to act as an organizer of popular opinion in an innovative way. It chose to do this through independent organizations like the Navy League, but understandably took fright when the latter used its popular resources for political campaigns against the government. On the whole, government remained suspicious of genuine popular agitation until a late stage before the First World War. As the Minister of War, General Heinrich von Goßler, had said to his colleagues in August 1900: 'auxiliary organizations with an agitational purpose' were not wanted.[46]

Moreover, as suggested above, the political parties were little better equipped than the state to provide an outlet for the political energies of newly activated strata in the localities: though they were in the process of reorganizing themselves at the centre, this was invariably done in a way which excluded the new men rather than admitting them, and in any case the process of readjustment

[46] Excerpt from the *Protokoll* of the Ministry of State, Aug. 27th 1900, ZStA Potsdam, Rkz., 2261: 38f. The Ministry was discussing a proposal (which it turned down) from the Navy League to hang posters in government buildings in support of German troops in China.

was extremely uneven, both within and between parties. These differences of propagandist adaptability became an object of urgent political debate in the aftermath of the 1903 elections, for though the tariff settlement had apparently cleared the path for co-operation against the Socialists, the actual outcome of the polls confirmed yet again both the chronic disunity of the bourgeois parties and the popular advance of the SPD. The rise in the latter's parliamentary strength from fifty-six to eighty-one seats made the question of anti-Socialist strategy an urgent priority for the right, particularly when industrial militancy also increased.[47] In such circumstances the minds of some old-style Conservatives turned once again to the idea of repression. In December 1903 Udo Graf von Stolberg-Wernigerode, an elder statesman of the Conservative Party and the Chairman of its Reichstag fraction, bemoaned the softness of the National Liberals and Centre and appealed to Bülow for a fresh 'legislative intervention of the state' against the SPD.

As always, such ideas found a sympathetic echo in some military circles, but Bülow himself remained carefully unimpressed by the demand for a new Anti-Socialist Law. The government's unhappy experiences in 1894–5 and 1897 with the Revolution Bill and the Prussian Law of Association had shown that the parliamentary basis for such a move was at the very least unpredictable, and the defeat of the Hard-Labour Bill in 1899 was a final warning against premature repetition. In his reply to Stolberg-Wernigerode, therefore, Bülow argued that a change of course in both the Centre and National Liberal Parties was a precondition for such a move. Otherwise, 'a procedure against the Social Democrats would be paralysed . . . by a conflict between the government and the bourgeois parties themselves'. At all costs Bülow wished to avoid the situation in which the government had to choose between 'victory of the revolution and *Staatsstreich* with absolutism'. A course of confrontation with the SPD would commit Bülow to a narrow parliamentary base of Conservatives and right-wing National Liberals at the very time that he was busily cultivating both the Centre and the left liberals. Accordingly, he advised Stolberg that the national parties should not always rely on the government to take the initiative, but should step in themselves.[48]

When Bülow made this remark he certainly knew that prominent adherents of *Sammlungspolitik* were preparing to do exactly that. Several independent centres of anti-Socialist propaganda pre-dated the elections of 1903—the regionally active 'Economic Defence League' in Harburg (set up in 1900), Friedrich Lange's 'National League for Reich Elections' formed in March 1902,

---

[47] See Saul, *Staat, Industrie, Arbeiterbewegung*, pp. 13–50.

[48] The Stolberg-Bülow exchange (Dec. 27th 1903, Jan. 7th 1904) has been referred to several times in existing work: e.g. D. Fricke, 'Der Reichsverband gegen die Sozialdemokratie von seiner Gründung bis zu den Reichstagswahlen 1907', *ZfG*, 7 (1959), p. 245; Witt, *Finanzpolitik*, p. 79; Saul, *Staat, Industrie, Arbeiterbewegung*, p. 34. The original may be found in ZStA Potsdam, Rkz., 1391/5.

and Max Lorenz's *Antisozialdemokratische Korrespondenz* sponsored by a group of Free Conservatives and right-wing National Liberals since early 1903 and financed largely by Krupp—and during the summer of 1903 several farther-reaching initiatives began to materialize.[49] The first of these came from Heinrich Fränkel, by this time a well-known freelance journalist specializing in anti-Socialist polemics, who issued a circular at the end of June 1903 calling for the formation of a 'Central Bureau for the Combating of Social Democracy'. A month later he had gained the support of many businessmen and landowners, together with some leading Conservatives and National Liberal parliamentarians.[50] By September a second group had formed, comprising mainly Free Conservatives, right-wing National Liberals and leading members of the CVDI, and the two initiatives coalesced for a joint conference in Halle on September 20th 1903. Meanwhile the progress of the Crimmitschau textile strike had galvanized employers into some unaccustomed organizational co-operation, and during December and January plans cohered for a national employers' association. The latter clearly gave added impetus to the idea of a new anti-Socialist propaganda agency; and after a further conference in Berlin in November, when Eduard von Liebert was adopted as Chairman of the venture, the Halle group announced the official foundation of the Imperial League Against Social Democracy at the start of January 1904. The thirty-three provisional committee-members included seven leading Conservatives, eight Free Conservatives and five National Liberals (all on the right), while eight had leading posts in employers' organizations or chambers of commerce, predominantly in coal, iron and steel. The new organization, which held its founding conference on May 9th 1904, was unambiguously an outgrowth of the conventional party-political right, formed by the tradition of *Sammlung* and the Cartel. Both the Centre and the left liberals were notably absent.[51]

At first the new organization grew slowly: by the end of 1904 there were only 2,879 individual members, a further 1,201 organized in seven local branches, and another 14,210 in corporately affiliated organizations (e.g. the Patriotic Association of Reuß j.L. with 2,700 members, the Central German Evangelical Workers' Associations with 2,100, and the Harburg Economic Defence League with around 4,000). In the next two years the total figures improved to 81,747 and 144,000 respectively, rising to a respectable total of

[49] For details of the three existing organizations, see Saul, *Staat, Industrie, Arbeiterbewegung*, p. 116, (notes 6–8).

[50] For details of Fränkel's initiative, see Saul, *Staat, Industrie, Arbeiterbewegung*, p. 117; the account in Hall, 'War of Words', pp. 30f., is garbled.

[51] This account follows that of F. Taylor, 'Foundation and Early Development of the Imperial League Against Social Democracy', unpub. MS. By comparison Saul's account (*Staat, Industrie, Arbeiterbewegung*, pp. 115–32) is disorganized and incomplete. Fricke, 'Reichsverband', is still a useful general introduction. Hall, 'War of Words', pp. 30ff., adds nothing new.

211,000 members by the end of 1909.[52] At first, as one Executive member said, the priority was 'simply to gather members by all means', and it was only by 1906 that 'the exact relationship of the affiliated organizations to the centre' was properly regulated.[53] By the end of that year the number of local branches had grown from only 91 in April to 287, rising to 702 by the end of 1909.[54]

Liebert remained Chairman of the Imperial League until the end of the Empire. He was assisted by an Executive, which numbered eight members in 1904 and thirteen by 1909, not including the salaried Secretary Albert Bovenschen, who was recruited from the Eastern Marches Society.[55] Like the wider Committee (forty-three members in September 1905), it consisted overwhelmingly of Conservatives, Free Conservatives and right-wing National Liberals, most of them big landowners, CVDI businessmen and commercial lawyers, with a smattering of radical nationalists (e.g. Lange, Wanckel, Kurd von Strantz and Sieg a retired Colonel from Wiesbaden).[56] The aim of the Imperial League, as Liebert defined it at the foundation, was to fight the SPD on two fronts: by working for anti-Socialist unity in elections, and by providing a system of social support for 'all those who are oppressed by Social Democracy', whether small businessmen, artisans or workers.[57]

By comparison with the *nationale Verbände*, amongst whom it can only partly be counted, the Imperial League Against Social Democracy was simultaneously the most ambitious of all the agitational pressure groups and the least able to break clear of the established party-political framework. At the level of

---

[52] Figures taken from Fricke, 'Reichsverband', p. 257, and Taylor, 'Foundation', p. 16. After 1904 the membership of corporately affiliated organizations was not separately recorded. In 1904 corporate members ranged from the large affiliates mentioned above to local branches of the Eastern Marches Society and a small railwaymen's club in Erfurt. By 1906 there were 340 in total, mainly veterans' and *Mittelstand* clubs.

[53] Dirksen, in the Committee Meeting of Dec. 12th 1904, minutes in ZStA Potsdam, Rkz., 1395/1, cit. by Taylor, 'Foundation', p. 16.

[54] Saul, *Staat, Industrie, Arbeiterbewegung*, p. 129.

[55] Heinrich von Tiedemann, Chairman of the Eastern Marches Society, had been involved in the Imperial League at a preparatory stage and was a member of its Committee. The original members of the Executive were as follows: Liebert, Bovenschen (as Secretary), the lawyer Hans Regula (for the Harburg Economic Defence League), Paul Hagemann (National Liberal lawyer from Thuringia), Wilhelm Hirsch (National Liberal Secretary of the Essen Chamber of Commerce), Julius Vorster (Free Conservative fertilizer manufacturer, Chairman of the protectionist Cologne Association of Industrialists, member of CVDI Directorate), Willy von Dirksen (Free Conservative parliamentarian), Karl von Arnim-Züsedom (Conservative parliamentarian). They were joined by Friedrich Lange (after the merger of his National League for Reich Elections in 1905), Carl Graf zu Dohna-Schlodien (Conservative landowner), Max Roetger (Chairman of CVDI), Wanckel (architect in Altenburg, leading associate of Lange in German-Union), and Hermann Graf von Arnim-Muskau (Free Conservative parliamentarian, formerly on the Pan-German Executive). Ibid., p. 453 (note 59).

[56] For a full list of Committee members, see the manifesto issued on Sept. 27th 1905, copy in BA-MA Freiburg, 3141, I. 3. 1.–12.

[57] Cited by Taylor, 'Foundation', p. 10.

propaganda, for instance, its literary output was prodigious: during the entire ten years of its peacetime existence the Imperial League distributed 47,067,961 copies of 170 different leaflets, together with 1,052,324 copies of more substantial pamphlets. Its substantial *Handbuch für nichtsozialdemokratische Wähler* sold 16,000 copies in three editions, and in 1909 it began publishing a popular *Nationaler Volkskalender*, whose distribution rose unevenly from 150,000 in 1910 to 330,000 in 1914.[58] Elections were a special focus for this activity, and in 1907 the Imperial League gave out a grand total of 10,149,330 leaflets. Its intercession performed a vital service for the bourgeois parties, for, as Bovenschen said, they were invariably still amateurs in matters of electoral organization. The National Liberals in particular 'had not the slightest idea how to handle an election by organizing the contact-men, distributing leaflets, supervising the electoral lists and working on the non-voters'.[59] In the Hannover by-election of June 1906 the Imperial League provided a constituency office of some hundred personnel, 104 mobile election centres, and a thousand volunteers for canvassing and leafleting.[60]

Such efforts were not confined to election times, and great importance was attached to creating a continuous organized presence within the working class itself. One expression of this concern was the so-called speakers' courses, in which potential agitators were taught how to lecture, chair meetings and popularize the movement's message: the first was held in December 1904 for thirty-six pupils, but by 1909 over a thousand were attending; in October 1907 this activity was extended to the provinces, with an attendance of some 6,000 in 1912–13, and in 1908 special courses were begun for teachers.[61] Following the example of the People's League for a Catholic Germany, workers themselves would ideally be recruited on to such courses, so that the fight against the SPD might devolve increasingly on to patriotic sections of the working class. According to Liebert, the Imperial League wished to train the 'more intelligent men from the workers' estate and the *Mittelstand*' who could communicate more naturally with their peers than could the 'educated man'.[62] A similar calculation lay behind the setting-up of 'National Labour Secretariats' to rival the SPD in the provision of legal advice and information on matters affecting work: by May 1909 only twenty-three of these existed, rising to 98 by the start of the war. They were meant to be staffed by working-class recruits trained on the speakers' courses, aided by the voluntary expertise of 'suitably

[58] Details from *10 Jahre Reichsverband (Festgabe der Hauptstelle des Reichsverbandes gegen die Sozialdemokratie)* (Berlin, 1914), pp. 52ff.
[59] Bovenschen to the Hagen National Liberal Party, Apr. 21st 1906, cit. in *Vorwärts*, Apr. 28th 1906.
[60] Saul, *Staat, Industrie, Arbeiterbewegung*, p. 129.
[61] Details ibid., p. 131, and Hall, 'War of Words', p. 32.
[62] See E. von Liebert, 'Der Reichsverband gegen die Sozialdemokratie', in *Konservative Monatschrift für das gesamte Leben der Gegenwart*, 1906, p. 631.

qualified members of the educated strata'. The aim as Bovenschen saw it, was to drive a patriotic 'wedge into the working estate'.[63]

In making contact with industrial workers the Imperial League experienced all the familiar difficulties, and succeeded best when a captive audience was at hand. Thus in 1910 it began sending leaflets through the post directly to workers on the recommendation of their employers, in order to protect them from Socialist reprisals. In early 1914 3,748 employers co-operated in this way, leading to the dispatch of 1,309,000 leaflets to a total of 460,000 workers: but the largest category of employers were farmers, while most of the workers were either unorganized agricultural labourers or the members of company unions in the engineering branches.[64] Moreover, when the Imperial League experimented with overtly political initiatives of its own by sponsoring the 'patriotic workers associations' in 1907, it encountered resistance from the big CVDI employers who opposed any semblance of autonomous working-class activity, however nominal, as the thin end of a trade-unionist wedge.[65]

This pinpointed a more general political handicap: both the left liberals and Centre were fairly solidly hostile from the beginning, but the Imperial League also provoked suspicions from the Conservatives and National Liberals as soon as it crossed the boundary between general anti-Socialist propaganda and specific political innovation. Thus when it began constructing a branch organization the Conservative leadership accused it of illegitimate competition and commented pointedly that it was no task of the Imperial League 'to weaken the organization of the old parties'. In the aftermath of the 1907 elections the Conservatives repeated these objections and denounced the Imperial League's drive to expand its local apparatus as the 'quite monstrous plan to create an organization which embraces all parties, or more accurately swallows them up'.[66] The reaction of the National Liberals was much the same: the decision to set up 'independent branches where political organizations of the national parties already exist' (i.e. in West Germany) would 'lead only to fragmentation and recriminations'.[67] Despite its contribution to the anti-Socialist victory of the 1907 elections, in other words, the Imperial League had simultaneously reached the threshold of its 'legitimate' activity. By intervening in the constituencies to organize united candidatures against the SPD, it had invaded the party-political domain, and its natural anxiety to build further on this success unavoidably threatened the integrity of the established parties. Powerless before

[63] See Bovenschen's memo of Dec. 1904, ZStA Potsdam, Rkz., 1395/1, cit. Taylor, 'Foundation', p. 25. Figures from Saul, *Staat, Industrie, Arbeiterbewegung*, p. 125.

[64] Ibid., p. 127.

[65] See F. Taylor, 'The Imperial League Against Social Democracy and the "National Workers' Movement" ', unpub. MS, esp. p. 20; Mattheier, *Die Gelben*, pp. 193–218; Saul, *Staat, Industrie, Arbeiterbewegung*, pp. 133–87.

[66] Ibid., p. 121.

[67] See *DortmZ*, May 13th 1907: 'From the Imperial League Against Social Democracy', for a detailed report.

Conservative and National Liberal objections, the Imperial League shelved its wider political ambitions and retreated into the less contentious practice of popular propaganda, abstaining completely from the Prussian Landtag elections of 1908.[68]

This contradiction had been present from the start in the two main initiatives from which the Imperial League had been born. Fränkel's idea of a 'Central Bureau' had been supported mainly by loyal party men: Conservatives like Oskar von Normann, Friedrich von Loebell (shortly to become Bülow's head of the Chancellory), Karl von Pappenheim-Liebenau, Hans Graf von Kanitz and Hans Freiherr von Maltzahn-Grimmen, and National Liberals like Theodor Habenicht (Party Chairman in royal Saxony), Hans Zabel (Secretary-General in Westphalia), and Adolf Metzger (Secretary in Württemberg). This group, for whom Arnim-Züsedom seems to have emerged as spokesman, viewed the proposed organization mainly as a national clearing-house for anti-Socialist literature, with no local apparatus to speak of. A second grouping, however, dominated by the major political voices of the heavy-industrial interest and some leading Free Conservatives, wanted much more than this.[69]

The differences were conveniently specified by Sieg, a retired colonel from Wiesbaden who attended the Halle conference in September 1904, and who identified himself with this second group. According to Sieg the envisaged foundation should be a mass agitational movement with an extensive local apparatus, an exact patriotic counterpart to the SPD and a means of defeating it politically. It would both sponsor patriotic workers for the Reichstag and establish local centres for legal advice and the disbursement of welfare. The national centre would concern itself mainly with propaganda and electoral finance, whilst local branches would organize resistance to 'Social-Democratic terrorism' on the ground. Taylor has summarized succinctly the differences between these two schemes:

> 'Sieg's extremely ambitious plan proposed much more than the setting-up of a mere "Anti-Socialist Centre" as envisaged by Arnim-Züsedom and his supporters. It was clearly hoped to create a large and vocal movement with its own mass base, intervening in all areas of political, economic and social life. The difference . . . was typified in the political and social situations of the protagonists . . . Sieg, a middle-class ex-officer in an urban area, involved in the Navy and Pan-German Leagues and without any clear party-political affiliations, was concerned with mobilizing the masses for the "national"

[68] Saul, *Staat, Industrie, Arbeiterbewegung*, p. 121.

[69] The provisional steering committee which emerged from the September meeting in Halle included key representatives of heavy industry in Rhineland-Westphalia (Hirsch, Beumer), Mansfeld (Hermann Schrader), and Silesia (Paul Ritter, for Pleß). The Free Conservatives included Zedlitz-Neukirch, Tiedemann, Dirksen, and Wilhelm Stockmann. Ibid., p. 122.

cause with whatever political instrument might come to hand—and the fact
that such an organization would clearly duplicate or even contest many of
the functions of the traditional parties caused him little concern. Arnim-
Züsedom, by contrast, was a patrician without affiliations to the existing
agitational organizations and a leading member of the Conservative Party,
which had clear sectional interests to defend and possessed in the Agrarian
League a mass adjunct which provided an efficient channel to its political
constituency. If according to Sieg's plan his new *Reichsverein* would be
"completely neutral" on the party-political plane, it was nevertheless stated
clearly that it would assume some of the responsibilities of the political
parties, which according to Sieg had shown "inadequacy" in the face of the
Socialist danger."[70]

In this way the experience of the Imperial League between 1904 and 1907
reproduced something like the radical-nationalist syndrome much closer to
the party-political centre of the old right. Though formed beneath the auspices
of the former Cartel parties and beholden to them for financial support, the
logic of the Imperial League's innovations signalled the growing obsolescence
of their accustomed politics. In other words, to develop the more vigorous
anti-Socialist practice demanded after the débâcle of the 1903 elections and
partially realized in 1907—to convert propaganda into political agitation—the
Imperial League necessarily outstepped the limits which the respective sectionalisms of the Conservatives and National Liberals had originally prescribed
for it. It tried increasingly to build its own organization and formulate its own
goals, and thereby anticipated in its agitational and electoral practice an anti-
Socialist unity which could only be forged from the destruction of the old
parties in a new unitary framework. The radical nationalists in the Navy
League and Pan-German League pushed in a similar political direction, though
here the ideal of unity was articulated more through the populist ideology than
through the grass-roots agitational practice.
      But in the end the Imperial League was inhibited by a fundamental constraint
of which the radical nationalists were by definition free. The former was an
instrument created and sustained by the party establishments themselves; and
while it also harboured more independent spirits like Lange, Bovenschen and
Liebert himself, when the party leaders called a halt it had little choice but to
pull back. The radical nationalists, on the other hand, who were constituted by
a deep antagonism to the very structure of *Honoratiorenpolitik* which most leading Imperial Leaguers inhabited, observed no such check. To that extent,
though the party-political implications of their activity were much less clear,
the untrammelled idealism of the radical nationalists carried them much
further into conflict with the practice of the old right than had been possible

[70] Taylor, 'Foundation', p. 5f.

for their colleagues in the Imperial League. During the conflicts of 1907–8 their oblique attack on the traditions of *Sammlung* supplied an impetus to the general radicalization of right-wing party politics which proved beyond the more central efforts of the Imperial League between 1904 and 1907.

PART III

7. 'A Rallying of all National Forces': Ideal and Reality

I

Superficially the tariff settlement of 1902 was a resounding victory for governmental *Sammlungspolitik*. When it approved the new tariffs on December 14th by a majority of 203 to 100, the so-called 'Kardorff-Majority' removed the main point of conflict between government and Conservatives and thereby realized a principal objective sketched out in 1897–8.[1] But two factors tempered this achievement. One was the fractious opposition of the Agrarian League, which still forced a third of the Conservatives present into the opposition lobby, and strained the party's tolerance of it virtually to breaking point.[2] But the other was the strategic position occupied by the Centre. A close relationship with the latter was certainly not at odds with government thinking in 1897, when Miquel's aim had been to 'establish the economic policies of Prince Bismarck from 1897, and therefore under all circumstances to win the Centre'.[3] But given the demagogy of the Agrarian League and the vacillations of the National Liberals in the intervening five years, the Centre had now supplanted the Cartel *de facto* as the fixed point in Bülow's parliamentary calculations. The government learned this pragmatically through a chain of parliamentary experience running from the passage of the Code of Civil Law, through the two Navy Laws and the defeat of the Hard-Labour Bill to the tariffs. It confirmed a long-term trend of German political life, as the SPD ate gradually into the parliamentary strength of the Cartel. Writing after the elections in 1898, Hohenlohe summarized the implications: 'The election statistics provide irrefutable evidence that it will not be possible in the foreseeable future to form a majority from the so-called national parties. One must therefore seek to win over one of the opposition parties. The only party which comes into

---

[1] See RT, Dec. 14th 1902, p. 7240. The Centre, National Liberal and Free Conservatives voted solidly in favour, whereas the Conservatives decided 30 for, 13 against. For the third reading, which lasted 14 days, see RT, pp. 7123–240. For brief descriptions of the negotiations: Barkin, *Controversy*, pp. 226–52; Stegmann, *Erben*, pp. 80–91; Witt, *Finanzpolitik*, pp. 63–74.

[2] See Fricke, 'Bund der Landwirte' in Fricke (Ed.), *Die burgerlichen Parteien*, p. 141; Puhle, *Agrarische Interessenpolitik*, pp. 223f.

[3] Heeringen to Tirpitz, Aug. 6th 1897, BA-MA Freiburg, Tirpitz Papers, N. 253, 4.

consideration here is the Centre, the overwhelming part of which is monarchist.'[4]

In other words, the government success in late 1902 owed less to the implementation of *Sammlungspolitik* as such than to a special relationship with the Centre. This was manifest in the outcome of the 1903 elections, when the Cartel parties suffered an even bigger débâcle than in 1898. The classic party of *Sammlung*, the Free Conservatives, had issued the familiar rallying slogans— 'the steadfast unity of all bourgeois elements . . . the common struggle of all state-preserving parties against the powers of the revolution, against Social Democracy'—but such appeals fell largely on stony ground.[5] As in 1898, with the same notable exceptions of the two Saxonies, parts of Thuringia and the Ruhr, the putative unity of the right was stretched simultaneously from both sides, for both agrarians and urban liberals invariably insisted on their own independent candidates. Despite the favourable tariff settlement, the Agrarian League was again the major disruptive factor. An important debate in *Der Tag* emphasized this several weeks before the poll: whilst Zedlitz-Neukirch called for unity against the SPD despite agrarian extremism, Hans Delbrück echoed the slogan 'Under all circumstances and at all costs *against* the Agrarian League' and insisted that 'rational politics will cease to be possible' if the latter won too many seats.[6] The basis for anti-Socialist unity was clearly no greater than in 1898. Individually, the position of the three Cartel parties held fairly steady—the two Conservative Parties each lost two seats and the National Liberals even gained five, bringing their respective totals to fifty-four, twenty-one and fifty-one—while the three left liberal groups dropped from forty-nine to thirty-six. But in the constituencies the will to compromise was lacking. The SPD's strength rose dramatically by twenty-five seats to a total of eighty-one, sweeping the board in royal Saxony with all but one of the twenty-three seats.

This re-emphasized the decisive importance of the Centre, with its solid bloc of a hundred seats. Unless the government was to embrace a course of confrontation with the Reichstag, it had to acquiesce in a pattern of parliamentary manoeuvre in which the Centre increasingly set the pace. In this situation, 'Centre votes were deployed partly to build up credit and goodwill with the government which could be drawn on in demanding specific legislative measures; more generally, to back their claims for "parity" with a demonstration that the Centre, like the Catholics it represented, was not an "enemy of the

---

[4] C. zu Hohenohe-Schillingsfürst, *Denkwürdigkeiten der Reichskanzlerzeit* (Stuttgart and Berlin, 1931), pp. 451–3. The best discussion of the Centre's graduation into a party of government is Blackbourn, 'Problem of Democratization'. See also R. Morsey, 'Die deutsche Katholiken und der Nationalstaat zwischen Kulturkampf und dem ersten Weltkrieg', *Historisches Jahrbuch*, 90 (1970), pp. 31–64.

[5] Free Conservative manifesto, from *MAZ*, May 1st 1903.

[6] This three-way debate between Zedlitz (Free Conservative), Delbrück (independent liberal-conservative) and Gustav Hartmann (left National Liberal, leader of Hirsch-Duncker trade unions), was reported in *WeimZ*, May 23rd 1903. The slogan echoed by Delbrück was issued by Hartmann.

Reich".[7] In the period between the mid-1890s and 1906 the Centre leadership emerged as the masters of parliamentary procedure. Far more than even the National Liberals they asserted the dignity of the Reichstag, applied themselves to the technicalities of committee-work and perfected the art of legislative compromise, particularly in matters of finance.[8] A fine practice of reciprocity with the government soon developed, of which Tirpitz, Bülow and Posadowsky were the official architects. Above all, the Centre wished to demonstrate its sense of responsibility in matters of state, so that the civil inequalities of Catholics might be overcome, not just in the question of the religious orders, but in the larger areas of state preferment and the allocation of national resources. Bülow used this skilfully. As he said in a private letter to the Centre aristocrat Ballestrem in April 1904: ' . . . it seems to me in the political interest highly important that it be shown . . . that the Centre is a state-preserving party, which is concerned for the welfare of the Reich in points of detail'.[9]

Given the Centre's solid commitment to parliamentary forms and National Liberal dislike of exceptional legislation, the government had little option but to tackle the problem of the SPD within the existing framework of the Constitution. As argued above, the foundation of the Imperial League Against Social Democracy in early 1904 was a partial recognition of this fact: though virulently anti-Socialist, in these first years it paradoxically accepted the constitutional basis of the SPD's political success, and only went over to the call for a new anti-Socialist law much later, between 1909 and 1911.[10] Moreover, while Bülow cultivated the Centre assiduously, this by no means exhausted his political repertoire, for his Chancellorship was equally notable for the conciliation of the left liberals, even before the decisive departure of the conservative-liberal Bloc in 1907. This produced a parliamentary practice of some fluidity, in which he governed eclectically by majorities of shifting complexion. This period also saw a certain strengthening of the parties' corporate identities. The Centre offers the clearest instance of this process. But from the early 1890s the left liberals were also emerging from their own ideological ghetto of 'Manchesterism' to explore new forms of constructive co-operation with the government, under the general banner of a new social liberalism. Similarly, the National Liberals were reaffirming their 'historic' character as a 'middle party', and the Conservatives merging more closely with the Agrarian League. This consolidation of specific party-political traditions ran counter to the logic of *Sammlungspolitik*, with its plea for unity and implied pursuit of a unitary organizational framework.

[7] Blackbourn, 'Problem of Democratization', p. 172.
[8] Ibid., pp. 172–6; also Zeender, *German Centre Party*, pp. 86f.
[9] Bülow to Ballestrem, Apr. 6th 1904, BA Coblenz, Bülow Papers, 94.
[10] See D. Stegmann, 'Zwischen Repression und Manipulation: Konservative Machteliten und Arbeiter- und Angestelltenbewegung 1910–1918. Ein Beitrag zur Vorgeschichte der DAP/NSDAP', *AfS*, XII (1972), esp. pp. 371ff., and *Erben*, pp. 246–8; Saul, *Staat, Industrie, Arbeiterbewegung*, pp. 306ff.

In the years following 1902–3, therefore, there was a kind of stabilization in the government's parliamentary position, though this offered no permanent solutions to the long-term problem of the Socialists. Strictly speaking this amounted to a suspension of *Sammlungspolitik*, where the latter is properly understood as the protectionist co-operation of industry and agriculture. This was true not in the sense that Bülow directly repudiated the language of *Sammlung*, but that its vocabulary was no longer appropriate for the immediate priorities of the government. To an extent this was a natural hiatus after the successful resolution of the tariff question, for the agrarians were now relatively contented. But more importantly, each of the major issues of these years—the negotiation of new commercial treaties, the Hibernia affair, the labour unrest, the Navy, colonies and above all the finance reform—in some way suggested—however obliquely—the long-term obsolescence of a specifically East-Elbian landed interest with privileged access to the state. After 1902 there was less immediate scope for *Sammlungspolitik* in the classic mould of Miquel. The issues were out of joint: either they were matters in which the agrarians had little pressing interest, or they pointed to a certain divergence from the interests of industry. In the most extreme cases, as with the need for financial reform, they even questioned the most bitterly defended agrarian immunities. In the end, therefore, Bülow faced the same problem confronted earlier by Bismarck, Caprivi and Miquel: namely, how to reconcile the Prussian Conservatives to the permanence of an industrial-capitalist economy and a broadly liberal polity. After Caprivi's hand-to-mouth liberal pragmatism Miquel had tried to revive Bismarck's recipe of economic protection and authoritarian anti-Socialism, but at the cost of postponing any reckoning with the landed interest's fiscal privileges. Thus, while Bülow reaped the short-term benefit of the tariffs, he was simultaneously burdened with the future political cost of an unsolved financial reform.

II

One group who felt themselves excluded by Bülow's political largesse were the radical nationalists. Here the Boer War had been a crucial watershed. Until 1900 relations between the Pan-Germans and the government had been good, permitting regular consultations on both major issues like the Navy and the Polish problem and more specific Pan-German initiatives over naval stations, German minorities abroad, colonization and so on.[11] Even after the public polemics of 1900–2, Hasse's personal access to Bülow remained good, especially in early 1904.[12] But from late 1900 the public relations between the League and

[11] e.g. Schilling, *Beiträge*, pp. 86ff.
[12] The evidence is presented ibid., p. 398. See especially, ZStA Potsdam, ADV, 26 (Committee of Mar. 15th 1901), and 31 (Committee of Dec. 7th 1901).

the government began to deteriorate under the impact of the Boer War. Divisions within the Pan-German ranks had already appeared at the Committee meeting of September 1900 in Leipzig, when Bülow's China policy and the Kaiser's personal influence had both come under criticism, but it was only after the visit of Paul Krüger to Cologne in November that the question of criticizing the government's foreign policy was properly aired. On November 2nd 1900 Krüger received a Pan-German delegation in Cologne amidst scenes of great patriotic jubilation, and Reismann-Grone expressed publicly the League's support for the Boer cause and its disgust at the government's decision not to receive him in Berlin. On December 8th the Pan-German Managing Committee met in Düsseldorf and approved a further deputation to Krüger, who by this time was in The Hague. But there were now certain disagreements concerning how far opposition to the government should be pushed. Lehr counselled moderation, so that Pan-German influence could be maintained. But Reismann-Grone and Claß were pressing hard for a more radical stance, and at this stage Hasse seems to have gone along with them.[13]

Bülow reacted to this Pan-German activity with an attack in the Reichstag on December 12th 1900, in which he patronized the League's good intentions and 'warm-hearted patriotism', while dismissing their political seriousness. His slighting reference to 'beer-bench politics' rankled for many years in Pan-German circles, but though this entrenched the 'national opposition' in their pro-Boer positions, it also successfully isolated them politically and began the process of re-establishing the government's credibility.[14] A renewal of tension with the government occurred in the late summer of 1902, when the defeated Boer generals Botha, De Wet and Delarey arrived in Europe on a goodwill mission. The Pan-Germans seized the chance to play hosts in Berlin, and Reismann-Grone handled the direct preparations for a massive reception on October 17th. As the day approached, Bülow applied pressure through both Arnim-Muskau and Stolberg-Wernigerode for a cancellation of the Berlin visit, and Hasse himself then added his voice. Claß and Reismann-Grone remained obdurate and carried their position in a hastily convened Committee meeting in Eisenach at the end of September.[15] At this point Bülow and Arnim-Muskau resorted to a subterfuge: when Reismann-Grone arrived at The Hague with the official invitation, he learned that De Wet had already been approached

---

[13] See the discussions in the Managing Committee on Sept. 8–9th 1900 and Dec. 8th 1900, ibid., 22 and 23; SA Essen, Reismann-Grone Papers, 10, IX. 1900. 2ff.; Claß, *Wider den Strom*, pp. 56ff.; Schilling, *Beiträge*, pp. 130ff., 390. A detailed study of German attitudes towards the Boers would be extremely valuable. In the meantime, see Anderson, *Background*, pp. 227–360.

[14] RT, Dec. 12th 1900, p. 475.

[15] The main source is Claß, *Wider den Strom*, pp. 66–8, as the minutes of the Managing Committee contain no record of the discussion: see ZStA Potsdam, ADV, 34. See also Anderson, *Background*, p. 340. According to Claß, Reismann-Grone, Samassa and Geiser joined him in opposing Hasse and Arnim-Muskau.

through a Captain Otto von Lossberg and asked to stay away.[16] Reismann repaired the damage and on the day of the reception in Berlin forced a 'showdown' in the Pan-German Committee. Arnim-Muskau was compelled to resign and was almost followed by Hasse.[17]

This was a vital juncture in the Pan-German League's political development. This was so in three senses. First, it confirmed the Pan-Germans in their diagnosis of official weakness. After the brief honeymoon of 1897–1900, when the government co-opted the Pan-German League into the campaign for the two Navy Laws, radical nationalists became less willing to suspend their disbelief in the government's sense of imperialist purpose. After the promising start with the seizure of Kiaochow in December 1897, Bülow had done little to realize Germany's 'place in the sun'. To the Pan-Germans the abortive discussions with Chamberlain and the British which stuttered along between 1897 and 1901 spelt only confusion, while the failure to support the Boers counted as a short-sighted betrayal of German interests to an overbearing British Empire. By the end of 1902 figures like Claß could see only a continuity of post-Bismarckian drift, a perception which increasingly conflated both foreign and domestic discontents into a single critique of the government—a directionless foreign policy, unnecessary conciliation of the Centre, failure to block the Socialists.

Earlier in this study it has been argued that radical nationalism derived much of its impetus from an unhappy encounter with the established structures of *Honoratiorenpolitik*. In the Navy League, and to a lesser extent in the Colonial Society and the Society for the Eastern Marches, that encounter occurred inside the respective organizations through a dynamic antagonism between 'old' and 'new' right, in which the nature of the conflict only gradually emerged. In the Pan-German League, on the other hand, the conventional *Honoratioren* were shed at an early stage, partly because the organization had originally been launched as a direct criticism of the party establishments which dominated the Colonial Society and seemed ready to acquiesce in the 'gutless' foreign policy of the Caprivi administration. In other words, by its very nature the Pan-German League offered less space for the honorific or non-activist mode of politics which appeared fairly naturally in the other *nationale Verbände*. The devious manoeuvres of Arnim-Muskau and Stolberg-Wernigerode in the autumn of 1902 may be seen as the last significant attempt of the old style

---

[16] Lossberg (1866–1914) left the Army in 1902 for a career in journalism, after having served in Africa and having fought with the Boers. He had attended the Managing Committee in Eisenach and proposed German backing for a new Boer rising from South-West Africa, but the Pan-Germans turned this down flat. Arnim then seems to have used Lossberg for a direct appeal to De Wet. See Claß, *Wider den Strom*, p. 68. See the detailed file on Lossberg, BA-MA Freiburg, 2248, 94067.

[17] SA Essen, Reismann-Grone Papers, 10, IX. 1902. 7; Claß, *Wider den Strom*, pp. 7of.; ZStA Potsdam, ADV, 35; Hartwig. *Zur Politik*, p. 100.

Honoratioren to define the League's practice, and their joint withdrawal from the Executive was a formal confirmation of their failure.[18]

This points to the second significant aspect of the events of 1902: afterwards the internal alignments of the League became much clearer. Proceeding from the recession of *Honoratiorenpolitik*, we may perhaps distinguish four main tendencies within the movement. The first was identified with Ernst Hasse himself: an old guard, many of them National Liberals, who saw the League mainly as an 'educational' organization committed to gaining a public hearing for the Pan-German 'point of view', but with little interest in any general renewal of party-political life. Though firmly committed to the *Primat der Nationalen*, Hasse experienced no difficulty in accepting the existing party divisions in domestic politics.[19] Indeed, he gave the League a deliberately low profile in the latter precisely to facilitate a broad appeal. There were three large areas in particular in which Hasse prevented the League from becoming embroiled: the confessional question, anti-semitism, and the land problem in the East. In the first two cases at least, Hasse had to resist the pressure of an important lobby, which constituted a second distinctive tendency in the movement. Based mainly in the Berlin branch, this was what Reismann-Grone called 'the influential radical-anti-semitic group in the League', led by the writers Fritz Bley and Paul Dehn. But though important at a general intellectual level, they never mustered sufficient strength to bring about changes of policy, and on two separate occasions failed to place candidates on the Managing Committee (1902 and 1904).[20] Roughly congruent with this group were those individuals who took up the cudgels for the Austrian *Los-von-Rom* movement: their strongest effort came in the spring of 1903 led by Dr Friedrich Hopf and J. F. Lehmann, but there was little general support for such an orientation.[21]

The third group comprised Free Conservative politicians who were interested mainly in forging a higher form of *Sammlungspolitik*. Historically they connected with the group around von der Heydt in 1892–3 which tried to launch a new National Party, and by 1903–4 they included individuals like Otto Arendt,

[18] Arnim-Muskau claimed in his formal letter of resignation to Hasse on Nov. 7th 1902 that he was leaving not because of political differences but through lack of time, but it seems fairly clear that the former was actually the case (ZStA Potsdam, ADV, 186). See the Managing Committee in Frankfurt am Main, Nov. 29th 1902, ibid., 36.

[19] See E. Hasse, *Deutsche Politik*, 2 vols. (Munich, 1906–8).

[20] For the general problem of anti-semitism in the Pan-German League, see Lohalm, *Völkischer Radikalismus*, pp. 32–56. For discussion of the 'radical-anti-semitic group', which also included Erich Stolte, see the Managing Committee minutes, Frankfurt am Main, Nov. 29th 1902, ZStA Potsdam, ADV, 36, and material in ibid., 188.

[21] Managing Committee of May 9th 1903, ibid., 39; Hasse to Reismann-Grone, Apr. 17th 1903, and Hasse to Lehmann, Oct. 21st 1903, ibid., 187; SA Essen, Reismann-Grone Papers, 10, IX. 1899. 3f.; Claß, *Wider den Strom*, p. 49. For the *Los-von-Rom* movement: L. Albertin, *Nationalismus und Protestantismus in der österreichischen Los von Rom Bewegung*, Diss. (Cologne, 1953); A. Whiteside, *The Socialism of Fools. Georg Ritter von Schönerer and Austrian Pan-Germanism* (Berkeley, 1975), pp. 243–62.

9

Wilhelm Schröder-Poggelow, Joachim Graf Pfeil and Eduard von Liebert. Their broad aim—to quote the motto of a periodical with which they were all later associated—was 'not to sharpen the conflicts in the German bourgeoisie but to moderate them, not to open new party-political wounds but to heal old ones'.[22] In principle their politics were close to those of Friedrich Lange, though without his incurable optimism. Founder of the German-Union and editor of the influential *Deutsche Zeitung*, Lange was fired by a consuming ambition to destroy the double domination of 'Ultramontanism and Social Democracy' by a 'national reform of our party-system'. Ultimately he aimed towards 'the idea of a great national party', but in the meantime hoped to initiate consultations between the existing 'parties of order'—'Conservatives, National Liberals, German-Social Party and the Agrarian League', as he put it.[23] To this end he had convened a conference in February 1897 with a view towards uniting those parties around a common 'Cartel-Committee' for the forthcoming elections.[24] Undeterred by lack of success, he repeated the attempt in the autumn of 1901. This time he conceived 'the plan of campaigning personally for the idea of a national union . . . by a series of great round-trips covering most of the Reich'.[25]

In five excursions lasting from two to five weeks each, Lange travelled through Schleswig-Holstein, Hannover, Mecklenburg, Pomerania, Posen, Prussian Saxony, Thuringia, Hessen-Nassau, Westphalia, Rhineland, the Palatinate, Hessen and Baden. His range extended from Hadersleben in the north to Constance in the south, and from Mönchen-Gladbach in the west to Thorn in the east. Altogether he visited 240 towns, an average of around three a day. They were chosen for the degree of disunity amongst the 'parties of order' or because they were particularly endangered by either Centre or SPD. In each town Lange used his contacts to arrange a meeting with the leading personalities: he would deliver an address of some forty-five minutes, followed normally by a vigorous debate. He was driven by the conviction that national politics had to be introduced more forcefully at the local level, for 'the German *Mittelstand* will only begin to relate to national politics and the interests of the Reich, when it can see some use for the latter arising from the local and neighbouring conditions. So—national politics under the parish-pump!'

Despite the expected indifference of the established parties, therefore, Lange set about building a nation-wide circuit of local contacts and on March 2nd 1902 constituted the National League for Reich Elections in Berlin. A manifesto carried the signatures of 130 contacts from the previous autumn's journeys, and argued that neither 'economic interests' nor the evangelical confession could provide an adequate basis for rallying the 'nationally-minded': for this

---

[22] Motto of *Das deutsche Volk*.
[23] Lange, *Reines Deutschtum*, pp. 430–3.
[24] Ibid., pp. 433f.; Claß, *Wider den Strom*, pp. 32f.
[25] Lange, *Reines Deutschtum*, pp. 436ff.

only 'national conviction' itself was appropriate. Four specific demands were formulated: the separation of all necessary defence expenditure from other political considerations, the implementation of a national finance reform, suppression of the national minorities inside Germany, and promotion of Germandom abroad. It was also stressed that no attack was intended on the existing Constitution or the provision of social welfare. Nor were the members of the new organization expected to abandon their existing parties. Without nominating its own candidates, it would simply act as the mediator between the 'national parties', intervening in those constituencies which were heavily divided between two or three broadly sympathetic parties.

Though its success was modest in the 1903 elections, Lange's National League for Reich Elections pointed the way for the future: it presaged the formation of the Imperial League Against Social Democracy in 1904 and anticipated the nationalist offensive in the 1907 elections. It was no accident that the group of Free Conservatives identified as the third distinctive tendency in the Pan-German League after 1902 should be playing central parts in both these later developments. But Lange was moving far too quickly: ideologically his attempt to embody the *Primat der Nationalen* in a specific practice of electoral unity was fascinating, but in 1902–3 far outpaced the more realistic expectations of men like Oktavio von Zedlitz-Neukirch, who were broadly sympathetic but much too conscious of surviving party traditions and their independence.[26] Moreover, the Free Conservative group were too deeply embedded in party politics to be carried away by thoughts of supra-party nationalist unity: their support for higher defence spending or an aggressive foreign policy was always tempered by the more prosaic calculation of the parliamentary consequences. To find an equivalent of Lange's concrete political strategy inside the Pan-German League proper we must look to the fourth distinctive tendency which emerged from the experiences of 1900–2.

This was also the third major significant aspect of the events surrounding the visit of the Boer generals in autumn 1902: they crystallized a new and more self-conscious radical-nationalist programme, which neither confined itself to the strictly foreign political sphere nor respected the autonomy of the party political arena. In other words, unlike Hasse its exponents recognized the need to develop domestic policies and eventually to restructure the entire party-political framework of the right, but at the same time lacked the party-political schooling which had earlier motivated the group around von der Heydt in 1892–3. To this extent the fourth tendency was composed of the radical nationalists proper who had no external affiliations to bind them: Heinrich Claß, Alfred Hugenberg, Paul Samassa, Georg von Stössel, Carl Klingemann,

---

[26] Zedlitz was a classic exponent of *Sammlungspolitik*. Significantly he appears to have had no close association with the Pan-German League, though he was right in the forefront of the movement for a new *Sammlung* after 1912, when the Pan-Germans were deeply involved.

Gustav Pezoldt and a few others.[27] More than this, they were actuated by a deep dislike for the 'dull and narrow-minded National Liberal party-framework' and a certain impatience with Hasse as a 'dyed-in-the-wool National Liberal'.[28] This group approached the 1903 elections in a mood of some optimism, for as Stössel argued, 'now that the economic strife has been removed by the certain acceptance of the tariff, the League can do great things for national unity'. Hasse opposed any official involvement with Lange's electoral organization as this would provoke too much internal opposition. But as Philipp Bonhard's important 'Memorandum concerning the domestic activity of the Pan-German League' revealed, with its stress on reconciling the bourgeois parties to common candidatures in marginal constituencies, Lange's aims were very close to the Pan-German's own. Moreover, as Stössel said, the SPD's excesses of obstruction during the Third Reading of the tariffs were an obvious argument for a Cartel in the coming elections.[29]

The actual results of the 1903 elections proved disappointing. Quite apart from the general disarray of the Cartel parties, the Pan-Germans saw their own number of affiliated deputies drop from forty-five to thirty-five. More important still was the quality of Pan-German representation: added to Lehr's death in 1901 Hasse's personal defeat in Leipzig deprived the League of spokesmen who were primarily Pan-Germans, for Claß was beaten in Alzey-Bingen and Stössel had been denied the nomination in Lehr's old constituency of Döbeln.[30] The optimism of the pre-election period—which had grown out of the successful agitation for the Navy and the populist buoyancy of the Boer campaigns—now turned to gloom. Hugenberg, a natural pessimist, wrote to Hasse that he 'could not escape the feeling that in virtually all spheres we are heading step by step for the national abyss', and Hasse voiced his assent.[31] Membership was stagnating. In 1901 it stood at the high point of 21,924. But by 1903 it was down to 19,068, and thereafter the decline was small and steady: 19,111 in 1904, 18,618 in 1905, 18,445 in 1906.[32] Moreover, a large paper membership often concealed practical inactivity: in October 1906 the Chairman of the branch in Karlsruhe resigned on the grounds that a handful of active members were carrying the whole burden of the administrative and agitational

[27] It was no accident that both Claß and Stössel had been closely associated with Lange in the 1890s before joining the Pan-Germans.

[28] Stössel to Claß, Jan. 2nd 1903 (ZStA Potsdam, ADV, 187), and Nov. 17th 1902 (ibid., 186).

[29] Stössel to Claß, Nov. 28th 1902, Dec. 2nd 1902, Dec. 23rd 1902; Claß to Hasse, Dec. 22nd 1902 (all ibid.). For a discussion of Bonhard's memorandum, see Hartwig, *Zur Politik*, pp. 107–9.

[30] Stössel to Claß, Jan. 2nd 1903, and Hasse's circular of July 23rd 1903, ZStA Potsdam, ADV, 187. For a full breakdown of Pan-German Reichstag deputies, see Schilling, *Beiträge*, pp. 519–24.

[31] Hasse to Hugenberg, Oct. 12th 1903, and Hasse to Ellenbeck, Nov. 10th 1903, ZStA Potsdam, ADV, 187.

[32] Wertheimer, *Pan-German League*, p. 45.

work.[33] Reismann-Grone, fresh from his chastening defeat in the Essen National Party, spoke frankly of a 'regression' in the Pan-German cause and confirmed that 'despite Klingemann's efforts even the Ruhr is ailing and falling to pieces'. Moreover, 'things are actually worse in the branches than the Executive can possibly realize. If this mood continues, . . . the number of members will drop much further and faster than has so far been the case.'[34]

Reismann-Grone was not alone in attributing this trend to the League's changed relationship with the government. He argued that under Bülow it had been 'systematically discredited and ruined from above, simply because the national opposition in the Boer War was inconvenient'. The Pan-Germans had been arraigned as 'dreamers and extremists' and had been 'worse treated than Social Democrats and Centre'.[35] Niemann echoed this view: the League's public status was so low because Bülow 'had managed to present (the Pan-Germans) as political children who were not to be taken seriously'. There were several responses to this predicament. One of the commonest was the call for a more intensive application to mundane practical work, with the issues carefully tailored to the peculiarities of different regions.[36] Equally common was a nostalgic hankering after the days of the two Navy Laws, and in 1904 Geiser, Niemann, Hopf and Hugenberg all urged a new naval agitation 'in the grandest style'.[37]

But there was a further response, which attempted to extract the positive value from the political isolation into which the League had been forced by Bülow. For instance, in April 1904 Hugenberg pointed out that 'the word "Pan-German" is no longer, as before, unclear and foggy, but by contrast acts as a challenge and an embarrassment'.[38] In this view the conflict with the government in 1902 had clarified the main thrust of Pan-German politics. In the past the League had been the victim of several elementary confusions in the press, being identified casually with any extreme nationalist and expansionist statement or with Schönerer's movement in Austria.[39] But now the Pan-Germans had been clearly associated with a series of pronounced radical-nationalist positions: an expanded Navy, a more vigorous drive for colonies, support for colonial settlers and German communities abroad, Germanization in the East, and more tentatively, a union of the 'national parties' against the SPD and the Centre. As Claß later observed: 'The experience during the Boer War, especially the fact that the official policy under Bülow had changed from that earlier proposed, the refusal to receive Krüger and the Boer generals, the

[33] Schilling, *Beiträge*, p. 373.
[34] Reismann-Grone to Hasse, no date (Apr. 1904), ZStA Potsdam, ADV, 43.
[35] Reismann-Grone to Hasse, Mar. 26th 1904, ibid.
[36] Niemann to Hasse, Apr. 1st 1904, and Hugenberg to Hasse, no date (Apr. 1904), ibid.
[37] Geiser to Hasse, Mar. 22nd 1904; Niemann to Hasse, Apr. 1st 1904; Hopf to Hasse, Apr. 4th 1904; Hugenberg to Hasse, no date (Apr. 1904), all ibid.
[38] Ibid.
[39] See Schilling, *Beiträge*, pp. 378f.

conciliatory attitude towards England—all these things had lightened for us younger men the work of a stronger emphasis on a national opposition.'[40]

In other words, the break with the government over the Boer War first constituted the Pan-Germans as an independent political factor on a stable basis. Naturally they had already regarded themselves as a 'national opposition' before this time, but the precise implications of this term had remained somewhat vague: it was only after 1902 that the group around Claß began specifying a strategy for the domestic political arena as well. The most important initiative in this respect was Claß's vigorous attack on the government at the annual Convention at Plauen in the autumn of 1903: published as a pamphlet under the title *Die Bilanz des neuen Kurses* (Munich, 1903), it was distributed to all members of the Reichstag and the state legislatures.[41] At the Council meeting of February 1904 in Berlin there was some criticism of this new departure, but an attempt to vote Hasse out of the Chair attracted only one vote. Replying to claims that attacks on the government, though in principle correct, were tactically misconceived, Claß insisted that 'the German people had suffered for years because the parties had abstained from principled criticisms on tactical grounds'. Liebert stressed that 'principled criticism is particularly necessary at the present time', while Dr Förster of Groß-Lichterfelde thought that Pan-German readiness to undertake such criticism was a 'godsend to the German people'. Dr Reuter of Hamburg argued that 'even a much sharper opposition was necessary for the national interest'.[42]

The immediate tactical consequence of the new orientation was a marked redirection of the League's efforts towards the party-political arena. As Stössel put it, 'the best elements of the Pan-German League everywhere must try to place themselves at the head of the patriotic clubs, electoral associations, Evangelical League etc. in their home town, in order to work there in a pronounced Pan-German sense'.[43] Rather than intervening publicly as an organization, the League should send its members to work discreetly and unobtrusively for Pan-German aims inside both the other *nationale Verbände* and the national parties themselves. This was what Hugenberg—the most extreme exponent of this tactic—variously called 'exploding bombs placed by an unknown hand' or cultivating the 'Pan-German bacilli'. He argued that the League should develop 'a double-face', one for the public and a true one known only to a small inner circle, which was determined 'to lay its cuckoo's egg everywhere' without at once claiming the public credit.[44] This was a far cry from Hasse's studied

[40] Claß, *Wider den Strom*, p. 91.

[41] See the detailed material concerning publication and distribution in ZStA Potsdam, ADV, 187, and in particular Hasse to Ellenbeck, Nov. 10th 1903.

[42] See the confidential *Verhandlungsbericht*, Feb. 21st 1904, ibid., 188.

[43] Stössel to Claß, Mar. 10th 1904, ibid.; see also Schilling, *Beiträge*, pp. 388f.

[44] Hugenberg to Hasse, no date (Apr. 1904), ZStA Potsdam, ADV, 43; Hugenberg to Claß, May 8th 1908, cit. A. Thimme, *Flucht in den Mythos. Die Deutschnationale Volkspartei und die Niederlage von 1918* (Göttingen, 1969), pp. 171f. The motif of the 'double face'

abstention from all domestic politics, with his indiscriminate dismissal of 'anti-semitism, the *Los-von-Rom* movement, the Wodan-cult, the anti-alcohol movement, purification of the language, the promotion of so-called German writing, agrarian politics, trading policy and most recently the League for Reich Elections'.[45] This was like discarding the baby with the bathwater. For as Claß and Stössel realized, the League could steer clear of the stormy waters of confessional politics—or the stagnant backwaters of racist eccentricity—without denying itself totally the materials of political success. The 'rightness' of Pan-German ideas was no longer enough: the League had to fight for their acceptance within the national parties.

III

In a striking sense the new Pan-German programme which gradually emerged from the altercations of 1902 represented what Bülow would have done if freed of certain basic constraints. Thus whilst angling for the nomination in the constituency of Döbeln in January 1903, Stössel outlined a programme which is worth quoting in full:

1. Solidly monarchist but still quite free and unprejudiced in criticizing the government.
2. Approval of all national expenditures within reasonable bounds, particularly for colonies and the fleet.
3. Energetic struggle against Poles, Danes, Frenchmen.
4. Likewise against the present power of the ultramontane party and its *claim* to be the only fully national group.
5. Therefore the drive for a national group of all parties as far as the *Freisinnige Vereinigung*, without imposing any conditions of an economic kind.
6. Struggle against Social Democracy *without any exceptional laws*.
7. Limitation of the power of our bureaucracy, particularly in the colonies.
8. Reich finance reform.

This programme is doubly interesting. It anticipated the actual experience of the Bülow Bloc between 1907 and 1909, and re-emphasized the potential contradictions between radical nationalism and the older tradition of *Samm-lungspolitik*. Elaborating on the above points, Stössel insisted that 'agriculture can and *must* be content with what has been achieved through the tariff'. Moreover, 'one must work for a growth and a strengthening of the peasant

---

reappears in Pan-German thinking at the end of the war, during the foundation of the *Deutschvölkischer Schutz- und Trutz-Bund*. See Lohalm, *Völkischer Radikalismus*, pp. 15–26, 86–8.

[45] Hasse's opening speech to the Eisenach Convention, May 25th 1902, *Kundgebungen, Beschlüsse und Forderungen des Alldeutschen Verbandes 1890–1902* (Munich, 1902), p. 94.

estate through the formation of tenant-farms in all provinces with excessive latifundia, so that the flight from the land and the labour-shortage come to an end and a healthy stock of recruits is guaranteed for our Army'.[46] Shortly before, Stössel had drawn a sharp contrast when discussing the Prussian Conservatives between 'the mass of the solid and patriotic population of the East' and the 'backward elements, with whom by conviction I myself will have not the slightest to do'.[47]

This was a decisive point, the most telling consequence at a party-political level of the radical-nationalist commitment. For not only did the latter enable its adherents to grasp the prickly nettle of the finance reform, it also permitted a more general critique of the landed interest East of the Elbe. This went right to the heart of *Sammlungspolitik* and its structural limitations as a strategy of government. For Miquel's policy in 1897 had been predicated on the conciliation of the big landowners at a time when agriculture contributed a declining share of the national product and the dominant ideology was permeated by notions of progress and industrial power. Businessmen, managers and professionals might accept agricultural protection in the general interests of anti-Socialist solidarity and the community of property, but there were limits to their tolerance. As we saw, in both 1898 and 1903 it proved impossible to hold the National Liberal Party solidly behind a programme of co-operation with the agrarian Conservatives, and in 1909 the collapse of the finance reform rallied even the most inveterate supporters of agrarian alliance to the banner of the anti-agrarian *Hansabund*.

From the early 1890s there had been a powerful left-liberal critique of agrarian privileges, which united hostility to tariffs with demands for tax reform, *Weltpolitik*, trade-union recognition and a renewal of social reform, and this programme even extended some way into the left wing of the National Liberals. One might also detect a general consensus amongst National Liberals as a whole that some form of finance reform had become unavoidable by the turn of the century, though the leadership continued to fudge the issue in the interests of the agrarian alliance. By contrast, the radical nationalists claimed the distinction of formulating the demand for a finance reform between 1900 and 1907 from an impeccably right-wing point of view. They did so not from naivety, but from a careful calculation of the requirements of an effective *Weltpolitik*, with an underlying ideology of progress which was vigorously bourgeois. Lacking the inhibitions of the parliamentary tacticians, they did not shy away from the political logic of their imperialism, for beyond a certain point rising expenditure on armaments and colonies necessitated a rationalization of national finances and in practice an attack on old agrarian immunities. Moreover, amongst the sophisticated ideologues of the Pan-German League there was also a more radical willingness to envisage a limited expropriation of

---

[46] Stössel to Claß, Jan. 2nd 1903, ZStA Potsdam, ADV, 187.
[47] Stössel to Claß, Nov. 17th 1903, ibid., 186.

big estates in the interests of promoting an independent peasantry, though this was an infinitely more delicate matter.

In other words, by 1907 the radical nationalists had helped raise the question of tax reform to a major priority on the government agenda. In so doing they simultaneously departed from the mainstream of *Sammlungspolitik* (which had depended on suppressing that very issue) and yet created a situation in which the basis for a more lasting unity of the right-wing parties could be laid. For the latter would never be possible until the Conservatives had swallowed the bitter pill of a finance reform. As Stössel's statements quoted above suggest, in some cases this was deliberate. But on the whole the contribution of the radical nationalists—particularly in the Navy League as we shall see—in precipitating this situation was much rather an objective consequence of their activity. More than anything else, it was the subtle political unity of 'national issues' (mainly the colonies and the Navy), finance reform and agrarian privilege which upset the comforting parliamentary equilibrium enjoyed by Bülow after 1903. On the one hand, the resistance of the Catholic peasantry and its spokesmen to the prospect of increased spending on the colonies and Navy was pushing the Centre reluctantly back into opposition; on the other hand, a break with the Centre would force Bülow into the alternative long demanded by the radical nationalists, namely a dissolution of the Reichstag and new elections beneath the nationalist banner. But the resulting nationalist coalition of liberals and Conservatives could only work if the latter finally agreed to a direct tax on landed income.

9*

8. The Radical-Nationalist Contribution

I

The Bülow Bloc proved to be a moment of fission in German politics. Between 1907 and 1909 conflicts were finally precipitated which had been building up since the 1890s. By departing dramatically from the established precepts of government—breaking with the Centre, swallowing the Cartel into a broader parliamentary bloc, and abandoning the old reserve towards radical nationalist mobilization—Bülow created a new situation, in which contradictions were harder to ignore. By bringing liberals and Conservatives together he ended by driving them apart. In particular, the strategic question of financial reform, which came to a head in 1908–9, exposed the full measure of agrarian intransigence and moved German liberals to a new reforming departure. During the Bloc liberals tasted the prospect of power and when the Conservatives flagrantly disregarded the principle of co-operation by rigidly defending the fiscal status quo, they took rapid measures to announce a new anti-agrarian course: a new organization, the Hanse-Union, achieved a united front of industry; the three left liberal groups combined by 1910 into a new German Progressive Party; and Ernst Bassermann steered the National Liberals in an avowedly anti-agrarian direction.

Potentially this was a far-reaching realignment of German politics.[1] It buried *Sammlungspolitik* as the appropriate or 'natural' strategy for government, though in the longer term, as we shall see, it enabled the transmutation of *Sammlung* into an expanded version of 'national opposition'.[2] Though immediately after the Bloc's collapse the Conservatives formed a 'Blue-Black' majority with the Centre, this had little tangible meaning, and by 1912 Conservative isolation in the Reichstag was apparent. Moreover, the anti-Socialist victory of 1907 proved short-lived, for in the 1912 elections the SPD enjoyed a massive resurgence of support and emerged as the largest party in the Reichstag, with 110 seats. Together the new anti-agrarian resolution of the National Liberals and the SPD landslide imposed a new logic on the government's

[1] The exact nature of this realignment and the weaknesses of the liberals' anti-agrarian orientation as a new reformist departure are discussed more fully in Ch. 9 below. Here I am concerned with the particular consequences for radical nationalism.

[2] This theme is taken up properly in Ch. 10.

parliamentary relations and ruled out the old neo-Bismarckian practice of 1897-1902: the Centre kept an inscrutable distance from any fixed alignment, while Bassermann served clear notice that his party was not to be had for any attack on trade unions, welfare or democratic rights. At most after 1912 the old Cartel could muster around 60 seats. In other words, the primary governing relationship of the Wilhelmine Empire, between the Prusso-German state and the landowning interest, was being brought into question.

Thus, though it started as an affirmation of nationalist solidarity, Bülow's Bloc ended by fragmenting the government's accustomed parliamentary support —first by turning on the Centre from December 1906 to January 1907, then encouraging the Liberals in a new critique of agrarian privilege, and finally (by the logic of the latter) permitting the Conservatives' incipient isolation. From the summer of 1911—when a crisis of foreign policy, a rightward shift of heavy industry and the approaching elections of 1912 imposed a new centrist tactic for the government of Theobald von Bethmann Hollweg (*Politik der Diagonale*) —the Conservatives slipped resentfully into opposition. They were joined by Free Conservatives, dissenting National Liberals, and assorted spokesmen of the *Mittelstand*. Moreover, in this situation Pan-Germans and naval radicals also found a place. As we have seen, radical nationalists pioneered a right-wing critique of government after 1890, and despite the broader animosity to the party *Honoratioren*, this became of evident use during the new conditions of right-wing weakness. During two major crises, in fact, that of the Navy League in 1907-8 and the Daily Telegraph Affair in the autumn of 1908, radical nationalists achieved something of a rupture in conventional conservative ideology. Though disquieting at the time, after 1909 this eased the re-combination of the right into a new unity of 'national opposition', where for the first time Conservatives also took their place.

Far from a constructive new departure, therefore, the Bülow Bloc ushered in a new period of difficulty for the government, where the old Bismarckian maxims no longer held. The particularities of that general situation will be taken up in more detail in the final chapters of this study. Here the main purpose is to consider the particular experience of the radical nationalists: how they related to the Bloc, how they tried to generalize the latter's importance, and how they contributed to the materials of a right-wing radicalization.

II

Bülow's decision to dissolve the Reichstag on December 13th 1906 was welcomed by radical nationalists of all descriptions.[3] After several months of rising controversy over the Centre's obstruction of colonial legislation, it came as a

[3] e.g. Rassow to Boy-Ed, Dec. 13th 1906, BA-MA Freiburg, 2257, 94137: 'The news has just arrived that the *Reichstag is dissolved!* I rejoiced with all my heart at the energy with which the Centre was at once dispatched.' Also Stern to Tirpitz, Dec. 16th 1906, ibid., 2240, 94040.

decisive attempt to build a new government majority from patriotic enthusiasm, and as such perfectly realized an old radical-nationalist dream. In particular, the Navy League activists had long insisted on the wider potential of their popular agitation, and the elections of 1907 were a perfect chance to prove the case. The context of the dissolution ensured that 'the honour of the German flag' would be 'in the foreground' of the campaigning, and the implied problem of creating 'an executive power standing above the parties' tempted the Navy League from its political reserve to pursue the chimerical goal of a peacetime nationalist hegemony.[4]

This was the first consequence of Bülow's action for the naval radicals: it enabled the dramatic consummation of their 'national' rhetoric, involved them in electoral agitation, and committed them firmly to the Bloc which emerged. Whether Bülow had thought through the implications of his decision or not, it quickly dictated a definite course of action, of which this was the most obvious constituent. Moreover, the dissolution would be an act of political frivolity without inaugurating an alternative governing bloc—a coalition 'from Kanitz, Liebermann and Hahn, to Kopsch, Naumann and Barth', as one National Liberal editorial put it. Bülow's main object became the 'pairing of the Conservative with the Liberal spirit', above all to convince the left liberals that the turn from the Centre meant a genuine liberal course. His declared object— of ending a situation where 'a single bourgeois party' (the Centre) 'could with the aid of the Social Democrats occupy a dominant position against the other bourgeois parties', and of building a strong liberal middle as an alternative— coincided with radical-nationalist expectations.[5] August Keim, by now the dominant voice in the Navy League Presidium, acclaimed the dissolution as the best national deed since the First Navy Law of 1898.

The main priority in the elections was the unity of the 'national parties': co-ordinating the campaigns and propaganda, rallying around common candidatures. Thus a number of non-party agencies were active in this sense, from the so-called 'Inter-Fractional Committee' (which distributed industrial finance amongst the various parties), the Committee *Patria* (a similar instance, more concerned with propaganda) and the Imperial League Against Social Democracy, to the veterans' associations and the specially created Colonial Action Committee (a group of academics, who mainly organized lectures in the style of the 1897-1900 naval campaigns).[6] But in the constituencies themselves

[4] Posadowsky to Bülow, Dec. 14th 1906, ZStA Potsdam, Rkz., 1794: 23ff.; Oberwinder, *Nationale Politik*, p. 35.

[5] Sources for quotations: *Hannoverscher Kurier*, Dec. 16th 1906; Bülow to Colonial Action Committee, Jan. 19th 1907, cit. G. Crothers, *The German Elections of 1907* (New York, 1941), p. 159; Bülow's 'New Year's Letter' to Liebert (as head of Imperial League Against Social Democracy), in B. von Bülow, *Reden*, II (Leipzig, 1910), pp. 451ff.

[6] For the operations of these other agencies: D. Fricke, 'Die Reichstagswahlen von 1907', *ZfG*, 9 (1961), pp. 538-76. See also the report of the Committee *Patria* to Bülow, Feb. 9th 1907, ZStA Potsdam, Rkz., 1798: 16-56.

the Navy League was by far the most active. It entered the campaign in response
to two presidential circulars from Otto zu Salm-Horstmar. The first was issued
six days after the dissolution, urging that everything be done within the limits
of the League's Constitution to ensure the return of a 'national' majority.
Accordingly, the Central Office sent election literature to the regions free of
charge (including a thousand copies of Gustav Frensson's *Peter Mohrs Fahrt
nach Südwest-Afrika*): by the first poll on January 25th 1907 twenty-one
million leaflets had gone out. This was closely synchronized with the advice of
Bülow's Imperial Chancellory, who also covered the Navy League's expenses
(75,000 marks by January 19th), for it was vital that the outlay remained unofficial. In addition the Chancellory gave Keim the names and addresses of
anyone writing in as a 'patriot'. At a more practical level the Navy Office
provided the labour for packaging the leaflets.[7]

The Navy League did far more than distribute literature. Despite Salm-
Horstmar's official disclaimer, Keim and the Central Office intervened consistently for the election of particular parties. In reality, of course, Salm's
circular was itself a licence for this type of activity, and a week later he
emphasized the pretence with a second circular, this time under his private
name. He appealed on members to turn out on election day lest the SPD win
by default, and listed thirty-four constituencies going marginally to the Social
Democrats in 1903. Working closely with the Chancellory, therefore, the
League's Central Office offered itself as an agency of conciliation between the
so-called 'patriotic parties'—Conservatives, Free Conservatives and National
Liberals, but also Anti-Semites, Agrarian League and left liberals. Where the
latter failed to agree on a common programme, the Navy League helped effect
a compromise. As Keim freely claimed after the elections, the favourable
outcome for the right owed much to the intervention of the League's activists,
who 'in a whole series of constituencies' exercised 'a mediatory and balancing
influence . . . where the union of the national parties was meeting with
difficulties'.[8]

The Navy League was most active in Central Germany, especially Thuringia
and Saxony. On December 27th 1906 Keim held a conference of activists
from the Thuringian states, Anhalt and royal Saxony in Weimar, and reported
to Bülow that three or four seats might be won from the SPD in Thuringia.
The next day he met spokesmen from south and west Germany in Frankfurt,
effected an arrangement between National Liberals and Democrats in the city
itself, and opened negotiations for all eight seats in the electoral district of
Cassel. By the end of December he reported a total of thirty-four seats which
might be taken from the Socialists. Early in January he was in Dresden, chairing
a meeting of Saxon naval activists and conferring with Gustav Stresemann and

[7] For references and further detail: Eley, 'German Navy League', pp. 267–9.
[8] A. Keim, *Die Wahlen und der Deutsche Flottenverein* (Berlin, 1907), Full references:
Eley, 'German Navy League', p. 269.

Paul Mehnert (leaders of the Saxon National Liberals and Conservatives):
there was a chance of taking six to ten seats from the SPD. Saxony and Thuringia had delivered the most dramatic SPD gains in 1903: twenty-two of the
twenty-three Saxon seats, with Gera, Greiz, Sonneberg, Gotha, Weimar,
Rudolstadt and Altenberg in Thuringia. Nine of these seats were marginal
constituencies earmarked by Salm's second circular. As this was also the
area of strongest radical engagement in the Navy League, it was scarcely
surprising that an activity of some intensity occurred.[9]

Events in Weimar-Apolda were typical. In 1903 the bourgeois parties had
failed to unite, and in the ensuing disorder the SPD had stolen the seat.[10] In
1907 things were even worse: National Liberals and Conservatives, who ran a
common man four years before, now split up and gravitated to the left liberals
and Anti-Semites respectively. On January 5th Walter Graef was nominated
by a broad right coalition of Conservatives, Agrarian League and three groups
on the radical right—German-Socials, Christian-Socials and German *Mittelstand* League. The same day the united liberals put up a Nuremberg school
inspector called Konrad Weiß. In this case Bülow's putative Conservative-
Liberal bloc was having a rough passage: the Conservatives declared their
public regrets, but the liberals retorted that 'the co-operation of all liberals' was
'the most effective and only instrument against Social Democracy'.[11] A week
later the Centre, a negligible force in this overwhelmingly Protestant area, also
announced its support for Graef against the 'unchristian SPD'.[12] A situation
reminiscent of 1903 was clearly emerging, despite the efforts to reach agreement
at the national level.

In Graef's second major rally he alleged that the liberals were prevented
from supporting him by a National–left liberal pact covering the whole of
Thuringia.[13] After an exhausting campaign—124 meetings in two weeks and
a further 52 in the last four days—Graef entered the second ballot with the
SPD.[14] At this point the Navy League's activists entered the scene. When
reconciliation was required between Graef and the beaten liberal alliance to
save the seat, an appeal was issued in the press two days before the run-off

[9] Ibid., p. 270.
[10] See the reports of the campaigning in *WeimZ*, Mar. 3rd and 5th, May 21st and 27th
1903. The parties concerned were the Conservatives, National Liberals, left liberals and
Agrarian League.
[11] *WeimZ*, Jan. 8th 1907.
[12] *WeimZ*, Jan. 15th 1907. The same alignments emerged in the sister seat of Eisenach,
where a National–left liberal coalition faced an alliance of Conservatives, Agrarian League
and five groups of the far right. The National Liberals had agreed to back Weiss, a left
liberal, for reciprocal backing in Eisenach. *WeimZ*, Jan. 23rd and 15th 1907.
[13] *WeimZ*, Jan. 11th 1907. One of Graef's most vocal backers was Hermann Gruner,
Secretary of the local *Mittelstand* Association and Treasurer of the Weimar Navy League.
Gruner had attended the League's Hamburg Congress as a delegate for Saxe-Weimar-
Eisenach.
[14] *WeimZ*, Jan. 23rd 1907.

calling for unity. It was signed by forty individuals calling themselves 'men of no clear party'. They included Flintzer (Chairman of the Navy League in Saxe-Weimar-Eisenach), Couvreur (Secretary), and two further leaders of the organization, Dr Knopf and Philipp Lämmerhirt.[15] This appeal was clearly the visible tip of a much larger campaign. It had its effect, for Graef was duly elected on February 5th 1907.

A more ambitious effort occurred in Dresden, where Friedrich Hopf formed a so-called 'National Committee' to mobilize popular support for the bourgeois parties. This was backed not only by the local Navy League and Pan-Germans, but also by the Colonial Society, German-Union, Eastern Marches Society, Imperial League Against Social Democracy, German-National Commercial Assistants Association, League of German Land-Reformers, Evangelical League, and two Evangelical workers' clubs.[16] Around the same time a German National Union was launched in Leipzig and Chemnitz and may have been linked to Hopf's initiative. Its aim was 'to emphasize the importance of *military, naval and world-political questions* for German-national politics (*deutschnationale Politik*), and to pursue these three goals by a *co-operation of all national parties*, all national men and women, without regard to party estate or confession'. Like Hopf's organization it survived the elections and issued an appeal in September 1907 for 'national' men and women to enter the 'national organizations'—Navy League, Imperial League Against Social Democracy, Colonial Society, Eastern Marches Society, Pan Germans, and so on.[17]

The Navy League also worked directly against the Centre. It backed the efforts of the Evangelical Workers' Association to sponsor its own candidates in eight or nine seats.[18] Keim was especially active in lending weight to the so-called 'national Catholic movement' in the West: several Catholics were standing against official Centre candidates and Keim aided their efforts by mobilizing naval activists in the areas concerned. The Manifesto by which national Catholics dissociated themselves from the Centre was signed by Dr Klein of Bonn (an elder statesman of the Navy League), Freiherr von Loë-Wissen (a former member of the Presidium), and J. Peters (one of Hermann Rassow's patrons in Elberfeld).[19] Moreover, Klein's colleague in the Bonn Navy League, Hamm, had long been a practising national Catholic in the

---

[15] These were the only identifiable signatories and the list certainly included other Navy Leaguers. Flintzer and Couvreur were among Keim's strongest supporters in 1907–8. Flintzer had also been original Chairman of the Weimar *Mittelstand* Association, one of Graef's sponsoring organizations: *WeimZ*, June 23rd and Nov. 20th 1904, Feb. 24th 1907.

[16] Circular issued Dec. 29th 1906 with additional material, ZStA Potsdam, Rkz., 1795, 1799. Hopf planned to extend the organization to all Saxony.

[17] *DortmZ*, Sept. 4th 1907.

[18] Keim to Loebell, Jan. 4th 1907, ZStA Potsdam, Rkz., 1807: 24ff.

[19] For a list of signatories: *DortmZ*, Jan. 12th 1907.

Rhineland, and now stood as the candidate of the united national parties in Neuß-Grevenbroich near Cologne.[20]

In the 1907 elections, therefore, the Navy League was the most important of several agencies engaged in co-ordinating the campaigns of the 'national parties' at a constituency level. There was close contact between Keim and the Inter-Fractional Committee, and at several points he interceded with the Chancellory for specific candidates. He sponsored the election of Eduard von Liebert in Borna (Saxony) and Stresemann in Annaberg-Schwarzenberg (also Saxony), and put the League's machinery at the disposal of the Free Conservatives in at least four constituencies scattered across the country (Danzig-Country, Pleß-Rybnik, Mörs-Rees and Zabern). Keim's achievement was officially recognized after the elections by the Kaiser himself.[21] The election results—the Centre was undiminished, but the new governing parties had a slight majority in their own right and the SPD plummeted from 81 to 43 seats[22] —seemed an impressive demonstration of the nationalist consciousness as assiduously cultivated by the Navy League's militant leaders. Keim and his colleagues inevitably saw them as a massive vindication for their agitational line. They emerged with hardened attitudes and inflated self-confidence. They now expected closer co-operation with the government in recognition of their services and a more positive response to their naval demands. As Keim told the Chancellory during the campaign:

> I must stress once again that it would be a great mistake to snub the Navy League . . . now that it has placed itself with manliness at the head of the national movement. One must now show the courage to own up publicly to one's friends, because reserve can only do harm.[23]

III

What, more exactly, was the Navy League's relation to the Bülow Bloc? As already suggested above, the elections of 1907, fought simultaneously against both the SPD and the Centre, were the dramatic consummation of a radical-nationalist dream. Naturally, the identification of the naval radicals with Bülow's new strategy also made for closer relations with the parties that composed his new majority: the two Conservative Parties, National Liberals, and to a much

[20] Report of a meeting addressed by Hamm in Rheinbach, *KVZ*, Jan. 22nd 1907. He was seconded here by von Trotha of Hagen, a leading supporter of Keim in 1908.

[21] Keim, *Erlebtes*, p. 118. Full references from Eley, 'German Navy League', p. 273.

[22] The Conservatives (54–60), Free Conservatives (21–24) and National Liberals (51–54) won slight gains, while the left liberals collectively recovered their 1898 strength (36–49). When the 16 Anti-Semites and Economic Unionists were added to this total of 187 with some of the 17 Independents, the new Bloc could claim a slight majority over the SPD (43), Centre (105), and the 30-odd particularists and national minorities.

[23] Keim to Günther, Jan. 15th 1907, ZStA Potsdam, Rkz., 1807; 39ff.

lesser extent the left liberals as well. This was the simple logic of the break with the Centre: it was necessary to support the Bloc to keep the Centre down. For if the Bloc fell, the nation would again feel 'the oppressive weight of the Centre's unrelenting fist in the fiercest fashion', and the party's power, which was 'hated by the German people', would be reimposed as a 'caudinian yoke on our nation's most vital interests.'[24] This sense of political identity for the Bloc ran very deep. It was no less than the logical culmination, in concrete political form, of the old demand for an ideal supra-party unity of the nation, based on the strict exclusion of all parties that denied the national consensus as the new Bloc chose to define it. The Bülow Bloc was 'founded on the basis of national questions' and 'precisely these questions' were to form its 'strongest cement'.[25] It was 'to facilitate a state power standing above the parties, free from all fraction tyranny', and a 'union of all patriots beneath the banner of the idea of the state', as one of August Keim's leading supporters put it.[26]

To specify the Bloc's significance for radical nationalism four particular points may be made. Most obviously perhaps, it provided the context in which the Navy League's internal divisions were bitterly revealed. The electoral involvement, notably the action against the Centre, did not go uncontested. In the view of an important minority, led by Freiherr von Würtzburg had based mainly in Bavaria and Berlin, this activity was flagrantly unconstitutional, as it breached the fundamental principle of non-partisanship and ranged the League against a particular party, the Centre. As we shall see, this opposition to the Presidium's line precipitated all the larger disagreements discussed in Chapter Five above. Though the conflict originated in 1904–5 in a particular difference over the terms of naval policy, this technical question soon disappeared into more basic issues of principle. As this study has argued, as an ideology radical nationalism began with a tension between political *arrivistes* and an existing party establishment, in a situation where the latter's material basis was fast disappearing. Expressed in the most general terms this led eventually to a frontal collision between an older patrician style of conducting politics and a new type of popular mobilization, and it was this larger conflict that now developed. In other words, the Navy League's radical nationalists were finally stampeded into an overt populist departure by the increasing irritant of a moderate opposition. The Bülow Bloc, and the inflamed expectations provoked by the 1907 elections, was the setting in which this could happen.

Secondly, the Bloc forged a closer relation to certain party politicians. Thus the special links with individual Free Conservatives were strengthened,

---

[24] Böhmer, *Bedeutung und Aufgabe des nationalen Blocks*, p. 19; Stern to Presidium, Apr. 23rd 1907, BHSA Munich, II, Ges. Berlin, 1158.

[25] *DortmZ*, Dec. 18th 1907: 'On the Crisis in the German Navy League'.

[26] Oberwinder, *Nationale Politik*, p. 35, and his address to the Dresden Navy League, Mar. 13th 1907, on 'The Role of the German Navy League in the Life of the Nation', reported by *Dresdner Anzeiger*, Mar. 14th 1907.

particularly by the election of Liebert, in which Keim had a particular part. But the general enthusiasm for the Bloc also fitted neatly with the efforts of National Liberals to appropriate the Navy League's popular following for their own ends. In September 1908, for instance, Gustav Stresemann advised Bassermann that the only reliable source of future support lay with the 'broad circles organized by the Navy League and Colonial Society and the sensible part of the Pan-Germans'.[27] He had developed this view two months before, arguing that only the 'leadership in national questions, especially those involving the colonies and the fleet', gave the National Liberals a genuine popular following:

> Economically we have no attractive power whatever: for big industry our social policy is too left-wing; the Agrarian League fights us because we didn't approve high enough tariffs for agriculture; the *Mittelstand* is whipped up against us on the grounds that we don't represent its interests strongly enough; and the urban bourgeoisie has a grudge against us just because we took a middle line on the tariffs. If we are ever surrounded in a political conflict, and if all these centrifugal forces operate at the same time, our party could split apart at the seams.

'We have always been at our best', Stresemann argued, 'when a national election slogan has led the people to our standard.' The party should harness the popular energies released by the Navy League by backing the demand for more ships. At least eighty per cent of naval activists were themselves National Liberals—in Thuringia, Hessen, Rhineland-Westphalia and Saxony 'the so-called supporters of Keim are drawn from the friends of our party'.[28]

These remarks were consistent with Stresemann's practice during the previous two years. A close associate of Keim from around 1905–6, he carefully identified himself with the Navy League's radical tendency. He sat on the executive for royal Saxony and worked closely with Hopf and Oberwinder. In the 1907 elections Keim interceded on his behalf in his Saxon constituency, and reaped the benefit of his support during the resulting controversy. He also came to Keim's defence in 1908 and agitated for the radical cause in the National Liberal Reichstag fraction. Stresemann was by no means alone in this respect. There seems to have been wide sympathy for Keim in National Liberal ranks, and the identification grew so close in 1908 that one observer compared the Navy League to a 'Young Liberal Conventicle'.[29]

[27] Memorandum of Sept. 5th 1908, cit. T. Eschenburg, *Das Kaiserreich auf dem Scheideweg* (Berlin, 1929), pp. 114ff.

[28] Stresemann to Editor of *Nat. lib. Korrespondenz*, June 21st 1908, ZStA Potsdam, Bassermann Papers, 9: 109ff.

[29] For full references: Eley, 'German Navy League', pp. 231f. The question of Stresemann's and the National Liberals' relation to radical nationalism will be discussed further in Ch. 9 below.

This radical-nationalist enthusiasm for the Bloc was not unreciprocated. Navy League and National Liberals were brought together by a mixture of ideological affinity and expediency. This was further cemented by the tendency to 'conjure up the spectre of Centre affiliations' behind the opposition of the Bavarian executive, for Keim's supporters argued with great success that behind Würtzburg 'stood the opponents of the national cause and of the Imperial Chancellor'.[30] A victory for the one was a victory for the other. Of this Bülow himself was keenly aware, for the Bloc was held in place by the same two factors—the nationalist consensus and enmity to the Centre. His unwillingness to allow the Centre to discredit the Navy League's nationalist vanguard gave Keim valuable assistance in 1907–8. In a sense radical nationalism embodied most exactly the political logic of Bülow's departure. When it came to uniting the discordant voices of Conservatives and Liberals the national factor revealed its limited efficacy. But for Keim and other radical nationalists this was the primary factor. Indeed, by concentrating so heavily on the 'national issue' of the Navy, by taking the patriotic rhetoric of the Bloc at face value, and by presenting a set of extreme demands, they helped expose the Bloc's concealed divisions. In this way the split in the Navy League foreshadowed that in the Bloc. By seeking to extend the latter's shaky nationalist foundations in a large-scale naval agitation the radicals posed the very question—financial reform—which finally brought it down.

This brings us to the third general point: the identity with the Bloc was at the same time a disjunction from the *Sammlung*. In December 1906 Bülow had broken decisively with an axiom of government politics since the 1890s—that the co-operation of the Centre was indispensable for a stable majority in the Reichstag. This insight was integral to Miquel's *Sammlungspolitik* in 1897, for any attempt to implement his neo-Bismarckian programme of protection and anti-Socialism was bound to fail without the Centre's consent. When the Navy League radicals embraced the new departure of 1907–9, therefore, they stood at odds not only with the Centre, but with the larger tradition of *Sammlungspolitik*. In his first programmatic statement after the elections Bülow paid formal homage to the *Schutz der nationalen Arbeit*, but conciliating the left liberals negated the practical import of this gesture: the concrete statements of legislative intent concerned only minor matters, the main drift being the appeasement of the liberal conscience.[31] This was precisely Bülow's problem. He had repudiated an older practice which privileged the landowning interest, without elaborating a viable alternative. The patriotic front of the elections

---

[30] Rassow to Boy-Ed, Jan. 20th 1908, BA-MA Freiburg, 2277, 94236; Oberwinder to Loebell, Jan. 6th 1908, ZStA Potsdam, Rkz., 2261: 225f. For many similar references: Eley, 'German Navy League', p. 232 (note 151).

[31] See RT, Feb. 25th 1907, pp. 35ff. The measures proposed by Bülow included a new law of association, reform of the criminal law, a new stock-exchange reform, and administrative economies.

was no long-term answer, for the Conservative-liberal alliance would founder
on the first serious question of economic policy (viz. the finance reform). Yet
beyond a certain point any liberal or technocratic attack on the landowners
would encounter the basic resistance of the monarchist state.

Radical nationalists paid little heed to such considerations. Heinrich Oberwinder attacked the Bismarckian Cartel as an unhealthy coalition of 'powerful
syndicates of entrepreneurs and big landowners', which owed its survival to
the 'social support' of the *Mittelstand* and other backward parts of the nation
'who, under the duress of the struggle for existence and their inability to
understand the course of economic development, wish to turn the latter back'.
The alternative to *Sammlung*, for which the radical nationalists had agitated
and which Bülow now gave them, was to end the 'plunder of antiquated party
doctrines' and to open a new phase of 'national policy, born by the free initiative
of the people'.[32] These remarks captured an important truth about the Navy
League's place in Germany's right-wing tradition: namely, the disjunction of
its radical nationalism from the notion of *Sammlung*, and the desire of its
activists to cast off the 'yoke of the Cartel'.[33] Though radical nationalists
often spoke of rallying all patriots into a single national bloc, this implied no
conception of *Sammlungspolitik* as properly understood. The term embraced
a special tradition of protectionist politics and was never used by the Navy
League to describe its own endeavours. It was perhaps less that most radical
nationalists consciously rejected the tradition of *Sammlung*, like Oberwinder
or Stresemann, than that they found it irrelevant to their concerns. To many
of them *Sammlungspolitik* was just part of the 'feeble-minded dogmatism' of
party life, which obstructed true nationalist consciousness.[34]

But beyond this general aversion to parliamentary discourse lay a particular
clash of ideology. August Keim distinguished himself from the conservative
practitioners of *Sammlung* by readily embracing industrialization as the essential
motor of German expansion in the world, as the precondition of an effective
Weltpolitik. This cardinal belief came from Keim's intimate collaboration with
Caprivi in 1892–3, for while subscribing to the Pan-German critique of the
latter's cautious foreign policy, Keim consistently defended his economic
measures. Like Caprivi he tried to unravel the political logic of industrial
growth, accepting the future obsolescence of agrarian privileges as a necessary
factor of economic 'modernization'.[35] This re-emphasizes the difficulty of
accommodating the naval movement to *Sammlungspolitik* and its conventions.
It enabled men like Keim, for instance, to support the finance reform in 1908–9

[32] Oberwinder, *Nationale Politik*, pp. 36, 54.

[33] Stresemann to Günther, Apr. 21st 1906, BA Coblenz, Stresemann Papers, 3053,
6824H.

[34] Heydweiller's circular, May 1907, StA Hamburg, DFV, III, 49.

[35] Keim, *Erlebtes*, pp. 6off., and his address to the Stuttgart Bismarck-Festival, Mar. 29th
1908, reported in full by *Schwäb. Merkur*, Mar. 31st 1908.

with no qualms of their political conscience.[36] It also, significantly, contrasted sharply with the attitudes of moderates like Würtzburg, who opposed the Navy League's involvement in the finance reform and had 'no desire to abandon agriculture by making Germany into a purely industrial state'.[37]

Radical nationalism cannot be grasped without stressing this alienation from normal party politics and the official organs of right-wing opinion. It was no accident that Keim's opponents had an orthodox schooling in the parties or the bureaucracy, men whose political vocabulary came naturally from the language of *Sammlung*. Keim's supporters, on the other hand, were invariably men of no particular party, who operated as outsiders, defining their politics from a critique of existing parties. The main form of their separation—this is the fourth point—was a special commitment to ideological integration. The belief that the Navy League had 'the special duty to cherish and foster the national sentiment and the national pride' was all-pervasive for a figure like Keim, encompassing every institution as a suitable vehicle, from 'princes, people and government', to 'school, house and family'.[38] This was almost an obsession with ideology, with the rhetoric of patriotism, and the myth of immutable national needs. It implied that all the problems of capitalist development could be solved by firmness of the national will and the union of all classes behind nationalist slogans. The jargon of 'national questions', 'national duties' and 'national concerns' conjured material want, social inequality, political repression and class conflict out of existence.[39] Otto Stern defined three pressing home problems in 1904—education, welfare and 'fighting the Polish danger'. All had marked nationalist overtones in his argument, but all took second place to the need to defend the fatherland against foreign threat.[40]

This mentality again distinguished radical nationalists from the orthodox party-political right. Where the latter laboured patiently for limited co-operation within the existing framework of the bourgeois parties, the former persisted in the delusion that unity could be forged from ideas alone. Keim's supporters believed that domestic unity could be achieved only 'in the sphere of foreign policy and overseas interests', for these questions alone could rally 'the political will' of the nation.[41] Instead there was only 'fragmentation', the 'vices inherited of weakness', and even worse, 'indifference' in 'all strata of the nation', not least amongst the 'educated classes'. It was only through an intensive campaign

[36] Ibid. Keim openly advocated finance reform as early as 1905: e.g. address to Gen. Board, Dec. 2nd 1905, *Verhandlungen*, pp. 1ff., BA-MA Freiburg, 2277, 94234. For the Navy League's general involvement in the campaign for the finance reform: Eley, 'German Navy League', p. 236.

[37] Würtzburg to Boy-Ed, Oct. 1st 1908, BA-MA Freiburg, 2278, 94239.

[38] See Keim's article 'On National Sentiment', *Die Flotte*, Jan. 1904.

[39] Titles of Keim's lectures on May 11th 1908 (Kaiserslautern), July 30th 1908 (Darmstadt), and Mar. 25th 1909 (Brunswick). See Keim, *Erlebtes*, p. 152.

[40] O. Stern, *Die Seemachtfragen der Gegenwart* (Berlin 1904), p. 45.

[41] Pan-German manifesto, Nov. 10th 1908, copy ZStA Potsdam, ADV, 67: 52.

of 'civic instruction' or 'a crusade of national education' that the 'development
of our inner unity and thereby the completion of the work of our national
unification', which began 'on the battlefields of France' from 'the blood-brother-
hood of the German tribes', could finally take place.[42] In a sense this was a
retreat into ideology, an evasion of the intractable problem of organizing a
united front of the bourgeois parties. Only by ignoring the divisions of interest
and ideas among the latter could the radical nationalists postulate an ideological
unity. This was a substitute for organizational reconstruction of the right.

Moreover, the supporters of Keim were seriously hampered in their self-
appointed task by the Navy League's own limited character: confined to naval
agitation alone, it could scarcely achieve a general nationalist reconstruction of
party-political life without effectively ceasing to be the German Navy League.
This virtually condemned the naval radicals to disillusionment, and many of
them (including Keim himself) were shocked from their blinkered confidence
only by the events of 1908 and the Navy League's great crisis. By affording an
ideal occasion for putting their integrative programme into practice, the 1907
elections triggered off the process. The radicals' open involvement in the
elections, even for the pursuit of non-sectarian ideals, helped explode the fiction
of the movement's party-political neutrality. The resulting controversy began
to jolt the radicals from their illusions and pushed them into explicit political
statements, though for propriety's sake they devised the formula of 'national-
political' activity to disguise the move. This was a critical development, which
hastened the inevitable decision: either the fictions of neutrality must be given
up and the Navy League publicly embrace politics, or else the wider ambition
must be discarded. The dilemma was accurately described by one sympathetic
commentary in the press. The confusion had only arisen in the first place, this
argued, because the radicals had set themselves wider ambitions, and 'great
national aims' of this kind were properly the responsibility of 'great national
parties'. The Navy League must face this reality, 'if only because in the last
resort things are involved which can only be achieved in a hard political
struggle'. In other words, the conflict in the Navy League only demonstrated
the pressing need for a new national *party*.[43]

In each of these four ways the Bülow Bloc had a special place in the radical-
nationalist formation and helped mature its self-consciousness: by providing
an impetus to the Navy League's internal conflict; by forming closer links
between the radical nationalists and certain party-politicians (particularly
National Liberals and Free Conservatives); by stressing a disjunction from the
specific tradition of *Sammlungspolitik*; and by strengthening the tendency to

[42] Manifesto published in *KZ*, June 1st 1909, calling for a 'crusade of national education',
and signed by 64 predominantly Pan-German intellectuals (academics, journalists, and non-
party politicians), including Claß, Keim, Liebert and other leaders of the League.

[43] *Westfälische Politische Nachrichten*, organ of the Westphalian National Liberals, cit.
DortmZ, Dec. 23rd 1907.

seek ideological solutions for political problems. To see how these features combined dynamically into a new populist departure, it is now necessary to turn in more detail to the Navy League's crisis of 1907–8.

B. THE CRISIS IN THE NAVY LEAGUE, 1907–8

I

The Navy League's great crisis was the manner in which a latent populist programme first assumed formal shape. In earlier years the conflict had been conducted in terms of the League's Constitution, the technicalities of its 'non-political' status, its methods of propaganda, and so on. But now the more basic questions of the movement's relationship with the government came to the fore and compelled radical nationalists to explicate their assumptions. In the Navy League radical nationalism emerged only from a dynamic process, in which activists faced the lessons of their practice. Most radicals—with notable exceptions like Heinrich Rippler, Heinrich Oberwinder and various Pan-Germans—acquired their populism from experiences within the movement itself. Events in 1907–8 forced the radicals into self-appraisal and faced them with political choices. The crisis quickened a process of radicalization which began in the elections of 1907. Moreover, as the potential became clearer, it drew the attention of certain Pan-Germans and other independent nationalists who had previously kept rather aloof. Their intervention on the side of the *Keimianer* (as the radicals became known) sharpened the process of radicalization.

Where did the conflict begin? Apart from general disputes over the form of propaganda ('educational' work *versus* political agitation) and the balance of centralism and federalism in the movement's Constitution, the argument initially centred on naval policy itself—namely the right of the Navy League's Presidium to develop an independent programme, different from that of the government.[44] In 1903 naval enthusiasts were already pushing for a more ambitious shipbuilding programme, and this demand was formally embodied in the Navy League's Dresden Resolution of April 1904. Several factors strengthened the tendency to a split from the government. One was the League's own agitational momentum, for by the end of 1903 it was clear that fresh demands were needed to maintain the activist *élan* and keep up recruitment. A second was the international situation. Naval radicals accused Tirpitz of neglecting the opportunity left by the Russian naval defeat of 1904, and throughout 1905–6 demanded a new Navy Bill to reinforce the German diplomatic offensive over Morocco. The 'burning question' of Germany's naval

---

[44] For lack of space, detailed discussion of the terms of the disagreements in the Navy League has been kept to a minimum. For a comprehensive account, see Eley, 'German Navy League', pp. 260–318.

striking power was the dominant theme of Navy League propaganda in these years.[45] Finally, the uncertainty in Navy Office planning until early 1905 made it hard to give the Navy League firm guidance on the content of propaganda. When the terms of the 1905 Bill were finally fixed it was naturally difficult to haul the Presidium back from its more extreme demands. The refusal of Tirpitz to take the latter into his confidence exacerbated a sense of alienation from official policy, and relations fast deteriorated.[46]

There were two decisive moments before 1907. One was in May 1905, when the Presidium defended its independence against an untimely intervention by the Kaiser, just before the annual Congress at Stuttgart.[47] This crystallized the alignments for the first time, and two distinct tendencies emerged: one radical in naval policy and critical of the government's parliamentary line, the other moderate and strictly governmental. The question of the League's independence was publicly debated for the first time, and the radicals emerged as the majority faction. The Presidium rightly suspected the leading moderates —Würtzburg in Bavaria, Hollmann in Berlin-Brandenburg—of intrigue with the government. Once a gap had opened between the League's demands and the Navy Office's actual requirements, Tirpitz had taken rapid steps to secure an ally: secret contacts were made with Würtzburg as early as May 1904, and these were vital in the following years. However, the Stuttgart Congress proved a triumphant vindication of the Presidium and moderate rebukes fell on deaf ears. The whole affair gave radical confidence a powerful boost, and the presence of Prince Heinrich (the Kaiser's brother and the League's national Patron) was treated as a demonstrative gesture of renewed Imperial support. For the Bavarians events had the opposite effect. Würtzburg had been moving towards an open break and his machinations had been instrumental in provoking the Kaiser's original intervention. His failure to unseat Keim from the Presidium was demoralizing, and shortly afterwards both he and Oldenbourg (the other Bavarian in the Presidium) resigned, with much bad feeling.[48]

The result was the lasting identification of the governmental standpoint with

[45] For detailed references: ibid., p. 226.

[46] Till early 1905 official thinking oscillated between reintroducing the six battle-cruisers struck out of the 1900 Bill and a more ambitious acceleration of the building tempo. By 1904 the Navy League was already demanding a third double squadron of battleships before 1912. For details of official planning: Berghahn, *Tirpitz-Plan*, pp. 325ff., 370ff., 448ff. For the specific problem of synchronizing propaganda and plan: Deist, *Flottenpolitik*, pp. 171ff.

[47] On May 5th 1905 the Kaiser telegraphed Salm that any trespass on the sphere of naval policy would itself be an infringement of the Imperial prerogative, whereupon both Keim and Menges resigned in protest. The Kaiser had acted impulsively, without the advice of Tirpitz or Bülow. Intensive negotiations dominated the week before the League's Stuttgart Congress on May 27th 1905, resulting in the reinstatement of Keim and Menges and a complete vindication of the Presidium's 'independent' stance. The story is told in detail in: Eley, 'German Navy League', pp. 260ff.; Deist, *Flottenpolitik*, pp. 181ff.

[48] For more detail: Eley, 'German Navy League', pp. 187ff.

'the schismatics from Bavaria and Berlin', as Oberwinder put it.[49] By securing his interests in the League through a fifth column, Tirpitz gave his opponents new weapons. Bavarian opposition to Congress decisions and Würtzburg's excessive zeal in putting the government's view allowed Keim to strengthen his standing with the membership by shifting the debate on to more favourable ground: he diverted attention from the original question and identified Würtzburg with disruption of the League's unity and the violation of majority decisions. Thus the tactical question of accommodating the government's wishes was systematically redefined as a matter of *principle*, concerning the Navy League's autonomy as an organ of popular opinion. The latter increasingly dominated the terms of debate. By 1907–8 it had completely supplanted the more limited question of synchronizing the movement's propaganda with the dictates of official policy.

The second decisive moment came at the end of 1905, with the General Board of December 12th. The context was provided by the slow progress of German interests in Morocco, alarmist talk of encirclement and British naval threat, and the new Bill introduced by Tirpitz, which fell far short of expectations. Keim launched a swingeing attack on the failure to replace inferior craft, or 'floating coffins' as he preferred to call them. In explaining the government's failure to produce an adequate Bill, moreover, he dismissed the foreign situation, shipyard capacity and lack of money. The only answer, he argued, lay with domestic considerations: a bigger Bill had been shelved for party-political reasons, and the League rejected party politics on principle. In this way, by using the fiction of objective *national* interests beyond the sphere of party debate, Keim adroitly avoided infringing the League's Constitution and yet in the same breath assumed a stance that was clearly partisan. This was a decisive step. For the first time the radicals announced their open opposition to the government. The Presidium's stance was now more directly political than ever before, and the old type of diffuse propaganda was finally discarded for a tightly organized campaign of pressure. This inevitably entailed a movement towards some parties and away from others. In particular, Keim accused Tirpitz of retreating before the parliamentary power of the Centre. Thus by coining the term 'national-political' to describe the League's activity, Keim contrived to attack the Centre without abandoning the statutory 'non-political' stance.[50]

The period spanning the Dresden Congress of 1904, the May crisis of 1905 and the General Board of December 1905, brought the Presidium and the Bavarian executive into sharp conflict for the first time. It began a process of rising animosity, in which both sides continually recharged their mutual suspicions. However, the brief juncture between Dresden and Stuttgart was the only point where the moderate position and its distinctive Bavarian version

---

[49] Oberwinder to Günther, Apr. 26th 1907, ZStA Potsdam, Rkz., 2261: 153.

[50] For detailed discussion of the Gen. Board of Dec. 1905: Eley, 'German Navy League', pp. 226f., 170ff.

were fully identical. Many who had earlier seen no danger in the Presidium's position were now spurred into action, but just at this point the Bavarians acquired particularist airs which alienated many potential supporters. Thus a third force of centrists gradually cohered: those concerned by radical excess, who condoned, however, neither the extreme opposition of the Bavarians nor its particularist overtones. Similarly, they supported an agitation beyond the confines of the existing shipbuilding programme, but drew the line at direct attacks on Tirpitz or the government. The typical spokesmen were Wilhelm Menges and Dürkheim-Montmartin: both saw the point of giving the membership goals of their own, yet avoided direct opposition to the official programme and kept the Navy Office fully informed of developments inside the Presidium. Menges withdrew from the latter at the end of 1905 rather than be a party to an agitation against Tirpitz, and reappeared in both 1907 and 1908 to mediate between warring factions.[51]

The centrists cohered more recognizably in the General Board of December 1905. Stengel, who put the intransigent Bavarian line, was backed only by Hollmann, whereas several individuals (e.g. Vopelius, Sering, vom Rath) counselled moderation on the Presidium without rejecting its proposals out of hand. As a group they lacked the extra pressure of the Centre Party's Bavarian hegemony to sharpen their hostility to Keim. Likewise, their identity with the Bülow Bloc after 1907 stopped them joining the Bavarian attack on Keim lest this damage the Bloc's prestige. They also suspected particularist motives behind the extremism of Bavarian demands in 1907. Though these factors muted their opposition in 1906–7, they stepped naturally into the breach when the Presidium resigned in January 1908, and played a vital part in the ensuing reconstruction. As individuals they were normally of high standing, often senior civil servants or party politicians. They included many elder statesmen of the movement (e.g. Menges, Klein, Dürkheim-Montmartin, Vopelius, Rassow), and prominent figures of the establishment, like Hermann Fürst Hatzfeld von Trachenberg, Victor Herzog von Ratibor, Ernst Fürst Hohenlohe-Langenburg, Otto Beutler, Friedrich Graf zu Eulenburg-Prassen, Georg Michaelis, Hans Delbrück, Otto von Manteuffel or the Bavarian Ambassador in Berlin, Hugo Graf von Lerchenfeld.[52]

---

[51] Ibid., pp. 263f.

[52] Hatzfeld was one of the richest of Silesia's aristocratic capitalists and a leading Free Conservative; in 1908 he was proposed by Vopelius as Salm's successor. Ratibor was also a Silesian grandee with big industrial holdings, and likewise a prominent Free Conservative: he was Chairman of the Silesian executive and resigned in 1908 in protest at Keim's election as Executive Chairman. Michaelis, his deputy in the Silesian Navy League and the future Imperial Chancellor, was the senior official in the Silesian provincial administration. Hohenlohe-Langenburg, who became Chairman of the Württemberg Navy League in 1908, was Head of the Colonial Department in 1905–6 and a leading Free Conservative. Beutler was Lord Mayor of Dresden, and like Manteuffel and Eulenburg-Prassen a leading Conservative politician. See ibid., p. 264 (note 16).

II

Though hostilities smouldered during 1906, reaching a rather confused climax at the Hamburg Congress in May, a full-scale crisis was only produced by the election involvement in January 1907.[53] Given the invincible position of the Centre Party in Bavaria, it was scarcely surprising that the Bavarian executive took exception to Salm-Horstmar's two circulars. While the elections were still in progress Würtzburg issued a contrary instruction to the Bavarian organization, and Salm-Horstmar prevented Keim from making an issue of this only with great difficulty. But when Keim heard that the branch of Wemding in Bavarian Swabia had disbanded in protest at the Presidium's electoral line, he reacted in typically inflammatory style, declaring that this was no loss to the movement and that 'any member of the Navy League who votes on this occasion for Centre-Poles-Guelphs-and-Social-Democracy is worthless for our national cause'.[54] The repercussions were immediate. Würtzburg protested to Tirpitz through Lerchenfeld, and Prince Rupprecht resigned as Bavarian Patron in protest at the League's 'political' activity. There followed a period of hectic negotiation: the Bavarians pressured Salm through Lerchenfeld, Tirpitz and their spokesman in the Presidium General von Spies, while Salm assured himself of Bülow's support. An open conflict was so far postponed, but could hardly be avoided. Keim would not budge, but Rupprecht would only withdraw his resignation if the General was removed.

Into this highly charged atmosphere came a series of dramatic disclosures in the Centre newspaper *Bayrischer Kurier*. Detailed extracts from letters sent by Keim to Navy League activists during the elections, acquired by a mixture of subterfuge, bribery and theft, now left no doubt that the League had been up to its neck in 'politics'.[55] The most compromising revelations concerned Keim's view of the Centre, and by extension of Catholicism. He urged one correspondent that all 'true Catholics' must seize the time to 'confess themselves opponents of the Centre's policies'. They should learn from the eight constituencies in the Rhineland, 'where true, highly regarded Catholics who are also members of the Navy League have set themselves against the Centre'. He told someone else that any member who shrank from attacking the Centre was useless to the movement. Similar letters had gone to Ludwig Weber, Otto Stern, Becker of Darmstadt, Dau of Neisse, Prof. von Savigny of Münster, and General von Liebermann of Cassel. Several times Keim came close to breaking the confessional taboo. He told Weber that the fight against the Centre was also against 'ultramontanism, the deadly enemy of the Evangelical confession'. The

[53] For events surrounding the Hamburg Congress: Deist, *Flottenpolitik*, pp. 189–96.

[54] Eley, 'German Navy League', p. 276, also for the following.

[55] For details of the acquisition of the letters, in which Matthias Erzberger played a key role: K. Epstein, *Matthias Erzberger and the Dilemma of German Democracy* (Princeton, 1959), pp. 57f. They were published mainly in two issues of the *BK*, Feb. 5th and 8th 1907.

phrase '*furor protestanticus*' for the nationalist campaign in Saxony became particularly notorious. He was alleged to have urged a pact with the SPD in Upper Silesia to defeat the Centre. For the Bavarian executive and its allies this seemed a perfect weapon to unseat Keim from his dominance in the Presidium.

But the strength of Keim's position—quite part from his support in the membership—was the indebtedness of Bülow. The Chancellor himself made this clear in an express dispatch to Pourtales, the Prussian Ambassador in Munich, who was pressing the Bavarian case. Bülow agreed that Keim's agitation was 'not without fault', but it was 'a political impossibliity to drop (him) now, immediately after the great services he undeniably provided in the election campaign'.[56] This was even clearer in the Reichstag debate of February 25th 1907, when the Centre and SPD launched a full-scale attack on the League. Bülow dismissed the charges of electoral manipulation and anti-clericalism, and delivered a powerful defence of Keim: 'he wished to acknowledge, loudly and gratefully, that Major-General Keim had placed his person in the service of a good cause in a selfless, self-sacrificing, tireless manner'. The elections had been fought not against the Centre as a confessional party, but against the 'misuse to which the Centre, backed by Social Democracy, had put its decisive position'. He attacked the party for making a gift of twelve seats to the SPD, 'the party of hostility to Christianity'.[57] In other words, Bülow could not afford to let Keim go. He was too closely identified with the Bloc, particularly by its opponents. Ten days before Matthias Erzberger had addressed a mass meeting in Berlin on the matter of the Navy League in the elections and had closed with the slogan: 'Out from this Organisation'. When a League supporter claimed the right of reply, pandemonium broke loose and he was ejected from the room. Two hundred of Keim's supporters rose in protest and left the meeting singing *Deutschland, Deutschland über alles*. The police dispersed the affray with difficulty.[58]

Keim's symbolic importance for the Bloc was the key factor in the situation. It prevented many moderates from joining a public atttack on the Presidium in case it rebounded to the advantage of the Centre. This applied to an important group of centrists in Berlin, who were mostly prominent Conservatives with leading positions on the Navy League's regional executives in the East.[59] Though basically sympathetic to the Bavarian position, they were unwilling to weaken the Bloc's prestige by advocating it in public, and agreed only to the massive application of private pressure for Keim's voluntary retirement. Keim

---

[56] Thermann to Pourtales, Feb. 15th 1907, PA-AA Bonn, Deutschland, 138, 5, Bd. 2.
[57] For a detailed description of the debate: Schilling, *Beiträge*, pp. 302ff.
[58] *DortmZ*, Feb. 16th 1907.
[59] e.g. Manteuffel (Berlin-Brandenburg), Eulenburg-Prassen (East Prussia), Freiherr von Maltzahn (Pomerania) and Ratibor (Silesia). They were also in close touch with Menges and Lerchenfeld.

exploited this reluctance to the full. On March 9th 1907 he told the Presidium 'that now he could go under no circumstances, precisely because no joy should be given to Erzberger and Bebel, and because such a step would be akin to desertion in battle'. He was totally unrepentant. The personal attacks on himself were 'Bavarian efforts to look after the Centre's business', which ended by 'suppressing the national idea'. 'Proceeding from the conviction that naval politics and national politics are inseparable', on the other hand, he had tried only 'to awaken and strengthen the national idea in order to serve the fatherland'.[60]

This situation persisted up to the Cologne Congress in May. Würtzburg and his colleagues remained bitterly hostile to Keim, but had to be content with exerting pressure behind the scenes through Lerchenfeld, the Navy Office and the centrists round Eulenburg-Prassen and Menges: an attempt to canvass the regional executives for a resolution censuring the Presidium was a dismal failure, attracting only fourteen of the fifty-two executives. By the time of the Congress, hopes of securing Keim's resignation had been abandoned—so far from retiring he had even been proposed as Executive Chairman, much to the Bavarians' disgust. Instead the moderate caucus in Berlin concentrated on reaffirming the 'non-political' character of the Navy League and on prohibiting a repetition of Keim's election involvement. But even this was doubtful. Spurred by the animosity of the Centre and reassured by Bülow's tacit support, Keim and the radicals were riding a wave of nationalist exhilaration. A month before the Congress Menges told Captain Karl Boy-Ed, who handled the Navy Office's relations with the League, that his fellow moderates now accepted that Keim would have an easy majority of delegates on his side.[61]

The Congress confirmed these suspicions. Keim was greeted with 'such a roar of applause and jubilation' that he was unable to begin his address for five minutes. He did not disappoint his admirers, issuing a vitriolic attack on those responsible for the theft of his letters, and calling for a new acceleration of the official naval programme.[62] In the General Board the previous day a compromise had been patched up behind closed doors, and this was now accepted as a unanimous resolution: it called in general terms for a quickening of the ship-building tempo and described the Navy League as 'a national organization standing above the conflicts of the confessions and parties'. This was just about enough for the Bavarians, and in accordance with the compromise in the General Board Würtzburg moved an informal rider to the official resolution. In view of assurances from Keim and Salm 'that the Navy League does not represent a national or political organization for or against the parties, but stands above the parties', he was withdrawing the Bavarian resolutions. Yet there was no formal redress for the Bavarian demands—there were no 'personal guarantees' for Prince Rupprecht, and there were no specific commitments to abstain from

---

[60] Eley, 'German Navy League', pp. 279f.
[61] Ibid., pp. 280ff.
[62] *Die Flotte*, June 1907, pp. 82ff.

elections. Moreover, the official resolution could perfectly easily sustain a radical 'national-political' interpretation. Above all, Keim remained, and he was more confident than ever.[63]

His survival had become a test of confidence in the Bülow Bloc. This was hammered home by the entire context of the Cologne Congress. The normal proposal for an honorary banquet for the Navy League delegates was defeated in the City Council by the opposition of the Centre, and the narrowness of the vote (eighteen to sixteen) suggested the deep gulf now separating the latter from the other bourgeois parties. Around the same time Wilhelm Becker, the long-serving Lord Mayor and a Navy League elder statesman, was forced out of office by his fellow National Liberals for having striven for an election agreement with the Centre.[64] A new confessional bitterness, which in areas north of Cologne produced a boycott of Catholics by Protestants, focused naturally around Keim's electoral exploits, and made it easier for his supporters to present his departure as a capitulation to the Centre.[65] Centre newspapers made great capital from the Congress and urged Catholics to leave the League. The Dortmund *Tremonia*, which had helped the SPD to a second ballot victory over the 'united national parties' in the city, was typical, insisting that all good Catholics had 'the moral and political duty of leaving the Navy League at once'.[66]

The press of the Bloc replied with statements of unequivocal support for Keim. Stresemann delivered a powerful tribute in the Congress itself, and a similar statement was made at the evening banquet by Hamm, his National Liberal colleague.[67] Keim claimed to have the confidential backing of the National Liberal Reichstag fraction.[68] His supporters in the League derived their strength from the new legitimacy conferred by the elections and the formation of the Bloc. In this sense the radicals had reached the height of their power in the naval movement, for the surrounding political context had enabled them to identify their success with a revival of the nationalist spirit in general. As Keim said: 'The meeting in Cologne was an imposing victory for the national cause', and the Navy League had 'proved itself a power of great importance for our public life'. Keim himself was obdurate. He was supposed to have said that 'Everything the Bavarians say is a swindle'.[69] Once again a final

---

[63] For a detailed analysis: Eley, 'German Navy League', pp. 282ff.

[64] *DortmZ*, May 10th 1907. Becker had close personal relations with Karl Trimborn, Centre deputy for Cologne, and his dismissal as Mayor was opposed by the Centre group. For his part in the elections: Fricke, 'Reichstagswahlen', p. 545.

[65] For reports of the boycott, and the comments of *Germania* holding Keim responsible: *DortmZ*, Feb. 28th 1907.

[66] *DortmZ*, May 13th 1907.

[67] *Die Flotte*, June 1907, pp. 101, 103.

[68] Keim to Günther, May 16th 1907, ZStA Potsdam, Rkz., 2261: 165, also for the following.

[69] The comment was overheard by Röper at Cologne and passed on to Würtzburg: Boy-Ed for Tirpitz, May 21st 1907, BA-MA Freiburg, Tirpitz Papers, N. 253, 9.

reckoning had been postponed, this time on terms even more favourable to the radicals.

III

Conflict exploded once more in December 1907. Both sides (now completely polarized around Würtzburg and Keim) had continued sniping during the summer, and this eventually produced a confrontation in which neither could give way. As an act of defiance—itself the product of minor Bavarian provocations—the Presidium ignored government counsels and elected Keim Executive Chairman. Prince Rupprecht immediately resigned as Bavarian Patron, the Presidium called an emergency Congress in Cassel for January 19th 1908, and both sides frantically rallied their support. At the Congress itself the Presidium stole the initiative by immediately announcing its collective resignation and successfully defined the issue as one of confidence in its leadership since Cologne. In a frenetic atmosphere of personal recriminations and emotive appeals to the movement's 'independence' the majority of delegates were clearly on Keim's side: the meeting ended with a radical vote of confidence and the Bavarians withdrawing from the Congress in protest. The following months saw an intricate process of manoeuvring in preparation for the next ordinary Congress, in Danzig in June. The maximum aim of the *Keimianer* was the re-election of the old Presidium, but this quickly proved impossible. Instead the centrists now emerged as the key grouping, with compromise as the order of the day. At Danzig Salm-Horstmar was briefly re-elected President, but after an audience with the Kaiser he declined. Keim and his lieutenants now left the Navy League completely to launch an independent 'National-Union', but by the end of September 1908 this had fizzled out. Peace was finally secured when Würtzburg and his two henchmen were pressured into resignation from the Bavarian executive. By this means—the embittered withdrawal of both protagonists, Würtzburg and Keim—the protracted conflict was resolved.[70]

What can we say about the significance of these events? First, the Cassel Congress was the first authoritative demonstration of the two sides' relative strength. Of the thirty-eight regional executives, twenty-seven committed themselves before the Congress: twenty-four expressed solidarity with the Presidium, though several accepted Keim's possible sacrifice for the sake of unity.[71] Only three—Baden, Berlin-Brandenburg, and Bavaria itself—opposed Keim's election. Of the rest, at least three supported the Presidium (Brunswick,

[70] The course of the crisis between Dec. 1907 and Oct. 1908 is discussed in exhaustive detail in Eley, 'German Navy League', pp. 286–318.

[71] Anhalt, Alsace-Lorraine, Gotha, Lippe-Detmold, Hessen, Mecklenburg, Oldenburg, Hannover, Hessen-Nassau, Hohenzollern, Pomerania, Rhineland, Westphalia, West Prussia, Reuß ä. L., Reuß j. L., Saxe-Altenburg, Saxe-Meiningen, Saxe-Weimar-Eisenach, Schaumburg-Lippe, Schwarzburg-Rudolstadt, Schwarzburg-Sondershausen, Waldeck-Pyrmont, Württemberg.

Lübeck and Hamburg), and three more (East Prussia, Silesia, Saxony) had strong radical lobbies.[72] Thus the radicals could reasonably claim about 175,000 of the League's 324,000 members, while their opponents had only 60,000. Yet this preponderance scarcely outlasted the Congress, for once the threat of an actual split materialized, a realignment took place. In particular, the third force of centrists finally took shape. Men like Vopelius, Klein and Hamm, respected elder statesmen, sought to prevent an irrevocable split. Hamm produced a compromise resolution with the likely support of Posen and Alsace-Lorraine, as well as his own colleagues from the Rhineland. As the 'three Bs' also committed their forty-one votes, this made a total of between sixty and seventy. It was less than a majority—the radical resolution had a total of seventy-nine delegates—but it did signify an important shift.[73]

Between Cassel and Danzig these centrists increasingly set the tone. Several initiatives coalesced in the proposal for a small unofficial conference in Dresden on March 14th. Here the mood was very different, and the twelve radicals failed to stamp their presence on the proceedings: outnumbering the six from Baden, Bavaria and Berlin-Brandenburg, they were offset by twelve new moderates.[74] Moreover, the issues of principle were suppressed, and the meeting produced a list for the new Presidium which proved a skilful blend of compromise: the key posts to complete outsiders, a balance in the two Vice-Presidencies, and the ordinary seats as consolation for the radicals.[75] Though the *Keimianer* rallied by calling an emergency General Board on April 12th, they made little impression on the composition of the list. Despite the initial election of Salm-Horstmar in Danzig, moreover, the latter corresponded closely to the actual shape of the new Presidium. When Salm turned down the Presidency, he was succeeded by the alternative candidate, Admiral Hans von Koester, who had already been adopted at Dresden.[76]

[72] No firm evidence is available for Bremen, Posen, Schleswig-Holstein, Prussian Saxony and Coburg.

[73] Of the remaining 55–65 delegates, a majority could be expected to support the radical resolution.

[74] The twelve radicals were Riesebieter (Oldenburg), Salmuth (Brunswick), Mayweg (Westphalia), Pflaum (Württemberg), Liebermann (Hessen-Nassau), Merck (Hessen), Flintzer (Weimar), Hammerstein (Rhineland), Schilbach (Reuß ä. L.), Jasper (Berlin-Brandenburg), Hopf (Saxony), and Pfeiffer (Rhineland). Their extreme opponents were Offenmüller, Dietz and Eichborn (Bavaria), Röper and Klewitz (Berlin-Brandenburg), and Cancrin (Baden). Busley, Ravené, Michaelis and Stentzel (Silesia), Schmidt (Alsace-Lorraine), and Knackfuß, Ritz, Hartmann, Hegemeister, Planitz and Beutler (all Saxony), could be regarded as new centrists.

[75] For details, Eley: 'German Navy League, pp. 301ff.

[76] The full composition of the new Presidium elected at Danzig was as follows: Köster (President); Liebermann and Theodor Körner of Bavaria (Vice-Presidents); Admiral Weber (Executive Chairman); Pflaum, Schweckendieck, Merck, Schilbach, Klein, Planitz, Thöne of Hannover, Schwarzzenberger of West Prussia, and Schmitz of Hamburg (ordinary members).

Superficially, therefore, the Danzig Congress in June 1908 seemed to have reimposed a comforting normality. Keim was definitely excluded, and the Navy Office had achieved virtually all its goals in the reconstruction of the Presidium, without a split or lasting secessions from the movement.[77] Though the old *Keimianer* still dominated the Danzig proceedings, they no longer controlled the League's key executive functions. Above all, their special relation to the Bloc had now been ruptured. In December 1907 Bülow's goodwill had crucially stiffened Keim's obduracy in the face of massive pressure from the Navy Office, but at a certain point Bülow had to give way, lest the radical-nationalist course begin to disturb the Bloc's stability, particularly with the finance reform and a new Navy Bill in the offing. After much prevarication Bülow eventually agreed to a public statement disavowing Keim on January 10th 1908, and after this the latter was clearly on his own.[78] In this way the Navy League seemed to have been reclaimed for a governmental standpoint. Moreover, the successful manoeuvring of the centrists, with their invisible network of contacts, looked very like a resurgence of the old *Honoratioren*.

This impression should be resisted. The post-Danzig settlement was very far from a victory for the old governmental standpoint. For one thing the whole climate of naval opinion had been decisively changed by the agitations of 1903-7, so that Tirpitz now began from quite different premises than before.[79] Furthermore, the radical-nationalist defence of the Navy League's independence established the inescapable context for Koester's Presidency, and the latter went to some lengths to demonstrate his good faith, adopting the rhetoric of the *Keimianer* and insisting that the League 'must run in front of the Navy Office rather than behind it'.[80] More specifically, the new Presidium met on September 9th 1908 to adopt a new agitational programme, and against the strenuous efforts of the Navy Office issued demands for a strengthening of the cruiser fleet. In justification Koester used arguments familiar to any prominent *Keimianer*. In other words, though the radicals were in partial retreat, they had done much to determine the terrain of the debate. As a result of radical efforts at Danzig the League was now officially a 'national-political' organization, and this registered an important ideological change. The *language* of right politics was different. As official spokesman for the Prussian government, Ernst von Jagow (Governor of West Prussia and Chairman of the Navy League's regional executive) gave striking testimony to this in his official address at Danzig:

The Navy League should not be an appendix of the Navy Office, but must be independent; it must possess the confidence of the whole German

[77] For official calculations, see the excellent analysis of Deist, *Flottenpolitik*, pp. 231ff.
[78] For a full description of this complex set of manoeuvres, see Eley, 'German Navy League', pp. 294ff., which supersedes the misleading account in Schilling, *Beiträge*, pp. 346ff.
[79] See esp. Berghahn, *Tirpitz-Plan*, pp. 505-92.
[80] Cancrin's report for Stabel, Mar. 16th 1908, GLA Karlsruhe, 69P, 1.

10

nation; it should not be regarded as an organ of the government, but as an expression of the will of the German people.[81]

Most of all, radical nationalism had emerged from the crisis with greatly enhanced confidence. In particular, the need for organization had forged a much stronger collective identity, especially after the Presidium's resignation, which deprived Keim of his previous apparatus. During December and January 1907–8 Keim spent much time rallying his supporters in the provinces, particularly in Thuringia and Central Germany. The small Thuringian states, Prussian and Grand Ducal Hessen, the Rhine-Ruhr, the Palatinate, Stuttgart and Munich emerged as particular centres of radical strength. Moreover, the radical presence was not confined to the regional executives. When Keim began a new offensive after the radical defeat in the April General Board, the main vehicle was the branches themselves. The General Board was condemned for acting 'without an appeal to the members', and branches were urged to call mass meetings to assess the mood of the 'masses' more accurately.[82] The most important initiative was in Mülheim-on-the-Ruhr, where the radical chairman Walter Hammerstein raised two demands: re-election of Keim and Salm-Horstmar, formal redefinition of the Navy League as a 'national-political' organization; if Danzig brought no redress, 'then we will secede . . .' A resolution was passed unanimously and sent to over 300 branches in West Germany.[83]

In the end the call for secession enjoyed only temporary and fragmented success. Once Salm had declined the Presidency, 152 branches left the League in fulfilment of an earlier ultimatum, accompanied by Keim himself, many individual radicals, the entire executive for Westphalia, and one whole region, Schwarzburg-Rudolstadt with 53 branches and 3,500 members.[84] But most of the radical executives preferred to temporize while the new Presidium revealed its credentials, and the secessions did not continue. Hammerstein launched an independent *Deutscher Flottenbund* in Mülheim, but this was presented only as a rallying-point, to keep the torch burning while the League clarified its internal relations. Keim had been planning to launch a more broadly-based 'National-Union' for several months, but when it came to the point at the end of July 1908 he held back the announcement, and tacitly acknowledged the declining prospects. In fact, most of Keim's supporters were pleasantly surprised by Koester's performance and the Presidium's new programme. As one statement observed, the latter 'corresponds in principle to the efforts of General Keim in so far as it goes beyond the terms of the Navy Law and presents further naval

[81] *Protokoll*, June 14th 1908, pp. 3f., BA-MA Freiburg, 2278, 94237.

[82] Statement published by a League member (possibly Trotha) in Hagen, 'Signal: "Stop" ', *RWZ*, Apr. 25th 1908.

[83] *RWZ*, May 22nd and 25th 1908; Trotha to Keim, May 22nd 1908, Keim Papers.

[84] *RWZ*, July 10th and 15th 1908; *WeimZ*, July 16th 1908; *DortmZ*, July 11th and 12th 1908; Boy-Ed for Tirpitz, July 4th 1908, BA-MA Freiburg, 2278, 94238.

demands'.[85] Finally, when a palace revolution in Bavaria eventually unseated Würtzburg and his two extreme supporters at the end of October 1908, most radicals returned to the fold.

Yet the campaign of the *Keimianer* retained a vital ideological effect. For it was in this period that radical-nationalist ideas of popular legitimacy—the critique of established political authority—first properly cohered. In December-January 1907–8 the attack on royal authority dramatized the process of radicalization, and it was now that all the charges of 'Byzantinism' and 'subservience' poured out against the moderates. A meeting of the Pan-German-dominated Berlin Colonial Society, addressed by Keim, Reventlow and Stresemann on December 10th 1907, had been particularly important in stoking this controversy. Reventlow attacked both the Kaiser and Tirpitz, and Stresemann was especially provocative, insisting that 'as an organ of one million national Germans the Navy League must be independent of all official constraints, even from high and the Highest quarters'; Keim was backed by the vast majority, and it hardly mattered if 'one person down there in Munich' (i.e. Prince Rupprecht) objected to his election.[86] This language became commonplace during 1908. The issue was whether the League should 'serve as upholstery', 'play the proud role of a gramophone' and be the 'advertising department' of the Navy Office, or else remain an 'independent national-political popular' organization. As Reismann-Grone put it: 'No diplomatic negotiations, no compromise. Either a national *Volksverein* with complete rights of self-determination or a split, a clean break from those who feel more at ease in the shadow of Court favour than beneath the sun of a free political life.'[87]

C. The Daily Telegraph Crisis and the Crystallization of a 'National Opposition'

I

For all the energies expended during the Navy League's crisis in 1907–8, there had been surprisingly little formal clarification. No clear statement had been agreed concerning the legitimate boundaries of agitation or relations with the state, and the Constitution was left exactly as before. Even the Danzig resolution, with its reference to the League's 'national-political status', to which the *Keimianer* attached such importance, was open to different interpretations: it appeared as an embodiment of *Keimianer* principle only in the light of Keim's previous practice, for in itself the 'national-political' formula was hardly less

[85] *WeimZ*, Oct. 3rd 1908.

[86] *KZ*, Dec. 12th 1907; Schilling, *Beiträge*, pp. 332f.

[87] Reventlow in *TR*, cit. *DortmZ*, Apr. 21st 1908: 'On the Road to Danzig'; Graf Paul von Hoensbroech, *RWZ*, July 13th 1908; *RWZ*, May 26th 1908: 'Don't Let Us Be Gagged'.

ambiguous than the old 'non-political' one. The only solid result of the long crisis, in fact, was the withdrawal of the two groups of enemies from the fore-front of the League's affairs: Keim and his most entrenched supporters on the one hand, Würtzburg and his two henchmen on the other.

But as we saw, both sides consciously adopted a larger set of loyalties. The *Keimianer* were linked to the Bloc and to a radical-nationalist ideal of anti-Socialist unity: they increasingly drew around themselves an interesting circle of National Liberals, some Free Conservatives, Pan-Germans and independent nationalists. On the other side Würtzburg was supported by the liberal-conservative establishments of south Germany, most of the ruling houses and their governments, the Navy Office, and at a distance the Centre.[88] In the crisis itself a larger complex of issues was quickly drawn in, with the radicals opposing not only the internal dissidents, but also the political forces behind them. As the crisis worsened the *Keimianer* went further and attacked the Navy Office, the Princes and even the conventional ideology of traditional monarchism itself. When this happened, many of Keim's ertswhile supporters gravitated towards the new centrist grouping of conciliators, because the anti-monarchist implications of his position crucially fractured the previous identity with the Bloc. This loss of sympathy exposed in sharper relief the basic features of the radical-nationalist position: a primary commitment to the German-national state as the supreme focus of political loyalty, a centralist rather than a federal view of the Empire (but German rather than Prussian), aggressive imperialism as a solvent of domestic disunity, the populist vision of a community of citizen-patriots.

In other words, it was the appropriation of the 'national-political' formula by a *particular* political tendency which caused the controversy. Hamm, for instance, frankly admitted that 'as soon as a Navy Bill is on the agenda, the movement must pursue party politics'.[89] The objections to the Navy League's 'political' involvement were purely relative, and men like Hamm, Rassow and Vopelius—all prominent centrists between Cassel and Danzig—made this clear by vigorously involving the League in the public agitation for the Finance Bill in 1908–9. They opposed Keim not for his political involvement as such, but because this was taking unacceptable directions. They identified the naval radicals with 'forces which have been working consciously or unconsciously, but systematically and tenaciously . . . for the inner decomposition of our people', which 'flow from that political group which calls itself, with more

[88] Württemberg provides a good example of this effect. Keim's supporters on the executive were mainly a younger generation of Protestant nationalist businessmen, sometimes politically independent, but normally National Liberal. They were restrained by the older ministerial establishment which originated in the German Party (i.e. likewise National Liberal, but formed in the earlier milieu of unification *Honoratiorenpolitik*), together with the high nobility around the ruling house. See especially the correspondence between Pflaum, a *Keimianer*, and Urach, the royal patron, who resigned in early 1908: HSA Stuttgart, E. 14, 1345.

[89] Statement in the Gen. Board, Apr. 12th 1908, ibid.

presumption than merit, Pan-German'.[90] They argued that this misappropriation of the term 'national' was dissipating the nation's energies in fruitless internal strife, an ironic commentary on the attempt to remove 'national politics' from party controversy. For Würtzburg the prospect of 'Keim, Reventlow, Liebert as sole spokesmen on national questions' was a national 'misfortune'. 'National-political' was only 'the slogan for justifying a struggle against the government and anyone who disagrees, and for the pursuit of demagogic chauvinism'.[91] The crisis in the Navy League, therefore, was put down to the thwarted ambitions of Pan-German extremists:

> We can see from the tenacity of the Pan-German elements in the Navy League and Colonial Society that they have decided on a struggle of life and death for their political influence in these previously unpolitical organizations. They have not yet managed to organize a political party, and as sparrows amongst the National Liberal starlings they are also ill at ease. So they defend their dominant positions in the Colonial Society and Navy League and the Evangelical Union with the courage of desperation.[92]

As cautioned earlier in this study, the relationship between the Navy League radicals and the Pan-Germans can easily be misunderstood. Many individual Pan-Germans were prominent supporters of Keim from an early stage, but they never represented anything remotely approaching an organized ginger-group within the Navy League.[93] Heinrich Rippler, J. F. Lehmann, Erwin von Dessauer and Friedrich Hopf were active as individuals, not as members of any tightly-knit Pan-German caucus. There were several reasons for this. One was an extreme fluidity in Pan-German thinking under Hasse. The Executive never reached a satisfactory consensus concerning relations with the Navy League, some members regarding it as a dangerous rival, others wanting to move it in a Pan-German direction. As late as 1905 Reismann-Grone still thought that the Navy League had usurped a role the Pan-Germans could perform perfectly well themselves.[94] Moreover, under Hasse the political implications of Pan-German ideology remained unclear. Membership of the

---

[90] *KVZ*: 'Is only the Army left?', reprinted in *Deutsche Volkszeitung*, July 19th 1908 as 'The "Pan-Germans" as Forces of Decomposition'.

[91] Würtzburg to Boy-Ed, Nov. 12th 1907, BA-MA Freiburg, 2277, 94235, and Würtzburg's memo, sent to Boy-Ed, July 3rd 1908, ibid., 2278, 94238.

[92] *KrZ*, cit. by *Berliner Volkszeitung*, Dec. 25th 1907: 'Conservatives against Pan-Germans'.

[93] There were *local* exceptions to this generalization, such as Munich, where Lehmann, Dessauer and Putz formed an important minority inside the Navy League's branch. The same was probably true of Berlin. See for instance the report of the Gen. Meeting for Berlin-Brandenburg, Jan. 11th 1908, *DortmZ*, Jan. 12th 1908. For some evidence of Pan-German organization in the Navy League, see the unsigned, undated shorthand notes (drafts for letters to Keim, Liebert and Dürkheim-Montmartin), authored possibly by Dessauer, loose-leaf in *Jahresbericht* 1905, BA Coblenz, ZSg. 1, 195/2.

[94] SA Essen, Reismann-Grone Papers, 10, IX. 1905. 2.

Pan-German League bore different meanings for different people: Hermann Rassow's membership had a different significance from that of the radical Friedrich Hopf or that of the Bavarian Richard Dumoulin Eckart.[95] Accordingly, there was no necessary connection between the *Keimianer* and the Pan-Germans until 1908. Keim himself had no ties with the latter until leaving the Presidium and many of his supporters were suspicious of the Pan-Germans.[96] Two factors made a convergence possible: the radicalizing effects of the 1908 crisis, and a sharper definition of political goals within the Pan-German League.

The first contacts were unofficial and resulted fairly naturally from the circumstances of the Navy League's crisis: some of Keim's most reliable backers were Pan-Germans and they inevitably tried 'to win his valuable energy for the Pan-German League'.[97] By mid-February 1908 Keim himself had joined the latter.[98] He was already searching for a new vehicle, and his closest associates began canvassing 'the possibility of fusing the Pan-German League with the great majority of the Navy League and perhaps other bodies as well'.[99] Discussion proceeded informally, co-ordinated by individual Pan-Germans of a Free Conservative background, including Liebert, Otto Arendt and Wilhelm Schröder-Poggelow, and involving members of the Colonial Society, Eastern Marches Society, Anti-Ultramontane League and several lesser groups. Friedrich Lange, who had floated similar schemes in 1897, 1902 and 1905, and who raised the idea again in the summer of 1909, was also involved.[100] But although the scheme made some headway in the Colonial

[95] Each representing a different current of the Navy League, they each held a seat in the Pan-German Board.

[96] See for instance: Pohl to Claß, July 20th 1908, ZStA Potsdam, ADV, 192; SA Essen, Reismann-Grone Papers, 10, IX. 1905. 2; Claß, *Wider den Strom*, pp. 156ff.; Neumann to Hasse, May 25th 1906, ZStA Potsdam, ADV, 45: 15.

[97] Klitzing to Claß, Jan. 30th 1908, ibid., 192: 23ff. Klitzing, who was Chairman of the Pan-German branch in Cologne, had made contact with Salm-Horstmar and found him sympathetic to the Pan-Germans. Keim's most important supporters in the press were the four leading Pan-German editors: Reismann-Grone (*RWZ*), Rippler (*TR*), Lange (*DZ*) and Liman (*LNN*).

[98] Claß to Keim, Feb. 17th 1908, ibid., 49.

[99] Schröder-Poggelow, statement to the Pan-German Executive, Feb. 8th 1908, ibid., 63: 11.

[100] Boy-Ed to Würtzburg, Mar. 12th 1908, BA-MA Freiburg, 2278, 94237; Loebell for Bülow, Feb. 28th 1908, ZStA Potsdam, Rkz., 2261: 260; statement by Stahlberg (head of the *Institut für Meereskunde*) to the Delegate Meeting of the Berlin-Brandenburg organization, June 21st 1908, reported in *RWZ*, June 22nd 1908. Liebert and Schröder-Poggelow were not originally acting as official representatives of the Pan-German League. For Lange's involvement, see ZStA Potsdam, ADV, 32: 1ff.; ibid., 33: 3ff.; ibid., 47: 6ff.; ibid., 48: 17; ibid., 71: 13; Claß, *Wider den Strom*, pp. 32f.; Lange to Bülow, Aug. 27th 1909, BA Coblenz, Bülow Papers, 108. Keim and Liebert were also involved with Lange in 1905: see SA Essen, Reismann-Grone Papers, 10, IX. 1905. 2; Erdmann to Boy-Ed, Feb. 12th 1908, BA-MA Freiburg, 2259, 94147. The shorthand notes referred to in note 93 above may have referred to the 1905 discussions: see BA Coblenz ,ZSg. 1, 195/2.

Society, the Pan-German leadership was unwilling to surrender its independence. After prolonged debate in the Pan-German Committee on February 8th 1908 the original plan for a 'great Overseas-Society' to provide 'greater impetus for the world-political and colonial tasks of the German people' was abandoned in favour of a less ambitious scheme for a 'National Co-ordinating Committee'.[101] A conference took place on March 9th to coincide with the Navy League's radical caucus the previous day, but the idea had plainly run out of steam by the end of March. Keim and Schröder-Poggelow were still proposing to launch the secessionist National-Union as the first step in the 'amalgamation of all *nationale Verbände* under a supreme command'—a '*Verband der Verbände*', as Keim put it. But the defeat of the naval radicals in the General Board was the final blow: Keim nurtured the idea a time longer, but its wider potential had gone.[102]

But Keim's ambition 'to unite as many of the national organizations as possible' had more than a passing importance.[103] It was a brief resurgence of an old chimerical dream of the German right, that of a single National Party campaigning on the 'national issues' alone. The formation of the Pan-German League in 1890–1 had been an expression of this ideology, as were the more ambitious schemes for a party-political refoundation in the winter of 1892–3. But the latter's failure showed precisely the lack of realism of ignoring the domestic arena in this way. Although this effectively confined the Pan-Germans under Hasse to the incubation of a radical-nationalist ideology, it could not prevent the intermittent recurrence of similar schemes: Friedrich Lange was their typical exponent, emerging at each critical conjuncture with a new plan for the unification of the right on the basis of 'national issues'. The Navy League under radical control harboured the same aspiration and the same belief in the *Primat des Nationalen*. Given this distinctive tradition, therefore, the development of Keim's politics after leaving the Navy League represents an important break. Not only was he compelled to recognize the inadequacy of a perspective derived from the naval issue alone: the failure to introduce additional planks to his platform through the 'amalgamation project' exposed the limitations of his conception still further, and pushed him into the concrete alternative of the Pan-Germans.

This was the final significance of the Navy League crisis in 1908: the coincidence of a dramatic political education for the *Keimianer* with a far-reaching political change in the Pan-German League, which committed the

---

[101] Executive *Protokoll*, Berlin, Feb. 8th 1908, ZStA Potsdam, ADV, 63: 8–21. Only Schröder-Poggelow and Liebert were unreservedly in favour of the original plan. Stössel, Reventlow and Klingemann were sympathetic but sceptical of success, while Reismann-Grone and Neumann would accept nothing more than a form of loose associtaion. Stolte and Itzenplitz were hostile, as presumably was Claß. See Claß to Reventlow, July 15th 1908, ibid., 192: 338f.

[102] For these details: Eley, 'German Navy League', p. 322 (notes 328–30.)

[103] Wilma von Plonski to Hollweg, July 25th 1910, BA-MA Freiburg, 2282, 94253.

latter to a systematic intervention in the domestic arena. The death of Hasse in January 1908 opened the way for a leadership which stressed concrete political agitation rather than 'national education work', and aimed for the infiltration of the *nationale Verbände* and the electoral committees of the 'national parties', the adoption of clear positions on domestic issues, and the castigation of the political establishment on all possible occasions. Its leading exponent was Claß himself, but he received vital support from other individuals whose influence grew with his own: Max Freiherr von Stössel, Ernst von Reventlow, Karl Itzenplitz, Carl Klingemann, Paul Samassa. During 1908 Claß worked consistently for the integration of any *Keimianer* secessionists directly into the Pan-German League, and to this end opposed any suggestion of an independent naval movement. Keim was elected to the Pan-German Committee and finally abandoned plans for a completely new organization. He was followed by others: Dr Gerhard became the Pan-Germans' new full-time Secretary in succession to Geiser, while Abbes, Deichmann and Major von Treyden of Rudolstadt were elected to the Council. Reismann-Grone, Itzenplitz and Klingemann drew many of Keim's supporters into the Pan-German stable, including Walther von Hammerstein in Mülheim. Gerhard made a rapid four-day tour of the radical strongholds in Thuringia, Hessen and Rhineland-Westphalia in October, and returned for more intensive recruitment in January–February 1909. In Schwarzburg-Rudolstadt entire branches joined the Pan-Germans.[104]

This went much deeper than formal association: it also reflected a vital juncture of ideology and political commitment, a common political experience and a shared dissatisfaction with the normal political process. The key factor was a common tendency towards 'national opposition': the willingness to embrace policies which conflicted directly with those of the Kaiser's appointed government. Pan-Germans and *Keimianer* were impelled together by a shared populist commitment, which sought to legitimate its opposition to the conservative governing establishment by a pseudo-democratic phraseology and the rhetorical mystification of the 'ordinary people'. Prince Rupprecht's opposition to the Presidium, the Kaiser's intervention in his favour and the hostile intrigues of the Navy Office all drove the radicals in this direction. The Daily Telegraph Crisis of November 1908, which unleashed a storm of outraged nationalism against the Kaiser, was a fitting climax to this political education of the *Keimianer*. It finally confronted radical nationalists with the logic of their opposition: 'revolt against the monarch' to preserve 'all the positive value which the monarchy has created'.[105] It emphasized the meaning of events in the Navy League as right-wing populists like Reismann-Grone understood

[104] *Keimianer* in Thuringia who became Pan-Germans included the two leaders in Schwarzburg-Rudolstadt, von Treyden and von Kleist, and Wichmann in Bernburg. For detailed references: Eley, 'German Navy League', pp. 324f. (notes 338–42).

[105] Redebold (Secretary of the Pan-German branch in Dortmund) to Claß, Nov. 3rd 1908, ibid., 62: 19ff.

them: 'that above the person must stand the dynasty, and above the dynasty the welfare of the people'.[106] For the strident aggression of the Pan-German reaction to the Kaiser's indiscretions cannot be completely understood outside the context of the crisis in the naval movement. As Walther Hammerstein told the Pan-German Committee: 'The Pan-German League can now take up the legacy of the Navy League. The reserves for the Pan-German League are already there, you must now rally the national-political elements from the Navy League.'[107]

II

The Daily Telegraph Crisis broke on October 28th 1908 when the British newspaper of that name published an article based on an interview with the Kaiser. Though conceived as a contribution to better Anglo-German relations, the latter was actually a model of indiscretion. The Kaiser complained of misrepresentation by the British press, accused the British government of rejecting his good offices during the Boer War, and generally adopted a mis-placed patronizing attitude on the subject of Anglo-German friendship. Though the reaction in Britain was unexceptional—the article simply confirmed existing views of Wilhelm II—in Germany the news was greeted with almost universal indignation. Public criticism—which extended from the SPD to the Conservatives—focused on two aspects of the article's publication. On the one hand there was disquiet that the interview had been approved in the first place (Bülow had passed the manuscript on to the Foreign Office without directly vetting it himself), and in this respect the affair led to a serious crisis in the relations between the Kaiser and his Chancellor. But on the other hand it precipitated an even worse crisis in the public status of the monarchy. Given a history of similar indiscretions, and coming so soon after the Eulenburg scandals, the Kaiser's irresponsible political dabblings inevitably provoked an angry outcry in the press and the parties. In a hectic two-week period—during which Bülow was under enormous pressure from all sides to assert his authority over the Kaiser and the latter entered a state of nervous collapse—there cohered an unprecedented consensus in criticism of the monarch.[108]

[106] Statement to Pan-German Executive, Leipzig, Nov. 4th 1908, *Protokoll*, ibid., 32.
[107] Ibid.: 36.
[108] For detailed treatments of the Daily Telegraph Affair, none of which properly recognize its *ideological* importance for the right, see the following: W. Schüssler, *Die Daily Telegraph Affäre. Fürst Bülow, Kaiser Wilhelm und die Krise des Zweiten Reiches 1908* (Göttingen, 1952); F. Hiller von Gaertringen, *Fürst Bülows Denkwürdigkeiten. Untersuchungen zu ihrer Entstehungsgeschichte und zu ihrer Kritik* (Tübingen, 1956); N. Rich, *Friedrich von Holstein* (Cambridge, 1965), II, pp. 753ff.; H. Rogge, *Holstein und Harden. Politisch-publizistisches Zusammenspiel zweier Außenseiter des Wilhelminischen Reichs* (Munich, 1959), pp. 359–416. The Eulenburg scandals can best be followed through Rogge, *Holstein und Harden*; otherwise we must await the appropriate volume of J. C. G. Röhl's edition of the Eulenburg Papers.
10*

The position of the bourgeois parties (as opposed to that of the SPD) on this matter was well stated by the left liberal Karl Schrader: 'We are not concerned in any way to weaken the authority of the Kaiser; on the contrary, our strong desire is to strengthen it in every way . . . accordingly, in the interests of the preservation of Imperial power and its dignity, we wish to recapture that old system (of the Bismarckian era).'[109] The main concern was defence of the Crown against the personal irresponsibility of the monarch, and only the SPD was prepared to think seriously of imposing formal constitutional constraints upon him. The attacks on Wilhelm II, from those of Heydebrand to those of Haussmann, were directed not at his allegedly 'unconstitutional' incursions into the sphere of Bülow's ministerial jurisdiction, but at 'the lack of a united stable leadership' in the government as a whole.[110] Accordingly, the main object was to strengthen the Chancellor's moral political authority in relation to the person of Wilhelm, by delivering the latter an admonitory political shock. This was the calculation behind the Conservative Party's unprecedented declaration of November 5th, and the gist of the crucial Reichstag debate of November 10th to 11th. When the Kaiser eventually issued a relatively contrite public statement on November 17th 1908, this object seemed to have been secured. Though the affair had finally shattered Bülow's relations with Wilhelm II, it proved a chastening experience for the latter. On only one future occasion, that of the Königsberg address of August 25th 1910, was one of his public statements again subjected to serious criticism in the Reichstag.[111]

The response of the Pan-Germans had been swift. On October 31st 1908—three days after the offending article appeared—a special meeting of the Committee was called to discuss its implications, and the next day as the crisis deepened this was brought forward ten days to November 4th to 5th. To emphasize the gravity of the situation invitations were also sent to all thirty-three Reichstag deputies who were members of the League and to sympathetic members of the press. When the meeting convened on the 4th the atmosphere was fraught. Pan-Germans shared the general outrage at the Kaiser's irresponsibility and joined the chorus of dismay that Bülow's government had failed to control his impulsive nature. But beyond this they brought to the Affair a dissenting tradition of nationalist opposition hardened by years of political exclusion. Claß and his colleagues saw Wilhelm II's indiscretions as regrettable confirmation of their own political acumen: the new crisis vindicated Pan-German criticisms of the government and delivered fresh evidence of the absence of political purpose. To salvage a sense of national honour the Kaiser should now be forced into the background and the Chancellor take careful

[109] TR, Nov. 10th 1908, p. 5414.
[110] E. Fehrenbach, *Wandlungen des deutschen Kaisergedankens 1871–1918* (Munich, 1969), p. 133. Ernst von Heydebrand und der Lasa was parliamentary leader of the Conservatives, Conrad Haußmann a leader of the South German People's Party.
[111] Fehrenbach, *Wandlungen*, p. 143.

note of the real feelings of the people. For this purpose a strong ideological lead from the Pan-Germans was even more vital than ever. After intensive discussion (and much disagreement) a series of resolutions were passed: that a direct petition be sent to the Kaiser, an extraordinary Convention be called later that month, and an appeal be issued to the German people (all proposed by Claß); that an open letter be sent to the Reichstag (Fick); that the League's public confidence be in practice withdrawn from Bülow (Simons); that a full-scale agitation be launched through mass meetings and lobbies of the press, politicians and princes (Pfeil and Reismann-Grone).

The second day was devoted to drafting the various documents. The petition to the Kaiser was dispatched on November 10th. The appeal to the nation was issued on the same day, but after complaints that the tone was too radical it was withdrawn and reissued in an amended form. By the time of the Convention on November 21st to 22nd, about a million copies of the appeal had been distributed, at a cost of 6,000 marks: 708,400 to newspapers, and 223,095 to the branches and individuals. The Convention passed a general resolution expressing the League's satisfaction that its long-standing critique of the government's foreign policy was now being properly aired in the press, the Reichstag and amongst the people at large. It urged that the debate be extended to 'the serious manifold damage perpetrated by the indulgence of personal rule in the domestic sphere' as well, but warned against any demand for constitutional change. If the Chancellor and the Reichstag lived up to their obligations, the existing Constitution was perfectly adequate to prevent the development of 'personal rule'. The real solution, it concluded, lay in a recharging of the national will.[112]

The discussion on November 4th had revealed some very interesting differences. Claß had given a strong lead by calling not only for the direct petition to the Kaiser (which was eventually accepted by the meeting), but also for the dismissal of Bülow (which was not). He also remarked that 'amongst the people the idea of excluding the Kaiser constitutionally from foreign policy has already surfaced'. The League could never support such a proposal, for it would create a permanent instrument of 'democratic parliamentary

[112] These details are taken from the minutes of the respective meetings and the accompanying texts and correspondence, in ZStA Potsdam, ADV, 67 & 68. See also the detailed account of the Convention in *TR*, Nov. 23rd 1908. The combined Executive and Managing Committee meeting of Nov. 4th to 5th was attended by the 4 members of the Executive (Claß, Liebert, Pfeil and Stössel), and 13 members of the Committee (Fick, Geiser, Gerhard, Hopf, Itzenplitz, Korodi, Lattmann, Petzoldt, Reismann-Grone, Reventlow, Stolte, Winter, J. F. Zeiss). They were joined by 4 Reichstag deputies (Karl Böhme, Friedrich Hanisch, Max Liebermann von Sonnenberg and Wilh. Schack, all of whom—together with Wilhelm Lattmann—sat for Hessian and Saxon constituencies in the Economic Union, a parliamentary alliance of the Anti-Semitic fractions), and three journalists (Eichler, Liman and Rippler). Hammerstein represented the *Keimianer* from the Navy League, and Paul Simons was invited as a senior ordinary member.

government'. In general he pressed hard for a principled initiative of 'national opposition', regardless of the possible consequences (e.g. loss of members). He was backed up by Stössel and Reventlow, and then by Itzenplitz, who laid particular stress on the opportunity for seizing the ideological initiative: 'We will take the wind from the Social Democrats' sails if we now travel the same path of sharpest criticism but in a national sense (Very true!). If the Reichstag does nothing, the people must act.' This met with general assent, but the call for Bülow's resignation encountered stiff opposition. Thus Liebert matched Claß for rhetoric—'Today, at this critical moment, when the entire German people is in a fever of excitement, the Reichstag speaks smugly of milk and cream'—but argued instead for strengthening Bülow's backbone against the Kaiser. He was supported by Pfeil and Reismann-Grone. In the end Claß's proposal for a direct petition was only passed by eight votes to seven, and the call for Bülow's dismissal defeated by the same figure. The next day saw similar differences over the text of the public appeal: Simons' original draft proved too sharp and had to be revised by Liebert, Pfeil and Stössel.[113]

In other words, the discussion of the Daily Telegraph Crisis saw the final coherence within the Pan-German League of the new leadership around Claß. The latter's association with Stössel now went back many years, but Reventlow and Itzenplitz were more recent recruits into the League's inner circles. To them should be added other key individuals, including Klingemann, Neumann, Samassa and Hugenberg, shortly to be joined by Keim, and somewhat later by Konstantin Frhr. von Gebsattel. The crucial impetus had been given by Claß's election as Chairman at the start of 1908 in succession to the deceased Hasse, and the new group could already be seen in action during the protracted resolution of the Navy League crisis. Claß had long been angling for a more dynamic political offensive by the League, and coming so conveniently after the radical-nationalist excitement of events in the naval movement, the Daily Telegraph Crisis was an admirable opportunity for equipping the Pan-Germans with a much stronger political profile. At a time when the popular credit of the government was fairly low in broad nationalist terms, a clear stance of 'national opposition' might conquer the Pan-Germans some valuable public space. In this sense the specific issue of Kaiser-Chancellor relations within the Imperial executive was less important to Claß than the ulterior motive of securing a new ideological lead for the Pan-German League. In this he was distinguished both from the more cautious tacticians like Liebert and Pfeil, who always kept one eye on the party-political scene and the stability of the Bülow Bloc, and from the purer idealists who had no sense of future political direction. Claß retained the older image of the League as an ideological vanguard (asserting a specifically Pan-German point of view, re-educating the public mind), but

[113] For the debate on Nov. 4th 1908, see the confidential *Verhandlungsbericht*, ZStA Potsdam, ADV, 67; 28–43; and for the debate over the draft, SA Essen, Reismann-Grone Papers, 10, IX. 08. 6f.

now combined it with a larger ambition for reconstituting the party political right.[114]

In the history of radical nationalism, therefore, the Daily Telegraph Affair was a vital moment, at which past struggles were recapitulated and their lessons recombined in a much clearer commitment to material political change. On the one hand, the old belief that 'domestic unity' could only be achieved 'in the area of foreign policy and overseas interests' was reaffirmed, and a call issued for 'the fusion of all healthy national forces into a workable, politically valuable organization in the struggle for the domestic and foreign interests of the German Reich'. On the other hand, that plea now carried an unmistakable populist inflection. The League insisted that a strong people must control its own foreign policy, and when the Chancellor 'has no backing in the Crown, he must be able to rely on a strong, organized public opinion'.[115] Claß now publicly questioned the legitimacy of traditional monarchy:

> The Chancellor-Crisis is now over, and we hope that the Kaiser-Crisis is also finished. The Kaiser must learn from recent events that a gulf has opened between him and the German people, that it is not the people's business to make that gulf disappear, but that every bond of loyalty has two sides, and that the *bond between Kaiser and people depends on mutual respect.*[116]

This was a vital departure, at which sections of the right finally burst the chains of royalist forbearance. A basis was now found, in a radical-nationalist conception of popular legitimacy, for opposing the government from the right. In this way the experience of the Navy League, which had been pragmatically forged, was properly articulated into a coherent political position.

In the process the two perspectives of radical nationalism—nationalist solutions for domestic problems, the populist critique of conventional bourgeois politics—became linked to a third, namely the nationalist coalescence of the right-wing parties. Under the anxious guidance of Claß the Pan-German League became increasingly oriented towards the domestic political arena, and contacts with big business and agriculture were assiduously strengthened. Moreover, as the old right's general confidence in Bethmann Hollweg gradually collapsed after 1911, and its leaders found themselves confronting a left-dominated

[114] After voting against the actions proposed by Claß on Nov. 4th, but then apparently participating in the final draft of the texts on the next day, both Liebert and Pfeil then protested at the radical form of the public statements. Liebert resigned, while Pfeil refused to attend the Convention in Leipzig on Nov. 21st 1908. See Claß to Klingemann, Nov. 25th 1908, ZStA Potsdam, ADV, 192: 434. Significantly Pfeil had tried to oppose Claß's election as Chairman by canvassing his own candidature, and Reismann-Grone had suspected Bülow's influence. See SA Essen, Reismann-Grone Papers, 10, IX. 08. 2.

[115] The quotations are taken from the text of the Appeal.

[116] Claß's address to the Extraordinary Convention, Leipzig, Nov. 22nd 1908, cit. *TR*, Nov. 23rd 1908.

Reichstag after the elections of 1912, the Pan-German critique of post-Bismarckian government acquired a new resonance. The old barriers of disapproval were slowly dismantled, and under unprecedented conditions of political weakness old and new right discovered a shared community in 'national opposition'. As we shall see, this opened a new perspective of realistic ideological leadership for the Pan-Germans, and after 1908 radical nationalism became increasingly embedded in a larger party-political project. As Hugenberg confided to his closest associate Leo Wegener:

> The recent events have returned me to a rather better political temper again . . . Now there is at least the *possibility* of improvement. If the Kaiser was now to declare (which he naturally won't do): Give me a group of parties in the Reichstag who are united over a). finance reform, b). grand reform of our bureaucracy, with *abolition of half our official activity* (as superfluous for a developed people) *and half our instances* (as superfluous for a bureaucracy which enjoys and deserves trust, including the judiciary) *and half our officials* (excluding *works*-administrations), c). concern for Army and Navy . . . colonial policy, and a *few other things too*, and I will let these parties *govern*, i.e. take the best people from them—if he did this we could arrive by a process of concentration at a viable national party, which would also regard the suffrage question etc. from a different angle. But hopefully we will reach the same goal by another slower route.[117]

[117] Hugenberg to Wegener, Nov. 15th 1908, BA Coblenz, Wegener Papers, 63.

PART IV

9. The Disunity of the Wilhelmine Power Bloc

I

Recent work has placed much stress on the political instability of the *Kaiserreich* in its last years of peace. The particular accent has varied, with some authors emphasizing 'ungovernability', others the polarization of political life into two hostile blocs of left and right, with others still arguing that the domestic crisis was so acute as to drive the government into the military adventure of July 1914. Whatever the exact terms of the argument, however, there has been fairly general agreement that by the eve of the war the Empire had found itself in some kind of political 'blind alley' or 'dead end'.[1] Wolfgang Mommsen has spoken of 'the almost complete deadlock of parliamentary politics' after 1912 and a 'stalemate between the various political groups' which 'was accompanied by sterile agitation and effectively blocked the way for any substantial change in the constitutional structure'.[2] This way of regarding Wilhelmine politics, of course, is directly linked to the larger problem of 'political modernization' and the prospects for genuine parliamentary reform before 1914. Recent discussion has always situated the particular crisis of 1912–14 in the larger context of the *Kaiserreich*'s 'permanent structural crisis'. Though the exact relation remains an object of much debate—particularly in the case of the July Crisis itself—Germany's imperialist foreign policy is now normally linked in some way to the compulsions of domestic instability. Thus Mommsen concludes his discussion of the problem by asserting that 'the causes of the First World War must be sought not in the blunders and miscalculations of the governments alone, but in the fact that Germany's governmental system, as well as Austria-Hungary's and Russia's, was no longer adequate in the face of rapid social change and the steady advance of mass politics'.[3]

To understand the nature of this pre-war political crisis it is necessary to recapitulate an argument mounted in the earlier stages of this book. Wilhelmine politics were shaped by the decomposition of the Bismarckian power bloc

---

[1] e.g. V. R. Berghahn, 'Das Kaiserreich in der Sackgasse', *NPL*, XVI (1971), pp. 494–506.
[2] W. J. Mommsen, 'Domestic Factors in German Foreign Policy before 1914', *CEH*, VI (1973), pp. 27f.
[3] Ibid., p. 43.

which had predominated since the 1860s, but which by the end of the 1880s was faced with new pressures it could not contain. Bismarck's extraordinary innovations of the unification years, which fractured existing Conservative assumptions and installed the Prussian monarchy at the head of a rather un-congenial liberal Empire, had realized pragmatically most of the major liberal demands, from the legal infrastructure of the national market and the appro-priate economic policies, to the *Kulturkampf* and the construction of the nation-state. Though not fully parliamentary the 1871 Constitution was liberal enough to nurture hopes of further advance, and in the meantime the federalist guaran-tees respected the autonomous liberal achievements of the non-Prussian states. Even the anti-Socialist and protectionist turn of 1878–9 scarcely affected this liberal ascendancy: alliance with the Conservative landowning interest seemed the natural form of bourgeois consolidation at this stage (particularly in the uncertainties of the depression), and the liberal hegemony continued unimpaired at the level of the regions and municipalities, while the emerging technocracy of experts, administrators and professional reformers soon established their dominance in the new fields of town planning, public health and general socia administration.[4] The real challenge came only later in the 1890s, when new contradictions appeared between different fractions of the ruling class, and when politics were placed on a new popular basis. These two sets of develop-ments constituted the long-term difficulties of the Wilhelmine state, and it is worth considering them in turn.

The post-Bismarckian governments were faced above all with the problem of constructing an adequate administrative practice for managing the affairs of a dynamic capitalist economy in the age of imperialism. This required close and increasing attention to whole new areas of state intervention, encompassing everything from the expansion of military and naval armaments and the improvement of national communications, to the educational system, public health, social welfare, taxation, the arbitration of disputes with labour, and a fully-fledged system of civil, criminal and commercial legality. The greatest single obstacle to this process in Germany was the residual power of the East Elbian landowning class and the enclaves of privilege it retained inside the state apparatus. Some of the latter—recruitment of state personnel from the Junkers, persistence of transmuted seigneurial jurisdictions, aristocratic domination of the officer corps—were less serious than others, and indeed might be identified in most developing capitalisms. But the most important were to be found at the political level proper: an entrenched position in the Prussian Constitution, and a system of protection negotiated through the

---

[4] N. O. Bullock's forthcoming study of the housing reform movement should cast important light on this neglected area. In the meantime, see D. Lindenlaub, *Richtungskämpfe im Verein für Sozialpolitik, Beihefte zu den Vierteljahreshefte für Sozial- und Wirtschaftgeschichte*, 52 and 53 (Weisbaden, 1967), and J. J. Sheehan, 'Liberalism and the City in Nineteenth Century Germany', *Past and Present*, 51 (1971), pp. 116–37.

elaboration of economic policy between 1879 and 1902. As we saw, Caprivi and Miquel had both been confronted by the political problem of an organized and extremely vocal landowning interest, but whereas Caprivi showed some pragmatic willingness to countenance infringements of established agrarian privilege, Miquel reverted to that older Bismarckian practice of which he had himself been a leading architect: the *Sammlungspolitik* of 1897 was a clear return to Bismarck's 'solidarity bloc' of 1879. When Bülow succeeded Miquel as the government's key man in 1900–1 he at first continued this line—fostering the co-operation of the organized protectionist interests in the CVDI and the older agrarian group of the VSWR, and working simultaneously for a corresponding parliamentary coalition of Conservatives, Free Conservatives, National Liberal Party and Centre.

As is now clear from recent historiography, agricultural protection presupposed a long-term alliance with key fractions of industrial capital who had a similar interest in closing the home market—namely, those in coal, iron and steel, textiles, paper and glass, refining and fertilizers, and heavy engineering, who formed the basis for the CVDI in 1876.[5] This political axis—the much-vaunted alliance of 'iron and rye'—was an element of relative stability in the structure of the *Kaiserreich*.[6] Though scarcely wholly advantageous for each other in straight economic terms (e.g. the iron tariff affected the needs of agriculture for cheap machinery, food tariffs adversely affected the industrial wages bill), these two sectionalisms were mutually reinforcing in the political arena. This was particularly marked during the campaigning over the impending tariff settlement in 1900–2, where protectionist self-interest of an unbending kind held heavy-industrialists to general co-operation with the big landowners and prevented any alternative link-up with the new exporting lobbies against the excesses of the Agrarian League.[7] But as agriculture's share in the composition of net domestic product fell by 1913 to under a quarter, the spokesmen of the CVDI became far less willing to tolerate the political extravagance of much agrarian agitation. A rift almost occurred over the Canal Bill in 1899, and further disagreements arose over stock-exchange and commercial legislation in 1904

---

[5] The best introduction to the CVDI is H. Nußbaum, 'Centralverband Deutscher Industrieller 1876–1919', in Fricke, *Die Bürgerlichen Parteien*, II, 850–71. Kaelble, *Industrielle Interessenpolitik*, should be used in conjunction with the relevant passages in Stegmann, *Erben*, esp. pp. 32ff., 146ff., 176ff., 208ff.

[6] Despite recent criticisms Stegmann has successfully shown this constancy. For his most recent statement: D. Stegmann, 'Hugenberg contra Stresemann. Die Politik der Industrieverbände am Ende des Kaiserreichs', *VfZ*, 24 (1976), pp. 329–78.

[7] See especially Bueck's address to the Gen. Meeting of the VDEStI, Jan. 10th 1901, BA Coblenz, R 131, 163, pp. 10–14; record of CVDI Directorate, no date (probably Oct. 31st 1899), where Bueck reported on efforts to counter the propaganda of the Central Office for the Preparation of Commercial Treaties, and minutes of CDVI Directorate, Jan 18th 1900, where opposition was expressed to the Agrarian League (both in SA Augsburg, Haßler Papers, 9a).

and 1907. Moreover, the resolution of the tariff question in 1902 removed the single most important factor binding the two interests together at the level of economic policy.[8]

In general, partly because of the general level of prosperity, the political co-operation with big agriculture ceased to be an immediate priority of the power-brokers in the CVDI. The latter's member firms were much more concerned with perfecting organizations for regulating markets and improving their control of the labour process, not least by continuing to exclude the trade unions. Between 1904 and 1911 200 new cartels were formed, of which the Steel Works Association of 1904 was the most important, and which generally hastened the process of reactive organization and counter-organization in specific sectors of the economy. Similarly, as the trade unions began to consolidate the advances achieved after the end of the depression in 1895–6, CVDI employers explored the full repertoire of repressive techniques for controlling the labour process—shop-floor discipline, black-lists and employer-run labour exchanges, centralized employers' organizations, anti-Socialist pressure groups, company unions and patriotic workers' clubs—but without demanding the national legislation against trade unions which had previously necessitated parliamentary dependence on the Conservatives. Moreover, after 1902–3 this facilitated new forms of co-operation with interests outside the CVDI itself, mainly in the field of export promotion. It was in this area that the long-run trends of industrial growth worked most strongly against a simple continuation of Miquel's agrarian *Sammlung*. The CVDI had always insisted in 1897–1902 that the new tariffs would have to accommodate industry's need for commercial treaties of long duration, and the renegotiation of the latter after 1904–5 quickly modified the agrarian triumph of 1902. In purely economic terms heavy industry was drawn increasingly into co-operation with the manufacturing interests which took its products and dominated a rising share of German trade. The CVDI's participation in the so-called *Interessengemeinschaft* in 1905–6 with the BdI and the Central Office for the Preparation of Commercial Treaties was a recognition of this trend.[9]

After 1902 it is possible to detect a tilting of the political balance away from agriculture and towards industry, as the changing structure of the economy began to impose new priorities on the state. One example was the growth of consultative arrangements which enmeshed the corporate interests within the

[8] Kaelble, *Industrielle Interessenpolitik*, pp. 128ff.; H. Horn, *Der Kampf um den Bau des Mittellandkanals. Eine politiologische Untersuchung über die Rolle eines wirtschaftlichen Interessenverbandes im Preußen Wilhelms II* (Cologne, 1964), esp. pp. 31ff., 39ff., 46ff., 90ff., 123ff.

[9] For a good general discussion of these trends: W. Gutsche, 'Probleme des Verhältnisses zwischen Monopolkapital und Staat in Deutschland vom Ende des 19. Jahrhunderts bis zum Vorabend des ersten Weltkrieges', in F. Klein, *Studien zum deutschen Imperialismus vor 1914* (Berlin, 1976), pp. 33–84.

structures of the state itself and necessarily took less cognisance of agriculture's traditional claims to primacy. The older Prussian agencies—e.g. the Statistical Offices, the Railway Council, the Advisory Committee for Waterways etc.— were important, but the main innovations were again made in the area of foreign trade, through the Colonial Council, the various tariff commissions and the expansion of the consulates. From 1904–5 there was increased industrial pressure for fresh concessions in this area, whether by adapting the old Economic Committee formed in 1897, by promoting bi-national economic contacts or by setting up a state Export Office.[10] Added to the ideologies of *Weltpolitik* and naval expansion this pressure for official sponsorship of foreign trade was bound to cause disquiet in agrarian ranks. But by far the most threatening aspect of industrial primacy in the economy was the inevitable pressure for political readjustments in the 'quasi-Constitution' of agrarian privilege, most notably in the areas of taxation and the Prussian suffrage. As recent literature has emphasized, it was above all the agrarians' successful sabotage of the Bülow finance reform in spring 1909, with its limited provision for direct taxation of landed incomes, which produced a temporary but none the less decisive fracture in the frayed neo-Bismarckian alliance of 1897. Agrarian intransigence strained the CVDI's public tolerance to breaking-point and created the necessary basis in the summer of 1909 for the launching of the Hanse-Union, the first general front of industrial, merchant and finance capital with an avowedly anti-agrarian direction.[11]

The Hanse-Union grew directly from the demise of the Bülow Bloc. Neither the liberal nor the Conservative participants in the latter had harboured many illusions concerning its long-term viability (though the liberals were more conscious of the advantages of their closer proximity to government), and each was perhaps mainly concerned that the odium for the Bloc's failure should lie with the other. Thus the agrarians had taken their decisions as early as September 2nd 1908 in the common 'Kolberg Programme' of the Agrarian League and Conservatives, but their public rejection of the proposed finance reform was not finally known until the end of March 1909. This already spelt the end of the Bülow Bloc, and by May 19th when the new Conservative-Centre majority formally replaced the contentious inheritance tax with a series of taxes on commercial transactions, the new battle-lines were already drawn.[12] A rally of *Mittelstand* organizations on April 13th attended by some 4,000 and addressed by the veteran 'social politician' Hans Freiherr von Berlepsch had given early warning of possible anti-agrarian initiatives, and on May 24th a

[10] Ibid., pp. 6off.
[11] The two essential works on the Hanse-Union are Stegmann, *Erben*, esp. pp. 176ff., and Mielke, *Hansa-Bund*.
[12] Witt, *Finanzpolitik*, pp. 229ff.; Stegmann, *Erben*, pp. 176ff.; B. Heckart, *From Basser-mann to Bebel. The Grand Bloc's Quest for Reform in the Kaiserreich, 1900–1914* (New Haven and London, 1974), pp. 77ff.

joint circular was issued in the names of Jacob Riesser (for the Central Association of German Bankers) and Max Roetger (the new Chairman of the CVDI and former Chairman of Krupp), calling for a general protest at a rally in Berlin on June 12th 1909. The meeting would inaugurate a new 'community of interest' amongst 'Germany's industry, trade and commerce', for the latter had 'finally exhausted their patience and (were) no longer willing to stand victim to laws which were dominated by the politics of one-sided economic interest'.[13]

The rally was attended by spokesmen for some hundred Chambers of Commerce and over 400 other business organizations, including both the CVDI and BdI. The speakers reflected the breadth of the meeting's composition: apart from Riesser himself they included the bankers Max von Schinckel and Franz von Mendelssohn, the heavy industrialist Emil Kirdorf, the electricity baron Emil Rathenau, the Chairman of the BdI Hermann Wirth, and the Berlin merchant Emil Jacob. The new organization which emerged, the Hanse-Union, was proclaimed as industry's answer to the Agrarian League, with the aim 'of protecting commerce, trade and industry against attacks and injuries of any kind . . . and of moderating the existing conflicts within their own ranks'. To this end membership was extended to 'every independent tradesman'. Moreover, as industrial, merchant and finance capital had become (it was claimed) the 'step-children of German law-making', a first priority was the election of sympathetic spokesmen to the Reichstag. The leading organs of the Hanse-Union—a Presidium of six, a Directorate of thirty-six, and the General Committee of at least a hundred—provided a cross-section through the structure of German capitalism, with strong representation for the big banks, heavy and light industry, large and small merchants, old and new *Mittelstand*. All regions were present, though there was perhaps a slight concentration of regions such as Berlin, the Rhineland, Saxony and Württemberg. The first Presidium comprised Riesser (President), Roetger (Vice-President), Albert Hirth (Chairman of the Association of Württemberg Industrialists and prominent in the BdI), Albert Steche (Chairman of the Leipzig branch of the Association of Saxon Industrialists, likewise prominent in the BdI), Rudolf Crasemann (a leading Hamburg exporter), and H. Richt (a master cabinet-maker and Chairman of the Central Committee of the United Guild Associations of Germany).[14]

The Hanse-Union was a development of the foremost importance. It was the single most significant product of the industrial-agrarian contradiction in Wilhelmine politics. Superficially it seemed to realize an old left-liberal dream of 'anti-feudal' unity, a new willingness in the economically active bourgeoisie to embrace what Max Weber had called the 'resolute pursuit of the consequences of our bourgeois-economic development' by assailing the remaining bastions of

[13] Stegmann, *Erben*, p. 178; Mielke, *Hansa-Bund*, pp. 31f.
[14] Details from Stegmann, *Erben*, pp. 178–32, and Mielke, *Hansa-Bund*, pp. 187–91.

agrarian privilege in the state.[15] Naumann had peddled this conception during the years of the National-Socials in 1896–1903, it lay at the basis of the more ambitious programmes advanced in the BdI, and was nurtured by most of those left liberals with any strategic vision of Germany's future political development.[16] Jacob Riesser—till 1905 Director of the *Darmstädter Bank* and thereafter the leading public spokesman for finance capital in general—certainly viewed the Hanse-Union in this light.[17] Perhaps the most systematic exposition of this perspective in immediate reaction to the foundation of the Hanse-Union in June 1909 came from the left liberal Franz von Liszt, a Berlin professor and Landtag deputy. Writing in the *Kölnische Zeitung* under the title 'Hanse-Union and Liberalism', he greeted the new organization as a first decisive blow against that 'Conservative domination in Prussia and thereby in the Reich' which had been inaugurated in 1879. The latter had its 'firm basis in the Cartel between the landowning interest and the raw materials industry', which had dictated the terms of economic policy and subordinated the whole of domestic politics in Prussia to the interests of the agrarian Conservatives. But now, Liszt argued, the decision of the CVDI to join the Hanse-Union marked a vital turning-point, for it finally enabled the full combination of all branches of progressive capital into an unprecedented anti-feudal alliance.[18]

Not the least of the features singled out by Liszt was the involvement of both old and new *Mittelstand* in the new enterprise. As mentioned above, one of the first big demonstrations against the Conservative defeat of the finance reform had occurred at a *Mittelstand* rally on April 13th, in which the German *Mittelstand* Association, the Saxon equivalent and a number of commercial organizations were all strongly represented. Feelings were running high in many sections of the traditional petty-bourgeoisie—Dietrich Hahn, who attended the April rally to put the Conservative case, was unceremoniously shouted down—and it was not surprising to find a significant presence of *Mittelstand* spokesmen in the new anti-agrarian coalition. Between them handicrafts, retailing, small business and commercial employees could probably claim some ten seats in the Hanse-Union's Directorate. Though his adherence to the new organization split his own movement and led eventually to a decisive new foundation to its right, the most important recruit from the old *Mittelstand*

---

[15] Kehr, *Battleship Building*, p. 454.

[16] For Naumann see the following pamphlets: *Flotte und Reaktion* (Berlin, 1899), esp. p. 15; *Weltpolitik und Sozialreform* (Schöneberg-Berlin, 1899), esp. pp. 14ff.; *Weltpolitik und Bürgerpolitik* (Hamburg, 1900). For the BdI: Ullmann, *Bund der Industriellen*, esp. pp. 165ff. For a good example of left liberal thinking: Gothein to Williger, Feb. 25th 1908, BA Coblenz, Gothein Papers, 34.

[17] See Riesser's major work on the German banks: *Die deutschen Großbanken und ihre Konzentration im Zusammenhange mit der Entwicklung der Gesamtwirtschaft in Deutschland* (3rd ed., Jena, 1910). See also the two articles in *DWZ*, July 15th and Aug. 1st 1909, and the more substantial *Der Hansa-Bund* (Jena, 1912).

[18] *KZ*, June 21st 1909.

was Carl Rahardt, Over-Master of the Berlin Carpenters Guild and since 1906 Chairman of the German *Mittelstand* Association. Rahardt also helped open the way to the United Guild Associations of Germany, who claimed a total membership of some 300,000. But in general the traditional petty-bourgeoisie was divided in its response to the Hanse-Union. The new *Mittelstand* was far more uniform in its sympathy. Here Riesser was able to secure the adherence of the Association of German Commercial Assistants (102,000 members in 1913), the Association for Commercial Clerks of 1858 (127,000 in 1913), the German Foremen's Association (62,000 in 1913), the Association of German Technicians (30,000), and many smaller groups, like the Society of German Salesmen or the Society of Travelling Salesmen of Berlin.[19]

This re-emphasized the difficulties of the power bloc: if the old alliance of 'iron and rye' no longer held good as the natural basis of the government's parliamentary practice, then the mood of the petty-bourgeoisie showed that the landowning interest could no longer assume the automatic support of a sub-ordinate popular mass. This compounded the political isolation of the landed interest, which resulted not just from an internal fractioning of the governing bloc, but also from a related dispersal of its popular support. Both processes had a structural cause, originally located in the 1890s, when Germany's accelerated passage into industrial capitalism began to create new contradictions in the social and political relations which had previously joined the Junkers to old industrial partners and a petty-bourgeois popular constituency. As argued in the earlier stages of this book, the popular mobilization of the 1890s tended to dissolve old habits of deference, and though the Conservative Party had been able by 1909 to absorb much of the rural and Anti-Semitic dissidence by means of the Agrarian League, its artful manufacture of a single 'agrarian interest' was never completely successful.[20] The entry of many *Mittelstand* politicians into the Hanse-Union showed that the traditions of anti-aristocracy were far from dead, and even those who stayed out (like Theodor Fritsch's important Saxon *Mittelstand* Association) still reaffirmed the need for a more equitable tax-system.[21] Similarly, the Hanse-Union deliberately cultivated the potential allegiance of the independent peasantry through the newly founded German Peasants' League, and though the latter could only claim some 50,000 members by 1914, it none the less embodied an important ideological

[19] For further detail: Mielke, *Hansa-Bund*, pp. 102–12 (old *Mittelstand*), 95–102 (new *Mittelstand*); Gellately, *Politics of Economic Despair*, pp. 165ff.; Stegmann, *Erben*, pp. 176ff. Figures are taken from Hohorst, Kocka, Ritter, *Sozialgeschichtliches Arbeitsbuch*, p. 138.

[20] In other words, though the Agrarian League successfully incorporated most of the independent Protestant farming movements of the 1890s (e.g. the Central German Peasants' Association), this invariably meant that conflicts were now acted out inside the organization itself. Most Agrarian League functionaries west of the Elbe walked a political tightrope between the dictates of agriculture's rational interest in the national parliamentary arena and the pressures of local farming lobbies.

[21] Gellately, *Politics of Economic Despair*, pp. 168f.

commitment which liberals had notably failed to make in the 1890s.[22] In general the anti-agrarian upturn of mid-1909 seemed to afford a vital opening for a new liberal politics, in which significant sections of the petty-bourgeoisie might be disengaged from their existing Conservative attachments and re-integrated into a new progressive bloc.

II

This raises the second long-term difficulty of the old power bloc. The first such difficulty—to recapitulate the preceding discussion—was the appearance of sharper contradictions between the leading fractions of the dominant classes: beginning under Caprivi in the early 1890s and at different times setting free traders against protectionists, manufacturers against primary suppliers, or small against big capital, these tended on the whole towards a political isolation of big agriculture. But simultaneously, the traditional relations of political subordination—the complex structures of informal *Honoratiorenpolitik*—which had previously ensured the electoral compliance of a popular mass, began to dissolve. It was this second problem—characterized above as a prolonged crisis of the power bloc's hegemonic capability—that proved particularly painful, for the most successful attempts at a sectoral solution tended only to worsen the power bloc's fractional disunity, radical nationalism by alienating the patricians of the Conservatives and Centre, the Agrarian League by sharpening the general bourgeois hostility to the special position of agriculture. In this situation the ability of the Hanse-Union to attract *Mittelstand* support was a development of extraordinary political importance, for when added to the novel combination of industrial, merchant and finance capital this popular potential raised the possibility of reconstituting the power bloc on an entirely new basis, against the agrarians.

In other words, the defeat of the finance reform and the foundation of the Hanse-Union nurtured hopes that the liberal parties might be able to re-establish their leadership over a popular coalition broad enough to capture the main direction of the state. There was a powerful sense in the leading circles in the Hanse-Union that the time for a decisive bourgeois politics had come, expressed most vividly perhaps in the title of Riesser's collected speeches, *Bürger Heraus!* or 'Citizens Arise!'.[23] As suggested above, the central thrust was a powerful indictment of the landed interest, articulated partly through the language of liberalism's historic anti-aristocratic critique, partly as an attack on the entrenched 'class-egoism' of agricultural privileges. As well as the demand for an equitable finance reform, there were commitments to

[22] The German Peasants' League is a badly neglected subject. The main source is H. Schwab, 'Deutscher Bauernbund', in Fricke (Ed.), *Die Bürgerlichen Parteien*, I, pp. 415–21.

[23] *Bürger Heraus! Ausgewählte Reden des Präsidenten des Hansa-Bundes Dr. Reisser* (Berlin, 1912).

systematic electoral activity and to breaking the power of the Agrarian League
by encouraging the independence of the smaller farmer. More guardedly, the
principle of the 'equality of all economic estates' which ran through the Union's
programme also entailed a commitment to reforming the Prussian three-class
franchise, though initially the plutocratic leanings of the CVDI representatives
required that this be played down.[24] In general Riesser insisted that the state be
made more responsive to the needs of industry and trade, and if pursued
consistently this would also involve 'the free development of a mature bourgeoisie, conscious of its strength and goals'. In terms reminiscent of Naumann's
at the turn of the century, Riesser argued that the question was whether
Germany 'should still be ruled and administered in whatever way after the
style of the long out-dated Prussian agrarian state', or whether 'burghers and
peasants' should at last be freed from their subjection to the power of the
Junkers.[25]

The party-political grouping to which the Hanse-Union potentially corresponded was a new liberal coalition, extending from the National Liberals to the
three left liberal fractions (themselves then in the process of unification), with
some support from the Centre and the likely toleration of the SPD. As Arthur
Rosenberg said, this would have been close to a German version of the
'Gladstonian coalition', whose absence was so large a measure of Germany's
distinctive political formation since the 1860s.[26] Of course a 'centre-left' of
this kind was never seriously on the cards before the First World War, because
(quite apart from the older ideological resistances) a series of regionally specific
antagonisms militated powerfully against any reformist intentions which might
conceivably emerge within the respective party leaderships. Liberal anti-
clericalism in the south-west and parts of the Rhineland, Centre dependence
south of the Main on the anti-liberal and anti-Socialist grievances of suffering
small producers, or the SPD's greater independence in most of northern
Germany, were the most obvious instances of these.[27] The same factors worked
against that other chimera of the pre-war years, the liberal-Socialist 'bloc from
Bassermann to Bebel'.[28] But the possibilities of a parliamentary regroupment
to match the new departure of the Hanse-Union might take other forms than
these. A closer relationship between the National Liberals and a reunited left

[24] See the programme published in Mielke, *Hansa-Bund*, pp. 200ff. The demand for
Prussian suffrage reform was given greater prominence after 1911.

[25] *Bürger Heraus!*, pp. 147f.

[26] A. Rosenberg, *Imperial Germany. Birth of the German Republic 1871–1914* (Oxford,
1931), p. 18. Rosenberg's idea was actually more specific than this, involving a coalition of
Centre, Progressives and SPD, and a considerable difference of emphasis. For a further discussion, see Blackbourn, 'Class and Politics', pp. 220ff.

[27] The best analysis of the contradictions keeping Centre and SPD apart in this way is
Blackbourn, 'Class and Politics'.

[28] Apart from Heckart, *Bassermann to Bebel*, see K. Wegner, 'Linksliberalismus im
wilhelminischen Deutschland und in der Weimarer Republik', *GG*, 4 (1978), pp. 120–37.

liberal party was the most modest and perhaps the closest at hand. Alternatively, more imaginative politicians might seek to capture the political logic of the 1907 elections, with their novel combination of radical nationalism, anti-Socialism and transmuted anticlericalism into a government strategy which was primarily ideological rather than economic. Arguably the Bülow Bloc delivered the materials of a more lasting coalition than actually resulted during 1907–9, based in the National Liberals as the leading fraction, probably some Free Conservatives, the left liberals and the extra-parliamentary movement of the *nationale Verbände*, and committed to a decisive 'modernizing' departure.

Bülow was clearly aware of these possibilities. Quite apart from the basic commitment to finance reform, which already entailed some break with the Conservatives, he also moved more tentatively in the area of Prussian suffrage reform: both his declaration of January 10th 1908 and his insistence nine months later that the speech from the throne should contain a further commitment were clear accommodations of liberal wishes.[29] Moreover, Bülow mounted a relatively new type of public campaign for the finance reform, doubly orchestrated through a special Economic Bureau in the Finance Office and Hamman's older apparatus of relations with the press.[30] The closest equivalent to this was the campaigning for the two Navy Bills in 1897–1900, and, like the Navy Office then, the Chancellory was drawn into closer relations both with the liberal parties and a wider spectrum of independent nationalist opinion.

This last factor—the legacy of having used the radical nationalists to run the official campaign in the 1907 elections—was perhaps the most interesting feature of Bülow's manoeuvres against the Conservatives after the summer of 1908. For the *nationale Verbände* were themselves highly active in the finance agitation. Most leading radical nationalists, from the old guard like Ernst Hasse to the recruits of experience like Keim or the more self-conscious ideologists like Stössel or Claß, had long admitted the importance of financial rationalization, and in the winter of 1908–9 quickly rose to the occasion. Here the key development was the 'Association for the Promotion of the Finance Reform' in October 1908, formed largely at the instigation of Ludwig Sevin, a young political scientist who had been active in the 1907 elections. Conceived as the catalyst for 'a great popular movement', this was to operate through the 'united local branches of the *nationale Verbände*', in close liaison with the Chancellory. As well as many National Liberals and a few dissident Conservatives, its sponsors included some familiar exponents of *nationale Politik*: Otto Arendt, Eduard von Liebert and Major-General Arthur von Loebell, a leader of the patriotic workers' movement and spokesman for the so-called Young

---

[29] Witt, *Finanzpolitik*, pp. 190f., 230f.

[30] Ibid., pp. 217ff. The new Economic Bureau was organized by Ernst von Halle, who ran the official propaganda for the Navy Office during the early years of the Tirpitz-Plan. See Deist, *Flottenpolitik*, esp. pp. 113ff.

Conservatives, a group which opposed the Conservative policy in 1909.[31]

This convergence of radical-nationalist and liberal politics on the issue of the finance reform—already presaged in the 1907 elections, as we saw—afforded, perhaps, a singular opportunity for rallying all those forces committed to a 'modernization' of the Empire's political structure. But it simultaneously indicated the *limited* 'progressive' potential of any liberal-nationalist bloc which might result. For the main impetus of the latter was not so much democratic (in the sense of a commitment to parliamentary controls, to universal suffrage in Prussia or to trade union recognition) as a desire for higher levels of 'national efficiency'. For radical nationalists this meant mobilizing the full financial resources of the state, overriding particularist and sectional divisions, strengthening the centralist as against the federal aspects of the Constitution, and promoting a sense of national citizenship. Similarly, most liberals were concerned with *Gleichberechtigung* or 'equality of status', namely the admission of the bourgeoisie to a share of political influence in the state commensurate with its importance in economy and society. Thus the basis on which the finance reform rallied the different fractions and tendencies of the bourgeoisie into a common programme was less 'democratic' than both anti-agrarian and national-ist. For this reason it is false to regard either the Bloc or the Hanse-Union as embodying real chances of formal 'parliamentarization'. As Witt has said, the issue was 'more modest' than this, namely:

. . . would the Conservatives, who enjoyed untrammelled domination in Prussia, but who were seriously weakened in the Reich, where they were cast back on the support of industry and its parliamentary arm the National Liberal Party together with that of the Centre, be sensible and freely renounce a part of their privileges in favour of the bourgeoisie?[32]

III

The importance of this point becomes clearer if we examine the National Liberals in more detail, for it was here that the fate of any reformist turn would finally be decided. In terms of political morale the National Liberals derived most benefit from the experience of the Bloc. From this time we may detect a notable invigoration of the party's inner life, for although an expansion of local organization had been facilitated by the new Constitution of 1905, it required the upswing of 1907–9 to supply the necessary impetus. In 1897 the number of local Associations was estimated rather optimistically as 400. But

---

[31] Details from Witt, *Finanzpolitik*, pp. 224ff. See also Rassow to Delbrück, Mar. 11th 1909, BA Coblenz, Delbrück Papers, 11.

[32] Witt, *Finanzpolitik*, p. 304. For liberal attitudes towards the Prussian suffrage question, see W. Gagel, *Die Wahlrechtsfrage in der Geschichte der deutschen liberalen Parteien 1848–1918*, esp. pp. 126ff.; also Heckart, *Bassermann to Bebel*, pp. 54–9, 154–60, 277–81.

during the life of the Bloc the figures rose from 940 to 1,285, and by the start of the war there were more than 2,000. By 1910 the party had 200,000 members, rising to 283,711 by 1915, with a well-developed regional organization in the Prussian provinces of Saxony, Hannover, Hessen-Nassau, the Rhineland and Westphalia, and in the historic strongholds of Baden, Württemberg, Hessen, the Palatinate, the rest of Bavaria and Saxony.[33] By comparison with the disastrous inactivity of the 1890s this registered a notable advance and at a time of continuing SPD gains assisted a valuable stabilization of the National Liberals' electoral position. Although the party's vote dropped by 0·9% between the 1907 and 1912 elections, it was still 1·1% higher than in 1898. By 1912 about 11·4% of all National Liberal voters were also members of the party, and as Nipperdey observes, this was an impressive achievement.[34]

This organizational growth was accompanied by a renewed sense of political direction. To an extent the origins of this could be traced back to the late 1890s, when Ernst Bassermann had inherited the national leadership as the known opponent of the 'Hard-Labour Bill' and other exceptional laws against the SPD. But the leftward tendency of this stance had been somewhat submerged in the concurrent preoccupations with the tariff settlement and the Navy Laws. More important was the ideological pressure of the Young Liberals, who from their origins in Cologne in 1898 spread through the Rhineland and the southwest to form a National Association in 1901: though small (some 2,500 members in 1900, over 10,000 by 1905, around 16–18,000 by 1914), they played a key role in structuring the discussion in the party and on the central questions of finance reform, social legislation, suffrage reform, co-operation with the left liberals and hostility to the agrarians clearly set the pace for Bassermann and the party centre.[35] But though there were important advances before 1907— e.g. the new Constitution of 1905 and Bassermann's official approval of pacts with the left liberals in the same year[36]—it was only the experience of the Bülow Bloc which really confirmed the new direction. Most obviously, the nationalist form of the 1907 elections corresponded exactly with the primary self-understanding of the National Liberals, who since the 1890s had been compelled, as we saw, to sublimate their internal disagreements in ardent celebration of their own contribution to Germany's national strength. Secondly, the Bloc brought the party much closer to the centre of governmental power. But thirdly, and most importantly, it derived a new buoyancy from the anti-agrarian upturn of 1909.

For this reason it is quite misleading to see the end of the Bloc as a defeat or a setback for the National Liberals. They might have been dislodged from the old government majority, but they responded by a powerful affirmation of

[33] Details from Nipperdey, *Organisation*, pp. 100f.
[34] Ibid., p. 102.
[35] Details ibid., pp. 96ff., and Eschenburg, *Kaiserreich*, pp. 11ff.
[36] *Allgemeiner Delegiertentag der Nationalliberalen Partei* (Berlin, 1905), II, pp. 30f.

liberal principle which laid the basis for an important revival of the party.[37]
In a sense this had been written into the relations of the Bloc since the summer
of 1908 at the latest, when the agrarians had waged an unrelenting campaign
against the National Liberals in the Prussian elections. This illustrated that the
latter would gain nothing by further compromises on matters like the finance
reform, for at present the 'Conservative-liberal fraternization' and 'the continued renunciation of a serious struggle against the Conservatives' led only to
'the self-castration of liberalism'.[38] Or as Bassermann remarked in July 1908
as news came in of agrarian excesses in the Landtag elections, 'we are paying
the cost of the Bloc policy'.[39] Accordingly, the final collapse of the Bülow Bloc,
though greeted by a storm of liberal outrage,[40] was seen at the same time as
clearing the way for genuine liberal policies in the party. At a special Congress
on July 4th 1909, three weeks after the launching of the Hanse-Union, Bassermann set a new anti-agrarian course, in which he invoked both Caprivi and a
new liberal era as the guiding slogans. To illustrate the new opportunities, he
pointed to the Hanse-Union, the German Peasants' League and the German
Mittelstand Association.[41]

In other words, there was a broad identity in the organizing ideas of both
the Hanse-Union and the National Liberal revival. If we are to understand
why the former failed to achieve its goals of *Gleichberechtigung*, in fact, it is
vital to appreciate why the related tendencies towards a larger refoundation
of German liberalism likewise evaporated before 1914. For to succeed at the level
of the state the project of a new progressive bloc also required an adequate
party-political articulation, and here the analysis of the National Liberal Party
becomes vital. To a great extent the National Liberals were prevented from
moving further to the left by the same factors that tended to immobilize the
Hanse-Union: on an industrial front the critical divisions—between the monopolies and small or medium capital, protectionists and exporters, intransigents
and conciliators on trade unionism—ran through the two organizations rather
than to their right. Most pointedly, the 'modernizers' around Bassermann were
always constrained by the pressure of a large right-wing in the Prussian party,
and here the CVDI industrialists wielded too much influence for the national

---

[37] This is naturally not to deny the existence of serious internal tensions in the National
Liberal Party after 1909, which by 1912 were leading increasingly in the direction of a split.
But it was precisely the rejuvenation of the party's reforming commitment which alienated
the old right wing and created the internal difficulties in the first place. Thus after 1909 it is
possible to speak of a simultaneous revival *and* crisis, in which the old industrial right found
itself increasingly isolated in the national party as a whole.

[38] Barth to Naumann, July 30th 1907, ZStA Potsdam, Naumann Papers, 143: 15f.

[39] Bassermann to Schiffer, July 1st 1908, BA Coblenz, Bassermann Papers, Kl. Erw.,
303–17.

[40] See the collection of quotations gathered from letters sent into the National Liberal
Central Office as a result of its stance on the finance reform: ZStA Potsdam, DVP, 1: 210–16.

[41] Cit. Eschenburg, *Kaiserreich*, p. 266.

leadership to envisage a break. Likewise, the spokesmen of the CVDI resisted any attempt in the Hanse-Union to extend feelers to labour, and were joined in this intransigence by many other elements as well. This was the Achilles' heel of Riesser's project. The CVDI had no intention of breaking with the agrarians: it joined the Hansa-Union in 1909 for tactical reasons (to teach the agrarians a lesson and to prevent the movement from getting out of hand), and in the summer of 1911 most of the heavy industrialists soon seceded.[42]

Moreover, if the CVDI would not join the Hanse-Union, the latter had little prospect of rallying the rest of the business world against it. Between 1895–6 and 1910–11 broad alliances against heavy industry had been possible in the campaigns against the tariffs, the Hard-Labour Bill or the cartels, based not only in small and medium capital, but also in the large shipping and manufacturing interests which required greater market control than the dominance of the protectionist and highly cartelized CVDI industries currently allowed. The Hibernia Affair in 1904–5 and the renewed cartel discussion of 1907–8 were perhaps the last major instances of this type.[43] The tariff negotiations in 1900–2 had already shown that there were clear limits to the opposition of a range of interests in shipping, electrical engineering and chemicals which formed the right wing of the anti-CVDI grouping, and it became increasingly difficult to interest them in common political action.[44] The big firms in these sectors found it easier to cope with heavy industry by acting unilaterally, through diversification, mergers and inter-penetration. Thus the advance of concentration in the heavy engineering and electro-technical industries had the effect of detaching key interests from the older loose anti-monopoly front, whilst the chemical industry preferred to straddle both the Hanse-Union and the CVDI. At the same time the gains of the SPD and the unions made even the more liberal employers wary of social or political concessions to labour. Taken together these factors reduced the anti-monopoly position to a rump of small and medium capitalists in the BdI and simultaneously severed it from a democratic politics of rapprochement with labour. Symptomatically, this easily permitted its degeneration into demagogic appeals to the petty-bourgeoisie, and by 1914 such moves were mounted largely by Conservatives, the Centre and spokesmen for the *Mittelstand*.[45]

[42] For the role of the CVDI in the National Liberal right, see Stegmann, *Erben*, pp. 159ff., 219ff., and for its attitude towards the Hanse-Union, ibid., pp. 176ff., 208ff., 239ff., and Mielke, *Hansa-Bund*, pp. 83ff.

[43] The most recent discussion of the former is the fine article by C. Medalen, 'State Monopoly Capitalism in Germany: The Hibernia Affair', *Past and Present*, 78 (Feb. 1978), pp. 82–112.

[44] For the position of these interests in the tariff negotiations: Stegmann, *Erben*, p. 88; Ullmann, *Bund der Industriellen*, pp. 189ff.

[45] See Gutsche, 'Probleme', p. 62, and Stegmann, 'Hugenberg contra Stresemann'. The best general study of anti-monopoly politics is H. Nußbaum, *Unternehmer gegen Monopole* (Berlin, 1966). For an exhaustive and highly instructive study of one instance: U. Brack,

Thus the difficulties of a viable reformism were partly to do with the developing structures of German monopoly capital: the latter increasingly enmeshed even the more liberal firms like the two electro-technical giants AEG and Siemens in networks of monopoly decision-making which owed nothing to liberal reform of the state, and may have made the latter seem redundant.[46] This re-emphasizes the power bloc's degree of fragmentation after the defeat of the finance reform. The old industrial-agrarian alliance was clearly in eclipse as the main basis of government, but important contradictions had prevented the broad front of industrial, merchant and finance capital from materializing in any stable parliamentary form. To compensate for these circumstances the wider popular resonance of the Hanse-Union's programme became even more vital, and despite the encouraging adherence of the *Mittelstand* groups and the progress of the Peasants' League, this could best be achieved by strengthening the left in the National Liberal Party. By this time, moreover, the organizational deficit which the National Liberals had incurred in the 1890s was finally being made good, and the quantitative expansion of the constituency apparatus noted above was also accompanied by a keener sense of popular politics. In this respect the debates and exhortations of the National Liberals reproduced the pattern of discussion inside the Navy League some years before to a striking degree. Young Liberals (who were also closely identified with the Navy League's radical leadership, it will be remembered) demanded greater involvement for local activists in the party's national organs, and simultaneously pressed for greater recruitment from the working class; they were opposed by the party establishment, who defended the regional autonomies of self-selecting *Honoratioren* and resisted any systematic appeal to the 'masses'.[47] In this situation the same potent antagonism against an unimaginative *Honoratiorenpolitik* was also present. As Gustav Stresemann put it at the Party Congress in October 1906, the National Liberals could not survive as a 'party of professors and businessmen', but needed 'to seek contact with all strata, with the artisans, with the workers, and even still more to convert our Associations into popular ones (*Volksvereinen*)'.[48]

As in the Navy League too, the National Liberals enjoyed little success in involving workers very actively in the party. In 1910 the official *Handbuch* claimed some 24,000 working-class members or 12% of the total, but they were

---

Deutsche Erdölpolitik vor 1914. Eine Fallstudie zu den Problemen der Marktbeherrschung und Staatsintervention im wilhelminischen Deutschland, (Diss. Hamburg, 1976), esp. pp. 390ff. See also Eley, 'Capitalism and the Wilhelmine State'.

[46] See especially H. Pogge von Strandmann, 'Widersprüche im Modernisierungsprozeß Deutschlands. Der Kampf der verarbeitenden Industrie gegen die Schwerindustrie', in Stegmann, Wendt, Witt, *Industrielle Gesellschaft*, pp. 225–40.

[47] Nipperdey, *Organisation*, pp. 102ff.; Reiss, *Bassermann zu Stresemann*, pp. 15ff.; Saul, *Staat, Industrie, Arbeiterbewegung*, pp. 171ff.

[48] *Allgemeiner Vertretertag der Nationalliberalen Partei* (Berlin, 1906), p. 54.

almost certainly mainly state employees or the members of Evangelical Workers' Associations and company unions.[49] In late 1912 Prof. Franz Moldenhauer, the head of the party in the Rhineland, urged the co-option on to local committees of 'representatives of all estates and circles, not just the prestigious and the rich, but also the less well off, workers, artisans, small officials etc.', but the next year there was only one worker, a turner, amongst the 47 members of the Provincial Executive.[50] It proved impossible to get workers adopted as candidates in elections, and this became a bitter bone of contention with the Evangelical Workers' Associations and Christian Trade Unions. Significantly, it was again the Young Liberals who tried most seriously to remedy the situation, but by mid-1903 even they had managed to form only three workers' clubs; somewhat later their efforts bore more fruit in south Germany, and by 1908 Bavaria claimed 34 Liberal Workers' Associations with some 6,000 members.[51] More ambitiously, the Duisburg textile industrialist Julius Liebreich, party Chairman in Duisburg-Mülheim-Oberhausen and a supporter of Bassermann in hostile territory, formed a 'Popular Association' which by 1912 had some 2,000 members. But Liebreich's achievement was exceptional and met with no support from his fellow industrialists in the Ruhr. On the contrary, the latter were ideologically fundamentally opposed to the idea, preferring instead the direct surveillance of their workers through the formation of company unions. This was a further instance, in fact, of how the party's heavy-industrial right seemed bent on conflict. Between 1909 and 1912 the number of company unions in the Ruhr rose from just one to 109, with a membership which rivalled that of the Free Trade Unions. In 1907–8 the same policy in the Saar had already caused bitter controversy in the party, and when the launching of the Hanse-Union linked these matters more closely to the surrounding questions of social reform after 1909, a serious public split could scarcely be delayed for very long.[52]

In the case of the working class, therefore, the new popular aspirations simply exacerbated existing divisions in the party and reproduced the tendency to caution in the leadership which characterized the Hanse-Union on the same question. For this reason the novel appeal to the new petty-bourgeoisie weighed all the heavier in National Liberal thinking. Here the importance of party-political intervention was well attested, for although the Hanse-Union strengthened its links with new *Mittelstand* (e.g. through the Employees' Committee formed in summer 1912), fears of reduced profitability led most of its leading members to resist ambitious moves in the region of white-collar welfare.[53] By comparison the National Liberals were better placed to respond to white-collar

[49] Nipperdey, *Organisation*, p. 104.
[50] Saul, *Staat, Industrie, Arbeiterbewegung*, pp. 171f.
[51] Details ibid., pp. 172ff.
[52] Details ibid., pp. 176ff. (Liebreich), 146ff. (growth of company unions), 174ff. (the Saar).
[53] See Mielke, *Hansa-Bund*, p. 98.

demands for special treatment, and here Stresemenn set the pace. In 1901 a wide spectrum of white-collar organizations had formed a Co-ordinating Committee to press for a state insurance scheme, and in 1906 Stresemann swung both the Association of Saxon Industrialists and the BdI round to its support.[54] In March 1907 he led a call in the Reichstag for government action and at the Party Congress later that year won the National Liberals' official support.[55] As a resolution of the BdI said, it was vital 'to strengthen the status-consciousness of the employees and thereby to prevent them from sinking into radical political and trade-unionist attitudes', and to this end white-collar workers should be given separate insurance provision rather than being simply incorporated into the existing schemes for the working class.[56] After complex negotiations the new Insurance Law passed its third reading in December 1911 and registered a notable success for the BdI and the National Liberals, against the opposition of the CVDI and the enforced abstention of the Hanse-Union.[57]

For Stresemann this represented a grand strategy of National Liberal survival. In an important memorandum to Bassermann in September 1908 he argued that the white-collar interest was the only one with which the party had significantly improved its relations, and this was a recurrent theme of his major speeches before 1914.[58] Though he also urged an interest in the 'patriotic working class' and the German Peasants' League, it was to 'a policy of going hand in hand with the great host of the employees' that he most frequently returned.[59] As he said in 1913: 'We live in the age of mass influence, and so industry must also try and rally the masses to itself, and through these masses to influence public opinion, legislation and the political parties that pay attention to these things.'[60] Statements such as these identify Stresemann as one of the few National Liberal politicians with a sense of popular politics comparable to that of the leading activists in the *nationale Verbände*, and, as we saw, he was closely identified with the populist agitation of the *Keimianer* in the Navy League in 1907-8. In an important sense these two features—the appeal to the new petty-bourgeoisie and the involvement with radical nationalism—formed a unity in Stresemann's politics, for the Navy League's popular constituency

---

[54] The affiliates of the Co-ordinating Committee included the right-wing German-National Commercial Assistants Association, a range of groups who later joined the Hanse-Union (Assoc. of German Commercial Assistants, Assoc. of Commercial Clerks of 1858, German Foremen's Assoc., Assoc. of German Technicians etc.), and smaller organizations like the General Society of Organists. See F. Taylor, '*Mittelstandspolitik* and the Insurance Law for *Angestellten* of 1911', unpub. MS, pp. 12f.; Ullmann, *Bund der Industriellen*, p. 216.

[55] Ibid., pp. 216f.

[56] Ibid., p. 220.

[57] Ibid., pp. 219ff.

[58] Eschenburg, *Kaiserreich*, pp. 114ff.

[59] G. Stresemann, *Wirtschaftspolitische Zeitfragen* (Dresden, 1911), pp. 194f.

[60] G. Stresemann, 'Probleme der deutschen Industrieentwicklung', in *Veröffentlichung des Bundes der Industriellen*, Heft 6 (Berlin, 1913), p. 37.

came in large part from exactly the same social strata. Moreover, it was only by stressing the national question in this way that the new white-collar strata could be successfully combined both with the interests of industry and the older liberal nationalism of the *Bildungsbürgertum*. As he said to Bassermann:

If there is anything to replace the drawing-power which we previously enjoyed as a party of the national conscience, then it is involvement in all those questions which today, in the age of the world economy, inspire the thinking circles of the people and especially the circles of youth and future generations. It is vital that we establish our leadership in matters concerning the colonies, the fleet and a more pointed foreign policy, so that we can win the broad circles organized by the Navy League and Colonial Society and the sensible part of the Pan-Germans. Amongst the liberal professions there are hundreds of thousands who in themselves stand outside the economic conflicts and do not care whether the tariff is ten or five marks, but who long for a strong national party they can respect . . . The preservation of the German Empire's position in the world economy is a lasting slogan . . . which will secure us enthusiastic supporters, whereas in the region of economic policy and as a party of the centre we will have to reckon with the greatest difficulties for the future.[61]

Gustav Stresemann was the characteristic figure of the new National Liberalism, for his career exemplifies all the major determinations from which the new orientation was formed. He was, for instance, himself of petty-bourgeois origins, the son of a Berlin beer-bottler, who hoisted himself into politics through a professional career in the pressure groups, by the insistent claims of his own achievements rather than the more genteel procedures of *Honoratiorenpolitik*. His first experience—organizing the Saxon chocolate lobby against the CVDI sugar cartel—provided a paradigm of later attacks on protection, price-fixing and the inter-penetration of industrial-agricultural interests. He built up the Association of Saxon Industrialists and on this basis was by 1907–8 the dominant figure in the BdI. Politically he was formed in Naumann's National-Socials, whose 1901 Congress he attended as the representative for Dresden at the age of twenty-three. He reacted against the Dresden liberal establishment and helped form a new National Liberal Association in the town, with close affinities to the Young Liberals.[62]

But it was as a public speaker for the Navy League that Stresemann first entered the national political stage, and as we saw, it was August Keim who assisted him into his first Reichstag seat in 1907.[63] It was on this dual basis—as a

[61] Eschenburg, *Kaiserreich*, pp. 116f.
[62] Details from: D. Warren, *The Red Kingdom of Saxony. Lobbying Grounds for Gustav Stresemann 1901–1909* (The Hague, 1964), pp. 25ff.; Heckart, *Bassermann to Bebel*, pp. 41f.
[63] For Stresemann's involvement in the naval question, see the following of his writings: *Das Interesse der sächsischen Volkswirtschaft an der Verstärkung der Flotte* (Dresden, 1905);

leading functionary of small manufacturing capital, as an aggressive exponent of radical nationalism—that he staked a claim to recognition in national politics. Moreover, as suggested above, in both spheres his politics were constituted by a relationship to the petty-bourgeoisie. The son of a small capitalist and himself a member of the new salariat, he was keenly aware that small capital could only gain its ends by entering the party-political arena and joining forces with the new *Mittelstand*. Conversely, he also argued that the National Liberals could only survive as an electoral force by sinking new roots in these same strata. To the project of popular liberalism which began to emerge from these calculations he brought a distinctive baggage of ideologies—land reform, hostility to the Junkers, and social imperialism from his days in the National-Socials, a populist nationalism from his time with the Navy League and Pan-Germans.[64]

IV

From this discussion it should be clear that the form of the National Liberal revival militated against a decisive turn to the left. Earlier in this book much stress was placed on a crisis of National Liberalism in the 1890s, when the party's traditional position in the Protestant countryside west of the Elbe began to break up. In many ways the most decisive shift in German politics in the Wilhelmine period (apart from the rise of the SPD) was the defection of the National Liberals' historic rural constituency, partly to the Agrarian League, partly to the Anti-Semites and radical particularists, and partly to the Centre. Without suggesting that the party could have responded in the manner of the Centre and Agrarian League, its failure to develop an adequate political response to this process had some vital effects. In particular, it failed to harness the activism of those strata of the petty-bourgeoisie who were its natural supporters, and thus created a space at a constituency level in which the independent nationalism of the *nationale Verbände* could flourish. Equally, when the National Liberals eventually set about recovering this lost popular ground, it was natural that they should turn to precisely the same groups of people. The appeal to the new *Mittelstand* was also a deliberate wager on its nationalist temper, an attempt to assimilate the enthusiasm generated by the Navy League and the other nationalist groups. Capitalizing on the buoyant nationalism of the Navy League's popular support and pandering to the self-esteem of white-collar workers were part of a single strategy, which aimed to create a new constituency for the National Liberals on the varied ground of the burgeoning

---

address to the Navy League Congress at Cologne on May 12th 1907, pub. as 'Flotte, Welt-wirtschaft und Volk', in *Wirtschaftspolitische Zeitfragen*, pp. 60–70; 'Aufgabe und Ziele der deutschen Flottenpolitik', ibid., pp. 103–13.

[64] In some ways the best guide to Stresemann's early political formation is still A. Thimme, *Gustav Stresemann. Eine politische Biographie zur Geschichte der Weimarer Republik* (Hannover-Frankfurt, 1959), pp. 12ff. See also Ullmann, *Bund der Industriellen*, pp. 99ff., 138ff.

managerial, professional and clerical strata. But unfortunately, like the social demands of the new petty-bourgeoisie, the politics of radical nationalism tended to foreclose the chances of a new left reformism. Instead of appropriating the popular success of the *nationale Verbände*, in fact, there was a sense in which the National Liberal Party had itself already been appropriated.

In other words, the lifeline to the petty-bourgeoisie also ran away from the working class. As Stresemann said, white-collar workers had 'always been true to the national cause and (had) helped fight our battles for the national idea', thus enabling a 'wall of *Mittelstand* strata' to be built against the SPD.[65] For Stresemann the appeal to these strata was not only a means of replacing support stolen by the Social Democrats, it was also meant to stiffen the backbone of directly anti-Socialist policies. This was the most fundamental obstacle of all to a full-blooded reformist departure after 1909: neither the Hanse-Union nor the National Liberals were ever prepared to co-operate nationally with the SPD until the special conditions after 1914 introduced some extra compulsions. At the most—the regional departure of the Baden Grand Bloc notwithstanding[66] —they were prepared to resist right-wing calls for fresh repressive measures, and to that extent clearly represented a more liberal position of much pragmatic value to the SPD. Thus Bassermann firmly resisted the rising pressure from within the CVDI after 1910 for new laws against strikes and pickets, and this undoubtedly helped crystallize an important centrist grouping in the Reichstag with the left liberals and the Centre. But particularly after the SPD landslide of 1912 and the resurgence of the right which followed, the Bassermann-Stresemann group were forced to face simultaneously left and right: parrying demands for fresh laws against the Socialists and trade unions, yet calling themselves for the vigorous application of existing legislation.[67]

Thus a number of factors conspired to restrict the real chances of a decisive reformist departure after 1909. The opposition of the big heavy-industrial firms in the CVDI made it difficult to overcome the inner-industrial contradictions of the Hanse-Union, and, as the years 1909–14 tended to confirm, the most likely resolution would in any case take an oligopolistic form damaging to the interests of small and medium capital.[68] Politically, moreover, the CVDI retained its links with agriculture, and on issues like protection, anti-Socialism and democratization in Prussia exerted a pressure through the National Liberal right which seriously constrained the more flexible group around Bassermann. This ruled out an opening towards the SPD, and though the Hanse-Union was willing to resist the extreme demands of the right no constructive programme for the incorporation of labour emerged. Similarly, the strategic presence of the big employers stopped Riesser and other liberals in the Hanse-Union from

[65] Cit. ibid., p. 142.
[66] See Heckart, *Bassermann to Bebel*, pp. 91ff.
[67] See especially Saul, *Staat, Industrie, Arbeiterbewegung*, pp. 350ff.
[68] See especially Pogge von Strandmann, 'Widersprüche'.

developing a proper policy of white-collar reform. Though this re-emphasized that change would have to come primarily in the political domain and though the National Liberals managed to achieve an important change of direction, however, the form of the latter likewise militated against rapprochement with the SPD. Both the wager on the new petty-bourgeoisie and the familiar stress on imperialism pushed in quite the opposite direction. On top of this the divisions of right and left continued to run through the National Liberals' own ranks, and the complex requirements of party unity also prevented a stronger leftward push.[69] In this sense the National Liberals united in their political dilemmas the familiar problems of the power bloc as a whole: the contradiction with agriculture moved them to the left, while the need for a new popular basis moved them simultaneously to the right.

There was one final limitation on the potential for a new progressive bloc: except under conditions of the most extreme crisis, as in October 1918, the government could never be expected to push through the required changes from above. This was clear enough from Bülow's last months in office. Though the Conservatives had irrevocably broken with the Bloc and had buried the parliamentary prospects of the Finance Bill, though the tendencies most closely identified with Bülow—the National Liberals and the *nationale Verbände* —were clamouring for decisive action, and though Bülow himself was implicitly encouraging them—he still shrank back from the brink of a final confrontation. The battle could only be waged further by dissolving the Reichstag and fighting an unprecedented election against the Conservatives, and although such a campaign would almost certainly have brought a substantial majority, Bülow could never have taken such a radical step. Ideology, precedent and the power of the monarchy necessarily constrained him. It would have reproduced a situation comparable to that of the 1860s, in which the Conservative position was undermined by a Bismarckian pattern of revolution from above, and the demands of the bourgeoisie for 'equality of status' met by a reform of the Prussian franchise—i.e. by dismantling the legal privileges which guaranteed the material foundations of Junker survival. Yet Bülow was no Bismarck (just as he was certainly no Gladstone), if only because he had the largest mass Socialist party in Europe at his back. In the end it was this factor above all else which held Bülow from a resolute 'modernizing' course, for any confrontation with the agrarians would automatically work to the advantage of the SPD, at the very least in a radically reformist sense. This exposed the largest single deficit in the politics of bourgeois reformism after 1909: in the absence of sympathetic co-operation from the government, it had no understanding of how to gain power in the state, or even a commitment to doing so.

The reformist left never solved the problem of its relations to the state. This compounded a situation of some confusion in the five years before the First World War, which was accurately captured by Bethmann Hollweg's shifting

[69] See Stegmann, *Erben*, pp. 219ff., 305ff.

pragmatism. For whereas the agrarians were left dangerously exposed by the momentary desertion of the CVDI and the apparent drifting away of the old petty-bourgeoisie, the new front of the bourgeoisie was itself riven by important contradictions and lacked anything approaching a unitary parliamentary representation. Anti-agrarianism proved an inadequate basis for a new progressive bloc of the centre-left. Internal conflicts, antagonism with labour and indifference towards the ultimate question of power in the state emphasized the complexity of the political situation: an evident crisis of the right, with no prospect of its resolution by a stronger grouping of the left. Bülow had shown a keen sense of this prospect:

> What will the Conservatives achieve if they actually split the Bloc? Confusion, bitterness and depression in broad Conservative circles, particularly in Central Germany, in the towns, amongst civil servants, petty-bourgeois etc.; a repetition of the Caprivi-course with concessions to the Poles and Guelphs; heavy predominance of the (in parliamentary terms) much stronger Centre over the Conservatives; real (not imaginary) concessions to liberal-democratic ideas in Prussia in order to protect the Party from the odium of a 'reactionary' regime of Junkers and priests. The Conservative Party will experience a setback comparable to that of the seventies. What will the agrarians achieve? The accusation of being wild egoists and of over-straining the bow for party-political motives as the Centre had done before 1907. In so far as they make themselves *de facto* dependent on the latter, they will lose their broad base in the *Mittelstand* and encourage in the Centre itself both the democratic influences and a freshly exaggerated social policy; for the Centre can never be agrarian alone.[70]

[70] Witt, *Finanzpolitik*, pp. 275f.

10. The Reconstitution of the Right

I

Bülow's prediction of Conservative isolation was amply justified by the elections of 1912. Though the agrarians had recovered their old industrial partners—a vital exodus of CVDI industrialists from the Hanse-Union occurred in summer 1911, accompanied by a more general drift of right-wing National Liberals disaffected with Bassermann—this proved no help at the polls. With 34·8% of the vote and 110 seats the SPD was incomparably the largest party, leaving the Centre trailing with 16·4% and a drop from 105 to 91 seats. The Conservatives were decimated by the loss of seventeen seats (60–43), and the Free Conservatives fell by ten to the all-time low of fourteen. The National Liberals and newly unified Progressive People's Party lost nine and seven seats respectively, returning totals of forty-five and forty-two. Though Stresemann was defeated, the Bassermann-tendency clearly dominated the National Liberal group, where the CVDI had at best four or five exponents. Likewise the Agrarian League had only five National Liberal supporters, by contrast with 1907 when 60% of the fraction were committed. Only 78 of the 213 candidates committed to the Agrarian League programme were actually elected, by comparison with 138 in 1907. Interestingly, the Hanse-Union claimed 88 deputies, almost wholly in the two Liberal parties. More ambiguously, the Imperial-German *Mittelstand* League set up in 1911 claimed a total of 103: 36 Conservatives and 7 Free Conservatives, 25 National Liberals, 21 Centre, 8 Economic Union, 1 Progressive and 5 Independents.[1]

This revelation of electoral weakness delivered a powerful shock to the party-political right. Between early 1912 and autumn 1913 an important regroupment took shape, stimulated by the politicized sectionalism of the CVDI, and involving an independent organization of the National Liberal right, new activity by the Free Conservatives, and a more conciliatory attitude in the Agrarian League. Common action occurred over demands for anti-strike legislation and a stop to social reform, while broad ideological communities were constructed on questions of imperialism and constitutional revision. By spring

---

[1] For details: J. Bertram, *Die Wahlen zum Deutschen Reichstag vom Jahre 1912* (Düsseldorf, 1964); M. V. Falk, 'The Reichstag Elections of 1912: A Statistical Study' (Ph.D. Diss. Iowa, 1976); Stegmann, *Erben*, pp. 258ff.

1913, in fact, calls for a new *Sammlung* of industry and agriculture, in conscious recollection of 1897–8 and 'the old brotherhood of arms' struck by Bismarck in 1879, were becoming commonplace. After an intensification of contacts they resulted in the co-called *Kartell der schaffenden Stände* (the 'Cartel of the Productive Estates') at the Third Annual Congress of the Imperial-German *Mittlestand* League in Leipzig on August 24th 1913. The host organization, the CVDI, the Agrarian League and the Union of Christian Peasants' Associations united publicly around a four-point programme: co-operation of the three groups, economic *Mittelstand*, industry and agriculture; preservation of 'authority' in all businesses; price guarantees and defence of the 'right to work' (i.e. strike-breaking), under the Bismarckian slogan of *Schutz der nationalen Arbeit* ('Protection of the National Labour'); and finally, opposition to Social Democracy and all Socialist ideas. This revealed the familiar contours of *Sammlungspolitik*: primacy of the 'productive estates' and their privileges, unconditional support for employers against trade-union pressure, intransigent opposition to Social Democracy and all democratic organizations.[2]

Against a background of incipient right-wing realignment, the *Kartell* takes on an obvious symptomatic importance, at the very least as a material representation of a certain political logic. Measured against the growing convergence of right-wing National Liberals, revitalized Free Conservatives and an agrarian Conservative leadership chastened by the outcome of the 1912 elections, it was a clear sign that the architects of *Sammlung* were again at work.[3] The keynote speeches at Leipzig were made by Hugo Kükelhaus for the *Mittelstand* League, Ferdinand Schweighoffer for the CVDI, Henning aus dem Winckel for the Agrarian League, and Wilhelm Kellermann, the Secretary-General of the Catholic Peasants' Associations. Eduard von Liebert for the Imperial League Against Social Democracy, Paul Fuhrmann for the National Liberal right, and leading representatives of Saxon Conservatives and National Liberals were present as guests. The ideological climate was avowedly reactionary, and aside from calls for laws against pickets and a veto on social reform, there was now

[2] For the proceedings of Aug. 24th 1913: *Bericht über den Dritten Reichsdeutschen Mittelstandstag* (Aug. 22nd–25th 1913) (Leipzig, 1913); Stegmann, *Erben*, pp. 362ff.; Gellately, *Politics of Economic Despair*, pp. 178ff. For the political background: Stegmann, *Erben*, pp. 305–27, 267–92, 352–60; Saul, *Staat, Industrie, Arbeiterbewegung*, pp. 306–81; Wernecke, *Wille zur Weltgeltung*, pp. 180ff.

[3] The Cartel's importance has been disputed by several authors. E.g. Kaelble, *Industrielle Interessenpolitik*, p. 204; Puhle, *Agrarkrise*, p. 58; H. A. Winkler, *Mittelstand, Demokratie und Nationalsozialismus. Die politische Entwicklung von Handwerk und Kleinhandel in der Weimarer Republik* (Cologne, 1972), pp. 53f.; Wehler, *Das Deutsche Kaiserreich*, p. 104; Mielke, *Hansa-Bund*, pp. 166–80. However, the analysis of Stegmann, *Erben*, and Saul, *Staat, Industrie, Arbeiterbewegung*, largely survives these criticisms. My own view is perhaps closest to that of G. Schmidt, 'Parlamentarisierung oder "Präventive Konterrevolution"? Die deutsche Innenpolitik im Spannungsfeld konservativer Sammlungsbewegungen und latenter Reformbestrebungen 1907–1914', in G. A. Ritter (Ed.), *Gesellschaft, Parlament und Regierung. Zur Geschichte des Parlamentarismus in Deutschland* (Düsseldorf, 1974), esp. pp. 274–8.

a new attack on the parliamentary Constitution. This signalled a new offensive
by the right, as Bassermann had gloomily predicted a fortnight before:

> . . . high-protection, water-tight tariffs, anti-Socialist laws, no suffrage
> reform in Prussia, at first an unobtrusive struggle against the national
> suffrage, struggle against all that is liberal, struggle against Bethmann-
> Delbrück, the yearning for the strong man. Of course all that is sheer
> madness, but in the end anything is possible with us.[4]

How strong was the continuity with 1897? Intimations of the past and
Bismarckian allusions permeated the Leipzig proceedings. The important
Saxon *Mittelstand* organ *Der Fortschritt* affirmed that 'the old Bismarckian
idea of a coalition of all state-preserving elements once again makes an opportune
appearance'. Schweighoffer invoked Bismarck as the 'greatest of all Germans',
while *Deutsche Volkswirtschaftliche Correspondenz*, *Deutsche Industrie-Zeitung*,
Deutsche Tageszeitung and *Hessische Landeszeitung* (organ of Heyl zu Herrnsheim, the right-wing National Liberal notable) all drew on Bismarck's essay in
the *Hamburger Nachrichten* of March 11th 1897, 'A Cartel of the Productive
Estates'.[5] In general the spectrum of support for the Leipzig rapprochement
broadly reproduced the public backing of Miquel's *Sammlungspolitik* fifteen
years before, with the major exceptions of a more self-consciously organized
National Liberal right and a far more conciliatory Agrarian League. Superficially
the continuity was imposing.

However, a number of important distinctions must be drawn. Most importantly, the Leipzig Cartel registered the declining importance of some old
party divisions, which in 1897–8 had considerably restricted the efficacy of the
Sammlung. The consolidation of jealously guarded party traditions—by a
combined argument from history and from the new conditions of the 1890s—
had militated powerfully against Miquel's strategy, and in the changed climate
after 1902–3 this was enough to place the idea of *Sammlung* completely on ice.
But after 1909 the important liberal revival (reorientation of the National
Liberals, launching of the Hanse-Union, left-liberal unification) removed some
of the obstacles to the co-operation of the right. Old party hostilities were
suppressed under the pressure of a left advance. Right-wing National Liberals
and agrarian Conservatives linked arms more tightly because parliamentary
dispositions left them no choice—not just because the SPD had 110 seats, but
because the National Liberal fraction had been won for a new anti-agrarian
course. The casualty was the traditional notion of the 'middle party', with its
sentimental postulate of ideological unity and ritual denial of 'one-sided
economic interest'. Men who rallied to an independent National Liberal

---

[4] Bassermann to Schönaich-Carolath, Aug. 6th 1913, in L. Maenner, *Prinz Heinrich zu
Schönaich-Carolath. Ein parlamentarisches Leben der wilhelminischen Zeit 1852–1920* (Berlin-
Stuttgart, 1931), p. 119.
[5] Stegmann, *Erben*, p. 387.

position in 1897–8 (i.e. a position historically distinct from that of the Conservatives) now felt a stronger community with the right: heavy industrialists in the Ruhr and Saar, big businessmen in Bavaria and Hamburg, landowners in Hannover and Hessen, old-style liberal patricians in most of Prussia.

Secondly, unlike its predecessor, the *Kartell der schaffenden Stände* was a triangular arrangement of industry, agriculture and *Mittelstand*. In 1897–8 the latter had been present mainly as a rhetorical ploy, a ritual concession to the demands of electoral popularity; by 1913 it was present as a public partner. In 1913 the Cartel was announced to the world at the Congress of the Imperial-German *Mittelstand* League; in March 1898 the Economic Manifesto had emerged from the private consultations of a handful of landowners and businessmen. Not only was the Agrarian League now at the centre rather than at the margins of the arrangement, but its mass membership was greatly augmented by the novel inclusion of the newly founded *Mittelstand* organization.[6] From August 1912 the latter was financed by the CVDI and Agrarian League to the tune of 15,000 marks a year, and its public rallies became occasions for demonstrative industrial-agrarian participation.[7] Of course, in August 1913 this delivered only a paper membership, a popular potential whose forms of material activation remained to be found. But the inclusion of the old *Mittelstand* was none the less vital. It showed that the old right was thinking more seriously about how to win popular support. It linked the practice of *Sammlungspolitik* for the first time to the prospect of a substantial popular movement. The officers had finally found their troops.

Thirdly, the new *Kartell* was further distinguished by a new interest in corporative representation. Reduced to a small minority in the Reichstag, the right turned on the superficial source of its declining fortunes, universal suffrage. Older habits of mind—liberal traditions of the qualified franchise, Conservative distaste for representative government—were easily mobilized at a time of political retrenchment, and corporative demands were sometimes only the atavistic desperation of old-style conservatives. But in 1912–13 the discussion also revealed some distinctive features. Interestingly, the lead came from the CVDI rather than the more predictable traditionalists. Proposals ranged from the simple nomination of more industrialists to the Prussian upper chamber, to the maximal solution of abolishing universal suffrage in the Reich, but by early 1914 a rough consensus had emerged for a new upper house as a counterweight to the 'democratic' Reichstag. Moreover, the new corporative speculations, oriented to representation by economic 'estates' or corporations, directly favoured the newly organized *Mittelstand*, often to the complete exclusion of the industrial working class from the company of legitimate interests.

[6] By 1913 the Agrarian League had 328,000 members, while in Aug. 1913 the *Mittelstand* League claimed 502,000 and in Dec. 1914 640,000. What these paper figures actually meant in practice is another question. For a cautionary remark: Mielke, *Hansa-Bund*, p. 292.

[7] Gellately, *Politics of Economic Despair*, p. 185.

To this extent, particularly for the more far-sighted politicians in the employers' movement, the Free Conservatives and Pan-Germans, the turn to corporative solutions was the ideological counterpart to the political coalescence with the *Mittelstand* League.[8]

But most crucially it signalled an incipient crisis in the legitimacy of parliamentary forms. In practice the late 1890s had begun a new period of relative parliamentary stabilization, when talk of *Staatsstreich* or the Anti-Socialist Law receded before pragmatic adjustment to universal suffrage and electoral politics. But the period after 1910–11 saw a resurgence of anti-parliamentary and repressive intent. This took a number of forms. The most concrete was the attack on the trade unions, with calls for specific legislation against pickets and a general toughening of the criminal law, thinly masking a 'Bismarckian' nostalgia for the comforting days of the Anti-Socialist Law.[9] Moreover, beyond the broad corporative sentiments in the CVDI were the more coherent ambitions of the Pan-Germans and other ideologues. Unquestionably the most controversial and widely discussed intervention was that of Heinrich Claß in the pseudonymous tract *Wenn ich der Kaiser wär*, published under the name Daniel Frymann in early 1912.[10] This was the first major Pan-German domestic initiative since the Daily Telegraph Crisis and installed the question of constitutional revision right at the centre of public debate. Extending deep into the inner circles of the CVDI, newly connected with the Agrarian League and reaching even to the entourage of the Crown Prince, the Pan-Germans' new influence re-emphasized the novelty of the 1913 Cartel. Whereas in 1897–1902 *Sammlungspolitik* was carefully adjusted to the existing political framework (working within the Constitution, tolerating the parliamentary commitments of liberals, accepting the need for broader alliance with the Centre), in 1913 the return to *Sammlung* was predicated on the desire to overturn that very same framework of pragmatic parliamentarism.[11]

However, it is important to remember that the right lost the battle for constitutional revision and failed to realize the corporative aims. For the most striking feature of the *Kartell der schaffenden Stände*—which above all else distinguished it from 1897—was not just its relative weakness in the Reichstag, but its divorce from the Imperial government. The Cartel was marked above

---

[8] Stegmann, *Erben*, pp. 368–80.

[9] Saul, *Staat, Industrie, Arbeiterbewegung*, pp. 306–94.

[10] For details of the publication: Stegmann, *Erben*, pp. 293–304. The full title was *Wenn ich der Kaiser wär. Politische Wahrheiten und Notwendigkeiten* (Leipzig, 1912). The author's real identity was a secret even to the leaders of the Pan-German League, and Claß confided only in Stössel and later Gebsattel. For the contents, see Kruck, *Geschichte*, pp. 59–65, and for the context, Claß, *Wider den Strom*, pp. 234ff.

[11] For the efforts of the Pan-Germans to influence the Court in a strategy of *Staatsstreich*, see H. Pogge von Strandmann, 'Staatsstreichpläne, Alldeutsche und Bethmann Hollweg', in I. Geiss and H. Pogge von Strandmann, *Die Erforderlichkeit des Unmöglichen. Deutschland am Vorabend des Ersten Weltkrieges* (Hamburg, 1965), pp. 5 ff.

all by its 'national opposition'. It began a period when the practice of government became increasingly relocated in the larger business of parliamentary management and the older 'natural' relationship to 'iron and rye' progressively strained. This did not mean that the state became fully 'parliamentarized' or that the government suddenly adopted the programme of the Hanse-Union and the National Liberal left. On the contrary, there were clear structural limits to the possible forms of accommodation with the left, and Bethmann Hollweg never lost sight of the monarchy's special relationship to the landowning class and its safeguards in the Prussian Constitution.[12] But it did mean that more attention was paid to the left's parliamentary dominance, which after 1912 increasingly set the pace of legislation and structured the options for government, and at the very least had to be neutralized. It was precisely the legitimacy of this necessary governmental practice that the 'national opposition' disputed, and though it retained important ministerial allies and enormous reserves of sympathy in the state apparatus as a whole, a new antagonism to government was now clear.

Measured against the previous history of the *Kaiserreich*, this rupture was a discontinuity of the profoundest importance. It brought a new contradiction into German politics, between a state structure which still formally gave a privileged status to the Prussian landowners and a political situation which ranged their political representatives *against* the appointed government. The constellation of forces this produced—a right grouping simultaneously rooted in leading fractions of industrial and agrarian capital and in the native organizations of the petty-bourgeoisie, committed to anti-democratic notions of state organization and deeply opposed to the existing government—already anticipated the basic scenario of the Weimar Republic. Isolated in the Reichstag, the right sought an alternative structure for protecting its interests. In so doing it disrupted the creeping legitimacy of parliamentary forms, complicated still further the chances of any limited 'liberalization' in the style of the Hanse-Union, and re-confirmed the disunity of the power bloc. In this way, the corporative turn both registered a further departure from 1897–1902, and established a lasting pattern for the future.

II

A further factor separating the coalition of 1913 from that of 1897 was the unifying role of radical-nationalist ideology. As argued in the main body of this book, such a role was previously precluded by a double set of contradictions. On the one hand, the main articulation of radical nationalism in the earlier period—colonialism, the big Navy and *Weltpolitik*—cut across the lines of the

---

[12] See esp. J. Schellenberg, 'Immediatbericht des preußischen Ministers des Innern v. Loebell vom 22.11.15. Dokumentation', *Jahrbuch für Geschichte*, I (1967), pp. 254f.

Sammlung and antagonized the agrarians. Piously affirming the essential harmony of industry and agriculture as the keystone of the social order, Miquel's supporters had no use for an ideology that stressed the very things they were trying to play down, namely the future primacy of industry, keeping the trade routes open, the progressive obsolescence of the Junkers and so on. But to make things worse, on the other hand, the *nationale Verbände* were captured by politicians who paid scant respect to the diplomatic, fiscal and parliamentary restraints observed by the government. When the main bearers of radical nationalism were driven by a populist critique of the old right and its patrician forms, such an ideology had little integrative value for the exponents of *Sammlung*.

This changed for a number of reasons. For the agrarians the most important was a general shift of imperialist priorities around 1910–11 from *Weltpolitik* back to continental policy. This diminished the obvious Conservative objection to radical nationalism—its identification with further industrial development— and reinstated the Army as the leading instrument of German aggrandisement. The gradual reversion to more traditional concerns of military security, after the fifteen-year hiatus of naval supremacy, may be detected as early as 1908, and was spurred by a series of important writings.[13] The first major signal was August Keim's address to the Pan-German Convention in 1910, when he called for an urgent expansion of the Army regardless of cost.[14] Keim's recent exploits in the Navy League gave this shift to the Army an added poignancy, and the pressure culminated appropriately in the formation of a new organization, the Defence League, under his Chairmanship in early 1912. Quite apart from the Army's historic place in Conservative affections, this implicit return to continental imperialism created a framework of thinking in which agrarian interests might be more easily satisfied. The prospect of eastward expansion brought a new vocabulary of imperialist speculation—territorial conquests, new living-space, settlement policies, the creation of a 'frontier peasantry', meeting the Russian threat—which was far more congenial to Conservative ears. Moreover, it was no accident that such talk coincided with the new attempts by Conservatives to devise a land policy for satisfying the smaller peasant. Radical nationalism's new militarist inflection, *Kontinentalpolitik* and internal colonization all combined neatly together.

These tendencies were dramatized by the second Moroccan Crisis in July– November 1911.[15] The disappointing outcome of the Agadir initiative—which

[13] The first was an essay by the pensioned Chief of Staff, Field-Marshall Alfred von Schlieffen, 'Der Krieg in der Gegenwart', published at the end of 1908. The major interventions were then the following: Frhr. von Falkenhausen, *Der große Krieg der Jetztzeit* (Berlin, 1909); H. von Freytag-Loringhoven, *Krieg und Politik in der Neuzeit* (Berlin, 1911); F. von Bernhardi, *Deutschland und der nächste Krieg*, and *Vom heutigen Kriege*, 2 vols. (both Berlin, 1912). See Pogge von Strandmann, 'Nationale Verbände', p. 309.

[14] *Alld. Bl.*, 1910, pp. 323–6.

[15] F. Fischer, *War of Illusions* (London, 1975), pp. 71ff.; Stegmann, *Erben*, pp. 216ff., 277ff.; and esp. Wernecke, *Wille zur Weltgeltung*, pp. 26–143.

for the Pan-Germans rankled particularly badly from their sense of having been 'used' and tricked by Kiderlen-Wächter, the Foreign Secretary—was accompanied by a storm of nationalist indignation in the right-wing press. The normal voices could be heard in criticism of the government, including the familiar Pan-German quartet, *Rheinisch-Westfälische Zeitung, Tägliche Rundschau, Deutsche Zeitung* and *Leipziger Neueste Nachrichten,* which had led the radical-nationalist defence of Keim in 1908. But this time the 'national opposition' enjoyed a much broader base. In particular, there were two direct attacks on the Kaiser himself, from sources which had been impeccably governmental during the *Keimianer* offensive of 1908: the one an article in the Free Conservative paper *Die Post,* the other a speech by the Conservative leader Ernst von Heydebrand und der Lasa in the crucial Reichstag debate of November 9th 1911.[16] The second Moroccan Crisis was the first occasion on which the traditional governmental parties—Conservatives, Free Conservatives and National Liberals—combined for a frontal attack on the government's foreign policy. Moreover, this hardening of nationalist resolution was systematically linked to a domestic-political calculation, the belief that the right's dwindling electoral support could only be restored by organized cultivation of the 'national idea'. These two factors—the simultaneous expectation and affirmation of war, the classic radical-nationalist recourse to ideological remedies for Germany's domestic disunity—were noted by Heinrich Claß at the height of the Moroccan Crisis in axiomatic form: 'War as the only cure for our people. The influence of foreign policy on domestic policy.'[17]

More than anything else it was the revelation of political weakness and the novelty of opposition to the government that drew the party establishments into the radical-nationalist camp. Naturally a genuine dismay at the government's apparent incompetence in foreign affairs contributed vitally to that very process of 'national opposition'. But the special conjunction with the radical nationalists —people, after all, who had been denounced as 'trouble-makers' only three years before—was mainly the product of common political adversity. Outraged at Bethmann Hollweg's lack of imperialist purpose, shaken by the 1912 elections, and bitterly critical of the government's observance of parliamentary constraints, Conservatives discovered a natural community with the Pan-Germans, who had been arguing these things since the 1890s. Moreover, inexorably confined electorally to the East Elbian heartlands, the Conservative Party was urgently in need of allies in the West, and as the National Liberals seemed set under Bassermann for an anti-agrarian course, minds turned instead towards attracting away some of their support. The National Liberal right was not much help in this respect, for outside Heyl zu

---

[16] *Die Post,* Aug. 4th 1911: 'Crisis and Withdrawal'; RT, Nov. 9th 1911, pp. 7721ff. Fischer justifiably describes the article in *Post* as 'sensational': *War of Illusions,* p. 83. For an exhaustive summary of the press reactions: Wernecke, *Wille zur Weltgeltung,* pp. 102ff.

[17] Note by Claß, summer 1911, cit. Hartwig, *Zur Politik,* p. 196.

Herrnsheim's Hessian fiefdom it was chronically lacking in electoral clout.

In this situation those radical nationalists with a base in the Free Conservative Party came into their own. From its foundation the latter had always shown two faces. The first was virtually indistinguishable from that of moderate Conservatives, particularly east of the Elbe, where the title might often be worn as a mere label of convenience, to distance the bearer from extreme agrarianism more than anything else. The other was a stronger and more systematized projection of the same stance, chosen by individuals with a principled attachment to the ideology of industrial-agrarian compromise. Typified by Wilhelm von Kardorff, who led the party till his death in 1907, this enabled the adherence of both right-wing industrialists and high aristocrats like the Catholic grandees of Silesia, earning it the reputation of the 'Bismarckian party *sans phrase*' or the 'step-sister of liberalism', the classic party of *Sammlung*.[18] Moreover, as we have seen, the major exponents of the latter— Kardorff himself, Arnim-Muskau, Arendt, Zedlitz-Neukirch, more latterly Liebert and Stössel—had a keen eye for the electoral potential of the 'national idea', and when the party began organizing itself properly for popular recruitment in 1911–12 this naturally played an important part.

But earlier there had been clear limits to the leaders' interest in such a course: both Kardorff and Arnim-Muskau had left the Pan-Germans over the Boer War, and the Silesian magnates with whom they were associated also opposed the movement towards national opposition after mid-1911. Furthermore, figures like Liebert and Zedlitz-Neukirch (who succeeded Kardorff at the party's head) carefully modulated their practice to the needs of the possible, and would move no faster than the existing pace of the party-political right would allow. Though the experience of the 1907 elections—anti-Socialism under nationalist slogans, the exemplary unity of the right in the constituencies—seemed to prove the value of a pronounced radical-nationalist course, the Free Conservative parliamentarians still counselled caution. Thus in the Imperial League Against Social Democracy—in party terms principally a Free Conservative outlet—the attempts to build on the promising success of the elections by setting up a branch organization and promoting 'patriotic workers' associations' were heavily modified after objections from the other right-wing parties and the CVDI.[19] Similarly, Free Conservatives were prominent in the efforts to patch up a compromise against the radical *Keimianer* in the Navy League, and Liebert

---

[18] The second phrase was used by the National Liberal deputy Rudolf von Campe in 'National Liberals and Free Conservatives', *NatZ*, Aug. 17th 1912. Contemporaries often expressed this relationship to *Sammlungspolitik* particularly directly: 'In national politics it (i.e. the Free Conservative Party) represents the Bismarckian policy of protection, and today is the political representative of the idea of the alliance between heavy industry organized economically in the CVDI and the Agrarian League.' Entry under 'Free Conservative Party', in *Politisch-wirtschaftspolitisches Konversations-lexicon* (Stuttgart, 1911), p. 178.

[19] See Mattheier, *Gelben*, pp. 193–218; Saul, *Staat, Industrie, Arbeiterbewegung*, p. 121; *DortmZ*, May 13th 1907: 'From the Imperial League Against Social Democracy'.

pleaded party responsibilities during the Pan-German initiative in the Daily Telegraph Affair. Even during the Moroccan Crisis, the vital watershed in this respect, the public turn to national opposition was only achieved at the expense of alienating the important Silesian magnates.[20]

Again, it was the growing antagonism between the government of Bethmann Hollweg and the old governmental parties of the Bismarckian Cartel which legitimated a stronger radical-nationalist profile for the Free Conservatives. By early 1912 they had emerged as the ideological pacemakers for a new *Sammlung*, active amongst both old *Mittelstand* and patriotic workers, and inscribing the possibility of the *Kartell der schaffenden Stände* on the public discourse of the right.[21] Many of the characteristic themes of radical nationalism now emerged, specified programmatically in the pages of the new party journal *Das neue Deutschland*. The Editor Grabowsky put the emphasis in the first issue on 'imperialism as an outlook on the world', and argued that 'Germany, riven at home, threatened from abroad, must find a battle-cry to rally all who are striving for the greatness and power of the Reich.'[22] As he said privately at the same time, the party 'finally wants to organize itself in a decisive progressive-conservative manner, and hopes thereby to call forth the great new conservative movement which should enable the educated strata to drive once again to the right'.[23] But imperialism could have this rallying function only as a 'popular idea' (*volkstümlicher Gedanke*), and as Andreas Koch, the Chairman of the Hamburg Conservative Union, said, this involved the repudiation of 'all *Honoratiorenpolitik*'.[24] It was in this context that Zedlitz-Neukirch called for the 'strengthening and extension of the national consciousness' as the 'priority of the hour', a priority moreover which could only be tackled with the 'indispensable' assistance of 'the nationalist pressure groups, Navy Leagues, Defence Leagues, Pan-Germans'.[25]

By 1913, therefore, the *nationale Verbände* found themselves in an enviable situation, which could scarcely have been anticipated five years before. At a time when German politics was increasingly marked by a deepening gulf between the conservative and liberal camps of the non-Socialist sector, radical nationalists found themselves fêted by both sides—by the new Bassermann-Stresemann leadership of the National Liberals as we saw, but also by the

[20] The leading opponent of the anti-governmental turn in the party was Hermann Hatzfeld zu Trachenberg, who had also been an important centrist figure in the Navy League. For his reaction to the offending article in *Die Post*, see Wernecke, *Wille zur Weltgeltung*, pp. 71f.

[21] See esp. E. Deetjen, *Freikonservativ! Die nationale Mittelpartei* (Ratibor, 1913).

[22] A. Grabowsky, 'Imperialism as an Outlook on the World', *Das neue Deutschland*, Oct. 5th 1912, pp. 12ff.

[23] Grabowsky to Fester, Oct. 16th 1912, BA Coblenz, Fester Papers, 96.

[24] A. Koch, 'The Future of the Free Conservative Party', *Das neue Deutschland*, Aug. 23rd 1913, p. 582.

[25] O. von Zedlitz-Neukirch, 'Foreign Policy and National Consciousness', ibid., Oct. 5th 1912, pp. 5ff. See also H. S. Weber, 'The Pan-German League', ibid., Feb. 7th 1914, pp. 231ff.

regenerate Free Conservatives. Moreover, though the relationship of the former to the radicals in the Navy League had been particularly strong, it is equally clear that many activists gravitated towards the latter. The most important of these was Eduard von Liebert, who played a leading part in most of the nationalist organizations. But many lesser examples could also be found. One was Ludwig Sevin, who became involved in the 1907 elections and then launched the Association for the Promotion of the Finance Reform in October 1908: in late 1912 he could be found amongst the first contributors to *Das neue Deutschland*.[26] Others like Ludwig Schaper had originally been National Liberals before passing through the radical-nationalist milieu: dying in 1914, he ended his career as the editor of a Free Conservative weekly.[27] This change of allegiance could often be dramatic. Fritz Stephan Neumann was a known anti-Socialist pamphleteer, and was also a regular contributor to the *Tägliche Rundschau* and *Schwäbischer Merkur* during their campaigns for Keim in 1908. By the end of 1910 he was working in the National Liberal Party's Central Office as editor of its official organs, but resigned in September 1912 because of the party's 'turn to the left'. After writing for *Hamburger Nachrichten*, *Das neue Deutschland* and *Berliner Neueste Nachrichten*, he took up a new post as joint editor of *Berliner Neueste Nachrichten* and *Deutsche Zeitung*, neatly symbolizing the union of Free Conservatives and Pan-Germans. Late in the summer of 1913 he campaigned vigorously for a 'Bloc of the Right' under the auspices of the Free Conservatives, what he called the 'union and integration of all forces of the people' and a 'rallying of all anti-democratic forces'.[28]

In the new period of right-wing coalescence after 1911 the radical nationalists may be said to have furnished the vital ideological perspectives. Between the 1890s and the collapse of the Bülow Bloc, the Pan-Germans in particular had provided a series of coherent right-wing positions which had been bitterly contested when originally advanced, but which now assumed an urgent topical relevance under the changed conditions of national opposition. This was most obvious in the case of the imperialist ideology and its putative domestic application. But the critique of the official foreign policy, in the cases of both the Pan-Germans and the Navy League radicals, had always been linked to a larger attack on the political establishment, from which the existing right-wing parties were not exempted. As this study has tried to argue, radical nationalism also entailed a populist commitment—a systematic appeal to the people, not just as a formality of public agitation, but as a constructive ideological assault

[26] L. Sevin, 'We No longer Wish to Be Politically Unrepresented', ibid., Oct. 5th 1912, pp. 6ff.

[27] See Saul, *Staat, Industrie, Arbeiterbewegung*, p. 466.

[28] For details of Neumann's career: Neumann to Tirpitz, Nov. 15th 1909, BA-MA Freiburg, 2299, 94353, enclosing a copy of his pamphlet, *Die Sozialdemokratie als Arbeitgeberin und Unternehmerin* (Berlin, 1909); Stegmann, *Erben*, pp. 322, 402; Guratzsch, *Macht durch Organisation*, pp. 251f., 415. During the war Neumann played an important journalistic role in the right-wing war aims movement.

on the old order, its parliamentary practices and forms of legitimacy. Further-more, the Pan-Germans were long-standing advocates of an alliance with the peasantry and traditional petty-bourgeoisie, cemented by land reform: the original plans for overseas colonization in the 1880s, Hugenberg's work in the co-operative movement east of the Elbe, and the more radical schemes for land redistribution and internal colonization were all expressions of this concern.[29] It was this populist commitment, with its characteristic petty-bourgeois inflection, that the party-political right, represented by a Free Conservative advance guard, now sought to appropriate.

In general the Pan-Germans were now much more tightly organized and much closer to the centre of the stage. This could already be seen from the composition of the Executive, which by 1913 consisted of individuals who were both more 'political' and better connected than before: Claß himself, Liebert and Stössel (both of whom held leading positions in the Free Conservative Party), the National Liberal Mülheim industrialist Karl Itzenplitz (a cousin of Hugo Stinnes and highly connected in the Ruhr), and August Keim. Moreover, the League had built a commanding position for itself in the right-wing press, expanding outwards from the old bases of Reismann-Grone, Rippler and Lange: partly by strategically placed individuals (e.g. Reventlow as foreign editor of the Agrarian League's *Deutsche Tageszeitung*, or Lutz Korodi as a regular contributor to *Preußische Jahrbücher*), partly as the beneficiary of far-reaching processes of concentration in the control of the press, in which Hugenberg had a key managerial role, and partly through the domination of journalists' organizations like the Berlin *Schriftstellerclub*.[30] Hugenberg's presence at the centre of the Ruhr oligopoly's political relations was also invaluable in gaining the League new access to industrial support, though this was not properly realized, either financially or politically, until after the outbreak of war.[31] Underlying each of these tendencies was a general reorientation of Pan-German activity towards the domestic arena, a development which Claß had fostered since 1902–3. Fortified by the close support of a united Executive, Claß acted from the firm conviction that the old methods of ideological propaganda—the

[29] See above all the programmatic essay by Hugenberg, 'A Pan-German Economic Policy', in *Alld. Bl.*, Apr. 30th 1899, repub. in *Zwanzig Jahre alldeutscher Arbeit und Kämpfe* (Leipzig, 1910), pp. 62–7. For Hugenberg's work in the East, see Guratzsch, *Macht durch Organisation*, pp. 26–63, 150–63, 363–79. For the ideological tradition of overseas settlement, see above all Bade, *Friedrich Fabri*.

[30] For the details of Pan-German influence in the press and in the *Schriftstellerclub*: Wernecke, *Wille zur Weltgeltung*, pp. 30, 37ff.; Junius Alter, 'Kampfjahre der Vorkriegszeit', MS, pp. 9–19, BA Coblenz, Junius Alter Papers, 6.

[31] In autumn 1912 Stössel made an important trip to the Ruhr to raise money for Claß's anonymous *Wenn ich der Kaiser wär*, and enjoyed a warm reception from Hugenberg (under-standably), Kirdorf, and so on, but with only moderate financial return. See Stegmann, *Erben*, pp. 297f. For the rapid accumulation of political support in the autumn of 1914, ibid., pp. 449ff.

repeated projection of the Pan-German 'point of view'—were no longer enough, no matter how skilful or massive the operation. The ability to impose Pan-German policies on an unwilling government first required the reorganization of the party-political right on a more favourable basis.

In other words, after 1908 the Pan-German League was directed by Claß as a fairly disciplined political formation, establishing its leadership amongst the *nationale Verbände* in a way which would have been unthinkable a few years before. A good illustration of this new situation was provided by the German Defence League, whose structure revealed an interesting set of contrasts with its predecessor the Navy League. For one thing, it was launched in December 1911 as a direct result of decisions taken in the Pan-German leadership, whereas in 1898 the Navy League was hatched without Pan-German participation and against their better wishes: in 1912 the Defence League was headed by a member of the Pan-German Executive (Keim), had several prominent Pan-Germans on its Committee (Emil Possehl, Heinrich Rippler, Dietrich Schäfer), and counted major Pan-Germans among the sponsors of its founding manifesto (e.g. Fritz Bley, Claß, Hopf, Klingemann, Langhans, Neumann, Salm-Horstmar, Thomsen); likewise the nationalist press was represented by the Treasurer Georg von Büxenstein and the normal run of radical-nationalist editors.[32] Moreover, though the National Liberals and Free Conservatives were carefully represented by Hermann Paasche and Otto von Dewitz as the two Vice-Chairmen, there was nothing like the profusion of senior party spokesmen which had originally decorated the leadership of the Navy League. The new organization, which grew from 33,000 members in May 1912 to 78,000 by June 1913 and 90,000 by the start of the war, with a further 260,000 in corporately affiliated organizations, was created for a specific purpose—to rally opinion for a rapid expansion of the Army—and was tightly integrated into the Pan-German League's overall political conception.[33]

Thus the Defence League was an independent foundation of the 'national opposition', in which the government had no real part. Though it had powerful allies inside the state apparatus, there was none of the close institutional

[32] Emil Possehl was an iron merchant and senator in Lübeck, with close connections to the *Deutsche Bank*. See his lecture 'Armed Forces and Economic Life', printed for private circulation and delivered in the first General Board of the Defence League on May 11th 1912, in E. Behm and J. Kuczynski, 'Arthur Dix: Propagandist der wirtschaftlichen Vorbereitung des Ersten Weltkrieges' (Appendix I), *JWG*, II (1970), pp. 83–9. Büxenstein was the influential Berlin publisher who managed the foundation of the *Deutsche Zeitungs-Gesellschaft* for the Conservative Party in 1908, which published *BNN* and *DZ*: details from Guratzsch, *Macht durch Organisation*, pp. 297ff. Amongst the other press-men were: Karl Elben (*Schwäb. Merkur*), J. Grauthoff (*LNN*), J. Hermes (*KrZ*), Heinrich Pohl (*Post*).

[33] Membership figures are taken from the relevant issues of the journal *Die Wehr*, June 1912 and June 1913. For details of the foundation: Keim, *Erlebtes*, pp. 165ff.; Wernecke, *Wille zur Weltgeltung*, pp. 174ff.; Fischer, *War of Illusions*, pp. 105–9; Claß, *Wider den Strom*. For a list of committee members and signatories of the founding manifesto: Keim, *Erlebtes*, pp. 174–6.

symbiosis which had characterized the foundations and subsequent histories of the Colonial Society, Eastern Marches Society and even the Navy League.[34] The talk was immediately of pressurizing the government, and whereas the Navy League's founders had carefully emphasized the superior competence of the Navy Office and the need to confine the propaganda to 'informative' and 'educational' work devoid of overt political content, the Defence League went straight away on to the offensive. No one took the part of a Hollmann or Würtzburg and demanded strict subordination of the League to the needs of the government. Nor did anyone put the case for a federalist structure, in which the key decisions about the form and content of agitation would devolve on to the League's regional committees. Both absences re-emphasized the organization's character as a Pan-German front and by comparison with the earlier nationalist groups marked a resounding victory for the radical-nationalist ideals of 'agitation', 'independence' and centralism. Above all, the structure and practice of the Defence League made no concessions to the old *Honoratiorenpolitik*. In simple sociological terms, of course, the founding circles reproduced the familiar pattern of academics, civil servants, respectable businessmen, landowners and generals, though the admixture of professional 'joiners' and other less prestigious people was perhaps larger than before, and four women also signed the manifesto. But most strikingly, the Defence League had no royal patron and no honorific President from the high aristocracy at its head.[35]

The Defence League's appearance was greeted by the normal chorus of right-wing approval.[36] The Conservative response initially revealed a residual distaste for the insubordinate posture of national opposition, arguing that it

[34] The League actually became co-opted into a political struggle *between* different government departments. The Chancellor and his collaborator Clemens von Delbrück (Imperial Secretary of the Interior) were embarrassed by the bellicose agitation and tried unsuccessfully to get the League declared a political organization (which would have debarred officers from joining). They were thwarted by an alliance of the Crown Prince, the Chief of Staff and the Prussian Minister of the Interior. Simultaneously the League was co-opted into a related conflict *within* the Army over the desirability of a further expansion, which would breach the aristocratic integrity of the officer corps and its traditions. In keeping with the general tenor of radical nationalism, Keim and the Defence League took emphatic sides for the 'modernizers' against the 'traditionalists' in this controversy. For details: Fischer, *War of Illusions*, pp. 108f.; Kitchen, *German Officer Corps*, pp. 137ff.; Groh, *Negative Integration*, pp. 385ff. My confidence in making this point has been greatly assisted by a prior reading of a forthcoming article by Roger Chickering.

[35] Until Chickering's work appears there is no detailed study of the Defence League. The above judgements are based mainly on a reading of *Die Wehr*, the most important pamphlets, and the file of correspondence between Keim and Claß in ZStA Potsdam, ADV, 406. See esp. *Warum muß Deutschland sein Heer verstärken?* (Berlin, 1912), and Keim to Bethmann Hollweg, Feb. 13th 1914, enclosing a copy of *Die Friedensbewegung und ihre Gefahren für das deutsche Volk* (Berlin, 1914), ZStA Potsdam, Rkz., 1415: 94.

[36] e.g. *RWZ*, Dec. 19th 1911; *DortmZ*, Dec. 27th 1911; *Post*, Dec. 19th 1911.

went against 'the Prussian grain to have to resort to organized pressure-group activity before our military administration can be held to the performance of its most vital and sacred duties'.[37] But under the sobering impact of the 1912 elections and the knowledge of an impending Army Bill the Conservatives soon swung round, and arguably the Defence League played a major part in enabling a closer relationship between the Pan-Germans and the agrarians.[38] The latter was perhaps the greatest single advance of the Pan-German position before the war, for Conservative suspicions of radical-nationalist land reform had always been a major obstacle to the League's acceptance in the right as a whole.[39] By the spring of 1913 close relations were being constructed with the leadership of the Agrarian League, and an important bilateral meeting was held in mid-June, at which Wangenheim raised the idea of 'a general union of all national forces outside the parliaments'. This relationship was cemented during the formation of the *Kartell der schaffenden Stände*, and a further small meeting of the two leaderships took place in Berlin on November 14th 1913. Concretely they agreed to co-operate closely in the delicate area of internal colonization, with Wangenheim as primary consultant to the Pan-Germans on such matters.[40] In the aftermath of the Leipzig accords between the CVDI, Agrarian League and *Mittelstand* League, the Pan-German Committee convened in Breslau to discuss the implications, and Claß put the case for the movement's careful integration into the new framework of right-wing co-operation. Senator Neumann reported on the discussion with the Agrarian League and affirmed Wangenheim's view that 'in the field of domestic politics a rallying of all state-preserving forces is needed against the growing democratization and atomization'.[41]

III

In these ways the years after 1909 represented an important period of transition in the history of the right. For despite recent emphasis on continuity, the evident re-combination of 'iron and rye' into a recognizable copy of the 1897 *Sammlung* should not disguise a vital process of intervening change. The *Kartell der schaffenden Stände* and the public discussion which surrounded it revealed clear tendencies towards a long-term re-foundation—in the right's organizational structure, in its class composition, in the breadth and forms of

[37] *KrZ*, Dec. 22nd 1911, cit. *DTZ*, Dec. 24th 1911.
[38] For the press reactions to the demand for a bigger Army: Wernecke, *Wille zur Weltgeltung*, pp. 174–243.
[39] See esp. *KrZ*, July 14th 1913: 'Conservatives and Pan-Germans'; Claß, *Wider den Strom*, p. 267; Stegmann, *Erben*, pp. 403, 325.
[40] Claß, *Wider den Strom*, p. 272; Stegmann, *Erben*, p. 356. Participants were Wangenheim, Oldenburg-Januschau, aus dem Winckel, Hahn and Wadehn for the Agrarian League; Breusing, Neumann and Claß for the Pan-Germans.
[41] Stegmann, *Erben*, pp. 389f., 343, 396f.

its popular appeal, in its relationship to the state, and in the terms of its ideological legitimation. Under conditions of unprecedented political weakness the big capitalists of the CVDI not only opted decisively for a renewal of the agrarian alliance and thereby repudiated the anti-agrarian departure of the Hanse-Union, they also contracted a new type of political arrangement with the independent organizations of the old petty-bourgeoisie. This was a novel descent into the political arena, not dissimilar in principle from the decision of big landowners to form the Agrarian League twenty years before.

But there was also an important difference. Though the process had been a difficult one, requiring a negotiated equilibrium with the interests of smaller producers which was also regionally contingent, the agrarians had none the less achieved their feat of popular incorporation with an organization which was directly under their own leadership. However complex and uneven the route, particularly in the first decade of 1893–1903, and however searching the implications for Conservative political practice, the Agrarian League had successfully contained both large and small producers in a single political apparatus. By contrast the CVDI were denied this advantage. In 1913 they pursued the goal of petty bourgeois incorporation by trying to influence formally independent organizations beyond their direct control. Naturally there were instances where the big bourgeoisie asserted an immediate paternalist control, and similar ambitions may be traced more uncertainly through the Imperial League Against Social Democracy and the attempts to form patriotic fronts in the working class. But even here the experiments with popular organization had a distressing habit of getting out of control. In general the backbone of *Mittelstand* mobilization was necessarily provided by the self-help initiatives of men like Kükelhaus. Though these were increasingly subsidized by big business—witness the financing of the Imperial-German *Mittelstand* League—grants of money were not automatically converted into subordinate political relations.

In other words, the exponents of *Sammlung* may have taken a new initiative in trying to equip themselves with an equivalent popular movement, but the *forms* of that popular politics, both organizationally and programmatically, were still rather ill-defined. The new self-consciousness of the traditional petty-bourgeoisie, equipped for the first time with a stable national organization to represent its independent interests, provided one element of uncertainty. The élitist *hauteur* of the industrial barons was clearly another. For though integrated at the level of ideology and politics, the leaders of the petty-bourgeoisie were certainly not admitted to the *Sammlung* as full participating partners, for this would have seemed too much like a democratic incorporation. Certain key spokesmen of the *Mittelstand* were taken in, but only on sufferance, and with a clear manipulative intent. The change had occurred very much at a level of ideology, in the sense that the necessity was now recognized of an appeal to the masses. But how that appeal might successfully be made, through which organizational forms, and—more to the point—without conceding too much to popular control, was entirely another matter.

Amongst the right the radical nationalists were perhaps the most firmly committed to the principle of popular mobilization, though the engaging naïvety of their expectations was often more striking than their material success. They had insisted since the 1890s that the right must re-ground its politics in a larger popular constituency and inaugurate a new practice of open competition with the Socialists: this demand was the more interesting for being pursued on the ideological terrain of the national idea rather than the economic ground of *Mittelstandspolitik* or material amelioration. Moreover, as we saw, it was raised in the form of an attack on the right-wing establishment, partly because the latter had refused to take up substantive radical-nationalist questions like faster naval expansion, but partly also because it failed to make its structures sufficiently adaptable to the new requirements of popular agitation. This deep ideological conservatism of the governing class helped create a new field of political contradictions, in which the radical nationalists complemented their anti-Socialism with a new hostility to traditional *Honoratiorenpolitik*. As well as calling for a new 'appeal to the people' as the main priority of the right, therefore, they now argued that this could only be achieved by reforming the latter's existing institutions. In this way the popular impetus of radical-nationalist politics became transformed into a rather subversive *populist* potential.

Furthermore, this important ideological struggle also occurred in a wider context of social change, through which the boundaries of political life were decisively redrawn. As the subordinate classes asserted new claims to political independence, the parties were forced into a new relationship with traditional supporters, and to retain the allegiance of the latter a new rhetoric, organization and agitational practice were required. Crucially assisted by the Catholic sub-culture and its 'ghetto mentality', the Centre Party responded best to these new tasks, but the Conservatives also experienced a similar renovation through the agency of the Agrarian League. In uneasy alliance with the Central German Anti-Semites, the Conservatives made themselves increasingly in the 1890s into a sounding-board for *Mittelstand* discontents, though without duplicating the organizational apparatus which in the shape of the Agrarian League already served the Protestant peasantry. To that extent the independent popular mobilization of the 1890s was partially assimilated to the existing framework of *formal* party allegiance. But the *very process* of that mediation had at the same time fundamentally transformed the content of the party's interior relations between leaders and led. Considered in relation to the Wilhelmine polity as a whole between the 1890s and the war, it may be taken as one instance of a general re-negotiation of the dominant ideology. Politically this corresponded to a decomposition of the Bismarckian system, socially to a 'reconstitution of the political nation'.

Viewed in these terms the *Kartell der schaffenden Stände* represented an important moment of re-composition. As argued above, the National Liberals lagged considerably behind in renewing their popular strength after the initial shocks of the 1890s, and when the Bassermann-Stresemann group did devise such a strategy under the auspices of the Bloc it led away from the basic positions of the right. Similarly, the Agrarian League proved inadequate for containing the aspirations of the old petty-bourgeoisie, and the reactions of the latter to the defeat of the finance reform served notice on the Conservatives that a new effort of popular incorporation was fast becoming necessary. The Leipzig accords of August 1913 and the organizational contacts which underpinned them indicated the forms of such a possibility. This was the moment at which the right manifestly applied the lessons of the previous two decades by demonstrating a renewed popular capability. This could be seen in the urgent propaganda of an Alexander Tille, in the increased promotion of tame workers' organizations, in the sponsorship of the old *Mittelstand*, and in the rapid emergence in the Conservative Party of figures like Wolfgang Kapp and Georg Wilhelm Schiele.[42] Most of all it could be seen in the heightened influence of the ideological vanguard of Free Conservatives and Pan-Germans. In this sense the Cartel was a moment of reconciliation for radical nationalists. It signalled a new political formation, in which the 'reconstitution of the political nation' and its consequences became properly articulated into the practice of the right as a

---

[42] Wolfgang Kapp (1858–1922) was the son of a famous liberal, Friedrich Kapp (see H.-U. Wehler, 'Vom radikalen Frühsozialismus des Vormärz zur liberalen Parteipolitik der Bismarckzeit: Friedrich Kapp, 1842–1884', in *Krisenherde*, pp. 237–58). After a successful career in the Prussian bureaucracy (Ministry of Agriculture) he became a leading member of the Conservative Party in East Prussia, where he also owned estates. From 1908 at the latest he was actively concerned with plans for promoting internal colonization and for consolidating the Conservative loyalties of agricultural workers and smaller peasants by means of an insurance movement. Though the relations were not always completely harmonious, he was also closely connected with the Hugenberg circle in this endeavour. By 1910 he was emerging as the leading propagandist for these ideas in the Conservative Party and was prominent in the discussions which spawned the Society for Internal Colonization. In 1913 he chaired the Association of Public Life-Assurance Agencies, conceived as a direct response to the SPD co-operative movement. During the war he rapidly emerged as a tireless exponent of a united 'national opposition' against Bethmann Hollweg's foreign and domestic programme, and became a leading architect of the Fatherland Party. He was distinguished from more traditional Conservatives by his sensitivity for the need to ground any popular appeal to the *Mittelstand* in specific programmes of material amelioration. There is no biography, and his politics are best approached through Stegmann, *Erben*, pp. 252f, 341ff, 326. Schiele was a close collaborator of Kapp both before and during the war: trained as an economist, he seems to have lived mainly from journalism (e.g. editor of *DVC* from 1916), and was the leading public propagandist for Kapp's ideas. He was later involved with Kapp in the ill-fated Putsch of 1920 against the Weimar Republic. For details of the latter, see J. Erger, *Der Kapp-Lüttwitz-Putsch. Ein Beitrag zur deutschen Innenpolitik* (Dusseldorf, 1967).

whole. Electorally weak and with diminished influence on government, the old industrial-agrarian alliance had none the less acquired the materials of its further self-preservation. Whether it could construct them into a stable political bloc was another question.

11. Looking Forward

I

Taking a long view, the history of the German right in the nineteenth century may be seen as the progressive isolation of the Prussian landowning interest and its declining ability to dictate the terms of government policy. The short-term consequence in the 1890s was a retreat into intensive sectional lobbying through the Agrarian League. But increasingly this entailed a search for new political allies, first by canalizing the grievances of smaller and medium producers into a common practice of agrarianism, and then by a more general courting of the old *Mittelstand*. In this way the requirements of political survival breached the aggressive autonomies of agrarian Conservatism as they appeared in the 1890s. Taken as a whole, the Wilhelmine period saw the absorption of Junker Conservatism into a much larger configuration of right politics. This was registered by the coalescence of 1911–13; the trend was accelerated during the war; and the process was formally completed by the dismantling of the Prussian Constitution in 1918. At the same time the right as a whole confronted more general problems of internal cohesion and popular legitimacy. Under the compulsion of a felt crisis on the eve of war, efforts were made to rebuild a firm political relationship with the petty-bourgeoisie and to rationalize it into a constructive right-wing departure. In this respect the *Kartell der schaffenden Stände* was an important sign that movement was afoot. Before concluding this study it is worth considering how far the tendencies to a firmer coalescence of the right were actually realized during the following decade.

A first important point concerns periodization. The main arguments of this book have been constructed around a three-fold distinction: an initial phase of bourgeois consolidation after unification, associated with Bismarck's anti-Socialist protectionist coalition of 'iron and rye'; the dissolution of this Bismarckian system during the 1890s, involving higher levels of self-mobilization of the subordinate classes and serious problems of popular integration for the right-wing parties; and finally, a new period of coalescence which began with the collapse of the Bülow Bloc in 1909. Though these were relatively autonomous political processes, moreover, they were finally determined with varying degrees of immediacy by larger social and economic factors, of which the passage from depression to a new period of expansion after 1895–6 was easily the most important. In the same way the successive experiences of war and revolution after 1914 had a vital part in structuring the context of right-wing politics, both by imposing new tasks and by creating a new decision-making environment. If the enormous climacteric of the war receives relatively little attention here —the war economy and the enhanced role of the state, the dislocation of peace-time incomes and living standards, the *Burgfrieden*, Bethmann Hollweg's 'new orientation' and the split in Social Democracy, the traumas of war-weariness and defeat—this is purely for reasons of space and delimitation of the analysis.[1]

In general the needs of the war bound the different elements of the right more tightly together. At a fundamental level this proceeded from the greater centralization and organization of the economy, as the state responded to the unexpected prolongation of the war with new corporative arrangements. More specifically, the co-ordination of war aims in opposition to the government— the institutionalization of 'national opposition' under changed conditions —spawned a whole series of *ad hoc* committees, propaganda centres, petitions, discussion circles and regular consultations among the parties and *Verbände*. Previously this kind of high politics had been conducted in the interstices of business, high society and other non-political transactions, whereas now it acquired its own distinctive political milieu. Tendencies in this direction could already be glimpsed on the eve of war, but it was the latter that supplied the final impetus. Henceforth the leading circles of both parties and pressure groups became closely integrated into unified milieux of right and left.[2]

II

What happened to the landowning interest after 1913? It was noticeable that in the Cartel discussions of summer 1913 it was the leaders of the Agrarian League that made the running from the Conservative side. It was true that in discussing the implications of the Leipzig accords the *Conservative Correspondenz* called for a 'Bloc of the Right' with 'Conservatives, Economic Reformers, Anti-Semites and National Liberal right', and that in the winter of 1913–14 Heydebrand was being heavily conciliatory towards the CVDI.[3] But where Wangenheim and Roesicke were clearly moving for a larger refoundation of the right, possibly on a unitary footing, Heydebrand wished to preserve the existing integrity of the Conservative Party—rather than seeing the latter

[1] Here I am explicitly concerned with a single specific question: viz. what happened to the forms of right-wing politics. There is an excellent introduction to the larger problems of the war in J. Kocka, *Klassengesellschaft im Krieg 1914–1918* (Göttingen, 1973).

[2] There is no good analysis of this change and no study of the new political clubs (e.g. Delbrück's 'Mittwochabend' which offered regular points of contact for members of different parties, businessmen, experts etc. For details of one discussion-circle that predated the war, viz. the 'World-Political Discussion Evenings' organized by Arthur Dix in 1913-14: Behm and Kuczynski, 'Arthur Dix', pp. 97–100.

[3] For details: Stegmann, *Erben*, pp. 400–8.

absorbed into a new coalition, he wished to assert its primacy by making it the natural refuge for the industrial right.[4] Claß and the Pan-Germans were fully aware of this problem, for though relations with the Agrarian League were now close and Pan-German roots were being sunk east of the Elbe for the first time, the Conservative leaders remained highly suspicious. As Gebsattel said, 'At the moment a new party is presumably still impossible', because for that the Conservative Party as a whole had to be won, and not just 'Kleist, Wangenheim, Wadehn'.[5] In other words, the old party loyalties remained strong, especially in the highest aristocratic circles. Here deference to monarchy also played its part, and one radical critic of the Conservative leadership complained bitterly of its failure to transform the old party into a 'great people's party' through attachment to 'a false royalism, which cannot separate the person of the monarch from the monarchist idea of the state'.[6] To this extent the institutional symbiosis of monarchy and landowning aristocracy remained an important reality of Wilhelmine politics right up to the collapse of 1918.

However, criticism of Heydebrand and Westarp for failing to take a stronger lead of 'national opposition' also signalled a break in the same relationship. In fact, in 1913–18 there was increasing tension between the tradition-conscious circumspection of the Conservatives' titular leadership and the more flexible practice of the agrarians around Wangenheim and Roesicke, with their national rather than East Elbian apparatus and long experience of alliance politics. From the outbreak of war the Agrarian League was intimately involved in the regular discussions of war aims, whereas the Conservative leadership noticeably kept its distance, particularly from the more organized manifestations of opposition to the government. The formation of the so-called 'Independent Committee' under Dietrich Schäfer is perhaps the best example, for it was only in mid-1916 that Westarp gave this his perfunctory support, a full year after the group first came together.[7] By early 1915 an alternative Conservative leadership could already be traced: not only the Agrarian Leaguers, but other members of the party with a growing affinity for the radical nationalists—Salm-Horstmar, Hertzberg-Lottin, Schiele, Graef, Grumme-Douglas, and above all Wolfgang Kapp. By the foundation of the new Fatherland Party in summer 1917 this was much clearer: launched from Königsberg in East Prussia under the guidance of Kapp, in conscious fulfilment of the promise of the Cartel, its leadership numbered none of the leading Conservative parliamentarians. Instead its

---

[4] See esp. the pamphlet by Otto von Pfister, *Deutschkonservativ!* (Berlin, 1913), which was aimed specifically at recruiting the support of West German industrialists.

[5] Gebsattel to Claß, Feb. 12th 1914, cit. Stegmann, *Erben*, p. 404.

[6] Hertzberg-Lottin to Westarp, July 3rd 1917, cit. ibid., p. 496.

[7] For details of the Independent Committee: K.-H. Schädlich, 'Der "Unabhängige Ausschuß für einen deutschen Frieden" als ein Zentrum der Annexionspropaganda des deutschen Imperialismus im ersten Weltkrieg', in F. Klein (Ed.), *Politik im Krieg 1914–1918* (Berlin, 1964), pp. 5off.; Stegmann, *Erben*, pp. 465–7.

organs were heavily dominated by recognized radical nationalists and their allies.[8]

In other words, the old Conservatives around Westarp were increasingly marooned on the bare institutions of 'Prussianism', defending formal traditions which their friends had fast abandoned. The 1918 Revolution completed this process. Once the Prussian Constitution was dismantled, East Elbian land-owners had to act quite differently, as an economic lobby like any other rather than as the political excrescence of a regional class structure with privileged access to the state. Lacking the security of that old organic connection, Agrarian Leaguers developed a fine awareness for the alternative sustenance of a larger political coalition: while Westarp worried over preserving the old Conservative organization during the foundation of the German-National People's Party in 1918–19, Wangenheim and Roesicke were busily incorporating the agrarian constituency in the new party. They adjusted far more quickly to the new political context, when the old alliance with the CVDI no longer held, where specifically Junker interests were forced into political retreat, and where the DNVP's urgent priority was the acquisition of a popular constituency.[9]

Thus though there may have been no serious attempt to expropriate the big estates east of the Elbe in the 1918 Revolution, there was a fundamental change in the landowners' ability to reproduce their economic power in the form of political influence in the state. From being structurally privileged in its access to state power, large-scale landed property was reduced to one fraction of the dominant classes among others, linked by channels of political representation to specific sectional organizations, whose practice was then articulated into one or more political parties. The effect was a decisive separation of agrarian politics from Conservatism of the traditional monarchist kind. The latter remained in certain sections of the aristocracy (e.g. in the circles that crystallized around Hindenburg after 1925), but on the whole agrarian organizations were distinguished throughout the 1920s by a pragmatic willingness to

[8] For the Fatherland Party we must await Dirk Stegmann's long-announced monograph. In the meantime see: K. Wortmann, *Geschichte der Deutschen Vaterlandspartei 1917–1918* (Halle, 1926); Stegmann, *Erben*, pp. 497ff.

[9] For the fate of the German Conservative Party in the DNVP: W. Liebe, *Die Deutschnationale Volkspartei 1918–1924* (Düsseldorf, 1956), pp. 25ff.; L. Hertzman, *DNVP. Right-Wing Opposition in the Weimar Republic, 1918–1924* (Lincoln, 1963), pp. 34–41, 64–71, 107ff., 180ff., 233ff.; A. Thimme, *Flucht in den Mythos. Die Deutschnationale Volkspartei und die Niederlage von 1918* (Göttingen, 1969), esp. pp. 9ff., 45ff., 141ff.; P.-C. Witt, 'Eine Denkschrift Otto Hoetzschs vom 5. November 1918', *VfZ*, 21 (1973), pp. 337–53. For agrarian politics after 1918: D. Gessner, *Agrarverbände in der Weimarer Republik* (Düsseldorf, 1976), pp. 13–82; G. A. Shellman, 'Land and Politics in Weimar Germany', (Ph.D. thesis, Iowa, 1975), esp. pp. 38–147; H. Muth, 'Die Entstehung der Bauern- und Landarbeiterräte im November 1918 und die Politik des Bundes der Landwirte', *VfZ*, 21 (1973), pp. 1–38; J. Fleming, *Landwirtschaftliche Interessen und Demokratie. Ländliche Gesellschaft, Agrarverbände und Staat 1890–1925* (Bonn, 1978).

fight for political concessions within the Weimar system. Though forced on to the defensive after 1918—preoccupied with containing the rural proletariat and renewing political relations with the independent peasantry—by 1924–5 the agrarians were pressing for governmental participation by the DNVP and reconstructing a framework of consultation with industry.[10] This completed a process registered by the Cartel in 1913: the growing independence of the agrarian movement from its comfortable basis in the Prussian Constitution—dramatically confirmed by the latter's destruction in 1918—and its re-integration within a larger bloc of the right.

III

The diminished ability of big landed property to set the context for the right in general was clearly revealed by the process of unification after 1913. By the outbreak of war little progress had yet been made: neither the Conservatives nor the National Liberal right were willing to take the plunge by forming a new party, and the commonest form of unity was still a coalescence on particular issues or in a particular locality.[11] But the war immediately drew the right more tightly together, initially in the autumn of 1914 to work out a common programme of war aims, later during 1915 because of its deepening hostility to the position of the government. The extreme circumstance of war accentuated the double stance of 'national opposition'—bitter criticism of the war effort abroad, angry denunciations of the 'new orientation' towards the Social Democrats at home. Early discussions in the winter of 1914–15 eventually cohered into the *Auskunftstelle Vereinigter Verbände* which held its first meeting on September 4th 1915, while around the same time the organization of the so-called 'Address of the Intellectuals' (presented to the Chancellor on July 8th 1915) laid the basis for what later became the Independent Committee for a German Peace (formally constituted on July 13th 1916). If the former provided mainly a co-ordinating centre for consultations and propaganda, the latter

[10] For this normalization of agrarian relations with the 'Weimar system', see especially Fleming, *Landwirtschaftliche Interessen*, and Gessner, *Agrarverbände*, pp. 13–82.

[11] Typical examples were the rally called by the sponsors of the patriotic workers' movement in June 1910, and the conference convened by Schwerin-Löwitz in Nov. 1912 to discuss the control of the agricultural labour force. The former was attended by representatives of all the future participants in the 1913 Cartel: the National Liberal right and the two Conservative Parties, the leading industries of the CVDI, the artisanate and other branches of the *Mittelstand*, the agrarians, the Pan-Germans (including Claß and Keim), and all the *nationale Verbände* (Saul, *Staat, Industrie, Arbeiterbewegung*, pp. 144f.). The latter was attended by representatives from the Agrarian League, the co-operative movement in the East, the insurance movement (in which Kapp was by now the moving spirit), other rural welfare organizations from the East, the veterans' clubs, the Defence League, and the Imperial League Against Social Democracy. (Fleming, *Landwirtschaftliche Interessen und Demokratie*, p. 72f.) The formation of the Prussia-Union in mid-1913 was an instance of a similar kind: Stegmann, *Erben*, pp. 421ff.

spawned a more ambitious programme of political agitation with a regional apparatus and local contacts. Both successfully rallied the full array of the organized right: radical Conservatives and right-wing National Liberals; Agrarian League, CVDI and *Mittelstand* League; ancillary agencies of *Sammlung* in east and west, like the Society for Internal Colonization or the German Association; the patriotic workers' movement; and the *nationale Verbände*. Most significantly, they were both directly influenced by Claß and the Pan-Germans, who had quickly installed themselves at the centre of the war aims movement.[12]

During this period there were two major impulses towards a unification of the whole right. The first came from the Pan-German League. There was already some pressure for a new party in summer 1915, when Otto-Helmut Hopfen, a confidant of Claß and friend of Keim, had proposed the conversion of the League into a full-scale party, under the title of *Deutscher Machtbund*. Claß was as yet unconvinced and continued cementing closer relations with the CVDI, eroding the suspicions of East Elbian Conservatives, and expanding the operations of the future Independent Committee. The provincial location of the Pan-German headquarters in Mainz and the large financial deficit constrained the movement's freedom of action considerably, and a major fund-raising operation was an urgent priority: the 'Salm Appeal' launched in February 1916 proved a success in this respect, and by June 1916 the League was comfortably installed in its new Berlin premises. Equipped with lucrative industrial contacts—for which Hugenberg's expanding communications empire bore no small responsibility—and with fresh contacts in Mecklenburg, Pomerania, and West and East Prussia, Claß was prepared by the spring of 1916 to explore the chances of a new unifying initiative. At first this was to take the form of a union of the *nationale Verbände* into a 'German People's Council', headed by Johann Albrecht of Mecklenburg or the recently dismissed Tirpitz. Though this specific plan was superseded, it achieved some reality in the summer of 1917 when Dietrich Schäfer formed the so-called Central Co-ordinating Office of the Patriotic Associations. This finally embodied an old radical-nationalist dream with a long history of thwarted ambitions, from the National-Party of 1892–3, through Friedrich Lange's many projects, to Keim's ill-fated *Verband der Verbände* in 1908.[13]

The second major impulse came from Wolfgang Kapp. As neither aristocratic traditionalist nor Agrarian Leaguer, but of unimpeachable bourgeois stock and the son of a famous liberal, closely identified with the active conciliation of the *Mittelstand*, Kapp represented the coming generation of Conservative

---

[12] Details taken mainly from Stegmann, *Erben*, pp. 449ff.

[13] For details: ibid., pp. 489ff. The Office had twenty-five affiliates, including the Pan-Germans, Agrarian League, Eastern Marches Society, Defence League, Society for Internal Colonization, Evangelical Union, the Independent Committee, and the national co-ordinating bodies of the patriotic workers' movement.

politicians. He was likewise at the centre of the war aims movement: speaker at the first great rally of business opinion on September 28th 1914, member of the *Auskunftstelle Vereinigter Verbände*, and close associate of Schäfer's Independent Committee. As the Pan-Germans prepared for a decisive initiative in the spring of 1916, moreover, Kapp published his so-called 'May-Memorandum', *Die nationalen Kreise und der Reichskanzler*, which united the foreign and domestic programmes of the 'national opposition' into a swingeing indictment of Beth-mann Hollweg. As well as the now familiar attack on the government's conduct of the war, he added the radical-nationalist critique of 'our ruinous party life' (only a victorious peace would hasten the 'concentration and reformation' of the party system), and insisted that only a 'truly popular domestic policy' could prevent the country from sinking into the 'democratic swamp' of a rapproche-ment with the SPD: welfare for the *Mittelstand*, rural settlement, housing reform and defence of the Prussian suffrage.[14] This inaugurated a period of quickening speculation. Schiele, Kapp's close associate, canvassed the idea of a 'new conservative party'. Gebsattel suggested a 'Conservative *Mittelstand* Party' or 'Conservative Citizens' Party'. Wangenheim observed that 'the future belongs to that party which can make itself into the mouthpiece and leader of the genuinely national-thinking circles of the German people'. Claß agreed: the goal was now 'foundation of the great national party'.[15]

The eventual outcome, in September 1917, was the launching of the Father-land Party. Though publicly restricted to foreign affairs alone and repudiating the desire to compete with the existing right-wing parties, this stood in evident lineage with the long tradition of *Sammlung*. Kapp originally wanted to launch the party from Friedrichsruh and considered the names 'Bismarck-Union', 'Bismarck-Party' and 'Hindenburg-Party' before settling on the final choice. It drew consciously on the past, with the 'combination Hi – Wa, Hirsch – Wangenheim, *Kartell der schaffenden Stände*, as invisible backbone'.[16] But the Fatherland Party also incorporated those fundamental changes which, as we saw, decisively separated the Cartel of 1913 from the previous experience of 1897, let alone from 1879.

Most obviously, it was constituted explicitly by the *Primat des Nationalen*, though it perhaps required the special circumstances of war to make this possible. Equally clearly it was constituted by an extreme stance of 'national opposition' —not only to the government's war aims, but also (though this was officially denied) to its programme of limited Prussian reform.[17] Though borne by the

[14] Ibid., p. 487.
[15] Ibid., p. 495.
[16] Kapp, cit. ibid., p. 499.
[17] The party's claim to be *above* 'party-political' matters (i.e. domestic policy) required that it deny any commitment to defend the existing Prussian suffrage, even though the Peace Resolution and the government's concession on the principle of Prussian reform had provided its double *raison d'être*. See esp. Tirpitz to Thimme, Oct. 10th 1917, BA Coblenz, Thimme Papers, 25: ' . . . the Party is ruled only by its Constitution, in which there is nothing about

12

subsidies of heavy industry and secure in the CVDI's general support, more-over, the party's leading organs were much more evenly composed than previous products of *Sammlung*, drawing not only on the typical *Honoratioren*, but also on the radical nationalists and spokesmen for the *Mittelstand*. Claß was involved with Kapp in the preparatory discussions, helped choose the original leadership, and took his place in the Inner Committee. Though the organic spokesmen of the petty-bourgeoisie were still kept at arm's length—figures like Jens Christian Jensen (the national chairman of the patriotic workers' movement), Heinrich Beythien (a leading functionary of the retailers' movement) or Kükelhaus sat not in the Inner Committee but in the broader executive organs —the dominant voices in the party were at least persons who felt that an appeal to the petty-bourgeoisie was vital. Above all, perhaps, the Fatherland Party claimed its own apparatus of popular recruitment, and by September 1918 had some 800,000 individual members organized into 2,536 local branches. In all of these ways the new party actually realized—in a single unitary organization— what the Cartel of 1913 had exhibited mainly as a series of potentials.[18]

Thus—given the obvious difficulty that it co-existed with the established parties of the right rather than replacing them—the Fatherland Party appeared a convincing answer to the right's problems. It simultaneously combined opposition to the government with extreme patriotism, it made a serious effort to incorporate the petty-bourgeoisie, and it had a broad popular basis in the country, which could only get stronger. Moreover, it seemed finally to have cracked one of the right's most abiding problems, namely how to circumvent the special position of the Junkers as an aristocratic landowning interest articu-lated into the structures of the Prussian monarchy. It has already been suggested above that Conservatives in the traditional Prussian mould were fast being out-flanked by those who were more sensitive to new contexts—Agrarian Leaguers who had to operate in a varied national setting, individual recruits to the Pan-Germans, a new generation of bourgeois activists like Kapp and Schiele—and the Fatherland Party now provided striking evidence that the re-formation of the right could proceed if necessary without the full co-operation of the Junkers. Wangenheim sat in its Inner Committee, but Conservative parliamentarians were notable mainly by their absence. Though Heydebrand and Westarp had convened discussions with right-wing National Liberals and CVDI business-men around a seven-point programme in September 1917 to oppose the Prussian

---

domestic policy or refusal of the Prussian suffrage reform . . . we have nothing to do with domestic policy, economic policy and social policy and we have no position on the Prussian suffrage reform, which in any case is running its course'. Tirpitz was First Chairman of the Fatherland Party, with Kapp as Second Chairman and Johann Albrecht von Mecklenburg as Honorary Chairman.

[18] For detailed references: Stegmann, *Erben*, pp. 499ff. For further detail on the attempts to develop a popular apparatus: Stegmann, 'Zwischen Repression und Manipulation', pp. 385ff.

reform and uphold 'authority', their intentions differed from those of Kapp. Their proposal 'to unite into a firm bloc all those with an interest in protecting the legitimate profit and property of the individual whether big or small',[19] envisaged a leading role for the existing Conservative Party and not the creation of a completely new structure. In this sense also the Fatherland Party represented the fulfilment of radical nationalism: the full maturity of a distinctively bourgeois nationalist politics, forced into a posture of defensive anti-democracy, but emancipated none the less from the demands of aristocratic accommodation.

This was even clearer in the formation of the DNVP in the hectic confusion of November 1918. Conceived, symbolically, at the funeral of the leading Free Conservative Karl Frhr. von Gamp-Massaunen, the new party was a hurried amalgam of Conservatives, Free Conservatives, Christian-Socials and Anti-Semites (re-combined into the German-*Völkisch* Party in March 1914), strengthened by the piecemeal affiliation of National Liberals, Pan-Germans and previously non-aligned nationalists— 'the reservoir for all those elements and party remnants who were not happy with the new course', as one DNVP deputy later put it.[20] But though the more pragmatic Conservatives had helped preside over this coalescence, Westarp and Heydebrand remained obdurately unco-operative: the latter remained disdainfully on his estates, while Westarp's insistence on preserving the integrity of the old Conservative organization almost sabotaged the negotiations at the last minute. The recalcitrant Conservative group took steps to strengthen their influence in the DNVP for the elections to the National Assembly in January 1919, but consistently refused to dissolve their separate organization. As in the period between 1913 and 1918, this contrasted with the attitude of Wangenheim and Roesicke, who quickly accepted the DNVP's primary claims. Moreover, the suspicions were mutual. Traditional Conservatives like Heydebrand were heavily compromised by association with the monarchy and its débâcle of defeat and abdication, so that the DNVP's public statements during 1918–19 urgently proclaimed the party's novelty. The taunt of dependence on the Junkers was the predictable basis of many left-wing attacks, and the charge which the DNVP's leaders most carefully resisted. Agriculture had no special place in the party's programme. This was true of the original manifesto on November 24th 1918 and those for the elections of 1919 and 1920, of Oskar Hergt's 'Programme of Order' in September 1919, and of the 'Basic Principles' adopted in April 1920.[21]

[19] This was Point One of the programme. See Stegmann, *Erben*, pp. 498f.

[20] General von Gallwitz, in a speech describing the party's foundation, Halle, Nov. 1920, cit. Liebe, *Deutsch-nationale Volkspartei*, p. 129.

[21] These are printed in full, ibid., pp. 107–21. Hergt, a civil servant and the last Prussian Finance Minister under the Empire in 1917–18, was the first Chairman of the DNVP from 1918 until his resignation at the end of 1924. For a portrait, see Thimme, *Flucht in den Mythos*, pp. 34–45.

The very name of the new party—'German-National People's Party'—doubly repudiated the specific legacy of Prussian Conservatism which Westarp and Heydebrand were so anxious to protect. On the one hand, it signalled the full incorporation of the Christian-Social movement into a larger party of the right. Though regionally important the latter never enjoyed significant influence in the old Conservative Party after the early 1890s, and the adherence of its leaders now gave the DNVP some welcome roots in the Christian labour movement. Between 1918 and 1924 the Christian-Socials were among the more stable elements of the party. More unpredictably the form of the party's title also registered the influence of the German-National Commercial Assistants' Association, though the political loyalties of that organization were quickly divided with Stresemann's German People's Party. Together these two groupings—backed up by the Anti-Semites and Pan-Germans—had insisted in November 1918 that the new foundation take the form of a *'People's Party'*.[22] But on the other hand, the option for the 'German-national' designation also signalled that Prussian traditions were being superseded. East Elbian Prussian Conservatism had been the largest of the entrenched particularisms of the *Kaiserreich* (though less noted perhaps than the more familiar instance of Bavaria) and its spokesmen had stubbornly defended the federalism of the Constitution against centralizing trends, particularly in financial affairs. This had been not the least of the reasons for Conservative suspicion of radical nationalism before 1909, and the DNVP's 'German-national' title (like its popular cast) must be counted an important victory of the latter over the former. As one old Prussian Conservative exclaimed in exasperation: 'What does German-national really mean? I am three times more of a Prussian than I am a German.'[23]

Thus it would be wrong to see the DNVP as a simple continuation of the 1913 Cartel. It certainly embodied the long-coveted ideal of an organizational unification. But the destruction of the Prussian Constitution had dislocated the landowning interest from its original position in the right: from being an immovable object, its political representation had been suddenly fragmented into disunity, before being re-integrated into a far more complicated political formation. Moreover, the DNVP was certainly no kind of final resolution for the previous divisions of the right. Most obviously, the foundation of Stresemann's DVP on December 15th 1918 registered the failure of the DNVP to establish itself as the undisputed refuge for right-wing National Liberals, and the new logic of compromise with organized labour led many of the old CVDI

[22] For the Christian-Social group, see esp. Hertzman, *DNVP*, pp. 173ff. For the German-National Commercial Assistants' Association: I. Hamel, *Völkischer Verband und nationale Gewerkschaft. Der Deutschnationale Handlungsgehilfen-Verband 1893–1933* (Frankfurt, 1967); L. E. Jones, 'The Crisis of White-Collar Interest Politics: Deutschnationaler Handlungsgehilfen-Verband and Deutsche Volkspartei in the World Economic Crisis', in Mommsen, Petzina, Weisbrod (Eds.), *Industrielles System*, pp. 811–23.

[23] General von Kleist of Wendisch-Tychow, cit. Liebe, *Deutschnationale Volkspartei*, p. 128.

to prefer the more 'liberal' alternative.[24] More importantly, in the long run, the new party failed to achieve any lasting integration of the petty-bourgeoisie. As a popular party (some 950,000 members in 1923, 21·4% of the popular vote in May 1924) it clearly enjoyed widespread support amongst both old and new *Mittelstand*.[25] But in two crucial respects the DNVP failed to establish its leadership amongst these strata: on the one hand it faced the competition of the *Wirtschaftspartei* (founded in September 1920), semi-independent agrarian deputies, and other organized expressions of the traditional petty-bourgeoisie;[26] on the other hand it quickly lost the ability to contain the unruly agitation of its *völkisch* wing, which seceded in late 1922 to form the German-*Völkisch*-Freedom-Party (DVFP).[27] Most ominously, this older tradition of Anti-Semitic politics was itself fast becoming superseded, for an entirely new milieu of *völkisch* activity was now being created, on a local basis and beneath the formal structures of the dominant right-wing party.[28]

In other words, the DNVP was a highly unstable synthesis. Its unification of the right had been achieved under the extreme duress of a revolutionary crisis, when the old assumptions had simply collapsed. The basis of co-operation was at first the elementary one of self-defence, and the forms of a more lasting integration proved hard to attain. The lingering autonomy of the Conservative group was a major obstacle between 1918 and 1923, and Westarp was only tempted into a more positive commitment of Conservative energies by the departure of rival groups: the original make-up of the DNVP was modified twice, first by the withdrawal of important Free Conservatives after the Kapp Putsch (Siegfried von Kardorff, Otto von Dewitz, Otto Arendt and Joh.

---

[24] The literature on the politics of industry during the Revolution and the foundation of the Republic is now enormous. The most important works are probably the following: F. Zunkel, *Industrie und Staatssozialismus. Der Kampf um die Wirtschaftsordnung in Deutschland 1914–1918* (Düsseldorf, 1974), esp. pp. 172–206; G. Feldman, *Iron and Steel in the German Inflation 1916–1923* (Princeton, 1977); Leopold, *Alfred Hugenberg*, pp. 11ff.; L. Döhn, *Politik und Interesse. Die Interessenstruktur der Deutschen Volkspartei* (Meisenheim, 1970).

[25] Liebe, *Deutschnationale Volkspartei*, pp. 33, 15ff.; Thimme, *Flucht in den Mythos*, pp. 26–32; T. Childers, 'The Social Bases of the National Socialist Vote', *JCH*, 11, 4 (1976), pp. 17–42.

[26] H. A. Winkler, *Mittelstand, Demokratie und Nationalsozialismus. Die politische Entwicklung von Handwerk und Kleinhandel in der Weimarer Republik* (Cologne, 1972); M. Schumacher *Mittelstandsfront und Republik. Die Wirtschaftspartei – Reichspartei des deutschen Mittelstandes 1919–1933* (Düsseldorf, 1972); M. Schumacher, 'Hausbesitz, Mittelstand und Wirtschaftspartei in der Weimarer Republik', in Mommsen, Petzina, Weisbrod (Eds.), *Industrielles System*, pp. 823–35; Heberle, *From Democracy to Nazism*, pp. 32ff.; Gessner, *Agrarverbände*, pp. 96ff.; J. Noakes, *The Nazi Party in Lower Saxony 1921–1933* (Oxford, 1971), pp. 108–20; Gellately, *Politics of Economic Despair*, pp. 197–209.

[27] Hertzman, *DNVP*, pp. 124–64; Liebe, *Deutschnationale Volkspartei*, pp. 61–73; H. Fenske, *Wahlrecht und Parteiensystem* (Frankfurt, 1972), pp. 241ff.

[28] Above all: Lohalm, *Völkischer Radikalismus*, and Noakes, *Nazi Party*, pp. 9–40.

Victor Bredt), and then by the *völkisch* secession of the autumn of 1922.[29] Furthermore, in the early years the DNVP executive exerted little control over its constituency parties, whose character embraced a diversity of right-wing formations. The first Congress of July 1919 tried to regularise relations with the local committees, but the proliferation of local *völkisch*, nationalist and para-military groups, each in a particular configuration with their local DNVP, continued to complicate this process. In a sense (for the first two elections of 1919 and 1920 at least) the process of negotiation and *ad hoc* compromise in the *Kaiserreich*, which had operated most successfully in the elections of 1907, was now institutionalized within the framework of a single party. Finally, the disorienting impact of the Revolution on the existing political loyalties of the bourgeoisie and petty-bourgeoisie should not be under-estimated. The same compulsions which at the top enabled a coalescence of the right into a single new party led at the base to the dispersal of the old popular constituencies of the component parties. For some years the DNVP was a party in search of a stable rank and file. To this extent it marked a simultaneous unification and fragmenta-tion of the right.

IV

What happened to the *nationale Verbände*? By contrast with the earlier period they had no specific history after 1918, in the sense that they made no distinctive contribution comparable to that of Wilhelmine radical nationalism. Individual radical nationalists continued to play leading roles in the DNVP—Hugenberg is the best-known example—and the Pan-Germans retained a position of influence in the same quarters.[30] But although the other pressure groups like-wise continued to exist during the Weimar Republic, the conditions of Germany's defeat in the First World War—loss of the colonies, drastic dis-armament and the loss of an offensive navy, the contraction of Germany's world-wide interests and the sense of global mission, the loss of territory and the creation of an independent Poland—transformed their conditions of existence. They were necessarily far more peripheral to the main concerns of German politics. For the Navy League the dislocation was the most painful: by 1925 membership had dwindled to less than 40,000, the idea of the Navy was discredited by the poor results of the war at sea, and to make matters worse the Navy was held guilty for spawning the naval mutinies that began the Revolu-tion.[31] Moreover, the radicalizing experience of the revolutionary civil war in

---

[29] Liebe, *Deutschnationale Volkspartei*, pp. 59–61; Hertzman, *DNVP*, pp. 112ff.

[30] Leopold, *Alfred Hugenberg*, pp. 27ff.; Thimme, *Flucht in den Mythos*, pp. 50–60; B. S. Chamberlain, 'The Enemy on the Right: The Alldeutscher Verband in the Weimar Republic, 1918–1926', (Ph.D. Thesis, Maryland, 1972).

[31] The literature on the *nationale Verbände* during the Weimar Republic is poorly developed. For the Navy League and Colonial Society, see Wulf, 'Deutscher Flottenverein', pp. 447f.,

1918–23 determined an entirely new mode of bourgeois politics, in which the more combative spirits now found a natural outlet through the para-military formations. In general the process of radical nationalism's integration into the right as a whole was completed by the formation of the DNVP. The end of the Empire and the collapse of the monarchy had finally generalized the politics of 'national opposition' to the right as a whole and in these new circumstances the *nationale Verbände* became subordinate instances in a much larger configuration.

The most enduring legacy of radical nationalism was a passionate belief in the *Primat des Nationalen*, the primacy of the national factor—the pervasive conviction that an objective 'national' interest dictated the ruthless subordination of all other issues to the resolute advancement of Germany's national power in all its manifold forms. This manner of thinking defined the most pressing object of political engagement in terms of nationalist re-education, or a 'crusade of national enlightenment', as one typical manifesto put it.[32] This belief in the power of ideas as the motive force of political action, in the principle that 'political actions are *finally determined* by people's political attitudes' as Tim Mason has put it,[33] implicitly denied both the importance and the legitimacy of material conflicts. Any attempt to project an alternative view of Germany's 'national' interests by suggesting the force of sectional considerations in the formulation of foreign policy was denounced as subversive and anti-national. Thus the Pan-Germans acknowledged that the nation was deeply divided on domestic policy 'through conflicting outlooks in relation to church and school and to economic, administrative and constitutional questions'. But this served only to entrench even further their conception of an objective national interest, embracing 'the great questions of the security of the fatherland, foreign policy, overseas trade, the protection of Germans abroad', and so on. The domestic divisions merely toughened the Pan-German League's image of itself as a movement able to articulate the real 'political will' of the people, unpolluted by selfish sectionalism.[34] By objective function, of course, this

---

and Müller and Fieber, 'Deutsche Kolonialgesellschaft', pp. 398ff. Otherwise, public discussion of naval and colonial policy may be traced through the following detailed studies: J. Dülffer, *Weimar, Hitler und die Marine. Reichspolitik und Flottenbau 1920–1939* (Düsseldorf, 1973), and K. Hildebrand, *Vom Reich zum Weltreich. Hitler, NSDAP und koloniale Fragen 1919–1945* (Munich, 1969). The Eastern Marches Society is better served. See the contribution by F.-H. Gentzen, 'Der Deutsche Ostmarkenverein von 1918 bis 1934', in Galos, Gentzen, Jacobczyk, *Hakatisten*, pp. 317–418, and K. Fiedor, *Antypolskie Organizacje W Niemczech, 1918–1933* (Wroclaw, 1973).

[32] *KZ*, June 1st 1909: 'Education for Citizenship', signed by sixty-four mainly Pan-German intellectuals, including Claß, Keim, Liebert, Langhans, Stössel, etc.

[33] T. Mason, 'The Legacy of 1918 for National Socialism', in A. J. Nicholls and E. Matthias (Eds.), *German Democracy and the Triumph of Hitler. Essays in Recent German History* (London, 1971), p. 222.

[34] Manifesto issued by the Pan-German League, Nov. 10th 1908, during the Daily Telegraph Crisis, text in ZStA Potsdam, ADV, 67: 52.

ideology was profoundly anti-Socialist and anti-democratic, though this should
not obscure the seriousness of the subjective commitment nor the effectivity of
the ideology *as an ideology*. Moreover, the double indignity of the Revolution
and Versailles in 1918–19 transformed the self-confident celebration of the
'national idea' into a passion of moral outrage at its violation. The political
myth of the 'war-guilt lie' and the 'stab in the back' by the 'November criminals'
deepened the propensity of the German right to construct their practice around
an ideology of the *Primat des Nationalen*.

Political failures were explained by inadequate application of the will and
imperfect understanding of 'national needs'. Confronted with the limited
success of their nationalist offensive, radical nationalists had no recourse but to
lament the so-called political 'immaturity' of the Germans, and at no time was
this retreat into ideology clearer than in the winter of 1918, when the right's
worst nightmares had materialized. Wolfgang Kapp left a graphic description
of this situation at the dissolution meeting of the Fatherland Party in December
1918:

> The bourgeois political and social order has been destroyed by the
> Revolution, the unity of the Empire is disintegrating, the Kaiser and the
> Princes have abdicated. Army and Navy are in complete dissolution, and we
> stand absolutely defenceless at home and abroad. Our enemies at home are
> turning this situation to their advantage. Part of the Eastern provinces are in
> the hands of the Poles and they are raising claims to some more, a Lithuanian
> movement has been formed, the Bolshevik threat is in the ascendant, and
> we have no means to prevent it. The people cannot be held by the banner,
> the ignominious armistice is concluded, the crime has been committed
> against the German people in that the Revolution has been unleashed at this
> very moment . . . The German Empire, the creation of Bismarck, has lasted
> for less than fifty years.

Kapp's explanation for this calamity sounded a familiar note: instead of
resisting, 'the bourgeoisie has gone to pieces, the internal disunity is on the
agenda just as it always has been, and in place of the united bourgeois bloc
from right to left there is complete fragmentation engineered by self-seeking
leaders'. The Revolution was caused neither by material problems nor by
genuine social unrest. The bourgeoisie's failure to resist came from moral
weakness and some strange, undefined political incapacity: 'if the German
people had been more politically mature, our efforts might have succeeded. But
it was not to be, our star has fallen, and with it the star of the fatherland.'[35]

----

[35] Kapp's statement in the dissolution meeting of the Fatherland Party's Imperial Committee, Dec. 10th 1918, *Protokoll*, BA Coblenz, Traub Papers, 48.

12. Conclusion: German Particularities

I

This study has tried to explore the central contradiction of Wilhelmine politics: namely the persistence of a state structure guaranteeing the historic privileges of a landowning interest, at a time when the capitalist transformation of German society, the diminishing role of agriculture in the economy and the antagonism of capital and labour were all demanding an adaptation of that state to entirely novel situations. Putting this slightly differently, we might argue that Wilhelmine politics was constituted by a double antagonism. On the one hand, the persistence of aristocratic survivals in an unreformed Prussian state necessarily created a field of political-ideological conflict with a liberal bourgeoisie increasingly conscious of its need for *Gleichberechtigung*, or equality of status. This was compounded by more specific grievances—e.g. the pressure of bourgeois Catholics for parity in civil opportunity and state preferment, and the growing conflict between the 'modernizing' aspirations of National Liberals in central Germany and the south-west and the more patrician cast of the Party in the north—which became articulated through a more self-conscious parliamentarianism in the Reichstag and made the dualism of Reich and Prussia increasingly hard to sustain.[1]

But on the other hand, we may point to the simultaneous existence of a precocious revolutionary Social Democratic Party, rooted in the explicit acknowledgment of class conflict and committed to a radical programme of reform far more extensive than anything the liberal bourgeoisie ever conceived. Whereas the pressure from the Socialist left was never sufficient to obscure completely the conflicts with the landowning interest (even at times of extreme crisis in the relations of capital and labour only certain fractions of the bourgeoisie were willing to enter a stable political alliance with the Junkers), it none the less always militated against the consistent pursuit of an anti-agrarian position. In other words, the simultaneous existence of these two separate fields of antagonism complicated the prospects of a further 'parliamentarization' of the state structure in the classic British mould. Indeed, for many years (from the late 1870s to at least the turn of the century) this helped to freeze liberal politics in a comfortable practice of class accommodation, in which the interests

[1] See esp. Blackbourn, 'Problem of Democratization', for discussion of this point.
12*

of landowners and bourgeoisie fused into a common structure of oligarchic political relations. *Honoratiorenpolitik*—to resume a second major theme of this book—was the institutional expression of this political, social and ideological accommodation of the bourgeoisie to aristocratic survivals.

However, this politics of accommodation was located in a very specific conjuncture, namely the immediate post-unification phase, when the legitimacy of the new nation-state and the legal infra-structure of Germany's capitalist development were both being consolidated. By the 1890s, and particularly with the beginning of the long expansion in 1895–6, a new period was starting, when the requirements of capital changed and the political compulsions were very different. The declining share of agriculture in the national product and the dramatically shifting demographic balance of town and country were the readiest measures of this change, and it was in the 1890s that the ideological dichotomy of *Industriestaat–Agrarstaat* properly dominated public discourse. Simultaneously, the same conditions of expanding industrial capitalism combined with the legalization of Socialist activities in 1890 to produce a new problem of organized labour. Within an expanding public sphere (e.g. through the growth of communications and expanding literacy) this new context produced new levels of political activity which the older party framework, both organizationally and ideologically, could no longer contain.

This created two sets of difficulties for the old Bismarckian power bloc. First, it produced an important renewal of bourgeois antagonism against the landowning interest. This took partly the form of particular economic grievances (e.g. the resentment of exporters at the high-tariff policy restored in 1897–1902), but also encompassed a wider social and political critique (e.g. as embodied eventually in the Hanse-Union of 1909). The consequence was a fractional disunity of the power bloc, which posed a serious problem for government: i.e. how to rationalize afresh the relations between the different fractions of agricultural, industrial, merchant and finance capital, by containing their conflicts within a manageable framework of political negotiation and by devising an appropriate governing majority for the Reichstag. But secondly, the 1890s witnessed an unprecedented politicization of the subordinate classes, which subjected the social relations on which traditional bourgeois politics depended to severe strain. As specific forms of this new popular mobilization (leaving aside the SPD's organization of industrial and craft workers) we may observe the following: new movements of peasant agriculture and traditional small business; the complex requirements of interest-politics in a heavily concentrated and cartelized economy; the self-confident maturity of the first generation of aspiring bourgeois and petty-bourgeois politicians to be completely moulded by the post-unification environment. In this situation the politics of the right were determined by a double long-term difficulty: a problem of the power bloc's internal unity, and a problem of its popular support.

This created a situation of intolerable complexity for the government. Under

Miquel and the early years of Bülow its response was to reconstruct the Bismarckian power bloc beneath the slogan of *Sammlungspolitik*. But the years after 1903 exposed this as a short-term expedient with no future in its existing form, and by 1912 this older basis of government—the Cartel in loose alliance with the Centre—was in complete dissolution. Institutional bases of Junker privilege naturally remained—viz. the Ministry of State, the Prussian Upper Chamber, the built-in Conservative majority in the Landtag, the recruitment of the local bureaucracy, and finally the monarchy itself, what Heydebrand called the 'pentagram in Prussia'[2]—but it was no longer possible to reproduce that simple dominance in the very different arena of the Reich. After the derisory showing of the old Cartel at the 1912 polls, the government of Bethmann Hollweg had no choice but to build tentative bridges to the reformist left. After 1909, in other words, it ceased to see the special relationship with the agrarians as an automatic priority, and the logic of this hand-to-mouth realignment damaged its relations with the right across the entire spectrum of policy. The pragmatic departure from old principles drove the right into growing extremities of 'national opposition' to the government, which culminated, as we saw, in the *Kartell der schaffenden Stände*.

With this the Wilhelmine state entered a definite crisis. Though it is by no means clear that there was no way out or that this led directly to a 'social-imperialist' gamble in July 1914, it none the less placed the government in an impossible situation. Severed from its accustomed relations with the right, it could not embrace a decisive departure to the left. As expressed above, this introduced a new contradiction into German politics, between a state structure which still formally guaranteed the privileges of the Prussian landowning interest, and a political line-up which ranged the latter's political spokesmen and their allies *against* the appointed government. But not only was the disunity of the power bloc re-confirmed in this more consolidated fashion. The logic of the situation was also forcing the right into a new populist departure. For to defend its position without the benefit of the old relation to the state, it was now resorting instead to an independent politics of popular mobilization *against* the government, and such an appeal to 'the people' was necessarily legitimated in quite new terms.

As the central chapters of this book have tried to argue, this departure was anticipated in the politics of the *nationale Verbände*. From the 1880s these organizations had provided a recurring pattern of right-wing dissidence which often upset the calculations of the government—the Boer War agitation and the naval radicalism of 1903–8 were the two best examples. But radical nationalism went much further than a series of specific disagreements over this or that aspect of official policy. It was radical not just because its demands were more extreme (e.g. for more ships, faster development of the colonies, harsher

[2] Heydebrand to Westarp, July 5th 1913, ZStA Potsdam, Westarp Papers, 1, cit. Fischer, *War of Illusions*, p. 190.

treatment of the Poles, a more 'German' foreign policy). It was also thoroughly hostile to the conventional way of doing things and was formed from a protracted conflict with the old governing establishment. In other words, radical nationalism was a highly distinctive ideological formation. Its exponents were a group of people for whom conventional orientations towards the parties or older 'corporate' institutions like the Army or the civil service mattered rather little: their main loyalty was to an idea of the nation materially embodied in a particular agitational practice which was certainly anti-Socialist and potentially anti-parliamentary.

When, under specific conditions of weakness after 1912, the old right swallowed its objections and combined with this dissidence in an enlarged 'national opposition', the consequences were accordingly profound. Conservative admission that 'tradition' could no longer be defended by traditional means was a triumphal vindication of radical-nationalist politics. It was also a measure of how far the landowners had been forced to sink their future in a larger political alliance, for the radical nationalists on their past showing were no mean critics of an extreme agrarian position. In fact, in this sense radical nationalism was an authentic product of the Wilhelmine conjuncture, deriving from both the latter's crucial particularities: not only was it motivated by the search for a nationalist counter-utopia to the SPD *Zukunftsstaat*, it was also thoroughly disrespectful of the Prussian landowners' special position in the state. Radical-nationalist criticism of classic Conservative positions had been a primary factor in the divisions of old and new right, and for this reason any new synthesis required Conservative acquiescence in a series of basic demands —tax reform, *Weltpolitik*, internal colonization, 'modernization' of the Army, and so on—which they had previously resisted. Under the novel circumstances of political weakness and isolation from the Imperial government after 1912 those terms began to be met.

This amounted to a fundamental radicalization of the right. If there was a single factor uniting the complex of changes this involved, moreover, it was an ideological commitment to the principle of mass politics. Furthermore, though this was in its general tendency consciously anti-democratic, it had only matured under the conditions of relative parliamentary stabilization after 1897, when the simple repression of Socialism ceased to be a viable option for the state and the containment of the left entered a phase of mainly ideological activity. In this new situation figures like August Keim and Hermann Rassow came into their own, enthroning the 'masses' at the centre of their rhetoric and perfecting a new practice of popular agitation. Between the 1890s and 1908–9, in other words, forces were unleashed which broke the bounds of the prevailing party framework. When they were gratefully reabsorbed into the structure of the latter under the new conditions of weakness and isolation after 1911–12, the effects were nothing less than transformative. It amounted to a definitive popularization of right-wing politics, and makes it possible to speak for the first time perhaps of a radical right.

II

This study has tried to look beyond simple notions of linear continuity—e.g. 'pre-industrial traditions', 'authoritarian and anti-democratic structures in state and society', 'susceptibility to authoritarian politics', or the defensive strategies of 'traditional power-élites'—which descend unchanged from the mid-nineteenth century down to the 1920s. Arguably the only fundamental continuity of this kind, though itself dynamic rather than unchanging, was the unevenly developing capitalist mode of production, with its social relations of subordination and exploitation, and its processes of reproduction. If we are to talk sensibly of the 'defence of the status quo' in Wilhelmine politics, it is on the latter that we must focus—viz. the property relations and the social relations of production—for otherwise we surrender our control of historical categories to the subjective perceptions of this or that group of Wilhelmine contemporaries: e.g. the Junker backwoodsman may have thought that he was defending the 'status quo', but his seigneurial and patriarchal ideals were already in the process of disappearance, while his anti-capitalist longings might well be contradicted by his own economic practice as a farmer. In this sense a 'tradition' is only as old as the practices and relations which embody and transform its meanings. In the case of the Prussian landowners and their place in Wilhelmine politics the feudal past was far less determining than a series of specific problems in the present, from the conditions of agricultural production and the control of rural labour, to the form of their relations with the various fractions of industrial capital or the politics of general agrarian mobilization. The same strictures apply to the other classes and class fractions in Wilhelmine society: the possible meanings and effectivity of a 'pre-industrial tradition' were strictly determined by the interior dynamics of the Wilhelmine conjuncture.

The dangers of a static notion of continuity are at their greatest perhaps in discussions of the Wilhelmine state, where the latter is taken to mean not just the central government institutions, but the general ensemble of state apparatuses (i.e. repressive, bureaucratic, ideological). For whereas the formal Constitution may have changed very little after 1871, the actual content of state relations necessarily changed in all manner of ways. One of the most important, as we saw, was precisely the declining ability after 1890 of the landowning class to dictate the terms of official policy, for as Germany's capitalist transformation proceeded the state appeared increasingly as a framework of institutions for containing and negotiating class antagonisms, i.e. as being itself located within a field of political conflict and therefore structurally incapable of servicing the 'pre-industrial domination' of a single class or fraction. The ability of the state to remain adaptable, to reproduce itself and to dispatch its functions was linked to an active process of political struggle—'a process of the continual renegotiation of relations between its constituent institutions or apparatuses, a process which also comprehends the internal reproduction of the institutions themselves, whether these be political parties, representative bodies, bureaucracies or whatever'.[3] For our purposes this was the more inescapable for occurring in the early stages of industrialization at a time of enormous social dislocation. In this sense it is the process of change that provides the continuity.

In other words, we are dealing not with a simple continuity (or survival) of structures, but with a complex continuity of problems. It makes little sense to speak of the ability of the landowning class (or the 'pre-industrial power-élite') to preserve 'the social and political status quo' in general, because the 'status quo' in that sense could never exist. Instead we need to think of more limited struggles to reproduce specific institutional relations (e.g. the Prussian three-class franchise, the aristocratic integrity of the officer corps, the dualism of Reich and Prussia, neo-seigneurial jurisdictions east of the Elbe, fiscal immunities, and so on), in a context of rapidly accelerating economic and social change which made this harder and harder to achieve. Though the problem remained the same (viz. aristocratic survivals in the structure of the state) and to that extent imposed an overall continuity on politics under the Empire, the possible range of solutions, the field of alliances and antagonisms, and the conditions under which the problem had to be addressed all changed fundamentally. Whereas in the post-unification phase of bourgeois consolidation it proved relatively easy to accommodate the bourgeoisie to aristocratic survivals, for instance, in the succeeding period of capitalist expansion this proved far more difficult. Moreover, the Bismarckian power bloc of 'iron and rye' (reproduced, as we saw, in local structures of *Honoratiorenpolitik*) had enjoyed the benefit of a relatively restricted public sphere. In the 1890s the latter's exclusiveness began to decompose, and the novel mobilization of the subordinate classes transformed the political context in which aristocratic privileges had to be defended.

It was this enlargement of the public sphere—a vital 'reconstitution of the political nation' in Blackbourn's phrase—that *specified* the Wilhelmine conjuncture. It initiated a far-reaching process of decomposition and recomposition in the life of the political parties, which confirmed them in a thoroughly new relationship to the freshly mobilized subordinate classes. In the case of the landowners this re-emphasized the difficulties of simply reproducing their traditional political influence in its old form, for not only did they have to fight much harder for the co-operation of the other dominant classes, they also had to devise new ways of winning popular support. Moreover, as well as seeking new allies in the peasantry and petty-bourgeoisie, the Junkers had to reconcile

[3] Caplan, 'Bureaucracy, Politics and the National Socialist State', p. 251.

themselves to the reality of constitutional government: after 1897 politics stabilized in a parliamentary mould, which strengthened 'not the Prussian-particularist and "feudal" features of the political status quo, but the national and bourgeois ones'.[4] For all of these reasons it makes little sense to speak any further of a 'pre-industrial power-élite' and its attempts to 'stabilize the system' as the dominant instance in Wilhelmine politics. For one thing this misunderstands the changing (and deteriorating) situation of the landowning class in the overall field of class relations and incorrectly theorizes its relation to the state. For another there was no 'system' in this sense to 'stabilize', for in the 1890s the Wilhelmine polity was only then being shaped.

It is extremely important, therefore, to grasp the dynamics of political change during the Second Reich. It is vital to get away from the notion that by the 're-foundation of the Reich' in 1878–9 the pattern of German politics was already fixed for the next four or even five decades. Such an approach effectively ignores the decomposition of the Bismarckian system in the 1890s and the complex social-historical process whereby the masses entered politics during that decade—it disqualifies the latter's importance and denies its transforming effects on the power bloc's hegemonic capability. Imprisoned within its own model of Wilhelmine politics as a manipulated system of institutionalized interventions *from above*, which successfully 'socialized' the masses into the prevailing 'structures of domination', this approach denies that the process of popular mobilization seriously affected the forms and possibilities of ruling-class politics. This assumes that the relationship of the so-called 'traditional élites' to the peasantry and petty-bourgeoisie was unproblematic—that the latter were painlessly eased into a straightforward subordinate relationship.[5] Yet, as this book has tried to argue, not only did the subordinate classes assert their own claims to vigorous independence, with crucial radicalizing effects on the bourgeois parties that tried to assimilate them (e.g. as in the Agrarian League), but the history of the *nationale Verbände* also revealed that certain junior and dissident politicians of the dominant classes were prepared to make a strong bid for their leadership. In other words, after the 1890s the relationship became problematic and unstable.

[4] Blackbourn, 'Problem of Democratization', p. 179.

[5] For a fuller critique, see G. H. Eley, 'Die "Kehrites" und das Kaiserreich: Bemerkungen zu einer aktuellen Kontroverse', *GG*, 4 (1978), pp. 91–107. See also Evans, 'Introduction', p. 23: 'Political processes, changes and influences are perceived as flowing downwards—though now from the elites who controlled the State, rather than from the socially vaguer entity of the State itself—not upwards from the people. The actions and beliefs of the masses are explained in terms of the influence exerted on them by manipulative elites at the top of society. The German Empire is presented as a puppet theatre, with Junkers and industrialists pulling the strings, and middle and lower classes dancing jerkily across the stage of history towards the final curtain of the Third Reich.' The image was used by H.-G. Zmarzlik, 'Das Kaiserreich in neuer Sicht?', *HZ*, 222, (1976), pp. 105–26.

III

Although the period opened by the *Kartell der schaffenden Stände* in 1913 saw the resolution of several long-standing difficulties in the position of the right—the re-integration of the landowning interest into a larger right-wing coalition on a non-privileged basis, the similar integration of a previously dissident radical nationalism, the achievement of a much higher level of organizational unity—the forms of this resolution were not without their own problems. In particular, the DNVP represented an extremely fragile unity, and although the revolutionary crisis of 1918 briefly soldered the various fractions of the dominant classes into an improvised defensive unity, the latter now had to be consolidated within a Republican state structure which was far less congenial. But by far the most serious of the DNVP's outstanding difficulties concerned its ability to devise an adequate popular practice under the new conditions of the strengthened parliamentary Constitution. One way of doing this was simply to accept the post-revolutionary situation, and on the whole the dominant classes did display a striking degree of flexibility in their pragmatic adjustment to the new context. But the simultaneous necessity of suppressing the attempts of the Socialist left to radicalize the revolutionary process also created an additional problem: namely, how to contain the counter-revolutionary ardour of the activist petty-bourgeoisie. This returns us to the problem of populism.

As I have tried to argue throughout this text, beginning in the 1890s the Wilhelmine power bloc experienced a long-term crisis of its hegemonic capability, deriving partly from its own lack of internal cohesion, partly from the independent self-mobilization of the subordinate classes outside the existing structures of political control. This meant not just a problem of popular *support* (i.e. as measured in the membership of organizations or the vote at elections), but also a problem of popular *legitimacy*. At a time when democratic forms of legitimacy were gaining increasing currency—not only through the SPD and the Free Trade Unions, but also through the practice and often the conscious programmes of the radicalized peasantry and petty-bourgeoisie—the dominant classes required a means of articulating such aspirations into a discourse of their own: i.e. a means of neutralizing popular democratic antagonisms by transforming them into objects of compromise within the limits of the system. One way of doing this was by a programme of radical parliamentary reform and trade union incorporation, but at the turn of the century this course had little backing amongst the dominant classes, and as we saw was badly blunted in its period of greater influence after 1909. Moreover, the party-political right, which represented the power bloc's leading fractions, proved unable to deliver any constructive alternative. In this situation radical nationalism, by a complex set of social-historical determinations, gradually materialized after 1900 as an extreme populist solution. Frustrated by the apparent immobility of the right-wing establishment and passionately committed to the national idea as an anti-Socialist panacea, Pan-Germans and naval radicals instated an appeal to the 'people in general' at the centre of their practice, in direct opposition to the conventional right and its traditions.

This radical-nationalist critique sprang from a crisis of confidence in the current politics of the power bloc—not just in the latter's policies and tactics (e.g. the failure to build enough battleships, or the failure to dissolve the Reichstag against the colonial opposition of the Centre and SPD), but in its willingness and ability to harness popular aspirations, and in the entire mode of politics (i.e. *Honoratiorenpolitik*) through which it was then constituted. At the moment of crisis, when the government and its conservative allies responded to the challenge of the *Keimianer* in the Navy League at the turn of 1907–8, the critique became pragmatically extended to the formal bases of conservative legitimacy themselves—dynasticism, federalism and monarchy. Though this stance of 'national opposition' was at first rejected by the party-political right, a series of events gradually forced a juncture: the Daily Telegraph Crisis damaged confidence in the Kaiser's personality almost irrevocably and severed the political defence of monarchy from deference to the existing monarch; the deterioration of Germany's European and world situation caused a collapse of confidence in the government's foreign policy; and the pragmatic accommodation of Bethmann Hollweg to the victory of the left in the 1912 elections sparked a related hostility to its domestic strategy as well. Moreover, the old leading fractions of the power bloc ('iron and rye') now experienced a crisis of political representation: not only were the old Cartel elements reduced to a parliamentary rump of some fifty seats, but the traditional vehicle of heavy-industrial politics, the National Liberal Party, had been captured in the Reichstag for a moderate reformist departure. In this situation of unprecedented weakness the radical-nationalist critique became serviceable for a larger grouping of interests.

Thus after 1911 the radical nationalists were successfully integrated into a larger right coalition, as old and new right buried their differences for common resistance to the left. This involved a virtual admission on the part of the former that radical measures were required to reconstitute its dominance in the power bloc and to recover some basis of support amongst the subordinate classes. Accordingly, as part of the attempt to recompose its unity in opposition to the Bethmann Hollweg government, the right also set out to legitimate its 'national opposition' by appropriating the radical nationalists' populist ambition. In other words, the incorporation of the *nationale Verbände* into the 1913 Cartel was not just a numerical addition of organizations with a large paper membership, but an ambitious political departure, for the leading radical nationalists were deeply committed to an ideal of systematic popular mobilization. This was no mere rhetoric. Though the populism of the Pan-Germans was elaborated as a universalizing vision explicitly divorced from class or sectional interests, it was also linked in the practice of the leading Pan-German politicians to a specific strategy of petty-bourgeois incorporation. This provided the double basis of the right's general radicalization: an anti-democratic populist offensive organized around the radical-nationalist counter-utopia, combined with the deliberate appeasement of the petty-bourgeoisie.

It is tempting to present this as manipulation—as a process engineered by the dominant classes on their own terms. There clearly were attempts to manufacture popular support in this way: e.g. the company unions and patriotic workers' associations, or certain strategies of the Agrarian League east of the Elbe. But manipulative interventions of this kind, conceived as the administrative incorporation of the masses within an unchanged authoritarian framework, betrayed little sensitivity for the problems of properly integrating the popular elements on a lasting basis. To be successful such a process of integration required that a certain relative autonomy be allowed to the latter, and this the traditional *Sammlungspolitiker* were reluctant to concede. By contrast the radical nationalists were far more sensitive to the needs of a genuine popular politics. They revealed this in every sphere of their practice—in their attitudes to organization, in their styles of propaganda and agitation, in their rhetoric, in their ideology, and especially in their relation to the traditional mode of *Honoratiorenpolitik*. Though often external to the petty-bourgeoisie in terms of their individual social standing—and therefore 'manipulators' in that crude sense—their appreciation of popular mobilization was formed by a direct encounter with the masses in their own agitational practice. Wilhelmine politics was in general increasingly dominated by men of this type—Hahn in the Agrarian League, Erzberger in the Centre, Stresemann in the regenerate National Liberals—and by 1913 they were also installed firmly at the centre of the reconstituted right.

However, during the old right's period of stagnation between the 1890s and 1909, the petty-bourgeoisie had also equipped itself with its own organizations, formed in vigorous independence from control by the dominant classes. Though the latter sought increasingly to influence their development (e.g. through the German Association or the Society for Internal Colonization and the various co-operative and insurance initiatives in the East), they could never be reduced to simple subordinate status. Most significantly, the traditional petty-bourgeoisie was now organized into a new national federation, the Imperial-German *Mittelstand* League, and this was admitted to the 1913 Cartel as an independent negotiating partner with its own distinct leadership. In other words, the petty-bourgeoisie had begun to generate its own stratum of politicians—whom one might characterize as organic intellectuals of the petty-bourgeoisie in Gramsci's sense—in the dense tangle of artisanal, retailing, co-operative and petty entrepreneurial organizations. By 1913 these had attained a level of self-consciousness which might easily frustrate any crude attempt at simple incorporation. As the organ of the *Mittelstand* League said of its participation in the Cartel: 'In reality, it is here for the first time that the *Mittelstand* as an accepted public power was recognized. Here were offered prospects and possibilities for development about which the *Mittelstand* had earlier hardly ventured to dream.'[6] In this mood the organized petty-bourgeoisie might easily bolt into an independent politics of its own if not given adequate recognition in the inner counsels of the dominant right-wing coalition.

In the aftermath of the war this problem became acute. Kapp, Claß and their allies in the Fatherland Party were certainly keen to strengthen the relationship to the old *Mittelstand*, but by the autumn of 1918 their efforts had not yet proceeded very far.[7] Similarly, although the DNVP made a deliberate attempt to embrace the extant organs of an independent *Mittelstand* politics, it proved unable to prevent the foundation of the *Wirtschaftspartei* in 1920 or the *völkisch* secession of 1922. Despite the presence of Pan-Germans and others at the centre of the right coalition who explicitly recognized the need for a new mass politics, it proved difficult to build further on the foundations of 1913. This was compounded by the special circumstances of the revolutionary conjuncture at the end of the war—the difficulty of reabsorbing the masses of persons mobilized for the war into the traditional political structures, and the paramilitary activation of petty-bourgeois support for the counter-revolution. In this situation the DNVP failed to hold the allegiance of the petty-bourgeoisie in a constructive political relationship. In this light the *Kartell der schaffenden Stände* assumes an extra significance: not for the last time the established German right chose at a moment of weakness to align itself with a movement of the petty-bourgeoisie which jealously asserted its own independence.

This was the most important continuity inaugurated by the Cartel: an unstable and contradictory relationship between the established right and the independent organs of the petty-bourgeoisie. On the one hand, it is clear that the DNVP failed to establish an undisputed leadership over the old *Mittelstand* in Protestant areas: not only was it competing with the *Wirtschaftspartei* and smaller economic splinter-groups, but there is also strong evidence that by 1924 it was already facing a long-term drift of *Mittelstand* support towards more radical right-wing alternatives. Though the DNVP showed continuing gains in both 1924 elections, these were achieved mainly at the expense of the DVP by appropriating the allegiance of the important white-collar constituency. By comparison it seems to have found that its role as a rallying-point for the traditional petty-bourgeoisie had already been partially usurped by the NSDAP and its equivalents.[8] But on the other hand, the DNVP also found itself

[6] *Reichsdeutsche Mittelstandsblätter*, Jan. 1914, cit. Gellately, *Politics of Economic Despair*, p. 193.

[7] See esp. Stegmann, 'Zwischen Repression und Manipulation', pp. 392ff.

[8] This seems to be the argument of Childers, 'Social Bases', pp. 20f.: 'The elections of 1924, therefore, appear to represent an important transitional stage in the evolution of voting preferences within the old middle class. Although a comparison of the May and December coefficients indicates a shift from the NSDAP toward its more moderate rivals, the voting pattern in cities with a high proportion of self-employed proprietors did not revert to the

undermined at its constituency base by a labyrinth of cross-cutting loyalties, as a multiplicity of locally-bounded *völkisch* groups gradually asserted their lasting independence. This was a new phenomenon, quite distinct from the older *völkisch* milieu at the end of the *Kaiserreich*, for which the DVFP was a final epitaph. The latter was described by Hitler in terms which suggested the nature of the disjunction: the phenomenon of the DVFP was

> similar to that of the 80s and 90s and, just as in those days, control over it was acquired by entirely honourable but fantastically naive scholars, professors, *Land-*, *Studien-* and *Justizräte*, in short middle-class idealists. It lacked the warm breath of youthful energy. The impetuous drive of enthusiastic hotheads was rejected as demagogy. As a result the new movement was a *völkisch* but not a popular movement.[9]

Whether or not this was an accurate sociological description of the pre-war Anti-Semitic movement, it certainly applied to the Pan-Germans and the activists of the *nationale Verbände*. As such it located a decisive limitation of their politics in the new post-war environment, where spontaneously generated *völkisch* movements—organic movements of the petty-bourgeoisie like the NSDAP—now contested their accustomed political space.[10]

In the end, therefore, this is a history without a conclusion. Although this study has tried to liberate the analysis of the Wilhelmine right from the proto-Nazi teleology into which it has normally been co-opted, it is impossible to close without addressing the problem of fascism, and here I have tried to propose a question rather than an answer. For, as suggested in the Introduction above, if we are to identify the conditions which *specified* fascism in Germany— i.e. its longer-term conditions of possibility—it makes some sense to examine the terms under which the subordinate classes were admitted to the political system. In this respect, as we have seen, due to the structural disunity and impaired hegemonic capability of the Wilhelmine power bloc, the right experienced a long-term difficulty of its popular legitimacy. The forms of the latter's

---

traditional liberal-conservative cleavage so evident in 1920. Moreover, as the coefficients for the election of 1928, a year of relative prosperity, tend to confirm, the fascist electoral tendencies which surfaced within the old middle class in May 1924 did not represent a spasmodic reaction to short-term economic crisis.'

[9] W. Jochmann, *Nationalsozialismus und Revolution. Dokumente* (Frankfurt, 1963), pp. 88f.

[10] This process may be traced most easily through the following: Noakes, *Nazi Party*, pp. 9–88, 108–20; Lohalm, *Völkischer Radikalismus*, esp. pp. 107–21, 176–255, 283–334; R. Lenman, 'Julius Streicher and the Origins of the NSDAP in Nuremberg, 1918–1923', in Nicholls and Matthias (Eds.), *German Democracy and the Triumph of Hitler*, pp. 129–59; G. Pridham, *Hitler's Rise to Power. The Nazi Movement in Bavaria, 1923–1933* (London, 1973), pp. 20ff., 42ff., 108f.; R. Phelps, ' "Before Hitler Came": Thule Society and Germanen Orden', *JMH*, 35 (1963), pp. 245–61, and 'Hitler and the Deutsche Arbeiterpartei', *AHR*, 68 (1962–3), pp. 974–86; Stegmann, 'Zwischen Repression und Manipulation', pp. 392–414; F. L. Carsten, *The Rise of Fascism* (London, 1967), pp. 82ff.

resolution, in both organization and ideology, were partially discovered in a difficult process of internecine conflict between the 1890s and 1908–9, when radical nationalists inaugurated a new populist offensive—i.e. a political struggle for the ideological leadership of the 'people in general'. However, the success of that offensive was in practice dependent on their ability to integrate the petty-bourgeoisie inside a new right-wing bloc, and though this was partly achieved for the traditional sectors in the 1913 Cartel, the latter still retained considerable political independence. The principal effect—viz. a structural instability in the relations of power bloc to petty-bourgeoisie—was arguably a vital condition of future possibility for the emergence of a German fascism.

Appendix 1. Chronology

1881	Aug.	General German School Society formed (renamed Society for Germandom Abroad, 1908).
1882	Dec.	Colonial League formed.
1884	Apr.	Society for German Colonization formed.
	Oct.	Elections under colonial slogan.
1887	Feb.	So-called 'Cartel Elections', with majority for two Conservative Parties and National Liberals.
	Dec.	Fusion of colonial groups into Colonial Society.
1890	Feb.	Elections, defeat of Cartel.
	Mar.	Fall of Bismarck, Caprivi Chancellor.
	Oct.	Anti-Socialist Law not renewed.
1891	Apr.	Pan-German League formed.
1893		Ernst Hasse takes over Pan-German League.
1894	Oct.	Hohenlohe succeeds Caprivi as Chancellor.
	Nov.	Society for the Eastern Marches formed.
1897	June	Conservative reconstruction of government under Miquel's slogan of *Sammlungspolitik*.
1898	Apr.	Passage of First Navy Law.
		Navy League formed.
	June	Elections, indifferent results for the right.
1899	Nov.	First crisis of Navy League.
1900	June	Passage of Second Navy Law.
	Oct.	Bülow succeeds Hohenlohe as Chancellor.
	Nov.	Krüger's visit to Cologne, where he receives Pan-German delegation.
	Dec.	Bülow denounces Pan-Germans in Reichstag.
1902	Oct.	Visit of Boer Generals to Berlin, producing crisis in Pan-German Leadership.
	Dec.	Passage of higher grain tariffs.
1903	June	Elections, with dramatic gains for SPD.
1904	Apr.	Navy League announces radical naval programme.
		Pan-Germans begin discussion of future aims.
	May	Imperial League Against Social Democracy formed.

1905	May	Crisis in Navy League's relations with government.
1906	June	Passage of Third Navy Law.
	Dec.	Bülow dissolves Reichstag on colonial issue.
1907	Jan.	Elections, with defeat for the SPD and heavy involvement by radical nationalists.
		Conservative-liberal Bülow Bloc formed against Centre Party and SPD.
	Feb.	Serious crisis in Navy League.
	May	Compromise at Navy League's Cologne Congress.
	Dec.	Renewed conflict in Navy League.
1908	Jan.	Emergency Navy League Congress at Cassel, with collective resignation of Presidium.
		Death of Hasse, Claß elected Chairman of Pan-German League.
	June	Danzig Congress of Navy League, with final exclusion of Keim from leadership.
		Transference of radical nationalists from Navy League to Pan-Germans.
	Nov.	Daily Telegraph Crisis and final consummation of radical nationalism as a 'national opposition'.
1909	Mar.	Collapse of Bülow Bloc.
	June	Hanse-Union formed.
		Final defeat of finance reform.
	July	Bülow succeeded by Bethmann Hollweg as Chancellor.
1911	July	Crisis over Morocco.
	Nov.	Reichstag debate on Morocco.
1912	Jan.	Defence League formed.
		Elections, with SPD landslide and collapse of right.
1913	Aug.	Proclamation of Cartel of the Productive Estates.

Appendix 2. Reichstag Elections 1887-1912 (No. of seats)

	1887	1890	1893	1898	1903	1907	1912
Conservatives	80	73	72	56	54	60	43
Free Conservatives	41	20	28	23	21	24	14
Anti-Semites & Others	3	7	21	31	22	33	19
Guelphs (Hannoverian Particularists)	4	11	7	9	6	1	5
Centre Party	98	106	96	102	100	105	91
National Liberals	99	42	53	46	51	54	45
Left Liberals	32	76	48	49	36	49	42
National Minorities (Poles, Danes, Alsace-Lorraine)	29	27	28	25	26	28	28
SPD	11	35	44	56	81	43	110
Total	397	397	397	397	397	397	397

NB

1 The chosen grouping of parties (into the right, Centre, Liberals, national minorities and SPD) is not the usual one. In most accounts the Guelphs, Anti-Semites etc. are kept apart from the Conservatives, while the National Liberals are grouped with the two Conservative Parties. However, though the latter method works for the 'Cartel Elections' of 1887, the main *tendency* of National Liberal politics thereafter was towards a far more centrist position, aligning them with the Catholic Centre in the 1890s and then increasingly with the left liberals as well. On the other hand, the Guelphs were in effect a conservative party of agrarian and *Mittelstand* interests, and normally voted accordingly. The category of 'Anti-Semites and others' includes an assortment of Independents and radical agrarian deputies who were often rogue Conservatives. Although this grouping of party categories also begs a number of questions, it is none the less more illuminating than the usual practice.

2 The category 'left liberals' includes basically three independent groupings who united in 1910 to form the Progressive People's Party: the *Freisinnige Vereinigung* and *Freisinnige Volkspartei* which originated in the left liberal split over support for the 1892 Army Bill, and the separate South German People's Party, based primarily in Württemberg.

Appendix 3. Comparative Membership of the Nationalist Pressure Groups

	Pan-German League	Navy League	Colonial Society	Society for the Eastern Marches	Society for Germandom Abroad	Defence League
1881					1,345	
1887			14,838			
1891	21,000		17,709		36,000	
1893	5,000		17,154			
1894	5,742		16,264			
1895	7,715		16,474	20,000	26,524	
1896	9,443		17,901	18,500		
1897	12,974		21,252	9,400		
1898	17,364	14,252	26,501			
1899	20,488	93,991	31,601			
1900	21,735	216,749	34,768	20,000	32,000	
1901	21,924	238,767	33,541			
1902		236,793	32,161			
1903	19,068	233,173	31,482	29,300		
1904	19,111	249,241	31,985		34,774	
1905	18,618	275,272	32,159			
1906	18,445	315,420	32,787	40,500		
1907		324,372	36,956			
1908		307,884	38,509			
1909		296,172	38,928			
1910		290,964	39,025	53,000	45,272	
1911		297,788	39,134			
1912	c.17,000	320,174	41,163			33,000
1913		331,910	42,212			78,000
1914		331,493	42,018	54,000	57,452	90,000

The following points should be noted:

1 The Navy League also enjoyed a huge additional membership from organizations who were corporately affiliated with local branches. In 1899 this amounted to 152,890, more than doubling by 1900 and rising steadily to 675,168 by 1908, to reach a total of 776,613 in 1914. In aggregate terms this gave the League well over a million members.

2 Both the Pan-Germans and the Colonial Society experienced striking gains in membership when campaigning on the naval issue between 1895 and 1900.

3 The Navy League took a significant drop in membership as a result of the crisis in 1907–8.

4 The turn away from 'world policy' back to 'continental policy' by the government after 1911 had no effect on the membership of the Colonial Society, which continued to rise.

Appendix 4. Regional Distribution of Radical Nationalist Strength during the Navy League Crisis of 1908

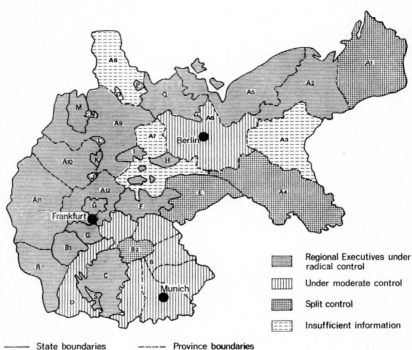

Regional Executives under radical control

Under moderate control

Split control

Insufficient information

———— State boundaries   ———— Province boundaries

Key
A Prussia
  A1 East Prussia
  A2 West Prussia
  A3 Posen
  A4 Silesia
  A5 Pomerania
  A6 Berlin-Brandenburg
  A7 Saxony
  A8 Schleswig-Holstein
  A9 Hanover

  A10 Westphalia
  A11 Rhineland
  A12 Hessen-Nassau
B Bavaria
  B1 Bavarian Palatinate
  B2 Bavarian Province of Central
    Franconia
C Württemberg
D Baden
E Saxony

F Thuringian states
G Hessen
H Anhalt
I Brunswick
J Waldeck-Pyrmolt
K Lippe-Detmold
L Schaumburg-Lippe

M Oldenburg
N Bremen
O Hamburg
P Lübeck
Q Mecklenburg
R Alsace-Lorraine
S Hohenzollern Territories

Appendix 5. From Empire to Republic: Changes in Party Organization

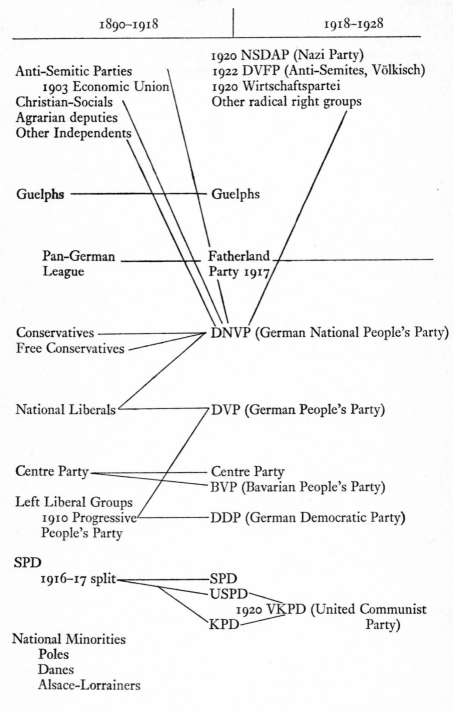

1890–1918 | 1918–1928

Anti-Semitic Parties
1903 Economic Union
Christian-Socials
Agrarian deputies
Other Independents

1920 NSDAP (Nazi Party)
1922 DVFP (Anti-Semites, Völkisch)
1920 Wirtschaftspartei
Other radical right groups

Guelphs ———————— Guelphs

Pan-German _____ Fatherland
League   Party 1917

Conservatives ———→ DNVP (German National People's Party)
Free Conservatives

National Liberals ———→ DVP (German People's Party)

Centre Party ———————— Centre Party
                                          BVP (Bavarian People's Party)

Left Liberal Groups
1910 Progressive ———————— DDP (German Democratic Party)
People's Party

SPD
1916–17 split ——————— SPD
                                    USPD
                                              1920 VKPD (United Communist
                                    KPD   Party)

National Minorities
Poles
Danes
Alsace-Lorrainers

Bibliographical Note

Many archives were visited for the purposes of this study and the following note is meant to provide only a general indication of the more important sources. Detailed reference is made in the footnotes, but otherwise specialists may care to consult my unpublished thesis, 'The German Navy League in German Politics, 1898–1914' (Sussex D.Phil., 1974), which contains a detailed breakdown.

For the general political background the most important sources were the files of the Imperial Chancellory in *Zentrales Staatsarchiv* Potsdam and of the Navy Office in *Bundesarchiv-Militärarchiv* Freiburg, together with numerous private papers. The most useful of the latter were in Potsdam (Bassermann, Kusserow, Naumann), Freiburg (Tirpitz, Müller, Knorr, Heeringen), and *Bundesarchiv* Coblenz (Bülow, Delbrück, Eulenburg, Gothein, Harden, Hohenlohe-Schillingsfürst A. & Chl., Junius Alter, Stresemann and Traub). In addition the Delbrück Papers were consulted in the *Deutsche Staatsbibliothek* Berlin, the Haßler Papers at *Stadtarchiv* Augsburg, and the Bachem Papers at *Stadtarchiv* Cologne. Industrial material was consulted mainly at the *Historisches Archiv der Gutehoffnungshütte* in Oberhausen and from the VDEStI files in Coblenz. For the nationalist pressure groups themselves, the single most important collections are the files of the Pan-German League in Potsdam and the governmental collections in Potsdam and Freiburg, together with the private papers of Keim, Wied and Reismann-Grone, which are in private hands. The Wegener Papers in Coblenz are also useful. Navy League records have survived haphazardly (the central archive was destroyed), mainly in state archives through the deposits of regional executives. Several are intact (Hamburg, Lübeck, Karlsruhe), but good collections can also be found in Marburg, Coblenz, Münster, Munich, Bremen, Wolfenbüttel, Bückeburg, Detmold and Stuttgart. The archive of the Navy League branch in Nuremberg is also intact (*Stadtarchiv* Nuremberg), and other branch materials can be found in *Stadtarchiv* Essen, *Landesarchiv* Saarbrücken, *Stadtarchiv* Wuppertal and the *Staatsarchive* in Münster and Detmold. Otherwise, both the general political scene (especially the conduct of elections) and the activities of the pressure groups can be successfully tracked through the records of the Prussian and other state bureaucracies: the most useful collections were in

BHSA Munich, HSA Stuttgart, HSA Marburg, SA Coblenz and SA Münster. The press was consulted mainly in the *Institut für Zeitungsforschung* in Dortmund, though miscellaneous collections of cuttings were also important. The more important dailies with national resonance were used systematically (e.g. *Kreuz-Zeitung, National-Zeitung, Kölnische Zeitung, Freisinnige Zeitung, Vorwärts*), as were strategic regional papers, such as *Rheinisch-Westfälische Zeitung* (for Reismann-Grone's Pan-German editorial perspective and details on the *nationale Verbände*), *Dortmunder Zeitung* (for an alternative National Liberal perspective in the same region), *Schwäbischer Merkur* (for radical nationalism in the South West), and *Weimarische Zeitung* (for events in Thuringia). The main pressure group journals were also used systematically, especially *Alldeutsche Blätter, Die Flotte* and *Deutsche Kolonialzeitung*. Innumerable pamphlets and leaflets were used, particularly the productions of the Pan-Germans and Navy League, but also the general corpus of naval and colonial propaganda from the period after 1895–6 and an enormous amount of anti-Socialist literature. A full list may be found in the bibliography to my thesis. Extensive use was made of the *Stenographische Berichte über die Verhandlungen des Deutschen Reichstags* (the Reichstag debates, abbreviated in the footnotes as RT), the usual reference works, and the memoir literature. Of the latter, H. Claß, *Wider den Strom* (Leipzig, 1932), A. Keim, *Erlebtes und Erstrebtes* (Hannover, 1925), and E. von Liebert, *Aus einem bewegten Leben* (Munich, 1925), were essential.

The secondary literature on the *nationale Verbände* is of variable value. By far the best general introduction is through the entries in the admirable G.D.R. handbook edited by D. Fricke, *Die Bürgerlichen Parteien in Deutschland*, 2 vols. (Leipzig, 1968–70). M. Wertheimer, *The Pan-German League, 1890–1914* (New York, 1924), is still most useful on the Pan-Germans, but must be treated with caution; of more recent work D. Stegmann, *Die Erben Bismarcks* (Cologne, 1970), and D. Guratzsch, *Macht durch Organisation* (Düsseldorf, 1974), present some vital material from the archives. For the colonial movement I have drawn mainly on the unpublished thesis by R. Pierard, 'The German Colonial Society 1882–1914' (Iowa, 1964), P. Anderson's resilient *The Background of Anti-English Feeling in Germany, 1890–1902* (New York, 1969), H. Pogge's 'The Kolonialrat, its Significance and Influence on German Politics from 1890 to 1906' (D.Phil Thesis, Oxford, 1966, shortly to be published), F. F. Müller, *Deutschland – Zanzibar – Ostafrika* (Berlin, 1959), and K. J. Bade's excellent *Friedrich Fabri und der Imperialismus in der Bismarckzeit* (Freiburg, 1975). The Eastern Marches Society is well served by a fine G.D.R.-Polish collaborative work, A. Galos, F.-H. Gentzen, W. Jacobczyk, *Die Hakatisten* (Berlin, 1966), and the older R. W. Tims, *Germanizing Prussian Poland* (New York, 1941). There is no work specifically on the Defence League, but both R. Chickering (Oregon) and S. Forster (Düsseldorf) are preparing major studies. For the Society for Germandom Abroad, there is G. Weidenfeller,

VDA. Verein für das Deutschtum im Ausland. Allgemeiner Deutscher Schulverein (1881–1918) (Frankfurt, 1976). Otherwise there is no work to speak of on cultural nationalism as an organized activity. The Navy League is treated comprehensively in my unpublished thesis, but W. Deist, *Flottenpolitik und Flottenpropaganda* (Stuttgart, 1976), is also an excellent guide. A more general work, K. Schilling, *Beiträge zu einer Geschichte des radikalen Nationalismus in der wilhelminischen Ära 1890–1909* (Diss., Cologne, 1967), is patchy, unanalytical and unreliable.

Otherwise, the reader is referred to the footnotes, which should make my main debts clear. The notes to the Introduction are intended as a detailed guide to the historiographical context, though they are by no means exhaustive. A handful of works have been indispensable, as will also be clear from the text: e.g. V. R. Berghahn's exhaustive analysis of naval policy, *Der Tirpitz-Plan* (Düsseldorf, 1971), and Deist's companion study of naval propaganda mentioned above; detailed monographs by D. Stegmann, *Die Erben Bismarcks*, (Cologne, 1970), P.-Chr. Witt, *Die Finanzpolitik des Deutschen Reiches von 1903 bis 1913* (Lübeck, 1970), and K. Saul, *Staat, Industrie, Arbeiterbewegung im Kaiserreich* (Düsseldorf, 1974); D. S. White's fine study of National Liberalism, *The Splintered Party* (Cambridge, Mass., 1976). I am particularly indebted to some unpublished manuscripts on the Imperial League Against Social Democracy by F. Taylor, and above all to D. G. Blackbourn's work on the Centre Party, which is a salutary lesson in how the history of politics ought to be written: 'The Centre Party in Wilhelmine Germany: the Example of Württemberg' (Cambridge Ph.D., 1976, shortly to be published by Yale University Press). Finally, the best guide to the current state of Wilhelmine historiography is now a collection of essays edited by R. J. Evans, *Society and Politics in Wilhelmine Germany* (London, 1978).

13

Index

DATE DUE

DEMCO 38-297